# Wills and Will-Making in Anglo-Saxon England

# YORK MEDIEVAL PRESS

York Medieval Press is published by the University of York's Centre for Medieval Studies in association with Boydell & Brewer Limited. Our objective is the promotion of innovative scholarship and fresh criticism on medieval culture. We have a special commitment to interdisciplinary study, in line with the Centre's belief that the future of Medieval Studies lies in those areas in which its major constituent disciplines at once inform and challenge each other.



All enquiries of an editorial kind, including suggestions for monographs and essay collections, should be addressed to: The Academic Editor, York Medieval Press, University of York, Centre for Medieval Studies, The King's Manor, York, YO1 7EP (E-mail: gmg501@york.ac.uk).

Publications of York Medieval Press are listed at the back of this volume.

# Wills and Will-Making in Anglo-Saxon England

Linda Tollerton

THE UNIVERSITY of York

YORK MEDIEVAL PRESS

First published 2011

A York Medieval Press publication
in association with The Boydell Press
an imprint of Boydell & Brewer Ltd
PO Box 9 Woodbridge Suffolk IP12 3DF UK
and of Boydell & Brewer Inc.
668 Mt Hope Avenue Rochester NY 14620 USA
website: www.boydellandbrewer.com
and with the
Centre for Medieval Studies, University of York

ISBN 978 1 903153 37 6

A CIP catalogue record for this book is available from the British Library



Printed in Great Britain by
CPI Antony Rowe, Chippenham and Eastbourne

# CONTENTS

# ILLUSTRATIONS

In memory of my parents, Ethel and Ronald Tollerton,
and of my brother, Steven

The publication of this book has been assisted by a grant from
The Scouloudi Foundation in association with the
Institute of Historical Research

# ACKNOWLEDGEMENTS

This book has had an extended gestation period, in the course of which I have accrued so many debts that it is impossible to acknowledge them all individually, but I am grateful to everyone who has supported my foray into Anglo-Saxon history.

Academically, I have one debt outstanding from my undergraduate years in Newcastle, where the teaching of Richard Bailey inspired in me a passion for the Anglo-Saxon period which has finally, forty years later, borne fruit. More recently, my MA in History at the University of York was supervised by the late Richard Fletcher, who encouraged me to pursue my burgeoning interest in wills. I have had opportunities to air preliminary ideas at York University's Centre for Medieval Studies, the Institute for Historical Research at the University of London, and the International Medieval Congress at the University of Leeds, and have benefited enormously from the questions and suggestions which resulted. I am grateful to Catherine Cubitt for support and wise advice over many years, and to Julia Crick, Sarah Foot and Kathryn Lowe for their generosity in sharing their research with me. I have also been grateful for the help of staff at the Brotherton Library, University of Leeds, at the British Library, Boston Spa, and particularly at York University Library.

I am further indebted to those who have contributed in various ways to the completion of the final draft. Map 1 was drawn by Chris Fern, and Map 2 is reproduced with the kind permission of Tim Pestell; Lorraine Painter created the spreadsheet which is Appendix 3. Anthony Stanforth helped me with the translation of academic German. Nicholas Brooks provided me with revised texts of wills in the archive of Christ Church, Canterbury, together with related commentaries, in advance of their publication in the forthcoming volume of the British Academy series. Stephen Baxter commented on Chapter 1, and gave me access to the unpublished notes on wills of the late Patrick Wormald, with whom I was privileged to discuss my ideas on several occasions. The generously detailed comments of an anonymous academic reader enabled me not only to avoid a number of errors, but also to sharpen both my thinking and my text. I have also appreciated the support, advice and sharp eyes of my editors: Jocelyn Wogan-Browne and Peter Biller at York Medieval Press, and Caroline Palmer and Rohais Haughton at Boydell & Brewer.

Finally, my greatest debt is to my parents, for their unfailing love and encouragement. My fascination with the past grew out of our family expeditions on Gliderways coaches to the ancient sites and monuments of the West Midlands. My mother taught me to imagine history, and my father was keen to help me explore it. Neither of them could have envisaged this book emerging from those childhood excursions, and it is my regret that they did not live to see its publication.

# ABBREVIATIONS

*Editions of Vernacular Wills*

| | |
|---|---|
| *Æthelgifu* | *The Will of Æthelgifu*, ed. and transl. D. Whitelock, with contributions by N. Ker and Lord Rennell (Oxford, 1968). |
| *Charters* (R) | *Anglo-Saxon Charters*, ed. and transl. A. J. Robertson (Cambridge, 1939). |
| *ECEE* | *The Early Charters of Eastern England*, ed. C. R. Hart (Leicester, 1966). |
| N&S | *The Crawford Collection of Early Documents and Charters*, ed. and transl. A. S. Napier and W. H. Stevenson (Oxford, 1895). |
| *SEHD* (H) | *Select English Historical Documents of the Ninth and Tenth Centuries*, ed. and transl. F. E. Harmer (Cambridge, 1914). |
| *Wills* (W) | *Anglo-Saxon Wills*, ed. and transl. D. Whitelock (Cambridge, 1930). |

*British Academy Charter Volumes*

| | |
|---|---|
| *Abingdon* | *Charters of Abingdon Abbey, Parts 1 and 2*, ed. S. E. Kelly, British Academy Anglo-Saxon Charter Series, vols. 7 and 8 (Oxford, 2000). |
| *Bath and Wells* | *Charters of Bath and Wells*, ed. S. E. Kelly, British Academy Anglo-Saxon Charter Series, vol. 13 (Oxford, 2007). |
| *Burton* | *Charters of Burton Abbey*, ed. P. Sawyer, British Academy Anglo-Saxon Charter Series, vol. 2 (Oxford, 1979). |
| *Bury* | *Charters of Bury St Edmunds Abbey, with St Benet at Holme*, ed. K. A. Lowe and S. Foot, British Academy Anglo-Saxon Charter Series (forthcoming). |
| *Christ Church* | *Charters of Christ Church, Canterbury*, ed. N. Brooks and S. E. Kelly, British Academy Anglo-Saxon Charter Series, vol. 18 (Oxford, forthcoming). |
| *Malmesbury* | *Charters of Malmesbury Abbey*, ed. S. E. Kelly, British Academy Anglo-Saxon Charter Series, vol. 11 (Oxford, 2005). |
| *New Minster* | *Charters of the New Minster, Winchester*, ed. S. Miller, British Academy Anglo-Saxon Charter Series, vol. 9 (Oxford, 2001). |
| *Peterborough* | *Charters of Peterborough Abbey*, ed. S. E. Kelly, British Academy Anglo-Saxon Charter Series, vol. 14 (Oxford, 2009). |

| | |
|---|---|
| *Rochester* | *Charters of Rochester*, ed. A. Campbell, British Academy Anglo-Saxon Charter Series, vol. 1 (Oxford, 1973). |
| *Selsey* | *Charters of Selsey*, ed. S. E. Kelly, British Academy Anglo-Saxon Charter Series, vol. 6 (Oxford, 1998). |
| *Shaftesbury* | *Charters of Shaftesbury Abbey*, ed. S. E. Kelly, British Academy Anglo-Saxon Charter Series, vol. 5 (Oxford, 1996). |
| *Sherborne* | *Charters of Sherborne*, ed. M. A. O'Donovan, British Academy Anglo-Saxon Charter Series, vol. 3 (Oxford, 1988). |
| *St Albans* | *Charters of St Albans*, ed. J. Crick, British Academy Anglo-Saxon Charter Series, vol. 12 (Oxford, 2007). |
| *St Augustine's* | *Charters of St Augustine's Abbey, Canterbury and Minster-in-Thanet*, ed. S. E. Kelly, British Academy Anglo-Saxon Charter Series, vol. 4 (Oxford, 1995). |
| *St Paul's* | *Charters of St Paul's, London*, ed. S. E. Kelly, British Academy Anglo-Saxon Charter Series, vol. 10 (Oxford, 2004). |
| Keynes, *Facsimiles* | *Facsimiles of Anglo-Saxon Charters*, ed. S. Keynes, British Academy Anglo-Saxon Charter Series, Supplementary vol. I (Oxford, 1991). |

*General Abbreviations*

| | |
|---|---|
| *ANS* | *Anglo-Norman Studies*. |
| *ASC* | *Anglo-Saxon Chronicle* (see Note on the References). |
| *ASC* C | *The Anglo-Saxon Chronicle, a Collaborative Edition, vol. 5: MS C, a Semi-Diplomatic Edition with Introduction and Indices*, ed. K. O'Brien O'Keeffe (Cambridge, 2001). |
| *ASC* D | *The Anglo-Saxon Chronicle, a Collaborative Edition, vol. 6: MS D, a Semi-Diplomatic Edition with Introduction and Indices*, ed. G. P. Cubbin (Cambridge, 1996). |
| *ASC* E | *The Anglo-Saxon Chronicle, a Collaborative Edition, vol. 7: MS E, a Semi-Diplomatic Edition with Introduction and Indices*, ed. S. Irvine (Cambridge, 2004). |
| *ASC* F | *The Anglo-Saxon Chronicle, a Collaborative Edition, vol. 8: MS F, a Semi-Diplomatic Edition with Introduction and Indices*, ed. P. S. Baker (Cambridge, 2000). |
| *ASE* | *Anglo-Saxon England*. |
| *Asser* | *Asser's Life of King Alfred*, ed. W. H. Stevenson (Oxford, 1904). |
| B&T | *An Anglo-Saxon Dictionary*, ed. J. Bosworth and T. Northcote Toller, 2 vols. (Oxford, 1898), with supplementary vol. by A. Campbell (Oxford, 1921). |
| BAR | British Archaeological Reports. |
| Birch | *Cartularium Saxonicum: a Collection of Charters Relating to* |

| | |
|---|---|
| | *Anglo-Saxon History*, ed. W. de Gray Birch, 3 vols. (London, 1885–1893). |
| *Blackwell Encyclopaedia* | *The Blackwell Encyclopaedia of Anglo-Saxon England*, ed. M. Lapidge, J. Blair, S. Keynes and D. Scragg (Oxford, 1999). |
| *C&S* | *Councils and Synods with other Documents relating to the English Church, I: AD 871–1204*, ed. D. Whitelock, M. Brett and C. N. L. Brooke, 2 vols. (Oxford, 1981), I (Part 1). |
| *CR* | *Chronicon Abbatiæ Rameseiensis*, ed. W. D. Macray (London, 1886), Rolls Series 83; reference by chapter number. |
| CUL | Cambridge University Library. |
| *The Danelaw* | Hart, C. R., *The Danelaw* (London, 1992). |
| DB | Domesday Book, cited in translation from the Alecto Historical Edition, ed. A. Williams and G. H. Martin (first published London, 1992, issued by Penguin books, 2002). |
| *DOEC* | *Dictionary of Old English Corpus*, ed. A. DiPaolo Healey and others, Toronto University Centre for Medieval Studies (electronic resource, in progress). |
| EETS | Early English Text Society. |
| *EHD* I | *English Historical Documents, I: c. 500–1042*, ed. and transl. D. Whitelock, 2nd edn (London, 1979). |
| *EHR* | *English Historical Review*. |
| *EME* | *Early Medieval Europe*. |
| Keynes, *Atlas* | *An Atlas of Attestations in Anglo-Saxon Charters c. 670–1066*, ed. S. Keynes (Cambridge, 2002). |
| Keynes and Lapidge | *Alfred the Great: Asser's Life of King Alfred and Other Contemporary Sources*, ed. and transl. S. Keynes and M. Lapidge (London, 1983). |
| *Laws*, ed. Attenborough | *The Laws of the Earliest English Kings*, ed. and transl. F. L. Attenborough (Cambridge, 1922). |
| *Laws*, ed. Robertson | *The Laws of the Kings of England from Edmund to Henry I, Part 1, Edmund to Canute*, ed. and transl. A. J. Robertson (Cambridge, 1925). |
| *LE* | *Liber Eliensis*, ed. E. O. Blake, Camden Society, 3rd series 92 (London, 1962); reference by book number (in Roman) and chapter number (in Arabic). |
| *Lib* | *Libellus quorundam insignium operum beati Æthelwoldi episcopi* (followed by chapter number). An edition is forthcoming: S. Keynes and A. Kennedy, *Anglo-Saxon Ely: Records of Ely Abbey and its Benefactors in the Tenth and Eleventh Centuries.* |
| MGH | Monumenta Germaniae Historica. |
| P&M | F. Pollock and F. W. Maitland, *The History of English Law Before the Time of Edward I*, 2 vols., 2nd edn (Cambridge, 1911). |

| | |
|---|---|
| S | *Anglo-Saxon Charters: an Annotated List and Bibliography*, ed. P. H. Sawyer (London, 1968). An updated version is available at: www.trin.cam.ac.uk/chartwww/> |
| *TRE* | *Tempore Regis Eadwardi* (indicating the tenurial position during the reign of King Edward the Confessor). |
| *TRHS* | *Transactions of the Royal Historical Society.* |
| *Writs* | *Anglo-Saxon Writs*, ed. and transl. F. E. Harmer, 2nd edn (Manchester, 1989). |

*Counties*

| | |
|---|---|
| Beds. | Bedfordshire |
| Berks. | Berkshire |
| Bucks. | Buckinghamshire |
| Cambs. | Cambridgeshire |
| Dors. | Dorset |
| Ex | Essex |
| Glos. | Gloucestershire |
| Hants. | Hampshire |
| Herts. | Hertfordshire |
| Hfds. | Herefordshire |
| Hunts. | Huntingdonshire |
| Kt | Kent |
| Leics. | Leicestershire |
| Lincs. | Lincolnshire |
| Mx | Middlesex |
| Nfk | Norfolk |
| Northants. | Northamptonshire |
| Notts. | Nottinghamshire |
| Oxon. | Oxfordshire |
| Sfk | Suffolk |
| Shrops. | Shropshire |
| Som. | Somerset |
| Staffs. | Staffordshire |
| Sy | Surrey |
| Wilts. | Wiltshire |
| Worcs. | Worcestershire |
| Yorks. | Yorkshire |

# NOTE ON THE REFERENCES

All charters are identified in the apparatus by the number allocated in Sawyer's *Handlist* (S).[1] In addition, wills edited by Napier and Stevenson, Harmer, Whitelock, Robertson and Hart are identified by the abbreviation given in the List of Abbreviations above, followed where relevant by the number of the document within the edition. Wills which have already appeared in British Academy charter volumes are further identified by archive (see the List of Abbreviations) and number within the volume. In general, texts and translations follow the currently available British Academy editions;[2] otherwise, they follow the individual editions cited in the List of Abbreviations and in footnotes.[3]

The *Anglo-Saxon Chronicle* is cited according to the adjusted dating as printed by Whitelock in *EHD* I, and subsequently as *The Anglo-Saxon Chronicle: a Revised Translation*, ed. D. Whitelock with D. C. Douglas and S. I. Tucker (London, 1961). Where reference to a particular version is necessary, or the original text quoted, the relevant volume in *The Anglo-Saxon Chronicle, a Collaborative Edition* (general editors D. Dumville and S. Keynes) is cited as given in the List of Abbreviations.

Domesday Book is cited in translation from the Alecto Historical Edition, ed. A. Williams and G. H. Martin (first published London, 1992, issued by Penguin books, 2002); Great Domesday is abbreviated as I, and Little Domesday as II, followed by the folio number.

Anglo-Saxon laws are cited by code and clause from the editions by Attenborough and Robertson given in the List of Abbreviations.

1 See the List of Abbreviations above. W39 (*Peterborough* 27), which is post-Conquest, is not included by Sawyer: see D. A. E. Pelteret, *Catalogue of English Post-Conquest Vernacular Documents* (Woodbridge, 1990), no. 68.

2 Currently both texts and translations of vernacular wills may be found in volumes 8 (*Abingdon*); 10 (*St Paul's*); 12 (*St Albans*); 13 (*Bath*); 14 (*Peterborough*); they will be included in the forthcoming vol. 18 (*Christ Church*). Vol. 9 (*New Minster*) prints texts with detailed summaries. Vol. 2 (*Burton*) includes a translation of the will of Wulfric Spott (S1536/W17, *Burton* 29) in the Introduction (pp. xv–xix). Volumes 1 (*Rochester*) and 4 (*St Augustine's*) print texts only.

3 I have generally followed individual editorial practice in quoting Old English texts, although I have silently omitted emendation signs and have replaced Old English wynn with the letter *w*.

# INTRODUCTION

It seems to have been the fate of Anglo-Saxon vernacular wills to be valued by scholars as a resource, yet neglected as a genre worthy of study in its own right. *The History of English Law*, published in 1898, describes Anglo-Saxon will-making as 'ill-defined', warranting only a few pages which seem largely designed to determine that it was neither the Roman testament nor the legal instrument of the later medieval period.[1] Since that date, only two detailed studies of the full corpus have appeared.

The first, published in 1963, is the important and wide-ranging survey by Sheehan.[2] He considers the Anglo-Saxon will from the point of view of the legal historian, placing it in the context of the Roman testament, the Germanic tradition of inheritance and the developments of the twelfth and thirteenth centuries. He examines the relationship between the Anglo-Saxon will and the two forms of *post obitum* disposition defined primarily by German legal historians: the *post obit* gift (a gift to take effect after the donor's death) and the *verba novissima* (deathbed gift).[3] However, the strength of his survey is that it recognises the individuality of the insular will, focusing on its transitional nature between the Roman testament and the canonical will of the post-Conquest period.

The second detailed study of the corpus, carried out by Lowe, was designed to evaluate the reliability of the transmission of texts by examining scribal techniques.[4] This study has been crucial in establishing the overall corpus and examining its integrity. The majority of the wills survive only in later copies, mainly in cartularies of the twelfth to fourteenth centuries, with very few surviving as contemporary or near-contemporary manuscripts. Even fewer survive in both forms, but where they do, Lowe has compared the versions in order to identify the problems experienced by the later copyists as they sought to create a working text, and the strategies they adopted to overcome them.[5] Where vernacular wills also survive in Latin versions,

1 F. Pollock and F. W. Maitland, *The History of English Law Before the Time of Edward I*, 2 vols., 2nd edn (Cambridge, 1911), II, 314–23 (p. 321).

2 M. M. Sheehan, *The Will in Medieval England* (Toronto, 1963).

3 For discussion of these terms see Sheehan, *The Will*, pp. 24–38.

4 K. A. Lowe, 'The Anglo-Saxon Vernacular Will: Studies in Texts and their Transmission' (unpublished doctoral thesis, University of Cambridge, 1990).

5 K. A. Lowe, '"As fre as thowt"?: some medieval copies and translations of Old English wills', *English Manuscript Studies 1100–1700* 4 (1993), 1–23; K. A. Lowe, 'Two thirteenth-century cartularies from Bury St Edmunds: a study in textual transmission', *Neuphilologische Mitteilungen* 93 (1992), 293–301.

Lowe's comparison of the texts reveals modifications often made by scribes who were inclined to omit details irrelevant to their purpose.[6] Lowe's work on the corpus has also enabled her to identify key characteristics of the vernacular will, and to explore its competence as an instrument of bequest.[7]

What has so far been lacking is a detailed study of the vernacular will as a social document. This is the more surprising given the availability of scholarly editions and translations. Nineteenth-century editors included wills in their voluminous editions of Anglo-Saxon charters, which were complemented by the facsimile volumes of contemporary single-sheet manuscripts.[8] However, the social significance of the wills was increasingly recognised as they began to be published with a detailed critical apparatus among editions of vernacular documents. The first such edition was that of Napier and Stevenson who, in 1895, published two vernacular wills from the Crawford collection of Anglo-Saxon charters, with notes primarily focused on the identification of places and people and the clarification of Old English vocabulary.[9] This was followed in 1914 by Harmer's selection of vernacular documents ranging from the early-ninth to the mid-tenth centuries, which included a number of important wills, not least that of King Alfred.[10] Here the commentary is extended to include discussion of dialect, with wide cross-referencing to supporting historical material.

A milestone was reached with the publication, sixteen years later, of the edition and translation of thirty-nine vernacular wills by Whitelock, which established beyond question that these documents constitute a genre worthy of study in their own right.[11] Her commentary on the wills and detailed indexing not only gave access to a valuable historical source, but revealed the complexity of the kindred and tenurial relationships in tenth- and eleventh-century England. Hazeltine's preface to Whitelock's edition considers the legal status of the Anglo-Saxon will, stressing the oral nature of the dispositive act (with its roots in Germanic tradition) which was itself binding, and

6 K. A. Lowe, 'Latin versions of Old English wills', *Legal History* 20.1 (1999), 1–24.

7 K. A. Lowe, 'The nature and effect of the vernacular will', *Legal History* 19.1 (1998), 23–61.

8 *Cartularium Saxonicum: a Collection of Charters Relating to Anglo-Saxon History*, ed. W. De Gray Birch, 3 vols. (London, 1885–93); *Codex Diplomaticus Ævi Saxonici*, ed. J. Kemble, 6 vols. (London, 1839–48); *Diplomatarium Anglicum Ævi Saxonici: a Collection of English Charters from the Reign of King Æthelstan of Kent AD 605, to that of William the Conqueror*, ed. B. Thorpe (London, 1865); *Facsimiles of Ancient Charters in the British Museum*, ed. E. A. Bond, 4 vols. (London, 1873–78); *Facsimiles of Anglo-Saxon Manuscripts*, ed. W. B. Sanders, Ordnance Survey, 3 vols. (Southampton, 1878–84).

9 *The Crawford Collection of Early Documents and Charters*, ed. A. S. Napier and W. H. Stevenson (Oxford, 1895) [N&S].

10 *Select English Historical Documents of the Ninth and Tenth Centuries*, ed. F. E. Harmer (Cambridge, 1914) [*SEHD*].

11 *Anglo-Saxon Wills*, ed. D. Whitelock (Cambridge, 1930) [*Wills*].

for which the document was merely an evidentiary record.[12] Seen from the viewpoint of the modern will, which itself has dispositive power, the Anglo-Saxon will presents problems of definition for legal historians, as illustrated by the title of Hazeltine's preface: 'Comments on the writings *known as* Anglo-Saxon wills' (my italics).

Whitelock's collection was supplemented by the wide-ranging edition of vernacular charters published by Robertson in 1939, which added a further sixteen wills to the canon.[13] A small number of documents has been published in individual editions in recent years,[14] and the ongoing British Academy charter series places the wills in the context of individual archives, providing collated texts with updated commentary.[15] However, earlier collections are likely to remain the bed-rock of the scholarship of wills until an edition of the full corpus appears, and I am greatly indebted to their erudition.

As legal historians, Sheehan and Hazeltine wrestled with the legal concept of *post obitum* disposition in relation to Anglo-Saxon wills, but the texts have proved a valuable source for a range of historical studies. A considerable number of such studies feature in the apparatus of this book, but a few will be highlighted here, representing important themes in recent research.

One area in which wills have been used as evidence is the study of land transmission, particularly in relation to the strategy of aristocratic families. The work of Wareham, in particular, has demonstrated that inheritance strategies could be used as a means of consolidating kinship bonds and establishing alliances; a bequest of land to the church, for example, was linked to commemorative rituals which played an important role in family identity, cementing the social relationship between church and laity.[16] A study by Williams of the family of Ealdorman Ælfhere of Mercia has drawn on the will

12 H. D. Hazeltine, 'Comments on the writings known as Anglo-Saxon wills', in *Wills*, pp. vii–xl (pp. viii–ix).

13 *Anglo-Saxon Charters*, ed. A. J. Robertson (Cambridge, 1939) [*Charters*].

14 'A new edition of the will of Wulfgyth', ed. K. A. Lowe, *Notes and Queries* n.s., 36 (1989), 295–8; *The Will of Æthelgifu*, ed. D. Whitelock, with contributions by N. Ker and Lord Rennell, The Roxburghe Club (Oxford, 1968) [*Æthelgifu*]; 'The will of Eadwine of Caddington', in S. Keynes, 'A lost cartulary of St Albans Abbey', *ASE* 22 (1993), 253–79 (pp. 275–9); 'The will of Wulf', ed. S. Keynes, *Old English Newsletter* 26.3 (1993), 16–21; S1608 (the will of Oswulf and Leofrun) is edited by C. R. Hart, *The Early Charters of Eastern England* (Leicester, 1966), no. 133 (pp. 86–9) [*ECEE*].

15 For the currently available volumes in the British Academy series which include wills see p. xiv, n. 2.

16 A. Wareham, 'The Aristocracy of East Anglia *c.* 930–1154: a Study of Family, Land and Government' (unpublished doctoral thesis, University of Birmingham, 1992); A. Wareham, 'Saint Oswald's family and kin', in *St Oswald of Worcester: Life and Influence*, ed. N. Brooks and C. Cubitt (Leicester, 1996), pp. 46–53; A. Wareham, 'The transformation of kinship and family in late Anglo-Saxon England', *EME* 10.3 (2002), 375–94; A. Wareham, *Lords and Communities in Early Medieval East Anglia* (Woodbridge, 2005).

of his brother Ælfheah in order to reconstruct the land-base on which their power rested, and an analysis of the ninth-century wills of King Alfred and Ealdorman Alfred by Wormald has identified the importance of the bequest of land in 'the politics of aristocratic family property', drawing attention to the likelihood that similar strategies – however difficult to identify – may be assumed in other wills.[17] Wormald's important unpublished work on land tenure and inheritance practice as it relates to wills is summarised in Appendix 5.

A second area of study which has drawn on vernacular wills is the examination of the position of women in Anglo-Saxon society. Stafford gives a succinct account of the ideology of 'a golden Age for women pre 1066' as viewed through the eyes of scholars of the nineteenth and early twentieth centuries, who saw women's wills as evidence for their independence and autonomy in land-holding in pre-Conquest England.[18] However, she shows that, in fact, such apparent independence can be illusory: women emerge into the documentary record as widows, and their bequests were often influenced by fathers or husbands. Women were significant in family strategy as 'conduits of land', and could be subject to royal interest or predation.[19] Stafford has also suggested that the need to specify and protect widows' dower from such royal interference was one factor prompting will-making in the tenth and eleventh centuries.[20] In identifying the majority of female donors as widows, Crick has argued that their wills should be seen in two contexts: that of family strategy for the transmission of land across generations, and that of women's responsibility for family commemoration, which is a significant feature of a number of wills.[21] She has also explored the tension that existed in the relationship of a widow with the property of the conjugal unit and the way in which this is reflected in will-making, emphasising the need to see both men's and women's wills in the context of family strategy.[22] In a further study of the bequest of movable wealth, Crick has questioned the

17 A. Williams, '*Princeps Merciorum gentis*: the family, career and connections of Ælfhere, ealdorman of the Mercians', *ASE* 10 (1981), 143–72; P. Wormald, '*On þa wæpnedhealfe*: kingship and royal property from Æthelwulf to Edward the Elder', in *Edward the Elder*, ed. N. J. Higham and D. Hill (London, 2001), pp. 264–279 (p. 277).

18 P. Stafford, 'Women and the Norman Conquest', *TRHS* 6th s., 4 (1994), 221–49 (p. 223).

19 Stafford, 'Women and the Norman Conquest', p. 232.

20 P. Stafford, 'Women in Domesday', *Reading Medieval Studies* 15 (1989), 74–94 (p. 88).

21 J. Crick, 'Women, posthumous benefaction and family strategy in pre-Conquest England', *Journal of British Studies* 38 (1999), 399–422.

22 J. Crick, 'Men women and widows: widowhood in pre-Conquest England', in *Widowhood in Medieval and Early Modern Europe*, ed. S. Cavallo and L. Warner (Harlow, 1999), pp. 24–36 (pp. 31–2), and 'Women, posthumous benefaction', p. 418.

stereotypical association of men and women with particular types of material goods, perceiving that 'men and women bequeath in unexpected ways'.[23]

Because a number of wills refer to movable wealth, sometimes specifying individual items in detail, they have also provided a useful source for art historians and archaeologists. Items such as jewellery, swords and furnishings may be paralleled in manuscript illustrations or extant objects, and descriptions of clothing bequeathed by women have been used to complement other evidence in the reconstruction of contemporary costume.[24] Such bequests have contributed to the profile of a society with considerable disposable wealth.[25]

A final example of an area of research in which wills, as vernacular documents, have been used as evidence is the debate concerning the degree to which Anglo-Saxon lay society was a literate culture. Kelly, in particular, has argued that documentation played an important role in secular life, and that use of the vernacular may imply a degree of literacy – or at least, a recognition among the laity of the value of documentation.[26] This is supported by Lowe's study of the chirograph, which examines evidence for the production of multiple copies of documents, including vernacular wills, some indicating that one copy was held by the lay donor.[27] Keynes has placed wills in the context of royal administration, alongside law codes, writs and the recording of legal proceedings, as evidence for the use of the vernacular for written communication between the government and the localities.[28]

The purpose of this book is to redress the balance by placing vernacular wills centre-stage and drawing on the contemporary context in order to elucidate their social role. Two factors are identified as significant in stimulating written will-making by a wealthy elite in the ninth, tenth and eleventh centuries: one was the complexity of issues relating to the transmission of land held by royal charter (*bocland*), and the other was the influence of the Church. The wills themselves, composed for a contemporary audience rather than for

23 J. Crick, 'Women, wills and moveable wealth in pre-Conquest England', in *Gender and Material Culture from Prehistory to the Present*, ed. M. Donald and L. Hurcombe (London, 2000), pp. 17–37 (p. 28).

24 C. R. Dodwell, *Anglo-Saxon Art: a New Perspective* (New York, 1982); G. R. Owen-Crocker, *Dress in Anglo-Saxon England*, revised edn (Manchester, 2004); D. A. Hinton, *Gold and Gilt, Pots and Pins: Possessions and People in Medieval Britain* (Oxford, 2005).

25 R. Fleming, 'The new wealth, the new rich and the new political style in late Anglo-Saxon England', *ANS* 23 (2000), 1–32.

26 S. E. Kelly, 'Anglo-Saxon lay society and the written word', in *The Uses of Literacy in Early Medieval Europe*, ed. R. McKitterick (Cambridge, 1990), pp. 36–62.

27 K. A. Lowe, 'Lay literacy in Anglo-Saxon England and the development of the chirograph', in *Anglo-Saxon Manuscripts and their Heritage*, ed. P. Pulsiano and E. M. Traherne (Aldershot, 1992), pp. 161–204. For the chirograph see Chap. 1, pp. 31–3 below.

28 S. Keynes, 'Royal government and the written word in late Anglo-Saxon England', in *Uses of Literacy*, ed. McKitterick, pp. 226–57.

a distant posterity, are often frustratingly vague and allusive; however, by establishing patterns of bequeathing, and by drawing on other resources, it is possible to shed light on the factors which influenced the men and women who, in anticipation of their own death, sought to make appropriate provision for the disposal of their property.

Chapter 1 addresses the nature of the evidence, establishing the corpus on which the research has been based, and taking into account the integrity of texts and the factors which are likely to have influenced their transmission within the archives of religious houses. The uneven distribution of wills, both chronologically across the ninth to eleventh centuries and geographically, is placed in the context of the religious and social climate which stimulated their production, and the circumstances which caused them to be preserved. The characteristics of form, structure and language of the wills are described, and their relationship with other forms of contemporary documentation, both Latin and vernacular, is considered. In addition, supplementary evidence for wills and will-making during this period is surveyed and evaluated, drawing on a range of Latin and vernacular sources. The chapter concludes with a discussion of the contemporary status of the Anglo-Saxon will, and its relationship with the modern legal instrument.

Anglo-Saxon wills generally lack notarial information, and are silent on the process by which they were produced. Chapter 2 collates evidence from a range of sources, including other vernacular documents and Latin chronicles, in order to reconstruct the likely sequence of events, from the oral declaration by an individual, through the documentation of the dispositions to the confirmation of the will on the donor's death. The Church is a ubiquitous presence, and it is in the archives of religious houses that these wills have been preserved. Since the records of land transactions from this period can be deficient, it is often difficult to establish whether the dispositions of a given will were completed; individual examples demonstrate both the effectiveness of the written will, and the potential problems which might undermine it.

Chapters 3 and 4 are concerned with the bequest of land, which is a feature of all Anglo-Saxon wills. Chapter 3 deals with the way in which such bequests were embedded in, and often prompted by, the important religious, cultural and political developments of the time, and were part of a strategy of land management which was crucial to the affirmation of aristocratic identity. Such influences are most evident in the wills of those in the very highest echelons of Anglo-Saxon society – royalty, ealdormen and bishops – who appear elsewhere in the historical record and for whose will-making contextual evidence is more likely to be available. Nevertheless, the wills of thegns may also give some hint of the circumstances in which they were made. The wills of the Bury archive, for example, are embedded in the contemporary local network, reflecting the complex tenurial patterns of tenth- and eleventh-century East Anglia, in which the bequest of land played a part. On a grander scale, the impact of the catastrophic events of 1066 upon the wills of donors who were living on the day King Edward was alive and dead, and upon their beneficiaries, can be detected in Domesday Book; indeed, it was probably this disaster which prompted the making of one of the last surviving Anglo-Saxon vernacular wills.[29]

Chapter 4 is concerned with the role played by the bequest of land in family strategy. The evidence suggests that the majority of those whose wills are extant were of thegnly rank or higher; the chapter therefore begins by showing the significance of land in establishing thegnly status, and hence the importance attached to its transmission. It is demonstrated that men and women were likely to make their wills at different points in the life-cycle – men in the fullness of family and public life, women in widowhood; since their bequests of land reflect different influences, the wills of these two groups are considered separately. Nevertheless, the wills of laymen and -women alike reveal a tension between the impulse which prompted the transmission of land within a kin group, and that which prompted pious bequests of land to the Church. The wills of both groups suggest the implementation of family strategy to deploy land to maximum advantage in both worldly and spiritual terms.

Movable wealth features in roughly half of the corpus, alongside bequests of land. Chapter 5 shows how donors may bequeath stock, slaves, coin, weapons, clothing, furnishings and items of precious metal, commensurate with their wealth and status. Such bequests were particularly likely to be omitted during the process of textual transmission, perhaps contributing to the uneven distribution pattern which suggests that women and churchmen were likely to bequeath a wider range of items than laymen. Comparison with burial deposits from the fifth to eighth centuries shows that certain items had long-standing gendered social symbolism, but the gendered patterns which emerge in wills may also be the result of men and women making their dispositions at different stages of the life-cycle: for men, the bequest of movable wealth may have been an assertion of public status, while for women, as widows, such bequests may have marked a particularly important change in social role. Overall, however, movable wealth in wills is strongly associated with the noble persona shared by both men and women, lay and religious, whether as donors or beneficiaries. This chapter also shows that, although in some respects movable wealth and land are bequeathed in different ways, both may be seen interacting with the system of gift exchange which has been recognised as an important element in early medieval society.

Chapter 6 explores how the wills of the wealthy laity, with their often substantial bequests to the Church, are related to the influence of powerful churchmen and, in the tenth century, to a changing religious ethos, with its emphasis on monasticism. The conventional, formulaic phrases used in

29 The will of Ulf and Madselin, 1066x1069 (W39, *Peterborough* 27).

wills to express the impulse which prompted bequests to the Church give little insight into the spiritual benefits which donors hoped for in return for their investment. One of the most significant areas of research for the understanding of this aspect of the vernacular will is that concerned with early medieval attitudes to death. Fundamental studies are those by Paxton and Geary, which examine the ritualisation of dying, death and commemoration and the changing relationship between the living and the dead in Europe during this period.[30] McLaughlin has shown how the developing liturgy for commemorating the dead in France between *c.* 750 and *c.* 1100 reflects the association between the laity and 'liturgical communities', and offers a valuable perspective on the relationship between the church and laity as it appears in Anglo-Saxon wills.[31] Whereas these studies are primarily concerned with Continental developments, that by Thompson focuses specifically on late Anglo-Saxon England, drawing on the evidence of diverse sources to examine the rituals associated with dying and death and placing them in the context of contemporary thought.[32] Medieval will-making in general has been related to the concept of the good death, which allowed the individual the opportunity to come to terms with both God and man before the end approached;[33] Thompson places particular emphasis on the importance of the concept of 'dying with decency' in later Anglo-Saxon England.[34] In this chapter, wills are considered in the context of the patronage of a prestigious religious house which, at least by the tenth century, had become a significant aspect of family identity among the Anglo-Saxon aristocracy. Those making bequests might expect to be included in the rituals commemorating benefactors which had developed within the prayer-cycle of celibate communities, and might also hope to obtain burial close to the relics of saints. Bequests of land were also made to the local or estate churches which had become intrinsic to thegnly status. In some cases laymen and -women had a proprietary interest in both church and clergy. Although little is known of the religious observance practised in such churches, there is some evidence that donors may again have expected commemoration as benefactors. The chapter concludes by considering the extent to which the pious bequests of the laity should be interpreted as a form of institutional piety, resulting from the production of wills under the aegis of the Church, or as a reflection of the personal piety of individual donors.

30 F. S. Paxton, *Christianising Death: the Creation of a Ritual Process in Early Medieval Europe* (Ithaca NY, 1990); P. J. Geary, *Living with the Dead in the Middle Ages* (Ithaca NY, 1994).

31 M. McLaughlin, *Consorting with Saints: Prayer for the Dead in Early Medieval France* (Ithaca NY, 1994), p. 21.

32 V. Thompson, *Dying and Death in Later Anglo-Saxon England* (Woodbridge, 2004).

33 P. Binski, *Medieval Death* (London, 1996), pp. 33–47.

34 Thompson, *Dying and Death*, Chap. 3.

One potentially fruitful area, the examination of Anglo-Saxon vernacular wills in the context of the Continental evidence, has not been pursued in this study for reasons summarised by Reuter in a paper which focused on the dispersal of movable wealth in the early medieval period:[35]

> The difficulty here is that there is no comprehensive survey of the wills which have survived from the early Middle Ages. ... There are perhaps a dozen Merovingian wills, which have been listed and discussed in a fine article by Ulrich Nonn, and a very small number of will-like documents from early medieval Italy and Spain ... Birgit Kasten and Goswin Spreckelmeyer have identified thirteen texts from the eighth and ninth centuries. But there is – to my knowledge – no study at all of surviving testaments from the post-Carolingian Frankish world, and at present one is reduced to impressionistic guesswork. For example, wills do not appear to have been at all prominent in the deposits of documents surviving from east and west Francia in the post-Carolingian era, but the absence of any survey makes it hard to say how rare they are. Emily Tabuteau's very thorough study of eleventh-century Norman law makes no mention of either wills or testaments, though she has extensive discussions of donations *post obitum.* The highly document-based monographs by Barbara Rosenwein on Cluny's lands, by Stephen White on donations to monasteries in western France and by Constance Bouchard on the nobility and the Burgundian church also do not mention wills. Testaments from the Ottonian era are very rare.[36]

As far as I am aware, the position remains unchanged, making access to Continental wills difficult. However, wherever possible, attention has been paid here to comparative documents, facilitated by two particularly valuable studies of individual ninth-century wills: that of the Frankish widow Erkanfrida, and that of Count Eberhard of Friuli and his wife Gisela.[37] In

35 T. Reuter, '"You can't take it with you": testaments, hoards and moveable wealth in Europe, 600–1100', in *Treasure in the Medieval West*, ed. E. Tyler (York, 2000), pp. 11–24 (pp. 20–1).

36 The studies referred to here are as follows: U. Nonn, 'Merowingische Testamente: Studien zum Fortleben einer römischen Urkundenform im Frankreich', *Archiv für Diplomatik* 18 (1972), 1–129; B. Kasten, 'Erbrechtliche Verfügungen des 8. und 9. Jahrhunderts', *Zeitschrift der Savigny-Stiftung für Rechtsgeschichte, germanistische Abteilung* 107 (1990), 236–338; G. Spreckelmeyer, 'Zur rechtlichen Funktion frühmittelalterlicher Testamente', in *Recht und Schrift im Mittelalter*, ed. P. Classen (Sigmaringen, 1977), pp. 91–113; E. Z. Tabuteau, *Transfers of Property in Eleventh-Century Norman Law* (Chapel Hill NC, 1988); B. Rosenwein, *To be the Neighbor of St Peter: the Social Meaning of Cluny's Property, 909–1049* (Ithaca NY, 1989); S. D. White, *Custom, Kinship and Gifts to Saints: the* Laudatio Parentum *in Western France, 1050–1150* (Chapel Hill NC, 1989); C. Bouchard, *Sword, Miter and Cloister: Nobility and the Church in Burgundy, 980–1198* (Ithaca NY, 1987). A further study which might be included here is M. Bull, *Knightly Piety and the Lay Response to the First Crusade: the Limousin and Gascony, c. 970-c. 1130* (Oxford, 1993).

37 J. Nelson, 'The wary widow', in *Property and Power in the Early Middle Ages*, ed. W. Davies and P. Fouracre (Cambridge, 1995), pp. 82–113, including an edition and translation of

addition, where parallels seem useful, reference has been made to a number of studies of will-making in later medieval Europe.

Since this book is concerned with the social rather than the legal aspect of Anglo-Saxon vernacular wills, I have sought to avoid undue complexity of terminology by placing technical terms and definitions in footnotes. I have retained the familiar term 'will' to refer to any document in which the completion of the gift or gifts is intended to be deferred until the death of the donor. However, as is shown in detail in Chapter 1, the genus 'will' includes three distinct species: the single-gift bequest (a gift to a single beneficiary to take effect on the death of the donor);[38] the multi-gift will, making a number of bequests to multiple beneficiaries, also to take effect on the death of the donor;[39] and the bequest-agreement, in which some form of arrangement is made by donor and beneficiary, acknowledging the beneficiary's claim on an estate while allowing the donor to retain a life interest in the land, with perhaps further designated lives, until such time as reversion to the beneficiary will take effect.[40] These terms (multi-gift will, single-gift bequest and bequest-agreement) will be used throughout where the distinction between the different types of document is germane to the discussion. The term *post obitum* distinguishes a gift intended to be completed after a donor's death from an *inter vivos* gift which is intended to take immediate effect. I have used the verb 'bequeath' in relation to both movable wealth and land.[41] Finally, in order to avoid overtones of the later testament which seem inappropriate here, I have avoided the word 'testator', preferring the more general term 'donor'.

the text; C. La Rocca and L. Provero, 'The dead and their gifts: the will of Count Eberhard of Friuli, and his wife, Gisela, daughter of Louis the Pious (863–64)', in *Rituals of Power from Late Antiquity to the Early Middle Ages*, ed. F. Theuws and J. L. Nelson (Leiden, 2000), pp. 225–80. Additional valuable studies: P. J. Geary, *Aristocracy in Provence: The Rhône Basin at the Dawn of the Carolingian Age* (Stuttgart, 1985); M. Innes, 'Charlemagne's will: piety, politics and the imperial succession', *EHR* 112 (1997), 833–55. Einhard's version of Charlemagne's will is readily available in the English translation by L. Thorpe, *Einhard and Notker the Stammerer: Two Lives of Charlemagne* (Harmondsworth, 1969), Book 5.

38 The equivalent of the *post obit* gift: Sheehan, *The Will*, p. 20. See Chap. 1, pp. 33–5 below for the single-gift bequest.

39 The term *cwide* is used by Sheehan to distinguish this form: *The Will*, pp. 39–47. Chap. 1, p. 27 below.

40 See Lowe, 'Nature and effect', p. 26 for the legal terms *precaria oblata* and *precaria remuneratoria*, and Chap. 1, pp. 24–36 below for further detail.

41 The verb 'devise' is the technically accurate term for the bequest of land.

# CHAPTER ONE

# Anglo-Saxon written wills: the nature of the evidence

The sixty-eight documents which make up the corpus of Anglo-Saxon vernacular wills on which this book is based survive in the archives of the religious houses which, almost invariably, were named as beneficiaries.[1] However, extant wills are unevenly distributed both chronologically and across archives, as Map 1 and Table 1 show, with none recorded further north than Burton-upon-Trent (Staffs.).[2] Ninth-century wills survive largely in the archive of Christ Church, Canterbury, dating between approximately 805 and 889;[3] six wills are extant, five as single sheet contemporary manuscripts, and one in a thirteenth-century cartulary associated with Christ Church.[4] In addition to this Christ Church group, a further three archives hold a single will: Rochester, and the New and Old Minsters at Winchester.[5] The documents can usually only be dated within broad parameters based on internal evidence or that of other sources, since notarial information is generally absent.[6] For example, the single-gift bequest of land at Eythorne (Kt) by the reeve Æthelnoth and his wife, Gænburg, can be dated to the pontificate of Archbishop

1 The exception is S1200/H7, *Christ Church* 90 from the archive of Christ Church, Canterbury, recording a bequest-agreement concerning land in which Christ Church had an interest: N. Brooks, *The Early History of the Church of Canterbury* (Leicester, 1984), pp. 147–8.

2 This issue is discussed by R. Fleming, *Kings and Lords in Conquest England* (Cambridge, 1991), pp. 18–20, in the context of the full range of Anglo-Saxon charters.

3 The earliest is the will of Æthelnoth and Gænburg (S1500/R3, *Christ Church* 39A, 805x824), and the latest that of Ealdorman Alfred (S1508/H10, *Christ Church* 96, 871x889).

4 Single sheets: S1500/R3, *Christ Church* 39A, 805x832; S1482/H2, *Christ Church* 70, 833x839; S1510/R6, *Christ Church* 78, 845x853; S1200/H7, *Christ Church* 90, 867x870; S1508/H10, *Christ Church* 96, 871x889. S1202/H8, *Christ Church* 95, *c.* 871, copied into London, Lambeth Palace MS 1212: *Medieval Cartularies of Great Britain: a Short Catalogue*, ed. G. R. C. Davis (London, 1958), no. 159.

5 Rochester: S1514/R9, *Rochester* 23, *c.* 855 (twelfth-century *Textus Roffensis*: *Cartularies*, ed. Davis, no. 817); Winchester, New Minster: S1507/H11, *New Minster* 1, 873x888 (the will of King Alfred, copied into the eleventh-century *Liber Vitae*: BL Stowe 944); Winchester, Old Minster: S1513/R17, *c.* 900 (copied into the twelfth-century *Codex Wintoniensis*: *Cartularies*, ed. Davis, no. 1042).

6 The exception is a single sheet from Westminster dated 998: S1522/N&S9 (Keynes, *Facsimiles*, no. 14).

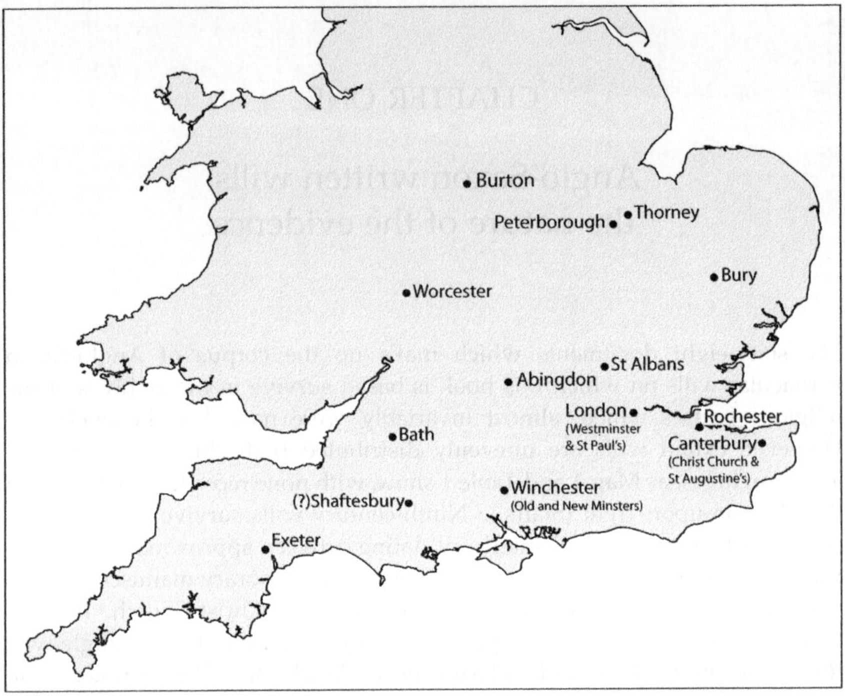


Map 1. The geographical distribution of Anglo-Saxon vernacular wills by archive (drawn by C. Fern)

Wulfred (805–832), who is named as beneficiary; however, the *terminus ante quem* may be refined to 824, when a charter records Wulfred's exchange of land at Eythorne.[7] The general lack of precision makes the chronology of the texts problematic; the will of Ceolwynn, for instance, copied into the twelfth-century *Codex Wintoniensis*, gives few clues, leading the editor to hazard an approximate date of *c*. 900.[8]

It is possible that some evidence of vernacular will-making may have been lost in the destruction of the archives of religious houses at the time of the Viking incursions, and the destruction of the Christ Church archive itself in 798 (in the course of the political upheaval which followed the death of King Offa in 796).[9] As the evidence stands, however, it seems likely that lay will-

7 S1266.

8 S1513/R17; *Charters*, p. 291.

9 P. Wormald, 'The ninth century', in *The Anglo-Saxons*, ed. J. Campbell (London, 1982), pp. 132–59, surveying the evidence for the Viking raids on pp. 144–5, and evaluating the disruption to the church on pp. 147–8. For the Vikings in Kent, see Brooks, *Early History*, p. 150. For changes in diocesan organisation in eastern England see J. Barrow, 'Survival and mutation: ecclesiastical institutions in the Danelaw in the ninth and tenth centuries',

**Table 1.** The numerical distribution of Anglo-Saxon vernacular wills by archive

| **Archive** | **wills dated before *c.* 900** | **dating margins** | **wills dated 924–*c.* 1070** | **dating margins** |
|---|---|---|---|---|
| Abingdon | | | 1 | 1003x1004 |
| Bath | | | 1 | 984x1016 |
| Burton | | | 1 | 1002x1004 |
| Bury | | | 20 | 942x1070 |
| *Canterbury:* | | | | |
| St Augustine's | | | 1 | 985x1006 |
| Christ Church | 6 | 805x889 | 8 | 958x1070 |
| Exeter | | | 1 | 1011x1015 |
| *London:* | | | | |
| St Paul's | | | 1 | *c.* 1000 |
| Westminster | | | 2 | 975x1016 |
| Peterborough | | | 1 | 1066x1069 |
| Rochester | 1 | *c.* 855 | 1 | 975x987 |
| ?Shaftesbury | | | 1 | *c.* 950 |
| St Albans | | | 4 | 956x1066 |
| Thorney | | | 1 | 1017x1035 |
| *Winchester:* | | | | |
| New Minster | 1 | ?896x899 | 8 | 932x*c.* 987 |
| Old Minster | 1 | *c.* 900 | 6 | 931x980 |
| Worcester | | | 1 | *c.* 1000 |

making in ninth-century Kent was associated with the energetic fund-raising of successive archbishops, particularly Wulfred (805–32) and Ceolnoth (833–70), whose names head the witness lists of wills from the archive at Christ Church at a time when royal patronage had virtually ceased to exist.[10] It is also likely that the documents were produced by the Christ Church scriptorium; the study by Brooks of a substantial number of contemporary single-sheet manuscripts preserved in this archive has identified the work of individual scribes, which includes two wills.[11] The absence of comparable evidence from

in *Cultures in Conflict: Scandinavian Settlement in England in the Ninth and Tenth Centuries* (Turnhout, 2000), ed. D. Hadley and J. D. Richards, pp. 155–76 (pp. 156–61).

10 On the context for their encouragement of lay patronage, see Brooks, *Early History*, pp. 132–42 for Wulfred and 146–7 for Ceolnoth. Wulfred witnesses S1500/R3, *Christ Church* 39A; Ceolnoth witnesses S1482/H2, S1510/R6 and S1200/H7 (*Christ Church* 70, 78, 90); their successor Æthelred (870–88) witnesses S1202/H8 and S1508/H10 (*Christ Church* 95, 96).

11 Brooks, *Early History*, pp. 170–4 on the scriptorium, and 359–62, nn. 67–94 on the manuscripts. The wills in question are S1482/H2, *Christ Church* 70, main text (Scribe 3) and S1510/R6, *Christ Church* 78 (Scribe 5).

other archives makes it difficult to demonstrate that this was general practice, but it seems the likeliest scenario.[12]

The Christ Church archive also provides important evidence that land bequeathed to the church had been acquired from the king by the donor – that is to say, it was bookland, over which the holder had the right of free disposition.[13] In some cases, the vernacular will and the royal charter granting the land which it bequeaths are physically related. For example, the bequest of the property to Christ Church by the reeve Æthelnoth and his wife is written on the same parchment as a copy of King Cuthred's charter of donation, made between 805 and 807, which grants land at Eythorne (Kt), the subject of the bequest, to Æthelnoth.[14] Both Latin grant and vernacular single-gift bequest are written in the same hand. Because the bequest cannot be dated precisely, it is difficult to know whether it is contemporary with the grant, or whether the original royal charter may have been copied for the purpose of adding the bequest.[15] A royal charter and the vernacular bequest bequeathing the land which it grants might also exist separately, as in the case of a charter of King Æthelwulf dated 845, granting land near Canterbury to his reeve, Badanoth Beotting, who, in his vernacular bequest, ascribes the origin of the property in question to the king;[16] both documents survive as contemporary single sheet manuscripts, and significantly – although existing separately – were written in the same hand, that of a scribe active at Christ Church in the middle years of the ninth century.[17] A similar association between royal charters and the bequest of land is suggested by the preservation of two wills in the twelfth-century *Textus Roffensis*, each of which is copied immediately following the relevant royal charter: one, the will of Dunn, is in the vernacular, while the other, that of Swithhun, is in Latin.[18]

12 The process of will-making is discussed in Chap. 2 below.

13 An admirably succinct account of the complex issue of land tenure in Anglo-Saxon England, including bookland, is given by A. Williams, 'Land tenure', *Blackwell Encyclopaedia*, pp. 277–8.

14 S1500/R3, *Christ Church* 39A, 803x824; S41. The Latin bequest of Dunwald (S1182/*EHD* I, no. 72, *St Augustine's* 12, 762) states that it was added to the royal charter.

15 The relationship between S41 and S1500/R3 is discussed in *Christ Church*, nos. 39 and 39A. See Keynes, *Facsimiles*, no. 18, p. 6 and S. Keynes, *The Diplomas of King Æthelred 'the Unready' 978–1016* (Cambridge, 1980), p. 121, n. 123 for the possible recopying of a charter in relation to a will (S1492/N&S10).

16 S296; S1510/R6, *Christ Church* 78 (845x853).

17 Identified as Scribe 5 by Brooks, *Early History*, p. 361, n. 70; A. Campbell, 'An Old English will', *Journal of English and Germanic Philology* 37 (1938), 133–52 (pp. 135–6). A tenth-century will (S1533/R26) which survives as a single sheet was at some point stitched to its related charter, S416: Lowe, 'Vernacular Will', p. 11.

18 The bequest of Dunn: S1514/R9, *c.* 855; related Latin charter: S315/*EHD* I, no. 89, 855 (both edited as *Rochester*, 23). The opening words of the bequest, *þas bōc* (this title-deed), seems also to imply that the charter and bequest were written on the same parchment, which Dunn had given to his wife. He stipulates at the end of the bequest that both *bōc*

There is a significant gap in the evidence at the turn of the tenth century. Apart from the uncertainly dated will of Ceolwynn, mentioned above,[19] and that of King Alfred which may date to the 890s, there are no extant wills between that of Ealdorman Alfred (871x889), and that of Wulfgar (931x939).[20] Given the association between the acquisition of land by royal charter and its bequest to the Church, the absence of wills at this juncture may be seen in the context of the general dearth of charters from the reigns of Alfred (871–899) and Edward the Elder (899–924), the reason for which has been much debated.[21] However, with the renewal of royal grants under King Æthelstan (924–939), possibly as the result of increasing political stability, a new sequence of wills begins. Although the origin of the estates bequeathed can only rarely be identified, there seems little doubt that wills continue to be concerned with acquired land, even if that acquisition took place in a previous generation; the first will in the new sequence, that of Wulfgar, bequeaths to the holy foundation at Kintbury (Berks.) land at Inkpen (also Berks.) which had first been acquired by his grandfather, Wulfhere (*þe hit ærest begeat*).[22]

The documents from the mid-tenth century to the Conquest are preserved in a wider range of archives, largely associated with houses reformed in the course of the tenth-century monastic revival.[23] This factor may contribute to the absence of evidence for written wills further north than Burton-upon-Trent

and *cwide* (will) should be kept at Rochester. The Latin will of Swithhun and related charter are edited as S157, *Rochester* 16.

19 N. 8.

20 S1508/H10, *Christ Church* 96 is dated on the basis of the accession of King Alfred, who is mentioned in the will, in 871, and the death of Archbishop Æthelred, who witnesses the will, in 889. S1533/R26 is dated on the basis of a royal charter (S416, 931) granting to Wulfgar land which features in the will, and his probable signature as ealdorman in 939 (*Charters*, p. 307). For King Alfred's will see Chap. 3 below.

21 For reviews of this topic, see Wormald, 'Kingship and royal property', pp. 274–6; S. Keynes, 'Edward, King of the Anglo-Saxons', in *Edward the Elder*, ed. Higham and Hill, pp. 40–66 (pp. 50–6); S. Keynes, 'England *c.* 900–1066', in *The New Cambridge Medieval History III: c. 900-c. 1024*, ed. T. Reuter (Cambridge, 1999), pp. 456–84 (pp. 465–6); D. Dumville, *Wessex and England from Alfred to Edgar: Six Essays on Political, Cultural and Ecclesiastical Revival* (Woodbridge, 1992), pp. 151–3; S. Keynes, 'The power of the written word: Alfredian England 871–899, in *Alfred the Great: Papers from the Eleventh-Centenary Conferences*, ed. T. Reuter (Aldershot, 2003), pp. 175–97 (pp. 191–2).

22 S1533/R26 (S379, 416). Other tenth- and eleventh-century wills bequeathing land held by royal charter: S1526/W1(S483); S1512/W7 (S571); S1484/W8 (S737, S738); S1485/W9 (S462, S585); S1505/W12 (S865); S1487/W13 (S794); S1494/W14 (S703); S1536/W17, *Burton* 29 (S886, and ?S577, *Burton* 11); S1492/N&S10 (S890). Four New Minster bequests (*New Minster*, 11, 14, 16, 21) are probably spurious, but each is related to an acceptable royal charter: S1509/R27 (S635); S1418/R28 (S505); S1419/R29 (S526); S1496/W6 (S536) (see *New Minster*, pp. xlvii-li). Æthelric of Bocking bequeaths land acquired by his father (S1501/W16[1], *Christ Church* 136), although no charter survives.

23 Exceptions: S1539/W3, possibly associated with the Shaftesbury archive, for which links with the reform are uncertain (see *Shaftesbury*, p. xvi, n. 17; S. Foot, *Veiled Women*, 2 vols. (Aldershot, 2000), II, 173–4); S1495/W22, *St Paul's* 22 and S1511/W11, *Rochester* 35 are

(Staffs.), a house which was established by Wulfric Spott, and endowed in his will dated 1002x1004.[24] The distribution across the archives is uneven (see Table One above); while most preserve one or two wills, and Christ Church, the Old and New Minsters at Winchester and St Albans a handful each, Bury St Edmunds preserves twenty. There is good reason to believe that a good deal of evidence has been lost. It is clear that, at least by the twelfth century, documents from the Anglo-Saxon period were in a state of decay in some archives – the archivist of Ramsey is particularly voluble on the subject – and are likely to have been discarded through illegibility, or perhaps irrelevance if a religious house had no interest in the land in question;[25] the Worcester monk Hemming describes Bishop Wulfstan (1062–1095, later St Wulfstan) sorting through early documents.[26] Although among the religious houses of eastern England only Bury has preserved a substantial number of wills from its re-founding at the beginning of the eleventh century, the evidence of Ramsey and Ely, considered below, suggests that more such documents may once have existed at other houses, such as Thorney, Crowland and Peterborough.

Various circumstances are likely to have influenced the survival of vernacular wills. They may have been preserved in the context of dispute, actual or potential. Abingdon, for example, preserves only the will of Archbishop Ælfric, 1003x1004, possibly because it was used in a late eleventh century dispute;[27] yet the Abingdon Chronicle contains a number of references to grants of property which may have been made in the form of vernacular wills.[28] A further reason for survival is that, as has been suggested above, some single-gift bequests may have been written on the same parchment as the royal charter donating the land in question, and were copied into cartularies in the course of recording the more significant document.[29] Thirdly, the

both from the archives of houses served by secular canons (see F. Barlow, *The English Church 1000–1066* (London, 1963), pp. 221–2, 219–20).

24 S1536/W17/*Burton* 29. Dumville, *Wessex and England*, pp. 31–7.

25 See p. 38 below.

26 *omnia antiquorum priuilegia et testamenta*: St Wulfstan's review of the Worcester archive is described by F. Tinti, *Sustaining Belief: the Church of Worcester from c. 870 to c. 1100* (Farnham, 2010), pp. 125–37 (quotation at p. 136, n. 164). The word *testamentum* was in general used to refer to any written document: Sheehan, *The Will*, p. 9.

27 S1488/W18, *Abingdon* 133; *Abingdon*, part 2, p. 520. Other wills linked to disputes are the wills of Brihtric and Ælfswith, S1511/W11, *Rochester* 35; Æthelric, S1471/R101, *Christ Church* 170 (see Brooks, *Early History*, pp. 147–8, 302–303 for issues surrounding the estate at Chart, Kent); Æthelgifu, S1497/*St Albans* 7 (the will recounts a dispute which had already taken place, and OE and Latin summaries survive in addition to the single sheet; Lowe, 'Latin versions', pp. 10–15).

28 *Abingdon*, part 2, Appendix I, pp. 579–83 and pp. xlix-l, on selective archiving and the vicissitudes to which muniments were vulnerable. See also *St Augustine's*, no. 38/S1502 and Appendix I, pp. 183–7, nos. iii, vii, viii, ix.

29 Possible examples are S1514/R9, *Rochester* 23; S1512/W7 (Old Minster, Winchester).

compilers of post-Conquest cartularies seeking to establish the pre-Conquest endowment and standing of their houses may have chosen to include wills of prestigious patrons; of the eight wills copied into the twelfth-century *Codex Wintoniensis*, for example, two are those of royal personages, and three were made by ealdormen.[30] Finally, the survival of twenty wills in the thirteenth-century Sacrist's Register from Bury seems to have been, at least in part, the result of particularly enthusiastic archiving.[31] Worcester, with its run of charters from *c.* 700, including vernacular leases, remains an anomaly: apart from the vernacular multi-gift will of Wulfgeat, which survives as a single-sheet and includes a bequest to the abbey of a brewing of malt,[32] the only evidence of interest in the documentation of bequests comes from five assorted texts preserved in the eleventh-century cartularies.[33] Both cartularies seem to have been compiled in response to specific circumstances. The earlier, known as the *Liber Wigorniensis*, dates to the pontificate of Archbishop Wulfstan (1002–1006), who held the bishopric of Worcester in plurality with the see of York; it may have been compiled in relation to the translation of the remains of St Oswald to the monastic church of St Mary *c.* 1002.[34] The

30 The ætheling Æthelstan (S1503/W20, *Christ Church* 142: two copies, in addition to the two surviving single-sheet versions); Ælfgifu, widow of King Eadwig (S1484/W8); ealdormen Ælfheah and Æthelwold (S1485/W9, S1504/H20), and Wulfgar, who probably became an ealdorman (S1533/R26: *Charters*, p. 307). See also A. R. Rumble, 'The purposes of the *Codex Wintoniensis*', *ANS* 4 (1981), 153–67.

31 Cambridge University Library MS Ff. 2.33; S. Foot, personal comment, and see *Bury* (forthcoming). For the sacrist William of Hoo, the likely compiler of this register, see R. M. Thomson, *The Archives of the Abbey of Bury St Edmunds* (Woodbridge, 1980), pp. 19–20, and no. 1296, pp. 148–9, for details of its contents.

32 S1534/W19.

33 BL Cotton Tiberius A. xiii. These texts are discussed below, as additional evidence for written bequest. They are: a dubious Latin bequest of King Offa (S146/*EHD* I, no. 78); an equally dubious burial payment by Wihburg (S1227); a Latin reference to an oral will-making in the context of a dispute (S1187/*EHD* I, no. 81); a Latin account of a death-bed will, possibly spurious (S1408); and a vernacular account of a dispute which may refer to a written will (S1458/R41). S1232/R113 may refer to a bequest-agreement, but in its present form it takes the form of an *inter vivos* grant: see *Charters*, p. 461; A. Williams, 'The spoliation of Worcester', *ANS* 19 (1996), 383–408 (pp. 386–7). For a succinct account of the Worcester sources, see J. Barrow, 'The chronology of forgery production at Worcester from *c.* 1000 to the early twelfth century', in *St Wulfstan and his World*, ed. J. Barrow and N. P. Brooks (Aldershot, 2005), pp. 105–122 (pp. 114–15); F. Tinti, 'From episcopal conception to monastic compilation: Hemming's Cartulary in context', *EME* 11.3 (2002), 233–61 (pp. 234–6). See also N.R. Ker, 'Hemming's cartulary: a description of the two Worcester cartularies in Cotton Tiberius A. XIII', in *Studies in Medieval History presented to F. M. Powicke*, ed. R. W. Hunt, W. A. Pantin and R. W. Southern (Oxford, 1948), pp. 49–75, reprinted in *Books, Collectors and Libraries: Studies in the Medieval Heritage*, ed. A. G. Watson (London, 1985), pp. 31–59.

34 Barrow, 'Forgery', p. 121; Tinti, 'Hemming's Cartulary', p. 235. The compilation of the *Liber Wigorniensis* is analysed by S. Baxter, 'Archbishop Wulfstan and the administration of God's property', in *Wulfstan, Archbishop of York: the Proceedings of the Second Alcuin*

second, dating to the later eleventh century and associated with the monk Hemming, seems to have been an attempt to establish the church's tenurial rights in the face of recent land appropriation by both lay and ecclesiastical lords, perhaps compiled in the context of the appointment of a new Norman bishop following the death of Bishop Wulfstan II in 1095.[35] Both cartularies preserve vernacular leases which record agreements between church and tenant similar to those found in bequest-agreements, but with the emphasis on the church's retention of control over the land, rather than the donor's.[36] If the Worcester archive included vernacular wills other than that of Wulfgeat among its *priuilegia et testamenta*,[37] the preservation or translation of such documents was apparently not regarded as significant for the purpose of the compilers in establishing title to land.

Twenty-two wills survive in manuscripts written before 1066.[38] However, the complexity of transmission is illustrated by the fact that a number of these cannot be taken at face value as records made at the time of the original transaction.[39] Some were copied in the pre-Conquest period, as in the case of the will of King Alfred, which was copied into the *Liber Vitæ* of the New Minster, Winchester, *c.* 1031.[40] The wills of the sisters Æthelflæd and Ælfflæd, made at least ten years apart, were written on the same parchment in the same hand of the early eleventh century, indicating that the earlier text, at least, is a later copy.[41] The will of Wulfric, preceded on a single sheet by King Æthelred's confirmation charter, is a late eleventh century copy.[42]

*Conference*, ed. M. Townend (Turnhout, 2004), pp. 161–205 (pp. 165–76); Tinti, *Sustaining Belief*, pp. 85–125.

35 Barrow, 'Forgery', p. 121; Tinti, 'Hemming's Cartulary', pp. 257–61. The compilation of Hemming's Cartulary is analysed by Tinti, *Sustaining Belief*, pp. 136–47.

36 For contractual elements in bequests of land see pp. 35–6 below. Kelly comments on the significance of perspective in the relationship between leases and gifts to the church ('Anglo-Saxon lay society', p. 48, n. 42). For the system of leasing at Worcester see V. King, 'St Oswald's tenants', in *St Oswald*, ed. Brooks and Cubitt, pp. 100–116 (pp. 100–103, 113–16); Tinti, *Sustaining Belief*, pp. 11–12.

37 See n. 26 above.

38 See Appendix 1A.

39 This section is indebted to the work of Lowe, particularly the catalogue of vernacular wills in the Appendix to her article, 'Nature and effect' and the analysis of manuscripts in her 'Vernacular Will', Chap. 1.

40 S1507/H11, *New Minster* 1.

41 S1494/W14, 962x991; S1486/W15, 1000x1002. Palaeographical evidence also suggests that the will of Leofwine (S1522/N&S9), dated 998, was copied in the mid-eleventh century: Keynes, *Facsimiles*, no. 14, p. 6. Other possible pre-conquest copies are S1539/W3, S1501/W13 and S1533/R26 (Lowe, '"As fre as thowt"?', p. 2, n. 4, and Lowe, 'Vernacular Will', pp. 12, 22–3); S1492/N&S10 (Keynes, *Facsimiles*, no. 18, p. 6 and Keynes, *Diplomas*, p. 121, n. 123; S1497/*St Albans* 7 (the evidence is surveyed by Crick, *St Albans*, pp. 152–3).The evidence for the will of Bishop Ælfric (S1489/W26) is less convincing: Lowe, 'Vernacular Will', pp. 21–2; *Wills*, pp. 181–2.

42 S1536/W17, *Burton* 29; S906, *Burton* 28. Lowe, 'Vernacular Will', p. 19; *Burton*, pp. ix–xx.

To add a further complication, there is evidence to believe that summaries and extracts of wills were already being made in the pre-Conquest period. A vernacular summary of the multi-gift will of Æthelgifu was written, together with a summary Latin translation, into a twelfth-century cartulary of St Albans, now lost, but transmitted via a recently-discovered seventeenth-century copy.[43] While it is likely that the twelfth-century scribe himself made the vernacular and Latin abstracts, the possibility must be considered that he copied and translated a vernacular summary which had been made in the pre-Conquest period; as Lowe has pointed out, since the vernacular abstract is close in form and content to other extant vernacular wills, this raises the further possibility that contemporary summaries may have been more common than now appears.[44] An eleventh-century vernacular bequest by Thurstan provides a further illustration of the complexities of transmission. He bequeaths an estate at Wimbish (Ex) to Christ Church, Canterbury, a transaction which survives in two separate contemporary manuscripts, both forming the upper portion of a chirograph and therefore not part of the same document.[45] However, the same bequest is also included in Thurstan's multi-gift will, which exists in a thirteenth-century copy from the Bury archive.[46] A further complexity is added: the two contemporary versions of Thurstan's bequest to Christ Church differ in detail. Both begin with a straightforward statement of bequest:

> *Þurstan geann þæs landes æt Wimbisc into xp̄es cyrcean for his sawle 7 for Leofware 7 for Æþelgyðe. þam hirede to fostre æfter Þurstanes dæge 7 æfter Æðelgyþe.*
>
> (Thurstan grants the estate at Wimbish, for his soul and for Leofwaru's and for Æthelgyth's, to Christ Church, for the sustenance of the community after Thurstan's day and after Æthelgyth's.)

However, they differ in the continuation. One reads as follows:

> *7 ælcon geare an pund to fulre sutelunge þa hwile þe we libban. 7 gelæste se hired æt xp̄es cyrcean swa hwæder swa he wille þam hirede into sc̄e Augustine þe twelf pund be getale oððe twa hide.*
>
> (And each year, as long as we live, a pound [shall be paid] as a sufficient proof [of this reversionary right]. And the community at Christ Church is

43 S1497/*St Albans* 7; Keynes, 'A lost cartulary', pp. 254–63. The vernacular and Latin abstracts are edited by Crick as *St Albans* 7A.

44 This issue is discussed in detail by Lowe, 'Latin versions', pp. 10–15. See also *St Albans*, pp. 159–60.

45 S1530/W30, *Christ Church* 166, 1042x1043, both manuscripts from the archive of Christ Church, Canterbury. For chirographs, see below n. 121.

46 S1531/W31, 1042x1045.

to pay to the community at St Augustine's whichever they prefer, twelve pounds by tale or two hides.)[47]

In the second version, the payment of rent to Christ Church is omitted, but the payment due to St Augustine's is retained; in addition, the option of the payment of two hides from the bequest to St Augustine's is included in the second version, and the twelve pounds excluded.[48] To account for this difference in emphasis between the two versions of the bequest, Lowe has suggested that the second document was produced for St Augustine's, which would have had no interest in the rent due to Christ Church but would have wished to preserve a record of the payment due from Christ Church to itself, as well as the preferred option.[49] Without the fortuitous survival of the multi-gift wills of Æthelgifu and Thurstan we would have a very limited view of the overall dispositions of these donors, based only on abbreviated texts. Lowe points out that the existence of abstracts of both wills serves as a reminder that the possibility of selective copying in the pre-Conquest period underlying other extant single-gift bequests or short multi-gift wills must be considered.[50]

A further forty-six wills – two thirds of the extant corpus – survive in post-Conquest manuscripts.[51] Through detailed comparison of wills surviving in both pre- and post-Conquest versions, Lowe has shown that the post-Conquest texts often have considerable integrity, although uncertain readings may result from later scribes' struggles with the unfamiliar orthography and syntax of Old English; scribes working in the twelfth century, possibly still reasonably familiar with the vernacular of the texts, were more likely to change their models than those working in later centuries.[52] For the purpose of the historian, therefore, post-Conquest copies may in general be regarded as useful working texts, although the possibility of truncation, in the form of the omission of witness lists, personal bequests and fine detail, must be borne in mind.[53] The vernacular and Latin abstracts of Æthelgifu's multi-gift will copied into the twelfth-century cartulary of St Alban's omit most bequests of chattels to secular beneficiaries.[54] Witness lists are particularly vulnerable

47 S1530/W30, *Christ Church* 166, Canterbury, DC, Chartae Antiquae C 70, s.xi$^{med}$.

48 S1530/W30, *Christ Church* 166, BL Cotton Augustus ii, 34, s.xi$^{med}$. The witness lists vary slightly, perhaps indicating that the documents were drawn up on different occasions.

49 For discussion of these texts and this suggestion, see Lowe, 'Nature and effect', pp. 32–3.

50 Lowe, 'Nature and effect', pp. 32–4.

51 Listed in Appendix 1B.

52 The relevant research has been carried out by Lowe: see in particular her articles 'Latin versions' and '"As fre as thowt"?'.

53 Truncation is more likely to take place in the twelfth century when texts are translated into Latin (Lowe, 'Latin versions', pp. 8–9, 10–15, 19, 20).

54 S1497/*St Albans*, 7. This amounts, as Lowe has pointed out, to twenty-four consecutive lines: see her detailed analysis of the texts in 'Latin versions', p. 11.

to truncation, surviving in twenty-three texts;[55] of these, twelve are single-sheet manuscripts, all but one probably contemporary with the transaction.[56] That more originally existed is suggested by the final sentence of the will of Wulfgyth: 'of this, King Edward and many others are witnesses' (*þisses is to ywithnesse Eadward king and manie oþre*).[57]

The possibility of post-Conquest forgery must also be considered.[58] In three cases where the texts are unsatisfactory in their present form the editors have argued that a genuine original probably underlies the later version, and that the dispositions may be trusted. The first is the will of Mantat the Anchorite, which survives in a fourteenth-century cartulary from Thorney Abbey and a later copy (dated 1558x1625) of the fourteenth-century text which, in part, seeks to replace with Standard West Saxon some of the Middle English forms in its model.[59] The second document is the bequest of Oswulf and Leofrun to Bury, which survives separately from the bulk of Bury wills, copied into a fifteenth-century Bury register known as the *Liber Albus*; although again the text shows signs of corruption, the editor argues in favour of an underlying authentic original.[60] This is equally possible in the case of the third document, Æthelflæd's single-gift bequest to St Paul's, which Kelly suggests may have been 'improved' in the light of a later dispute.[61] A further four short texts from the archive of the New Minster, Winchester, have also been included in the corpus, although their authenticity has been questioned by their most recent editor on the grounds of late linguistic forms and suspicious similarity in wording.[62] These texts may be of dubious value as evidence for pre-Conquest bequests, but they reveal that post-Conquest forgers at the New

55 See Appendix 1. This number excludes the duplicate contemporary versions of S1530/W30, *Christ Church* 166 and S1503/W20, *Christ Church* 142.

56 The exception is S1501/W16[1], *Christ Church* 136, where the hand is later than the date of the will (*Christ Church*, forthcoming). In addition, S1455/R62, *St Augustine's* 31 was written in a contemporary hand into a gospel book associated with St Augustine's Abbey.

57 S1535/W32, *Christ Church* 176. For the view that not all wills were witnessed, see *Æthelgifu*, p. 20.

58 See Keynes, *Diplomas*, pp. 4–6 for discussion of reasons for, and the range of, post-Conquest forgery; forgery at twelfth-century Worcester is discussed by J. Barrow, 'How the twelfth-century monks of Worcester perceived their past', in *The Perception of the Past in Twelfth-Century Europe*, ed. P. Magdalino (London, 1992), pp. 53–74, *passim* (with references to other Benedictine houses at p. 73, n. 83).

59 S1523/W23, 1017x1035, edited by Whitelock from the later manuscript, and by Hart from the cartulary (*ECEE*, pp. 204–206); Lowe, 'Vernacular Will', p. 37.

60 S1608, 1044x1052, *ECEE*, no. 133 (pp. 86–91, together with a Latin translation which follows it in the manuscript); BL MS Harley 1005, fol. 105; Davis, *Cartularies*, no. 105.

61 S1495/W22, *St Paul's* 22, *c.* 1000; *St Paul's*, pp. 188–91.

62 S1509/R27, 932x939; S1418/R28, 946x953; S1419/R29, 947x955; S1496/W6, 957x *c.* 958 (*New Minster* 11, 14, 16, 21, with authenticity discussed on pp. xlvii–li. King Alfred's bequest to Shaftesbury (S357/R13, *Shaftesbury* 7) has been omitted from the corpus as spurious (*Shaftesbury*, pp. 29–30).

Minster had an awareness of, and respect for, the pre-Conquest vernacular will as useful evidence in establishing title to land.

## The form and language of the documents

Although it has been shown above that the royal charter granting land and the document which bequeathed it may be closely related, differences in style and form reflect their divergence in status and purpose. As Keynes has succinctly written, 'the charter was addressed in Latin to posterity, defining the estate and establishing its privileged purpose'.[63] It carried the imprimatur of royal power, was vested with religious authority, and was an important symbol of rights in land.[64] The will, however, has more in common with the royal writ, which was written in the vernacular and, again in Keynes's words, 'addressed in the vernacular to contemporaries, making it known that an estate had changed hands'.[65] Multi-gift wills at least, which are often directed to the king, might usefully be seen in the context of correspondence.[66]

The earliest will to address the king and court is that of Ealdorman Alfred, which begins:

> *Ic Elfred dux hatu writan 7 cyðan an ðyssum gewrite Elfrede regi 7 allum his weotum 7 geweotan, 7 ec swylce minum megum 7 minum gefeorum, þa men þe ic mines erfes 7 mines boclondes seolest onn, ðet is þonne Werburg min wif 7 uncer gemene bearn.*

63 S. Keynes, 'Charters and writs', in *Blackwell Encyclopaedia*, pp. 99–100 (p. 100).

64 For an interpretation of the ideological aspect of the royal charter see C. Insley, 'Where did all the charters go?', *ANS* 24 (2001), 109–27. Reference to the *boc*, or title-deed, as a symbol of ownership features in a number of wills: S1506/R32, *Christ Church* 121; S1471/R101, *Christ Church* 170; S1524/W5; S1512/W7; S1514/R9, *Rochester* 23; S1511/W11, *Rochester* 35; S1539/W3. For the role of the royal charter in land transactions see Kelly, 'Anglo-Saxon lay society', pp. 43–6.

65 Keynes, 'Charters and writs', p. 100. For the development and use of the writ, see *Writs*, pp. 10–24. See also R. Sharpe, 'The use of writs in the eleventh-century', *ASE* 32 (2003), 247–91 (pp. 247–53). However, Sheehan described a development from eighth- and ninth-century wills, which were strongly under the influence of the charter, to the 'informal narrative style' of the tenth and eleventh centuries: Sheehan, *The Will*, pp. 56–9.

66 Asser uses the term *epistola* in referring to King Æthelwulf's will: *Asser*, chap. 16, line 6. See also the letter recorded in *LE* from Godgifu to Bishop Ælfric and Abbot Leofric of Ely, making a bequest (*LE* II, 83); the Latin text was perhaps translated from the vernacular. P. Stafford describes the will as 'a dialogue between nobles and royal power': *Unification and Conquest: a Political and Social History of England in the Tenth and Eleventh Centuries* (London, 1989), p. 160. On informal letter survival see M. Garrison, '"Send more socks": on mentality and the preservation context of medieval letters', in *New Approaches to Medieval Communication*, ed. M. Mostert (Turnhout, 1999), pp. 69–99, and M. Garrison, 'Letter collections', in *Blackwell Encyclopaedia*, pp. 283–4.

(I, Ealdorman Alfred, order to be written and declared in this deed to King Alfred and to all his councillors and advisors, and also to my kinsmen and to my friends, the persons on whom I most happily bestow my inheritance and my bookland, that is indeed to Wærburh my wife and our joint child.)[67]

A number of wills show stylistic parallels with the writ. A good example is Ealdorman Æthelmær's will, which begins in the third person, as is usually the case in writs:

*Æðelmær ealdorman cyð on ðysum gewrite his cynehlaforde and eallum his freondum [hwæt] his cwyde wæs to his nyhstan dæge.*

(The Ealdorman Æthelmær in this document informs his royal lord and all his friends [what] his will was on his last day.)[68]

The text then shifts to the first person for the dispositions which follow, again following the pattern of writs.[69] The verb *cyðan* (to make known), often found in both wills and writs, is also found in the opening of the early tenth century Fonthill letter, written to King Edward by Ealdorman Ordlaf between 900 and 924 in the context of a dispute.[70] Wills couched in the first person often share with the Fonthill letter the impression of a strong personal voice.[71] Ordlaf, arguing his case that King Alfred's judgment in the dispute concerning land at Fonthill should be respected, is rhetorically forthright:

*7 leof, hwonne bið engu spæc geendedu gif mon ne mæg nowðer ne mid feo ne mid aða geendigan? Oððe gif mon ælcne dom wile onwendan ðe Ælfred cing gesette, hwonne habbe we ðonne gemotad?*

67 S1508/H10, *Christ Church* 96, 871x889. The ætheling Æthelstan also addresses the *witan*.

68 S1498/W10, *New Minster* 25. Other wills addressed to the king, although not necessarily at the beginning of the text: S1504/H20; S1484/W8; S1505/W12; S1494/W14; S1486/W15; S1536/W17, *Burton* 29; S1538/W21, *Bath and Wells* 21; S1523/W23. S1521/W29 is addressed to the queen. S1534/W19 addresses the king by proxy. S1519/W34 addresses Earl Harold, and S1491/W4, *New Minster* 18 addresses Ealdorman Ælfheah.

69 The will of Leofgifu (S1521/W29, 1035x1044) actually uses the conventional writ greeting, uniquely addressing the queen: *Leofgifu gret hyre leuedi* (Leofgifu greets her lady). See also the will of Mantat the Anchorite (S1523/W23, 1017x1035), dubious in its present form. For greetings in writs, see *Writs*, pp. 61–2.

70 S1445/H18, *EHD* I, no. 102. Text and translation are from S. Keynes, 'The Fonthill letter', in *Words, Texts and Manuscript: Studies in Anglo-Saxon culture presented to Helmut Gneuss*, ed. M. Korhammer (Cambridge, 1992), pp. 53–97 (p. 63). See *Writs*, pp. 63–4 for discussion of the relevant opening formulae in writs; examples are S1064/*Writs* 2, and Queen Ælfthryth's letter to Archbishop Ælfric and Ealdorman Æthelweard (S1242/*Writs* 108). For use of *cyðan* in wills, see S1539/W3; S1498/W10, *New Minster* 25; S1501/W16[1], *Christ Church* 136; S1538/W21, *Bath and Wells* 21; S1523/W23; S1528/W25; S1530/W30, *Christ Church* 166; S1531/W31; S1516/W33; S1499/W35.

71 For use of the first person in wills see n. 95 below.

(And, Sir, when will any suit be closed if one can end it neither with money nor with an oath? And if one wishes to change every judgement which King Alfred gave, when shall we have finished disputing?)[72]

Ælfhelm, addressing his will either to King Edward ('the Martyr', 975–978), or, more probably, his half-brother and successor, Æthelred (978–1016), concludes his dispositions with equal forthrightness:

> *Nu bydde Ic þe leof hlaford. ꝥ min cwyde standan mote. 7 ꝥ þu ne geþauige. ꝥ hine man mid wuo wende. god is min gewyta ic wæs þinum fæder swa gehyrsum swa ic fyrmest myhte. 7 fullice hold on mode. 7 on mægene. 7 þe æfre on fullon hyldon hold. 7 on fulre luue. þæs me is god gewyta.*
>
> (Now I pray you, dear lord, that my will may stand, and that you will not permit it to be wrongfully altered. God is my witness that I was as obedient to your father as ever I could be, and thoroughly loyal in thought and in deed, and was ever faithful to you with perfect loyalty and devotion; of this God is my witness.)[73]

This assertion of loyalty, particularly in the turbulent times which followed the death of King Edgar, suggests that Ælfhelm had good reason to be anxious about royal support for his will.

Wills also share their use of the vernacular with other documents which recorded the transactions of everyday life, such as marriage agreements, estate inventories and gild statutes.[74] While the level of lay literacy may be disputed, there is no doubt that, at least by the tenth century, the vernacular was well established as a vital and effective means of written communication in both church and lay circles, and it is in this overall context that wills may best be understood.

In terms of form, surviving will documents may be divided into three groups, as noted above:[75] the multi-gift will, the single-gift bequest, and the bequest-agreement, a group in which the element of contract is a pronounced feature. These groups will be described separately.

### The multi-gift will

This group of documents is characterised by gifts to multiple beneficiaries which are to take effect after the death of the donor. Although most include no information concerning the date or place of the proceedings they record, by the mid-tenth century multi-gift wills had developed a more or less consistent formal structure which corresponds in broad terms with that of the

72 S1445/H18; Keynes, 'The Fonthill letter', section 8, p. 76.

73 S1487/W13, 975x1016.

74 Kelly surveys vernacular documents in the context of lay literacy: 'Anglo-Saxon lay society', pp. 46–62.

75 Introduction, p. 10.

Latin charter: introductory clauses, dispositive section, sanction and witness list.[76]

The ecclesiastical influence on the documents is evident in two features. The first is the inclusion in a number of contemporary single sheets of a chrismon, a pictorial form of invocation reinforcing the ecclesiastical authority of the text, which may be lost in later copies of the documents.[77] The second is the sanction, which survives in twenty-nine texts, usually as the final or penultimate clause.[78] It invokes spiritual retribution upon those who might attempt to alter the will and interfere with the donor's intentions, but may also include a reservation of the donor's right of revocation. There may also be a reference to the king's power over the will, with the hope that he will exercise it on the donor's behalf – in Æthelgifu's case, reference is made to both king and queen:

> *Heo ne anbit na hyre cynehlaforde ne hire hlæfdian ac gif hwa bidde ꝥ ðes cwide standan ne mote wurðe he aworpen on þa wynstran hand þonne se hæland his dom deme 7 he wurðe gode swa lað swa iudas þæs þy hyne selfne aheng buton hio hit get self awende 7 þa ne lybben þe hit nu becweden ys.*
>
> (She does not expect it [i.e. a challenge to her will] of her lord and lady; but if anyone ask that this will may not be allowed to stand, may he be cast on the left hand when the Saviour pronounces his judgement and may he be as hateful to God as was Judas, who hanged himself, unless she herself change it hereafter, and those be not alive to whom it is now bequeathed.)[79]

Wulfric Spott similarly expresses his confidence in the king's support for his will, excluding him from the sanction:

76 One document is dated: S1522/N&S9, 998; S1511/W11, *Rochester 35* (973x987) incorporates the place of the declaration, along with a witness list, in the preamble to the will. For a description of charter form and a concise general account, see Keynes, 'Charters and writs', p. 99; *EHD* I, pp. 369–84. King, 'St Oswald's tenants', p. 102, points to diplomatic parallels between charters and the Worcester leases, some of which survive in the vernacular.

77 Single-sheet manuscripts including a chrismon: S1508/H10, *Christ Church* 96; S1522/N&S9; S1533/R26; S1534/W19; S1482/H2, *Christ Church* 70; S1489/W26; S1492/N&S10; S1497/*St Albans* 7; S1503/W20, *Christ Church* 142. S1536/W17, *Burton* 29 has the abbreviation IND (*in nomine domini*). See Keynes, *Diplomas*, p. 4 for the loss of pictorial invocations in cartulary copies.

78 On sanction clauses in charters see S. Hamilton, 'Remedies for "Great Transgressions": penance and excommunication in late Anglo-Saxon England', in *Pastoral Care in Late Anglo-Saxon England*, ed. F. Tinti (Woodbridge, 2005), pp. 83–105 (pp. 100–102). On sanction clauses in wills see B. Danet and B. Bogoch, ' "Whoever alters this, may God turn his face from him on the day of judgement": curses in Anglo-Saxon legal documents', *The Journal of American Folklore* 105 no. 416 (1992), 132–65.

79 S1497/*St Albans* 7.

*7 god ælmihtig hine awende of eallum godes dreame. 7 of ealra cristenra gemanan. se ðe þis awende. butan hit min an cynehlaford sy. 7 ic hopyge to him swa godan. 7 swa mildheortan þ he hit nylle sylf don. ne eac nanum oþrum menn geþafian.*

(And whoever perverts this, may God remove him from all God's joy and from the communion of all Christians, unless it be my royal lord alone, and I believe him to be so good and gracious that he will not himself do it, nor permit any other man to do it.)[80]

The notification which begins most wills is a brief opening clause identifying the donor, and stating the intention to bequeath property.[81] A limited number of verbs is used to declare the donor's purpose, usually *cyðan* (to make known, proclaim), widely used in writs, or *sweotelian* (to make clear, declare). There may be no addressee, but, as has been shown, some donors address the king.[82] They may request his permission to make a will, as in the case of Wulfwaru:

*Ic Wulfwaru bidde minne leofan hlaford Æþelred kyning him to ælmyssan. þ ic mote beon mine cwydes wyrðe.*

(I, Wulfwaru, pray my dear lord King Æthelred, of his charity, that I may be entitled to make my will.)[83]

Others request the king's support for the will, allowing their dispositions to stand:

*Þis is Æþelwoldis cwyde. þæt is ærest þæt he bitt his cynehlaford for godes lufon and for his cynescipe þæt his cwyde standen mote on þæm þingon þe he æt þe gegearnod hæfþ and æt þinum foregengan.*

(This is Æthelwold's will. First he prays his royal lord for the love of God and the sake of his kingly dignity that his will relating to those things which he has acquired from you and from your predecessors may stand.)[84]

Some address a wider audience, as in the case of Ealdorman Alfred, quoted above, and Ealdorman Æthelmær, who 'informs his royal lord and all his

80 S1536/W17, *Burton* 29. See also S1487/W13 for a similar exclusion of the king.

81 See Keynes, *Diplomas*, pp. 111–14, for the use of notification clauses in some royal charters; forms of notification in vernacular documents are discussed in *Writs*, pp. 15–16. Three wills recorded in Latin in the Ramsey Chronicle preserve notification clauses: S1807/*CR* 34; S1808/*CR* 35; S1810/*CR* 31.

82 N. 68 above. In two cases the document begins unceremoniously with the phrase *ic an* (I grant): S1496/W6; S1533/R26.

83 S1538/W21, *Bath and Wells* 21. Other examples: S1485/W9, and S1484/W8 for a third person version of this sentence. S1483/W2 and S1503/W20, *Christ Church* 142 refer to permission already granted.

84 S1505/W12, *New Minster* 29. See also S1494/W14; S1486/W15. In two cases this request is placed at the end of the will: S1511/W11, *Rochester* 35; S1487/W13.

friends' of his will.[85] It is at this stage in the will that the *post obitum* intention is usually made clear. The document may be described as X's *cwide*, a term which, as Lowe has shown, usually occurs in charters in relation to bequest;[86] the second law-code of King Cnut legislates concerning the man who dies *cwydeleas*, indicating that, by the 1020s at least, the word referred to a will (although not necessarily a written one).[87] The *post obitum* nature of dispositions may also be signalled by the use of the phrase *æfter X's dæge*, indicating that the gifts are to take effect on the death of the donor; X may be the name of the donor or the first- or third-person pronoun.[88] The notification clause may also include donors' reasons for their will-making. Four donors refer to a prospective pilgrimage.[89] Pious motives, such as concern for the soul's welfare,[90] or a sense of spiritual as well as secular responsibility, may be adduced.[91] Bishop Theodred reflects on the debt of prayer he owes to those from whom he had received property.[92] Some donors identify the source of their property,[93] or reflect on their temporary tenure in this world.[94]

The dispositive sections of the documents as we have them show evidence of scribal redrafting of the oral dispositions which underlie them. Although the majority are in the first person, using the present tense, perhaps reflecting the practice of the writ, in other instances the donor's dispositions are reported, using the third person and past tense.[95] Switches between third and first person from clause to clause may occur, perhaps as the result of the

85 S1498/W10, *New Minster* 25: *cyð... his cynehlaford and eallum his freondum*. Other wills notifying friends (no doubt also including kin): S1536/W17, *Burton* 29; S1807/*CR* 34; S1808/*CR* 35. S1531/W31 and S1499/W35 notify 'all men' (*alle manne*).

86 Lowe, 'Vernacular Will', p. 163, n. 4, citing two exceptions: S1089 and S1047. An exception cited by Sheehan as an *inter vivos* gift (S357/R13) is almost certainly a late forgery: see *Shaftesbury*, no. 7. The name of the document probably derives from the oral nature of the transaction which it represents: Hazeltine, 'Comments', pp. xii-xiii, n. 1; B&T shows that both the noun *cwide* and the verb *becweðan* may refer to oral as well as written acts.

87 II Cnut, 70.

88 In some instances the *post obitum* intention becomes clear later in the text: S1508/H10, *Christ Church* 96; S1487/W13; S1486/W15; S1503/W20, *Christ Church* 142; S1537/W27; S1531/W31; S1525/W38. In two cases the deferment of the dispositions is implicit in the text: S1489/W26; S1523/W23.

89 S1500/R3, *Christ Church* 39A; S1487/W13; S1486/W15; W39/*Peterborough* 27. See also the Latin will of Dunwald, S1182/*St Augustine's* 12.

90 The phrase 'for my soul' does not necessarily imply *post obitum* intention: see S1232/R118 for an *inter vivos* grant using this phrase.

91 S1525/W38; S1490/W28; S1519/W34; W39/*Peterborough* 27.

92 S1526/W1.

93 S1503/W20, *Christ Church* 142; S1489/W26.

94 S1531/W31; S1516/W33; S1501/W16[1], *Christ Church* 136.

95 A study of 62 wills by B. Danet and B. Bogoch has identified 59% written entirely or almost entirely in the first person and 40% written entirely or almost entirely in the third person: 'Orality, literacy and performativity in Anglo-Saxon wills', in *Language and the Law*, ed. J. Gibbons (London, 1994), pp. 100–35 (pp. 111–112, and Table 3.1).

correlation of dispositive acts which took place on different occasions, now to be incorporated in a multi-gift document.[96] Other explanations may be scribal confusion as to the stance taken in relation to an oral transaction,[97] or simply textual convention in which such shifts of person were irrelevant.[98]

The organisation of the dispositive sections across the corpus of multi-gift wills is striking enough in most documents to indicate scribal management of what were probably notes taken at an oral declaration.[99] The dispositive verb is usually *geunnan* (to give, grant), although *becweðan* occurs occasionally in tenth- and eleventh-century texts.[100] Cohesion is usually effective: the opening clause is signalled by a variant of the phrase *þæt is ærest* (that is first), and each new bequest by the word or symbol 'and'.[101] Where listing of estates is featured, it is clearly signposted. For example, Wulfric's will incorporates a list of estates he intends to bequeath to Burton Abbey:

> *And þys synd þa land þe ic geann into Byrtune. þ is ærest …*
>
> (And these are the estates which I grant to Burton: that is first …)[102]

The word 'and' precedes each subsequent estate, which may simply be named or identified with brief additional details. Such verbal pointers are important in establishing the coherence of the written text, and would be vital in assisting the comprehension of an audience at a public reading. The dispositions themselves are, in general, clearly structured, suggesting careful drafting of the document. It is usually possible to identify a grouping of bequests to royalty (including heriot, or inheritance payment to the king, which is given in more or less detail);[103] to religious houses; to named churchmen or members of the

96 *Writs*, pp. 61–3. For example, S1516/W33 shifts from first to third person to incorporate an agreement, and the joint will W39/*Peterborough* 27 uses first person for the male voice and third person for the female. See also Chap. 2 below for the multiple dispositive acts of Siferth of Downham. For changes of person in the Fonthill letter see Keynes, 'The Fonthill Letter', section 12, p. 85, with comments on p. 7, and for an alternative view M. Boynton and S. Reynolds, 'The author of the Fonthill letter', *ASE* 25 (1996), 91–5.

97 Danet and Bogoch, 'Orality', p. 111; Hazeltine, 'Comments', pp. xxx-xxxi. Change of person is found in: S1487/W13; S1534/W19; S1484/W8; S1485/W9; S1511/W11, *Rochester* 35; S1505/W12; S1515/H21, *New Minster* 17; S1517/*St Albans* 15; W39/*Peterborough* 27 (and briefly in S1539/W3; S1526/W1; S1527/W24). S1537/W27 shifts from passive to first person. A similar phenomenon has been noted in early thirteenth century wills from Genoa: S. Epstein, *Wills and Wealth in Medieval Genoa* (Cambridge, 1984), p. 22.

98 *Writs*, pp. 61–2.

99 A possible exception is S1509/W3, in which the organisation of complex bequests is tenuous.

100 S1490/W28; S1539/W3; S1505/W12, *New Minster* 29; S1495/W22, *St Paul's* 22. It is used consistently in S1488/W18, *Abingdon* 133.

101 Danet and Bogoch, 'Orality', p. 118.

102 S1536/W17, *Burton* 29, and S1486/W15 for similar signposting of lists.

103 For heriot see Chap. 5 below.

nobility; and to the donor's kindred or household. In the wills of laymen, the rights of wives are often particularly prominent. Similarly, where significant numbers of chattels are concerned, they will usually be dealt with separately from the gifts of land. Occasionally it is possible to identify a clear grouping of estates by origin, as in the will of Æthelgifu, where a group of estates in Northamptonshire (Weedon, Watford and Thrupp), probably inherited from her own kindred, are dealt with as a unit following distribution of the bulk of the estates, which were probably inherited from her husband.[104] Individual gifts of land may be modified in a number of ways by a statement of powers. For example, the reservation of an estate, or part of it, for one or two lives may be specified, with details of the ultimate reversion; terms of tenure may be described, perhaps with reference to a food-rent to be paid to the church, non-alienation by the beneficiary or rights of access.[105] Since no Anglo-Saxon formulary survives, and may never have existed, it seems likely that scribes used conventional alliterative formulas, perhaps related to land transactions conducted orally, such as *swa ful and swa forð* (as fully as) and *mid mete and mid mannum* (with stock and men), to signify the terms on which land was to be transferred.[106] Something of the history of the estate – particularly where it had been contentious – may be given;[107] and the donor's right to bequeath may be established by some account of the land's origin.[108] Manumission and almsgiving may be stipulated in relation to a particular gift, or at the end of the dispositive section as an overall instruction.[109]

104 *Æthelgifu*, pp. 28–9.

105 S1528/W25 uses the phrase *[mid] ingong and vtgong* (with ingress and egress). This may be formulaic, but it is tempting to see this sole usage in the wills as relating to an actual or potential dispute (see Chap. 3, pp. 129–31 below).

106 Keynes, *Diplomas*, pp. 115–17. For the use of alliterative phrases in a range of vernacular documents see *Writs*, pp. 85–92 (esp. at p. 87). *Swa ful and swa forð* indicates that the full rights as held by the donor – generally not specified in detail – are to be conveyed to the beneficiary. The phrase *mid mete and mannum* seems to encapsulate what appears to have been the regular practice of transferring stock and slaves with an estate. See S1487/W13; S1512/W7; S1498/W10, *New Minster* 25; S1486/W15; S1536/W17, *Burton* 29; S1538/W21, *Bath and Wells* 21; S1465/R86, *Christ Church* 153; S1224/R97; S1471/R101, *Christ Church* 170. The phrase occurs in the lease S1062/R118 and the writ S1242 (*Writs* 108). On the use of such alliterative or rhyming phrases to enhance the performativity of the will see B. Danet and B. Bogoch, 'From oral ceremony to written document: the transitional language of Anglo-Saxon wills', *Language and Communication* 12 no. 2 (1992), 95–122.

107 A good example is S1519/W34, where Ketel refers to a successfully-defended lawsuit. See also S1527/W24.

108 S1503/W20, *Christ Church* 142 and S1489/W26 refer to the purchase of land; S1538/W21, *Bath and Wells* 21, S1533/R26 and S1501/W16[1], *Christ Church* 136 refer to inheritance, and S1534/W19 to the purchase of land with the money belonging to the donor's wife.

109 The bequest of movable wealth, including stock, and manumission are discussed in Chap. 5 below.

One aspect of these documents which makes their interpretation difficult for the modern historian is the context-dependent nature of the dispositions.[110] In general, donors are simply identified by name, with the occasional title such as 'ealdorman' or 'bishop'; beneficiaries may, in addition, be identified by relationship with the donor. Estates are identified by name, with little additional detail, in contrast with the detailed boundary clauses characteristic of the royal charter;[111] even where a section of an estate is reserved from the main bequest, no further information may be given than the number of hides, possibly the name of the current holder, or occasionally brief topographical detail. For example, Thurstan bequeaths an estate at Harlow (Ex) to the religious house of Bury St Edmunds, with the exception of 'the half hide which Ælfwine had at Ealing Bridge, and except the homestead which Ælfgar occupies and the spur of land which belongs to it'.[112] A similar style can be seen in the bequest of chattels. Although some items are clearly described, much of the language used is subjective; for example, donors refer to their best sword, horse, linen or apparel, apparently placing reliance on the knowledge of family or members of the household to fulfil the gift; Bishop Ælfric relies on his stewards' knowledge of which members of the household were entitled to receive a bequest of coin.[113] Similarly, in giving instructions for manumission, some donors (particularly women) are very specific, naming slaves to be freed, but in other cases, where half of the slaves on a given estate are to be freed for the donor's soul, there is no indication of how the choice is to be made. It is likely that there were customary practices governing the selection procedure: the multi-gift will of Æthelstan Mannessune, recorded in Latin in the Ramsey Chronicle, describes how thirteen of every thirty counted men were to be chosen by lot for manumission at the crossroads.[114] Characteristically, the documents can afford to be allusive because they rely on current shared knowledge within the kindred, the household and the wider community, which would enable the donors' dispositions to be interpreted.[115]

Witness lists attest to the oral and public nature of will-making, but, since they were particularly vulnerable in the copying process, it is likely that more

110 Danet and Bogoch, 'Orality', pp. 119–27.

111 Only two wills include a boundary clause. S1513/R17 is a cartulary copy (see Lowe, 'Vernacular Will', pp. 63–5). S1486/W15 has bounds (for three estates only) added, in a different hand, to the composite contemporary parchment which includes S1494/W14 (*Wills*, p. 145).

112 S1531/W31: *þe halue hide þe Ælfwine hauede at Gildenebrigge. and buten þat tuft þe Alfgor on sit and þat hoo. þerto.*

113 S1489/W26 (*mine cnihtas þa mina stiwardas witan*). Danet and Bogoch, 'Orality', pp. 120–6. See also: S1497/*St Albans* 7; S1538/W21, *Bath and Wells* 21; S1539/W3; S1526/W1.

114 *CR* 33. Manumission and the bequest of slaves are discussed in Chap. 5 below.

115 Danet and Bogoch refer to the 'decoding' of the text through knowledge shared within a community: 'Orality', p. 120.

witness lists once existed.[116] Where they do survive, they are usually found, variously set out, at the end of the document.[117] Some lists are extensive, suggesting public gatherings in the presence of royalty or – more usually – high-ranking churchmen. One contemporary manuscript from the archive of Christ Church, Canterbury, lists churchmen from Christ Church (including the archbishop) and from St Augustine's, Canterbury (including the abbot), a number of laymen (at least one of whom was a king's thegn), and adds the three *geferscipas innanburwara 7 utanburhwara 7 micle mættan* (three Canterbury fraternities).[118] Other witness lists are brief, perhaps representing those attending a deathbed.[119] The status of witnesses is often given and, in general, as in royal charters, a hierarchy is observed: senior churchmen and ealdormen precede lower-ranking churchmen and laymen.

Boundary clauses are not usually a feature of multi-gift wills.[120] Since these are concerned with a number of estates bequeathed to different beneficiaries, the inclusion of bounds would have been unwieldy and impractical. In addition, since bounds were often added to royal charters, they may have been superfluous in wills which, as has been suggested above, do not seem to have acted as evidence of title.

Wills were, in all likelihood, generally produced in multiple copies. Some pre-Conquest manuscripts survive as chirographs, where duplication or triplication on a single sheet is indicated by the letters CHIROGRAPHUM written between the copies and then cut through.[121] No matching portions

116 See pp. 20–1 above. The role of witnesses is discussed in Chap. 2 below.

117 S1511/W11, *Rochester* 35 uncharacteristically incorporates the witness list into the notification clause of the will, and adds – again uncharacteristically – the place where the will was declared. This format may reflect the fact that the will is related to the resolution of a long-running dispute concerning land at Snodland, Bromley and Fawkham (Kent): see Chap. 4, pp. 161–5 below.

118 S1506/R32, *Christ Church* 121: 'fellowships of those living within and outside the town and the many diners'. For the terminology here see *Charters*, pp. 316–17; for a detailed discussion of the social groups involved and the significance of this witness list, see Brooks, *Early History*, pp. 28–30, 237. S1531/W31, copied into the thirteenth-century Bury cartulary, lists witnesses in four counties.

119 E.g. the wills of the ætheling Æthelstan (S1503/W20, *Christ Church* 142) and Bishop Ælfwold (S1492/N&S10): see *Wills*, p. 129. The possibility that these are deathbed wills is discussed below, Chap. 2, pp. 66–7.

120 The multi-gift will of Ælfflæd (S1486/W15), a single-sheet manuscript including the will of her sister Æthelflæd, has the bounds of three of the estates bequeathed to the religious house at Stoke-by-Nayland added in a different – although contemporary – hand (*Wills*, pp. 145–6). Bounds also follow the cartulary copy of the single-gift bequest of Ceolwyn (S1513/R17).

121 The term 'chirograph' is used here in the specific sense of a document originally created in this way; for a description of the procedure, see the account of the will-making of Siferth of Downham in Chap. 2 below. The form and use of the chirograph in Anglo-Saxon England, with particular relation to wills, have been explored by Lowe, 'Lay literacy': see pp. 170–1 for discussion of the form, and 185–203 for a list. See also Kelly,

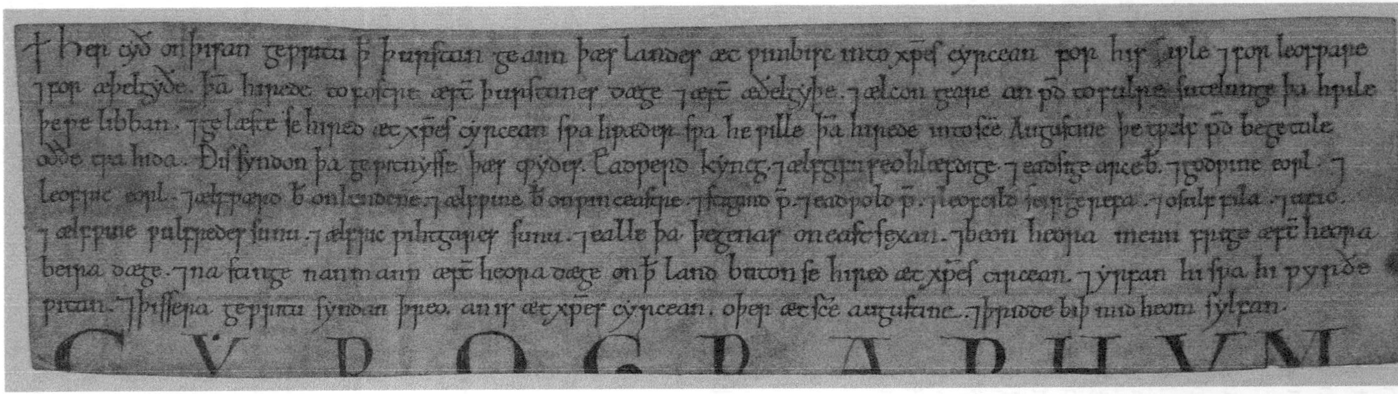

**Figure 1.** The single-gift bequest of Thurstan (S1530/W30, *Christ Church* 166, 1042x1043). Canterbury, DC, Chartae Antiquae C70, a contemporary single-sheet parchment (the upper portion of a chirograph). Reproduced with the permission of Canterbury Cathedral Archives.

survive, although S1530/W30 (the single-gift bequest of Thurstan) exists in two upper portions of different contemporary chirographs.[122] A number of documents, including those preserved in cartulary copies, incorporate at the end what Lowe has termed a 'marker clause': that is to say, a clause which indicates that the document exists in two or three copies, and usually giving the destination of each copy.[123] Such marker clauses occasionally survive translation into Latin.[124] In general, copies are held by one or two of the principal religious beneficiaries – perhaps one of them the house responsible for the drawing up of the will – and the donor. In the case of Leofgifu, the king holds one copy:

> *Nu sinden þise write þre. on is mid þise kinges halidome. and oþer at seynt Eadmunde. 7 þridde mid Leofgiue seluen.*
>
> (Now there are three of these documents. One is in the king's sanctuary; and the second is at St Edmunds; and the third with Leofgifu herself.)[125]

Lowe has suggested that the use of the marker clause in the chirograph became a particular feature of the eleventh century, when it was becoming increasingly important to indicate in the text the holders of the various copies.[126]

When the multi-gift will emerges in the mid-tenth century it does so as a fully formed, cogent instrument capable of fulfilling its purpose of recording complex *post obitum* dispositions, and combining a formal affiliation with the royal charter with the functional immediacy of the vernacular. The process which led to the creation of the documents is reconstructed in Chapter Two.

## The single-gift bequest

A number of documents recording a gift or gifts of land to a single beneficiary share many of the formal and linguistic features of the multi-gift will (see

'Anglo-Saxon lay society', pp. 49–50. For more general use of the term in post-Conquest sources see Hazeltine, 'Comments', pp. xxiii-xxv (esp. at p. xxiv, n. 2).

122 Other examples of chirographs: S1471/R101, *Christ Church* 170; S1487/W13; S1503/W20, *Christ Church* 142; S1506/R32, *Christ Church* 121; S1522/N&S9; S1534/W19. S1810/*CR* 31 translates into Latin a vernacular bequest which was originally divided into three parts (*in tribus partibus divisum*).

123 The term is used by Lowe, 'Lay literacy', p. 171. Marker clauses are found in: S1510/R6, *Christ Church* 78; S1528/W25; S1465/R86, *Christ Church* 153; S1521/W29; S1527/W24; S1224/R92; S1531/W31; S1468/R97; S1470/R100; S1516/W33. S1530/W30, *Christ Church* 166 and S1471/R101, *Christ Church* 170 are chirographs which also include a marker clause.

124 S1810/*CR* 31; S1520/*LE* II, 88.

125 S1521/W29. This is also the case in S1520/*LE* II, 88, the will of Leofgifu.

126 Lowe, 'Lay literacy', pp. 175–6.

Appendix One). Several include a witness list,[127] and/or a sanction.[128] Most use language characteristic of the multi-gift will: a brief notification uses the verbs *cyðan* or *sweotelian* in relation to the donor's name;[129] the dispositive verb is *geunnan;*[130] and cohesion features are similar. Most use the formula *æfter X's dæg* to indicate deferment of the gift.[131] Occasional marker clauses are added, indicating that at least one other copy was made.[132] The bequests often include details typical of the multi-gift will. For example, donors may state the reason for the gift;[133] they may add conditions, or terms of tenure;[134] or they may state the origin of the property.[135]

The relationship between single-gift bequests and multi-gift wills is difficult to establish.[136] While some were probably free-standing, it may be that some were, as has been suggested above, extracts from a longer document;[137] the bequest of land by Ordnoth and his wife to the Old Minster, Winchester, was only part of a multi-gift declaration made before the community:

> *He 7 is* [sic] *wif cwædan on heora gewitnesse þ is* [sic] *æhta gangan on his freonda hand ofer his deg se ðel þe he cweþe.*
>
> (He and his wife announced in their presence that the part of his possessions which he stated was to go into his friends' possession after his death.)

The bequests to the donors' *freonda* need not necessarily, of course, have been written down; Ealdorman Æthelwold refers to dispositions which were to be carried out 'just as I have instructed the friends to whom I have been speaking'.[138] The complex relationship between the two extant single-gift versions of Thurstan's bequest of the estate at Wimbish (Ex) to Christ Church, Canterbury, discussed above, and the same gift as recorded in his multi-gift

127 S1530/W30, *Christ Church* 166; S1495/W22, *St Paul's* 22; S1512/W7; S1500/R3, *Christ Church* 39A; S1510/R6, *Christ Church* 78. That of S1234/R116, *Christ Church* 183 has been truncated. The authenticity of S1509/R27 is dubious (see n. 62 above).

128 S1495/W22, *St Paul's* 22; S1499/W35; S1529/W36. S1500/R3, *Christ Church* 39A has a clause prohibiting changes to the dispositions recorded in the document.

129 S1530/W30, *Christ Church* 166; S1495/W22, *St Paul's* 22; S1499/W35; S1512/W7; S1524/W5; S1510/R6, *Christ Church* 78; S1234/R116, *Christ Church* 183; 1513/R17.

130 Except S1510/R6, *Christ Church* 78 (*agifan*); S1495/W22, *St Paul's* 22 (*becweðan*); S1500/R3, *Christ Church* 39A (*arædan:* 'settle, decree').

131 Except S1495/W22, *St Paul's* 22 (*cwide*); S1499/W35 (gift placed in the context of the overall *cwide* in the prohibition clause/anathema).

132 S1530/W30, *Christ Church* 166; S1510/R6, *Christ Church* 78.

133 S1495/W22, *St Paul's* 22; S1530/W30, *Christ Church* 166.

134 S1234/R116, *Christ Church* 183; S1510/R6, *Christ Church* 78; S1530/W30, *Christ Church* 166.

135 S1513/R17.

136 Lowe, 'Nature and effect', pp. 30–3.

137 See p. 20 above.

138 S1524/W5; S1504/H20: *swa swa ic nu þam freondum sæde þæ ic to spræc.*

will, is also difficult to establish.[139] The dating of both the bequest and the will depends on the known dates of witnesses: for example, Stigand attests both versions of the bequest as priest; since he became bishop of Elmham in 1043, and is styled as such in the witness list of the will, it might be assumed that the will post-dates the bequest.[140] Unfortunately, Stigand was briefly deposed in the same year, so this assumption is uncertain. The fact that the bequest appears in the multi-gift will in the first person, and the single-gift version is couched in the third person, might suggest that the single-gift document was made as an abstract for individual beneficiaries (Christ Church and St Augustine's, Canterbury);[141] the multi-gift will is preserved in the Bury archive. This group, consisting of a multi-gift will and two versions of a single bequest contained within, it demonstrates the complexity of documentation which might surround will-making.

## The bequest-agreement

Like single-gift bequests, bequest-agreements are solely concerned with land transactions.[142] They share the features of the multi-gift wills and single-gift bequests described above: the majority include witness lists,[143] and were made in multiple copies;[144] two include anathemas.[145] The term *æfter X's dæg* is generally used to indicate deferment of completion, and in two cases the transaction is referred to as a *cwide*.[146] A distinctive feature of this group, as it has been identified by Lowe, is the element of contract between donor and beneficiary; characteristically, these documents include the terms *foreweard* or *geðinge* (both with the sense of 'agreement' or 'contract'), suggesting the bilateral nature of the transaction.[147]

The arrangements recorded in these documents vary in complexity, often involving the immediate transfer of rights in the land to the beneficiary, with

139 See pp. 19–20; S1530/W30, *Christ Church* 166, 1042x1043; S1531/W31, 1042x1044/1045.

140 For discussion of dating issues see *Wills*, pp. 189, 192.

141 Lowe's interpretation of the variations between the two versions of the single-gift bequest is given above, p. 20.

142 This group has been identified and discussed by Lowe, 'Nature and effect', pp. 28–9: S1200/H7, *Christ Church* 90; S1202/H8, *Christ Church* 95; S1224/R92; S1234/R116, *Christ Church* 183; S1455/R62, *St Augustine's* 31; S1471/R101, *Christ Church* 170; S1506/R32, *Christ Church* 121. See also S1465/R86, *Christ Church* 153; S1470/R100; S1474/R105; S1235/*St Albans* 17.

143 Lowe notes this as a distinguishing feature of the bequest-agreement: 'Nature and effect', p. 28.

144 This is generally indicated by a marker clause, although S1506/R32, *Christ Church* 121 survives as part of a chirograph.

145 S1470/R100; S1471/R101, *Christ Church* 170.

146 S1506/R32, *Christ Church* 121; S1465/R86, *Christ Church* 153.

147 Lowe, 'Nature and effect', p. 28.

reacquisition by the donor for a specified number of lives.[148] In some instances, this involves the immediate handing over of the *boc* (title-deed) to the beneficiary as a token of the gift.[149] In other instances, the donor is to pay a stipulated rent, either in coin or produce, in return for the use of the land for one or more lives;[150] in one case the donor made an estate over to the church and 'bought it [back]' (*hit gebohte*) for two lives on the payment of four pounds and an annual food-rent.[151] Occasionally, donors may impose the payment of rent on their successors, effectively recognising the completion of the gift on their own death.[152] The ultimate outcome is that the land reverts in full to the beneficiary at the end of the stated term.[153] The agreement (*forwarde*) between Wulfgeat and his wife and Bury represents a recurring pattern, whereby a community leases land to a grantee for one or more lives (in this case, for the lives of Wulfgeat and his wife, and Ælfwine and his wife), with reversion to the community along with one or more of the grantee's own estates.[154] Such bilateral arrangements may also occur in multi-gift wills alongside the unilateral bequests. A good example of the fluidity of the form is the multi-gift will of Ulf and Madselin, which announces itself as a *foreweard* and incorporates a number of contractual arrangements (including a mortgage agreement which the donors made with Bishop Ealdred before going on pilgrimage) as well as straightforward unilateral bequests.[155]

## Other evidence for vernacular will-making

Evidence from a number of sources indicates that more vernacular wills once existed than are now extant. While such evidence needs to be treated with caution, overall it endorses the significance of the role of the vernacular will

148 The forms of agreement described here equate to those identified by legal historians in Continental documents: *precaria oblata* and *precaria remuneratoria*; for a description of these categories and their relevance to Anglo-Saxon wills see Lowe, 'Nature and effect', p. 26, and K. A. Lowe, 'Wills', *Blackwell Encyclopaedia*, pp. 478–80.

149 As in: S1506/R32, *Christ Church* 121; S1471/R101, *Christ Church* 170; S1524/W5; S1512/W7; S1514/R9, *Rochester* 23.

150 S1530/W30, *Christ Church* 166; S1455/R62, *St Augustine's* 31; S1465/R86, *Christ Church* 153.

151 S1465/R86, *Christ Church* 153 (*forwyrd*).

152 For example, S1506/R6, *Christ Church* 78; S1487/*St Albans* 7; S1511/W11, Rochester 35; S1538/W21, Bath and Wells 21; S1484/W8; S1202/H8, *Christ Church* 95; S1506/R32, *Christ Church* 121, a contemporary manuscript which bears an endorsement confirming the agreement with the donor's successor.

153 Sheehan, *The Will*, pp. 25–7.

154 S1470/R100.

155 W39/*Peterborough* 27 (1066x1068). A similar mortgage arrangement features in the single-gift bequest of Æthelnoth and Gænburg – an agreement in everything but name (S1500/R3, *Christ Church* 39A).

in later Anglo-Saxon society, and often provides a valuable perspective on aspects of the will-making process.

### Latin chronicles: the *Liber Eliensis* and *Chronicon Abbatiæ Rameseiensis*

The twelfth-century chronicles associated with the fenland abbeys of Ely and Ramsey are a particularly rich source of information on the bequest of land, with good evidence to suggest that their compilers drew on a substantial body of pre-Conquest vernacular documentation.

Although the early religious house at Ely, founded by St Æthelthryth in the later seventh century, was probably destroyed during Viking incursions *c.* 870, the shrine survived, and formed the focus of the abbey's refoundation under the aegis of Bishop Æthelwold *c.* 970.[156] The *Liber Eliensis*, a history of the abbey, was compiled between 1131 and 1174, drawing on a variety of sources.[157] Most significant for the present study is Book Two, which incorporates an earlier Latin text describing the endowment and land transactions of the abbey between its refoundation in 970 and the late 980s. The text in question, the *Libellus quorundam insignium operum beati Æthelwoldi episcopi* (referred to as the *Libellus*), is also preserved separately in two twelfth-century manuscripts; in its turn it was based on an Old English source, the precise nature of which is unclear.[158] Book Two of the *Liber Eliensis* draws on its Latin predecessor as far as chapter forty-nine, but later chapters also incorporate references to bequests which may have originated in vernacular documents.[159]

Ramsey Abbey, on the other hand, was newly founded *c.* 966 by Æthelwine, Ealdorman of East Anglia (962–992), in association with Bishop Oswald of Worcester.[160] The *Chronicon Abbatiæ Rameseiensis* (here referred to as the Ramsey Chronicle) is a *liber benefactorum*, probably compiled *c.* 1170 (a date

156 For the abbey's history see S. Keynes, 'Ely Abbey 672–1109', in *A History of Ely Cathedral*, ed. P. Meadows and N. Ramsay (Woodbridge, 2003), pp. 2–58.

157 *LE*, pp. xxviii–xlix. Quotations are from *LE*. English translations are taken from *Liber Eliensis: a History of the Isle of Ely from the Seventh Century to the Twelfth*, transl. J. Fairweather (Woodbridge, 2005), unless otherwise stated.

158 For the *Libellus* see *LE*, p. xxxiv and Appendix A, pp. 395–6; A. Kennedy, 'Law and litigation in the *Libellus Æthelwoldi episcopi*', *ASE* 24 (1995), 131–83; Keynes, 'Ely Cathedral', pp. 5–9. An edition of the *Libellus* is forthcoming: S. Keynes and A. Kennedy, *Anglo-Saxon Ely: Records of Ely Abbey and its Benefactors in the Tenth and Eleventh Centuries*. Reference to the *Libellus* are made by chapter, in conjunction with *LE* (e.g. *LE* II, 47/*Lib* 58).

159 See Appendix 2 below. For discussion of Ely cartularies see *LE*, pp. xxxix–xlii. In two cases, vernacular wills including the bequests to Ely recorded in the chronicle survive in other archives (S1486/W15, *LE* II, 63; S1487/W13, *LE* II, 73).

160 The abbey's foundation and history is summarised by J. Blair, 'Ramsey Abbey', *Blackwell Encyclopaedia*, pp. 385–6.

based on the latest material recorded).[161] The compiler drew on a number of sources, including Byrhtferth's life of St Oswald, written at Ramsey between 997 and 1002, and perhaps a hypothetical Latin chronicle for the period *c.* 958 to *c.* 992 by the same author, but his main evidence for the abbey's benefactors from its foundation *c.* 966 consisted of the pre-Conquest charters stored in the abbey's archive, which appear to have been disintegrating.[162] He declares his intention to translate them for future reference, and so that donors will continue to be commemorated even if the lands they gave had been lost to the abbey.[163] These charters seem to have included a number of multi-gift wills and single-gift bequests which are duly translated and incorporated in the text.

The *Liber Eliensis* and the *Chronicon Rameseiensis* may be placed in the tradition of local histories written particularly in the south of England in the reigns of Stephen (1135–1154) and Henry II (1154–1189), when 'the lawlessness of the nobility and the expanding claims of the crown threatened and challenged vested interests'.[164] Whereas some archives – such as Rochester – preserved their ancient charters in cartularies, others embedded the material in narrative.[165] The Ely and Ramsey chronicles record the endowment of two important fenland abbeys at a time when the religious reforms of the tenth century prompted significant transfers of land from the laity to the church. It has been calculated, for example, that the founders of Ramsey, Bishop Oswald and Ealdorman Æthelwine, were responsible for the transfer of over one hundred hides of land.[166] Bishop Æthelwold, lacking the patronage available to Oswald, mounted a vigorous pursuit of land for his church at Ely, frequently driving a hard bargain, as the *Liber Eliensis* reveals.[167] From 975,

161 *CR*, p. xxii. Quotations are from *CR*. Translations of chapters 1–60 are taken from *Ramsey Abbey's Book of Benefactors*, Parts I and II, transl. S. B. Edgington and others (Huntingdon, 1998 and 2001); translations of other chapters are my own. Bequests are listed in Appendix 2 below.

162 For the sources of *CR* see A. Gransden, *Historical Writing in England c. 550-c. 1307* (London, 1974), pp. 273–5; *Byrhtferth's Enchiridion*, ed. P. S. Baker and M. Lapidge (Oxford, 1995), pp. xxxii-xxxiii. For the date of Byrhtnoth's *Vita Oswaldi* see M. Lapidge, 'Byrhtferth and Oswald', in *St Oswald*, ed. Brooks and Cubitt, p. 65, and pp. 76–8 for the hypothetical Latin chronicle. For the compiler's references to the deteriorating charters see *CR* 1, 39.

163 *CR* 1, 23, 30, 106.

164 Gransden, *Historical Writing*, p. 269. See also Rumble, '*Codex Wintoniensis*', pp. 157–8.

165 See Lowe, 'Latin versions', p. 4, for discussion of format, and for the integrity of charter material. For eleventh-century monastic chronicles, see P. J. Geary, *Phantoms of Remembrance* (Princeton NJ, 1994), Chap. 4; Tinti, 'Hemming's cartulary', pp. 234–5, describes the different approaches in the two eleventh-century Worcester cartularies (see also Tinti, *Sustaining Belief*, pp. 147–50).

166 J. A. Raftis, *The Estates of Ramsey Abbey* (Toronto, 1957), p. 7.

167 For Ely's acquisition of land see E. Miller, *The Abbey and Bishopric of Ely: the Social History of an Ecclesiastical Estate from the Tenth to the Early Fourteenth Century* (Cambridge, 1951), pp. 16–25; Keynes, 'Ely Cathedral', p. 26.

following the death of King Edgar, supporter of the monastic reform, church lands were less secure. Ely, in particular, faced a number of disputes; the *Liber Eliensis* catalogues the estates lost to the abbey in the succeeding century.[168] The Ramsey compiler bemoans the loss of abbey lands, some of which were redistributed in 1066 or lost in later political turbulence.[169] It may have been the absence from the archive of royal charters giving title which prompted renewed interest in pre-Conquest vernacular documentation related to particular estates.

Since the chronicles may well be regarded as partisan, it is difficult to be sure to what extent their evidence can be taken at face value. An imaginative approach to the compilation of evidence was not unknown: in the Ramsey Chronicle, for example, the royal confirmation charter purportedly issued by Edgar in 974 and the writ of King Edward granting extensive judicial and financial rights to the abbey are indeed forgeries.[170] However, there seems good reason to accept that a pre-Conquest vernacular record of land transactions, including bequests, existed at Ely, and was finally incorporated into the twelfth-century *Liber Eliensis*. By implication, the existence of an archive of vernacular documents, as asserted by the Ramsey compiler, is credible. As Appendix Two shows, vernacular wills which include bequests to both Ramsey and Ely occasionally survive in different archives. Unfortunately, it is not always easy to correlate the evidence, as in the case of the Ramsey Chronicle's record that Ælfhelm and his wife, Æffe, granted land at Hatley and Potton (Beds.) to Ramsey Abbey – apparently *inter vivos* – for the sake of their souls; reference is made to the evidence of the *præsentis paginæ*, which was duly witnessed.[171] In spite of the fact that Potton and two hides at Hatley appear to have been inherited by Æffe through the will of her father, Æthelstan Mannessune (also recorded in the Ramsey Chronicle), Ælfhelm himself, in his own multi-gift will which is extant as a contemporary single sheet, bequeaths Hatley and Potton to two brothers, Ælfmær and Ælfstan, rather than to Ramsey.[172] A further complication is added by an entry in a gospel book associated with Ely, which records Ælfhelm's grant of one hide at Potton to his goldsmith, also called Leofsige, and possibly the beneficiary of that name who was to inherit remaining land at Hatley in Æthelstan Mannes-

168 E.g. *LE* II, 42–47/*Lib* 53–57.

169 *CR* 1, 23, 79, 89, 107.

170 S798, *CR* 111 (*ECEE*, no. 18); S1109, *CR* 97 (*Writs* 61). See also A. Williams, 'Thegnly piety and patronage in the late Old English kingdom', *ANS* 24 (2001), 1–24 (pp. 3–4) for a view which inclines to scepticism, and n. 165 above.

171 *CR* 34.

172 *CR* 33, *c.* 986; S1487/W13, 975x1016. Æffe was to have a life interest in Potton, which would revert to Æthelstan's nephew 'if he could establish title to it' (*dirationare posset*) which, according to the Ramsey chronicler, he failed to do (*CR* 34).

sune's will.[173] Various valiant attempts have been made to disentangle the convoluted threads of these relationships and transactions.[174] They may represent negotiations and subdivisions of estates of which we have no record, or the Ramsey Chronicle entry recording the gift of Ælfhelm and Æffe may be an example of wishful thinking; there is no other indication that Ramsey had an interest in land at Hatley or Potton.[175]

Formal and stylistic parallels between a number of the Latin versions of bequests and vernacular wills increase the probability that original Old English documents were indeed the source for the chronicle accounts. The Latin phrasing may be reminiscent of that found in extant vernacular texts, as where bequests are made for the soul of the donor *pro anime suae*, rendering Old English *for his sawle*.[176] References to bequest for the souls of relatives or ancestors may also be paralleled: *pro ... antecessorum suorum animabus* may render Old English *for ure aldre soule*. The phrase *pretium sepulturae* may translate Old English *saulsceat* (soul-scot, or burial dues), a term found in vernacular wills and laws.[177] Similarly, Gode's bequest to Ramsey is to take effect *post dies suos*, rendering Old English *æfter his dæge*.[178] The vernacular term *heregeat* (heriot) occurs once, glossed by the compiler as *relevatio haereditatis*.[179] One rare example of an extended Latin will included in the *Liber Eliensis* is that of Leofflæd, which parallels the form of vernacular multi-gift documents as it is outlined above.[180] It begins with a notification clause, addressed to King Cnut (1016–1035), followed by dispositive clauses, and concludes with a sanction clause and reference to the triplication of the document:

> *Hec scripto tripliciter consignantur. Unum est apud Ely, aliud in thesaurus regis, tertium Leofleda habet.*
>
> (These things are recorded in a document written out in triplicate. There is one at Ely, another is in the king's treasury and Leofflæd possesses the third.)[181]

173 S1218a/R71; *Catalogue of Manuscripts Containing Anglo-Saxon* ed. N. R. Ker (Oxford, 1957), no. 22.

174 *Wills*, pp. 133–7; *Charters*, pp. 388–9; C. R. Hart, 'Eadnoth, first abbot of Ramsey and the foundation of Chatteris and St Ives', *Proceedings of the Cambridge Antiquarian Society* 56–7 (1964), 61–7, revised and reprinted in Hart, *The Danelaw*, pp. 613–23 (pp. 619–20); Wareham, 'St Oswald's family and kin', pp. 51–3.

175 Potton was held by the king in 1066, and by Countess Judith in 1086; Cockayne Hatley was held by Earl Tostig, and in 1086 it belonged to the countess's manor of Potton: DB I, fol. 217v.

176 As in *CR* 53 and S1487/W13 (p. 30, line 20). See also *CR* 35, 107 and S1512/W27 for variants.

177 *CR* 107 (p. 175) and e.g. I Æthelstan, 4.

178 *CR* 55 and S1487/W13 (*Wills*, p. 30, line 26).

179 *CR* 63. For heriot, see Chap. 5, pp. 190–4 below.

180 *LE* II, 88; see pp. 24–33 above.

181 Anathemas are found in *CR* 31, 33, 35, 42, 107.

The occasional survival of such distribution details, together with passing references by the *Liber Eliensis* compiler to the documentation of bequests, adds weight to the likelihood that vernacular wills were preserved in both archives.[182]

As in the case of vernacular wills, dating of individual transactions recorded in the chronicles is often insecure, but it is clear that the majority of bequests occurred in the latter part of the tenth century, the years immediately following the foundation of Ramsey and the re-foundation of Ely, suggesting that the initial impetus for bequest came from the influence of the founders. Nevertheless, bequests and *post obitum* agreements continued to be a significant source of monastic land into the eleventh century.[183]

By comparing Latin versions of pre-Conquest wills in chronicles and cartularies with the related vernacular texts which occasionally survive, Lowe has shown that translators were likely to select and adapt the original material.[184] Unlike their fourteenth- and fifteenth-century successors, twelfth-century scribes seem to have been sufficiently literate in the vernacular to edit as well as translate the text before them, often omitting bequests not directly relevant to their purpose.[185] Many references to *post obitum* disposition in both the Ely and Ramsey chronicles are brief, occasionally made in passing in the course of the narrative. The Ramsey compiler acknowledges truncation where information is irrelevant to the community; following the Latin translation of bequests of land by Godric to the abbey and to his younger son he writes:

> *Præter hæc quoque plurima alia dona quæ aliis concessit in eodem scripto reperimus, quæ quia nos minime contingebant in figuris Anglicis neglecta remanserunt.*
>
> (In addition to these, we find in the same writing many other gifts which he [Godric] granted to others, [which] have remained neglected in English letters because they are of little concern to us.)[186]

182 *CR* 31; *LE* II, 11/*Lib* 12 (the detailed account of the will-making of Siferth of Downham, discussed in Chap. 2 below); *LE* II, 70. The Latin term 'chirograph' used in the rubrics and introductions to documents in both the *LE* and *CR* does not necessarily have the specific meaning of duplication or triplication: Hazeltine ('Comments', p. xxiv, n. 2) cites evidence that Norman writers used the term *chirograph* as a 'terminus technicus' to designate Anglo-Saxon documents; see Kennedy, 'Law and litigation', p. 162, n. 120 for usage of the term in the *Libellus*. See Appendix 2 below for references to the documentation of bequests in *LE*.

183 Miller, *Ely*, pp. 16–18, 21–2; Raftis, *Ramsey*, pp. 6–7, 13–15.

184 Lowe, 'Latin versions', *passim*, to which this account is indebted. See Appendix 2 below for vernacular wills from other archives underlying *LE* or *CR* Latin versions.

185 Lowe, '"*As fre as thowt*'?", pp. 18–20.

186 *CR* 63 (my translation); Lowe, 'Latin versions', p. 2. The compiler also records that *Acleya*, bequeathed by Godric to his son Eadnoth, was subsequently bequeathed by the latter to Ramsey.

The scribe appears to have had before him Godric's vernacular multi-gift will, presumably incorporating bequests to beneficiaries other than Ramsey; he tells us that he had also included in his translation Godric's bequest of *Acleya* (Oakley, Nfk) to his younger son, Eadnoth, because Eadnoth subsequently bequeathed the land to the abbey. There is also frequent indication in the chronicle accounts that witness lists have been truncated. For example, in the Ramsey Chronicle the donors Ærnketel and Wulfrun address *Æthelredo regi domino nostro et omnibus suis de Eboraco et de Notingeham*.[187] Occasionally a more detailed list of names survives, perhaps where the bequest has been (or may be) subject to dispute. The account in the Ramsey Chronicle of the negotiations concerning the will of Æthelstan Mannessune which took place a year after his death is a case in point: witnesses include Æthelsige, son of Ealdorman Æthelstan, Leofric, son of Ealdorman Æthelwine, other named individuals 'and many more' (*et aliorum multorum*).[188]

The evidence for vernacular will-making preserved in these chronicles is a particularly valuable supplement to that of the surviving wills because the narrative context which is often provided – particularly by the Ely compiler – is generally absent from the vernacular documents. Such context is especially important in establishing circumstances in which wills were made or challenged, offering glimpses of the relationship between lay donors, their kindred, and the church.

**Latin documents**

The evidence of a small number of Latin documents for both individual bequests and other aspects of *post obitum* disposition also complements that of the vernacular wills (see Appendix 1C).

The earliest is dated 762: Dunwald's bequest of a residence (*villam*) in Canterbury to the church of St Peter and St Paul (later to become St Augustine's monastery).[189] Although the text survives only in a thirteenth-century cartulary associated with St Augustine's, it makes it clear that Dunwald originally added his bequest to the royal charter which granted him land, and which has not survived.[190] The most recent editor has noted the formal relationship of this bequest to that of the contemporary land charter.[191] The document adopts a narrative style, with Dunwald made to explain the reason for his grant: he has been given the task of taking money to Rome for the soul of

187 'Our lord King Æthelred and all his people of York and Nottingham'; *CR* 38. This parallels the summary phrase concluding the vernacular will of Wulfgyth (S1535/W32, *Christ Church* 176), surviving only in a twelfth-century copy: *þisses to ywithnesse Eadward king and manie oþre*. See also *LE* II, 67. Lowe, 'Latin versions', p. 19.

188 *CR* 33.

189 S1182/ *St Augustine's* 12, *EHD* I, no. 72.

190 See nn. 14–18, 22 above for further examples of this practice.

191 *St Augustine's*, pp. 49–50.

his patron, King Æthelberht of Kent. He bequeaths a specific property 'in the market-place at the Queen's gate' to the church, unless he should make the gift in his life-time, terms which suggest that he hoped to enjoy his property on his return, but recognised the dangers of the journey before him. He asserts that the king granted him this and other property with freedom of disposal, and explains that he has recorded this bequest on that charter. In addition, he has 'caused to be set out this deed of my donation and have strengthened it with my own hand' (*hunc libellum huiusce donationis mee describi feci et manu propria roboraui*) in order to prevent dispute, and possibly, as Kelly has suggested, to take account of the fact that his bequest involved only one of the estates named in the royal charter of donation.[192] The witness list follows, including the names of Archbishop Bregowine and Abbot Jænberht of St Augustine's as well as that of the donor.[193]

A further Canterbury document – this time from the archive of Christ Church – is the will of the priest Werhard, a kinsman of Archbishop Wulfred (805–832). The text survives in Latin (with later interpolations), but may have been based on a vernacular original.[194] The interest of this document lies in Werhard's bequest of the acquired property of Archbishop Wulfred, who, according to the will, bequeathed a life interest in these extensive estates to his kinsman before its reversion to Christ Church, along with Werhard's own patrimony; Brooks suggests that Werhard's will reflects the influence of a Mercian noble family at Christ Church over two generations.[195]

Two further Latin documents concerned with the bequest of land are preserved in the eleventh-century Worcester cartularies.[196] The first, preserved in the later eleventh-century cartulary attributed to Hemming, is an account

192 *St Augustine's*, p. 49.

193 For possible truncation of the witness list, see *St Augustine's*, p. 50.

194 This survives in the Christ Church, Canterbury cartulary (S1414, *Christ Church* 64, *c.* 833), printed in *Diplomatarium*, ed.Thorpe, pp. 466–8; for the manuscript details and diplomatic discussion, together with the suggestion that this is based on a vernacular original, see Brooks, *Early History*, Appendix A, p. 323. This may also be the case with S1502/*St Augustine's* 38, the Latin single-gift bequest of Æthelric Bigga to St Augustine's, which supplements Æthelric's vernacular bequest-agreement with Christ Church, S1471/R101, *Christ Church* 170 and has parallels with vernacular bequests: *St Augustine's*, p. 133.

195 The case is made by Brooks, *Early History*, pp. 139–42. Archbishop Wulfred, his kinsman Werhard and King Coenwulf of Mercia, from whom Wulfred acquired much of the land, were all commemorated at Christ Church on 9 Kal April, apparently linked by this benefaction: R. Fleming, 'Christ Church's sisters and brothers: an edition and discussion of Canterbury *obit* lists', in *The Culture of Christendom: Essays in Medieval History in Memory of Denis L. T. Bethell*, ed. M. A. Meyer (London, 1993), pp. 115–53 (p. 127).

196 For the compilation of the early eleventh century *Liber Wigorniensis* and late eleventh century cartulary associated with Hemming see nn. 34, 35 above.

of proceedings at two synods which took place at *Clofesho* and *Acleia*.[197] Although this document is dated 804 in the opening clause, it incorporates information from a further synod which took place no later than 807, indicating that the first section, at least, was written retrospectively.[198] The whole is couched in the first person. Æthelric, son of Æthelmund, relates that he appeared before a synod at *Clofesho* to justify his right to dispose freely of land at Westbury-on-Trym (Glos.), which he had inherited from his father, and which seems to have been the subject of dispute.[199] On examination of his title-deeds (*libris*), the synod ruled in his favour. Æthelric then left his land in trust with friends while he went on pilgrimage.[200] The account goes on to relate that, a few years after reclaiming his land, Æthelric attended another synod and declared his will, which is then quoted. He grants estates to the church of Deerhurst (Glos.), where he wishes to be buried (and which may have been a family foundation), subject to the condition that the community fulfilled its vows (*vota*) as promised; the church at Gloucester is to receive thirty hides; a certain Wærferth is to have a life interest in two estates, with reversion to Worcester; and Æthelric's mother, Ceolburh, who became abbess of the religious house at Berkeley (Glos.), is to hold Westbury for her lifetime, together with land at Stoke, with reversion to Worcester.[201] Æthelric places Ceolburh's claim to the land in the protection of Worcester and the Archbishop of Canterbury, who witnessed the transaction, and copies of the document were lodged with the Bishop of Lichfield (also named as a witness) and two of Æthelric's loyal friends.

The second Worcester document, preserved in the earlier of the eleventh-century cartularies, is also concerned with land at Westbury, recording King

197 S1187/*EHD* I, no. 81; BL Cotton Tiberius A xiii fols. 49–50, 198v–199v (Hemming's Cartulary); Davis, *Cartularies*, no. 1068 (2). The Latin text may be found in *Diplomatarium*, ed. Thorpe, pp. 54–5.

198 For issues surrounding dating, see P. Wormald, 'Charters, law and the settlement of disputes', in *The Settlement of Disputes in Early Medieval Europe*, ed. W. Davies and P. Fouracre (Cambridge, 1986), pp. 149–68, reprinted in P. Wormald, *Legal Culture in the Medieval West: Law as Text, Image and Experience* (London, 1999), pp. 289–311 (p. 295, n. 26); C. Cubitt, *Anglo-Saxon Church Councils c. 650-c. 850* (Leicester, 1995), p. 281.

199 Ealdorman Æthelmund's death is recorded in the *ASC* s.a. 802. S139 (793x796) records a grant of land at Westbury to Æthelmund by King Offa: see below. This synod probably gives the document its date of 804.

200 The land appears to have been mortgaged, since, on his return, Æthelric repaid the money he owed to those holding his land. See a similar arrangement in the eleventh-century will of Ulf and Madselin (W39/*Peterborough* 27).

201 Wormald, 'Charters, law', p. 296. Stoke may be Stoke Bishop (Glos.) or Stoke Prior (Worcs.): P. Sims-Williams, *Religion and Literature in Western England, 600–800* (Cambridge, 1990), pp. 175–6; Wormald, 'Charters, law', pp. 310–11. For Gloucester and Deerhurst see Tinti, *Sustaining Belief*, pp. 230–9. The Abbess Ceolburh whose death is recorded in the *ASC* s.a. 807 may have been Æthelric's mother, which determines the *terminus ante quem* for the synod at which Æthelric declared his bequests (Cubitt, *Church Councils*, p. 281).

Offa's bequest of sixty hides at Westbury and twenty hides at Henbury (Glos.) to Worcester, reserving a life interest for his son Ecgberht.[202] The bequest is made for Offa's soul, and the souls of his parents, details of food-rent due from the estate are given, and a witness list follows, including the names of Offa and his son, Archbishop Æthelheard and further church and lay dignitaries. Although this text has generally been accepted as authentic, Whitelock pointed out that 'it is difficult to reconcile' this bequest of Westbury with Æthelric's claim in S1187 on what appears to be the same estate.[203] To add a further complication, a contemporary single-sheet manuscript survives recording Offa's grant of fifty-five hides at Westbury to Æthelric's father, Æthelmund.[204] As Wormald remarked in his discussion of these documents, 'these are what diplomatists usually consider suspicious circumstances'.[205]

Wormald suggested that the documentation surrounding the bequest of Westbury by Æthelric and Offa was created in the Worcester scriptorium in the early ninth century, in response to a dispute which is recorded in a further document copied into Hemming's Cartulary.[206] According to the document in question, in 824 the 'Berkeley people', possibly members of Ceolburh's own community, whose encroachment on the Westbury estate Æthelric had apparently envisaged in his will, challenged Worcester's claim on the land.[207] The dispute was brought before a further council at *Clofesho*, where Bishop Heahberht of Worcester produced documents (*libris*) in support of his claim, and reference was made to Æthelric's bequest. The council found in favour of Worcester. Although considerable emphasis seems to have been placed on documentary evidence in the adjudication of this dispute, it is unclear whether S1187 was indeed included in the bishop's evidence presented to the council. If it was compiled for this purpose, it must be assumed that the procedure of lay will-making which it describes was familiar not only in the Worcester scriptorium, but also to those adjudicating, and that the documentation of such bequests was admissible for consideration. However, if a royal charter in Worcester's favour (S146) had indeed been concocted in the scriptorium to strengthen its claim to Westbury, it seems that the record of the will was regarded, in itself, as being of limited value in establishing title.[208] The

202 S146/*EHD* I, no. 78 (*Diplomatarium*, ed.Thorpe, pp. 39–40); British Museum Cotton Tiberius A xiii fol. 48; Davis, *Cartularies*, no. 1068 (1).

203 *EHD* I, p. 512.

204 S139, 793x796; Cubitt, *Church Councils*, p. 274.

205 'Charters, law', p. 296. The documentation relating to this estate is also discussed by Tinti, *Sustaining Belief*, pp. 203–6.

206 S1433/*EHD* I, no. 84 (*Diplomatarium*, ed. Thorpe, pp. 67–9); BL Cotton Tiberius A. xiii fols. 47–48; Davis, *Cartularies*, no. 1068 (2). For Wormald's case see his 'Charters, law', pp. 296–8.

207 Sims-Williams, *Religion and Literature*, p. 176.

208 Wormald argues that S146, Offa's putative bequest of Westbury to Worcester, was adapted from a near-contemporary charter, which included food-rent details and an

use of Latin in S1187 to record Æthelric's dispositions, which would undoubtedly have been made in the vernacular, suggests that at the beginning of the ninth century the vernacular written will, already established at Canterbury, had not found favour at Worcester.[209]

**Other references to wills and will-making**

References also exist to written wills which no longer survive, although it is not clear whether they were written in Latin or the vernacular. In Asser's Life of King Alfred we are told that two years after Alfred's father, King Æthelwulf (839–858), returned from Rome *c.* 856, he made a will:

> ... *cogitans de suo ad universitatis viam transitu, ne sui filii post patris obitum indebite inter se disceptarent, hereditariam, immo commendatoriam, scribi imperavit epistolam.*
>
> (... as he reflected on his going the way of all flesh, he had a testamentary – or rather advisory – epistle drawn up so that his sons should not quarrel unnecessarily among themselves after the death of their father.)[210]

Asser summarises the king's dispositions, which included the divison of the kingdom between his two eldest sons, the division of his own inheritance (*propriae hereditatis*) among his sons, daughters and kinsmen, the distribution of money, and the provision for alms and pious gifts.[211] Æthelwulf's youngest son, King Alfred, ordered his father's *yrfegewrit* to be read before a meeting of the *witan*, apparently as evidence of his right to inherit the family land, but it is difficult to determine the relationship between the two documents; nevertheless, Alfred clearly felt that such a document (genuine or spurious) would strengthen his case.[212]

appropriate witness list: 'Charters, law', p. 296–97; Sims-Williams, *Religion and Literature*, p. 174, n. 147. For the possible use of forged charters of Offa to defend valuable assets 'accumulated through small benefactions' at St Albans, see J. Crick, 'Offa, Ælfric and the refoundation of St Albans', in *Alban and St Albans: Roman and Medieval Architecture, Art and Archaeology*, ed. M. Henig and P. Lindley, The British Archaeological Association Conference Transactions 25 (Leeds, 2001), 78–84 (esp. p. 83).

209 See the discussion of the Worcester archive above, n. 33 and pp. 17–18, and S1446/H15, with its possible reference to a will (below pp. 49–50). A further document, the burial payment of Wihburg (S1227, 1046x1062), also recorded in Hemming's Cartulary, is a forgery in its present form but is significant as evidence of interest in recording bequests at Worcester in the eleventh century (Tinti, 'Hemming's Cartulary', pp. 253–4).

210 *Asser*, chap. 16, p.14; Keynes and Lapidge (London, 1983), p. 72 (although I have substituted 'epistle' for their 'document' in the translation of *epistola*: see n. 66 above).

211 *Asser*, chap. 16.

212 S1507/H11, *New Minster* 1. King Alfred's will, together with the account of the council meeting which precedes it (at which Æthelwulf's *yrfegewrit* was read), is discussed in Chap. 3 below.

Two further written wills may once have existed. It appears that Ealdorman Oswulf made a written will since a document dated 844, an account of the final settlement of an ongoing challenge to Oswulf's dispositions, refers to the *altera kartula* which recorded his will.[213] Although the will itself does not survive, other documents recording his gifts to the church are extant, making the existence of a will granting property in reversion to the church inherently likely.[214] A similar brief reference, this time to a *testamentum*, occurs in the account of a disputed bequest at Worcester recorded by Hemming.[215] We are told that, as he lay dying, Toki, a king's thegn, bequeathed land *testamento* to Bishop Ealdred (1046–1061); this *testamentum* was challenged by Toki's son, Aki, who, in the presence of a prestigious gathering, accepted eight marks of gold from the bishop in return for relinquishing his claim on the property.[216]

One of the difficulties is that references in the sources to a bequest or will-making do not always make it clear whether documentation is involved. For example, in the tale of a land-owning woman incorporated into Lantfred's Life of St Swithun, written between 971 and 981, she was urged to 'put her estates in order before death came upon her', but there is no evidence of the drawing up of a written will.[217] A similar problem arises in the interpretation of a law concerned with will-making: the second code of King Cnut, dated *c.*1020, refers to the possibility of a man dying intestate (*cwydeleas*), with the implication that this is undesirable:

213 S1439, 844 (*Diplomatarium*, ed. Thorpe, pp. 96–100). This document is lost, surviving only in a transcript. For Oswulf's death 810x820 see J. Crick, 'Church, land and local nobility: the case of Ealdorman Oswulf', *Bulletin of the Institute of Historical Research* 61 (1988), 251–69 (pp. 254–8), and Cubitt, *Church Councils*, p. 283.

214 S153, 798; S1188/H1, 805x810. For discussion of the complex documentation surrounding transactions involving Oswulf, see *SEHD*, pp. 69–70; Crick, 'Church, land', *passim*; Cubitt, *Church Councils*, p. 283.

215 S1408, 1052x1056 (*Codex Diplomaticus*, ed. Kemble, IV, no. 805). This text may be dubious as it stands, but 'may well contain authentic material': A. G. Kennedy, 'Disputes about *bocland*: the forum for their adjudication', *ASE* 14 (1985), 175–95 (pp. 194–5, n. 74). It survives in BL Cotton Tiberius A. xiii, fol. 178rv ( Hemming's Cartulary: see n. 35 above).

216 Tinti suggests that the three hides at Teddington (Worcs.) which formed part of Toki's bequest may have been leased over more than one generation: *Sustaining Belief*, p. 178. There is no mention of the use of documentary evidence by Bishop Ealdred in support of his case, in contrast with Bishop Heahberht's *libris* produced in asserting Worcester's title to Westbury (p. 45 above).

217 *Omnes itaque uicini, affines et famuli ad eam accedentes, hortabantur eam gementes, ut proprias disponeret possessiones antequam necis interitus aduentaret, quoniam arbitrabantur eam cito obituram*: *The Cult of St Swithun*, ed. and transl. M. Lapidge, Winchester Studies 4, ii, (Oxford 2003), pp. 290–3, and p. 236 for dating. See also S1476/R114, *c.* 1053, an agreement between the Old Minster, Winchester, and Wulfweard, concerning land which Queen Ælfgifu bequeathed (*bæcweð*) to both parties: no documentary evidence was apparently produced to support the claim of the monks to this land in 1086 (*Charters*, p. 462).

> *Gyf of ðysum life man gewite cwydeleas, sy hit ðurh his gymelyste, sy hyt ðurh færlicne deaþ, ðonne ne teo se laford nan mare on his æhte butan his rihtan heregeate.*
>
> (If a man departs from this life intestate, whether through negligence or through sudden death, his lord shall take no more from his property than his legal heriot.)[218]

Although the term *cwide* is used in a number of written wills to refer to the document, in this context it could equally refer to the oral process.[219] Cnut's law is more concerned with the effect of intestacy than with the manner of will-making. A clause in the law of King Alfred seems to imply that documentary evidence of a man's intentions with regard to the transmission of land through inheritance *may* be available, but is too vague to constitute a reference to a written will.[220] Similarly, a number of writs of King Edward (1042–1066) addressed to the shire confirm bequests, but again there is usually no evidence of a written will;[221] in only one case – Edward's writ confirming the will of Ælfric Modercope – does the will itself survive as a post-Conquest copy in the Bury archive.[222]

Given the potentially contentious nature of the bequest of land, reference to written wills or will-making might be expected to feature prominently in the surviving accounts of disputes concerned with inheritance; the combative formula from the late tenth or early eleventh century known as *Hit Becwæð* appears to be an assertion of a beneficiary's right to hold land which he has inherited from one whose ancestors had acquired it, and who had the right to bequeath it freely.[223] However, as has already been shown in relation to the dispute concerning Westbury, where such references to the documentation of bequests occur, there is limited evidence to suggest that a will was actually produced in support of a claim. In two cases an *yrfegewrit* is produced as evidence. In the first, already mentioned above, the *yrfegewrit* produced by King Alfred before the *witan* may have been related to his father's will as

218 II Cnut, 70: *Laws*, ed. Robertson, pp. 208–209.

219 See n. 86 above for the term *cwide*.

220 Alfred, 41: *gif hær bið gewrit oððe gewitnes* (if there is documentary or other evidence).

221 *Writs* 2 (S1064), 12 (S1072), 17 (S1077), 22 (S1082), 111(S1153); doubtful or spurious: 74 (S1118), 84 (S1128), 93 (S1137), 112 (S1154).

222 *Writs* 22 (S1082); S1490/W28.

223 *Hit Becwæð* is translated and discussed by P. Wormald, *The Making of English Law: King Alfred to the Twelfth Century* (Oxford, 1999), pp. 384–5; the Old English text is printed in *Die Gesetze der Angelsachsen*, ed. F. Liebermann, 3 vols. (Halle, 1898–1916), I, 400. Disputes concerning inheritance listed in P. Wormald, 'A handlist of Anglo-Saxon lawsuits', *ASE* 17 (1988), 247–81, reprinted in Wormald, *Legal Culture*, pp. 253–87: nos. 57, 58 (S877/*EHD* I, no. 120); 89 (S1077, *Writs* 17); 32 (S1211/*SEHD* 23); 86 (S1404/*Writs* 3); 90 (S1408); 40 (S1447/R44); 47 (S1458/R41: in this case, a will is made in triplicate, but not apparently used in evidence); 85(S1474/R105). In addition, S1446/H15.

described by Asser.[224] In the second case, a vernacular account of a dispute copied into the earlier of the eleventh-century Worcester cartularies, the *yrfegewrit* may have taken the form of an agreement. In the early years of the ninth century, a dispute arose concerning land at Sodbury (Glos.) between the church of Worcester and the descendants of Eadbold, to whom Bishop Mildred (743–775) had granted this episcopal estate, to be held by his family as long as they could supply men prepared and qualified to take orders (*þe godcundes hades beon walde 7 þæs wyrðe wære*).[225] By the time of Bishop Wærferth (873–915), this was no longer the case, but the family still held the land. Wærferth eventually brought his case to the court of Ealdorman Æthelred of Mercia, citing as evidence the *erfegewrit* of Eastmund, who had inherited the estate from the original recipient Eadbald, and who, on his death, 'gave command in the name of God, that the man who succeeded to the estate should succeed thereto on the condition laid down by Bishop Mildred; but if he were so presumptuous to violate it, he should know that he would be found guilty before God's throne'.[226] A settlement was negotiated, and we are told, in the bishop's words:

> *7 ic þa mid mira higna leafe æt Weogornaceastre him sealde þæt lond on ece erfe 7 þa bec 7 þæt Eastmundes erfegewrit 7 eac ure agen rædengewrit þæt wære him to þam gerade þæt land to læten þe mon ælce gere gesylle fiftene scillingas clænes feos to Tettanbyrg þam bisceope.*
>
> (Then, with the leave of my community at Worcester, I gave him the estate as a perpetual heritage, together with the charters, and Eastmund's testament [*erfegewrit*], and also our own written agreement that the estate should be made over to him on condition that fifteen shillings of good money should be given every year to the bishop at Tetbury.)

Eastmund's *erfegewrit* is not extant, but the early eleventh century Worcester cartulary preserves an account of similar arrangements made between *c.* 781 and 800 by a certain Abbot Headda for his *hereditatem*. Headda held land in endowment of a family monastery at Dowdeswell (Glos.); if his heirs failed to produce a man in holy orders to maintain the monastery, it and the land were to revert to the community at Worcester in order to prevent them falling under lay control (*numquam laicorum subdetur*).[227] This text does not take the

224 See n. 212 above.

225 S1446/H15, *c.* 903; BL Cotton Tiberius A. xiii fols. 56r–57r (*Liber Wigorniensis*). It seems that Sodbury supported a family church, possibly a monastery: Sims-Williams, *Religion and Literature*, pp. 156–7.

226 *þam men þe to þam lande fenge, þæt he þonne on þa ilcan wise to fenge þe Mired bisceop bebead; gif he þonne to þan gedyrstig wære þæt he þæt abræce, þæt he wiste hine scyldigne beforan Godes heahsetle æt þam miclan dome.*

227 S1413; BL Cotton Tiberius A. xiii fol. 26rv (s.x[1]), printed in *Cartularium*, ed. Birch, no. 283.

form of a bequest; rather, it is an agreement between Headda and the bishopric of Worcester intended to safeguard the integrity of the family monastery. It is likely that Bishop Wærferth's *erfegewrit* was a similar document, either a genuine record of Eastmund's intentions, or a fabrication created for the occasion.[228]

A third example of the role which a written will might play in a dispute, even though, in this case, the document does not seem to have been used in formal proceedings, is drawn from the *Liber Eliensis*. The estate of Easter (Ex) had been granted to Ely, along with two other estates, by the widow Godgifu; the gift was confirmed by her will, written in English.[229] However, during the abbacy of Wulfric (*c.* 1045–*c.* 1065) Easter was appropriated by Æsgar the Staller, who remained impervious to requests for its restoration, and continued to hold it even after the community appealed to the king.[230] The monks duly 'proceeded to strike him with the javelin of excommunication' (*iaculo anatematis eum ferire adgressi sunt*) on a daily basis. This spiritual weapon was combined with a persistent publicity campaign, in the course of which two documents were 'publicly exhibited' (*publice ostendente*). One was King Edward's writ, confirming the terms of Wulfric's abbacy and his undisputed right to the property held by Ely.[231] The second document was Godgifu's will (*testamentum donantis*). The forum for this publicity is unclear. It is equally unclear whether the excommunication or public opprobrium influenced the outcome, since the king intervened (*a rege correptus*) and, 'returning to his senses' (*in se reversus*), Æsgar entered into an agreement with the abbot and community whereby he would hold the estate for his lifetime.[232] While the rhetoric of the twelfth-century writer obscures procedural detail, his incorporation of the will into the community's armoury against Æsgar reveals, at the very least, post-Conquest interest in such documents as evidence in support of what, in this instance, proved to be an ongoing dispute.[233]

228 See above n. 206 for the suggestion of forgery in support of Worcester's claim in the dispute concerning the will of Æthelric.

229 *LE* II, 81: *et in testamento Anglice confirmavit*. The gift is dated to the abbacy of Leofric (1022–1029?).

230 The account of these proceedings is given in *LE* II, 96.

231 The Ely compiler incorporates a vernacular text of this writ in II, 95, with a Latin translation in 95a. See also *Writs* 47.

232 The Latin translation of the English agreement is given in *LE* II, 96.

233 See Blake, *LE*, p. 166, n. 1 for reservations about the integrity of this account. Harmer accepts the royal writ as an authentic copy: *Writs*, pp. 222–4. DB shows that Easter was held by Æsgar in 1066, and by Geoffrey de Mandeville in 1086, although it was then being claimed by the abbot with the support of the Hundred: II, fol. 60v.

## The Anglo-Saxon will from a modern perspective

Although the Anglo-Saxon will would hardly be recognised as a legal instrument in modern law, Hazeltine regarded it as a forerunner of the modern document,[234] and Sheehan noted that certain features already occurring in a number of Anglo-Saxon wills would become important in the twelfth-century canonical will.[235] In this respect two features are particularly significant.

The first such element is the concept of the executor, which emerged formally in the thirteenth century.[236] A number of Anglo-Saxon wills incorporate references to named individuals who hold some measure of responsibility for the implementation of the donor's intentions. Their responsibility falls short of representing the testator, which was the role of the later executor,[237] but such individuals may be regarded as having *mund*, or protection, over the will itself or some of its provisions.[238] It is generally the king who is asked to protect the overall implementation of the will.[239] The king may also be asked to interest himself in specific issues, such as the protection of a religious foundation,[240] or the welfare of a donor's retainers who would be otherwise unprotected.[241] The church, either in the form of a religious community or a named individual, may be asked to take similar responsibilities,[242] occasionally with specific reference to a local church bequeathed or patronised by the donor.[243] Laymen may also be named: noblemen,[244] high-ranking thegns[245] and brothers[246] are all designated as having a role in the protection and implementation of donors' dispositions. In three cases, men are required to carry

234 Hazeltine, 'Comments', p. vii.

235 Sheehan, *The Will*, pp. 46–7.

236 P&M, II, 334; Sheehan, *The Will*, pp. 148–62.

237 See Sheehan, *The Will*, p. 155 on the role of the executor, and E. R. Archer and B.E. Ferme, 'Testamentary procedure with special reference to the executrix', *Reading Medieval Studies* 15 (1989), 3–34.

238 Sheehan distinguishes between the roles of executor and protector (*The Will*, pp. 43–4); see also Hazeltine, 'Comments', p. xxxvi, and P&M, II, 321–2.

239 S1483/W2; S1505/W12; S1487/W13; S1511/W11, *Rochester* 35*; S1497/*St Albans* 7; S1523/W23*. (*indicates a combined request to king and queen. S1521/W29 addresses the queen only).

240 S1486/W15; S1536/W17, *Burton* 29.

241 S1484/W8. The king is also asked to be the *freond* of Wulfgeat's wife and daughter (S1534/W19).

242 S1490/W28; S1482/H2, *Christ Church* 70; S1510/R6, *Christ Church* 78; S1501/W16[1], *Christ Church* 136; S1500/R3, *Christ Church* 39A.

243 S1521/W29? (difficult reading); S1525/W37; S1234/R116, *Christ Church* 183; S1536/W17/*Burton* 29.

244 S1486/W15; S1490/W28; S1491/W4, *New Minster* 18.

245 S1490/W28; S1531/W31 (a business partner).

246 S1490/W28; S1482/H2, *Christ Church* 70; S1536/W17, *Burton* 29; S1517/*St Albans* 15.

out financial transactions on the donor's death.[247] The role of these functionaries in the implementation of the will was crucial, often recognised by the donor through bequests to those named.

A further element found in the Anglo-Saxon will which was to prove fundamental in the later will is the right of revocation, which is retained by some donors.[248] For example, the will of King Alfred records that he destroyed all previous documents, and that of Æthelgifu includes a rider recognising specifically that the death of beneficiaries would require changes to her dispositions.[249] Such examples imply that the revocation clause represented a genuinely available option. It was certainly so perceived by Eadsige, a monk at Christ Church, Canterbury, who, with the support of King Cnut, was destined to become archbishop; he explicitly holds the threat of revocation over the Christ Church community if they should fail to support him.[250] The option of revocation may, on this evidence, have been a useful influence over potential beneficiaries.[251]

Nevertheless, the differences between the Anglo-Saxon vernacular will and the legal instrument familiar to us today emphasise the way in which the earlier document was very much a product of its own social context.[252] In the first place, the modern will has performative powers enshrined in the document itself, whereas the Anglo-Saxon will appears to have had no inherent power to enact the dispositions which it contained; its function was evidentiary, the oral and public aspect of the transaction retaining primacy.[253] However, it has been suggested by Danet and Bogoch that Anglo-Saxon written wills should be seen as transitional; the incorporation of certain

247 The brothers of the ætheling Æthelstan (S1503/W20, *Christ Church* 142) and Ælfric Modercope (S1490/W28); the business partner (*felage*) of Thurstan (S1531/W31), who is required to oversee distribution of alms.

248 Revocability is a feature of the modern will. Hazeltine ('Comments', p. xi, n. 2) argues that any revocation would involve renegotiation with the donee; Sheehan argues for varying degrees of revocability (*The Will*, pp. 45–6); Lowe ('Nature and effect', p. 37) accepts revocability in certain circumstances. The principle of revocation is discussed by Sheehan, *The Will*, pp. 142–7.

249 S1508/H11, *New Minster* 1; S1497/*St Albans* 7. See also S1499/W35 for Bishop Æthelmær's reference to the possibility of changing his will. The donor's reservation of the right to revoke may be incorporated in the anathema as in S1483/W2; S1521/W29; S1531/W31; S1491/W4, *New Minster* 18; S1497/*St Albans* 7.

250 S1465/R86, *Christ Church* 153; see Chap. 3, pp. 125–6 below.

251 See also Wulfgar (S1533/R26), who makes bequests subject to the obedience (the verb is *gehyran*) of the beneficiaries. Ordnoth and his wife (S1524/W5) reserve the right to reclaim a landbook from the Old Minster, Winchester, to make any necessary corrections.

252 The differences between the Anglo-Saxon will and its modern counterpart are discussed by Danet and Bogoch, 'Orality', pp. 105–106.

253 Sheehan, *The Will*, p. 19; Hazeltine, 'Comments', pp. viii-ix; Keynes, 'Royal government', p. 256; Kennedy, 'Law and litigation', p. 173; M. T. Clanchy, *From Memory to Written Record: England 1066–1307*, 2nd edn (Oxford, 1993), pp. 294–5.

language features, such as references to the act of writing itself, indicates that scribes were seeking to invest the documents with performative powers.[254] Documentation certainly provided useful memoranda of both the dispositions made and the witnesses present at the time that the will was declared, and the limited evidence for the use of wills in the context of disputed inheritance does not necessarily mean that they had no part to play. As Heidecker has proposed for the role of Carolingian charters in disputes, wills may have contributed towards 'making an argument prevail in court', while not, in themselves, constituting 'an infallible definitive argument'.[255]

It is not only in its evidentiary nature that the Anglo-Saxon will differs from the modern will. A further important difference is the contractual, or bilateral, element which is often a feature of the earlier document, incorporating agreements related to land which often had complex ramifications.[256] Attention has also been drawn to the apparent paradox inherent in the common will phrase 'I give after my day' (*ic an æfter min dæg*), which would be untenable as a concept in later law but which captured for an Anglo-Saxon donor and audience both the declaration of intent and the deferment of the gift.[257]

It is also the case that Anglo-Saxon wills do not have the ambulatory quality of the modern will – that is, the quality of disposing of residual property, or that which accrued after the will was declared.[258] In fact, the significant link between will-making and bookland demonstrated earlier in this chapter suggests that the Anglo-Saxon will was not necessarily concerned with the disposition of an individual's entire property, but that its focus was likely to be the transmission of land granted by royal charter with freedom of disposition.[259] That those holding such land might indeed wish to influ-

254 On the performative aspect of wills see Danet and Bogoch, 'From oral ceremony to written document', pp. 98–114.

255 K. Heidecker, 'Communication by written texts in court cases: some charter evidence (*ca* 800-*ca* 1100)', in Mostert, *New Approaches*, pp. 101–26 (p. 124, with an example of this procedure in relation to a charter in ninth-century Burgundy at p. 114).

256 Hazeltine, 'Comments', pp. i, xviii–xxiii; Sheehan, *The Will*, pp. 27–9.

257 Hazeltine, 'Comments', pp. viii, xi–xii; P&M, II, 317–18.

258 Sheehan, *The Will*, p. 46. Possible instances are S1485/W9 (the bequest of residue to a wife); S1526/W1 (Bishop Theodred refers to the acquisition of further property but no indication is given as to how such property is to be distributed); S1501/W16[1], *Christ Church* 136 where Æthelric bequeaths a life interest in 'all that I leave' (*ealles þæs þe ic lefe*).

259 See pp. 14–15 above. The distinction between bookland and other property is discussed by P. Wormald, *Bede and the Conversion of England: the Charter Evidence*, Jarrow Lecture (1984), pp. 19–23, reprinted in P. Wormald, ed. S. Baxter, *The Times of Bede: Studies in Early English Christian Society and its Historian* (Oxford, 2006), pp. 135–66 (pp. 153–7); Wormald, 'Kingship and royal property', pp. 264–5; S. Reynolds, *Fiefs and Vassals: the Medieval Evidence Reinterpreted* (Oxford, 1994), pp. 324–31. For Wormald's proposal that most property disposed of by will was likely to have been bookland see his 'Kingship and royal property', pp. 264–8; his unpublished notes containing material preparatory to the second volume of his two-volume study *The Making of English Law* (deposited

ence its transmission is illustrated by King Alfred's law, possibly dating from *c.* 886,[260] referring to an individual's right to place restrictions on the alienation of bookland from the kindred through a recognised public procedure:[261]

Cl. 41: *[Be boclande]*

*Se mon se ðe bocland hæbbe, 7 him his mægas læfden, þonne setton we, þæt he hit ne moste sellan of his mægburge, gif þær bið gewrit oððe gewitnes, ðæt hit ðara manna forbod wære þe hit on fruman gestrindon 7 þara þe hit him sealdon, þæt he swa ne mote; 7 þæt þonne on cyninges 7 on biscopes gewitnesse gerecce beforan his mægum.*

(We have further established, that a man who holds land by title-deed, which his kinsmen have left him, shall not be allowed to give it out of his kindred, if there is documentary or [other] evidence that the power to do so is forbidden by the men who first acquired it, or by those who gave it to him. And he [an owner at some time] might declare it [the limitation] before his kinsmen in the presence of the king and bishop.)[262]

The royal interest in arrangements for the transmission of bookland which is apparent here is acknowledged in multi-gift wills, with their requests for the king's permission that donors' bequests should be implemented.[263]

Unlike a modern lawyer, in drawing up a will the Church was not a disinterested party. With a single exception, all wills bequeath property, often land, to the Church.[264] The influence of the Church is reflected in the form and

in the archives of King's College, London) contain further material concerned with land tenure and inheritance practice as they relate to wills (summarised in Appendix 5 below).

260 For dating see Keynes and Lapidge, p. 304 and Wormald, *English Law*, pp. 281, 286, 425–6. Also relevant is the date of Fulk's letter to Alfred, which may have influenced Alfred's preface to the code and suggests a link between Alfred and Hincmar of Rheims via Grimbald (see Keynes and Lapidge, p. 182 for dating to *c.* 886, and pp. 182–6 for the translated text). This appears to be one of a series of clauses which Alfred himself introduced into his code, alongside legislation derived from his predecessors (Wormald, *English Law*, p. 282).

261 King Alfred placed such restrictions on the transmission of land in his own will (see Chap. 3, pp. 89–90 below). It is unclear whether his practice informed Clause 41, or was influenced by it (see Wormald, *English Law*, p. 282; Keynes and Lapidge, p. 309, n. 24).

262 The phrasing is ambiguous, but I have followed the translation of Kennedy ('Disputes', pp. 179–80), who argues that the clause allows for the public establishment of a limitation by a holder of bookland. See also Keynes and Lapidge, pp. 168, 309 nn. 24, 25. Attenborough's translation reads '[and he who contests such an alienation] shall make a declaration to this effect in the presence of his kindred, with the king and bishop as witnesses' (*Laws*, p. 83); this places the initiative with a litigant attempting to prevent alienation in the case of dispute.

263 For the process of royal confirmation of wills, see Chap. 2, pp. 67–70 below; for heriot, a different aspect of royal interest, see Chap. 5, pp. 190–4 below.

264 The exception is S1200/H7, *Christ Church* 90 (867x870), Cynethryth's bequest-agreement to her late husband's kinsman of land at Chart (Kt), in which Christ Church,

language of the documents, as well as in their preservation in the archives of the beneficiary religious houses. However, in the ninth century donors were already including in their wills bequests of land as well as movable wealth to a range of lay beneficiaries, particularly kindred. By the tenth century the vernacular will had developed a sophisticated form, and was valued by the nobility as an aspect of inheritance strategy. It is also likely that the wealthy laity, living in a society in which vernacular documents played an increasing role, were aware of the advantages of having a written record of their dispositions; the documents show that, like modern testators, a number of donors held a copy in their own archives.[265]

The Ramsey chronicler, introducing his catalogue of pre-Conquest *post obitum* gifts to the abbey, extols the virtues of 'the ancients raised in better times' (*antiquorum … quos meliora saecula procrearunt*) who, unlike those of his own day, not only gave thought to the welfare of their souls by making provision while in full health for pious bequests to the Church, but also had their provisions publicly documented.[266] The process by which this was carried out is the subject of the next chapter.

Canterbury, had a long-standing interest: Brooks, *Early History*, pp. 147–8; S1471/R101, *Christ Church* 170; Chap. 4, p. 161 below.

265 Kelly, 'Anglo-Saxon lay society, pp. 47–62; Keynes, 'Royal government', pp. 248–55.

266 *CR* 30.

# CHAPTER TWO

# The process of will-making

Since the vernacular wills themselves provide little insight into the process which produced them, any attempt to reconstruct that process must draw on other contemporary documents as well as narrative sources. One text is particularly valuable: the account in the twelfth-century *Liber Eliensis* of a sequence of *post obitum* dispositions made by a certain Siferth of Downham (Cambs.). Bishop Æthelwold's accumulation of land at Downham was not without incident, as in the case of many of Æthelwold's land deals; this appears to have prompted the compiler of the earlier *Libellus,* on which the chronicle account is based, to include a considerable amount of circumstantial detail for the transactions in support of Ely's title to the land, including, incidentally, Siferth's will-making.[1]

The oral aspect of the will-making process is well demonstrated in the account of Siferth's declaration of two *post obitum* gifts at Ely, made on separate occasions, with considerable emphasis placed on the oral declaration before witnesses at every stage in these proceedings. His first declaration, which took place between 975 and 978, was made before particularly distinguished company:[2]

> *Nec multo post Siverthus de Dunham defractus viribus vergensque in senium, infirmitate pedum, que podagra dicitur, graviter contrahebatur. Qui eo tempore, quo beatus Æðelwoldus Æðelredum, futurum regem tunc vero comitem, et matrem suam [Ælftreðam reginam] et Alfricum Cild et plures maiores natu Anglie ad Hely secum adduxerat, venit cum coniuge sua nomine Wlfled ad episcopum et ei coram prememoratis notificavit se post diem suum duas hydas quas in Dunham habuit Deo sancteque Æðeldriðe pro anima sua daturum ibique se dixit sortitum esse locum sepulture sue rogavitque omnes qui aderant, ut super hac re sibi testificarentur.*

1 *LE* II, 11–12/*Lib* 10–12. For the sources of the *LE* account see Chap. 1, n. 158 above. The role of dispute – actual or potential – in prompting thorough recording of transactions is discussed by Lowe, 'Lay literacy', pp. 172–3.

2 This declaration was made in the presence of Æthelred, described as 'the future king but at that time an earl' (*futurum regem tunc vero comitem*), placing it before his accession in 978, although Blake questions the accuracy of the statement (*LE*, p. 86, n. 3); *LE* II, 78 places the event during the reign of Æthelred's half-brother, Edward. Translations are taken from *Liber Eliensis*, transl. Fairweather, unless otherwise stated; for problems of interpreting the Latin text, see ibid., pp. xxv–xxvii.

(Not long afterwards Siferth of Downham, incapacitated and declining into the feebleness of old age, was seriously afflicted by a disease of the feet which is called gout. At the time when the blessed Æthelwold had brought with him to Ely Æthelred, the future king but at that time an earl, and his mother, Queen Ælfthryth,[3] and Ælfric *Cild* and many of the senior men of England, this man, with his wife, Wulfflæd by name, came to the bishop. In the presence of the people already mentioned, he informed him that on his death he would give the two hides which he possessed at Downham to God and St Æthelthryth, for the sake of his soul, and said that he had chosen that as the place of his burial,[4] and asked all those present to be witnesses to this matter.)[5]

This forum for Siferth's first bequest was an august gathering. The presence of Queen Ælfthryth may reflect both her own family connexions and land interests in East Anglia, and her alliance with Bishop Æthelwold.[6] Ælfric *Cild* was a man of considerable standing, possibly the brother-in-law of Ealdorman Ælfhere of Mercia, whom he succeeded as ealdorman in 983.[7] Siferth's presence in such company indicates his own status, and perhaps his relationship with Bishop Æthelwold's great ally, the reeve Wulfstan of Dalham.[8] It is unclear how many bequests were declared before such prestigious company, but some will-making does seem to have taken place, or the wills published, in the presence of the king and men of the highest rank, as in the case of the vernacular single-gift bequest of Thurstan to Christ Church, Canterbury, made between 1042 and 1043; each of the two contemporary chirographs has a witness list including King Edward (the Confessor), his mother, Ælfgifu, two ealdormen, Archbishop Eadsige of Canterbury, two bishops, two priests, the sheriff of Essex and three named laymen, at least one of whom (Ælfric, son of Wihtgar) was a substantial landholder in East Anglia.[9]

3 Ælfthryth (d. *c.* 1000) was the second wife of King Edgar. Her name is added only in one manuscript (*LE*, p. 86, n. *j*).

4 My emendation; Fairweather has 'he had chosen the place of his burial there' (p. 110).

5 *LE* II, 11.

6 For the alliance between Ælfthryth and Bishop Æthelwold, see B. Yorke, 'Æthelwold and the politics of the tenth century', in *Bishop Æthelwold: his Career and Influence*, ed. B. Yorke (Woodbridge, 1997), pp. 81–6. For her links with East Anglia see P. Stafford, *Queen Emma and Queen Edith: Queenship and Women's Power in Eleventh-Century England* (Oxford, 1997), p. 133, n. 194; Wareham, *Lords and Communities*, p. 19.

7 Ælfric became ealdorman of Mercia in 983, and was banished for treason in 985/6: M. A. L. Locherbie-Cameron, 'The men named in the poem', in *The Battle of Maldon AD 991*, ed. D. Scragg (Oxford, 1991), pp. 238–49 (p. 241); he also witnesses transactions in *LE* II, 7, 46/*Lib* 5, 57, and *CR* 51.

8 Siferth may have been the son-in-law of Wulfstan: Wareham, *Lords and Communities*, pp. 34, 39; for Wulfstan, see Keynes, 'Ely Abbey', pp. 17, 19 and Kennedy, 'Law and litigation', p. 146.

9 For details of the witnesses, see *Wills*, pp. 190–2, and p. 188 for Ælfric. One of the manuscripts (BL Cotton Augustus II, 34) adds two further witnesses: Ælfric, Archbishop of York, and Ælfgar, son of Ealdorman Leofric.

The audience for Siferth's second declaration at Ely was less prestigious, and perhaps more typical:

*Alio quoque tempore, post mortem scilicet Godingi de Gretune, venit secundo idem vir ad Hely, ubi noverat illum esse sepultum, rogavitque fratres, ut eum ad sepulturam illius ducerent. Nam erat ei familiarissimus. Quo cum venissent, vocavit ad se abbatem et Ædricum et Leovricum de Berle et Levingum de Trumpentune innotuitque eis, quod sui karissimi et fidelissimi amici ibi essent sepulti et quod ipse nimia infirmitate depressus morti appropinquasset, 'ideoque', inquid, 'o karissimi mei, volo ut conventio mea coram vobis renovetur, videlicet quomodo hic elegi mihi locum sepulture mee et post diem meum Deo et sancte Æðeldriðe dedi duas hydas, quas in Dunham habeo, et filie mee duas hydas do in Wilbertune et precor, o amici mei, ut hoc oblivioni non tradatis, immo, ubi necesse fuerit, illud recognoscatis'.*

(On another occasion also, after the death of Goding of Gretton, the same man came a second time to Ely, where he knew Goding had been buried, and asked the brothers to take him to his burial place. For he used to be a very dear friend to him. When they arrived there, he called the abbot to him, and Eadric, and Leofric of *Berle*, and Lyfing of Trumpington, and made it known to them, that his most dear and faithful friends were buried there, and that he himself, weighed down by his extreme infirmity, was coming close to death. 'And therefore,' he said, 'most dear people, I desire that my agreement be renewed before you, namely how I have chosen my place of burial here, and have given to God and St Æthelthryth, after my day is over, the two hides which I have at Downham, and how I give to my daughter two hides at Wilburton. And I beg, my friends, that you do not cast this into oblivion, but rather, when it becomes necessary, you acknowledge it.')

On this occasion, the abbot and three laymen of some local standing were present: Eadric, Leofric of *Berle* and Lyfing of Trumpington. Eadric may be the man who attended Siferth's death-bed, who at that point in the narrative is described as an important member of Ealdorman Æthelwine's retinue (*unus de proceribus Aieluuini alderman*);[10] Leofric of *Berle* appears elsewhere in the *Liber Eliensis* as one of a group of men with legal responsibilities;[11] and Lyfing (*Levingum*) may possibly be the man (*Leovingo*) who witnesses an exchange of land between Abbot Byrhtnoth and Ælfric.[12] This emphasis on local witness is apparent when, on his return home, Siferth seems to have reiterated his dispositions at a further public meeting:

*Item eodem die remeando domum renovavit eandem conventionem coram melioribus eiusdem provincie ultra Upuuere in loco, qui dicitur Hyravicstouue.*

10 See n. 33 below.

11 *legales viri* (*LE* II, 8/*Lib* 6). For the role of such men see Kennedy, 'Law and litigation', pp. 158–9.

12 *LE* II, 11/*Lib* 13. Such identifications are hazardous, given the proliferation of similar names throughout Book Two of *LE*.

(Similarly, on his return home that day, he renewed this agreement in the presence of the better people of his region beyond Upware, in the place which is called *Hyravicstouue*.)

Siferth ensured that his bequests were publicised in the appropriate locale, before gatherings which would be required to adjudicate should dispute arise.[13] This procedure sheds light on the even more relentless repetition accorded to Thurstan's vernacular multi-gift will, which was publicised across the four counties in which his land lay: witnesses are listed for Norfolk, Suffolk, Cambridgeshire and Essex, including Earl Harold and Bishop Stigand, two sheriffs, as well as a range of church- and laymen.[14] The importance of such publication is endorsed by the formula *Hit Becwæð*, of the late tenth or early eleventh century, which includes the assertion 'there is no man alive who ever heard that [the land] was claimed or craved in hundred or any other meeting, in market-place or church congregation as long as he [the deceased donor of the land] lived'.[15]

The role of the church as a place of public gathering, where will-making may on a number of occasions, as here, have taken place, is demonstrated elsewhere in Book Two of the *Liber Eliensis*. For example, a meeting was convened at the northern entrance to the church by the reeve Wulfstan of Dalham, accompanied by *barones* (men of rank), and attended by representatives of two hundreds; before this gathering Ogga of Mildenhall announced his intention to bequeath land to the church, before being persuaded by Wulfstan to convert his bequest into an *inter vivos* gift.[16]

13 DB I, fols. 191v-192r assigns Downham and Wilburton to different hundreds, both meeting at Witchford; by the thirteenth century, Downham belonged to Ely hundred, and Wilburton to Witchford. For the hundreds of Ely and Witchford, see Miller, *Ely*, pp. 14, 31–3, 219–21. For general comment see Kennedy, 'Law and litigation', p. 140, and p. 142 for the convening of such meetings to resolve disputes.

14 S1531/W31; the multi-gift will includes the bequest to Christ Church, Canterbury, which also exists separately as two chirographs (S1530/W30, *Christ Church* 166; see Chap. 1, n. 45 above). For the identity of these witnesses, see *Wills*, pp. 196–7. This witness list is a rare survival in the thirteenth-century Bury Sacrist's Register into which it was copied.

15 *Nis æni man on life, ðe æfre gehyrde, ðæt man cwydde oððon crafode hine on hundrede oððon ahwar on gemote, on ceapstowe oþþe on cyricware, ða hwile þe he lifde*: *Gesetze*, ed. Liebermann, I, 400, para. 3.1; transl. Wormald, *English Law*, p. 385 (see Chap. 1, n. 223 above).

16 *LE* II, 18/*Lib* 27; *CR* 89. See also *LE* II, 12/*Lib* 15 for a hundred meeting inside the north gate of the churchyard at Ely. For Ely and Cambridge as important centres for public procedures, see Kennedy, 'Law and litigation', p. 139. The late eleventh century historian Eadmer reports meetings held at the south door of the south tower at pre-Conquest Christ Church, Canterbury: H. M. Taylor, 'The Anglo-Saxon church at Canterbury', *Archaeological Journal* 126 (1969), 101–29, including the relevant text (p. 129, para. 15g) and translation (p. 125, para. 15g), following R. Willis, *The Architectural History of Canterbury Cathedral* (London, 1845). *CR* 89 records a bequest made by Wulfwine son of Ælfwine *in capitulo fratrum apud Ramesiam in vigilia Pentecostes* (in the chapter [meeting] of the brothers at Ramsey on the eve of Pentecost).

However, the bequest of an unnamed woman, preserved in an account known as the Herefordshire Lawsuit, was not made before a public gathering but at her own residence.[17] In this text we are told of a dispute which took place during the reign of Cnut (1016–1035) between a mother and son concerning land at Wellington and Cradley (Hfds.). Edwin, Enniaun's son, claimed the land held by his unnamed mother, and took his case to the shire court. Although she was residing at Fawley (Hfds.), only ten miles from the meeting of the shire court which was convened at Aylton, near Ledbury (Hfds.), she was represented in court by Thurkil the White, a local landowner, and husband of her kinswoman, Leofflæd.[18] Since he was unfamiliar with the claim (*talu*), the court dispatched three thegns, Leofwine of Frome, Æthelsige the Red and Winsige the seaman, to take the woman's testimony concerning her claim to the land at issue:

> *Ða sæde heo ꝥ heo nan land hæfde þe him aht to gebyrede . 7 gebealh heo swiðe eorlice wið hire sunu . 7 gecleopade ða Leoflæde hire magan to hire Ðurcilles wif . 7 beforan heom to hire þus cwæð . her sit Leoflæde min mæge þe ic geann ægðer ge mines landes . ge mines goldes . ge ræglæs . ge reafes . ge ealles þe ic ah æfter minon dæge . 7 heo syððan to þam þegnon cwæþ . doð þegnlice . 7 wel abeodað mine ærende to þam gemote beforan eallum þam godan mannum . 7 cyðaþ heom hwæm ic mines landes geunnen hæbbe . 7 ealre minre æhte . 7 minan agenan sunu næfre nan þing . 7 biddað heom beon þisses to gewitnesse: . And heo þa swæ dydon . ridon to þam gemote . 7 cyðdon eallon þam godan mannum hwæt heo on heom geled hæfde. Ða astod Ðurcil hwita up on þam gemote . 7 bæd ealle þa þægnas syllan his wife þa landes clæne . þe hire mage hire ge-uðe . 7 heo swa dydon.*

> (Then she said that she had no land that in any way belonged to him, and was strongly incensed against her son, and summoned to her her kinswoman, Leofflæd, Thurkil's wife, and in front of them said to her as follows: 'Here sits Leofflæd, my kinswoman, to whom, after my death, I grant my land and my gold, my clothing and my raiment and all that I possess.' And then she said to the thegns: 'Act like thegns, and duly announce my message to the meeting before all the worthy men, and tell them to whom I have granted my land and all my property, and not a thing to my own son, and ask them to be witnesses of this.' And they did so; they rode to the meeting and informed all the worthy men of the charge that she had laid

17 S1462/R78, *EHD* I, no. 135. The text was written into an eighth-century gospel book at Hereford in a script contemporary with the transaction: *Catalogue of Manuscripts of Hereford Cathedral Library*, ed. R. A. B. Mynors and R. M. Thomson (Cambridge 1993), p. 65; Ker, *Catalogue*, no. 119.

18 For Leofflæd and Thurkil: *Charters*, pp. 400–401; Stafford, 'Women and the Norman Conquest', pp. 241–2. For another example of a woman represented by an advocate in court see S939/W16[2], *Christ Church* 137, where Æthelric's widow was represented by Archbishop Ælfric (see p. 71 below). Ælfflæd also designates a *forespeca* (advocate) and *mundiend* (protector) in S1486/W15. However, *LE* also gives examples of women who were present in court: see, for example, *LE* II, 11a, 18/*Lib* 14, 27.

upon them. Then Thurkil the White stood up in the meeting and asked all the thegns to give his wife the lands unreservedly which her kinswoman had granted her, and they did so.)

The vivid use of first person speech in this account, as in the case of Siferth's two bequests at Ely and many vernacular wills, highlights the significance of the oral act. It is the oral witness of the three thegns which is accepted by the court (although Thurkil's part in the proceedings is not given); and however informal the woman's declaration may appear, it is endorsed by the full witness of the shire court. On this occasion, the witnesses included not only Bishop Æthelstan of Hereford, Ealdorman Ranig, the sheriff, and other local dignitaries and thegns, but also Tofi the Proud who, we are told, had come to the court on the king's business.

In spite of the focus on the oral proceedings in these accounts, documentation was an important feature, and seems to have been firmly under the aegis of the church, adding spiritual protection to the transaction.[19] Vernacular wills were not only stored in the archives of religious houses, but were in all likelihood written by scribes of beneficiary churches: it has been shown above, for example, that ninth-century bequests to Christ Church, Canterbury, were recorded by scribes active at the Christ Church scriptorium.[20] Furthermore, at the behest of Thurkil (who was an interested party, since his wife was the beneficiary of the bequest), the judgment of the Herefordshire court was recorded in the eighth-century gospel book at Hereford Cathedral where it survives today; Domesday Book records that this community held Cradley, one of the estates in question, in 1066.[21] Even though there is no mention of Siferth's bequests at Ely being documented, the *Libellus* compiler's apparent access to witness lists suggests that a written record was indeed made.

The account of Siferth's two visits to Ely endorses the evidence of the vernacular wills that *post obitum* disposition could take place over time, and involve different transactions.[22] Although Siferth's health was declining, his death was not imminent. He was able to travel to Ely twice, make a formal

19 Surviving witness-lists include at least one churchman, in most cases demonstrably associated with a beneficiary house. In only one case is there evidence that a document may have been written in other circumstances: S1533/W26 (the will of Wulfgar) is a contemporary single sheet, written in the hand of a scribe associated with the royal estate at Great Bedwyn: M. B. Parkes, 'A fragment of an early-tenth-century Anglo-Saxon manuscript and its significance', *ASE* 12 (1983), 129–40 ( p. 137, n. 51); Keynes, 'Royal government', p. 252, n. 102.

20 Chap. 1, n. 11 above ; Brooks, *Early History*, pp. 168–74, 360–1 (nn. 70–82).

21 Hereford Cathedral P. i. 2, fol. 134rv, a blank space at the end of the final quire (Ker, *Catalogue*, no. 119a); *Charters*, p. 401. Twelve hides at Cradley were in the hands of the cathedral chapter in 1066, and Thurkil held Wellington: DB I, fols. 182r, 187r.

22 Kennedy, considering a range of examples, concludes that they were 'made probably in old age, but at some leisure, not at the very end of testators' lives': 'Law and litigation', p. 166.

declaration, and on the second occasion address a further gathering – apparently on the same day – at some distance from Ely.[23] However, his increasing infirmity made it desirable to order his affairs in preparation for death.[24] In contrast, the will of Wulfgar makes it absolutely clear that he expects to live long enough to monitor the behaviour of his beneficiaries, and to make further bequests:

> *7 ic an þæs landes æt Butermere ofer minne dæg Byrhtsige twegea hida 7 Ceolstanes sunum anes gif hie me oð ðæt on ryht gehieraþ 7 ic cweðe on wordum be Æscmere on minum geongum magum swelce me betst gehieraþ.*
>
> (And I grant two hides of the estate at Buttermere, after my death, to Brihtsige and one to Ceolstan's sons, if they show me due obedience until then. And I shall verbally bequeath *Æscmere* to such of my young kinsmen who obey me best.)[25]

The phrase *on wordum* indicates that oral bequests remained an option, and could supplement dispositions which were documented. Other wills also suggest that the donors expected longer life through the inclusion of a revocation clause, or a clause allowing for the birth of an heir.[26] Ealdorman Ælfheah seems to consider the possibility that his wife may not outlive him, since his bequest to her will take effect 'if she live longer than I'.[27] Will-making need not have been prompted by failing health, but by a number of factors which made the ordering of affairs advisable, such as remarriage, pilgrimage, widowhood or the decision to found a monastery.[28] Bishop Ælfsige seems to have made his will before setting out for Rome to collect his pallium – a journey from which he failed to return, having met his death crossing the Alps.[29] The *Liber Eliensis* tells the dramatic story of Leofwine, who made his will as part of the expiation of his matricide, and went on to live to old age.[30]

23 Upware is about fifteen miles south of Ely, on the River Cam. Even if Siferth travelled by boat, this was a considerable undertaking.

24 Following illness, Bishop Wilfrid spent eighteen months settling his affairs: *The Life of Bishop Wilfrid by Eddius Stephanus*, ed. and transl. B. Colgrave (Cambridge, 1927), chap. 63, pp. 136–7.

25 S1533/R26. Eadsige's bequest to Christ Church, Canterbury (S1465/R86, *Christ Church* 153) is contingent upon the co-operation of the community; he reserves the right to change it (see Brooks, *Early History*, p. 295 and Chap. 3, p. 126 below for the circumstances).

26 S1483/W2, S1531/W31, S1497/*St Albans* 7; King Alfred changed his will at least once: S1507/H11, *New Minster* 1. S1482/H2, *Christ Church* 70, S1508/H10, *Christ Church* 96 and S1500/R3, *Christ Church* 39A suggest the possibility of an heir.

27 S1485/W9: *gyf heo leng beoð þonne ic.*

28 S1508/H10, *Christ Church* 96; W39/*Peterborough* 27, S1525/W38, S1519/W34; S1536/W17, *Burton* 29. The widow Godgifu made a will on her husband's death granting land to Ely (*LE* II, 81), and made a further bequest when she was dying (*LE* II, 83).

29 S1491/W4, *New Minster* 18: see *Wills*, p. 114, and Chap. 3, pp. 116–17 below.

30 *LE* II, 81, 60; these examples are cited and discussed, with others, by Kennedy, 'Law and litigation', pp. 166–7.

The acquisition of bookland may itself have prompted the recipient to make at least a single-gift bequest of that land: as has been shown in Chapter One, a substantial number of wills bequeath at least one estate granted to the donor by the king.[31]

The account of Siferth's *verba novissima* – his final disposition, made on his death-bed – is a particularly valuable description of the procedure involved in the drawing up of a will. Although in recounting Siferth's final will-making, the *Liber Eliensis* compiler shows no interest in the spiritual aspect of his passing, it is possible that Siferth's final dispositions were made in the course of the administration of the last rites. The vernacular rubric incorporated in a surviving *ordo* for ministering to the sick and dying includes the instruction:

> *Æfter þam þe se mettruma his þing becwedene hæfð, underfo se mæssepreost his andetnesse.*
>
> (After the sick person has bequeathed his property, the priest shall receive his confession.)[32]

However, it is the procedure rather than the ritual which is the focus of the Ely account:

> *Deinde cum idem vir, videlicet Siverthus de Dunham, prevalente infirmitate, mortis horam sibi ingruere sensissed* [sic] *et apud Lindune absque spe recuperande sanitatis iacuisset, misit pro abbate Brihtnoto et pro fratribus ecclesie. Aderantque ibi Æluricus de Wicham, Ældstanus et filius suus Wine, Leovricus, Brihtelmus, Alfelmus de Redeuuinclen et Ædricus, unus de proceribus Aieluuini alderman, et Osuuoldus presbiter et Sexferdus cum filio suo. Tunc Brihtnotus abbas testamentum huius Siferdi coram uxore et coram filia sua coramque omnibus supramemoratis fecit scribi in tribus cyrographis coramque cunctis fecit recitari lectumque fecit incidi unamque partem cyrographi retinuit Siuerdus, alteram autem dedit abbati.*
>
> (Then when this same man, Siferth of Downham, with sickness overpowering him, had come to feel that death was approaching, and had taken to his bed at Linden without hope of recovering his health, he sent for Abbot Byrhtnoth and for the brothers of the church. And there were present Ælfric of Witcham, Ealdstan and his son Wine, Leofric, Byrhthelm, Ælfhelm of *Redeuuinclen* and Eadric, one of Ealdorman Æthelwine's high-ranking men,

31 See Chap. 1, pp. 14–15, nn. 14–18, 22 for the link between royal charters and wills.

32 Bodleian Laud Misc. 482 (dated s.xi$^{med}$ by Ker, *Catalogue*, no. 343); the text is printed by B. Fehr, 'Altenglische Ritualtexte für Krankenbesuch, heilige Ölung und Begräbnis', in *Texte und Forschungen zur Englischen Kulturgeschichte: Festgabe für Felix Liebermann*, ed. Heinrich Boehmer and others (Halle, 1921), pp. 46–67 (see p. 54 for this rubric). I am indebted for this reference to Dr V. Thompson, who discusses the manuscript and its significance in her *Dying and Death*, Chap. 3 (esp. pp. 67–81).

> and the priest Oswald, and Seaxferth with his son.[33] Then Abbot Byrhtnoth arranged for the will of Siferth to be written down in a tripartite chirograph, in the presence of his wife and daughter and all the people mentioned above, and had it read out before them all. When it was read, he had it cut, and Siferth kept one part of the chirograph, giving the second part to the abbot.)

Great emphasis is placed on Abbot Byrhtnoth's meticulous approach to the recording of Siferth's final wishes; the recording is done at his behest, the text is read before those present, again emphasising the oral and vernacular aspect of the transaction. Of particular significance is the description of the preparation, cutting and distribution of a chirograph, a type of document widely used to record business matters, including leases and dispute settlements, as well as wills.[34] The process by which Abbot Byrhtnoth organised the documentation of Siferth's dispositions reflects the interest and resources of the church, although it is unclear where the chirograph was drawn up: was one of the accompanying brothers an accomplished scribe, or was the document drawn up in the Ely scriptorium on the basis of notes made at Siferth's bedside? [35] Although the impetus for the documentation of bequests seems to come from the church, lay value for such written record is clear: Siferth himself distributes the copies, keeping one himself; and in the account of the Herefordshire Lawsuit it is Thurkil who rides to Hereford Cathedral to have the court's judgment recorded in the gospel book. It is also possible to envisage lay archives which contained documents recording a range of such vernacular transactions, perhaps made over time; for example, marker clauses in the documents indicate that Thurstan and his wife held copies both of their single-gift bequest to Christ Church *and* of his multi-gift will which included it.[36]

The prosaic account of Siferth's final dispositions is in marked contrast to the topoi which feature in descriptions of the death of saints and bishops, which are concerned to enhance the spiritual qualities of their subjects. A bishop, for example, is likely to be credited by his biographer with divine

33 Ælfric of Witcham, Sexferth and Wine, son of Ealdstan also feature elsewhere in local transactions: *LE* II, 11 33, 34/*Lib* 10, 43, 45. See above n. 10 for Eadric witnessing Siferth's second declaration at Ely.

34 The phrase *in tribus cyrographis* [lit: 'in three chirographs'] shows that, for this scribe, the term *chirograph* did not necessarily imply duplication or (as is clear from the context here) triplication on a single sheet of parchment: see Chap. 1, nn. 121, 182. For vernacular wills surviving as chirographs see Chap. 1, n. 122.

35 A similar procedure may be presumed in the account of a death-bed will made before Archbishop Dunstan in the course of a dispute involving St Andrew's, Rochester (S1458/R41, *Rochester* 34) 960x988).

36 S1462/R78; S1530/W30, *Christ Church* 166; S1531/W31. For marker clauses see Chap. 1, n. 123 above. See Kelly, 'Anglo-Saxon lay society', pp. 36–62, especially at pp. 46–51, for the increasing role of vernacular documentation in the context of lay literacy.

intimation of impending death, allowing him time to order the affairs of his diocese and to distribute his wealth.[37] For Bishop Wilfrid, however, like Siferth, ailing health was the trigger which prompted the distribution of his goods. Shortly before his death in 709, Wilfrid ordered his treasure to be brought before him and, with two abbots and 'some very faithful brethren' (*fratribus valde fidelibus*) as witnesses, he divided the gold, silver and precious stones into four parts: one part was to be sent to churches in Rome for the sake of his soul; another was to be distributed among the poor; the third part was to be divided between the abbots of Hexham and Ripon; and the final part was to be distributed among those who had been closest to him in his work and his exile, and to whom he had given no land.[38] Wilfrid then had enough strength to set off on a journey south, publishing the bequests he had made among the abbots of the houses he visited, and distributing land and coin 'as though ... he were sharing his inheritance among his heirs before his death'.[39] At the monastery of Oundle, Wilfrid became mortally ill; he blessed those attending him, who sang psalms at his bedside until he died.[40] The eighth-century account of the death of Bede in 735 by his pupil Cuthbert emphasises his cheerfulness and resilience in the face of death, as he recited the psalter and quoted from the gospels, working to the last on his translation of St John's gospel in his determination to benefit 'my children' (*pueri mei*).[41] To those assembled around his bed he offered comfort, distributing the little he had in the way of personal property – pepper, *oraria* (napkins?) and incense – among the priests of the monastery where he had spent his life, and died, we are told, sitting on the floor of his cell, in the place where he used to pray, singing God's praises.[42] If Siferth disposed of his movable wealth on his deathbed, such a distribution held no interest for the Ely compiler. In fact, he includes no details of Siferth's final dispositions; since his main concern was Ely's title to Downham, the compiler perhaps relied on the circumstantial detail of Siferth's previous bequests of Downham to substantiate Ely's

37 G. Scheibelreiter, 'The death of the bishop in the Early Middle Ages', in *The End of Strife*, ed. D. Loades (Edinburgh, 1984), pp. 32–43; Reuter, 'Testaments, hoards', pp. 17–18, with examples.

38 *Life of Bishop Wilfrid*, ed. Colgrave, chap. 63, pp. 136–7.

39 *Quasi ... ante obitum suum haereditatem haeredibus dispertiens*; ibid., chap. 65, pp. 140–1.

40 Ibid.

41 *Bede's Ecclesiastical History of the English Church and People*, ed. and transl. B. Colgrave and R. A. B. Mynors (Oxford, 1969), pp. 580–7 (p. 582).

42 Ibid., pp. 584–5. For discussion and examples of the ritual surrounding the death of a monk see C. Cubitt, 'Monastic memory and identity in early Anglo-Saxon England', in *Social Identity in Early Medieval Britain*, ed. W. O. Frazer and A. Tyrrell (London, 2000), pp. 253–76 (p. 269). The *Liber Eliensis* account of the death of St Æthelfryth is a further example of the topos (*LE* I, 20–21). For tenth-century monastic practice see *Regularis Concordia Anglicae Nationis Monachorum Sanctimonialiumque*, ed. and transl. T. Symons (London, 1953), chap. 12, pp. 64–8.

claim, and sought to emphasise the close bond between donor and church by recounting the abbot's presence at the deathbed formalities.

Without a narrative context, it is difficult to distinguish vernacular deathbed wills from those made at leisure.[43] In some instances, the phrasing may suggest that the documents represent dispositions made *in extremis*. For example, the will of Ealdorman Æthelmær announces that it was declared 'on his last day' (*his nyhstan dæge*), a phrase which seems to imply that Æthelmær, if not actually on his death-bed, believed that this would be his final will.[44] Equally enigmatic is the evidence for the imminent death of the ætheling Æthelstan, eldest son of King Æthelred, which arises principally from a clause near the end of the will:

> *Nu þancige Ic minon fæder mid ealre eadmodnesse on Godes ælmihtiges naman þære andsware. þe he me sende on frigedæg. æfter middessumeres mæssedæge. be Ælfgare. Ælffan suna. þ wæs. þ he me cydde. mines fæder worde. þ ic moste be Godes leafe. 7 be his. geunnan minre are. 7 minra æhta. swa me mæst ræd þuhte.*
>
> (Now I thank my father in all humility, in the name of Almighty God, for the answer which he sent me on the Friday after the feast of midsummer by Ælfgar, Æffa's son; which, as he told me in my father's words, was that I might, by God's leave and his, grant my estates and my possessions as seemed to me most advisable.)

It seems likely that Æthelstan died on Friday, 25 June in 1014, the day on which his father's permission was received, or very shortly afterwards.[45] A third example is Bishop Ælfwold's will, which was made between 1011, the date of his final attestation of a royal charter, and 1015, when his successor's signature first appears.[46] Again the evidence rests on a single clause in which he bequeaths a ship to the king:

> *He is eall gearo butan þam hanon he hine wolde ful gearwian his hlaforde to gerisnum gif him god uðe.*
>
> (It is all ready except for the rowlocks. He would like to prepare it fully in a style fit for his lord if God would allow him.)[47]

His anxiety that he may not live to see the completion of his ship may imply

43 For chronicle evidence of other wills made *in extremis* see *LE* II, 11, 21 59, 61, 81, 83 (*Lib* 32); *CR* 28 (pp. 53, 54), 51, 53, 103 (p. 169), 107 (pp. 175–6).

44 S1498/W10, *New Minster* 25. The phrase is used at the end of the preamble to S1507/H11, *New Minster* 1, the will of King Alfred, with the implication that his present dispositions were not necessarily those which would apply on 'his last day'.

45 S1503/W20/*Christ Church* 142; the date of Æthelstan's death is discussed by Keynes, *Diplomas*, p. 267, and see Chap. 3, p. 99 below.

46 S1492/N&S10. These dating parameters are suggested by Keynes, *Diplomas*, p. 121, n. 123.

47 Translation from *EHD* I, p. 581.

that his death is imminent; it may also be the pious hope of a religious man. However, additional support for the theory that at least two of these three documents may be deathbed wills comes from the inclusion of short witness lists, possibly representing a private gathering, appropriate for a deathbed, rather than the public forum suited to their rank: that of Ælfwold was witnessed by five men, all beneficiaries of the will, two of whom were kinsmen, two priests and one a monk;[48] that of Æthelstan names as witnesses his brother Edmund, Bishop Ælfsige of Winchester, Abbot Brihtmær of the New Minster, Winchester, and Ælfmær, Ælfric's son, all of whom are beneficiaries (if this Ælfmær is to be identified with at least one of the other Ælfmærs mentioned in the will).[49] Both of these wills survive as contemporary single sheets, reducing the likelihood that the lists have been truncated by a later copyist. In addition, the wills of all three donors (Æthelmær, Æthelstan and Ælfwold) include detailed bequests of movable wealth which look remarkably like the winding up of a man's affairs: Bishop Ælfwold makes a range of bequests of stock, furnishings, coin and books to beneficiaries who include members of the nobility, kin, a scribe, and his retainers (*hiredmen*); Æthelstan bequeaths swords, horses and a trumpet; and Æthelmær distributes coin to a range of religious foundations. Like Ælfwold, Æthelstan recognises outstanding debts and makes arrangements for them to be dealt with, and, again like Ælfwold, both Æthelstan and Æthelmær acknowledge members of their household: Æthelmær intends five pounds to be divided among his servants; Æthelstan names, among others, his sword polisher (*swurdhwitan*) and staghuntsman (*headeorhunton*) as beneficiaries.[50]

The final stage in the will-making process is the confirmation of the dispositions by secular authority. The evidence of the vernacular wills suggests that this was the prerogative of the king, but the third section of Siferth's chirograph was sent, instead, to Ealdorman Æthelwine:

> *Tertiam [partem] vero misit statim per prefatum Brihthelmum Æieluuino alderman, qui tunc temporis deiebat in Ely, et petiit ab eo, ut suum testamentum ita stare concessisset*[51] *quomodo abbas illud scripserat et ordinaverat apud Lindune coram predictorum testimonio virorum. Cum itaque Aieluuinus alderman hoc audisset et cyrographum vidisset, remisit illico ad eum Wlnothum de Stouue cum Brihtelmo sciscitatusque est ab eo quid aut quomodo vellet de testamento suo. Qui mox per*

48 For the formal ritual surrounding a bishop's deathbed see Scheibelreiter, 'The death of the bishop', p. 37.

49 See *Wills*, p. 170; such problems of identification recur throughout the wills. See pp. 63–4 above for the list of those attending Siferth's death-bed.

50 For the deathbed distribution see Reuter, 'Testaments, hoards', p. 18. Such distributions are particularly rare in the wills of laymen: see Chap. 5, p. 221 below.

51 The Latin phrase *petiit … ut suum testamentum ita stare concessisset* probably reflects the phrase *he bitt þæt his cwyde standan mote* (he asked that his will might stand) found in vernacular wills.

> *eosdem renuntiavit ei sic suum testamentum absque omni contradictione vel mutatione se velle stare, sicuti prefatus abbas illud in cyrographo posuerat. Quod ut Aieluuinus alderman audivit, totum concessit ut staret, sicuti ipse Siverhtus testatus erat.*
>
> (The third part he sent at once by the aforesaid Byrhthelm to Ealdorman Æthelwine, who at that time was dwelling at Ely, and asked him to allow his will to stand, just as the abbot had written it and set it down at Linden in the witness of the aforementioned men. And so when Ealdorman Æthelwine heard this and saw the chirograph, he sent Wulfnoth of Stowe back there to him with Byrhthelm and asked him what he wanted concerning his will and with what conditions. Siferth soon sent the reply to Æthelwine through Wulfnoth and Byrhthelm that he wished his will to stand free from challenge or alteration as the aforesaid abbot had set it down in the chirograph. When Ealdorman Æthelwine heard this, he granted that it should stand in its entirety, in accordance with the attestation that Siferth himself gave.)

Æthelwine (ealdorman of East Anglia 962–992) is ubiquitous in the pages of the *Liber Eliensis* as both litigant and adjudicator.[52] His presence at Ely on this occasion may be accounted for by his tendency to use it as an administrative centre.[53] He held great power in the region – he has been described as 'a virtual plenipotentiary', and as such may have had considerable influence over the bequest of land.[54] It is also possible, however, that Siferth was not a king's thegn, and that his heriot was due, not to the king, but to Æthelwine himself. Ketel, whose vernacular will of the mid eleventh century is the only one extant including a heriot clause which identifies the donor as a lesser thegn, owes his heriot to Archbishop Stigand, and places his will under the protection of Stigand and Earl Harold, both of whom were significant landowners in East Anglia.[55] If the procedure Æthelwine adopted in validating Siferth's will is correctly reported, it seems unnecessarily long-winded: he appears to have required further oral confirmation from Siferth, even though one of the messengers who brought him the will was present at the declaration. This is an illustration of oral confirmation privileged above the written word, but it smacks of bureaucracy – the Anglo-Saxon equivalent of forms in triplicate – or the Ely compiler's anxiety to reinforce the legitimacy of the abbey's claim to the land.[56] The will of the ætheling Æthelstan certainly presumes a formal, public reading of his dispositions:

52 Wareham, *Lords and Communities*, pp. 21–7; Æthelwine is venerated in *CR* as founder and patron.

53 Kennedy, 'Law and litigation', p. 144.

54 Kennedy, 'Law and litigation', p. 145, with a warning on p. 137 that the picture given by the *Libellus* may be local to East Anglia and Cambridgeshire.

55 S1519/W34. Ketel is described as a thegn of Stigand in relation to one of his estates: DB II, fol. 254r. Chap. 4 below focuses on the status of donors.

56 Kennedy, 'Law and litigation', p. 173: 'As a class of evidence [documents] were locked

*Nu bidde ic. ealle þa witan. þe mine cwyde gehyron rædan. ægðer ge gehadode. ge læwede. þ hi beon on fultume. þ min cwyde standan mote. swa mines fæder leaf. on minon cwyde stænt.*

(Now I pray all the councillors, both ecclesiastical and lay, who may hear my will read, that they will help to secure that my will may stand, as my father's permission stands in my will.)

The wording of this clause indicates that Æthelstan expected that his will would be ratified, as Keynes puts it, as 'part of the routine business of government'.[57] This was essentially an oral procedure, but some documentary evidence of such proceedings survives. Leofgifu's will refers to one copy of the document being kept 'with the king's relics' (*mid þise kinges halidome*).[58] King Æthelred's confirmation of the will of Wulfric Spott, which endowed Burton Abbey, was issued in 1004 with the subscriptions of what appears to be a full council.[59] In addition, a series of writs was issued by Edward the Confessor to local courts confirming publicly, probably on the death of the donor, the right to bequeath.[60] One example is the writ confirming the joint bequest of Tole and her late husband, Urk, to their church at Abbotsbury (Dorset):

(+ *Eadweard kyng gret Hermann . b̄ . 7 Harold eorl 7 ealle mine þegenas on Dorsætan freondlice. 7 ic cyðe eow þ hit is min fulla unna þ Tole min mann Urkes lafe þ heo becweðe hire land 7 ehta into Sc̄e Petre æt Abbodesbyrig swa swa hire leofest sy be minan fullan geleafan swa full 7 swa forð swa þa forewirda ær gewrhte* [sic] *wæran þ hit sceolde æfter heora begra dage hire 7 Urkes hire hlafordes for heora sawle gan into þam haligan mynstre. Nu wille ic þ heora cwide stande swa swa hit geforewird wes. on godre manna gewitnesse þe þar wið weran.*

(+ King Edward sends friendly greetings to Bishop Herman and Earl Harold and all my thegns in Dorset. And I inform you that Tole my man Urk's widow has my full permission to bequeath her land and possessions to St Peter's at Abbotsbury, as best pleases her, with my full consent, as fully and completely as it was arranged by the agreements previously made, that it should after the death of both of them – her death and that of Urk

into the wider complex of oral procedures and, it would seem, treated essentially as another witness of the claims in whose support they were produced.' Keynes, 'Royal government', p. 256.

57 Keynes, 'Royal government', p. 254; Ealdorman Alfred also addresses his will to the *witan*: S1508/H10, *Christ Church* 96.

58 S1521/W29. Eadric the Tall sent a copy of his will to King Edgar (*LE* II, 27/*Lib* 38): p. 72 below.

59 S906 precedes a copy of the will (S1536/W17, *Burton* 29) on a single parchment: they appear to be late eleventh century copies (*Burton*, pp. xix–xx).

60 *Writs* 2 (S1064), 12 (S1072), 17 (S1077), 22 (S1082), 111(S1153); doubtful or spurious: 74 (S1118), 84 (S1128), 93 (S1137), 112 (S1154).

her lord – pass into the possession of the holy monastery for [the benefit of] their souls. Now my will is that their bequest shall remain in force in accordance with the agreements made with the cognisance of good men who were present.)[61]

The death of Urk had clearly prompted a review of his *post obitum* dispositions, possibly in association with Tole's payment of his heriot.[62] It seems likely that the previous agreement reached before witnesses, to which the writ refers, was the original declaration of those intentions – in other words, the bequest to St Peter's. The significance of the king's confirmation of bequests may be illustrated by an account in Domesday Book of evidence given by the jurors concerning an estate at Fawler (Berks.):

> About this manor the shire testifies that Eadric, who used to hold it, gave it over to his son, who was a monk in Abingdon, to hold it at farm and to provide him [Eadric] with the necessaries of life for as long as he lived [and] after his death to have the manor; therefore the men of the shire do not know that it belongs to the abbey, and they have seen neither the King's writ nor seal concerning it. The abbot on the other hand testifies that *TRE* [Eadric's son] transferred the manor to the church to which he belonged, and concerning this he has the writ and seal of King Edward, according to the testimony of all his monks.[63]

The abbey's claim to the land hinges, apparently, not on the possession of a landbook, nor on written evidence of the original bequest, but on the king's confirmation. By the mid-eleventh century at least, therefore, the royal writ confirmed the transmission of bookland following a bequest.[64]

That the king had the potential power to interfere with the inheritance process is revealed obliquely in the expressions of confidence which appear in some wills that he will not exercise that right.[65] Forfeiture could certainly be an issue, as is demonstrated by the documentation surrounding the will of Æthelric of Bocking. His multi-gift will, made between 961 and 995, stipulates the heriot due from a king's thegn close to the king in the Danelaw.[66] Nothing further is known about him, beyond the fact that, at the time of his death, he stood accused of treachery: the document recording King Æthelred's confirmation of the will relates that Æthelred believed Æthelric to have been involved in treacherous negotiations with Swein 'that he should

61 S1064/*Writs* 2, 1058x1066. Although this writ survives only in a post-Conquest copy, it is regarded as a copy of an authentic original by Harmer (*Writs*, pp. 117, 119).

62 As described in S939/W16[2], *Christ Church* 137: see below p. 71.

63 DB I, fol. 59r.

64 *Facsimiles of English Royal Writs to AD 1100: presented to V. H. Galbraith*, ed. T. A. M. Bishop and P. Chaplais (Oxford, 1957), p. xi; Sharpe, 'The use of writs', pp. 247–8.

65 S1487/W13; S1497/*St Albans*, 7; S1536/W17, *Burton* 29.

66 S1501/W16[1], *Christ Church* 137.

be received in Essex when he first came there in the fleet'.[67] We are told that Archbishop Sigeric, 'for the sake of the estate at Bocking',[68] had acted as Æthelric's advocate (*forespeca*) with the king – apparently before Æthelric's death – but to no avail. By the time of Æthelric's death, 'he was neither cleared of the charge, nor was the crime atoned for'.[69] Æthelric's widow brought the heriot of her late husband to Cookham (Berks.), where the king was holding a full council. Æthelred seems to have been intransigent, reasserting the accusation of treachery against Æthelric and refusing permission for the will to stand. Archbishop Sigeric had died, so the widow turned to his successor, Ælfric, and a certain Æthelmær for their advocacy;[70] she promised her morning-gift to Christ Church 'for the king and all his people' (*for ðone cincg. 7 ealne his leodscype*) in an attempt to persuade the king to drop his 'terrible accusation' (*egeslican onspæce*) and allow Æthelric's will to stand. The document – presumably written on behalf of Christ Church – celebrates the king's consent, and ends with an extensive witness list.[71] The widow would retain the life interest in her husband's property which he had been anxious to secure for her by his will, bequeathing an estate to Bishop Ælfstan (of London) in the hope of gaining his protection; and Christ Church acquired her morning-gift, as well as the reversion of Bocking. Archbishop Dunstan had earlier been less successful in his negotiations with King Edgar. In the course of recounting the convoluted history of the estates of Sunbury (Mx) and Send (Sy), a contemporary document relates that one of the principals in the drama, Ecgferth, bequeathed Sunbury to Dunstan, on the understanding that he would act as guardian (*to mundgenne*) for Ecgferth's widow and child.[72] When Ecgferth died, the archbishop went to the king 'and reminded him of the guardianship and of his cognisance',[73] only to be told, 'My councillors have declared all Ecgferth's property forfeit, by the sword which hung on his hip when he was drowned'.[74] Refusing even Dunstan's offer to pay

67 *þ man sceolde on Eastsexon Swegen underfon ða he ærest þyder mid flotan com.* S939/W16[2], 995x999, which survives as the central section of a contemporary tripartite chirograph, also in the Christ Church archive. The date of the campaign in question is uncertain, but see N. Brooks, 'Treason in Essex in the 990s: the case of Æthelric of Bocking' (forthcoming) for a survey of the political context.

68 *For ðæs landes þingon æt Boccinge*, which Æthelric bequeathed to Christ Church following his wife's life interest. S1218 is a twelfth-century cartulary version of this bequest (in Latin) in which Æthelric's wife is named as Leofwyn.

69 *þa wæs he þisse spæce ægþer ge on life. ge æfter ungeladod ge ungebett.*

70 Possibly Ealdorman Æthelmær who was named as advocate in the will of Ælfflæd (S1486/W15): n. 110 below.

71 Copies were held by Christ Church, by Æthelric's widow, and 'in the king's sanctuary' (*æt þæs cinges haligdome*).

72 S1447/R44, *c.* 950x968.

73 *Myngude þære munde 7 his gewitnesse.*

74 *Mine witan hæbbað ætrecð Ecgferðe ealle his are . þurh þ swyrd þe him on hype hangode þa he adranc.* The circumstances are obscure; see *Charters*, p. 338 for a survey of possibilities,

Ecgfrith's wergild as compensation, the king then granted the land to his own kinsman, Ealdorman Ælfheah, and Dunstan was finally able to acquire it only through a costly purchase.[75]

The transfer of property to the beneficiary completed a bequest. In the case of land, this required the transfer of the title-deed, and the payment of heriot. The *Liber Eliensis* provides a good example of this procedure.[76] We are told that before Eadric the Tall (*Longus*) died he made his will, which included a bequest to the king of an estate at Hauxton (Cambs.), and sent a copy to King Edgar. After Eadric's death, Bishop Æthelwold bought four and a half hides at Hauxton and three hides at Newton (Cambs.) from the king, but within a month the king died, before Eadric's heriot had been paid and the charters for the estates obtained.[77] Eadric's brother, Ælfwold, and other kinsmen held onto the charters of both estates, claiming that Newton was a separate estate, and not part of the bequest; the bishop, on the other hand, claimed that Newton had been bequeathed by Eadric as part of the estate at Hauxton. This dispute rumbled on for many years, to be resolved only by the intervention of Ealdorman Byrhtnoth, who negotiated a settlement at some cost to the church.[78] Some vernacular wills recognise the significance of the *boc*. For example, Wynflæd's bequest of an estate to her daughter stipulates that the *boc* will be handed over on her death:

> *7 hio becwið Æðelflæde hyre dehter … þ land æt Ebbelesburnan 7 þa boc on ece yrfe to ateonne swa hyre leofosð sy.*
>
> (And she bequeaths to her daughter Æthelflæd … the estate at Ebbesborne and the title-deed as a perpetual inheritance to dispose of as she pleases.)[79]

Similarly, Æthelweard arranges that the title-deed should be handed to Christ Church, Canterbury, with the estate at Ickham (Kent), on its reversion.[80] Others transfer the *boc* to the beneficiary at the time when the will is declared

including the suggestion that the sword was the symbol of a royal official (see the will of Ealdorman Ælfgar, S1483/W2, for what is possibly a sword of office, and Chap. 5, pp. 194–6 below for further discussion of the significance of swords).

75 Edgar's grant to Ælfheah is S702, 962 (see S1485/W9 for Ælfheah's will). Forfeiture may underlie the bequest of Inkpen (Berks.) by Wulfgar (S1533/R26): the estate was granted to Wulfgar's grandfather and forfeited by his father, Wulfhere (S362/*EHD* I, no. 100); it is unclear how Wulfgar reacquired it.

76 *LE* II, 27/*Lib* 38.

77 *Deinde vero infra unum mensem, priusquam episcopus et abbas cyrographa … habuissent et antequam relevationes date fuissent de illis terris, exuit hominem Ædgarus rex.*

78 Ælfwold surrendered the charters, in return for two Ely estates, and 30 mancuses paid by Byrhtnoth; the abbot had already granted an estate to Ealdorman Æthelwine, whose negotiations came to nothing. A similar impasse is implied in *CR* 103, where Abbot Ælfwine resorts to bribing the king and queen.

79 S1539/W3. See also S1511/W11, *Rochester* 35.

80 S1506/R32, *Christ Church* 121; see Chap. 4, p. 161 below for details of this bequest.

– *to swutelunge* (as evidence), in the words of the bequest of Ordnoth and his wife to the Old Minster, Winchester.[81]

The care with which donors sought to protect their dispositions – publicising them well, commending them to the king, invoking the power of the church through sanctions – indicates that the inheritance of land could be contentious. For example, land which had been leased by the church on specific terms to a layman might be bequeathed within the family of the tenant beyond the terms of the agreement, and could prove difficult to regain.[82] The dispute described above, between Ely and the kinsmen of Eadric the Tall, illustrates how bequests to the church might be challenged by a donor's kin.[83] This is well illustrated by the will of Æthelgifu, which recounts how her husband's kinsmen 'did not allow her' (*ne gelefde hire*) to bequeath property left to her by her husband with freedom of disposition.[84] The identity of Æthelgifu's husband is uncertain; he may have been the Æthelric credited with the gift of Gaddesden to St Albans in the endorsement of a lost charter associated with the documentation surrounding Æthelgifu's will.[85] The dating of the will and the events it records is equally uncertain, but it seems likely that the will itself was drawn up during the minority of the ætheling Æthelstan (perhaps between 985 and 1002), referring to a dispute which took place a number of years earlier, possibly in the 950s.[86] The will records that the dispute was heard at a joint meeting of the shires of Bedford and Hertford:[87]

> *Þa lædde heo að to Hyccan .xx. hund aða þær wæs Ælfere on 7 Ælfsige .l.d 7 Byrnric wæs þa gerefa 7 ealle þa yldestan men to Bedanforda 7 to Heortforda 7*

81 S1524/W5; these donors reserve the right to retrieve the document when necessary in order to make corrections (*rihtinge*). Dunn has given the *boc* to his wife, but stipulates that it is to be kept with the will in the Rochester archive (S1514/R9); both documents were copied into the *Textus Roffensis* (*Rochester*, 23). See also S1471/R101, *Christ Church* 170 and S1511/W7.

82 S1404/*Writs* 3 (with discussion by Harmer at pp. 122–3); S1446/H15 (see Chap. 1, pp. 49–50 above).

83 S1077/*Writs* 17 reinstates such land apparently lost to Bury (see also Hart, *ECEE*, pp. 90–1), and S1408 records a challenge by Aki, Toki's son, to his father's bequest to Bishop Ealdred of Worcester (see Chap. 1, p. 47 above).

84 S1497/*St Albans* 7. Both S1474/R105, *Sherborne* 17 and S1458/R41, *Rochester* 34 record disputes between brothers, apparently over inherited land, which in the case of the latter extends to involve kin by marriage. The extended and violent dispute within a family recorded in S877, *New Minster* 31 may also have originated in inheritance. In the Herefordshire Lawsuit, Enniaun's case against his mother seems to hinge on her right to bequeath the estates in question – probably inherited from her husband – freely (S1462/R78: pp. 60–1 above).

85 S1497/*St Albans* 7A(d); Crick, *St Albans* pp. 93–4.

86 The evidence is surveyed by Crick, *St Albans*, pp. 92–4.

87 Kennedy has argued that, in general, the adjudication of disputes concerning *bocland* was the responsibility of local courts: 'Disputes', pp. 181–6.

*heora wif ufonan þone cwide 7 þær [ … ] þa of ærdo[.]de Eadelm hire hlafordes swustur sunu hire lond hire æt Standune.*

(Then she [Æthelgifu] produced an oath at Hitchin (Beds.), twenty hundred oaths: there were included Ælfhere and Ælfsige *cild* and Byrnric who was then reeve and all the chief men belonging to Bedford and Hertford, and their wives. In spite of the will and [text illegible], Eadelm, the son of her lord's sister, dispossessed her of her land at Standon [Herts.].)[88]

Crick has shown that Ælfhere, if he is the ealdorman of that name styled *dux* in witness lists from 956, Ælfsige *cild* and Byrnric attest a number of charters together during the reign of Eadwig (955–959), which provides a possible indicator of the date of the dispute.[89] The illegibility of the text at a crucial point makes it difficult to be sure of the outcome, but the phrasing seems to indicate that the court found in Æthelgifu's favour. However, Eadelm, her husband's sister's son, appears to have flouted not only her husband's will but also the court's ruling. Eadelm seized her estate at Standon, prompting Æthelgifu to refer her case to the king:[90]

*Þa sohte ic þæne cing 7 gesealde. hym .xx. punda þa agef he me myn lond on his unþonc.*

(Then I appealed to the king, and gave him twenty pounds; then he gave me back my land against his will.)

To whom did Æthelgifu pay twenty pounds? The plethora of third person male pronouns obscures the meaning. As the translation stands above, the payment may have been made to the king, an interpretation supported by the story preserved in the Ramsey *Chronicon* of Abbot Ælfwine paying twenty gold marks to King Edward (the Confessor) and five to Queen Edith in order to earn a favourable judgment when Æthelwine Niger's bequest to Ramsey

88 S1497/*St Albans* 7.

89 *St Albans*, p. 93. Crick rejects as unlikely the possibility that Ælfhere was unstyled in the will in error, preferring the explanation that he had not yet been promoted to ealdorman, thus placing the dispute before that event.

90 For theoretical discouragement of premature recourse to the king in disputes see II Cnut, 17–20 which prescribes three hearings in the hundred court, and one in the shire court before a case could be taken to the king; see P. Wormald, 'Giving God and king their due: conflict and its regulation in the early English state', *Settimana di Studio del Centro Italiano di Studi sull' alto Medioevo* 44 (1997), 549–90, reprinted in Wormald, *Legal Culture*, pp. 333–57 (pp. 346–8). The only other direct appeals to the king relating to bequests which I have been able to find are *CR* 103 and S1447/R44, but see also the king's intervention in the dispute recorded in S877/R63, *New Minster* 31 (*EHD* I, no. 120), which may have involved inheritance: *New Minster*, pp. 150–2, and S. Keynes, 'Crime and punishment in the reign of King Æthelred the Unready', in *People and Places in Northern Europe: Studies presented to Peter Hayes Sawyer*, ed. I. Wood and N. Lund (Woodbridge, 1991), pp. 67–81 (pp. 78–9).

was disputed by his cousin.[91] However, since it has been shown above how the dispute over the bequest of Eadric the Tall was resolved only on payment of significant compensation by Abbot Brihtwine to the claimants, it possible that Æthelgifu paid the twenty pounds to her husband's nephew in order to persuade him to withdraw his claim to the estate.[92] Whether in return for payment or at the king's instigation, it was presumably Eadelm who (however reluctantly) returned the land to Æthelgifu.

The fact that the inheritance process could be hard-fought and expensive may account for the apparent increase in written will-making, hedged with such protection – secular and spiritual – as was available. Given the limitations of the evidence, it is difficult to assess the extent to which the process was effective, but in a number of cases bequests seem to have been completed.[93] Domesday Book provides some examples: in 1066 Æthelgyth, widow of Thurstan, was holding land bequeathed to her by her husband's will; Thurkil the White was holding one of the estates (Wellington) bequeathed to his wife, Leofflæd, by the unnamed widow in Herefordshire; and four hides at Downham were held by the abbot of Ely.[94] Editorial detective work among registers and cartularies has provided examples of monastic houses holding lands bequeathed to them in extant written wills.[95] Occasional charters of confirmation exist: in his will, Archbishop Ælfric asks the king to endorse an arrangement with St Alban's Abbey whereby the king would receive the unidentified estate of *Eadulfingtune* in return for confirming the abbey's rights at Kingsbury (Herts.), which was duly done, as the extant royal charter shows.[96] Rarely, estates may be tracked by other means: a document from St Paul's, London, dating probably to c. 1000 and known as the Ship List, stipulates the naval levy due from specific estates, including estates bequeathed

91 *CR* 103. (The translation is that of Whitelock, *Æthelgifu*, pp. 14–15, followed by Crick, *St Albans*, p. 151).

92 *LE* II, 27/*Lib* 38.

93 Lowe discusses the competence of the vernacular will in 'Nature and effect', pp. 41–7.

94 S1531/W31; M. A. Meyer, 'Women's estates in later Anglo-Saxon England: the politics of possession', *Haskins Society Journal* 3 (1991), 111–29 (pp. 118–19); *Wills*, pp. 190, 195–6. For Thurkil, who had presumably inherited from his wife, see *Charters*, p. 401; DB I, fol. 192r.

95 For example, Whitelock shows that Christ Church, Canterbury, apparently received Stisted (Ex), bequeathed in S1535/W32, *Christ Church* 176 and Hollingbourne (Kt), bequeathed in S1503/W20, *Christ Church* 142 (*Wills*, pp. 198, 169). Such research is now greatly facilitated by the work of editors in the ongoing British Academy Anglo-Saxon charter series.

96 S1488/W18, *Abingdon* 133, 1003x1004; S912, *St Albans* 11, 1005; the integrity of the charter and its relationship with the will are discussed by Crick, *St Albans*, pp. 183, 186–7; Keynes, 'A lost cartulary', p. 265. See also S906, the confirmation charter of Wulfric Spott's endowment of Burton Abbey, S1536/W17 (*Burton* 28, 29).

by Bishop Theodred in the mid-tenth century;[97] and land at Roydon (Nfk), bequeathed by Thurketel of Palgrave to his wife, Leofcwen, subsequently reappears in Bishop Ælfric's will with the information that he had bought it from a certain Leofwyn – presumably Thurketel's widow.[98]

Nevertheless, difficulties could arise in effecting the donor's dispositions. Two such difficulties – obstruction by the king and successful challenge, particularly likely to be mounted by kindred – have already been considered above.[99] Political circumstances may have been a factor in some cases. For example, the apparent failure of some estates bequeathed to Burton Abbey by Wulfric Spott either to reach their destination or to be retained by the abbey may be related to the fact that Wulfric's brother Ælfhelm, Ealdorman of Northumbria, fell from power within four years of Wulfric's death.[100] In addition, some wills were disrupted by the Norman Conquest: where donors were still alive in 1066, their lands were often reallocated, overriding their dispositions.[101] But it is also possible that apparent non-completion of a donor's bequests could be the result of renegotiation between the beneficiary and an interested party. That this was a recognised procedure is demonstrated by the reference in the bequest-agreement between Æthelric and Archbishop Eadsige that the donor's friends (*freonda*) should have the opportunity to 'continue to hold the estates, agreeably to the archbishop, at a fair rent or in accordance with other such arrangements as may be devised at the time with the existing archbishop'.[102] Ceolwynn makes provision for the estate which she bequeaths to the Old Minster, Winchester, to be exchanged for one 'which is nearer to them and more convenient'.[103] A non-testamentary agreement dated between 975 and 978 shows a certain Ælfwine carrying out such a negotiation with Bishop Æthelwold and the community of the Old Minster, Winchester.[104]

97 S1526/W1; *St Paul's* 25, items 1, 2, and 3 (and see also items 16, 28 and 32 for discussion of other bequests).

98 S1527/W24, dated to the mid-eleventh century, but probably before 1038, in relation to S1489/W26 which is dated to the reign of Harold Harefoot (1035/1037–1040).

99 See pp. 70–2, 73–5 above.

100 S1536/W17, *Burton* 29. Keynes, *Diplomas*, pp. 211–14; *Burton*, pp. xliv–xlv; Baxter, *Earls*, pp. 180–2; Fleming, *Kings and Lords*, pp. 42–8, with discussion of Wulfric's bequests at p. 44; Chap. 4, p. 143 below. Further examples: S1486/W15 (Chap. 6, pp. 270–1 below); S1503/W20, *Christ Church* 142 (Chap. 3, p. 105 below).

101 S1531/W31 (the reversion of land following the death of Thurstan's widow, Æthelgyth); 1516/W33; S1519/W34; W39/*Peterborough* 27; S1235/*St Albans* 17.

102 *Þa land furþor on þæs arcebisceopes gemede ofgan mage . to rihtan gafole . oððe to oþran forewyrdan . swa hit man þænne findan mage wið þone arcebisceop þe þanne libbe*; S1471/R101, *Christ Church* 170, *c.* 1045. The ninth-century wills of Ealdorman Alfred (S1508/H10, *Christ Church* 96) and King Alfred (S1507/H11, *New Minster* 1) make provision for kinsmen to buy land bequeathed to women.

103 *Ðæ him gehændre beo 7 behefre*; S1513/R17. See also S1514/R9, *Rochester* 23 for a similar arrangement.

104 S1376/R53.

Ælfwine's ancestors had bequeathed an estate at Moredon (Wilts.) to their heirs, on condition that they pay an annual food-rent to the Old Minster. Ælfwine's father, Ælfsige, handed (*betehte*) the land to the Old Minster 'because of the food-rent' (*forða feormæ*) – possibly it proved too onerous. Ælfwine reacquired this land, giving to the Old Minster, in exchange, family property within the city walls of Winchester, along with the *boc*. The agreement is witnessed, and four copies were made.[105] It is therefore possible that discrepancies which arise in the fulfilment of a donor's intentions may have no more sinister explanation than a business transaction for which no records survive. It is also possible that completion of a donor's bequests might be delayed by kin, with or without the agreement of the beneficiaries. At the end of his will, Ealdorman Ælfgar requests the king to ensure that his children should not be allowed to set his will aside.[106] The king's protection is often invoked by donors, but this phrasing is unique, hinting that Ælfgar may have had specific concerns. He bequeaths a life interest in Cockfield and Lavenham (Sfk), and Peldon and Mersea and Greenstead (Ex) to his older daughter, Æthelflæd; Cockfield is to revert to Bury, and the remainder to Stoke-by-Nayland (Sfk). As Æthelflæd's will shows, she not only retained a life interest in these estates, but in her turn bequeathed a life interest in them to her sister, Ælfflæd, and her sister's husband, Byrhtnoth.[107] It is Ælfflæd's will which fulfils Ælfgar's intentions.[108]

However, the vulnerability of *post obitum* disposition is illustrated by the will of Ælfflæd, Ælfgar's younger daughter and last in the family line.[109] She reiterates bequests made by her father and older sister to the religious house at Stoke-by-Nayland, of which her family were patrons, requesting King Æthelred to protect both the 'holy foundation' (*þa halgan stowæ*) at Stoke and the family endowment of it. But in addition, Ælfflæd enlists the support of powerful men both for her bequests and for the family foundation, as the final clauses in her will show:

> *7 ic gean Æðelmære æaldorman þes landes æt Lellinge ofer mine deg mid mete. 7 mid mannum. æalswa hit stent on þet gerad þ he beo on minum life min fulla freod. 7 forespreca. 7 mira manna. 7 efter minum dege beo þara halgan stowe. 7 peræ are ful freod. 7 forespeca æt Stocæ þe min yldran on restaþ. 7 ic gean þes landes æt*

105 S1232/R113 recounts similar negotiations between Wulfweard the White and the Old Minster, Winchester, concerning a bequest of Queen Ælfgifu-Emma.

106 S1483/W2, 946xc.951: *werken min bern þat he werken þat he nefre ne mugen forwerken mine quide.*

107 S1494/W14, 962x991 (?after 975).

108 S1486/W15, 1000x1002. Lowe suggests that this delay in reversion may have been negotiated with the beneficiaries: 'Nature and effect', pp. 41–4. For re-donation by successive donors see Chap. 4, pp. 159–60, and for detailed discussion of these wills see Chap. 6, pp. 235–7.

109 S1486/W15.

> *Lissingtune Eðelmere mines ... mid mete. 7 mid mannum ealswa hit stent. 7 hine eadmodlice bidde þ he min fulla freod. 7 mundiend beo on minum dege. 7 efter minum dege gefelste þ min cwide 7 mira yldran standan mote.*
>
> (And I grant to the ealdorman Æthelmær the estate at Lawling after my death, with its produce and its men, just as it stands, on condition that during my life he shall be a true friend and advocate to me and to my men, and after my death, be a true friend and advocate of the holy foundation at Stoke, where my ancestors lie buried, and its property. And I grant the estate at Liston to Æthelmær my [...] with the produce and with the men just as it stands, and humbly pray him that he will be my true friend and protector during my life, and after my death will help to secure that my will and my ancestors' wills may stand.)

Ealdorman Æthelmær was probably the son of Æthelweard, ealdorman of the Western Shires, whom he succeeded.[110] He was influential at the court of King Æthelred,[111] and is probably to be identified with the Æthelmær whose support was enlisted by the widow of Æthelric of Bocking in her attempt to defend her husband's will.[112] As it turned out, Ælfflæd's concerns were justified. While family bequests to larger houses, such as Christ Church, Canterbury, Bury and Ely all seem to have reached their destination,[113] Domesday Book reveals that the estates bequeathed to Stoke by Ælfgar and his daughters were in lay hands in 1066.[114]

The evidence presented in this chapter suggests that the process by which vernacular wills were produced was both sophisticated and flexible. Oral procedures were paramount at every stage, but each stage was capable of generating documentation: the single-gift bequest or multi-gift will made in advance of mortal illness, the deathbed disposition, the confirmation by the

110 For this identification of Ealdorman Æthelmær see *Wills*, pp. 144–5 and Wareham, *Lords and Communities*, p. 58; for the possibility that his title is a later insertion, see Keynes, *Diplomas*, p. 210, n. 203. The second Æthelmær is unidentified.

111 For Æthelmær's influence at court, see Keynes, *Diplomas*, pp. 191–3, 209–13.

112 See n. 70 above.

113 In 1066 Christ Church held Monks Eleigh (Sfk) (DB II, fol. 373r), and Bury held Cockfield (DB II, fol. 359r). *LE* II, 63, 64 refer to the bequest of Lavenham by Æthelflæd and Ælfflæd. St Paul's was also holding rights in *Tidwoldingtune* (Heybridge, Ex) bequeathed by Ælfgar and Haddam (Herts.) bequeathed by Æthelflæd (*Wills*, pp. 140, 143; *St Paul's*, pp. 94–5).

114 *Wills*, p. 105; DB II, fol. 401r. Hart suggests that Peldon and Mersea had entered the royal fisc: C. R. Hart, 'The Mersea charter of Edward the Confessor', *Essex Archaeology and History* 12 (1980), 94–102, revised and reprinted in Hart, *The Danelaw*, pp. 495–508 (p. 502, n. 24). See also Fleming, *Kings and Lords*, p. 46; S. Keynes, 'A tale of two kings: Alfred the Great and Æthelred the Unready', *TRHS* 5th s., 36 (1986), 195–217 (p. 207, n. 43). For Freston, Stoke, Withermarsh, Polstead, Stratford (all Sfk), see DB II, fols. 395v, 401rv, 402r. Colne and Tey (Ex) cannot be precisely identified, but all likely places were in lay hands in 1066. The endowment of family churches and religious houses is discussed below in Chap. 6.

king of bequests of land, and the records of inheritance disputes. Multi-gift wills, at least, were intended to be produced and read aloud at a public gathering. Their content was a matter of public debate, the issue a matter for the king and the local courts.

The process of will-making placed the donor at the centre of interlocking social networks. One of these relationships – that with the Church – seems all-pervasive, providing the practical framework of witness, documentation, advocacy, and perhaps forum for will-making, as well as the spiritual rites associated with the deathbed.[115] But the secular networks were equally important. The will, reflecting the donor's relationship with his or her lord, also reflected his or her place in the social hierarchy and the responsibilities attendant upon it. Perhaps of more immediate significance for thegns was the local network, based upon the areas where the donor held land; it was the witness of those attending the hundred and shire courts which would be crucial in influencing the outcome of any disputes which might arise in relation to the will, and it was within the network of the kindred that such disputes were most likely to arise, and where the personal responsibilities of the donor lay.

The will-making process recognised the vulnerability of *post obitum* disposition, and such protection as it offered – whether secular or spiritual – was invoked by the donor. In preparing for death, donors entrusted their dispositions, which were carefully considered, not only to individuals who survived them, but to the institutional authority of the king and church.

115 For ecclesiastical involvement in the production of royal charters, see the postscript to the survey of Anglo-Saxon charter scholarship by Brooks: N. Brooks, 'Anglo-Saxon charters: the work of the last twenty years', *ASE* 3 (1974), 211–31, reprinted with a postscript in N. Brooks, *Anglo-Saxon Myths: State and Church 400–1066* (London, 2000), pp. 181–215 (pp. 208–9).

# CHAPTER THREE

# Politics, power and the bequest of land

Land was at the heart of wealth and status in Anglo-Saxon England, and the seriousness with which its transmission was viewed is demonstrated by the process of will-making described in the previous chapter, hedged around as it was with witnesses, documentation and the protection of king and church. It can often be difficult to determine the factors which influenced donors' decisions, hampered as we are by the limited information in the sources about the donors themselves, their beneficiaries and the history of the estates. However, where donors belonged to the highest echelons of Anglo-Saxon society both they and their families feature more frequently in the historical record, providing a clearer context for their bequests.[1] Among those holding secular office are two kings and five ealdormen, along with lesser figures who came within their orbit: a king's son, women who were associated with the royal family, and the daughters of an ealdorman. A second group held high ecclesiastical office; the bequests of five bishops, an archbishop and two further potential archbishops must be placed in the context not only of their responsibilities within the church, but also of their role as major landholders and political figures.[2] If the bequests of this elite group reveal the particular influence of their political roles, and the power which they wielded, the wills of lesser men reveal in various ways the significance of the local political network as well as, in some instances, the impact of the political upheavals of the time.

It will become clear in this chapter that, although there were some fundamental concerns shared by the donors whose bequests of land are considered here, their dispositions were often a response to individual circumstances.

### The bequest of land in royal wills

The wills of only two kings survive: that of Alfred, datable to the last quarter of the ninth century, and of Eadred, made between 951 and 955. Both are

1 These donors account for roughly thirty per cent of the corpus.

2 The grants of the priests Æthelnoth and Eadwulf (S1418/R28, S1419/R29) have been omitted here as of dubious *post obitum* status and likely post-Conquest productions: *New Minster*, nos. 14, 16 and pp. lvii-li.

preserved as later copies in the archive of the New Minster, Winchester, founded by Edward the Elder in 901.[3] The very different circumstances, both political and personal, in which these kings drew up their wills influenced not only the nature of their dispositions, but also the tone and form of the documents.

## King Alfred's will

The document known as King Alfred's will was probably drawn up in response to a dispute concerning his tenure of family land.[4] It falls into two parts, the second demarcated in the eleventh-century copy by a large initial I. The first part – a preamble to the will proper – consists of Alfred's account as presented to the *witan* at *Langandene* (unid.) of the sequence of events which led to his inheritance of the family property, and includes the outcome of the council meeting which considered his right to inherit; the second part is the will itself. The first part must have been drawn up between Alfred's accession in 871, and the death of Archbishop Æthelred (d. 888), who is named in the opening paragraph of Part One among those privy to Alfred's deliberations concerning his inheritance.[5] It is likely that the will which now follows the preamble was made by Alfred in the later years of his reign, possibly the 890s, replacing at least one earlier will, to which he refers in the text:[6]

> *Þonne hæfde ic ær on oðre wisan awriten ymbe min yrfe þa ic hæfde mare feoh 7 ma maga. 7 hæfde monegum mannum þa gewritu oðfæst 7 on þæs ylcan gewitnesse hy wæron awritene. þonne hæbbe ic nu forbærned þa ealdan þe ic geahsian mihte.*
>
> (Now I had previously written differently concerning my inheritance, when I had more property and more kinsmen, and I had entrusted the documents

3 Although the twelfth-century historian William of Malmesbury refers to a *testamentum* of King Edward the Elder, he gives no further information other than to assert that the king named his son, Æthelstan, as his successor: *William of Malmesbury: Gesta Regum Anglorum*, ed. and transl. R. A. B. Mynors, R. M. Thomson and M. Winterbottom (Oxford, 1998), ii. 133 (*EHD* I, no. 8, p. 305).

4 S1507/H11, *New Minster* 1; translations are quoted from Keynes and Lapidge, pp. 174–8. The text was copied into the New Minster *Liber Vitae*, written in 1031: BL Stowe 944 (fols. 29v-33r); Davis, *Cartularies*, no. 1050; Ker, *Catalogue*, no. 274. See *New Minster*, p. 10 for the form of the document. It is reproduced in *Facsimiles*, ed. Sanders, III, no. 22 and *The Making of England*, ed. L. Webster and J. Backhouse (London, 1991), no. 240.

5 On dating, see *New Minster*, pp. 11–12; Keynes and Lapidge, pp. 173–4.

6 A date in the 890s depends on the use in the opening sentence of the title *Ælfred Westseaxena cincg*, a designation shared by a charter of 898 (S350), and on the identification of Ecgwulf, mentioned in the will as having held land at Lower Hurstbourne from Alfred, with the *cynges horsþegn* of that name whose death is recorded in the *ASC* s.a. 896; Keynes and Lapidge, p. 289, n. 34. The case for this dating of the will is made by J. L. Nelson, 'Reconstructing a royal family: reflections on Alfred, from Asser, chapter 2' in *People and Places*, ed. Wood and Lund, pp. 47–66 (p. 59, n. 68, p. 64. For Alfred's regnal styles see Keynes and Lapidge, p. 227, n. 1.

to many men, and they were written with the same witness. Accordingly, I have now burned all the old ones I could discover.)

It seems likely that the replacement will became linked to the original preamble in the course of later copying.

Part One of the document begins by announcing Alfred's intention to establish his claim to family property:

*Ic Ælfred cingc mid Godes gife 7 mid geþeahtunge Ætheredes ercebisceopes 7 ealra Westseaxena witena gewitnesse, smeade ymbe minre sawle þearfe 7 ymbe min yrfe þæt me God 7 mine yldran forgeafon 7 ymbe þ yrfe þæt Aðulf cincg min fæder us þrim gebroðrum becwæð.*

(I, King Alfred, by the grace of God and on consultation with Archbishop Æthelred and with the witness of all the councillors of the West Saxons, have been enquiring about the needs of my soul and about my inheritance which God and my elders gave to me, and about the inheritance which my father King Æthelwulf bequeathed to us three brothers.)[7]

This enquiry appears to have been prompted by a challenge mounted by – or on the part of – his 'young kinsmen' (*mægcild*), most probably his nephews, whose father, Æthelred, Alfred had succeeded on the throne in 871. The pious opening clause is followed by Alfred's presentation of his case, with the witness of the *witan* emphasised throughout, suggesting that his evidence was given during the formal hearing of a dispute. Needless to say, in spite of what Wormald described as Alfred's 'rebarbatively detailed' account of this sequence of negotiations and bequests, interpretation of the evidence is not straightforward.[8]

Alfred begins by referring to his father's bequest of his *yrfe*, which was to be shared among Æthelbald, his eldest son, Æthelred, the third son, and Alfred himself, as the youngest.[9] According to Alfred, the second son, Æthelberht, was not included in Æthelwulf's distribution of property.[10] Alfred states that King Æthelwulf's intention was that the brother who lived longest

7 This discussion of both the property transactions recounted by Alfred and his dispositions is indebted to the detailed analysis by Wormald, 'Kingship and royal property', pp. 268–77.

8 Wormald, 'Kingship and royal property', p. 270.

9 Wormald, 'Kingship and royal property', pp. 264–8 discusses the term *yrfe* in relation to inherited land. Alfred's bequests of movable wealth are discussed in Chap. 5 below.

10 It has been suggested that Æthelwulf may have been concerned to protect the interests of his younger sons, who were still minors, establishing Æthelbald as guardian: A. Williams, 'Some notes and considerations on problems connected with the English royal succession, 860–1066', *ANS* 1 (1978), 144–67 (p. 146). See also D. Dumville, 'The ætheling: a study in Anglo-Saxon constitutional history', *ASE* 8 (1979), 1–33 (pp. 23–4); A. P. Smyth, *King Alfred the Great* (Oxford, 1995), pp. 416–18; P. Stafford, 'Succession and inheritance: a gendered perspective on Alfred's family history', in *Alfred the Great*, ed. Reuter, pp. 251–64 (pp. 256–7)

would inherit 'everything' (*eallum*). However, Alfred's version of his father's *post obitum* arrangements is, in this respect, at variance with that included by Asser in his Life of Alfred, written in 893, which makes no such stipulation.[11] Asser's account of the events leading up to King Æthelwulf's will-making begins with his journey to Rome in 855, leaving Wessex itself in the hands of his eldest surviving son, Æthelbald, and the eastern kingdom of Kent, Sussex and Essex in those of his second son, Æthelberht. At this time, his two youngest sons, Æthelred and Alfred, were still children, ineligible to rule.[12] When Æthelwulf returned a year later, together with his new young wife, Judith, daughter of the Frankish king Charles the Bald, he encountered considerable political tension, possibly exacerbated by his marriage: Asser reports a coup led by his eldest son, Æthelbald, who was ultimately established in Wessex, while Æthelwulf himself seems to have displaced Æthelberht in the eastern kingdom.[13] It was at this point, according to Asser, that Æthelwulf 'had a testamentary – or rather advisory – epistle drawn up'.[14] The precise political arrangements are unclear, as is the extent to which Æthelwulf 's 'advice' was in fact a recognition of the status quo, but having just returned from the court of Charles the Bald he was in a good position to be aware of the potential threat to the West Saxon kingdom from conflict within the family.[15]

As far as can be judged from Asser's account, Æthelwulf's will confirmed the division of the kingdom into west and east between his two eldest sons, Æthelbald and Æthelberht respectively, which seems already to have taken place.[16] In addition, Æthelwulf also provided for division of his 'own inheritance' (*propriae hereditatis*) between his sons, his daughter and his kinsmen

11 *Asser*, chap. 16; the date of composition is provided by Asser's reference to the king's current age in chap. 91.

12 Keynes and Lapidge, p. 314, n. 4; Williams, 'Royal succession', pp. 145–6; D. P. Kirby, *Earliest English Kings* (London, 1991), p. 200.

13 *Asser*, chap. 12; Keynes and Lapidge, pp. 234, n. 26. Kirby, *Earliest English Kings*, p. 201, suggests that the western kingdom was itself partitioned between Æthelbald and Æthelwulf.

14 *hereditariam, immo commendatoriam, scribi imperavit epistolam*: *Asser*, chap. 16 (and see Chap. 1, n. 210 above). For the equation of the will with the so-called Decimation – the booking of the tenth part of his land – by King Æthelwulf, reported in *ASC* s.a. 855–858, and the dating of the will *before* his departure for Rome, see Smyth, *King Alfred the Great*, pp. 403–409. For a review of the evidence see Stafford, 'Succession and inheritance', p. 256, n. 17.

15 Keynes and Lapidge, p. 237, n. 33; the struggles of Charles the Bald are recounted by J. Nelson, 'The Frankish kingdoms 814–898: the West', in *The New Cambridge Medieval History II: c. 700-c. 900*, ed. R. McKitterick (Cambridge, 1995), pp. 110–41 (pp. 121–5).

16 Dumville, 'The ætheling', p. 23; Stafford argues that Æthelwulf's will reflects a family settlement: 'Succession and inheritance', p. 256.

(*propinquos*);[17] the proportions of this distribution are not given, but the land was also burdened with alms for the benefit of Æthelwulf's soul, in that his successors were instructed to feed and clothe one poor man for every ten hides of *hereditariam terram suam* (his hereditary land), as long as it remained in cultivation.

Æthelwulf died in 858, and at this point, Alfred's preamble picks up the story. Æthelbald, the eldest son, died without issue in 860, whereupon Æthelberht, Æthelwulf's second son, assumed the throne of a united Wessex.[18] Alfred's enigmatic comment on events at that time probably conceals some intense negotiations among the surviving brothers:

> *7 wit Æþered* [sic] *mid ealra Westseaxena witena gewitnesse uncerne dæl oðfæstan Æþelbyrhte cingce uncrum mæge on þa gerædene þe he hit eft gedyde unc swa gewylde swa hit þa wæs þa wit hit him oðfæstan, 7 he þa swa dyde ge þæt yrfe ge ꝥ he mid uncre gemanan begeat 7 þæt he sylf gestrynde.*
>
> (And Æthelred and I, with the witness of all the councillors of the West Saxons, entrusted our share to our kinsman King Æthelberht, on condition that he would restore it to us as much under our control as it was when we entrusted it to him; and then he did so, both that inheritance and what he had obtained from the use of our joint property, as well as that which he had himself acquired.)

In due course, the throne passed to the next brother in line, Æthelred, on Æthelberht's death in 866.[19] A similar agreement was reached between Æthelred, on his accession, and Alfred, the remaining brother. Alfred attempted to gain *minne dæl*, referring presumably to the 'share' of the inheritance (*yrfe*) which he and Æthelred had allowed Æthelberht to use during his reign, but Æthelred claimed that it could not be done:

> *Þa sæde he me ꝥ he naht eaðe ne mihte todælan forþon he hæfde ful oft ær ongefangen, 7 he cwæð þæs þe he on uncrum gemanan gebruce 7 gestrynde æfter his dæge he nanum menn sel ne uðe þonne me. 7 ic þæs þa wæs wel geþafa.*
>
> (He then told me that he could not divide it at all easily, for he had attempted to do so many times before; and he said that after his lifetime he would give

17 His instructions also included the distribution of 'such money as should remain after his death' (*pecuniarum, quae post se superessent*): for *post obitum* distribution of royal treasure see Chap. 5, pp. 198–201 below.

18 Williams, 'Royal succession', pp. 146–7; Keynes and Lapidge, p. 314, n. 3; Dumville, 'The ætheling', pp. 22–4.

19 There is no mention of Æthelberht having direct heirs, so the succession was apparently unchallenged. See Dumville, 'The ætheling', pp. 23–5 for factors influencing the succession.

to no person sooner than to me whatever he held as our joint property and whatever he acquired. And I was then readily a supporter of that.)[20]

The negotiations were carried out between the brothers 'in the presence of all our councillors' (*beforan urum witum eallum*); Alfred's use of the phrase *æfter his dæge* – characteristic of wills – emphasises the element of *post obitum* gift. It seems likely that at this stage, Alfred was in a strong position to inherit the throne, as well as the accumulated family inheritance, which now consisted of all that King Æthelwulf had bequeathed to his sons.[21] This is reinforced by the outcome of further negotiations which took place at *Swinbeorg* (unid.), at some time between Alfred's marriage in 868 and the spring of 871, when Æthelred died.[22] The threat of Viking attack, and perhaps changing personal circumstances, required a review of existing arrangements for the transmission of the property and the throne. Asser's dramatic account of the battles fought by the brothers to protect their kingdom vividly suggests the context for this agreement:[23] the urgency was to provide for a strong adult king, a role that Æthelred's eldest son was too young to fulfil, and a united Wessex to withstand the increasing vigour of the Viking raids. The agreement added further convolutions to the transmission of the family property:

> *Þa gecwædon wit on Westseaxena witena gewitnesse þæt swaðer uncer leng wære, þe he geuðe oðres bearnum þara landa þe wyt sylfe begeaton 7 þara landa þe unc Aðulf cinge forgeaf be Aðelbolde lifiendum butan þam þe he us þrim gebroðrum gecwæð. 7 þæs uncer ægðer oþrum his wedd sealde swaðer uncer leng lifede þæt se fenge ægþer ge to lande ge to madmum 7 to eallum his æhtum butan þam dæle þe uncer gehwæðer his bearnum becwæð.*
>
> (We agreed in the witness of the councillors of the West Saxons that whichever of us should live longer should give to the other's children the lands which we ourselves had obtained, and the lands which King Æthelwulf gave to us during Æthelbald's lifetime, except those which he bequeathed to us three brothers. And each of us gave to the other his pledge, that whichever of us lived longer should succeed both to the lands and to the treasures

20 Precisely why the property could not be divided is obscure; the difficulty may be linked to the terms of King Æthelwulf's will: Keynes and Lapidge, p. 315, n. 7.

21 For a schematic outline of these manoeuvres, see Wormald, 'Kingship and royal property', p. 269, table 19.1. For Alfred as heir apparent (*secundarius*), see *Asser*, chap. 29; Keynes and Lapidge, p. 240, n. 56 and p. 315, n. 7; Dumville, 'The ætheling', pp. 24–5.

22 The dates 870x871 are proposed by Keynes and Lapidge, p. 315, n. 9. Concern is expressed by both brothers for the welfare of their progeny; Alfred married in 868, and Æthelred, at least, probably had children, since his eldest son was about ten years older than Alfred's: B.Yorke, 'Edward as ætheling', in *Edward the Elder*, ed. Higham and Hill, pp. 25–39 (p. 30). For the family tensions underlying this agreement see Stafford, 'Succession and inheritance', pp. 259–60.

23 *Asser*, chaps. 35–40.

and to all the other's possessions except that part which each of us had bequeathed to his children.)[24]

In the event, the survivor was Alfred, who inherited the obligation to provide for his nephews, Æthelred's children, by granting to them land which he had himself acquired, as well as his share of land which, we now discover, he and Æthelred had received *inter vivos* from their father, presumably to maintain them in their minority.[25] Alfred succeeded to the accumulated family property bequeathed to the three brothers by Æthelwulf, and that property accrued by Æthelberht during his tenure which had passed to his brothers by agreement. Alfred also succeeded to the throne.

Alfred's claim to the family property, according to this complex account, was based on a series of negotiations with his brothers which were primarily intended to maintain a united Wessex. Although the document tells us that Alfred took King Æthelwulf's *yrfegewrit* to the assembly at *Langandene*, where it was read aloud, if this was the will as summarised by Asser, it is difficult to see how it would support Alfred's case. Nevertheless, the use of such a document sheds valuable light on the role of written evidence – and specifically here, what may have been a will – in a dispute.[26] But Alfred had a further argument to make in support of his position: the delay in the challenge. He reminds the council that, when his brother died, 'no-one made known to me any will or testimony showing that the position was other than as we had previously agreed before witnesses';[27] it was only now that 'we heard many disputes about the inheritance'.[28] No specific details are given of the challenge mounted by Æthelred's sons, but it seems likely that – just as Alfred had tried to claim his *dæl* from Æthelred – his nephews were claiming a share in the core family inheritance, perhaps with implications for their ultimate throneworthiness on Alfred's death. While Alfred's two eldest brothers seem to have died without issue, easing the transition of both throne and inheritance laterally, from brother to brother, the situation was now much more volatile, with the sons of both Æthelred and Alfred as potential claimants. It was his position in relation to the transmission of the inheritance which Alfred sought to assert at the council meeting at *Langandene*, insisting that he

24 See Wormald's schematic analysis, 'Kingship and royal property', p. 269, table 19.1.

25 It is not clear whether this grant was to take effect immediately or on Alfred's death, nor is it clear what was to happen to Æthelred's acquired land: Wormald, 'Kingship and royal property', pp. 269–70.

26 For other possible examples, see Chap.1, pp. 48–50 above.

27 *Þa ne cydde me nan mann nan yrfegewrit ne nane gewitnesse þ hit ænig oðer wære butan swa wit on gewitnesse ær gecwædon.*

28 *Þa gehyrde we nu manegu yrfe geflitu.* A dispute in tenth-century East Anglia, reported by *LE*, hinged on the failure of the claimants to make their case during the lifetime of their kinsman: *LE* II, 18/*Lib* 27. The formula *Hit Becwæð* makes a similar point (see Chap. 2, n. 15).

wished to know what was right according to the *folcriht* (common law), 'lest any man should say that I treated my young kinsmen wrongfully, the older or the younger'.[29]

Alfred urged his councillors to 'expound the common law' (*folcriht arehton*), reassuring them that 'I would never bear a grudge against any one of them because they declared what was right'.[30] Part One of the document concludes with the *witan's* judgment in Alfred's favour:

> *7 hy þa ealle to rihte gerehton 7 cwædon þ nan rihtre riht geþencan ne mihtan, ne on þam yrfegewrite gehyran nu hit eall agan is þæron oð þine hand, þonne þu hit becweðe 7 sylle swa gesibre hand swa fremdre swaðer þe leofre sy.*
>
> (And then they all pronounced what was right, and said that they could not conceive any juster title, nor could they find one in the will. 'Now everything therein has come into your possession, so you may bequeath it and give it into the hand of kinsman or stranger, whichever you prefer'.)

Given the fact that inheritance disputes often arose within the kindred, as has been shown in the previous chapter, this seems to be a recipe for discord – and so it was to prove, even though Alfred was more circumspect in his bequests than this judgment allowed. In fact, the only land which Alfred bequeathed away from his kindred was to the Church: he fulfilled his father's bequest of Chisledon (Wilts.) and Lower Hurstbourne (Hants.) to the church at Winchester, together with *sundorfeoh* (private property) of his own at Lower Hurstbourne, which was in the hands of Ecgwulf.[31]

Part Two of the document, Alfred's will itself, may, as has been suggested above, date to the last years of his reign – possibly to the period after 896 when the new wave of Viking attacks had been repulsed. This was not his first will; in the text he refers to at least one previous document which he had distributed and has now recalled, destroying copies which he could find and declaring null those which he could not.[32] But with another military crisis and great feats in consolidating the kingdom behind him, Alfred may have faced a different problem, which prompted the making of a new will: that of the succession. Wormald suggests that, as far as land is concerned, Alfred's bequests seem intended 'to limit dissipation of the family's landed assets and to restrict them to those members in a position to bid construc-

29 *Þy læs ænig man cweðe þ ic mine mægcild oððe yldran oððe gingran mid wo fordemde.* Æthelred had two sons, Æthelhelm and Æthelwold, both named in Alfred's will: see below.

30 *Ic hyra nefre nænne ne oncuðe forþon þe hy on riht spræcan.*

31 See above n. 6 for the identity of Ecgwulf. The community had rescinded their right to the reversion this property, but it was regranted to them by Alfred in S354; the complex negotiations surrounding the reversion are discussed by S. Keynes, 'The West Saxon charters of King Æthelwulf and his sons', *EHR* 109 (1994), 1109–49 (pp. 1137–8).

32 *Þonne hæbbe ic nu forbærned þa ealdan þe ic geahsian mihte. Gif hyra hwylc funden bið ne forstent þæt naht, forþam ic wille þæt hit nu þus sy mid Godes fultume.*

tively ... for the throne'.[33] The first aspect of this dynastic strategy is Alfred's preferential treatment of his own sons in the distribution of land, probably family property derived from kings Æthelwulf and Æthelberht.[34] The principal beneficiary is Alfred's eldest son, Edward, who is to receive fourteen estates stretching from the West Country, through Hampshire and Wiltshire, to Surrey, together with two groups of bookland, one probably in the West Country, given its affinity in the list with estates in Devon and Cornwall,[35] and the other consisting of 'all the booklands which I have in Kent' (*ealle þa bocland þe ic on Cent hæbbe*). Alfred's younger son, Æthelweard, is to receive seventeen estates distributed through the West Country, Hampshire and Wiltshire. In contrast, Alfred bequeaths significantly fewer estates to his nephews: the elder, Æthelhelm, is to receive eight estates, and the younger, Æthelwold, three. Furthermore, these estates are largely restricted to Sussex and Surrey, peripheral to the Wessex heartlands, and may have been land due to Alfred's nephews under the *Swinbeorg* agreement.[36] Such an unequal distribution would enhance the throneworthiness of Alfred's sons, Edward in particular, over that of their cousins.[37] Æthelred's sons were most certainly in a position to 'bid constructively' for the throne on their uncle's death; they were older than their cousins, and as sons of the older brother may have had a strong claim.[38] The resentment of Æthelwold may be surmised from his rebellion against his cousin following Edward's accession in 899. Edward was twice forced to march against Æthelwold and his supporters, and the matter was only resolved – possibly with some opprobrium attached to Edward – in 903, with the death of Æthelwold in battle.[39]

33 Wormald, 'Kingship and royal property', p. 271. It is generally agreed that the will itself is not concerned with what has been termed 'royal demesne', which was inalienable: *New Minster*, p. 11; Wormald, 'Kingship and royal property', p. 268; Keynes and Lapidge, p. 314, n. 3; Smyth, *King Alfred the Great*, pp. 409–14.

34 Wormald draws attention to the will's emphasis on this property: 'Kingship and royal property', p. 270 (identified as A1 in his Table 19.1). Alfred's bequests of land are tabulated in ibid., pp 272–3, table 19.2, and mapped by Keynes and Lapidge, p. 176.

35 Keynes and Lapidge, p. 317, n. 20.

36 Wormald, 'Kingship and royal property', p. 270; Yorke, 'Edward', p. 30; Keynes and Lapidge, p. 173. The western part of the kingdom was described by Asser as more important (*principalior*) than the eastern, which had on two occasions been held by the heir apparent as a sub-kingdom (*Asser*, chap. 12); now it was stripped of the lands in Kent, which were bequeathed to Edward.

37 Yorke, 'Edward', pp. 29–35; Keynes, 'Edward', p. 48. Dumville points to the lack of 'institutional provision for the succession of a dedicated heir': 'The ætheling', p. 24.

38 Yorke ('Edward', p. 31) points out that Æthelwold witnesses above Edward in one of Alfred's charters dated to the 890s (S356), suggesting seniority; both are designated *filius regis* (Æthelhelm's absence may suggest that he predeceased Alfred). See also Williams, 'Royal succession', p. 149, and for discussion of the role of the will in the transmission of the kingship, pp. 152–3.

39 The story is told in the *ASC* s.a. 903, although the events probably took place at the end

The second aspect of Alfred's dynastic strategy is his favouring of the male line in order to avoid dispersal of the family land. This is evident in the bequests to his son and nephews, and, in addition, his bequest of seven estates in Sussex to his kinsman Osferth, about whom little is known, in spite of his prominence in witness lists in the reigns of Edward and Æthelstan.[40] Although Alfred ensures that his wife and daughters are provided for – Ealhswith, his wife, is to receive three estates, and a further six are shared among his three daughters, all in central Wessex – he places explicit restrictions on the transmission of the land:

> *7 ic wylle þa menn þe ic mine boclande becweden hæbbe þæt hy hit ne asyllan of minum cynne ofer heora dæg, ac ic wylle ofer hyra dæg þæt hit gange on þa nyhstan hand me butan hyra hwylc bearn hæbbe þonne is me leofast þæt hit gange on þæt stryned on þa wæpned healfe þa hwile þe ænig þæs wyrðe sy. Min yldra fæder hæfde gecweden his land on þa spere healfe næs on þa spinl* [sic] *healfe þonne gif ic gesealde ænigre wif handa ꝥ he gestrynde þonne forgyldan mine magas. 7 gif hy hit be þan libbendan habban wyllan gif hit elles sy gange hit ofer hyra dæg swa swa we ær gecweden hæfdon. Forþon ic cweðe þæt hi hit gyldan forþon hy foð to minum þe ic syllan mot swa wif handa swa wæpned handa swaðer ic wylle.*
>
> (And I desire that the persons to whom I have bequeathed my bookland should not dispose of it outside my kindred after their lifetime, but I desire that after their lifetime it should pass to my nearest of kin, unless any of them have children; then I should prefer that it should pass to the child in the male line as long as any is worthy of it. My grandfather had bequeathed his land on the spear side and not on the spindle side. If, then, I have given to any one on the female side what he acquired, my kinsmen are to pay for it, if they wish to have it during the lifetime [of the holders]; otherwise, it should go after their lifetime as we have previously stated. For this reason I say they are to pay for it, because they are receiving my property, which I may give on the female side as well as on the male side, whichever I please.)

Although Alfred insists on his right to grant property 'on the female side' (*wif handa*), he makes provision for kinsmen to acquire it by payment during the woman's tenure. In stipulating that the property should remain in the male line, Alfred claims that he is following the precedent set by his grandfather, Ecgberht. He anticipates the possibility that his beneficiaries may have no direct male heirs; in that case, their inheritance would revert to his 'nearest kin' (*þa nyhstan hand me*). This type of limitation on the alienation of land

of 902 (*EHD* I, p. 208, n. 5). For the suggestion of some stigma attached to Edward, see Keynes, 'England', p. 461.

40 Keynes, *Atlas*, Table XXXIa (last attestation 934). He shares the Os- prefix with members of Alfred's maternal kin; it has been suggested that he may have been Alfred's illegitimate son since he is styled *frater regis* in S1286 (904), a charter of Edward (Nelson, 'Reconstructing a royal family', pp. 59–61). See Keynes and Lapidge, p. 322, n. 79 for the view that this styling is an error.

from the kindred also features in Alfred's law-code, possibly dated *c.* 886, and in the exactly contemporary will of Ealdorman Alfred.[41]

If the distribution of land in Alfred's will is seen as the culmination of a complex dynastic strategy designed to consolidate the power-base of the royal house of Wessex, it appears to have been remarkably successful. Æthelwold's challenge to Edward's succession which, at least in part, the will must have provoked, was short-lived, and seems to have won little support within Wessex. It is likely that most of the eleven estates bequeathed to Æthelwold and his older brother, Æthelhelm, reverted to the king, since at least seven were in royal hands in 1066.[42] In addition, Domesday Book shows that half of the named estates bequeathed to Alfred's sons remained *terra regis* in 1066, together with two estates in Sussex bequeathed to Osferth.[43] Some estates seem to have become associated with the endowment of queens or æthelings: both Wantage and Lambourn (Berks.), for example, bequeathed by Alfred to his wife, were later associated respectively with Queen Eadgifu, mother of King Eadred, and Æthelflæd of Damerham, second wife of King Edmund.[44] The land *æt Dene*, probably East or West Dean (Sx), bequeathed by Alfred to his younger son, seems later to have been known as *Æthelingadene*,[45] and Rotherfield (Sx), bequeathed to Osferth, may be the estate which features in the early eleventh century will of the ætheling Æthelstan.[46]

## King Eadred's will

The will of Alfred's grandson, King Eadred (946–955), was made, in very different circumstances, in the latter years of his reign, during which he seems to have been dogged by ill health to the point where he may have been forced to delegate some aspects of government.[47] Since Eadred appears to have

41 S1508/H10, *Christ Church* 96, 870x889. For Alfred's law see Chap. 1, p. 54 and nn. 260, 262 above. Similar limitations are placed on the transmission of land in the earlier will of Abba (S1482/H2, *Christ Church* 70, 833x839).

42 Beeding, Beddingham, Eastbourne, Steyning (Sussex: DB I, fols. 20v, 28rv); Godalming, Guildford (Surrey: DB I, fols. 30rv). Guildford probably including Eashing (Keynes and Lapidge, p. 322, n. 74). Dubious charters indicate that a further two may have returned to the king: Aldingbourne is claimed to have been returned to the church at Selsey by King Eadwig (S1291; *Selsey*, no. 20, and pp. lxix–lxxiii); Crondall was granted to the Old Minster, Winchester, by King Edgar (S820). The tenurial history of the estates named in the will is tabulated by Wormald, 'Kingship and royal property', pp. 272–3, table 19.2; see also the notes on each estate in Keynes and Lapidge, pp. 317–23.

43 The evidence and its implications are discussed by Wormald, 'Kingship and royal property', pp. 271–4.

44 Keynes and Lapidge, p. 323, nn. 88, 89; Stafford, *Queen Emma and Queen Edith*, p. 129, nn. 161, 162.

45 Keynes and Lapidge, p. 319, n. 41; Keynes, *Diplomas*, p. 187, n. 117.

46 S1503/W20, *Christ Church* 142 (*Hyðerafelda*: the identification is uncertain).

47 S1515/H21, *New Minster* 17, 951x955. The will was copied into the fifteenth-century *Liber Abbatiae*: Earl of Macclesfield, Sherburn Castle (fol. 22); Davis, *Cartularies*, no. 1051. The

remained unmarried and childless, the only throneworthy princes of the next generation were Eadwig and Edgar, the sons of Eadred's older brother and predecessor, King Edmund (939–946). The succession may already have been subject to negotiation: on Eadred's death, only one of the æthelings, Eadwig, had reached adulthood, but was still very young (probably about fifteen).[48]

Eadred's bequests of land are as strategic as those of his grandfather. The churches to which he bequeaths a number of estates were all royal foundations at Winchester.[49] The Old Minster, the New Minster, and *Nunnaminster*, all churches with royal associations, are to receive three estates each: the Old Minster, which had been associated with the kings of Wessex since the seventh century and had been the original burial place of Eadred's grandfather, King Alfred, was to receive Downton, Damerham and Calne (all Wilts.); the New Minster, the building of which was instigated by Alfred but completed by his son and Eadred's father, King Edward, who had been buried there in 924, was to receive Wherwell, Andover, Kingsclere (all Hants.); and the *Nunnaminster*, again built by King Edward on land associated with his mother, Ealhswith (and which housed Eadred's sister, Eadburh, who had entered the nunnery), was to receive Thatcham (Berks.), Shalbourne and Bradford (both Wilts.).[50] These estates are not bequeathed with explicit reference to the welfare of Eadred's soul, or requests for prayers for himself and his ancestors, as is characteristic of wills, nor is it clear that he intended one of the Winchester churches as his place of burial, although he was actually buried at the Old Minster.[51] It seems that, through these bequests, Eadred intended to reinforce

earlier date is established by the bequest to Bishop Ælfsige, who acceded to Winchester in 951. Eadred's ill health is reported in the earliest Life of St Dunstan, *Memorials of St Dunstan*, ed. W. Stubbs, Rolls Series 63 (1874) chap. 20, p. 31. For Eadred's delegation of authority see S. Miller, 'Eadred', in *Blackwell Encyclopaedia*, p. 150, and *New Minster*, p. 80; for the absence of Eadred's attestations in the 950s see Keynes, *Diplomas*, pp. 46–8.

48 Williams, 'Royal succession', pp. 151, 155. The division of the kingdom between the two æthelings which subsequently took place may have been expedient: N. Brooks, 'The career of St Dunstan', in *St Dunstan: his Life, Times and Cult*, ed. N. Ramsay, M. Sparks and T. Tatton-Brown (Woodbridge, 1992), pp. 1–23 (pp. 18–20); Keynes, 'England', p. 478; Williams, 'Royal succession', pp. 155–6.

49 The will begins with the bequest of treasure 'to the place where he wishes that his body should rest' (*into þære stowe þær he wile his lic reste*), without naming the church: see Chap. 5, n. 114 below for Eadred's bequests of treasure to the church.

50 Foot, *Veiled Women*, II, 243–5.

51 *New Minster*, p. 79. Eadred's parents had been buried at New Minster, to which his grandfather's body had been moved on its completion; his immediate predecessor, Edmund, had been buried at Glastonbury, and Æthelstan at Malmesbury. It is possible that Eadred had intended to be buried at Glastonbury, which he had patronised: A. Thacker, 'Dynastic monasteries and family cults: Edward the Elder's sainted kindred', in *Edward the Elder*, ed. Higham and Hill, pp. 248–63 (p. 256); *Abingdon*, part 1, xxxvi–xxxvii. He was remembered as a 'friend and champion' (*amator et defensor*) of the Old Minster in *Wulfstan of Winchester: the Life of St Æthelwold*, ed. and transl. M. Lapidge and M. Winterbottom (Oxford, 1991), chap. 10.

the relationship between the royal dynasty and what were effectively royal *Eigenklöster*.[52]

Eadred's only other bequest of land is made to his mother, Queen Eadgifu. She had been prominent at court during the reign of Edmund, and continued to be so under Eadred, perhaps exerting particular influence during his illness.[53] She was to receive three named estates which all had strong royal associations: Amesbury (Wilts.), which had been bequeathed by King Alfred to his younger son, Æthelweard; Wantage (Berks.), which Alfred had bequeathed to his wife, Ealhswith; and Basing (Hants.), which (according to a dubious charter) King Edmund had granted to his priest, Æthelnoth.[54] Eadred's bequest may have been part of a strategy to use a pool of estates for the endowment of royal women.[55] However, Eadgifu was also to receive 'all the booklands which I have in Sussex, Surrey and Kent, and all those which she has previously had', a bequest which may have been politically sensitive.[56] It seems likely that Eadred was bequeathing to his mother bookland associated with the eastern sub-kingdom which had been divided by Alfred, who left estates in Kent to his eldest son, Edward, Eadgifu's husband, and estates in Surrey and Sussex to his nephews, Æthelhelm and Æthelwold, and his kinsman Osferth. These estates may have reverted to the royal fisc under the terms of his will which imposed limits on alienation from the kindred.[57] The bequest of this land to Eadgifu appears to have been a significant gesture; Brooks has suggested that, given the minority of the younger ætheling, Edgar, Eadgifu was holding these estates on his behalf, and given the fact that the bequest reunited the lands associated with the sub-kingdom, this would have given him a powerful base from which to establish a claim to the throne.[58] It is also possible that Eadgifu's high profile at court during the reign of her two sons, Edmund and Eadred, and her close association with St Dunstan, whose influence under Eadred had increased, established her as a potentially key figure under the new regime, given Eadwig's youth on his accession in 955.[59]

52 This strategy is in marked contrast to King Æthelstan's uneasy relationship with Winchester: *New Minster*, pp. xxviii–xxx.

53 Stafford, *Queen Emma and Queen Edith*, p. 199; Keynes, *Atlas*, Table XXXIa.

54 S505, 945, *New Minster* 13. A forged charter records Æthelnoth's subsequent bequest of the land to the New Minster: S1418/R28, *New Minster* 14. Basing was still in royal hands *TRE* (DB I, fol. 45r), as were Amesbury and Wantage (DB I, fols. 64v and 57r).

55 Stafford, *Queen Emma and Queen Edith*, pp. 129–30.

56 *7 ealra minra boclanda þe ic on Suðseaxum hæbbe 7 on Suðrigum 7 on Cent, 7 ealra þæra þe hio ær hæfde.* Eadred had granted land at Felpham (Sx) to Eadgifu in 953 (S562); Alfred had bequeathed land here to his kinsman, Osferth.

57 Æthelwold's land would have been particularly vulnerable following his defeated rebellion.

58 Brooks, 'Career', p. 14,

59 P. Stafford, 'The king's wife in Wessex 800–1066', *Past and Present* 91(1981), 3–27 (pp. 25–6). It has been suggested that Eadgifu acted as quasi-regent in Kent: P. Stafford, 'Eadgifu', in *Blackwell Encyclopaedia*, p. 149; idem, *Queen Emma and Queen Edith*, pp.

That this bequest of land to Eadgifu was felt to be a significant – and possibly provocative – gesture, either by the new king, Eadwig, or his advisers, seems clear from the events which followed. Eadgifu lost her influence at court; her charter attestations cease, and a document of *c.* 959, recording Eadgifu's grant of land to Christ Church, Canterbury, following her reinstatement on the accession of Edgar, remarks that when Eadred died she was 'despoiled of all her property' (*man Eadgife berypte ælcere are*), and suggests that Eadwig did not support her when her claim to the land was disputed.[60]

Eadred's bequests to the church also seem to have fallen foul of the changing political climate. Four of the nine estates were in the hands of the church in 1066, but not always the correct church, and not, apparently, via Eadred's will: King Æthelred restored Downton to the Old Minster in 997, and granted Bradford (bequeathed by Eadred to the *Nunnaminster*) to Shaftesbury in 1001; Wherwell Abbey's claim to land at Wherwell (which should have been in the hands of the New Minster) was probably confirmed by Æthelred in 1002.[61] Damerham reached Glastonbury, rather than the Old Minster as Eadred intended, via the will of the former queen, Æthelflæd, widow of King Edmund, which post-dated that of Eadred.[62] The remaining five estates were held by the king, one of them – Thatcham – having been bequeathed to King Edgar by Ealdorman Ælfheah, suggesting that it had fallen into lay hands after Eadred's death.[63] Like his great-grandfather Æthelwulf, Eadred placed a burden of alms upon all the land he bequeathed:

> *Þonne wille ic ðæt man nime to ælcan þissa hama twelf ælmesmen, 7 gif hwæt hera ænigan getide, sette man þær oþerne to. 7 stande þis eal þa hwile þe Cristendom beo, Gode to lofe, 7 minra sawle æleisnesse. 7 gif þis hwa don nelle, þonne gange þæt land in þær min lic reste.*

189, 201. For an overview of the political aspects of Eadwig's accession, see Stafford, *Unification and Conquest*, pp. 47–8; Yorke, 'Æthelwold', pp. 74–9; Keynes, 'England', pp. 476–9.

60 Keynes, *Atlas*, Table XXXIa; S1211/H23.

61 S891; S899; S904. *New Minster*, pp. 78–9.

62 S1494/W14, 962x991. King Edmund had granted Æthelflæd a life interest in Damerham, with reversion to Glastonbury (S513, 944x946). The complex history of this estate is discussed by L. Abrams, *Anglo-Saxon Glastonbury: Church and Endowment* (Woodbridge, 1996), pp. 105–6.

63 S1485/W9, *c.* 968x971 (DB I, fol. 43r).The history of Kingsclere is also difficult to interpret: Alfred bequeathed land there to his daughter, who became abbess of Shaftesbury (*Asser*, chap. 98); in a will pre-dating that of Eadred, Ealdorman Æthelwold, who was closely associated with the court of King Edmund, bequeathed land acquired from his lord, including an estate at Kingsclere, which was to go to his nephew (S1504/H20, 946x947; *SEHD*, p. 117). Æthelwold regularly attests the charters of King Edmund: Keynes, *Atlas*, Tables XLII, XLV. (DB I, fol. 43r). For Calne, Andover and Shalbourne see DB I, fols. 64v, 39r, 73r.

(Further, I desire that twelve almsmen be chosen on each of these estates, and if anything should happen to any of them, another is to be put in his place; and all this is to hold as long as Christianity endures, to the glory of God and the redemption of my soul; and if anyone refuses to carry it out, then that land is to revert to the place where my body shall rest.)

It seems unlikely, in the circumstances, that this was respected.

All of the estates bequeathed by Eadred to Eadgifu were held by or of the king in 1066; although Edgar reinstated her to her property, land which she held as dowager queen would, in all likelihood, have reverted to the crown on her death, in accordance with the restrictions placed on women's inheritance of land by Alfred.[64] The wills of two former queens suggest that the transmission of estates designated for the support of royal women continued to to be circumscribed.

## Æthelflæd's will

Æthelflæd, daughter of Ealdorman Ælfgar, was the second wife and widow of King Edmund.[65] One version of the *Anglo-Saxon Chronicle,* noting the circumstances of King Edmund's death, refers to her as Æthelflæd of Damerham, an estate granted to her for life by the king, with reversion to Glastonbury.[66] This sobriquet may indicate that she spent her years as dowager queen in retirement at the religious house which King Alfred's will indicates was in existence on this estate.[67] She does not seem to have attended court, although her stepson, King Edgar, granted her an estate at Chelsworth (Sfk) in 962, suggesting continuing goodwill if not direct contact.[68] Æthelflæd made her will

64 There is a hint in *LE* II, 31/*Lib* 41 that Eadgifu made a will which has not survived: the compiler refers to her bequest of Holland (Ex), which she had purchased, to a noblewoman, Ælfthryth, who in turn gave the land to Ely.

65 Edmund's first wife, by whom he had two sons, Eadwig and Edgar, died in 944: *The Chronicle of Æthelweard*, ed. and transl. A. Campbell (London, 1962), Book 4, chap. 6 (p. 54). Ælfgar's will is extant: S1483/W2. Æthelflæd's connections and her will are discussed by Wareham, *Lords and Communities*, pp. 53–6.

66 *ASC* D, s.a. 946; S513, 944x946, granting a life interest in Damerham and Martin (Hants.) and Pentridge (Dt) to Æthelflæd, with reversion to Glastonbury.

67 King Alfred bequeaths to the community at Damerham its landbooks, and freedom to choose its lord (S1507/H11, *New Minster* 1; Stafford, *Queen Emma and Queen Edith*, p. 95, n. 125. *LE* II, 64 suggests that Æthelflæd may have remarried, describing her as the widow of Ealdorman Æthelstan (Rota); *Wills*, p. 138; C. R. Hart, 'The ealdordom of Essex', in *An Essex Tribute: Essays presented to Frederick G. Emmerson*, ed. K. Neale (London, 1987), pp. 57–73, 76–85, revised and reprinted in Hart, *The Danelaw*, pp. 115–40 (p. 127). This is doubted by Stafford, *Queen Emma and Queen Edith*, p. 134, n. 200, and Wareham, *Lords and Communities*, pp. 53–4, n. 30.

68 S703. See also S1795, *St Paul's* 17, an entry from a lost register of St Paul's, London, recording King Edgar's permission for Æthelflæd, his father's widow, to give Hadham (Herts.) to the church. The name Æthelflæd which occurs in the witness list of S549 may be an error: *Burton*, p. 14.

between the date of this charter, 962, and the death of Ealdorman Byrhtnoth, one of the beneficiaries, at Maldon in 991, although her bequest on behalf of King Edgar's soul may indicate 975, the year of his death, as the *terminus post quem*.[69] With the exception of a gift of chattels to the king and the distribution of men and stock, the will is concerned solely with the disposition of land. Apart from Chelsworth, which she held in her own right (bequeathing it to Bury St Edmund's), Æthelflæd bequeaths two distinct groups of land: estates which she had inherited from her father, mainly in Suffolk and Essex, and those which she seems to have held as dowager queen.[70] This latter group of estates, sited in Berkshire – Lambourn, Cholsey and Reading – is bequeathed to the king, apparently returning royal land which Æthelflæd held as dower: Lambourn had been bequeathed by King Alfred to his wife;[71] Cholsey was held by the dowager queen Ælfthryth before she gave it to her son Æthelred in 996;[72] Reading was still in the hands of the king in 1066, and its significance as former dower land may have influenced the refoundation of a religious house there in the twelfth century.[73] The royal estate at Damerham, in which Æthelflæd had been granted a life interest by her husband, King Edmund, is bequeathed to Glastonbury on his instructions.[74]

## Ælfgifu's will

Although categorical evidence is lacking, it is widely agreed that Ælfgifu was the wife of King Eadwig (955–959), separated from him by Archbishop Oda in 958 on grounds of consanguinity.[75] A further possibility is that she may herself have belonged to a separate branch of the royal house; she bequeaths property, in a context which suggests that they may be siblings, to an Æthelweard, who may be the ealdorman and chronicler of that name, and who himself claimed descent from the older brother of King Alfred, Æthelred I.[76]

69 S1494/W14. The will is a later copy, preceding the will of Æthelflæd's sister, Ælfflæd (S1486/W15, 1000x1002) on a single sheet of parchment, both documents written in a hand of the early eleventh century: BL MS Harley Charter 43 C4 (*Wills*, p. 137).

70 Æthelflæd's bequests of her inherited land are discussed in Chap. 6, p. 236 below.

71 Its history is charted by Stafford, *Queen Emma and Queen Edith*, p. 129, n. 162.

72 S877/*EHD* I, no.120: Stafford, *Queen Emma and Queen Edith*, p. 129, n. 163.

73 P. Stafford, '*Cherchez la femme*: queens, queens' lands and nunneries: missing links in the foundation of Reading Abbey', *History* 85 (2000), 4–27 (pp. 10–18).

74 See n. 62 above. *TRE* Glastonbury held both Damerham and Pentridge (DBI, fols. 66v, 77v). Abrams, *Glastonbury*, p. 105.

75 *ASC* D, s.a. 958. For the identification, see *Wills*, p. 119, and among recent commentators Stafford, *Queen Emma and Queen Edith*, p. 127; *Abingdon*, part 2, pp. 315–16, 417; Yorke, 'Æthelwold', pp. 76–7; C. R. Hart, 'The will of Ælfgifu', in Hart, *The Danelaw*, pp. 455–65 (p. 464).

76 *Wills*, p. 119; *Æthelweard*, ed. Campbell, Prologue (p. 2), and Book 4, chap. 2 (p. 39). Ælfgifu bequeaths a life interest in Mongewell (Oxon.) and Berkhampstead (Herts.) to Ælfweard, Æthelweard and Ælfwaru (identified as her sister in a separate bequest), with reversion to the Old Minster, Winchester.

Such a relationship would give weight to the grounds of consanguinity on which her separation from King Eadwig was based, and would also account for King Edgar's description of her as a kinswoman in two charters in her favour.[77] Yorke has suggested that Ælfgifu's bequest to Bishop Æthelwold, with a request for his prayers for her and her mother, was made in recognition of Æthelwold's intervention on her behalf, perhaps securing for her a land endowment appropriate to her status as a former queen.[78] Ælfgifu made her will between 966 and 975, bequeathing a number of estates directly into royal hands or to churches with royal associations.[79] The bulk of this property lay in Buckinghamshire, peripheral to the Wessex heartland.[80] Six estates, four of them in Buckinghamshire, are bequeathed to the king,[81] and one to the ætheling.[82] A further five estates are bequeathed to religious houses with royal associations: the Old Minster, Winchester, where Ælfgifu wished to be buried (Princes Risborough, Bucks.); the New Minster (Bledlow, Bucks.); Romsey, re-established by Edgar in 967 (Whaddon, Bucks.); Bath, which in 975 was the site of King Edgar's coronation in 973 (*æt Wicham*, possibly Wickham, Cambs.); and Abingdon, established by King Eadred 950x955 (Chesham, Bucks.).

Much of the land which Ælfgifu bequeathed to the church seems to have been in lay – often royal – hands by 1066, although this does not necessarily mean that the will was ineffective: in at least two cases – Chesham, bequeathed to Abingdon, and Bledlow, bequeathed to the New Minster – the estates may have been sold or exchanged 'as part of the active management of the endowment'.[83] Many of the estates bequeathed in the will, whether to lay or religious beneficiaries, were held by the family of Earl Godwine in 1066.[84] Princes Risborough (bequeathed to the Old Minster) was held by the future

77 S737 and S738.

78 Yorke, 'Æthelwold', p. 80.

79 S1484/W8, surviving in the twelfth-century *Codex Wintoniensis* (BL Additional MS 15350, fol. 96rv). The dating parameters are provided by a royal charter in her favour (S738) and the death of King Edgar, who gave an estate to Ely which had been bequeathed to him by Ælfgifu (*LE* II, 47; *Wills*, p. 118).

80 Stafford, *Queen Emma and Queen Edith*, p. 131; D. Hill, *An Atlas of Anglo-Saxon England* (Oxford, 1981), maps 145–161.

81 Wing, Haversham, Marsworth and Linslade (which was granted to Ælfgifu by Edgar in 966: S737); Gussage (Dorset); Hatfield (Essex or Cambs.).

82 Newnham Murren (Oxon.), also granted to Ælfgifu by Edgar in 966 (S738). The ætheling in question is probably Edmund, Edgar's eldest son by his second wife: Yorke, 'Æthelwold', p. 84.

83 *Abingdon*, part 1, p. clxv. See also *New Minster*, p. 121. Bledlow and Whaddon were held of King Edward *TRE* (DB I, fols. 146r, 147v); Chesham was held of Queen Edith (DB I, fol. 150v); Earl Harold held Princes Risborough (DB I, fol. 143r).

84 For the view that this represents either a failure to honour Ælfgifu's bequests, or the dispossession of her family under Cnut after 1017, see Fleming, *Kings and Lords*, p. 44.

king, Earl Harold;[85] Haversham (bequeathed to the king) by Countess Gytha, Earl Godwine's widow and Harold's mother;[86] men of Harold held Whaddon and Wing (both held by Edward *Cild*), Berkhamstead[87] and possibly Gussage[88] (both held by Eadmær); and men of Queen Edith, Godwine's daughter, held Chesham and Linslade.[89] If Ælfgifu's estates were not royal land to begin with, they largely became so.[90]

In the absence of evidence for the will-making of kings other than Alfred and Eadred, it is tempting to speculate that their wills arose from a particular set of circumstances – perhaps political exigence. Use of the vernacular indicates that the wills were intended for a lay as well as an ecclesiastical audience, such as the *witan*. It is equally tempting to see them as a strategy proposed by the powerful churchmen present at each court.[91] Archbishop Æthelred, named by Alfred in the opening clause of the preamble to his will as privy to his deliberations, also witnessed the contemporary will of Ealdorman Alfred.[92] Dunstan, abbot of Glastonbury, was an important presence at Eadred's court; although the degree of his influence is uncertain he seems to have been sufficiently embroiled in court politics to warrant exile under Eadwig's regime.[93] If later kings saw the advantage of will-making as a political strategy, the evidence has not survived.

## The will of the ætheling Æthelstan

The final extant royal will – that of the ætheling Æthelstan, the eldest son of King Æthelred by his first wife – was made at a time of political turmoil in England. The Danish king, Swegn, mounted a determined campaign to seize the English throne, which culminated in the submission of Northumbria, Lindsey and the Five Boroughs at Gainsborough in 1013, followed by the rest

85 DB I, fol. 143r.

86 DB I, fol. 148r.

87 DB I, fol. 136v, but see Stafford, *Queen Emma and Queen Edith*, p. 131 for identification of this estate with Little Berkhamstead, which was held by three people from the king (DB I, fol. 142r).

88 Gussage All Saints was held by Eadmær *TRE* (DB I, fol. 79v).

89 DB I, fol. 150v.

90 It is possible that Harold acquired estates in Buckinghamshire through his tenure of the ealdordom of East Anglia (*c.* 1044–1053), which may, by the later tenth century, have subsumed the estates of Oxfordshire and Buckinghamshire formerly associated with ealdormen of Mercia; the valuation of Princes Risborough in Domesday Book may also suggest that it had once been a royal manor: A. Williams, 'Land and power in the eleventh century: the estates of Harold Godwineson', *ANS* 3 (1980), 171–87 (p. 174). Stafford has argued that Ælfgifu's lands contributed to the expansion of the queen's estate in later Anglo-Saxon England: *Queen Emma and Queen Edith*, pp. 131, 134.

91 For example, see Keynes, 'The written word', p. 1.

92 S1508/H10, *Christ Church* 96, 870x889.

93 *New Minster*, p. 80; Brooks, 'Career', pp. 14–15; Keynes, 'England,', pp. 474–6; *Memorials*, ed. Stubbs, chap. 20, p. 31 (*EHD* I, no. 234, pp. 901–2).

of England. King Æthelred, his second wife, Emma, and their two young sons fled into exile, until Æthelred was reinstated in the following year on Swegn's death.[94] This restoration of the royal house merely staved off an impending succession crisis: although Æthelstan was the eldest ætheling, with what must have been perceived as a strong claim to the throne, Swegn's son Cnut would pursue his own claim based on his father's conquest.[95] Not only that, but a later tradition asserted that the throneworthiness of Edward, Æthelred's first son by Emma, had been generally recognised before his birth, displacing the sons of Æthelred's first marriage; whatever the truth of this, the existence of further æthelings from this marriage may have created tensions within the royal family.[96] This volatile situation was exacerbated by the factionalism within the English aristocracy, and the apparently malign influence of Eadric Streona at court.[97] The disaffection of leading families in the North, the East Midlands and East Anglia contributed to the capitulation to Swegn in 1013.[98] There is no evidence for the whereabouts or activities of the three eldest æthelings during King Æthelred's exile in 1013/1014, and they may have maintained links with the North through their mother's family;[99] the actions of the middle brother, Edmund, following the murder of the northern thegns Siferth and Morcar in 1015 – marrying Siferth's widow, taking possession of the brothers' estates, and collecting an army in the North – suggest that this was the case.[100] However, there are few hints of these upheavals in Æthelstan's will, which is likely to have been made in the summer following his father's reinstatement to the throne.

There is evidence to suggest that the will was drawn up as Æthelstan lay on his deathbed.[101] Although his date of birth is uncertain, he is unlikely to

94 *ASC* s.a. 1013, 1014. For an overview of political developments, see Stafford, *Unification and Conquest*, pp. 65–8.

95 Stafford, *Unification and Conquest*, pp. 71–1.

96 *Vita Ædwardi Regis qui apud Westmonasterium requiescit*, ed. and transl. F. Barlow (London, 1962), pp. 7–8, 60. The case is discussed by F. Barlow, *Edward the Confessor* (London, 1970), pp. 31–8.

97 The tensions at court are described in relation to royal charters by Keynes, *Diplomas*, pp. 209–14. They are most vividly evoked by R. Fletcher, *Blood Feud: Murder and Revenge in Anglo-Saxon England* (London, 2003), particularly at pp. 73–85 for the period in question. For Eadric see Keynes, 'A tale of two kings', pp. 213–17.

98 Stafford, *Unification and Conquest*, p. 66.

99 Ælfgifu was Æthelred's first wife, and the mother of the surviving æthelings, Æthelstan, Edmund and Eadwig. It is possible that she was the daughter of Earl Thored of Northumbria: Keynes, p. 187, n. 118; *EHD* I, p. 48; Stafford, *Queen Emma and Queen Edith*, p. 85. For Earl Thored, see Fletcher, *Bloodfeud*, pp. 70–2, 82.

100 *ASC* s.a. 1015, 1016.

101 See Chap. 2, p. 66 above. S1503/W20, *Christ Church* 142 survives in two manuscripts of the early eleventh century, both from the archive of Christ Church, Canterbury: BL Stowe Charter 37 (the upper portion of a chirograph); Canterbury, DC, Chartae Antiquae H 68, which preserves the step from a wrapping tie (*Facsimiles*, ed. Sanders, I, 18).

have been born before *c.* 985, when his father reached his majority and may then have married.[102] Æthelstan begins attesting royal charters in 993 (S876), and continues to do so until 1013 (S931), appearing consistently above his brothers in the witness lists.[103] He must have predeceased Morcar and Siferth, who are mentioned in his will and were probably the chief thegns of the Seven Boroughs who were murdered in 1015. A good case has been made for his death in the year 1014, making him little more than twenty years old: his obit was recorded at Christ Church, Canterbury, as 25 June, with no year given;[104] the will itself tells us that Æthelstan received his father's permission to bequeath his property 'on the Friday after Midsummer' (*on frigedæg. æfter middessummeres mæssedæge*), which, in 1014, indeed fell on 25 June.[105] If Æthelstan did receive his father's permission on the day of his death, the will – which is extremely detailed and complex – may have been drawn up in anticipation of its arrival, since the clause recording the names of the messengers uncharacteristically appears after the bequests, rather than before.[106]

Æthelstan's bequests of land are those of a wealthy aristocrat. He bequeaths twenty-one estates, and unspecified land in East Anglia, recognising the Church, his male kin, members of his household and other individuals, in the process revealing a male-dominated world, an impression reinforced by his bequests of horses and weaponry.[107] The dispositive section of his will begins with bequests of land to the Church. Like King Eadred, Æthelstan recognises the royal houses at Winchester, bequeathing to the Old Minster three estates which he had actually bought or leased from his father. Two of these estates – Adderbury (Oxon.) and Marlow (Cambs.) – are to be given 'with my body [to the place] where I shall rest'.[108] In each case, Æthelstan is careful to state

102 At this time, Æthelred seems to have emerged from a period of regency; his mother, Queen Ælfthryth, ceases to attest charters, and regular grants to the laity begin: Keynes, *Diplomas*, pp. 174–6; Stafford, *Queen Emma and Queen Edith*, p. 189 and n. 127.

103 Keynes, *Atlas*, Table LIX.

104 BL Arundel 68, fol. 32r; Davis, *Catalogue*, no. 187: register of the fourteenth-fifteenth centuries associated with Christ Church.

105 The case is made by Keynes, *Diplomas*, p. 267, and accepted by Brooks and Kelly, *Christ Church* 142; a case has also been made for Æthelstan's death at the battle of Sherston in 1016: M. K. Lawson, *Cnut: the Danes in England in the Early Eleventh Century* (London, 1973), p. 79, n. 76.

106 Compare S1483/W2; S1485/W9.

107 His bequests of movable wealth are discussed in Chap. 5, pp. 194–6, 218–19 below. The only women mentioned in his will are his foster-mother, Ælfswith, who receives an estate 'for her just deserts', and his grandmother, Queen Ælfthryth, who brought him up and whose soul is to benefit from his bequests to the church.

108 *in mid me . þær ic me reste*. The text is ambiguous here: it is unclear whether Adderbury alone, or both estates, are linked with his burial (see *Wills*, p. 169); however, since the third estate, Morden, is granted on a different premise, it seems more likely that Marlow was linked with Adderbury. Brooks and Kelly suggest that the attendance of the bishop of Winchester and the abbot of the New Minster at Æthelstan's will-making may indicate that he died in the city (*Christ Church* 142).

the respective history of the estates: he had bought them from his father for two hundred gold mancuses by weight (*be gewihte*) plus five pounds of silver (Adderbury), and two hundred and fifty gold mancuses by weight (Marlow). The third estate – Morden (Cambs.) – is land which Æthelstan held from his father on lease (*þe min fæder me to let*), so the alienation of it to the Old Minster was subject to his father's consent:

> *7 ic hine þæs bidde for Godes lufan. 7 for Sc̄a Marian. 7 for Sc̄e Petres. ꝥ hit standan mote.*
>
> (And I entreat him that it may stand, for the love of God and of St Mary and of St Peter.)[109]

In addition, one estate (for which no history is given) is granted to the *Nunnaminster*.[110] Christ Church, Canterbury, is to receive Garrington and Hollingbourne, the only two estates in Kent bequeathed by Æthelstan.[111]

Æthelstan goes on to make bequests of land to his father and brother. No history of their acquisition is given, and in most cases identification is difficult. Of the three estates bequeathed to the king, *Norðtune*, as Whitelock points out, could be one of a number of Nortons, suggesting Chipping Norton (Oxon.), perhaps because of its proximity to the second estate, Mollington (Oxon.);[112] from the third estate, Chalton (Hants.), Æthelstan reserves eight hides for his *cnihte* (servant), Ælfmær, who may (or may not) be the Ælfmær of other bequests and who witnesses the will.[113] Even more obscure are the lands which Æthelstan bequeaths to his brother, Edmund: 'the estates which I own in East Anglia (?)' (*þara landa þe ic ahte on East Englan* [sic]), and the estate *æt Peacesdele*.[114] Because of the opaque history of most of these estates, it is difficult to know whether Æthelstan was bequeathing to his father and

109 Æthelstan's bequest of Hambledon (Hants.?) to Ælfmær is also specifically subject to his father's consent, raising the possibility that it, too, may have been held by Æthelstan on lease (see below).

110 Rotherfield (Sx or Oxon.?). King Alfred bequeathed an estate at Rotherfield to his kinsman Osferth, which may have reverted to the crown (see above n. 46). Æthelstan recognises the New Minster with the gift of a silver cauldron.

111 Hollingbourne is granted with the reservation of one ploughland (*sulunge*) for Siferth, who may or may not be the Siferth who is a further beneficiary. Whitelock comments that the small amount of land involved here, and its southern location, make it unlikely that this Siferth is to be identified with the northern thegn (*Wills*, p. 169).

112 *Wills*, p. 170.

113 *Wills*, p. 170.

114 *Æt Peacesdele* was originally identified as the Peak District (Derbs.) by Whitelock, following Mawer (*Wills*, p. 171); she subsequently accepted Pegsdon (Beds.) as more likely, following Ekwall, and noting that the annual food rent payable to Ely from this estate could be transported by the River Ouse (*Æthelgifu*, p. 23). However, this identification is questioned by Brooks and Kelly, who point out the significance of the lead and iron resources of the Peak District for Anglo-Saxon kings (*Christ Church* 142).

brother land which he held in his own right, or land which he held as one of the æthelings.[115]

Æthelstan uses the bequest of land to acknowledge others who were close to him. His foster-mother, Ælfswith, is to receive 'for her great deserts' (*for hire myclon geearnungon*) an estate at Weston (unid.) which Æthelstan bought from his father for two hundred and fifty gold mancuses. His chaplain, Ælfwine, is to receive an estate *æt Heorulfestune* (unid.), and the Siferth who is to receive Hockliffe (Beds.) is probably the thegn of the Seven Boroughs who, with his brother, Morcar, held land in Yorkshire and the East Midlands, and was murdered in 1015.[116] Æthelstan's seneschal (*discþegn*) Ælfmær is granted eight hides at Catherington (Hants.) which, as Whitelock pointed out, lies within two miles of the eight hides to be reserved for an Ælfmær *cniht* from the estate at Chalton bequeathed to the king, suggesting that the *cniht* and the *discþegn* are identical.[117] The Ælfmær, son of Ælfric, who witnesses the will is likely to be just such a responsible member of the household.

Although remaining bequests of land are enigmatic, involving some degree of speculation in the identification of beneficiaries, or place-names, or both, it is possible that they involve estates which Æthelstan had acquired as a result of forfeiture arising from judicial proceedings. In two instances, Æthelstan appears to be restoring land which had for some reason been forfeit:

> *7 ic ann Leofstane Leofwines breðer. Cwattes. þære landare. þe ic of his breðer nam. 7 ic geann Leommære. æt Biggrafan þæs landes þe ic him ær of nam.*
>
> (And I grant to Leofstan, the brother of Leofwine, Quatt (Shrops.), the landed property which I had taken from his brother. And to Leofmær of Bygrave (Herts.) I grant the land which I have taken from him.)[118]

The circumstances are, as usual, obscure: it appears from the wording that Æthelstan himself was responsible for these confiscations, and that his

115 That such land existed is implied by a charter of Æthelred, which twice refers to 'lands belonging to the kings' sons' (*terras ad regios pertinentes filios*): S937, *Abingdon* 129, probably 999; *EHD* I, no. 123. The estates include Bedwyn (Hants.), Hurstbourne and Burbage (Wilts.). Keynes, *Diplomas*, p. 256.

116 *Wills*, pp. 155, 172; *ASC* s.a. 1015. Although Morcar is not a beneficiary, the will refers to the fact that he is in possession of a coat of mail which Æthelstan bequeaths to the king.

117 *Wills*, p. 170. She also suggests that since the Hambledon bequeathed to a further Ælfmær, subject to the king's permission, may be the Hampshire place of that name, within five miles of Chalton, all three Ælfmærs constitute the same beneficiary. This identification has been questioned by Brooks and Kelly (*Christ Church* 142), and Hambledon (Bucks.) proposed; this Ælfmær is therefore likely to be a different beneficiary.

118 The identification of Quatt is made by Brooks and Kelly, *Christ Church* 142. Little may be said about the bequest of three hides *æt Lutegaresheale* (unid.) to Godwine *Drefelan* (the Sniveller or Driveller), whose nickname is otherwise unrecorded (*Wills*, p. 173).

final will-making provided an opportunity to make reparation.[119] Forfeiture may also lie behind Æthelstan's bequest of land *æt Cumtune* to Godwine, son of Wulfnoth, if this Wulfnoth is to be identified with the Wulfnoth *Cild* who, in 1009, virtually single-handedly brought about the disruption of the English fleet which had been constructed on the orders of King Æthelred in a desperate attempt to resist the Viking marauders.[120] The story is full of drama: the fleet had gathered at Sandwich, when Brihtric, brother of Eadric Streona, made accusations against Wulfnoth *Cild* to the king; Wulfnoth enticed twenty ships from the fleet, and went on to ravage the south coast. Brihtric led eighty ships in pursuit of Wulfnoth, but they were wrecked in a great storm, and Wulfnoth burnt them. The rest of the fleet disbanded and, as the chronicler remarks sadly, 'let the toil of all the nation thus lightly come to naught'.[121] It would be surprising if Wulfnoth's estates were *not* forfeit in such circumstances, and it is conceivable that one of them should have found its way into the hands of the ætheling. Several *Chronicle* accounts describe Wulfnoth as 'the South Saxon', and one identifies him additionally as the father of Earl Godwine, who was to come to prominence in the reign of Cnut.[122] Unfortunately, the estate in question cannot be identified with any certainty, although Domesday Book records that Earl Godwine held ten hides at Compton in Sussex.[123]

The final bequest provides further grounds for speculation. Æthelstan grants an estate at Tewin (Herts.) to Ælfweard and Lyfing, of whom nothing further is known. An estate at Tewin is also bequeathed by Æthelgifu, whose multi-gift will, dated between 956 and 1002, disposes of land in Hertfordshire, Bedfordshire and Northamptonshire.[124] It is, of course, possible that these were two different estates.[125] However, Æthelgifu's principal beneficiary, who is to receive Tewin, is a certain Leofsige, apparently a minor at this stage; Æthelgifu commends him to the queen (*hire hlæfdigan)*, possibly Queen Ælfthryth, King Æthelred's mother, requesting her to watch over (*bewite*) him

119 Land at Bygrave was held in 1066 by Leofmær – possibly a son or relative of the Leofmær to whom land (unnamed, but possibly Bygrave itself) was returned in the will: DB I, fol. 135r; *Wills*, p. 173.

120 The events are related in *ASC* s.a. 1009.

121 *ASC* C, D, E, F: *7 leton ealles þeodscipes geswincg þus leohtlice forwurðan* (text from E; transl. *EHD* I).

122 Wulfnoth is identified as a South Saxon in *ASC* D, E, F; only F (interlineated) identifies him as the father of Godwine; Lawson, *Cnut*, pp. 176–7; Williams, 'Land and power', pp. 176–7, 186–7; S. Keynes, 'Cnut's earls', in *The Reign of Cnut, King of England, Denmark and Norway*, ed. A. R. Rumble (London, 1994), pp. 43–88 (pp. 70–4).

123 DB I, fol. 24r.

124 S1497/*St Albans*, 7.

125 Two estates are recorded in DB I, fols. 135r, 141r; see Lord Rennell in *Æthelgifu*, p. 69. Whitelock points out (*Æthelgifu*, p. 23) that Æthelstan's will disposes of land in Æthelgifu's neighbourhood: Bygrave (Herts.); Hockliffe (Beds.); and, if identification is correct, Pegsdon (Beds.) and Steeple Morden (Cambs.).

and to allow him to serve the ætheling (possibly the young Æthelstan, who was brought up by Ælfthryth, his grandmother).[126] Whether this Leofsige, who may have entered the ætheling's household, is to be identified with the ealdorman of that name who had been an official in the royal household, was promoted to ealdorman, and banished in 1002 for the murder of the king's reeve during a quarrel, is a moot point.[127] These links are tenuous, to say the least, but it does not seem beyond the bounds of possibility that Æthelstan had acquired an estate forfeited by a former member of his household.

If Æthelstan's bequests of land reveal the complex tenurial arrangements and relationships central to aristocratic life, his will has also been interpreted in terms of contemporary politics, emphasising the tension between Æthelstan and his father and seeing the will as an attempt to influence Æthelred's policies.[128] It is possible that Æthelstan had become a focus for those in the North and Midlands at odds with the king and his key adviser, Eadric Streona. Some of those named in the will, apparently as Æthelstan's associates, were embroiled in the opposition to Æthelred's regime: the brothers Siferth and Morcar, who held land in Yorkshire and the East Midlands, paid with their lives on Æthelred's return to power in 1015;[129] Godwine – if the beneficiary of land *æt Cumtune* is correctly identified as the later earl who came to prominence under Cnut – was the son of a rebel.[130] Æthelstan bequeaths to his father horses given to him by Thurbrand (possibly Thurbrand the Hold of Yorkshire, who murdered Earl Uhtred, perhaps at Cnut's behest) and Leofwine (possibly Earl Leofwine of the Hwicce, who held office under both Æthelred and Cnut).[131] However, the king is also to receive a sword which belonged to Ulfketel, possibly the East Anglian thegn who put up a spirited defence against the Danes and eventually died at *Assandun* in 1016.[132] Æthelstan's bequests of six pounds to Shaftesbury Abbey, the burial place of his uncle, Edward the Martyr, in 978, whose death allowed Æthelred to accede to the

126 It is impossible to be certain of these identifications, since the will itself is not specific, and uncertain dating compounds the problem of chronological relationships. See Crick, *St Albans*, pp. 92–4 for a survey of the evidence.

127 *ASC* s.a. 1002; the events of the quarrel are recounted in S926. The identification is accepted by Stafford, *Queen Emma and Queen Edith*, pp. 218–19, and Hart, 'The ealdordom of Essex', pp. 136–7. For a sceptical view, see *Æthelgifu*, pp. 24–6.

128 This political reading is developed by N. J. Higham, *The Death of Anglo-Saxon England* (Stroud, 1997), particularly at pp. 42–7, 56–7.

129 *ASC* s.a. 1015; for the political context of these killings see Fletcher, *Bloodfeud*, pp. 81–3. Higham, *Death of Anglo-Saxon England*, p. 57. For Siferth and Morcar see n. 116 above.

130 The identifications are suggested by Higham, *Death of Anglo-Saxon England*, p. 43. For Whitelock's comments and reservations see *Wills*, pp. 170–1.

131 Higham, *Death of Anglo-Saxon England*, p. 43. For Thurbrand, see Fletcher, *Bloodfeud*, pp. 1–4, 51, 114–15; for Leofwine, see Keynes, 'Cnut's earls', pp. 74–5 and S. Baxter, *The Earls of Mercia: Lordship and Power in Late Anglo-Saxon England* (Oxford, 2007), pp. 17–28.

132 Higham, *Death of Anglo-Saxon England*, p. 43; Keynes, *Diplomas*, p. 208 and n. 199; *ASC* s.a. 1004, 1010, 1016.

throne, may also be construed as criticism of his father's putative implication in the murder of his half-brother, although there is no evidence to link Æthelred directly with this crime and, by 1001, Shaftesbury had become the site of a royal cult.[133] Similarly, Æthelstan's bequests of land and war-gear to his brother, including the sword which belonged to King Offa, may anticipate the militant stance which Edmund was eventually to take;[134] Edmund both witnessed the will and was given responsibility for implementing certain details, suggesting a close relationship between the brothers.

Æthelstan's will undoubtedly reveals a warrior prince with a considerable household and connexions with a potentially disaffected aristocracy. It is likely that tensions concerning the succession simmered within the royal family, exacerbated by the consecration of Emma, Æthelred's second queen, which enhanced the throneworthiness of her sons in relation to that of Æthelstan and his brothers.[135] However, the extent to which the will reveals the 'deep dissensions' between Æthelred and his father detected by Higham is debatable.[136] This view sees Æthelstan's repeated requests addressed to the king that his bequests should be allowed to stand as evidence that he distrusted his father.[137] However, in each case the request is attached to the bequest of a specific estate. One was held by Æthelstan on lease from the king, as the will tells us (Morden, bequeathed to the Old Minster, Winchester, for the souls of both Æthelstan and his father). The other estate – Hambledon (probably Bucks.) – is granted by Æthelstan (subject to his father's permission) to a certain Ælfmær as land which he had previously held (*þe he ær ahte*); could this be the restitution of a further forfeit estate? However this may be, Æthelstan's requests for the king's consent apply to bequests each of which constitutes a special case, not to the overall will. Similarly, although (as Higham points out) Æthelstan was likely to have enemies at court,[138] his address to the *witan*, invoking support for his will, need not have been made as a special plea in anticipation of the king's opposition, but as a formal acknowledgement of the regular procedure.[139] It is also difficult to ignore the affectionate tone of the will which, like a number of wills recorded in the first person, retains the impression of a strong personal voice, notwithstanding

133 Higham, *Death of Anglo-Saxon England*, p. 42; Keynes, *Diplomas*, pp. 163–74; *Shaftesbury*, p. xiv with references. The arguments vindicating Æthelred are developed by S. Ridyard, *The Royal Saints of Anglo-Saxon England: a Study of West Saxon and East Anglian Cult* (Cambridge, 1989), pp. 155–71.

134 Higham, *Death of Anglo-Saxon England*, p. 43.

135 P. Stafford, 'The reign of Æthelred II: a study in the limitations on royal policy and power', in *Ethelred the Unready: Papers from the Millenary Conference*, ed. D. Hill, BAR British Series 59 (1978), pp. 15–37 (pp. 35–7).

136 Higham, *Death of Anglo-Saxon England*, p. 44.

137 Higham, *Death of Anglo-Saxon England*, pp. 41–2.

138 Higham, *Death of Anglo-Saxon England*, p. 42.

139 The clause addressing the *witan* is quoted in Chap. 2, p. 69 above.

scribal mediation.[140] For example, Æthelstan refers warmly to both his foster-mother and grandmother; the king himself is referred to consistently as 'my father', becoming 'my dear father' (*leofan fæder*) in the valedictory clause of the will, where his soul is included among those to benefit from Æthelstan's pious gifts. It is possible to dismiss such terminology as political expedience, but it is equally possible to consider the warmth with which Æthelstan addresses his father as a gesture of reconciliation at the point of death. After all, it must have been clear to Æthelstan that the soul of the elderly, ailing and beleaguered king would soon be as much in need of prayer as his own.

It is difficult to ascertain the extent to which Æthelstan's bequests took effect, given the uncertainties of identification outlined above. In 1066, the Old Minster, Winchester, held two of the three estates (Adderbury and Morden) which it should have received under Æthelstan's will;[141] and Christ Church, Canterbury, held Hollingbourne, preserving, in addition to copies of the will, an entry in a gospel book recording King Æthelred's confirmation of his son's bequest.[142] Remaining estates bequeathed to the church were either in lay hands, or cannot be traced.[143] In general, it is impossible to detect the completion of bequests to the laity unless land is subsequently granted to the church, which does not seem to have been the case here.[144] Furthermore, the political upheavals which followed Æthelstan's death made his bequests to the laity particularly vulnerable.[145]

## The bequest of land by ealdormen

The wills of five ealdormen are extant. That of Ealdorman Alfred is contemporary with that of King Alfred, dated to the latter ninth century; those of the ealdormen Ælfgar, Æthelwold, Ælfheah and Æthelmær span roughly (given the uncertainty of dating parameters) the third quarter of the tenth century.[146] Although under King Alfred the office of ealdorman seems to have been

140 E.g. S1497/*St Albans*, 7; S1487/W13; S1491/W4, *New Minster* 18.

141 DB I, fol. 4v.

142 BL Cotton Claudius A iii fol. 3v; Brooks, *Early History*, p. 385, n. 92; the estate was confirmed to the archbishop by King Edward in S1047/R95, 1042x1066.

143 Marlow (bequeathed to the Old Minster) was in various lay hands in 1066 (DB I, fols. 144v, 150r, 151r, 152r). Garrington (bequeathed to Christ Church, Canterbury), was also in lay hands (DB I, fol. 12r). The *Nunnaminster* had no record of land at Rotherfield *TRE* (*Wills*, p. 169), but Rotherfield (Sx) was in the hands of Earl Godwine (DB I, fol. 16r).

144 See above n. 119 for evidence for the fulfilment of the bequest to Leofmær of Bygrave.

145 See, for example, K. Mack, 'Changing thegns: Cnut's conquest and the English aristocracy', *Albion* 16 (1984), 375–87; Fleming, *Kings and Lords*, p. 44.

146 S1508/H10, *Christ Church* 96, 871x889 (Alfred); S1483/W2, 946xc.951 (Ælfgar); S1504/H20, 946x947 (Æthelwold); S1485/W9, *c.* 968x971/2 (Ælfheah); S1498/W10, *New Minster* 25, 971x983 (Æthelmær).

largely administrative, restricted mainly to the individual shires of Wessex, it developed through time so that, by the tenth century, ealdormen held sway as powerful magnates over wider territory.[147]

A good illustration is the extent of the landed property of Ælfheah, ealdorman of central Wessex 959–971/2, which has been analysed in detail by Williams.[148] He bequeaths twenty estates in seven counties, for which the hidage of nine, amounting to 309 hides, can be established; but by assuming that estates mentioned in the will for which hidage is not available would be of roughly equivalent value, and taking account of other estates known to have been held by Ælfheah which do not appear in the will, the value of his land overall has been estimated at a total of 700 hides. That ealdormen were well placed to increase their personal holdings in land is demonstrated by the will of Æthelmær, ealdorman between 940 and 946 of what may have been the former sub-kingdom of Wessex which included Sussex, Surrey, Kent, and possibly Essex,[149] who bequeaths land confiscated from a certain Lufa; Æthelmær had bought it from the king *æt Cyrthugtune* for one hundred and twenty gold mancuses, a transaction witnessed by all his *geferena* (companions), as well as Bishop Æthelwold.[150]

However, there are hints of a submerged tenurial complexity, with some of the estates bequeathed by ealdormen possibly held on lease from the king. This has the implication that, in these instances, it is the remaining leasehold which is being bequeathed, rather than permanent rights in the land. The opening clause of Ealdorman Æthelwold's will refers to 'the landed properties which I have earned from my lord' (*þa landare þe ic æt mine hlaforde geearnode*), which implies that Æthelwold held these estates by royal charter. He begins by bequeathing Wylye (Wilts.) to the Old Minster, Winchester, and goes on to bequeath a number of estates to his kinsmen.[151] It is the final clause which raises questions about the nature of his tenure of at least some of these estates:

147 For the office of ealdorman see H. R. Loyn, *The Governance of Anglo-Saxon England 500–1087* (London, 1984), pp. 75–7; P. Stafford, 'Ealdorman', in *Blackwell Encyclopaedia*, pp. 152–3. For the role of ealdormen and earls in the tenth and eleventh centuries see Baxter, *Earls*, pp. 74–85, and for the fluctuation in the structure of eleventh-century earldoms pp. 62–71.

148 For the calculations which follow, see Williams, '*Princeps Merciorum gentis*', pp. 150–4. Ælfheah's death is given as 971 by John of Worcester (*Wills*, p. 121); however, his final charter attestation is S784 (972): Keynes, *Atlas*, Table LVI.

149 Hart, 'Ealdordom of Essex', p. 125; C. R. Hart, 'Athelstan "Half King" and his family', *ASE* 2 (1973), 115–38, 143–4, revised and reprinted in Hart, *The Danelaw*, pp. 569–604 (p. 573).

150 This bequest, to the New Minster, Winchester, is confirmed by a charter of King Æthelred dated 982 (S842, *New Minster* 26).

151 S1504/H20. For the suggestion that Wylye was bookland originally granted to an ancestor of Æthelwold, see Hart, 'Athelstan "Half King"', p. 573, n. 14.

*7 eall þæt yrfe þæ ic hæbbe on lænelandum, þonne wylle ic þæt þæt sie gedeled for mine sawle swa swa ic nu þam freondum sæde þæ ic to spræc.*

(And I desire that all the stock that I hold on [my] leased land should be distributed for the good of my soul, as I have just instructed the friends to whom I have been speaking.)[152]

As so often, the text is enigmatic. Æthelwold may be referring to estates not mentioned in the will, over which he had no right of bequest beyond the accrued stock, but it is possible to interpret this clause as referring to some of the estates specified in the will, which may have constituted the leased lands in question; some were certainly held by or of the king in 1066.[153] Rather more secure evidence for leasehold is found in a charter of King Eadwig, granting rights in land at Wroughton (Wilts.) to Ealdorman Ælfheah, with permission to designate a single successor (after which the land would presumably revert to the king); in his will, Ælfheah bequeaths the estate to the Old Minster, Winchester, with no reference to the terms on which it was held.[154]

Apart from their status by right of office, these tenth-century ealdormen were undoubtedly part of a high-ranking kindred network.[155] Three can be shown to be linked to powerful dynasties, including royal houses, by blood or by affinity.[156] Ælfgar is not designated ealdorman in his will, but attests charters as *dux* between 945 and 951, and seems to have been based in Essex,

152 Harmer's translation of the text interprets *yrfe* as referring to the leasehold property itself (*SEHD*, p. 119); I have preferred the meaning 'stock' (B&T *yrfe*) since the distribution of stock is referred to in other wills when the land itself is not within the donor's gift (see Chap. 5, pp. 180–2 below), and would fit the context here.

153 Of the eight estates in question, one is unidentified, and one uncertain (*æt Æscesdune* may be Ashdown, Berks.); in 1066, Ogbourne (Wilts.), Broadwater (Sx) and Kingsclere (Hants.) were held by or of the king (DB I, fols. 65v, 28v, 50r); Cheam (Surrey) was held by the archbishop of Canterbury (DB I, fol. 30v); Washington (Sx) was held by Earl Gyrth (DB I, fol. 28r); and South Newton was held by the royal nunnery at Wilton (DB I, fol. 68r, and Edgar's confirmation S766). The later evidence for 'comital manors' linked to earldoms is surveyed by Baxter, *Earls*, pp. 141–5.

154 S585 (956). For the identification of the place-name *æt Ællændune* as Wroughton and a brief history of the estate, see *Malmesbury*, pp. 183–4. The designation of the beneficiary is ambiguous; Kelly interprets the phrase *he gean his drihtne for his sawlæ þæarfæ þæs landæs æt Ællændune* as a gift to the king (*Malmesbury*, p. 183), but since the bequest is made for Ælfheah's soul and is immediately followed by a bequest to the Old Minster, and since the usual terms for the king in wills are *cyning* and *hlaford*, I suggest that *drihten* here refers to God (as in S1531/W31, S1535/W32, *Christ Church* 176 and S1499/W35). An estate at Wroughton was held by the bishop of Winchester in 1066 (DB I, fol. 65v).

155 Fleming, *Kings and Lords*, pp. 23–32, with a schematic genealogy at p. 24, fig. 2.1.

156 Nothing is known of Alfred beyond the likelihood that he was ealdorman of Surrey from 853 (*SEHD*, p. 88); he is entitled *dux* in his will. Æthelmær's connexions are equally obscure beyond his tenure of the ealdormanry of Hampshire 977–82 (*New Minster*, p. 119); his heriot equates to that of an ealdorman, and he is entitled such in his will: N. Brooks, 'Arms, status and warfare in late-Saxon England', in *Ethelred the*

where he may have had ancestral roots.[157] His status may be detected through the alliances made by his daughters: the older, Æthelflæd, was the second wife of King Edmund; the younger, Ælfflæd, was the wife of Byrhtnoth, a man of great wealth in East Anglia, who became ealdorman of Essex in 956 and died at the Battle of Maldon in 991.[158] Æthelwold and Ælfheah, both termed *ealdorman* in their wills and paying the appropriate heriot, were not only men of significance in their own right, but were also linked to the most powerful aristocratic families of the mid-tenth century. Æthelwold was the brother of Æthelstan, known as Half-King, ealdorman of East Anglia 932–956, whose wife fostered the young Prince Edgar and whose son, Æthelwine, later known as *amicus dei*, became ealdorman of East Anglia in 962.[159] Ælfheah was the brother of Ælfhere, ealdorman of Mercia and one of the key figures in King Edgar's reign.[160] This family seems to have been related to the royal house of Wessex, since in a number of charters Ælfheah, Ælfhere and their brother, Ælfwine are designated kinsmen of the king.[161] In addition, Ælfheah names as a beneficiary his kinsman Æthelweard, probably the ealdorman and chronicler of that name who himself claimed royal descent, and who may have been the brother of the former queen Ælfgifu.[162] There is also a hint that Ælfheah's wife, Ælfswith, was herself of royal blood.[163]

Since the office of ealdorman was, by the tenth century, a political appointment, and given the high public profile of these men, it is likely that political factors influenced their bequests.[164] Such factors can be detected in the will of Ælfheah, whose position in the reign of King Edgar was politically ambiguous. As has already been shown, Ælfheah was the brother of Ælfhere,

*Unready*, ed. Hill, pp. 81–103, reprinted in N. Brooks, *Communities and Warfare 700–1400* (London, 2000), pp. 138–61 (p. 148).

157 *ASC* D refers to Ælfgar as ealdorman s.a. 946; Hart, 'Ealdordom of Essex', p. 127; his heriot is that of a king's thegn under King Eadred: Brooks, 'Arms, status', p. 150.

158 Hart, 'Ealdordom of Essex', pp. 131–5, with the suggestion that he may have been descended from the Mercian royal house at p. 131; M. A. L. Locherbie-Cameron, 'Byrhtnoth and his family', in *The Battle of Maldon*, ed. Scragg, pp. 253–62 (pp. 253–5).

159 Hart, 'Athelstan "Half King"', pp. 579, 597.

160 Williams, '*Princeps Merciorum gentis*', pp. 147–58.

161 S555, S564, S582, S585, S586, S702, S802; Williams, '*Princeps Merciorum gentis*', p. 145, n. 4.

162 *Æthelweard*, ed. Campbell, Book 4, chap. 2, p. 39; n. 76 above.

163 S662 (955x959) includes a vernacular note identifying Ælfswith as Eadwig's *magan*. S462 (940) grants land to 'Elswith my kinsman and minister': Whitelock suggests scribal omission of Ælfheah's name (*Wills*, p. 125), but Abrams prefers a corruption of the name Ælfsige (*Glastonbury*, p. 55); see also Fleming, *Kings and Lords*, pp. 29–30 and n. 64. Possible royal kinship for the family of Æthelstan Half-King depends upon unreliable comments in the *Vita Oswaldi* and *CR*: Fleming, *Kings and Lords*, p. 30, n. 71, but see Hart, 'Athelstan "Half King"', p. 570.

164 For the political role of tenth-century ealdormen see Stafford, 'Ealdorman', *Blackwell Encyclopaedia*, p. 152.

ealdorman of Mercia.[165] In the political upheaval of 957, when the kingdom was divided between King Eadwig and his brother Edgar, Ælfhere remained in Mercia with Edgar, succeeding to his father's ealdormanry. Ælfheah, however, remained in Wessex, possibly serving as Eadwig's seneschal until 959, when he first attests as ealdorman.[166] He benefited from the generosity of Eadwig, receiving estates in Wiltshire by royal charters which described him as the king's esteemed or faithful *minister*.[167] It may have been at this time that Ælfheah's friendship with Bishop Ælfsige of Winchester was established.[168] Since Ælfsige was a secular cleric in an increasingly monastic church, Ælfheah's alliance with him was politically sensitive. When the kingdom was reunited under Edgar on Eadwig's death in 959, Ælfhere and Ælfheah were embroiled in the political tensions which surrounded issues of the royal succession and religious reforms – Ælfhere was later to be regarded as anti-monastic, although this label would seem to oversimplify the factors underlying the violence which erupted on the death of King Edgar.[169] Nevertheless, Ælfheah seems to have established himself at Edgar's court, attesting charters consistently, in second or third place, between 959 and 970, and receiving grants of land from the king.[170] He bequeaths seven estates in Buckinghamshire, Berkshire and Wiltshire to King Edgar, in addition to his heriot.[171] However, further bequests are unequivocal in demonstrating his allegiance to the faction dominated by Bishop Æthelwold and Edgar's queen, Ælfthryth, which sought to establish the primary claim to the throne of Edmund and Æthelred, her sons by Edgar, excluding Edgar's son, Edward, by his previous wife.[172] The text of Ælfheah's will refers to Ælfthryth as his *gefædere*,[173] and to the older ætheling (Edmund), who is granted coin and a sword, as 'the king's

165 See n. 160 above.

166 For this and what follows, see Williams, '*Princeps Merciorum gentis*', pp. 148–9 and n. 29.

167 S585 (956): *æt Ellendune* (Wroughton) to *meo fideli ministro ac propinquo*; S586 (959): land on the River Nadder to *meo dilecto ministro ac propinquo*; S639, *Abingdon* 75 (957), granting land in Berks. to Ælfheah, is dubious.

168 Ælfsige refers to this friendship in his will S1491/W4, *New Minster* 18 (see p. 118 below).

169 Williams, '*Princeps Merciorum gentis*', pp. 149, 160–72.

170 Keynes, *Atlas*, Table LVI, but note also the outlying attestation of S784 (972). Charters in Ælfheah's favour are S702 (962; see also S1447/R44) and, jointly with his wife, S747 (967).

171 Worth, Thatcham, Cookham (Berks.); Chelworth in Cricklade, Inglesham (Wilts.); Aylesbury, Wendover (Bucks.). All estates except Inglesham, which is not listed separately in DB, were held by or of the king in 1066 (DB I, fols. 56v, 58r, 74r, 143r). Land at Inglesham was bequeathed by Æthelmær, ealdorman of Hampshire 977–982, to his son; for possible identification of this estate see *New Minster*, p. 120.

172 For an overview of the political issues, see Yorke, 'Æthelwold', pp. 75–87 and Stafford, *Unification and Conflict*, pp. 44–61. For the political affiliations of Ælfheah and his family see Williams, '*Princeps Merciorum gentis*', pp. 148–50, 155–9.

173 This term may refer to the spiritual kinship between godparents or between godparent and parent, as well as to that between godparent and child (B&T, supp. (1); *Wills*, p. 123). Either of the first two meanings would be appropriate in this context.

son and hers', a distinction which pointedly fails to acknowledge the existence of Edward. Both Ælfthryth and the younger ætheling (presumably Æthelred, future king) are granted a single estate.[174] In making this bequest, Ælfheah also allied himself with the queen's staunch supporter, Bishop Æthelwold, who witnessed the will. Interestingly, another witness was Ealdorman Æthelwine, who had succeeded his father, Æthelstan Half-King, as ealdorman of East Anglia, and who had been raised as the foster-brother of the ætheling Edgar; Æthelwine was committed, along with Archbishop Dunstan, to the succession of the eldest ætheling, Edward.[175] Ælfheah's bequests thus seem to have carried a powerful political charge. Williams has commented that the confrontation which took place in 975 between these two aristocratic families 'must have been long brewing';[176] Ælfheah's partisan will, made several years before Edgar's death, is evidence that this was indeed the case.

The absence of further multi-gift wills made by ealdormen, and the concentration of extant documents within a short span of the tenth century, makes it likely that vernacular will-making at this social level was stimulated by the activities of a small group of well-connected and influential churchmen – Oswald, Dunstan and Æthelwold – just as the active fund-raising of archbishops of Canterbury seems to have prompted a series of bequests to Christ Church in ninth-century Kent.[177] The bequest of land to the Church features in four of the five wills, the exception being that of Ealdorman Alfred, who alienates no land to the Church in his multi-gift will; however, in a separate bequest-agreement with Christ Church, Canterbury he is to gain a life interest in the community's estate of Croydon (Sy) in return for the reversion of his own estate at Chartham (Kt) on his death.[178] The difference in emphasis in the remaining four wills is revealing. Ælfgar, making his will before the full impact of the monastic reform, was primarily concerned to endow a local community at Stoke-by-Nayland (Sfk) with which his family was associated, with additional reversionary bequests to Bury, Christ Church, Canterbury (both served at this time by secular communities), and the nunnery at Barking. His older daughter, Æthelflæd, was charged to bequeath the estate of Ditton (Cambs.), in which she was to hold a life interest, to a 'holy place' (*halegan stowe*) of her choice; making her will most probably after the death of King Edgar in 975, she chose Ely, refounded *c.* 970 by Bishop Æthelwold, rather than the secular houses patronised by her father.[179] In contrast with Ælfgar's

174 *Æt Scyræburnan* (?Shirburn) and Walkhampstead (later Godstone, Sy) respectively.

175 Yorke, 'Æthelwold', pp. 84–5; Hart, 'Athelstan "Half King"', p. 579.

176 Williams, '*Princeps Merciorum gentis*', p. 160, and pp. 160–70 for the political context.

177 For the high-ranking connexions of the three key figures of the Reform, roughly co-terminous with the period covered by these wills, see: Wareham, 'Saint Oswald's family and kin', pp. 47–9; Brooks, 'Career', pp. 5–12; Yorke, 'Æthelwold', pp. 68–9.

178 S1202/H8, *Christ Church* 95, 870x879; Brooks, *Early History*, pp. 151–2, and p. 355, n. 78 for dating.

179 S1494/W14. For Æthelflæd's bequests as former queen, see p. 95 above.

patronage of unreformed houses, the remaining ealdormen bequeath land to reformed churches with strong royal associations. For example, Ælfheah bequeaths two estates to the Old Minster, Winchester, from which the secular clergy were expelled in 964; and one estate each to Bath and Malmesbury, both houses restored or reformed under King Edgar.[180] In addition, land at Batcombe (Som.) would revert to Glastonbury, a house strongly associated with Archbishop Dunstan, after the lives of Ælfheah's wife, son and brothers.[181]

It is Ælfheah who makes the most substantial bequests of land to the church, bequeathing directly or by reversion five of the twenty estates named in the will – a total of one hundred and thirty hides. Based on the estimation of his overall wealth given above, this amounts to about 19 per cent of his landed property. This is indeed a substantial investment of land 'on behalf of his soul's need' (*for his saulæ þæarfæ*), but perhaps the generosity of bequests of land to the Church by Æthelwold, Ælfheah and Æthelmær should not be overestimated. Ælfheah's bequests to the Old Minster, Winchester, for example, amount to effective recycling: he had only a life interest in Crondall (Hants.), bequeathed to him by Bishop Ælfsige, who had stipulated reversion to the Old Minster on Ælfheah's death and, as has been suggested above, Ælfheah may have held Wroughton on lease, bequeathing the remaining leasehold to the Old Minster rather than full rights in the land. The total of Æthelmær's estates cannot be determined accurately, since he grants unspecified land to his wife, but of the four named estates in the will, only one (confiscated land which he had acquired from the king) is to go directly to the New Minster, Winchester, as his burial payment; a further estate – South Tidworth (Hants.) – which he bequeaths to his wife would revert there on her death, for both of their souls, and the remaining two were bequeathed to his sons. Of the nine estates bequeathed by Ealdorman Æthelwold, only one – Wylye (Wilts.) – is granted to the church in return for prayers on his behalf.

The fact that there are no extant written wills by ealdormen from the eleventh century may reflect the serendipity of survival. However, it may also reflect a changed approach at this social level to the deployment of land.[182] The political changes which began in the closing decade of Æthelred's reign and gathered momentum under Cnut (1016–1035) disrupted the closely-entwined aristocratic network which had dominated the tenth century.[183] Patronage of

180 *ASC* A, F, s.a. 964; *Bath and Wells*, pp. 13–17; *Malmesbury*, p. 24. Æthelwold bequeaths an estate to the Old Minster, and Æthelmær to the New Minster, Winchester. For the royal associations of these churches, see p. 91 above.

181 *For urnæ fædær and for uræ modor and for us eallæ*. See Chap. 6, pp. 233–5 below.

182 Insley, 'Where did all the charters go?', pp. 126–7. See also Wareham, *Lords and Communities*, p. 129.

183 Keynes, *Diplomas*, pp. 209–28; Keynes, 'Cnut's earls', pp. 78–88; Mack, 'Changing thegns', pp. 377–8; Fleming, *Kings and Lords*, pp. 32–52. The exceptional survivor was the family of Ealdorman Leofwine of Mercia: Baxter, *Earls*, Chap. 2.

the church continued under the new regime, but it had few roots in the tradition of close family links with individual religious houses, often spanning several generations, which had underpinned the political alliances and family strategy of the tenth-century aristocracy.[184] The bequest of land had been an important element in the articulation of this relationship, and the impulse for the documentation of the complex dispositions of powerful men.[185] If, for the new aristocracy, the bequest of land was largely supplanted in the eleventh century by *inter vivos* gift, the written will had lost its relevance.[186]

## The bequest of land by churchmen

Whereas the surviving multi-gift wills of ealdormen are concentrated between the years 946 and 983, those of five bishops – Theodred, Ælfsige, Ælfwold, Ælfric, and Æthelmær – and Archbishop Ælfric span the last century of Anglo-Saxon England.[187] In addition, two bequest-agreements survive, made by men who were subsequently elevated to the episcopate: the priest Eadsige, who became archbishop in 1038, and Stigand, who – if the identification is correct – became Bishop of East Anglia in 1043, and archbishop in 1052.[188] The multi-gift will of Ulf has been excluded from the discussion here, since his status is uncertain: Keynes tentatively identified him as the bishop of Dorchester appointed in 1046, partly on the basis of his pious bequests, while acknowledging that he might equally have been a pious layman; the latter view is preferred by Crick in her recent survey of the evidence.[189] This difficulty of distinguishing between the will of a pious layman and a bishop demonstrates the close relationship between secular and spiritual lordship, which is further illustrated by the fact that all five bishops making multi-gift

184 Lawson, *Cnut*, pp. 117–60.

185 Chap. 4, pp. 156–65 below examines the relationship between the Church, family strategy and the written will.

186 The role of *inter vivos* endowment of the Church in the strategy of Earl Leofric of Mercia (*c.* 1020–1057) is surveyed by Baxter, *Earls*, Chap. 5; he notes the apparent absence of written bequests in the family at p. 139. See also the account of the role of Tovi the Proud and Harold Godwineson in the endowment of Waltham Abbey: *The Waltham Chronicle*, ed. and transl. L. Watkiss and M. Chibnall (Oxford, 1994), pp. xiii-xxv.

187 Bishops Theodred (S1526/W1, 942x*c.*951), Ælfsige (S1491/W4, *New Minster* 18, 951x958), Ælfwold (S1492/N&S10, 1011x1015), Ælfric (S1489/W26, 1035x1040), Æthelmær (S1499/W35, 1047x1070); Archbishop Ælfric (S1488/W18, *Abingdon* 133, 1002x1005).

188 S1465/R86, *Christ Church* 153, *c.* 1032 (the date is derived from a late list of Canterbury benefactors: *Charters*, p. 419); S1224/R92, *c.* 1040.

189 S1532/*St Albans* 13, 1026x1046; Keynes, 'The will of Wulf', p. 20; *St Albans*, pp. 203–4. Omitted from this discussion as spurious are S1418/R28, *New Minster* 14 and S1419/R29, *New Minster* 16, the single gift bequests of the priests Æthelnoth and Eadwulf (see Chap. 1, n. 62 above). For the eccentric will of Mantat the Anchorite (S1523/W23) see Chap. 6, p. 274 below.

wills make provision for the payment of their heriot to the king. The *Regularis Concordia* of *c.* 973, the monastic customary probably compiled by Bishop Æthelwold, explicitly forbids payment of heriot by abbots and abbesses, but the fact that bishops do not seem to have been relieved of such payment perhaps illustrates the secular aspect of their position.[190] Archbishop Ælfric and bishops Theodred and Ælfwold all specify substantial war-gear to be made over to the king, Theodred referring to this as his heriot; Archbishop Ælfric makes additional provision for his due heriot payment; Bishop Ælfric grants two marks of gold to the king without direct reference to heriot, although a significant gap in the manuscript at this point may indicate the omission of military items;[191] and Bishop Ælfsige simply refers to his heriot payment, without further detail. Bishops therefore seem to have shared with their high-ranking secular counterparts the customary payment of heriot in order to secure the terms of the will.

As is the case in the wills of ealdormen, land is at the heart of these documents, and, similarly, had been acquired in a number of ways. For example, Bishop Ælfric of East Anglia bequeaths land which he had acquired by royal grant;[192] by purchase;[193] and by gift.[194] Like ealdormen, bishops were involved in complex leasing arrangements, which are more or less visible: we are told explicitly that Bishop Ælfsige is returning land at Taunton (Som.) leased to him by the king, but it is also possible that he was holding land at Highclere and 'the two Worthys' (all Hants.) as the second tenant of a four-life lease.[195] A number of the wills distinguish between land held by bishops in their own right, through acquisition or inheritance, and that held by right of office. This is most clearly seen in the will of Bishop Theodred, who held the see of London together with that of Suffolk, and who is specific in bequeathing only acquired stock from land attached to the bishoprics, transmitting the estates to his successor intact.

190 *Regularis Concordia*, ed. Symons, chap. 69. The itemisation of heriot rates due from different social ranks in II Cnut, 71 does not mention bishops. Heriot payments are discussed in Chap. 5 below.

191 *Wills*, p. 72, n. 4. Although this survives as a single sheet written in an eleventh-century hand, Whitelock argues, on the basis of omissions and insertions in the text, that it may be a later copy (*Wills*, p. 181–2); alternatively, it could be a draft.

192 No charter is extant for Worlingworth (Sfk), but charters do survive for land bequeathed by bishops Theodred (Southery: S483) and Ælfwold (Sandford: S997). Bishop Ælfsige was granted land at Highclere in the dubious S565 (*New Minster*, p. 83).

193 Moulton (Sfk) and Roydon (Nfk). Estates had been purchased by Bishop Theodred (a messuage in Ipswich), Archbishop Ælfric (Wallingford and land in London), Eadsige (Orpington, for '80 marks of white silver by the standard of the husting').

194 Fenland given to him by Thurlac and Ælfric. The messuage in Norwich was probably also a gift, since the will refers to those who granted (*geuðan*) it to him.

195 S595; *New Minster*, p. 84. See below pp. 124–5 for the complexity of leasing arrangements in S1465/R86, *Christ Church* 153, S1486/R97 and S1499/W35.

The wills of these churchmen reflect the complexity of their social role, their often considerable landholdings, and a range of approaches to the *post obitum* disposition of their property in response to specific historical and personal circumstances.[196] For example, two mid tenth century bishops, given very different profiles by the twelfth-century historian William of Malmesbury, made very different wills as the tide of ecclesiastical reform was gathering momentum.

The earlier of the two is the exemplary Bishop Theodred of London, who first attests a royal charter in 926, and appears to have died between 951 and 953, when his successor begins to subscribe.[197] He also held the see of Suffolk.[198] There can be little doubt of his prestige at court: he acted as an emissary of the king on at least two occasions, and was a leading signatory of royal charters from 935.[199] William of Malmesbury, in his twelfth-century history of English bishops, extolled his virtues:[200]

> *Cognomen Boni uulgo sortitum pro prerogatiua uirtutum. Vno excidisse magis errore quam crimine, quod fures apud Sanctum Edmundum deprehensos, quos conatibus irritis martir inuisibili nodo astrinxerat, seueritati legum addixerit, patibulis adiudicatos. Sed de facto recogitantem piguisse, totoque uite tempore post haec exercuisse penitentiam, culpa mordente conscientiam. Eius corpus iuxta fenestram criptae locatum est in edito, pretereuntibus conspicuo.*
>
> (His pre-eminent virtues won him the nickname of 'the Good'. He had one lapse (they say), more an error than a crime, in that he handed over to the rigour of execution on the gallows thieves caught at St Edmunds, whom the martyr had bound by an invisible knot during their abortive attempt. Second thoughts led to a revulsion of feeling, and for the rest of his life he did penance, while the misdeed nagged at his conscience. His body was placed high up near the window of the crypt, for passers-by to see.)[201]

196 Since Bishop Ælfwold, in what was probably a deathbed will (S1492/N&S10) bequeaths only one estate, to his episcopal church, his dispositions are discussed in Chap. 5 below.

197 S1526/W1, 942x *c*.951, preserved in the fourteenth-century Bury Sacrist's Register; for the dates of his tenure and of the will see *St Paul's*, pp. 90, 116–18. This account of Theodred's career is based on D. Whitelock, *Some Anglo-Saxon Bishops of London*, Chambers Memorial Lecture (London, 1974), pp. 17–21, and *St Paul's*, pp. 116–18.

198 The history of the diocesan organisation at this time is obscure: *Wills*, p. 99; J. Campbell, 'The East Anglian sees before the conquest', in *Norwich Cathedral: Church, City and Diocese*, ed. I. Atherton, E. Fernie, C. Harper-Bill and H. Smith (London, 1996), pp. 3–21 (pp. 3–15), reprinted in J. Campbell, *The Anglo-Saxon State* (London, 2000), pp. 107–27 (pp. 107–124). See also *St Paul's*, pp. 29, 90.

199 See VI Æthelstan, 12.1 and Ælfgar's will (S1483/W2) for Theodred as emissary; Whitelock, *Anglo-Saxon Bishops*, pp.17–18; *St Paul's*, ed. Kelly, p. 31; Keynes, *Atlas*, Tables XXXVII, XLI, XLIV.

200 Texts and translations are taken from *William of Malmesbury: Gesta Pontificum Anglorum*, ed. and transl. M. Winterbottom and R. M. Thomson (Oxford, 2006).

201 *Gesta Pontificum*, ii.73.16. Whitelock remarks on the surprising absence of commemoration of Theodred at St Paul's: *Anglo-Saxon Bishops*, p. 21.

Theodred's public status is reflected in his bequest to the king of three estates, two in Cambridgeshire and one in Norfolk, along with a substantial heriot payment. His will is equally exemplary; he had amassed considerable property in East Anglia, which he distributes among his diocesan churches and his kindred.[202]

In his ecclesiastical role as bishop of London, Theodred bequeaths four estates to St Paul's: Southery (Nfk), and *Chich* (later St Osyth), Tillingham and Dunmow (all in Essex). Similarly, he bequeaths two estates, Horham (Sfk) and *æt Elyngtone* (possibly Athelington, Sfk) to his *bishopriche* at Hoxne (Sfk), which remained one of the two episcopal seats of the diocese of East Anglia.[203] In each case, the grant is made specifically to the community, with the apparent intention of distinguishing these estates from the property of the bishop.[204] In addition, Theodred is careful to identify the demesne lands of the bishop in each diocese, bequeathing only the acquired stock on these estates to be distributed on his behalf.[205] In spite of the changing religious climate, as well as making bequests to his episcopal churches Theodred recognises the significance of Mendham and St Edmund's at Bury, two of the local minsters served by secular communities which flourished in pre-Reform East Anglia. There is no other reference to a community (*godes hewen*) at Mendham (Sfk); it is to receive two estates (Shotford and Mettingham, both Sfk), as well as one hide reserved from the estate at Mendham (which Theodred bequeaths to his nephew, Osgot) along with the minster itself.[206] However, the community of canons tending the relics of St Edmund had, at the beginning of the

202 It is tempting to see King Edmund's grant of Southery (S483) in 942 as the stimulus for Theodred's will-making, for Theodred refers to 'what I have acquired and may yet acquire' (*þe ic begeten habbe 7 get bigete*). Apart from this grant and his purchase of a messuage in Ipswich the origins of Theodred's lands are obscure (Whitelock, *Anglo-Saxon Bishops*, p. 20). For the view that this was his personal property see *St Paul's*, p. 91; see T. Pestell, *Landscapes of Monastic Foundation: the Establishment of Religious Houses in East Anglia c. 650–1200* (Woodbridge, 2004), pp. 85–6 for the possibility that some was land leased from the church, and C. R. Hart, 'The St Paul's estates in Essex', in Hart, *The Danelaw*, pp. 205–20 (p. 213), for the view that Theodred was confirming the canons' rights in the Essex property, rather than granting it anew.

203 *Wills*, p. 102; Whitelock, *Anglo-Saxon Bishops*, p. 18.

204 On this distinction see *St Paul's*, pp. 82, 93–4. *Chich* (St Osyth) is granted to St Paul's *to bedlonde*: Whitelock (*Wills*, p. 101) draws attention to the gloss of O.E. *beodland* as *terras dono ad refectorium fratribus* (B&T, Supp.). However, only Tillingham was in the hands of the canons of St Paul's in 1066; St Osyth was held by the bishop (DB II, fol. 11r).

205 Fulham (Mx) and Dengie (Ex) remained property of the Bishop of London in 1066: DB I, fol. 127v; II, fol. 24r (Fulham was excluded from the division of stock). Hoxne was held by Bishop Æthelmær of East Anglia *TRE*: DB II, fol. 379r. For this as demesne see *St Paul's*, pp. 92–3.

206 Bury held Mendham itself *TRE*, including a church with 20 acres: DB II, fol. 368rv. References to other local religious communities may be found in the wills of Ealdorman Ælfgar and his daughters (S1483/W2, S1494/W14, S1486/W15): Stoke-by-Nayland, Hadleigh and Sudbury (Sfk), and West Mersea (Ex).

tenth century, transferred to the site at *Bedricesweorð*, which would later be refounded as the monastery of Bury St Edmund's. This royal cult attracted considerable local support, and the bequest of four estates for his soul's welfare by a high-ranking churchman, at a time when the monastic revival was gathering momentum, is a reflection of its increasing importance.[207]

The bulk of Theodred's property lay in Suffolk, and the fact that he bequeaths a number of these estates to his collateral kindred suggests that his family may have originated in this area:[208] seven named estates with *alle þe smale londe þat þereto bereð* (all the small estates that belong to them), plus the messuage in Ipswich, are to go to his principal beneficiary, his sister's son, Osgot; and five estates are bequeathed among three further kinsmen – his sister's son, Offa, Offa's brother, and Osgot, Eadulf's son.[209] In its recognition of both public and private responsibilities, Theodred's will seems unexceptional.

In contrast, not only does Bishop Ælfsige of Winchester provide William of Malmesbury with an opportunity to indulge his pleasure in a good story, but his will is a rather different proposition from that of Theodred.[210] Ælfsige was appointed bishop of Winchester in 951, attested the charters of King Eadwig regularly, and on the death of Archbishop Oda (probably in 958), while the kingdom was still divided between Eadwig and Edgar, was elevated to Canterbury.[211] As a secular cleric his reputation did not fare well in the hands of William, whose highly-coloured account of Ælfsige's rise and fall could not be further from the approving tone of his biography of Theodred:

> *[Ælfsige] paratis aduocatis, quorum manus palpauerat, subreptoque regis Edgari edicto, Cantiam intrusus est. Primoque exceptionis die non abstinuit quin furias mente confotas euomeret, tumulum beati uir pede pulsans, animam voce lacessens … Sed illo exacto die, cum rabiei efflator cubili se dedisset, uidit beati uiri effigiem astantem et improperare conuitium et uelox minari exitium. Ille, qui uolatico fantasmate se derideri putaret, nichilominus ad recipiendum pallium Romam per Alpes contendebat. Ibi niuali frigore gelatus, nichil aliud remedii comminisci potuit quam ut exinteratorum equorum adhuc spirantibus extis immergeret pedes, quibus*

207 Other bequests seem to suggest his awareness of and support for the gathering tide of reform: he grants five pounds to Glastonbury, already reformed under Dunstan, and fifty mancuses of gold to the dowager queen Eadgifu, who was strongly identified with the reform movement.

208 This is considered by Pestell, *Landscapes*, p. 84; see Whitelock, *Anglo-Saxon Bishops*, pp. 19–20 for the suggestion that he may have had German connexions.

209 A certain Wulfstan, otherwise unidentified, is to receive one estate.

210 S1491/W4, *New Minster* 18, 951x958, preserved in the fifteenth-century *Liber Abbatiae* of the New Minster. The former *terminus post quem* of S1491 was 955, based on a charter (S565) granting the estate of Highclere to Ælfsige, now recognised as dubious: *New Minster*, p. 83.

211 The year of Oda's death is unclear, although 958 is most likely: Williams, '*Princeps Merciorum gentis*', p. 149; Brooks, *Early History*, pp. 237–8; Keynes, *Atlas*, Table XLVIII.

*Sancti sepulcrum uiolauerat. Sed nec sic algore tepente in mortem anima fugiente diriguit.*

([Ælfsige] got supporters together by greasing their palms, forged an edict from King Edgar, and was foisted upon Canterbury. On the first day of his reception there, he could not refrain from spewing out the bile that he had been fostering in his heart. He stamped on the grave of the blessed Oda, and abused his soul ... But that day over, when he had vented his rage and taken himself off to bed, he saw at the bedside the ghostly likeness of the blessed man, reproaching him for his insults and threatening him with a swift demise. He imagined this was but the mockery of some fleeting phantom, and was not deterred from setting off across the Alps to receive the pallium at Rome. Amid the cold snows he froze up. The only remedy he could contrive was to plunge his feet into the still breathing vitals of horses he had had disembowelled – the feet with which he had insulted the saint's tomb. Not even by these means could he warm himself up; his spirit departed, and he froze to death.)[212]

Within five years of Ælfsige's death, Bishop Æthelwold had expelled the secular canons from the cathedral and replaced them with monks. While the account of the canons' licentious behaviour in Wulfstan's *Vita Sancti Æthelwoldi* is no doubt exaggerated, it illustrates the tensions between the secular and monastic wings of the church.[213]

Ælfsige's will was, in all likelihood, drawn up in 958, in anticipation of the dangers of his journey to Rome to collect his pallium.[214] His episcopal church – the Old Minster, Winchester – is his principal ecclesiastical beneficiary. It is to receive only one estate directly – Ringwood (Hants.), which is subject to an unspecified previous agreement; in addition, Crondall and Tichbourne (Hants.), bequeathed respectively to Ealdorman Ælfheah and Wulfric Cufing for their lives, are to revert there. Like Theodred, Ælfsige bequeaths land to his kindred. His 'young kinsman' (*mægcnafan*) is to receive a life interest in Abbot's Ann (Hants.), with reversion to the New Minster.[215] 'The two Worthys' (probably Headbourne and Martyr Worthy, Hants.), Highclere (Hants.) and the other lands which had been held by Ælfsige's father would also revert to this 'young kinsman' after the lives of Ælfsige's kinswoman (*magan*) and sister.[216] Here, like Theodred, Ælfsige seems to be recognising the claims of collateral kin.

212 *Gesta Pontificum*, ed. Winterbottom and Thomson, i.17. 5–6; see Brooks, *Early History*, p. 375, n. 98 for the source of this story. I am indebted to Miller, *New Minster*, p. 83, for this and other references concerning Ælfsige.

213 *Wulfstan's Life of St Æthelwold*, ed. Lapidge and Winterbottom, chap. 16.

214 For such dangers, see Barlow, *The English Church 1000–1066*, p. 298, n. 7.

215 For the complex history of Ælfsige's estates see *New Minster*, p. 84.

216 The identity of Wulfric of Wickham and Ælfwig, who are each bequeathed an estate (in Ælfwig's case in reversion following the death of 'the widow' – presumably the current

However, the plot thickens. The kinswoman (*magan*) and young kinsman (*mægcnafan*) named as beneficiaries in his will were, in all likelihood, his wife and son, since the Godwine of Worthy who died in battle in 1001 is identified as Bishop Ælfsige's son in the *Anglo-Saxon Chronicle* account; he presumably acquired the cognomen on inheriting the life interest in 'the two Worthys' bequeathed to him in Ælfsige's will.[217] He was also to receive the reversion of Ælfsige's patrimonial land, which was to be held for her life by the woman who may have been Ælfsige's wife and Godwine's mother. Ælfsige's family might well have been an embarrassment to him in the contemporary climate, with its increasing emphasis on monastic chastity – hence the anonymity of the terminology.

If this identification of Godwine of Worthy, who was killed in 1001, as Ælfsige's son and the 'young kinsman' of the will, is correct, he must have been very young at the time of his father's death, and Ælfsige may have had good reason to be anxious about securing his inheritance. Furthermore, his own position as a secular cleric in turbulent political times may have made his dispositions vulnerable. It is therefore significant that, although he stipulates payment of his heriot and returns a leased estate (Taunton, Som.) to the king, it is to his friend Ealdorman Ælfheah that he makes a direct appeal for the protection of his will:

> *Þonne bidde ic minnan leofan freond Ælfheah þæt þu bewite ægþer ge þa land ge þa þe mine magas sien, and ꝥ þu ne geþafige þæt man þis on ænig oþer wænde.*
>
> (Then I pray my dear friend Ælfheah, that you will watch over both the estates, and those who are my kinsmen, and that you will never permit anyone to alter this in any way.)

In return for his support of Ælfsige's dispositions, Ælfheah is to receive a life interest in the substantial estate of Crondall (Hants.), which would revert to the Old Minster on his death.[218] Ælfsige's will seems to have stood, possibly through the support of Ælfheah, who lived on until 971/2: Godwine must have inherited land at the Worthys to have acquired his cognomen; Crondall was held by the Old Minster in 1066;[219] and Abbot's Ann was in the hands of the New Minster, presumably having reverted on Godwine's death, as stipulated by Ælfsige.[220] Although Ælfsige's will reflects the secular nature of his episcopate, there seems little reason to see his bequests as endorsing the castigation of his reputation by William of Malmesbury. William remarked of

holder), cannot be established. For Wulfric Cufing, who is to receive a life interest in Tichbourne, see *Wills*, pp. 115–16.

217 *ASC* A, s.a. 1001; *Wills*, pp. 114–15; Williams, *'Princeps Merciorum gentis'*, p. 149.

218 Ælfheah bequeathed Crondall to the Old Minster in his own will (1485/W9). For the political context for this friendship see p. 109 above.

219 DB I, fol. 41r.

220 For the history of Abbot's Ann, see *New Minster*, pp. 29–30.

a later archbishop, Stigand, 'he had no means of knowing how badly he was erring, but thought church business was conducted just like public affairs'.[221] Without the negative refraction of the monastic viewpoint, Ælfsige's will shows him fulfilling his responsibilities, both public and private, with reasonable integrity.

A further two contrasting wills – that of Archbisop Ælfric, made between 1002 and 1005, and Bishop Ælfric of East Anglia, made between 1035 and 1040 – are those of career churchmen operating in very different circumstances.

Archbishop Ælfric was closely associated with the monastic reform movement.[222] He was a monk at Abingdon, abbot of the reformed abbey of St Alban's, became bishop of Ramsbury in 990, and was archbishop of Canterbury from 995 until his death on 16 November 1005. At Abingdon, at the heart of the reformed church, he was remembered as a 'beacon among bishops',[223] yet he continued to hold the see of Ramsbury in plurality with Canterbury, and passed the abbacy of St Alban's to his brother, Leofric.[224] A secular dimension to his career is suggested by his bequest of considerable amounts of war-gear, including ships, reflecting the state of military alert which characterised this period of King Æthelred's reign as he struggled to mobilise the country against the Viking raiders.[225] Ælfric was known to have influence with King Æthelred; both the widow of Æthelric of Bocking, in her battle to persuade the king to allow her late husband's will to stand, and the wealthy landowner Wulfric Spott, who endowed the abbey of Burton in his will, sought Ælfric's advocacy at court.[226] In the words of Brooks, he was an archbishop 'whose career reveals a characteristic mixture of the virtues of the monastery and the acquisitiveness of the noble', features which are reflected in his will.[227]

It is possible that Ælfric's family originated in Gloucestershire, since he bequeaths two estates in that county (Fidington and Newton) to his sisters

221 *Nesciret quantum delinqueret, rem aecclesiasticorum negotiorum sicut publicorum actitari existimans.* (*Gesta Pontificum*, ed. Winterbottom and Thomson, i. 23. 3).

222 S1488/W18, *Abingdon* 133. This account of his career draws on *C&S*, pp. 237–8; *Wills*, pp. 160–1; *Abingdon*, part 2, p. 520; Brooks, *Early History*, pp. 286–7; *St Albans*, pp. 20–1.

223 *Inter pontifices rutilans ceu mystica lampas*; from an eleventh-century Abingdon epitaph, *C&S*, p. 237, n. 2.

224 For evidence of his links with the reform movement see *St Albans*, pp. 20–1.

225 As did Ælfwold, bishop of Crediton 987–1011/15 (the date of his death – and of his will – is uncertain): S1492/N&S10 (*C&S*, no. 51; *EHD* I, no. 122). The document survives as a contemporary single sheet: Keynes, *Facsimiles*, no. 18. Dating parameters of 1011x1015 have been suggested by Keynes, *Diplomas*, p. 121, n. 123. Ælfwold's successor, Eadnoth, first attests in 1015 (S934: Keynes, *Atlas* LXb). Ælfwold's bequests of movable wealth are considered in Chap. 5 below.

226 S939/W16[2], *Christ Church* 137; S1536/W17, *Burton* 29. Brooks, *Early History*, p. 286. See also *St Albans*, p. 21.

227 *Early History*, p. 286. S1488/W18, *Abingdon* 133, 1002x1005, preserved in the thirteenth-century Abingdon cartulary BL Cotton Claudius B vi. For dating see *Abingdon*, part 2, p. 520.

and their children. It seems that the family was wealthy: the will itself refers to Ælfric's purchase of two estates – Wallingford (Berks.) and an estate in London – while other charter evidence shows that he had purchased land at Dumbleton (Glos.), which also features in the will.[228] That Ælfric remitted money owed to him by the people of Kent, Middlesex and Surrey indicates that he had used his wealth to alleviate the pressure on those struggling to pay off the Danish raiders, a form of almsgiving and magnanimity available only to the most wealthy; it is also to be found in the will of King Eadred, who bequeathed a considerable sum 'for the redemption of his soul, and for the good of his people, that they may be able to purchase for themselves relief from want and from the heathen army, if they need to do so'.[229]

Ælfric's bequests can be compared not only with the multi-gift wills of other churchmen, but also those of ealdormen. Like Bishop Theodred, he recognises the claims of collateral kin – in this instance, those of his sisters and their children, who are to receive two estates; the additional instruction that 'the land of Ælfheah, Esne's son, is always to remain in his family', implies that Ælfheah has a life interest in an estate which is part of patrimonial land, and which is to revert to Ælfric's family on Ælfheah's death.[230] Whereas ealdormen may bequeath land to religious foundations to which they have a family or political commitment, Ælfric, like Theodred (and Bishop Ælfric of East Anglia, whose will is discussed below), distributes land among religious houses with which he was associated during his career: Abingdon is to receive Dumbleton (Glos.), reserving three hides for a certain Ælfnoth with reversion to the church after his death; Christ Church, Canterbury, is to receive Westwell and Bourne (both Kt) and Risborough (Bucks.) *to saulsceat* (as burial payment); St Alban's is to receive Tew (Oxon.) subject to an agreement with the current tenant (see below), and an estate in London; and Cholsey is to receive the reversion of Wallingford (Berks.) on the death of the current holder.[231]

These bequests, together with manumission of all men penally enslaved during his tenure and gifts of movable wealth to St Alban's make this a thoroughly appropriate, if not overtly pious, will. There are no requests for

228 S901, *Abingdon* 132. Wulfric Spott bequeathed to Ælfric land at Dumbleton which he had received by royal charter (S886; S1536/W17, *Burton* 29, 1002x1004); see *Abingdon*, part 2, pp. 517–20 for the relationship between these two parcels of land. *Eadingtune* (unidentified) had also been the subject of financial negotiations between Ælfric's brother, Leofric, and the king (see below). S916, *St Albans* 12 also shows Ælfric and Leofric purchasing forfeited land to endow St Alban's.

229 *... his sawla to anliesnesse 7 his ðeodscipe to þearfe ... to þan ðæt hi mege magan hungor 7 hæþenne here him fram aceapian gif hie beþurfan.*

230 *7 Ælfheages land Esnes suna ga a on his cyn*; this suggests the restricted transmission already seen in the wills of King Alfred and Ealdorman Alfred (n. 41 above).

231 Cholsey was in the diocese of Ramsbury: see *Abingdon*, part 2, p. 521 for the possible involvement of Ælfric in its foundation under King Æthelred.

prayers for Ælfric's soul, as in the case of Theodred. Indeed, it is a marked feature of this will that it encapsulates a number of negotiations and agreements concerning land which Ælfric took care to set forth in some detail, and which reveal a role in business affairs typical of a secular magnate. He refers to the purchase of two estates, one at Wallingford (Berks.) and one in London, which he bequeaths to the church. In addition, we have a glimpse of the archbishop at the centre of a web of tenants. He reiterates the terms of his agreement with Ceolric concerning Tew, which is to remain in place on the estate's reversion to St Alban's at Ælfric's death: Ceolric is holding part of the estate for his life, and a further seven and a half hides on lease, for which he paid the archbishop five pounds and fifty mancuses of gold; on Ceolric's death, the entire estate would revert to St Alban's, together with Osney (Oxon.) – presumably an estate held by Ceolric in his own right.[232] Ælfric seems not only to have been capable of driving a hard bargain, but also to have had an eye for detail: in bequeathing a life interest in three hides at Dumbleton to Ælfnoth, Ælfric adds ten oxen and two men, with the stipulation that 'they are to be subject to the lordship to which the land belongs', and must revert to Abingdon with the land on Ælfnoth's death.[233] However, his acumen and influence are most clearly seen in his direct address to the king concerning an unresolved land transaction relating to St Alban's:

> *7 he wilnode gif hit his lafordes willa wære þ he gefæstnode into sc̄e Albane þ land æt Cynges byrig 7 fenge sylf wið þam. eft to Eadulfingtune.*
>
> (And he wishes, if it were his lord's will, that he would confirm to St Albans the estate at Kingsbury, and himself retake possession of *Eadulfingtune* in return.)

We learn more details about this transaction from a charter of King Æthelred, dated 1005. Abbot Leofric, Ælfric's brother, had given two hundred pounds of gold and silver to the king for the purpose of paying Danegeld; in return, as a pledge, the king had granted him fifty-five hides at *Eadulfinctun* and six hides (probably the Kingsbury of the will) near St Albans.[234] The charter goes on to record the resolution of the transaction, which may have been prompted by the request in Ælfric's will: Leofric was now returning *Eadulfinctun* to the king, and had paid an additional two hundred pounds in order to retain the six hides.[235]

232 See Chap. 1, p. 36 above for this type of reversionary agreement.

233 *7 filgan hi þam laford scype þe þ land to hyre.*

234 S912, *St Albans* 11. This transaction must have taken place after *c.* 993, when Leofric succeeded his brother as abbot (*St Albans*, p. 186). For the identification of the estates, see *St Albans*, pp. 186–8, and *Abingdon*, part 2, p. 521.

235 This charter is not witnessed by Ælfric, suggesting that he may have been dead by the time it was issued: Keynes, *Diplomas*, pp. 260–1.

If the will of Archbishop Ælfric shows a churchman operating at the highest social and political level, that of Bishop Ælfric, made between 1035 and 1040 (during the reign of Harold Harefoot, who is mentioned in the will), gives the impression of a landowner at the heart of a network of local transactions and tenancies.[236] As has already been pointed out, Bishop Ælfric had acquired his estates through royal charter, gift and purchase.[237] With one exception, all the estates and beneficiary houses named in the will were within East Anglia.[238] Ælfric recognises his episcopal seats at Elmham (Nfk) and Hoxne (Sfk), both served by secular canons, with gifts of fenland, valued at one thousand pence in the case of Hoxne, with that bequeathed to Elmham perhaps worth something similar.[239] His most substantial bequest is to Bury, which had been refounded as a monastery by King Cnut, and had risen considerably in prestige; the house is to receive three estates, a messuage in Norwich, and a mill.[240] In addition, the monks are to pay sixty pounds for the estates at Titchwell and Docking (Nfk). Specific members of the Bury community are also named: Ufi the prior (*prouast*), who is to have a share in Egmere (Nfk); Leofstan the dean (*dæcane*) receives Grimston (Nfk) with full rights, and the monk Edwin the mill at Guist (Nfk).[241] It appears that Ælfric preferred to entrust responsibility for intercession on behalf of his soul to the monks of Bury, rather than to the canons of his episcopal churches: Worlingworth is bequeathed to Bury for the souls of Ælfric and the king, by whom (as the will tells us) it was granted to Ælfric, and the messuage in Norwich for Ælfric's soul and the souls of those who gave him the property. Two further estates in Norfolk (Fersfield and Walsingham) are to be sold 'as dearly as possible' (*swa man derast mage*) to fund bequests in coin and payment of debts. The local tenor of Ælfric's will is heightened by the inclusion of details of the origins of property, and the naming of former owners.[242]

236 S1489/W26. The possibility of two bishops of this name serving consecutively as bishops of East Anglia is discussed by Whitelock, *Wills*, p. 180; Campbell, 'East Anglian sees', p. 121, favours the Ælfric who died in 1038, an appointee of Cnut.

237 See nn. 192–4 above.

238 The exception is the messuage in London, bequeathed to St Peter's – possibly Westminster. It must be assumed that fenland bequeathed in the will was also local.

239 Campbell, 'East Anglian sees', (p. 121) notes the disparity between these gifts and Ælfric's bequests of five pounds each (or twelve hundred pence) to Ely, St Benedict at Holme, and even his tailor (*sæmestre*).

240 The refoundation took place *c.* 1020: Lawson, *Cnut*, pp. 142–3 and n. 108.

241 Leofstan witnesses the will of the local landowner Thurstan (S1531/W31). The priest Ælfwig, who receives Roydon, may also have been a member of the Bury community, since land there is listed under the lands of the abbot in DB (II, fol. 211v). Moulton (Sfk) is bequeathed to Sibriht, apparently a layman; land here was in the hands of Stigand *TRE* (DB II, fol. 372r). The affiliation of Ælfwine 'my priest at Walsingham', who is to share Egmere, is unclear.

242 The mill at Guist had been owned by Ringwaru; a further mill is identified by the name of its former owner Wulfnoth; and Ælfric had bought land at Roydon from Leofwyn,

Three further documents from the Bury archive reveal more clearly how churchmen might become embroiled in complex land transactions, sometimes for their own advantage. A brief excursion into the career of Stigand, archbishop of Canterbury, will provide a context.[243] Stigand had strong East Anglian connexions; his family held substantial property in Norwich, and Stigand himself continued to acquire land in this area.[244] He came to favour under Cnut, who appointed him royal priest at the church of *Assandun* in 1020. He became bishop of Elmham in 1043, was promoted to Winchester in 1047, and finally to Canterbury in 1052, a position he held until his deposition in 1070. On his elevation to Winchester, his brother, Æthelmær, succeeded him in the vacant see of Elmham which he, too, held until 1070, when he shared Stigand's downfall. Both men were secular clerics, and lived worldly lives: Æthelmær was married, with a son, and Stigand, apart from playing an active role in the politics of Edward's reign, accumulated huge personal wealth.[245] Smith has pointed out that Stigand's holdings are 'difficult to disentangle' from those of the bishopric and those of Bury, but he acquired at least some of his land – either legitimately, by purchase or lease, or illegitimately, by encroachment – from religious houses, including Bury.[246] A bequest-agreement copied into the Bury Sacrist's Register gives a glimpse of this relationship before Stigand became bishop.[247] Under this agreement, Stigand has leased an estate at Playford (Sfk) to his priest, Ælfgar, for his lifetime, with reversion to Stigand on his death; after the death of both Stigand and Ælfgar, the estate is to revert to Bury. The document was drawn up in duplicate, with one copy held by Stigand, and the other by Bury, and the transaction was apparently carried out in a prestigious forum, if the witness list is to be trusted: Bishop Ælfric and Abbot Ufi head the list, followed by a series of laymen who appear elsewhere in charters and appear to be important local figures – Ælfwine, Wulfweard's son, Ælfric, Wihtgar's son, Eadric (possibly of Laxfield), Ordgar

the widow of Thurketel of Palgrave, who had inherited it from her husband (S1527/W24).

243 For a summary of Stigand's career see M. F. Smith, 'Archbishop Stigand and the eye of the needle', *ANS* 16 (1994), 199–219 (pp. 199–204).

244 Stigand's property holdings, based on the Domesday survey, are surveyed by Smith, 'Archbishop Stigand', *passim*.

245 Æthelmær's wife is referred to in DB II, fol. 195r, and his son, Sæman, in a lease of Stigand in favour of Æthelmær (S1402/R106); Smith, 'Archbishop Stigand', pp. 200–202, 204.

246 Smith, 'Archbishop Stigand', p. 206.

247 S1224/R92, dated 1040 in a fourteenth-century Bury list of benefactors (*Charters*, p. 424; Davis, *Cartularies*, no.119). Stigand is given no attribution, which led Robertson (*Charters*, p. 424) to suggest that this was not the later archbishop, but a layman who also benefited under the will of Leofgifu (S1521/W29). However, since both transactions involve land in East Anglia, and given the archbishop's known relationship with Bury, the balance seems to be in favour of identifying both men with the clerical Stigand (see *Wills*, p. 188).

and Leofmær – as well as members of the Bury community and 'many more' witnesses.[248] There is no further evidence of such bequest-agreements on his part, or indeed of his will, but Stigand marches with some persistence through wills of the mid-eleventh century. He appears as a beneficiary in three wills: that of Leofgifu, in which he is bequeathed land at Willesham (Sfk);[249] that of Thurstan, a wealthy East Anglian landowner, who bequeaths half a mark of gold to Bishop Stigand, along with Earl Harold;[250] and that of Ketel, from whom the archbishop was to receive land at East Harling (Nfk), together with Ketel's heriot payment.[251] He also appears as a witness of three transactions concerning the bequest of land in East Anglia, including both Thurstan's multi-gift will and single-gift bequest;[252] the third transaction is a reversionary bequest-agreement between Æthelmær, 'the bishop's brother', and Abbot Ufi and the Bury community, drawn up between 1043 and 1044.[253] According to this document, Æthelmær had paid one mark of gold to the abbey for a life interest in 'the little estate' at Swanton (Nfk), which would revert to Bury on his death, together with the half estate (*halfe lond*) at Hindolveston (Nfk), which seems to have been his own property.[254] However, what appears to have been a straightforward bequest-agreement is complicated by the evidence of a further document, drawn up between 1047 and 1070, once Æthelmær had become bishop.[255] This document records Æthelmær's gift of four estates, together with fifty marks of silver, to Bury. Two of these estates are Swanton and Hindolveston, which were the subject of the previous agreement, but in addition Æthelmær grants estates at Langham and Hindringham (both Nfk). At first sight this looks like a straightforward *inter vivos* grant;[256] however, in the final clause the text refers to the document as Æthelmær's *cuide*, and the earlier bequest-agreement makes it clear that at least two of the estates, Swanton and Hindolveston, were intended to revert to Bury on Æthelmær's death. The fact that Æthelmær was still in possession of at least

248 For details of these landowners see *Charters*, pp. 425–6. Stigand's name appears between ecclesiastical and secular attestations.

249 S1521/W29, 1035x1044, but probably before 1043 since Stigand is unstyled; see n. 247 above for the identification with the future archbishop.

250 S1531/W31, 1043x1045. Harold also had significant landed interest in East Anglia.

251 S1519/W34, 1052x1066. Ketel is named in DB as a thegn of Stigand in relation to an estate at Walsingham (Nfk): II, fol. 254r; *Wills*, p. 198.

252 S1530/W30, *Christ Church* 166, 1042x1043, as priest; S1531/W31, 1043x1045, as bishop.

253 S1486/R97, 1043x1044, as bishop. Also as bishop he also holds one copy of a bequest-agreement S1470/R100 involving Bury.

254 The document was originally in duplicate, copies held by Æthelmær and Bury. Again the witness list is prestigious, including, after Stigand, Abbot Ufi, Leofstan the Dean (a beneficiary under Bishop Ælfric's will), Abbot Leofsige of Ely, Abbot Ælfsige of Holme, and local lay dignitaries: *Charters*, p. 432. Pestell, *Landscapes*, pp. 121–2 draws attention to the close relationship between these fenland communities.

255 S1499/W35, 1047x1070.

256 *Wills*, p. 402, and noted by Lowe, 'Nature and effect', pp 24–5.

two of the four estates in 1066 is further indication that the completion of this transaction was intended to be deferred until his death.[257] The inclusion of Swanton and Hindolveston in the later document (S1499/W35), without reference to the previous bequest-agreement (S1486/R97), confirms the possibility that other transactions which appear to be straightforward bequests may actually be ratifications of existing agreements for which documentation has been lost.[258] However this may be, these three documents suggest that the brothers Stigand and Æthelmær, established as both secular and ecclesiastical magnates in East Anglia, used the reversionary bequest-agreement to their advantage; as William of Malmesbury commented, it indeed seems that both of them 'thought church business was conducted just like public affairs'.[259]

The role that the bequest of land could play in secular and ecclesiastical politics is illustrated by the will of Eadsige, bishop-elect. Eadsige was a royal priest who, in the early 1030s, seems to have been chosen by Cnut for eventual elevation to the see of Canterbury; as part of this process, he was consecrated bishop in 1035, and acted as assistant to the ailing Archbishop Æthelnoth until his own succession in 1038.[260] The document survives only in later copies, but is probably to be dated between 1032 and 1035, before Eadsige became a bishop.[261] It is unusual in that it combines an *inter vivos* grant with *post obitum* dispositions, all concerning land in Kent. Two estates – Berwick and Orpington – are granted to Christ Church, Canterbury, during his lifetime.[262] Palster and Wittersham are to revert to the Christ Church community following his own death and that of his brother, Edwin.[263] The arrangement concerning the estates at Appledore and Warehorne is more complex: Eadsige has granted Appledore to Christ Church, but has paid the community four pounds in order that he and Edwin should have the use of it for their lifetimes, with payment of an annual food-rent; he has also paid four pounds to the community for the use of Warehorne for his lifetime and that of Edwin. Both estates would revert to Christ Church on the death of both brothers.

257 Æthelmær certainly held Swanton and Hindringham (DB II, fol. 192r), and probably Hindolveston and Langham (DB II, fols. 192v, 194r), since all four estates were held by the bishop of Thetford in 1086.

258 See S1536/W17, *Burton* 29 for Wulfric's bequest of land at Acton to Burton Abbey for two lives *ealswa þa foreword sprecað*.

259 See *Gesta Pontificum*, ed. Winterbottom and Thomson, i. 23. 3, quoted above at n. 221.

260 Brooks, *Early History*, pp. 258, 295–6.

261 S1465/R86, *Christ Church* 153. A fifteenth-century list of benefactors gives the date 1032 for Eadsige's gifts, but the main Christ Church cartulary (Lambeth Palace 1212; Davis, *Cartularies*, no. 159) gives 1035: Brooks, *Early History*, p. 387, n. 117.

262 In effect Eadsige was transferring the lease of Berwick to Christ Church at this stage: this bequest pre-dates S974 (1035) in which Cnut grants Berwick to Eadsige, now styled bishop, with full rights. Eadsige had bought Orpington for eighty marks of silver at the husting, but it is not clear whether this also refers to a lease.

263 Edwin is identified as the archbishop's brother in the witness list of S1400/R108.

On the face of it, this series of gifts seems to be an act of piety; the text records that the estates are given to Christ Church for the good of Eadsige's soul. However, it might more appropriately be termed an act of bribery. To begin with, we are told that 'King Cnut and the Lady Ælfgifu granted permission to Eadsige their priest, when he became a monk, to dispose of the estate at Appledore as pleased him best'.[264] This could be no more than the conventional permission of the king, were it not for the fact that Eadsige's becoming a monk was a means of insinuating a royal priest into the Christ Church community.[265] Not only this, the document ends with an explicit threat:

> *Đises cwides he geunn ðam Hirede to þam forwyrdan þ hi æfre hine wel healdan, 7 him holde beon on life 7 æfter life, 7 gif hi mid ænegan unrede wið hine ðas forwyrd tobrecan, þænne stande hit on his agenan gewealde hu he siþþan his agen ateon wille.*
>
> (He [Eadsige] grants this bequest to the community on condition that they always give him staunch support and are loyal to him during his life and death. And if by any folly they break this agreement with him, it shall be in his own power to decide how he will then dispose of his property.)

It is noteworthy that Eadsige's agreements with Christ Church are made specifically with the community, and his grants are for their benefit – Orpington as *scrudland*, or land to provide clothing for the community, and Palster and Wittersham *to fostorlande*, to provide food.[266] This agreement provided all parties with some advantage: Eadsige and his brother gained the use of valuable land; the Christ Church community had the long-term prospect of the reversion of land, as well as immediate food-rent and coin, to reconcile them to this royal priest introduced as a member of the community and archbishop-elect; and Cnut was successful in placing his own man in a position to gain the highest ecclesiastical office.[267]

It is likely that more wills and bequest-agreements were made by high-ranking churchmen than have survived.[268] It is significant, for instance, that the will of Archbishop Ælfric was preserved, not at Canterbury or St

264 *Cnut cyng 7Ælfgifu seo hlæfdige geuþan Eadsige heora preost ða he gecyrde to munece þ he moste ateon þ land æt Apoldre swa him sylfan leofast wære.*

265 Brooks, *Early History*, p. 295.

266 In 1086 Appledore, Warehorne and Orpington were listed as land of the archbishop's monks (DB I, fols. 5r, 4v); Berwick was held of the archbishop (DB I, fol. 4v). Wittersham has no separate entry, but Palster was in the hands of the bishop of Bayeux (DB I, fol. 10v); Robertson points out that the pre-Conquest tenant is given as Eadwig the priest, and suggests a scribal error for Eadwine, possibly Eadsige's brother (*Charters*, p. 419).

267 Brooks, *Early History*, pp. 258, 295–6, and, for the political problems of Eadsige's pontificate 1038–1050, pp. 298–303.

268 The list of Bishop Leofric's gifts to Exeter recorded in a gospel book in a hand of *c.* 1070 may include bequests: *Charters*, Appendix 1, no. 1 (Bodleian Library, MS Auct. D. 2. 16 (2719), fols. 1–2v; Ker, *Catalogue*, no. 291).

Alban's, but at Abingdon, possibly because the estate of Dumbleton, with which it is concerned, later became the subject of dispute.[269] Similarly, that of Bishop Ælfsige was not preserved at the Old Minster, Winchester, in spite of its interest in several properties mentioned in the will, but at the New Minster.[270] What emerges from those documents which have survived is that, in spite of their spiritual role, bishops were as preoccupied with the acquisition, manipulation and transmission of land as any secular lord. As spiritual magnates, they endowed their churches through the bequest of land; as secular magnates, they deployed land through their bequests for the benefit of their kin and for political purposes.

## The bequest of land and the local network

This chapter has so far been concerned with those who lived their lives, and made their bequests, in the glare of public life at the highest social and political level. The wills of thegns, however, show that the bequest of land was of considerable significance and interest in a local context.[271] The *Liber Eliensis*, for instance, tells us that Siferth of Downham announced his dispositions not only at Ely, but also at a local forum near his home.[272] The few witness lists which have been preserved in wills record the presence of local thegns as well as local churchmen when the will was declared or read aloud. Thurstan's single-gift bequest of Wimbish (Ex) to Christ Church, Canterbury is attested not only by named local thegns, of whom one (Ælfric, Wihtgar's son) administered royal land in East Anglia, and another (Leofcild) was the shire-reeve of Essex, but also by *ealle þa þegenas on Eastsexan*;[273] his multi-gift will lists witnesses in Norfolk, Suffolk, Cambridgeshire and Essex, all shires where he held land, again including Leofcild among the Essex witnesses and Ordgar, the shire-reeve of Cambridgeshire, among the witnesses of that county.[274] The same principle of local witness seems to have applied in towns: the port-reeve of London attests Brihtmær's bequest of his homestead at Gracechurch

269 *Abingdon*, part 2, pp. 519–20.

270 *New Minster*, p. 84.

271 For the significance of land in establishing thegnly status see Chap. 4, pp. 140–1 below.

272 Chap. 2, pp. 58–9 above.

273 S1530/W30, *Christ Church* 166, surviving as a contemporary single sheet. Ælfric witnesses S1084, 1078 (see also *CR* 103, where he challenges the will of a kinsman); he was a royal servant (Stafford, *Queen Emma and Queen Edith*, p. 110). For remaining witnesses see *Wills*, pp. 188, 192.

274 S1531/W31, surviving as a thirteenth-century cartulary copy. For remaining witnesses see *Wills*, pp. 196–7. These lists suggest that both the bequest and will of Thurstan were read aloud at meetings of the shire; see also S1462/R78 for the presence of the shire-reeve at the hearing concerning the bequest of land in Herefordshire. The witnesses of Siferth's will-making included local lawmen: see Chap. 2, n. 11 above.

Map 2. The landholding of Benedictine monasteries in East Anglia as recorded in Domesday Book, reproduced with the permission of T. Pestell from his *Landscapes of Monastic Foundation: the Establishment of Religious Houses in East Anglia, c. 650–1200* (Woodbridge, 2004), Fig. 24.

to Christ Church, Canterbury, while the witnesses of Æthelweard's bequest-agreement with Christ Church concerning Ickham included a gathering of those living both within and without the city walls (*innanburwara 7 utanburhwara*), and the *micle mættan* – possibly a gild – as well as representatives of the church communities.[275]

Any change in land tenure was potentially of local significance, but the bequest of land to the church contributed to the profound social and economic impact of the great monastic houses on their local region, as studies of Continental land transactions have demonstrated. The work of Innes on

275 S1234/R116, *Christ Church* 183; S1506/R32, *Christ Church* 121 (the terminology here is discussed by Robertson, *Charters*, pp. 316–17, and Brooks and Kelly, *Christ Church*, no. 87).

the charters of the Middle Rhine Valley between 400 and 1000 has shown how the Church had become 'an important patron and social actor from the level of the elite to that of the village'.[276] Attention has been drawn by Rosenwein to the importance of land donations to the abbey of Cluny as a means of establishing social cohesion in an otherwise fragmented society.[277] Similarly, in his study of early medieval East Anglia Wareham has explored the significance of lordly patronage of the church 'in serving to consolidate local and regional frameworks'.[278]

In tenth- and eleventh-century East Anglia it must indeed have been very difficult for those holding land to avoid being a neighbour of at least one of the powerful monastic houses which pursued vigorous policies of land acquisition. The activities of Bishop Æthelwold at Ely, ably supported by Abbot Byrhtnoth, reveal the hard-headed approach to land acquisition adopted by some churchmen seeking to establish a land-base for their houses.[279] A study by Raftis of the economic history of Ramsey Abbey has suggested that, between them, Ealdorman Æthelwine and Bishop Oswald were involved in transferring over 100 hides of land to the new house; by 1086, Ramsey held roughly 318 hides and 28 carucates in measurable land, as well as fisheries, urban property and a number of estates which cannot be measured.[280] The impact of such land transfer must also be seen in the context of the foundation or refoundation and land endowment of neighbouring houses at Crowland, St Neots, Peterborough and Thorney, all of which contributed to the density of monastic landholding (see Map 2).[281]

Both the *Liber Eliensis* and *Chronicon Rameseiensis* show the respective houses embroiled in local land disputes. Abbots of major houses wielded considerable power, with contacts at court and in the higher echelons of the church: for example, Ramsey abbots witnessed royal charters from the accession of Æthelred to the death of Edward the Confessor (that is, from 978–1066), and Ramsey provided three bishops of Dorchester and a bishop of London between 1006 and 1049.[282] Ramsey's influence at court is demonstrated by the account of the challenge mounted to the will of Æthelwine the Black, probably made *c.* 1049, in which he bequeathed four estates to Ramsey.

276 M. Innes, *State and Society in the Early Middle Ages: the Middle Rhine Valley 400–1000* (Cambridge, 2000), p. 49.

277 Rosenwein, *To Be the Neighbor of St Peter*, p. 75.

278 *Lords and Communities*, p. 23.

279 For alleged extortion involving Bishop Æthelwold, see *LE* II, 10/*Lib* 8.

280 Raftis, *Ramsey*, p. 7.

281 Peterborough, Thorney and Crowland were founded/refounded *c.* 970, and St Neots 975x984: Pestell, *Landscapes*, pp. 107, 122.

282 Keynes, *Atlas*, Tables LX1–LXVII; Barlow, *The English Church 1000–1066*, pp. 102–103, 219. For an account of a local dispute in early medieval Italy illustrating the power of the Church see R. Balzaretti, 'The monastery of Sant' Ambrogio and dispute settlement in early medieval Milan', *EME* 3.1 (1994), 1–18.

His kinsman, Ælfric son of Wihtgar, an influential landowner in Suffolk, claimed to be the rightful heir to the land since the king had not confirmed the bequest. Royal support for Ramsey was bought by Abbot Ælfwine's gift of twenty gold marks to King Edward, and five to Queen Edith. There may also have been a political dimension to this decision, since Ælfric had been a high-ranking servant of Queen Emma, and the decision to favour Ramsey may signal a shift of royal favour under the new regime, with the monks well placed to extend their own influence.[283] Where disputes were heard in the shire court, the church was strongly represented, as in the case of the dispute between Sherborne Abbey and Care, Toki's son, concerning land at Holcombe (Dev.) heard *c.* 1046 by the shire court of Devon.[284] The simplest explanation of yet another enigmatic document is that Toki had bequeathed the estate to his son Ulf, but on Toki's death Ulf's brothers challenged his inheritance and occupied the land. Care, one of the brothers, presumably represented their case in the shire court. Ulf's interest was represented by the community of Sherborne Abbey, supported by Bishop Ælfwold of Dorset. The Devon court – which included Earl Godwine, father of the future King Harold, Bishop Lyfing and the abbots of Tavistock and Buckfast – confirmed Ulf's life interest in the land, with reversion to Sherborne Abbey on his death. The court ordered the other brothers to leave the land. Here, the influence of the abbey in the shire court triumphed, at the expense of the kindred.[285]

One will hints at the tensions which could arise between the laity and their monastic neighbours. Thurketel of Palgrave made his multi-gift will at some point in the early years of the eleventh century, probably before 1038.[286] It does not specify a heriot payment, so there is no means of identifying his status other than by the bequests he makes: he names six estates on the border between Norfolk and Suffolk, suggesting that he may have been a substantial property owner like Ketel, inhabiting that murky area between lesser and king's thegn. Thurketel makes a bequest to Bury for his soul, but the final dispositive clause suggests the potential for dispute between lay landholders and a major religious house:

> *And þe mor þe ic 7 þo munekes soken ymbe min del fremannen to note so he er deden . er daye 7 after daye.*

283 *CR* 103; Stafford, *Queen Edith and Queen Emma*, pp. 112, 150 for a possible political dimension. The evidence for bribery in the *Libellus* is discussed by Kennedy, 'Law and litigation', p. 153.

284 S1474/R105, *Sherborne* 17. III Edgar 5. 2 stipulates the presence of the bishop as well as the ealdorman at the shire court.

285 O'Donovan suggests that Holcombe may have been in the gift of King Cnut, leased to Toki as a loyal follower (*Sherborne*, p. 59).

286 S1527/W24.

(And [I grant] the moor, about my portion of which the monks and I contended, for freemen to use, both before my death and after it, as they did before.)

Although this clause is characteristically context-dependent, relying on contemporary local knowledge for its interpretation, some of the background to it may be deduced. The abbey of Bury seems to have encroached on moorland over which Thurketel had some rights, infringing established local custom, perhaps of free grazing. The past tense of the Old English verb *sacan* (to strive or contend) implies that the dispute had been resolved, possibly in a local court.[287] Thurketel's formal grant of land to local freemen in his will presumably represents a ratification of the settlement reached with the abbey, which was to hold one copy of the document (Thurketel and the bishop were to hold further copies). It is conceivable that the will was drawn up in the context of such a settlement.

The wills of thegns preserved in the Bury archive reflect vividly the complex tenurial issues which pertained in East Anglia at this time. Many show a process of subdivision of parcels of land, often with portions reserved from a main bequest to endow a local church. This is spectacularly the case in the will of Edwin. The document as it now stands consists of a list of Edwin's gifts of land to the church, incorporating an agreement with his nephew, Ketel, which would result in the reversion of estates at Thorpe and Melton (both Nfk) to Bury and Holme respectively.[288] Although the details are not absolutely clear to the modern reader, Edwin grants small parcels of land to fifteen local churches (in one case to the *ealde kirke*, possibly at Wreningham, Nfk). In some cases, land is reserved from the main estate (see Table 2). In one instance, as in a number of wills, a local landmark is cited to clarify the boundaries of land parcels: at Bergh, Edwin bequeaths to Ely land south of the *kinges strete*, a Roman road, reserving ten hides for Bergh church; land north of the *strete* is distributed among four other local churches, including Apton, with which Bergh (Nfk) was later to be united.[289] Ketel identifies a rather less permanent boundary for land which he bequeaths to the church: 'where the enclosure (*geard*) reaches Leofric's hedge (*hyge*)'.[290]

The will of Thurketel of Palgrave provides further evidence for the subdivision of estates.[291] It includes bequests recognising the claims of his wife

287 *Sacan* has as one of its meanings the legal sense of bringing a suit (B&T, *sacan* III).

288 S1516/W33. There is the possibility that Thorpe was held on a two-life lease from Bury, since Edwin refers to Ketel's payment of an agreed rent; see Ketel's will (S1519/W34) for reference to this agreement, and DB II, fol. 204v.

289 Roman roads as landmarks also occur in S1501/W16[1] and S1522/N&S9. Today, Street Farm, Bergh Apton, may mark the line of this boundary. St Martin's, Apton, was demolished in the nineteenth century.

290 S1519/W34.

291 S1527/W24.

**Table 2.** Edwin's bequests of land in Norfolk to local churches (S1516/W33)

| Estate bequeathed | Main beneficiary church | Local beneficiary church |
|---|---|---|
| Algarsthorpe | Bury | Algarsthorpe (10 acres) |
| Little Melton | Holme | Little Melton (10 acres) |
| Bergh (south of king's street) | Ely (except the north enclosure at *Appelsco*) | Bergh (10 acres)<br>Apton (half turf-pit with access 2 rods wide) |
| Bergh (north of king's street)[1] | | Apton (10 acres)<br>Holverstone (4 acres)<br>Blyford (4 acres)<br>Sparham (4 acres) |
| Great Melton | Holme (reversion) | Great Melton (land owned by Thurweard[2] + Edwin Ecgferth's son) |
| Thorpe[3] | Bury (reversion) | Ashwell (8 acres) |
| Wreningham | | 'old church' (8 acres)<br>Fundenhall (2 acres)<br>Nayland (2 acres) |

1 It is unclear whether Ely is also to receive land north of the street.

2 *At Metheltone into þere kirke þe Þurwerd ahte*: the context suggests that Thurweard owned the land, not the church.

3 Later joined to Ashwell as Ashwell Thorpe.

and male kin, and men of unspecified relationship who hold land from him, possibly at the level of lesser thegn – Osbeorn, Ælfwold and Wulfwine.[292] He also grants freedom and some rights in their landholding (however nominal those rights may have been in practice) to 'his men' who were tied to the land.[293] In addition, Thurketel endows a local estate church, as well as making bequests to the bishop and the community at Bury. Of the five estates bequeathed, only one is a simple grant – that of Wingfield (Sfk), which is bequeathed to Thurketel's brother's sons, Ulfketel and Thurketel. Three estates are subdivided. Palgrave (Sfk) is granted to St Edmund at Bury for Thurketel's soul, but fifteen acres at Palgrave, with a toft, is bequeathed to

292 Thurketel's heriot is not given; see Chap. 4, p. 141 below for the qualification for the status of king's thegn, including men under him holding five hides.

293 Each of them was to have his homestead (*toft*), his cow and his corn (see Chap. 5, nn. 40–42 below).

Leofcwen, his wife. Following this clause come three further bequests which may also refer to Palgrave:

> *And Wlwine habbe þat lond þe he mines hafde. 7 Alfwold habbe mid ton þe he her hauede .XVI. acres mid tofte mid alle. And Osebern habbe þat lond beside Thrandestone þat ic þer hauede.*
>
> (And Wulfwine is to have that land of mine which he held. And Ælfwold, as well as the ten (?) which he had before, is to have sixteen acres with a toft and everything. And Osbeorn is to have the land near Thrandeston which I have had there.)

It is unclear from the context whether these estates are to be regarded as separate from Palgrave, or subdivisions within it, as was presumably the case with the parcel of land which Thurketel bequeathed to his wife.[294] If the latter was the case, Palgrave may have been divided among as many as five beneficiaries.[295] Roydon (Nfk) is also subdivided, this time into three parcels, but here we find references to what appears to be the local field system: half is bequeathed to Thurketel's wife, according to an agreement (*to þat forwarde þat we spreken habben*); a further parcel is bequeathed to the estate church at Roydon (the middle furlong at Roydon hill (*berh*), *Scortland* and the priest's toft); and a further twenty acres are granted to Leofric, Thurketel's nephew (*neue*), Godwine, Thurketel's kinsman, and Wulfwine and his brother. Whether these bequests constituted the whole of Thurketel's holdings at Roydon is unclear.[296] A further estate, Whittingham (Sfk), is to be divided between the community at Bury and the bishop. In contrast, Thurketel bequeaths to his wife an estate at Shimpling (Nfk) which has actually been consolidated after its acquisition from two sources: part of it was *ceapland* (purchased land), and part of it was given to him on their marriage – presumably as part of a marriage agreement.

This group of Bury wills also reveals that the complexity of the local hierarchy complemented the complexity of local landholding. This is best illustrated by the will of Ketel, who was still alive in 1066, when his lands were sequestered. He stipulates a heriot payment which identifies him as a lesser thegn in the Danelaw; this is to be paid to Archbishop Stigand, 'my lord', to whom Ketel also bequeaths an estate at Harling (Nfk), and his status as a thegn of Stigand is confirmed by a Domesday entry for one of his estates

294 Thrandeston is very close to Palgrave, and may have shared a boundary.

295 Bury held 4 carucates at Palgrave *TRE*, with 28 men holding '2 carucates less 12 acres' (DB II, fol. 361r).

296 For the open field system see O. Rackham, *The History of the Countryside: the Classic History of Britain's Landscape, Flora and Fauna* (London, 1986; reprinted London, 2000), pp. 164–179; D. Hooke, *The Landscape of Anglo-Saxon England* (Leicester, 1998), esp. Chap. 6 and pp. 115–31.

(Walsingham in East Carleton, Nfk) where he is described as such.[297] Nevertheless, the same entry shows that he was substantial enough to have a free man holding seventy-five acres at East Carleton. Matters are further complicated by a separate Domesday reference to him as a thegn of King Edward in relation to his land at Onehouse (Sfk).[298] The penultimate dispositive clause in Ketel's will, addressed to Earl Harold, hints at the complex tenurial arrangements which could exist between lord and man:

> *And ic an þe lond at Fretinge after þat ilke forwarde þat þu þe self and Stigand Archebiscop mine louerd wrouhten.*
>
> (And I grant the estate at Frating according to the agreement which you yourself and Archbishop Stigand my lord made.)

The nature of this agreement is, of course, obscure at this distance, but it is possible that Ketel was holding only a life interest in the land.[299] Like Thurketel of Palgrave, Ketel also uses his will to state his claim to land which had been subject to dispute, appealing to Earl Harold in his will for protection of an estate *æt Moran* (unid.) occupied by his enemies (*mine vnwinan*), bequeathing to Harold half the estate in question. He asserts that he and his wife acquired the land 'in the witness of God and many men' (*on godes witnesse and mani manne*), and had since 'neither lost it by lawsuit nor forfeited it' (*nawer ne forswat ne forspilde*).[300] It seems that, whereas for ealdormen the bequest of land was likely to be influenced by high politics, for thegns it was likely to be embedded in the local network.[301]

## The impact of the Norman Conquest

A few multi-gift wills reveal vividly the impact of the catastrophe of 1066. A number made in the 1040s and 1050s were overtaken by events, and failed

297 DB II, fol. 254.

298 DB II, fol. 416v. For such multiple commendation see, for example, Williams, 'Land and power', pp. 178–81; and, for the complexities of tenure in DB, C. P. Lewis, 'The Domesday jurors', *Haskins Society Journal* 5 (1993), 17–44 (pp. 24–32).

299 Ketel held Frating (Ex) as a manor and two hides in 1066 (DB II, fol. 75v). Both Stigand and Harold were significant landholders in East Anglia; Williams, 'Land and power', pp. 172–4 for Harold's holdings in 1066, and p. 176 for commendation to him; Stigand's power is summarized by Barlow, *The English Church 1000–1066*, pp. 78–9, and linked to 'Godwine ambitions in East Anglia' by E. John, 'The end of Anglo-Saxon England', in *The Anglo-Saxons*, ed. Campbell, pp. 214–39 (p. 230).

300 *Forswat* is probably a scribal misreading of *forsp[r]ac*, from *for-sp[r]ecan*, B&T, II: to lose that which is the subject of a [law]suit; *forspillan*, B&T, III: to lose. For this phrase see *Wills*, p. 204 and S981/R85, l. 12. I am indebted to Dr K. A. Lowe for advice on this point.

301 Wareham argues for the emergence of a local gentry in East Anglia in the first third of the eleventh century: *Lords and Communities*, Chap. 5.

to take effect. Thurstan, making his will between 1043 and 1045, bequeathed 'everything which I have in Norfolk', to his wife, confirming their marriage agreement;[302] in addition she would receive two estates in Essex (Pentlow and Ashdon) apparently outright, as well as a life interest in others bequeathed to the church or to individual priests.[303] Æthelgyth survived her husband, and was in possession of her substantial inheritance in 1066.[304] However, by 1086 her lands had been re-allocated, most to Ralph Bainard, and some probably to Reynold, son of Ivo.[305] Land which should have reverted to the Church on her death remained in the hands of her Norman successor. The wills of Æthelgyth's contemporaries Edwin and Ketel were also overtaken by the events of 1066; both were in possession of their land on the day King Edward was alive and dead, and both were displaced by Normans.[306]

The multi-gift will of Ulf and Madselin, drawn up in the aftermath of the Conquest, between November 1066 and 1069, gives some sense of the effect on individuals.[307] It announces itself as a *foreweard* (agreement), made in advance of the donors' pilgrimage to Jerusalem, and a number of the dispositions are indeed of the nature of agreements. Although little is known of Ulf, the limited evidence which is available reveals him as a man of status in the Danelaw. His family seems to have held land primarily in Lincolnshire: his father, Tope, had held an estate at Kilmington, where Ulf also had land; his mother, Eadgifu, was holding a number of estates in Lincolnshire in 1066, including two, Messingham and Kettleby, which are mentioned as in her possession when the will was drawn up;[308] his brother, Halfdan, also named in the will, similarly held land in Lincolnshire.[309] Ulf and his brother were kinsmen of Abbot Brand of Peterborough, with whom the fortunes of the family became entwined in the difficult years after the Conquest.[310] Ulf

302 S1531/W31: the phrase is *to munde and to maldage*, a Scandinavian formula (*Wills*, p. 195).

303 Wimbish (Ex), Shouldham (Nfk). Kedington (Sfk) was to be shared by Thurstan's chaplain and priest, and a further named priest.

304 This has been estimated at 60 hides, valued at about £120: Meyer, 'Women's estates', p. 118.

305 *Wills*, p. 190.

306 S1516/W33; S1519/W34. See also S1235/*St Albans* 17.

307 W39/*Peterborough* 27; Pelteret, *Catalogue*, no. 68: surviving in the twelfth-century section of the *Liber Niger*, a Peterborough register (Davis, *Cartularies*, no. 754). The dating parameters are provided by the appointment of Brand, who features in the will, as abbot of Peterborough in November 1066, and his death in 1069; Whitelock suggests that the *terminus ante quem* may be refined to 1068 (*Wills*, p. 207), but see *Peterborough*, pp. 314–15.

308 DB I, fol. 362rv.

309 DB I, fol. 344rv.

310 Fleming, *Kings and Lords*, pp. 139–40; *Peterborough*, pp. 118–19.

himself held property valued at approximately £105 *TRE*.[311] Nothing at all is known of his wife, Madselin, beyond this document.

The will itself gives no hint of the turbulent political situation in which it was declared. The dispositions are complex, taking account of the spiritual needs of the donors and the need to protect family land. The first dispositive clause bequeaths land at Carlton, Bytham and Sempringham (all Lincs.) to the fenland abbeys of Peterborough, Crowland and Ramsey respectively, for the redemption of the donors' souls. An unexceptional arrangement, were it not for the fact that, according to Domesday Book, these estates were held *TRE* by Morcar, who became Earl of Northumbria in 1065. It is unclear upon what grounds Ulf and Madselin were in a position to bequeath these estates to the Church, although the most likely explanation is that they were commended to Morcar and held the land from him.[312]

The second dispositive clause confirms a series of transactions between Ulf and Archbishop Ealdred of York. First, it records Ulf's sale of two estates – Lenton (formerly Lavington, Lincs.) and Hardwick in Witchley (Northants., formerly Lincs.) – to the archbishop.[313] That this sale actually took place is confirmed by the evidence of the wapentake at a Lincolnshire *clamor*, recorded in Domesday Book.[314] The second transaction between Ulf and the archbishop involves a mortgage: Ealdred held a mortgage on Ulf's land at Skillington (Lincs.), Hoby (Leics.) and Morton (unid.), having paid eight marks of gold to Ulf which would be repaid, and the land reclaimed, if he and Madselin returned safely from pilgrimage.[315] A contingency plan had been agreed: in the event of Ealdred's death, Ulf's kinsman Abbot Brand would take over the mortgage; Ulf's bequest to Brand of an estate at Manthorpe (Lincs.), is probably an acknowledgement of his support in the mortgage negotiations.

At this point, the will changes focus to record a series of dispositions made

311 Fleming, *Kings and Lords*, Table 5.1, p. 175. For the suggestion that he was a royal seneschal see A. C. E. Welby, 'Ulf of Lincolnshire before and after the Conquest', *Lincolnshire Notes and Queries* 14 (1917), 196–200 (p. 197). He is listed among witnesses to King William's confirmation of King Edgar's charter S787, *Peterborough* 16f (spurious in its present form, but possibly incorporating authentic material: *Peterborough*, p. 315).

312 *Peterborough*, p. 315; Baxter, *Earls*, p. 267.

313 Ealdred is referred to as bishop in the will, but had become archbishop in 1061. For the identification of these estates see *Peterborough*, pp. 316–17.

314 At some point the archbishop had been disseised of these estates, but had then been reseised: the wapentake confirm that they had seen the king's seal: DB I, fol. 376v; *Peterborough*, pp. 314–15.

315 See S1500/R3, *Christ Church* 39A for a similar arrangement with Archbishop Wulfred of Canterbury to fund a pilgrimage; S1187/*EHD* I, no. 81 records Æthelric, son of Æthelmund's mortgaging of his land, and reclaiming it on his return from pilgrimage. Hoby was held by Ulf in 1066 (DB I, fol. 236r), but Skillington was held by Morcar (DB I, fol. 340r). *Peterborough*, p. 317.

by Ulf and Madselin, individually or jointly.[316] Ulf makes further grants to kinsmen: *Willaby* (Wilby, Northants?) to Siferth, and Claxby (Lincs.) to his brother, Halfdan. The Ingemund who is granted *Coringatune* (Kilmington, Lincs.?) is possibly also a kinsman.[317] A further estate (Limber, Lincs.) is granted to his servants (*mine cnihtas*). Madselin bequeaths an estate (Stoke Rochford, Lincs.) to her kinswoman, Leofgifu. Both husband and wife record what appear to be reversionary agreements: Madselin has granted Stroxton (Lincs.) to Ingemund, and in return he has granted her the west hall at Winterton (Lincs.);[318] Ulf has granted his land at Kettleby and Keelby Cotes to his mother, and she has granted to him a separate estate at Kettleby, and Messingham.[319] Further pious gifts are recorded: an estate at Ormsby to St Mary's Church (both Lincs.), a foundation endowed by Earl Leofric of Mercia and his wife Godgifu; Madselin's estate *æt Lohtune* (Laughton, Lincs?) to Thorney; and proceeds from the sale of Overton (Leics?) to be distributed on behalf of the donors' souls.

It is clear that a number of gifts recorded in this document were intended by the donors to take effect *post obitum*: estates are to revert to Peterborough, Crowland and Ramsey 'after their day, for the redemption of their souls'; Overton is to be sold to subsidise a pious distribution; Madselin's land 'which she has' at Laughton is to revert to Thorney; and Ulf's gifts of land to Ingemund, and to be shared by his servants, are specifically to take effect if he fails to return from his journey. In contrast, the arrangements for the sale and mortgage of estates to fund the pilgrimage were already in place when the document was drawn up. The status of other gifts is less clear, although the use of the perfect tense of the verb *geunnan* suggests that these, too, had already taken effect. For example, Ulf states that 'I have granted' (*ic hæbbe geunnan*) land to Abbot Brand and Siferth, and Madselin 'has granted' (*hafað geunnan*) land to her kinswoman; Ulf 'has granted' estates to his mother, while she 'has granted' estates to him in return.[320] The document therefore seems to be an amalgam of bequests and the confirmation of *inter vivos* transactions.

The agreements between Madselin and Ingemund and Ulf and his mother may be paralleled by Ketel's arrangements with his sisters in advance of his own pilgrimage. He makes provision for the reversion of estates to them, together with a mark of gold, in the event of his death; the fact that the same

316 Ulf continues to appear in the first person, but Madselin is designated only by the third person pronoun.

317 For the identification of these estates see *Peterborough*, pp. 317–18.

318 Both estates granted by Madselin – Stoke Rochford and Stoxton – were held by Morcar in 1066: DB I, fol. 360v. Such an arrangement with Ingemund suggests that he was a kinsman.

319 Eadgifu was holding these two estates in 1066: DB I, fol. 362r.

320 Kelly notes that DB records Ulf's sale of four and a half hides at Ormsby to St Mary's, Stow, which was holding the land on his death, suggesting that this gift, too, had already been completed: *Peterborough*, p. 317; DB I, 376r: *clamores*.

arrangement allows him to inherit from them, should they pre-decease him, indicates that he had every intention of continuing to hold his own land should he return safely from his journey.[321] Perhaps Ulf and Madselin had come to similar arrangements with their own kin, the land in question to be held in guardianship for them – in other words, their grants may have awarded temporary tenure rather than outright gift.

While it is impossible to be certain about the context in which Ulf and Madselin made their dispositions, a strong possibility, given the dating parameters of the will, must be the aftermath of the rebellion against King William which took place in the North in 1068.[322] The fact that they appear to have been holding land from Earl Morcar who, with his brother, Edwin, had submitted to William after the Conquest, suggests their allegiance to him. The role of these earls in the rebellion of 1068 is unclear, but their position and that of their men may have been compromised by events.[323] This seems to have been the case with Ulf's brother, Halfdan, to whom the brothers' kinsman, Abbot Brand, leased an estate because he had been dispossessed, losing his lands to the bishop of Lincoln.[324] Brand himself, having offered allegiance to Edgar Ætheling on the abbey's behalf, was in a precarious position, retaining his position only on a payment of forty marks of gold to King William.[325] At the time when the will was drawn up, Ulf's mother, Eadgifu, was still in possession of her estates, but she, too, would ultimately be dispossessed. For Ulf and Madselin, pilgrimage may have seemed the best option, offering at least the hope of better times and an opportunity to reclaim their land.

It is a testimony to the strength of the tradition of vernacular will-making that, even at this time of confusion, danger and insecurity, Ulf and Madselin had recourse to it as a means of ordering their affairs. Their will may have been preserved in Peterborough records as evidence of the community's claim to land which it never received: most of Ulf's property, including the estate at Carlton bequeathed to Peterborough, went to Drogo de Beuvrière.[326] It is not known whether Ulf and Madselin undertook their pilgrimage, nor, if they did, whether they returned. Nor is it known at what point they realised that their careful dispositions on behalf of their souls and their kindred had been in vain.

321 S1519/W34, 1052x1066.

322 *The Ecclesiastical History of Orderic Vitalis: Vol. II, Books III and IV*, ed. and transl. M. Chibnall (Oxford, 1969), pp. 215–19; Fletcher, *Bloodfeud*, pp. 171–4; Baxter, *Earls*, pp. 273–8; A. Williams, *The English and the Norman Conquest* (Woodbridge, 1995), pp. 32–9.

323 Williams, *The English and the Norman Conquest*, p. 53.

324 DB I, fol. 360rv; Fleming, *Kings and Lords*, pp. 140–1, 165 and n. 104. Halfdan's dispossession must have taken place before Brand's death in 1069.

325 *Peterborough*, p. 118.

326 *Peterborough*, pp. 316–17.

## The bequest of land in context

This chapter has shown how bequests of land reflect the complex networks of allegiance and power to which these donors belonged. Since it seems likely that most wills were made in advance of mortal illness and were declared publicly, the dispositions they contained were an assertion of wealth and status which was likely to reverberate for the remaining years of a donor's life.

It is also clear that individual donors were often responding to specific circumstances in bequeathing land, taking account of religious and political change, dynastic considerations or local tenurial issues. Through their bequests they might seek to articulate, manipulate, reinforce or protect relationships with individuals or institutions. This might be seen on a grand scale, as in the wills of King Alfred, Ealdorman Ælfheah or Archbishop Ælfric; but it is also evident in the wills of lesser men such as Thurketel of Palgrave or Ketel whose bequests negotiate the complexities of local tenurial issues and the local hierarchy. There is a particular poignancy in the bequests of Bishop Ælfsige and Ulf and Madselin who, in different ways, used their wills to navigate turbulent political waters.

The focus in this chapter has been largely on the public and political aspects of the bequest of land. In contrast, the next chapter focuses on a very different, more personal aspect: considerations of family.

# CHAPTER FOUR

# Lay bequest of land: pious gifts and family strategy

For lay donors across the full social spectrum, two factors consistently influenced bequests of land: the Church and the family. The alienation of land to the Church for spiritual benefit, for individual or family commemoration, needed to be balanced with the needs, or expectations, of the kindred. The way in which men and women managed these apparently conflicting claims in their wills is the focus of this chapter.

Compared with the kings, ealdormen and bishops whose wills were the primary focus of the previous chapter, the majority of lay donors were of lower social status, rarely featuring in the historical record beyond their wills.[1] The detailed heriot clauses included in the wills of some male donors, approximating to the tariffs set out in the law of King Cnut, indicate that they most probably belonged to the rank of king's thegn, or thegn closer to the king in the Danelaw.[2] In only one case – that of Ketel – is the payment that of a lesser thegn in the Danelaw.[3] For thegns, as for ealdormen, land was crucial in establishing their status. This is demonstrated by two texts associated with Archbishop Wulfstan of York (1002–1023).[4] The first, known as *Geþyncðo*, establishes the basic qualification for promotion from ceorl to thegn:

> *7 gif ceorl geþeah, þæt he hæfde fullice fif hida agenes landes,* ***cirican 7 kycenan****, bell****hus*** *7 burhgeat, setl 7 sundernote on cynges healle, þonne wæs he þanon forð þegenrihtes weorðe.*
>
> (And if a ceorl prospered, [so] that he possessed fully five hides of land of his own, (a church and a kitchen), a bell(tower) and a gatehouse, a seat

1 Twenty-six male and thirteen female donors, with eight wills made jointly by men and women. S1482/H2, *Christ Church* 70 is generally regarded as a joint will; since the multi-gift will is attributed to Abba, and is written in a different hand from the endorsement in the name of his wife, Heregyth, they are treated here as individual donors.

2 II Cnut, 71.1–71.5. S1490/W28; S1487/W13; S1501/W16[1], *Christ Church* 136; S1505/W12; S1517/*St Albans* 15; S1519/W34; S1531/W31; S1534/W19; S1536/W17/*Burton* 29; S1537/W27. Joint: S1511/W11/*Rochester* 35. For heriot tariffs and wider discussion of heriot see Chap. 5, pp. 190–3 below.

3 S1519/W34.

4 For the relationship between these two texts, and their association with Archbishop Wulfstan, see Wormald, *English Law*, pp. 391–4.

and a special office in the king's hall, then was he henceforth entitled to the rights of a thegn).[5]

The significance of the five hides of land is emphasised in the second text, *Norðleoda laga*:

> *And þeah he geþeo, þæt he hæbbe helm 7 byrnan 7 golde fæted sweord, gif he þæt land nafað, he bið ceorl swa þeah.*
>
> (And even if he prospers [so] that he possesses a helmet and a coat of mail and a gold-plated sword, if he has not the land, he is a ceorl all the same.)[6]

Further promotion could also be achieved, according to *Geþyncðo*:

> *7 gif þegen geþeah, þæt he þenode cynge 7 his radstefne rad on his hirede, gif se þonne hæfde þegen, þe him filigde, þe to cinges* ***utware fif*** *hida hæfde 7 on cinges sele his hlaforde þenode 7 þriwa mid his ærende gefore to cinge, se moste siððan mid his foraðe his hlaford aspelian* ***æt mistlicon neodan*** *7 his onspæce geræcan mid rihte, swa hwær swa he þorfte.*
>
> (And the thegn who prospered, [so] that he served the king and rode in his household band on his missions, if he himself had a thegn who followed him, possessing five hides on which he discharged the king's dues, and who attended his lord in the king's hall, and had thrice gone on his errand to the king – then he was afterwards allowed to represent his lord with his preliminary oath at various necessities, and legally obtain [his right to pursue a] charge, wherever he needed.)[7]

Again, a vital element is the land qualification, this time on the part of the follower. Although it is often difficult to be precise about the hidage of the estates bequeathed in wills, and the documents do not necessarily dispose of a donor's entire landed property, the significance of the bequest of land in terms of status, not only for the donor but also for potential beneficiaries, was considerable.

The physical world of this landed class is a vivid element in wills, reflecting not only the description in *Geþyncðo*, but also the evidence of archaeology. When donors bequeath a residence, we might envisage a manorial complex of the type excavated at sites such as Goltho (Lincs.) and Raunds (North-

5 *Geþyncðo*, chap. 2: Liebermann, *Gesetze*, I, 456; *EHD* I, no. 51a (p. 468). The sections in bold are found only in the twelfth-century *Liber Roffensis*. I have amended Whitelock's 'castle gate' to 'gatehouse' following A. Williams, '"A bell-house and a burh-geat": lordly residences in England before the Norman Conquest', in *Medieval Knighthood* IV, ed. C. Harper-Bill and R. Harvey (Woodbridge, 1992), pp. 221–40 (p. 227); see also S. Draper, 'The significance of OE *burh* in Anglo-Saxon England', in *Anglo-Saxon Studies in Archaeology and History* 15, ed. S. Crawford and H. Hamerow (Oxford, 2008), pp. 240–53 (p. 245).

6 *Norðleoda laga*, chap. 10: Liebermann, *Gesetze*, I, 460; *EHD* I, no. 51b (p. 469).

7 *Geþyncðo*, chap. 3: Liebermann, *Gesetze*, I, p. 456; *EHD* I, no. 51a (p. 468).

ants.): a hall with separate domestic buildings within an enclosure, with an associated church.[8] In two wills donors bequeath a *heafodbotl*, probably the principal residence, and possibly the administrative centre, of an estate.[9] Estate churches may feature in wills, either as beneficiaries, as in the wills of Edwin and his nephew Ketel, or as bequeathed property, as in the case of Brihtmær's church of All Hallows.[10] The complexity of estate structure is illustrated by the bequest of tofts, and references to meadowland, fenland, woodland and moorland, as well as cultivated land.[11] The personnel necessary for the running of such estates feature regularly in wills as beneficiaries, and occasionally as chattels: priests, reeves, men and women of the household, some with specialist functions, receive chattels, freedom and land. Leofgifu grants land to two reeves (*reue*) and three stewards (*stiward*) as well as her household priest (*hirdprest*); Ælfhelm Polga bequeaths half a stud to *minan geferan þe me mid ridað* (my companions who ride with me); Wynflæd refers to enslaved women who served as weaver and seamstress, and Æthelgifu to swineherds, a goldsmith, a huntsman and a dairymaid.[12] In addition to their rural estates, donors may hold property in one of the burgeoning towns: for example, Æthelric Bigga agrees the reversion to the Church of the *haga* (tenement) which he had built in Canterbury.[13]

It seems likely that many of these thegnly donors were linked to wide-ranging aristocratic kindred networks.[14] The Mercian landholder Wulfric Spott, for example, whose will is dated between 1002 and 1004, may have

8 G. Beresford, 'Goltho Manor, Lincolnshire: the buildings and their surrounding defences c. 850–1150', *ANS* 4 (1981), 13–36; A. Boddington, *Raunds Furnells: the Anglo-Saxon Church and Churchyard*, English Heritage Archaeological Report 7 (London, 1996). The evidence has been surveyed by Williams, '"Bell-house"', *passim*, and J. Blair, 'Hall and chamber: English domestic planning 1000–1250', in *Manorial Domestic Buildings in England and Northern France*, ed. G. Meirion-Jones and M. Jones (London, 1993), pp. 1–16 (pp. 1–9). For the *burh* as a high-status enclosure see Draper, 'The OE *burh*', p. 248. Residences are bequeathed in: S1234/R116, *Christ Church* 183 (*homstal*); S1497/*St Albans* 7 (*staðol*); S1593/W3 (*worþige*); see also the reference to Ælfgar's 'houses and court' (*domos suas et curiam*) at Burwell in *CR* 25.

9 S1538/W21, *Bath and Wells* 21 and S1522/N&S9. Thurstan's estate at Shouldham (Nfk) is divided into two halls: the *Midelhalle* and the *Northhalle*; a third (south) hall is implied, and may be indicated in DB II, fols. 250v-251r, 231r (S1531/W31); Williams, '"Bell-house"', p. 228. See also W39/*Peterborough* 27, where the 'west hall' is the subject of an exchange.

10 S1516/W33; S1519/W34; S1234/R116, *Christ Church* 183. For proprietary churches, see Chap. 6, pp. 261–4 below.

11 See, for example, S1490/W28; S1527/W24; S1528/W25; S1501/W16[1], *Christ Church* 136; S1534/W19. S1531/W31 refers to a deer-enclosure (*derhage*) and a stud. Æthelgifu's estate at Standon (Herts.) included a vineyard (S1497/*St Albans* 7).

12 S1521/W29; S1487/W13; S1539/W3; S1497/*St Albans* 7. For slaves in wills see Chap. 5, pp. 183–6 below.

13 S1471/R101, *Christ Church* 170.

14 See Chap. 3, pp. 107–8 above for the kindred networks of ealdormen.

been the son of Wulfrun, whose abduction from Tamworth by Olaf Guthfrithson is recorded in the Anglo-Saxon Chronicle for 943, and who is credited with founding a religious house at Wolverhampton.[15] Wulfric seems not to have held office, but is referred to by the king in the charter confirming his endowment of Burton Abbey as *nobilis progeniei minister* (a thegn of noble lineage); his heriot is not fully specified, but approximates to that of a king's thegn.[16] His brother Ælfhelm, a beneficiary of the will and one of its designated protectors, was the ealdorman of Northumbria killed – possibly by Eadric Streona – in 1006, after Wulfric's death; Wulfric's nephews, Ufegeat and Wulfheah, also beneficiaries, were blinded.[17] Morcar, the thegn of the Seven Boroughs who fell foul of Eadric in 1015, was the father of Wulfric's goddaughter, and may have been married to Wulfric's niece; he was certainly a substantial beneficiary of land under the will.[18] Given the turmoil of the latter years of Æthelred's reign, it is tempting to see Wulfric's bequest of eleven estates to Morcar as a political gesture as well as one of family solidarity.[19]

The East Anglian landholder Thurstan, like Wulfric, stipulates the heriot of a king's thegn, but one appropriate to a thegn closer to the king in the Danelaw.[20] He belonged to a dynasty established in East Anglia over three generations, and with a history of patronage of the fenland abbey of Ely which was recorded in the *Liber Eliensis*.[21] Through the family of his mother and grandmother he could claim kindred with Byrhtnoth, Ealdorman of Essex and patron of Ely, whose descent from the Mercian royal house has been postulated;[22] he could claim affinity with the family of Ealdorman Ælfgar through Byrhtnoth's marriage to Ælfgar's daughter, Ælfflæd, whose

15 S1536/W17, *Burton* 29. S1380, which records the endowment of Wolverhampton by Wulfrun, may be spurious. For the likely identity of individuals associated with Wulfric see *Burton*, pp. xxi–xxiii, xxxviii–xliii and *Wills*, pp. 152–3. See also K. A. Lowe, 'Never say *nefa* again: problems of translation in Old English charters', *Neuphilologische Mitteilungen* 94 (1993), 27–35 (pp. 29–30).

16 S906, *Burton* 28, 1004. The payment of 200 mancuses as part of his heriot, as opposed to the 50 required by the tariff, may be a commutation of some of the weapons required, but may also reflect his noble birth: *Burton*, p. xx.

17 *ASC* s.a. 1006.

18 *Burton*, p. xliii; *ASC* s.a. 1015. Morcar and Siferth are named in the will of the ætheling Æthelstan (S1503/W20, *Christ Church* 142; see Chap. 3, pp. 101, 103).

19 Wulfric's only direct descendant named in the will is his *earman dehter*, who is granted a life interest in two estates. His brother Ælfhelm is granted four estates, his nephew Wulfheah three, sharing in addition lands 'between the Ribble and the Mersey, and in Wirral' with his father, while Ufegeat, Wulfheah's brother, receives only one.

20 S1531/W31, 1043x1045. The complexities of these tariffs are discussed in Chap. 5, pp. 191–3 below.

21 See Locherbie-Cameron, 'Byrhtnoth', *passim*, with a reconstructed family tree at pp. 253–62. Byrhtnoth's kindred and their relationship with Ely are discussed by Wareham, *Lords and Communities*, Chap. 4, with an extended family tree on p. 48.

22 Hart, 'The ealdordom of Essex', p. 131; Locherbie-Cameron, 'Byrhtnoth', p. 253.

older sister was the second wife of King Edmund; and through his father, Lustwine, he may have been linked to the powerful East Anglian family of Æthelstan Mannessune. Two of Thurstan's ancestors died in battle against the Danes: his maternal great-grandfather, Ealdorman Byrhtnoth, was killed at Maldon in 991, and his maternal grandfather, Oswig, died at Ringmere in 1010.[23] The *Liber Eliensis* records the generosity of Thurstan's parents, listing estates which they bequeathed to the abbey.[24]

Some donors acquired wealth and status from service to royalty or the aristocracy. For example, the ninth-century wills of Abba and Æthelnoth describe them as reeves, the latter designated reeve of Eastry, a royal estate.[25] Leofgifu, whose will is addressed to the queen rather than the king, was in the service of Queen Emma, as was her kinsman Ælfric, son of Wihtgar, a beneficiary of the will.[26] Another aspect of service on the part of one donor is preserved incidentally in the account of the miracles of St Edmund, written *c.* 1100 by Hermann, probably a monk at Bury. Hermann records that Ælfwyn, a recluse at St Benedict at Holme, was the daughter of Thurketel Heyng who bequeathed land to Bury and St Benedict at Holme probably in the second quarter of the eleventh century; Ælfwyn told him that her father had collected tax for King Swegn before the latter's death in 1014, upon which Thurketel is said to have returned the money.[27] In addition, patterns of charter attestation show some male donors in regular attendance at court, as in the case of Wulfric Spott, who witnesses charters of King Æthelred from the 980s to his death *c.* 1002.[28]

Many thegns remain shadowy figures, in some cases known only from their wills, but they nevertheless held, and bequeathed, substantial amounts of land, sharing with ealdormen preoccupations concerning its disposal, particularly in respect of their endowment of the Church and the pattern of bequests to kin. A few documents show husbands and wives acting together, usually to bequeath land to the Church, but a small group of women emerges in widowhood to make bequests of land independently. This chapter shows

23 *ASC* s.a. 991, 1010.

24 *LE* II, 89. A number of these estates also feature in Thurstan's will; see p. 160 below.

25 S1482/H2, *Christ Church* 70; S1500/R3, *Christ Church* 39A. See also King Cuthred's charter in Æthelnoth's favour (S41) which styles him *praefectus meus*.

26 S1521/W29; Stafford, *Queen Emma and Queen Edith*, pp. 110, 112, 181 n. 95; C. R. Hart, 'The Eastern Danelaw', in Hart, *The Danelaw*, pp. 25–113 (p. 69).

27 S1528/W25. *Wills*, p. 180; *Heremanni Archidiaconi Miracula Sancti Eadmundi*, ed. F. Liebermann, *Ungedruckte Anglo-Normannische Geschichtsquellen* (Strasbourg, 1879), pp. 203–81 (chap. 8); for the date of Hermann's text see A. Gransden, 'The legends and traditions concerning the origins of the Abbey of Bury St Edmunds', *EHR* 394 (1984), 1–24, (p. 5). See Lawson, *Cnut*, pp. 25–7 for Swegn's activities in England, and *ASC* s.a. 1013 for his demands for payment.

28 *Burton*, pp. xxxviii–xxxix; Keynes, *Atlas*, Table LXIII.

men and women, generally making their wills at different points in the life-cycle, responding to a range of different factors in making their dispositions.[29]

## The bequest of land by laymen

As in the case of ealdormen, thegns bequeath land which may have been acquired in a number of ways.[30] The will of Wulfric Spott, although it is uncharacteristic in the sheer number of estates of which it disposes, illustrates this well, referring to land acquired through purchase, gift, inheritance and royal charter, as well as that held by lease.[31] Occasional references by other donors show similar origins for the estates bequeathed, and some royal charters exist granting the estates which feature in wills.[32]

In a study of widowhood in pre-Conquest England, Crick has suggested that the death of a wife may have been a significant factor in prompting the will-making of laymen, identifying a group of ten male donors who make *inter vivos* grants or wills as widowers, the wills referring to daughters, but without mention of either wives or sons.[33] The implications of this, as Crick points out, may be that the absence of a son, with no expectation that one

29 The following discussion is based on the analysis of wills in my published doctoral thesis: L. Tollerton Hall, 'Wills and Will-Making in Late Anglo-Saxon England' (University of York, 2005), Chap. 3.

30 S1487/W13; S1490/W28; S1471/R101, *Christ Church* 170; S1501/W16[1], *Christ Church* 136; S1506/R32, *Christ Church* 121; S1505/W12; S1510/R6, *Christ Church*, 78; S1234/R116, *Christ Church* 183; S1512/W7; S1514/R9, *Rochester* 23; S1516/W33; S1517/*St Albans* 15; S1455/R62; S1519/W34; S1522/N&S9; S1527/W24; S1528/W25; S1530/W30, *Christ Church* 166 and S1531/W31 (same donor); S1532/*St Albans* 13; S1533/R26; S1534/W19; S1536/W17, *Burton* 29; S1537/W27. The will of Abba (S1482/H2, *Christ Church* 70) is included; his wife's bequest appears as a separate endorsement in a different hand: Brooks, *Early History*, p. 360, n. 70. S1509/R27 and S1496/W6 (*New Minster* 11, 21) are excluded on grounds of forgery.

31 S1536/W17, *Burton* 29: godfather's gift of Elford and Oakley (see *CR* 33 for a gift made at the font); *þæs þe Scegð me becwæð* (that which Scegth bequeathed to me); Appleby, *þe ic gebohte mid minum feo* (that I bought with my money); reversion to the church of leased land *æt Actune*, Longdon and Bupton. The charter by which Wulfric acquired Dumbleton (Glos.) is S886.

32 Inheritance: S1501/W16[1], *Christ Church* 136; purchase: S1534/W19, S1487/W13, S1517/*St Albans* 15, S1527/W24 (the donor also refers to land received when he married his wife). S1471/R101, *Christ Church* 170 grants a *haga* built by the donor. Wills bequeathing land held by charter: S1510/R6, *Christ Church* 78 (land near Canterbury, S296); S1512/W7 (Rimpton, S571); S1505/W12, *New Minster* 29 (Manningford, S865, *New Minster* 28); S1487/W13 (Wratting, S794); S1533/R26 (Ham and Collingbourne, S416 and S379, *New Minster* 8).

33 Crick, 'Men, women and widows', pp. 30–1. The wills identified are: S1519/W34, S1483/W2, S1536/W17, *Burton* 29; S1533/R26, although the contemporary endorsement recording Wulfgar's gift to the Old Minster need not necessarily indicate that his wife had predeceased him.

would be born, could have stimulated the making of a written will in order to protect the donor's *post obitum* dispositions where there was no apparent heir.[34] While widowhood may indeed have been an important factor, when the evidence of this sample of documents is placed in the context of the full corpus of vernacular wills by individual male donors, it seems unlikely that the death of a spouse was the only factor which prompted male will-making. King Alfred's will, of course, bequeaths considerable quantities of land to his wife, sons and daughters, but both ealdormen and thegns show consistent concern to bequeath land within the conjugal unit.[35] Three ealdormen and almost half of the thegns whose wills are extant bequeath land to their wives; in addition, three lay male donors whose bequests are recorded in the Ramsey Chronicle refer to wives.[36] Eight male donors bequeath land to daughters,[37] and eight make bequests to sons.[38] As far as the evidence goes, these categories do not seem to be mutually exclusive; laymen may make bequests to wives and daughters, wives and sons, or to all three.[39] It therefore seems that the motives for will-making were more complex than might at first appear.

An important factor influencing the bequests of a number of laymen was the need to specify the claims on land of wives and daughters, whose interests may have been vulnerable to predation, particularly from male kin, on the death of the donor.[40] This is made particularly clear in the opening clause of Ealdorman Alfred's will, in which he states that he wishes to notify the king and *witan* of 'the persons on whom I most happily bestow my inherit-

34 Crick, 'Men, women and widows', pp. 31–2.

35 For King Alfred's bequests of land see Chap. 3, pp. 87–90 above; they are not included in the analysis here, although his bequests to kin are not uncharacteristic.

36 Ealdormen: S1498/W10, *New Minster* 25; S1485/W9; S1508/H10, *Christ Church* 96. Thegns: S1482/H2, *Christ Church* 70; S1538/R26; S1501/W16[1], *Christ Church* 136; S1534/W19; S1531/W31; S1527/W24; S1528/W25; S1487/W13; S1234/R116, *Christ Church* 183; S1510/R6, *Christ Church* 78; S1517/*St Albans* 15; S1505/W12. *CR* 33, 34, 53 (Æthelstan Mannessune, Ælfwold, Godwine).

37 Ealdormen: S1508/H10, *Christ Church* 96; S1483/W2. Thegns: S1487/W13; S1234/R116, *Christ Church* 183; S1528/W25; S1536/W17, *Burton* 29; S1534/W19; S1519/W34 (stepdaughter).

38 Ealdormen: S1498/W10, *New Minster* 25; S1485/W9; S1508/H10, *Christ Church* 96. Thegns: S1471/R101, *Christ Church* 170; S1539/W13; S1234/R116, *Christ Church* 183; S1517/*St Albans* 15; S1505/W12. S1508/H10, *Christ Church* 96 also makes provision for a future son, and S1482/H2, *Christ Church* 70 refers to the prospect of a future child .

39 Wives and daughters: S1534/W19, S1528/W25; wives and sons: S1517/*St Albans* 15, and S1505/W12; S1485/W9; S1498/W10, *New Minster* 25; all three: S1487/W13, S1234/R116, *Christ Church* 183; S1508/H10, *Christ Church* 96 (and see *CR* 33, the will of Æthelstan Mannessune). S1483/W2 bequeaths to daughters only (it is possible that the Æthelweard and Wiswith for whom prayers are to be said in this will are the late son and wife of Ealdorman Ælfgar).

40 For disputes see p. 73 above and p. 168 below. For the bequest of land to wives and daughters see nn. 36, 37 above.

ance and my bookland' – namely his wife and daughter.[41] Alfred goes on to bequeath six estates, totalling 104 hides, to Wærburh, his wife, and his daughter, Ealhthryth, 'our joint child' (*uncer gemene bearn*).[42] On Wærburh's death, two of these estates, totalling 38 hides (Sanderstead and Selsdon, and Lingfield, Surrey) are to go uncontested (*unbefliten*) to Ealhthryth, and then to her child (*bearn*) if she should have one;[43] if Alfred's kinsmen wish to acquire the remainder of Ealhthryth's estates, she is to receive compensation for them. Ealhthryth's interests are also protected in Alfred's bequest-agreement with Christ Church, Canterbury, in which Alfred bequeaths his estate at Chartham (Kt) to Christ Church in return for a life interest in the community's estate of Croydon (Sy); Alfred stipulates that on his death Ealhthryth is to have first refusal of leasing Chartham from the community.[44]

In at least three instances, bequests of land to wives are linked to marriage agreements, which sought to secure a woman's property in widowhood, and could involve her being endowed with land by her husband and her own kindred. A widow's position was defined in the law-code of King Cnut, which states:

> *And sitte ælc wuduwe werleas twelf monað 7 ceose heo syððan þæt heo sylf wille. 7 gyf heo ðonne binnon ðæs geares fæce wer geceose, ðonne ðolie heo ðære morgengeafe 7 ealre þære æhtan ðe heo þurh þone ærran were heafde, 7 fon þa nyxtan frynd to þam lande 7 to þam æhte þæt heo ær hæfde.*
>
> (And every widow shall remain twelve months without a husband, and she shall afterwards choose what she herself desires. And if within the space of a year she chooses a husband, she shall lose her morning-gift and all the property which she had from her first husband, and his nearest relatives shall take the land and the property which she had held.)[45]

The contemporary procedural text known as *Be Wifmannes Beweddunge*, dating to the time of Archbishop Wulfstan (1002–1023), states that the prospective bridegroom is to make a gift in return for the woman's acceptance of his offer of marriage, and then announce 'what he grants her if she should live longer than he' (*hwæs he hire geunne gif heo læng sy ðonne he*).[46] Furthermore, the wife

41 S1508/H10, *Christ Church* 96: *þa men þe ic mines erfes 7 mines boclondes seolest onn.* For the full text see Chap. 1, pp. 22–3.

42 Sanderstead and Selsdon (listed as a joint estate), Clapham, Horsley (Sy); Westerham, Longfield (?), Nettlestead (Kt).

43 The terms *bearn* and *cild* occasionally occur; although these are not gender-specific they may refer to sons in the context of wills: L. Lancaster, 'Kinship in Anglo-Saxon society, parts 1 and 2', *British Journal of Sociology* 9 (1958), 230–50, 359–77 (p. 236). See S1483/W2, S1528/W25.

44 S1202/H8, *Christ Church* 95.

45 II Cnut, 73–73a.

46 Wormald, *English Law*, p. 386–7; printed with translation in *C&S*, pp. 427–31(quotation at p. 429).

is to be entitled to half the property (*yrfe*) on widowhood (all of it if they should have a child) unless she should remarry, whereupon the agreement would become void.[47]

Two contemporary marriage agreements survive, representing individual negotiations. The first is an account of an agreement between Godwine and Brihtric, made at Kingston before an assembly including King Cnut, the community of Christ Church, Canterbury, and lay witnesses. It begins in the past tense and the third person, recording that the bridegroom, Godwine, offered gold as an inducement to the woman to accept him, and two estates, thirty oxen, twenty cows, ten horses and ten slaves, presumably as her endowment.[48] Following the witness list for this transaction, we are given a further list of those who stood surety when the bride was brought from Brightling (presumably her home); the text then changes to the first person and present tense, representing the words of the bride's father, Brihtric, who confirms that what he has granted to the couple (which is unspecified) is to be held by the surviving partner (*7 swa hwæðer heora læng libbe fo to eallan ætan ge on ðam lande þe ic heom gaf ge o ælcon þingan*).[49] Brihtric retained a copy of the document. There is no indication on what terms Godwine's grant of land to his prospective wife was made: it is possible that if she survived him, she would hold land from both her husband and her father in her own right.

The second marriage agreement to survive asserts that the woman is to have free disposal of one estate as well as a life interest in others.[50] It records the agreement made between Archbishop Wulfstan and Wulfric, who offered marriage to the archbishop's sister. Wulfric promises his wife two estates for her lifetime, a leasehold estate for three lives from the abbey at Winchcombe, and an estate in her own right to dispose of freely (*to gyfene 7 to syllenne ðam ðe hire leofest wære on dæge 7 æfter dæge ðær hire leofest wære*); he also promises her (*behet hire*) fifty mancuses of gold, thirty men and thirty horses.

Reference to such agreements is found in a number of laymen's wills. Thurketel of Palgrave grants to his wife, among other estates, 'the other which I received when I married her; and half Roydon ... on those terms which we have agreed' (*7 þat oþer þat ic mid hire nam and half Reydone ... to þat forwarde þat we spreken habben*).[51] Thurketel Heyng refers explicitly to his wife's freedom of disposition:

47 As would apparently be the case if the widow of Eadwine of Caddington were to remarry: S1517/*St Albans* 15.

48 S1461/R77, 1016x1020. The manuscript has been lost, the text surviving only in an eighteenth-century version. The document was produced in triplicate, one copy held by Brihtric, the bride's father.

49 The change of pronoun may indicate the amalgamation of two separate documents representing different stages of the transaction.

50 S1459/R76, 1014x1016. This manuscript has also been lost.

51 S1527/W24.

**Table 3.** Ælfhelm's bequests of land to his wife (S1487/W13, 975x1016)

***Her morning-gift:***
Baddow (Ex)
Burstead (Ex)
Stratford (Sfk)
Enhale (Cambs.): 3 hides

***Land he gave her 'when we first came together':***
Wilbraham (Cambs.): 2 hides[1]
Rayne (Ex): ? 2 hides[1]

***By agreement:***
Half of the stock at each estate (*tun*) irrespective of holder, 'as it was granted to her'.

***Additional bequests:***

| | |
|---|---|
| Carlton (Cambs.) | |
| Gestingthorpe (Ex): | *heafodbotl*, all the property on it and *mid mete 7 mid mannum*[2] |
| | woodland and open land shared with her daughter (and her daughter's husband?) |
| | reserved bequest to priest |
| Conington (Cambs.): | half the estate shared with daughter (reserving 4.5 hides which are bequeathed elsewhere) |
| Troston (Sfk): | stud shared with 'my companions who ride with me' |
| | half of 'what is on the woodland' shared with daughter. |

1 The context suggests that, in both cases, the land is bequeathed fully stocked (*7 þ þærto lið*).
2 *Heafodbotl*: principal residence; *mid mete 7 mid mannum*: see Chap. 1, n. 106 for this formula.

*An mine wyues del euere unbesaken to gyfen and to habben þer hire leuest be.*

(And my wife's portion is to be ever uncontested, for her to hold or give where she pleases.)[52]

The will of Ælfhelm Polga shows the degree to which a wife's inheritance from her husband might be the result of prior agreement, itemising six estates related to their marriage (see Table 3). Unfortunately, no indication of the terms of these agreements is given, so it is unclear whether his wife was free

52 S1528/W25.

to dispose of at least some of them, as was the wife of Thurketel Heyng, or whether they would revert to the Church or Ælfhelm's kin on her death.[53]

Bequests of land by male donors to wives and daughters are generally, although not invariably, for life, in most cases with reversion to the Church.[54] These women therefore inherited responsibility for land which was committed to earn spiritual benefit for the soul of the donor, and perhaps those of his kin, as well as their own. Ealdorman Ælfheah expresses his confidence in his wife's integrity:

> *Þonnæ an ic Ælfsithæ minon wifæ gyf heo leng beoð þonne ic and it swa gehylt swa ic hiræ truwan to hæbbe ealra þara oðæra landa þæ ic læfæ.*
>
> (Then to my wife Ælfswith, if she live longer than I and holds the property in accordance with the trust I have in her, I grant all the other estates which I leave.)

If Ælfswith is the *vidua sanctimonialis* who receives land from King Edgar in 970, it is possible that she did indeed survive her husband, and may have become a vowess in widowhood.[55] Overall, the amount of land bequeathed to daughters is relatively small – usually limited to one or two estates – but the daughters of Ealdorman Ælfgar inherited responsibility both for the administration of considerable property destined in his will for reversion to the Church, and for the fulfilment of his bequests, probably in the absence of a son.[56]

One factor which does not seem to have influenced either ealdormen or thegns in their bequest of land was the creation of an heir in the sense of an individual who would succeed to the bulk of the donor's property.[57] Where sons are named in wills they receive remarkably little land. Ealdorman Ælfheah, whose enormous landed property has been described above, bequeaths only one estate each to his sons Godwine and Ælfweard.[58] Ealdorman Æthelmær's

53 Other wills referring to agreements are S1508/H10, *Christ Church* 96 (*word gecweodu*); S1498/W10, *New Minster* 25 (*wedde*). S1482/H2, *Christ Church* 70 incorporates a similar agreement.

54 Exceptions: S1534/W19, *c.* 1003; S1508/H10, *Christ Church* 96; S1487/W13. Abba's land, granted to his widow, is to pass in the male line, reverting to the Church in the absence of a male heir (S1482/H2, *Christ Church* 70). The intended fate after her life of the estates bequeathed to his wife by Eadwine of Caddington is unclear (S1517/*St Albans* 15; Keynes, 'A lost cartulary', p. 278).

55 S775; Foot, *Veiled Women*, I, 182–3; Abrams, *Glastonbury*, p. 143 and n. 4. However, Ælfheah's attestation of S784, a charter dated 972 (see Chap. 3, n. 170) presents a problem with this identification.

56 S1483/W2; the Æthelweard whose soul is mentioned in the will may be Ælfgar's late son. See Chap. 6, pp. 235–6 below for details of Ælfgar's bequests.

57 Sheehan, *The Will*, p. 151; P&M II, pp. 316–17.

58 S1485/W9. See Chap. 3, p. 106 above for Ælfheah's property.

sons similarly receive one estate each.[59] Thegns' dispositions follow a similar pattern. In three instances, estates are to be held in usufruct by sons, with reversion to the Church.[60] For example, Æthelwold's son is to have only one hide, together with a *lecge* (possibly a scabbard); this is in the context of a bequest to Æthelwold's wife of a life interest in ten hides at Manningford (Wilts.), which was granted to Æthelwold by King Æthelred and which, on her death, is to revert to the church rather than to Æthelwold's son.[61] In Ælfhelm's will, which has been discussed above in relation to marriage agreements, both wife and son appear as beneficiaries; Ælfhelm's son, Ælfgar, is granted two estates in usufruct, with the proviso that he in turn bequeath them to a religious foundation of his choice – paltry indeed, compared with Ælfhelm's bequests to his wife Æffe.[62] In two other wills mentioning both wife and son the pattern is less extreme, but consistent.[63] There is, however, a notable exception: Eadwine of Caddington bequeaths seven estates, one as usufruct, to his son, Leofwine, who was still a minor; his wife is granted two estates and, by implication, responsibility for Leofwine's property during his minority. Should she remarry, she would lose the two estates, and responsibility for Leofwine's land would be transferred to Æthelwine, probably Eadwine's brother.[64]

Ealdorman Alfred's bequest of land to his son is particularly difficult to interpret:

> *Ond ic selle Eðelwalde minum sunu III hida boclondes ... 7 gif se cyning him geunnan wille þes folclondes to ðem boclonde, þonne hebbe he 7 bruce.*
>
> (And I give to Æthelwold, my son, three hides of bookland ... and if the king will grant him the folkland along with the bookland, let him have it and enjoy it.)

If this bequest of three hides, in the context of Alfred's bequest of land amounting to 104 hides to his wife and daughter, seems parsimonious, the reference to *folcland*, that elusive category of landholding which has generated considerable debate among historians,[65] does little to clarify Alfred's

59 S1498/W10.

60 S1234/R116, *Christ Church* 183: Brihtmær's wife, son and daughter hold the homestead and church with reversion to Christ Church, Canterbury; S1471/R101, *Christ Church* 170: Æthelric's son has a life interest in two estates and a messuage with reversion to Christ Church, Canterbury; S1539/W13: Ælfhelm's son is to have two estates and may choose to which foundation they should revert on his death.

61 S1505/W12; S865. The will can only be dated in relation to this charter.

62 Table 3 above.

63 S1505/W12; S1485/W9 (wife to receive residue).

64 S1517/*St Albans* 15.

65 For example, see F. W. Maitland, *Domesday Book and Beyond: Three Essays in the Early History of England* (Cambridge, 1897, repr. 1907), Essay II: 'England Before the Conquest', section 2, pp. 244–58; E. John, *Land Tenure in Early England*, 2nd edn (Leicester, 1964);

intentions. While it is clear that the folkland in question was subject to different tenurial arrangements from Alfred's bookland, and remained in the gift of the king, the precise nature of that tenure or of the transaction envisaged by Alfred in this clause is obscure. Maitland's interpretation was that Alfred himself was in possession of the folkland,[66] but the will's most recent editors suggest that Æthelwold himself may have been in possession, holding the land from the king, and that Alfred envisaged the possibility that the king would convert it into bookland, with rights of free disposal, for Æthelwold's benefit.[67] Perhaps Alfred used the opportunity in his will, which is addressed directly to the king, to support his son's interest in the land. The actual amount of the folkland may have been relatively small, since Alfred instructs Wærburh to offer Æthelwold compensation of a single estate, should he be denied the folkland:[68]

> *Gif hit þet ne sio, þonne selle hio him swa hwaðer swa hio wille swa ðet lond an Horsalege swa ðet an Leangafelda.*
>
> (If that shall not be, then [Wærburh] is to give him whichever she pleases, either the land at Horsley [10 hides] or that at Lingfield [six hides].[69]

It is therefore possible that, with the three hides of bookland inherited from his father and the gift of Horsley by Wærburh, Æthelwold would benefit to a maximum of thirteen hides under his father's will. However, Alfred makes further provision that if a nearer male heir (*gesibbra erfeweard … wepnedhades*) should be born to him, then all of Alfred's property would devolve upon him.

Various proposals have been put forward to account for this meagre treatment of Æthelwold. Since the will makes it clear that Æthelwold, unlike Ealhthryth, is not a child of his father's present marriage, he may have been illegitimate, his claim on his father's property secondary to a 'nearer', or legitimate, heir.[70] Alternatively, he may have been sufficiently provided for on the

E. John, *Orbis Britanniae and Other Studies* (Leicester, 1966), pp. 64–127; S. Reynolds, 'Bookland, folkland and fiefs', *ANS* 14 (1992), 211–27; Reynolds, *Fiefs and Vassals*, pp. 324–5; Keynes, *Diplomas*, pp. 31–2; Wormald, 'Kingship and royal property', pp. 264–8; R. Faith, *The English Peasantry and the Growth of Lordship* (Leicester, 1997), pp. 89–90; Kennedy, 'Disputes', pp. 175–9.

66 Maitland, *Domesday Book and Beyond*, p. 246.

67 Brooks and Kelly, *Christ Church* 96. The possibility of folkland used as an aspect of royal patronage is discussed by Baxter, *Earls*, pp. 145–9, esp. at p. 147.

68 The point is made by Brooks and Kelly, *Christ Church* 96.

69 Lingfield was bequeathed to Wærburh, with reversion to Ealhthryth, and then to her child or Alfred's nearest paternal kinsman; Horsley would follow the same route but had to be purchased from Ealhthryth by any member of Alfred's paternal kin who wished to acquire it.

70 Maitland, *Domesday Book and Beyond*, p. 246. Ealhthryth is distinguished as the child of Alfred and Wærhburh.

death of his mother or his father's remarriage, or by some other means.[71] Since Alfred twice refers to his daughter as 'our joint child' – that is, of himself and Wærburh – a further possibility is that Alfred's will is primarily concerned with bookland which he acquired through his marriage with Wærburh, on which Æthelwold would have no claim.[72] Frustrating though this conundrum may be for the modern historian, the lack of detail concerning Æthelwold reinforces Alfred's assertion at the beginning of the will that he is primarily concerned with bequests to his present wife and their daughter; Æthelwold's inheritance is, in this respect, marginal.

Alfred is also concerned with the potential claim of patrilineal kinsmen on the land which he has bequeathed to Wærburh and Ealhthryth.[73] Among the estates which he bequeaths to his wife and daughter he identifies two groups: one (Sanderstead, and Selsdon with Lingfield) are to pass to Ealhthryth on Wærburh's death, and to her child (*bearn*), should she have one; if not, they are to pass to the nearest kin in Alfred's paternal line. Remaining estates (Westerham, Clapham, Horsley and Nettlestead) are to be held by Ealhthryth (again on her mother's death), but Alfred's wider paternal kin would have the right to purchase them from her.[74] In general, ealdormen and thegns making bequests of land to collateral kin place similar emphasis on the male line. This is illustrated by the ninth-century will of the reeve Abba:

> *7 gif mine broðar ærfeweard gestrionen ðe londes weorðe sie þonne ann ic ðem londes. Gif hie ne gestrionen oððа him sylfum ælles hwæt sele æfter hiora dege ann ic his Freoðomunde gif he ðonne lifes bið. Gif him elles hwæt sæleð ðonne ann ic his minra swæstarsuna swælcum se hit geðian wile 7 him gifeðe bið.*

> (And if my brothers beget an heir fit to hold land, then I give the land to him. If they have no heir, or if anything happens to him (or them), after their death I give it to Freothomund, if he be alive at the time. If anything happens to him, then I give it to whichever of my sisters' sons is willing to receive it and to him be it granted.)[75]

71 *SEHD*, pp. 90–1; Harmer suggests that Æthelwold may already have been holding property through right of office: an Æthelwold *dux* witnesses Ealdorman Alfred's bequest-agreement with Archbishop Alfred, although he is placed above Alfred in the list (S1202/H8, *Christ Church* 95), and the Ealdorman Æthelwold whose death is recorded in *ASC* s.a. 888 is identified in the Chronicle of Æthelweard as the ealdorman of Kent (*Æthelweard*, ed. Campbell, p. 47). This identification is doubted by Brooks and Kelly, *Christ Church* 96. Wormald, 'Kingship and royal property', p. 267 suggests that Æthelwold had heritable property, as opposed to bookland.

72 *Christ Church* 96.

73 The parameters of Anglo-Saxon kinship are outlined by Lancaster, 'Kinship', pp. 232–9.

74 For this principle of limitation in the will and law of King Alfred, see Chap. 1, p. 54 and Chap. 3, p. 89. For the view that these two groups constitute the *ærfe* (inherited land) and *bocland* distinguished by Alfred in the opening clause see *Christ Church* 96.

75 S1482/H2, *Christ Church* 70. Freothomund is unidentified, although his position in the line of heirs suggests that he is likely to have been a kinsman.

**Table 4.** Schematic representation of lay male bequest of land to kin

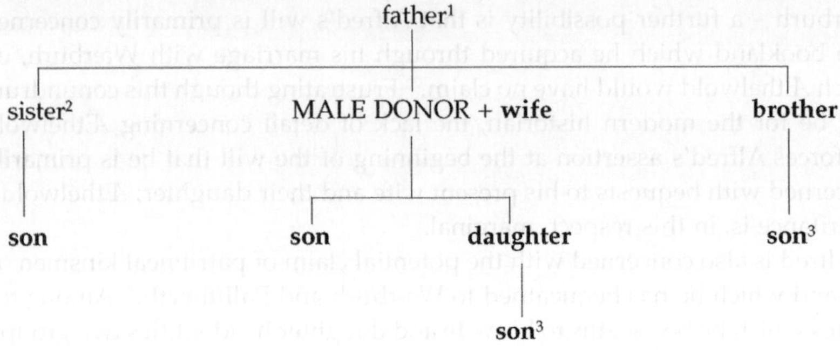


**Beneficiaries shown in bold**

1 S1508/H10, *Christ Church* 96 possibly transmits land in the maternal line; S1519/W34 refers to agreements with maternal uncles; S1531/31 bequeaths usufruct in land to a maternal aunt; the donor's mother receives land in S1483/W2.

2 S1519/W34 includes bequest-agreements with sisters.

3 See p. 147, n. 43 for the terms *cild* and *bearn* possibly referring to sons in this context.

The same principle is also seen operating in the eleventh-century will of Eadwine of Caddington; in the eventuality of his son's death, his brother's sons were to inherit Sundon and Caddington, and his sister's son was to receive a further estate, which would all then pass 'within my kindred, always in the male line' (*innon mine cynn æfre on þa sperhand*).[76] Not only is there a tendency to favour the male line, but the range of kinship, in so far as it can be identified, tends to be limited to siblings and their offspring (see Table 4).[77] Two ealdormen and nine thegns bequeath land to collateral kin within these parameters.[78] Sons appear rarely as beneficiaries of land in wills where collateral kinsmen are to inherit, which may suggest that male kin were to benefit in the absence of a direct male descendant, as appears to be the case in the will of Abba, quoted above; nevertheless, sons and collateral kinsmen do occasionally feature together, indicating that the existence of a

76 S1517/*St Albans* 15.

77 The term *mæg* may refer to close kinship: Lancaster, 'Kinship', p. 237.

78 Ealdormen: S1504/H20; S1485/W9. Thegns: S1482/H2, *Christ Church* 70; S1537/W27; S1536/W17, *Burton* 29; S1487/W13; S1517/*St Albans* 15; S1527/W24; S1519/W34; S1516/W33. Kinsmen are named by two ealdormen where the degree of kinship is uncertain (S1508/H10, *Christ Church* 96; S1483/W2).

direct male heir did not necessarily exclude the wider male kin from a claim on land.[79]

Collateral kinsmen, like sons, in most cases receive one or two estates, a pattern seen in the will of Ælfhelm Polga.[80] His son, Ælfgar, receives a life interest in two estates (Whepstead and Walton, Sfk), with reversion to the church of his choice. Ælfhelm goes on to make a series of bequests to kinsmen. Two of his brothers are named: Ælfhelm (the Younger) is to receive two estates (Ickleton, Cambs. and *Maworth*, unid.), and Wulfmær, one estate (Barnham, Sfk?); in addition, Troston (Sfk) is to be divided between Ælfhelm's three brothers, although the third is not named. Ælfhelm's nephews, Æthelric and Ælfwold, sons of the younger Ælfhelm, are to share four hides reserved from the estate at Conington (Cambs.), half of which is granted to Ælfhelm's wife and daughter; in addition, Ælfwold is granted land at Troston currently held byÆthelric. Finally, Ælfhelm refers to arrangements involving his kinsman Leofsige, who is to receive Littlebury (Ex), subject to a previous agreement made before the ealdorman, and the estate at Stockton (Nfk?), which is to be shared with his wife, and for which he must pay one hundred mancuses of gold to subsidise Ælfhelm's heriot.[81]

This pattern of relatively small bequests of land within the male kindred, and limited bequests to sons in particular, requires explanation. It is unlikely that wills dispose of a donor's entire property.[82] Wormald proposed that land held on terms other than by *boc* may have been transmitted by 'normative customs';[83] Crick further suggests that such routes for the transmission of property may not have required documentation, or that documentation was not preserved because the Church had no interest in the transaction.[84] While these explanations are inherently probable, they do not entirely address the very specific parameters of land distribution by laymen described above. However, if the bequest of land to kinsmen by male donors is viewed from the perspective of alienation to the Church rather than inheritance practice, it becomes clear that, at least by the tenth century, the beneficiaries constitute precisely that group of male kin who are likely to have had an interest in the land had it not been alienated as a pious gift, particularly where such

79 Both sons and collateral kin appear as beneficiaries in S1485/W9, S1508/H10, *Christ Church* 96 and S1487/W13. See also *CR* 33 where Æthelstan Mannessune bequeaths land to his son (conditionally), to his brother's son and to his kinsman Leofsige.

80 S1487/W13.

81 The kinship is not specified in the will, but Leofsige is identified in the Ramsey Chronicle as Ælfhelm's *agnato* (*CR* 34): for a survey of the evidence see Locherbie-Cameron, 'Byrhtnoth', p. 26, n. 17. See *Wills*, pp. 133–4 for family ramifications and references; Robertson identifies Wulfmær as Ælfhelm's brother: *Charters*, p. 388.

82 Lowe, 'Nature and effect', pp. 37–9. Ealdorman Ælfheah had received estates by royal charter which do not appear in his will (Williams, '*Princeps Merciorum gentis*', pp. 152–3).

83 Wormald, 'Kingship and royal property', p. 267.

84 Crick, 'Women, posthumous benefaction', p. 407.

land had been acquired in a previous generation and was beginning to be perceived as inherited property.[85] Seen from this perspective, the distribution of land in the wills of male donors looks more like a family settlement intended to avoid contention rather than a unilateral act of generosity.[86] It may also reflect the settlement stipulated in the law of Cnut if a man *should* die intestate: his lord, to whom his heriot is due, is responsible for ensuring that the man's property (*æht*) is distributed among his wife, children and close kinsmen (*neahmagon*), 'each according to the share which belongs to him'.[87] Although in theory the holder of bookland had the right of free disposition, the reality of family claims may have imposed constraints.[88]

The pattern of land distribution among kin in the wills of male donors may be illuminated by comparison with documents recording the *laudatio parentum*, a process which was prevalent in Western France in the latter half of the eleventh century and the first half of the twelfth by which a kindred group gave formal consent to the gift of land to the Church.[89] Unlike wills, these were *inter vivos* gifts, often made before senior members of the beneficiary religious community in the presence of consenting members of the donor's close family, wider kindred and other interested parties.[90] The process of granting land with the *laudatio parentum* is likely to have been prompted by concern to avoid dispute over the alienation of land to the church; care was taken to record the presence of relatives giving the *laudatio*, and considerable effort was expended by the church to gain the consent of those interested parties who were not present.[91]Although the documents themselves are different in form from Anglo-Saxon wills, and record *inter vivos* rather than deferred gifts, the similarity in distribution between the kin giving the *laudatio* and those named as beneficiaries of land in the wills of male donors is marked.[92]

85 P. J. Geary, 'Exchange and interaction between the living and the dead', published as 'Echanges et relations entre les vivants et les morts dans la société du haut Moyen Age', *Droit et Cultures* 12 (1986), 3–18, translated in Geary, *Living With the Dead*, pp. 77–92 (pp. 81–2).

86 Reynolds, *Fiefs and Vassals*, p. 328.

87 *Ælcon be ðære mæðe ðe him to gebyrige*: II Cnut, 70.1.

88 An extract from a lost charter of Archbishop Wulfred (805x832) asserts a person's right to control his bookland: printed with a revised translation by K. A. Lowe, 'William Somner, S1622, and the editing of Old English charters', *Neophilologus* 83 (1999), 291–7 (p. 295); for imposed limitations see n. 74 above.

89 The key study is White, *Custom, Kinship*.

90 White, *Custom, Kinship*, p. 34.

91 White, *Custom, Kinship*, pp. 43–55, 62–8.

92 Kin may occasionally be identified in the surviving witness lists of lay wills: S1506/R32, *Christ Church* 121 (son); S1455/R62, *St Augustine's* 31 (father); S1234/R116, *Christ Church* 183 (son?: *St Paul's*, p. 229); S1485/W9 (brother, sister's son); S1511/W11, *Rochester* 35 (unspecified kinsmen and ? a kinswoman); S1202/H8, *Christ Church* 95 (agreement: son?); S1508/H10, *Christ Church* 96 (son, wife and unspecified kinsman); S1503/W20,

White's study has shown that the consenting kin for the *laudatio* was generally drawn from the descendants of the donor's two sets of grandparents, tending to limit the kin within the range of first cousin; the consent of spouses, children and siblings was more frequent than that of, for example, matrilineal kin or other *affines*;[93] and overall, consenting groups had a clear male bias, with eight males for every five females, seventeen consenting brothers for every four sisters, and for every male child of the donor's brother or sister consenting, only one female child did so. There is also evidence to suggest that patrilineal kin dominated the consenting groups.[94] In addition, the kin giving the *laudatio* is mainly restricted to two or three generations.[95] Beneficiaries within a similar range of kinship receive land in the wills of male donors (see Table Four above), with the implication that, for the purposes of the transmission of land, kinship was relatively narrowly defined.[96] White's analysis of those giving the *laudatio* also shows that male donors rarely appear elsewhere in the lists of consenting kin as fathers, and never as grandfathers; he suggests that men would normally expect to retain their authority over land until death, when they would be succeeded by a son or other male heir.[97] It is possible that the survival of a relatively greater number of wills made by male donors than by women indicates that, among the Anglo-Saxon nobility, rights in land were similarly vested in a senior male figure within a kin group for his lifetime, with the attendant responsibility for arranging its distribution after his death.

In both the *laudatio parentum* and Anglo-Saxon will-making the procedure recognised and reaffirmed the role of key members of the kin group, a

*Christ Church* 142 (brother). Bishop Ælfwold's will was witnessed by his brother-in-law and an unspecified kinsman (S1492/N&S10).

93 The composition of the consenting group may have varied according to the origin of the property which was being alienated to the Church, so that, for example, *affines* were likely to consent when a donor alienated land which was his wife's through inheritance from her own kin, through dowry or by marriage agreement; this may be related to the tradition that land should be offered to the Church for the souls of those from whom it had been acquired: White, *Custom, Kinship*, pp. 113–17, 124.

94 White, *Custom, Kinship*, pp. 96–8 and 109–11 for the choice and ranking of consenting kin. Wareham argues for an increasing emphasis on agnatic kinship from the tenth century in his 'Transformation of kinship'.

95 This may reflect low life expectancy, or the need for individuals to have reached an appropriate age: White, *Custom, Kinship*, pp. 114–15.

96 J. Crick, 'Posthumous obligation and family identity', in *Social Identity*, ed. Frazer and Tyrrell, pp. 193–208 (p. 201 and n. 54). For the significance of the conjugal couple, their progenitors, siblings and offspring in relation to three-generation kinship see P. Stafford, 'Kinship and women in the world of Maldon: Byrhtnoth and his family', in *The Battle of Maldon: Fiction and Fact*, ed. J. Cooper (London, 1993), pp. 225–35 (pp. 225–7); for a similar pattern of land transmission, R. Le Jan, *Famille et pouvoir dans le monde franc (vii^e–x^e siècle): essai d'anthropologie sociale* (Paris, 1995), pp. 236–42.

97 White, *Custom, Kinship*, p. 115.

strategy which may be glimpsed at work in the vernacular will of Wulfgar.[98] This was a man of some prestige, witnessing charters as *minister* from about 928 to 938, and then as ealdorman of Eastern Wessex from 939 to 948.[99] He bequeaths two estates – Ham and Collingbourne (both Wilts.), which he held in his own right, to the New and Old Minsters, Winchester, respectively.[100] However, he also bequeaths inherited family land. First, he bequeaths a life interest in Inkpen (Berks.) to his wife Æffe, with reversion to a local religious foundation at Kintbury (Berks.), which is otherwise unknown; he refers to the fact that this estate was first acquired by his grandfather, Wulfhere, who had himself been an ealdorman (probably of the same area). The bequest to the church is made on behalf of Wulfgar's own soul, that of Wulfric (probably his father), and that of Wulfhere; during her tenure, Æffe is required to pay an annual food-rent to Kintbury on their behalf.[101] It seems likely that Wulfgar's family had established a close relationship with this local foundation, similar to that of Ealdorman Ælfgar's family with Stoke-by-Nayland. The will of Ælfflæd, Ælfgar's younger daughter, refers to her ancestors' endowment of the 'holy place' (*halgan stowæ*) with land at Stoke, and Ælfgar's references to 'our' ancestors suggest that the family link with Stoke was established at least by his parents' generation.[102]

A second estate bequeathed by Wulfgar had also been acquired by his grandfather Wulfhere, who received Buttermere (Wilts.), including *æt Æscmere*, from King Æthelred of Wessex in 863.[103] However, the terms of Wulfgar's bequests are, in this instance, very different:

> *7 ic an þæs landes æt Butermere ofer mine dæg Byrhtsige twegea hida 7 Ceolstanes sunum anes gif hie me oð ðæt on ryht gehieraþ*
>
> (And I grant two hides of the estate at Buttermere, after my death, to Brihtsige and one to Ceolstan's sons, if they show me due obedience until then.)

As so often, crucial information is lacking, but the context seems to imply that Brihtsige and the sons of Ceolstan were Wulfgar's kinsmen who owed him respect and allegiance. In addition, land *æt Cræft* (unid.) is bequeathed to

98 White, *Custom, Kinship*, pp. 160–71; S1533/R26, 931x939.

99 Wulfgar is unstyled in his will, suggesting that it was drawn up before he became ealdorman *c.* 939. For biographical details see *Charters*, pp. 307–308.

100 S416 (931) records King Æthelstan's grant of Ham to Wulfgar; S379 (921), granting Collingbourne in the name of King Edward, is spurious as it stands: see *New Minster*, no. 8 and p. 49.

101 Wulfhere attests as ealdorman between 854 and 871x877; S362 (*EHD* I, no. 100) suggests that his land was forfeit for desertion of King Alfred. See *Charters*, p. 267. Nothing is known of Wulfgar's father.

102 S1483/W2 (9946x*c.* 951); S1494/W14 (962x991); S1486/W15 (1000x1002). For detail of the bequests to the church by Ælfgar and his daughters see Chap. 6, pp. 235–7 below.

103 S336.

Wynsige and Ælfsige, and Denford (Berks.) to Cynestan and Æthelstan, all of whom may also have been Wulfgar's kinsmen, since the bequests are conditional on the same terms of obedience. These bequests have been formally documented and published in his will, but Wulfgar keeps *Æscmere* in reserve:

> *7 ic cweþe on wordum be Æscmere on minum geongum magum swelce me betst gehieraþ.*
>
> (And I shall verbally bequeath *Æscmere* to such of my young kinsmen as obey me best.)

The phrase *on wordum* implies that Wulfgar envisages further oral dispositions, subject to the co-operation of his 'young kinsmen'. There would have been no point in stipulating such conditions if the kinsmen concerned had been unaware of them. Wulfgar appears here as a figure of seniority and authority among his kindred, exercising his right to dispose of bookland as he sees fit, and in the process exacting some measure of allegiance from his male kindred – perhaps including support for his bequests to his wife and to the church – as the price of his bequests. That some donors anticipated a challenge from kindred is clear: for example, Wulfric Spott's bequest of an estate to his nephew, Ufegeat, is made 'in the hope that he may be a better friend and supporter to the monastery [of Burton]'.[104]

Both the *laudatio* and the Anglo-Saxon will show that the alienation of land to the Church was indeed a family matter. In the case of the former, White has suggested that it was 'a formal act more similar to giving than to witnessing'; in a sense, the whole consenting group participated in the gift, and benefited from the attendant spiritual rewards.[105] A similar ethos may be proposed for the kin-group featuring as beneficiaries of land in the wills of Anglo-Saxon male donors, since it can be shown that bequests of land were often made to churches which had links with the donor's kindred over time.[106] Thurstan's bequests to Ely, for example, may be seen in the light of his family's patronage of Ely over four generations. His descent from Ealdorman Byrhtnoth, a much-honoured benefactor of Ely, has already been established.[107] The *Liber Eliensis* preserves the multi-gift will of Leofflæd, Byrhtnoth's daughter and Thurstan's grandmother, granting land to Ely, and lists the estates granted

104 S1536/W17, *Burton* 29: *on þ gerad þ he freond 7 fultum þe betere sy into þære stowe.* See also Ælfgar's request to the king to prevent his children's interference in his bequests (S1483/W2, and Chap. 2, n. 106 above).

105 White, *Custom, Kinship*, pp. 46, 160–1. This aspect of the bequest of land to the church is discussed in Chap. 6 below.

106 Male donors usually bequeath between one and three estates to the church. The exceptions are Thurstan (S1531/W31), who bequeaths eight not including bequests to local churches, and Wulfric Spott (S1536/W17, *Burton* 29), who endows his foundation at Burton-upon-Trent with more than forty-eight.

107 See pp. 143–4 above.

by his parents, Leofwaru, Leofflæd's daughter, and her husband Lustwine.[108] A number of these estates feature in Thurstan's will, with no reference to the prior donations of his ancestors: Wetheringsett, (Sfk), Knapwell (Cambs.) and Weston (Ex), all previously granted to Ely by Leofflæd or his parents, are to revert to Ely after his life or, in the case of Weston, after the life of Æthelswith, possibly his maternal aunt, to whom he bequeaths a life interest.[109] A similar sequence of re-donation may be seen in the wills of Ealdorman Ælfgar and his daughters.[110] The reiteration by Æthelflæd and Ælfflæd of their father's reversionary bequests to the church reinforces the family link with the beneficiary foundations – a strategy which has been identified in gifts of land to Cluny.[111] Other wills and chronicle evidence attest to such links between families and particular beneficiary houses. The Ramsey Chronicle, for instance, records a sequence of bequests by Æthelstan Mannessune and his family which spans three generations.[112]

Continuing links between donors' families and beneficiary churches were established not only by bequests of land, but also by bequest-agreements. Male donors bequeathing land to the church frequently arrange for members of the conjugal family and the wider kin to have usufruct, with reversion to the church after one or two lives. In effect, this meant that the donor's immediate kin gained the benefit of the land in the short term, often with the possibility of negotiating an agreement with the church for further lives, while the church might hold the title-deeds, or gain an annual rent, with the anticipation of ultimate reversion of the land. A donor might require an annual food-rent to be paid to the beneficiary church by those holding the land, as in the case of Wulfgar, above, as an acknowledgement of the church's interest in the land and in order to gain immediate spiritual benefits for his soul after death.

108 *LE* II, 88, 89.

109 *LE* II, 88; Æthelswith had entered a religious house under the aegis of Ely (*Wills*, p. 193). Other estates granted to Ely by his parents are diverted by Thurstan: Wimbish is bequeathed to Christ Church, Canterbury, and others to his partner (Borough Green – subject to agreement), his wife Æthelgyth (Pentlow, Ashdon), or to be shared between his priest and two chaplains after his death and Æthelgyth's (Kedington). *LE* (not usually reticent on such matters) gives no indication of a dispute, so it is possible that an agreement had been reached between Thurstan and the Ely community, whereby Thurstan continued to hold the land: Lowe, 'Nature and effect', pp. 44–6.

110 S1483/W2, 1494/W14, S1486/W15; see Chap. 6, pp. 235–7 below for details of these bequests.

111 Rosenwein, *To Be the Neighbor*, pp. 122–5, with specific examples at pp. 49–65. See also Chap. 6, pp. 233–5 below.

112 *CR* 33, 34, 54, 62, 63, 106, 107. For this family's links with Ramsey see Hart, 'Eadnoth'. The will of Wulfgar (S1533/R26), discussed above (pp. 158–9), shows ancestral links with Kintbury; Ealdorman Ealhhere and his family endowed Christ Church, Canterbury (S1195/H5, S1198/H6; Brooks, *Early History*, pp. 148–9). The link between Glastonbury and the family of Ealdorman Ælfheah (S1485/W9) is explored in Chap. 6, pp. 233–5 below.

On the death of the donor, further negotiations between the kindred and the beneficiary church were often required, as shown in the bequest-agreement between Æthelweard and the archbishop and community of Christ Church, Canterbury, concerning Ickham (Kt).[113] Æthelweard has negotiated that, on his death, the estate will pass to a certain Eadric for his lifetime, if he is still alive, and if not, to Æthelgifu – the relationships are unstated – presumably with reversion to Christ Church. A single payment of five pounds and an annual food-rent are to be paid by the heir, who would be entitled to the proceeds of justice. Should both Eadric and Æthelgifu predecease Æthelweard, the estate and *boc* would be 'delivered up' (*agifan*) with his body 'on his own behalf and for [the benefit of] those from whom the land came'.[114] In the context of similar agreements, this suggests that Ickham was family land which Æthelweard had inherited, and which was to earn spiritual benefit for him and his ancestors.[115] A contemporary endorsement, which indicates that Eadric did indeed survive to inherit and make his own agreement (*gerednæs*) with the community, records the payment of his five pounds and confirms the terms on which he was to hold the land.

The potential for further negotiation between a donor's kin and a beneficiary church concerning bequeathed land is included in the detailed account of Archbishop Eadsige's reversionary agreement with the thegn Æthelric Bigga and his son, Esbearn, relating to land at Chart (Kent). Although at the time of the transaction the estate was in the hands of Æthelric, the document sets out Christ Church's claim in a way that suggests that Chart had been the subject of a dispute.[116] The terms were that Æthelric should hold Chart until his death, when it would revert to the archbishop in order to provide food and clothing for the community, and earn spiritual benefit both for Æthelric and the archbishop. The title-deeds of the estate were handed over by Æthelric, *to ecere ælmessan* (in perpetual alms). In addition, Æthelric and Esbearn would continue to enjoy their own estates of Milton and Stowting, and a *haga* in the town, which would revert to the church after their lives, unless 'their friends' (*heora freonda*) could come to some arrangement with the archbishop. Failing this, the land would be lost to Æthelric's kindred.[117]

This view of the bequest of land as an aspect of family strategy is relevant to the multi-gift will of Brihtric and his wife, Ælfswith, dated between 973

113 S1506/R32, *Christ Church* 121.

114 *For hine 7 for ða ðe him . land fram com.*

115 For the view that Æthelweard was leasing the land from Christ Church, and that the payment of rent applied also to him, see *Christ Church* 121.

116 S1471/R101, *Christ Church* 170; Brooks, *Early History*, pp. 147–8, 302–303.

117 For a similar arrangement see S1202/H8, *Christ Church* 95, and the account of such negotiations between an interested party and the church in S1376/R53 (discussed in Chap. 2, pp. 76–7 above).

**Table 5.** A summary of the dispute concerning the estates of Snodland, Bromley and Fawkham (Kt), indicating likely points for the making of the will S1511/W11, *Rochester* 35

| | | |
|---|---|---|
| ***Before 958*** | | **Evidence** |
| Ælfhere in possession of Snodland (Kt) | | S1511/W11[1] |
| – he bequeaths Snodland to St Andrew's, Rochester (possibly reserving a life interest for his wife Æscwyn) | | |
| – Æscwyn hands the title-deeds (*becc*) to Rochester | | S1457/R59[2] |
| Title-deeds stolen (by priests) and sold to Ælfric, son of Ælfhere and Æscwyn | | S1457/R59 |
| Ælfric bequeaths a life interest in Snodland to his wife Brihtwaru, with reversion to Rochester (witnessed by Archbishop Oda, d. 958) | | S1511/W11 |
| – the reversion of Fawkham and Bromley (Kt) after her death may also have been bequeathed on this occasion | | S1511/W11[3] |
| ***Before 975*** | | |
| Ælfric dies: his widow holds the title-deeds | [WILL?] | S1457/R59 |
| Bishop Ælfstan (964–994?) claims deeds of Snodland | | S1457/R59 |
| – awarded the deeds by a court in the presence of King Edgar | | |
| – Brihtwaru's property at Bromley and Fawkham forfeit to the king for theft | | |
| – Brihtwaru hands over the deeds of Bromley & Fawkham | | |
| – the bishop buys these estates from the king & grants usufruct to Brihtwaru | [WILL?] | |
| ***After 975: the death of King Edgar*** | | |
| Brihtric (a kinsman of Brihtwaru) compels/urges (*genedde*) her to re-possess the estates | | S1457/R59 |
| – public hearing before Ealdorman Eadwine (of Sussex: d. 982) finds in favour of Brihtwaru | | |
| – Bishop Ælfstan forced to relinquish deeds | [WILL?] | |
| ***987*** | | |
| King Æthelred grants Bromley to his *minister* Æthelsige | | S864[4] |

1 *Rochester* 35 (973x987): the will of Brihtric and Ælfswith.

2 *Rochester* 36 (980x987): record of dispute (for dating see *Rochester*, pp. xxiv–xxv).

3 The reversion of these estates was bequeathed to Rochester on behalf of Ælfric and his ancestors; like Snodland, they may have been inherited land in which Brihtwaru had a life interest.

4 *Rochester* 30 (987). Bromley was restored to Rochester by Æthelred in 998 (S893, *Rochester* 32). Snodland seems to have been re-acquired by Bishop Godwine, 995–1005/6 (S1456, *Rochester* 37; *Charters*, no. 69). All three estates were held by Rochester in 1086: DB I, fol. 5v.

and 987, which is preserved in the twelfth-century *Textus Roffensis*.[118] It seems to have been drawn up in the context of a dispute between the family of a certain Ælfric and the Rochester community concerning three estates in Kent, although the will's precise relationship with the dispute proceedings is unclear. Nothing is known about the donors beyond the will, and the documentation surrounding the dispute is so complex that a synopsis of the key events relevant to the present discussion is set out in tabular form (see Table 5).[119] Three points for the making of the will, incorporating arrangements concerning the disputed estates, in relation to the chronology of the unfolding dispute seem possible, and are indicated in the Table. The earliest places it before 975, in advance of the court case at which the deeds of Snodland were awarded to Rochester in the presence of King Edgar, and Brihtwaru's estates of Fawkham and Bromley were forfeit.[120] Alternatively, it may have been made *after* the court case, when the bishop agreed to grant usufruct (*ðara lande bryces*) of Bromley and Fawkham (and, possibly, Snodland – the Rochester account is ambiguous on this detail) to Brihtwaru; a reversionary agreement between Brihtwaru and the abbot at this point is likely.[121] Thirdly, the will could have been a response to the finding of the shire court after 975, when the abbot was to return the title-deeds (again the estates are unspecified) to Brihtwaru; given Brihtric's apparent involvement in Brihtwaru's challenge at this point, perhaps mounted in the context of the upsurgence of unrest in the aftermath of Edgar's death, the appearance of a reversionary clause for the estates in his will would make sense, reflecting a settlement with the abbot which is not recorded elsewhere.[122]

The will itself gives no indication that it is dealing with property subject to dispute, but at its heart is the reversion of the estates of Snodland, Bromley and Fawkham (Kt) to the church of Rochester on the death of Brihtwaru, the widow of Ælfric:

> *7 þæt land æt Fealcnaham. æfter Byrhwara dæge. into Sancte Andree. for Ælfric hire hlaford. 7 his yldran. swa heora cwide wæs. 7 Bromleah. æfter Brihtwara dæge. into Sancte Andrea. swa Ælfric hire hlaford hit becwæð. for hine 7 his yldran. 7*

118 S1511/W11, *Rochester* 35. The dating is that of Whitelock (*Wills*, p. 129); a *terminus post quem* of 964 has been proposed by C. Flight, 'Four vernacular texts from the pre-Conquest archive of Rochester Cathedral', *Archaeologia Cantiana* 115 (1995), 121–53 (pp. 126–7).

119 Accounts of the dispute, and various interpretations of the evidence, may be found in *Wills*, pp. 128–9; Wormald, 'Charters, law', pp. 298–301; Flight, 'Four vernacular texts', pp. 126–37. The authenticity of documents surrounding the dispute is discussed in *Rochester*, pp. xxiv–xxv; for errors in S1457/R59 (*Rochester* 36) which suggest some creativity on the part of the scribe see *Charters*, p. 367.

120 The argument is developed by Flight, 'Four texts', pp. 126–7, 129–33.

121 S1457/R59, *Rochester* 36.

122 Wormald suggests that Brihtric was 'smitten by conscience' at this point: 'Charters, law', p. 299.

*Snodingcland eac. into Sancte Andrea. æfter hire dæge. swa Ælfhere hit becwæð. Ælfrices fæder. 7 he seoððan.*

(And after Brihtwaru's day, the estate at Fawkham [is to go] to St Andrew's for her husband Ælfric and his ancestors, in accordance with their will; and Bromley after Brihtwaru's day to St Andrew's as her husband Ælfric bequeathed it, for him and his ancestors; and Snodland also to St Andrew's after her day, as Ælfhere, Ælfric's father, bequeathed it, and Ælfric afterwards.)

The relationship between Brihtwaru and Brihtric and Ælfswith is unstated, as is the reason for the inclusion of this arrangement in the will. The emphasis in this clause is on commemoration of Brihtwaru's husband and his predecessors, and on the fact that this reversion is the fulfilment of their pious bequests; it is possible that Brihtwaru's interest in this land may have been the result of a marriage agreement, although this is nowhere stated. Furthermore, we are told not only that Ælfhere, Brihtwaru's father-in-law, bequeathed Snodland to Rochester, but that his son Ælfric, Brihtwaru's husband, also did so; the names of prestigious witnesses to Ælfric's bequest are given, including the former queen, Eadgifu, widow of Edward the Elder and grandmother of King Edgar, and Archbishop Oda.[123] Although the Brihtric of the will is nowhere explicitly identified as Brihtwaru's kinsman, the inclusion of these arrangements in the will seems best explained by assuming that this was the case, and that he was involved in the dispute as her kinsman of that name mentioned in S1457/R59, perhaps (as Whitelock suggests) as her advocate (see Table 5).[124]

There is a hint in the first clause of the will that it may indeed have been linked with a family response to the dispute. This clause announces that the document is the 'final will' (*nihsta cwide*) of Brihtric and his wife, Ælfswith, declared at Meopham (Kt), which lies about thirty miles from Rochester amid the other estates named in the will.[125] Such location of the will-making proceedings is unique in the corpus, and suggests an extraordinary event. This impression is enhanced by the fact that the declaration was made 'in the presence of their relations' (*on heora maga gewitnæsse*). We are then given a list of names of these male relatives, including Brihtric himself, adding Brihtwaru as 'Ælfric's widow', and culminating with the name of Bishop Ælfstan of Rochester, a key figure in the dispute, as Table 5 shows. Of the eight men named, all except Wine the priest and Ælfgar of Meopham are beneficiaries

123 Since Archbishop Oda died in 958, this bequest has a clear *terminus ante quem*. Two other witnesses, Ælfheah and Ælfric, Ælfstan's sons, feature in a dispute with Rochester over land at Wouldham, near Snodland (S1458/R41, 960x988).

124 *Wills*, p. 129. Whitelock identifies the Brihtric of the will and of the dispute as a single individual (*Wills*, p. 128); Flight sees them as different men ('Four vernacular texts', p. 134, n. 22). For male advocacy for a woman in a dispute see Chap. 2, p. 71 above.

125 Flight, 'Four vernacular texts', figs. 1 and 2, pp. 130, 136.

of land in the will.[126] In each bequest, there is a strong emphasis on family land, suggesting a family strategy in operation: Wulfheah is granted Birling (Kt), and must pay one thousand pence to Rochester on behalf of Brihtric and Ælfswith and their ancestors; the brothers Wulfstan Ucca and Wulfsige receive Walkingstead (in Godstone, Sy) and Wateringbury (Kt) respectively, with the stipulation that the estates must remain in their family; and the brothers Wulfheah and Ælfheah receive Harrietsham (Kt) on the same terms, dividing the *inland* and the *utland* between them. A similar proviso is attached to the bequest of *Hæslholt* to Sired, and to that of Titsey (Sy), along with the title-deed, to Wulfsige.[127] It is tempting to see these bequests as a means of gaining the support of the key male kin of Brihtric and Brihtwaru for a settlement with Rochester. It is also important to note that Brihtric and Ælfswith stipulate the payment of food-rent to Rochester from each of the estates bequeathed to these kinsmen, engaging the beneficiaries in an ongoing relationship with the church, and in family commemoration.[128]

However vexed the interpretation of this group of documents may be, the will seems to represent not only the bequests of Brihtric and Ælfswith, but also the commitment of a kin-group to the completion of the pious bequest of two of their number: Ælfric's father, Ælfhere, who bequeathed the land to Rochester in the first place, and Ælfric himself, Brihtwaru's husband, who endorsed that bequest.

For laymen, the bequest of land within the kindred was influenced by two main factors: the desire to protect the interests of wives and daughters, and the advisability of an equitable distribution among close kinsmen which would engage their support for the proposed alienation of land to the Church. Such bequests to kinsmen may also, of course, have reduced the risk of a challenge to the tenure of women. Underlying both factors was the pious gift – the reversion of land held in usufruct by wives and daughters, and the direct alienation of one or more estates to the Church for the spiritual advantage of both donor and kin-group. For women, the parameters for the bequest of land were, in many ways, different.

126 Two Wulfsiges are distinguished in the list, as brother of Wulfstan Ucca and *se blaca* respectively, but are not distinguished in the body of the will, although it seems likely that both were beneficiaries (see below).

127 Probably *se blaca*, since the other Wulfsige seems to be linked with his brother both in the bequest of land and in the responsibility for the distribution of alms on behalf of the donors.

128 They also bequeath Meopham to Christ Church, Canterbury. For the bequest of movable wealth in this will see Chap. 5, pp. 209–11 below.

## The bequest of land by women

A few women appear as joint donors with their husbands in a number of single-gift bequests which assert the right of both partners to a life interest in land before its reversion to the Church.[129] The documents often take the form of an agreement, as in the *foreweard* between Wulfgeat and his wife and the abbot and community of Bury: the donors are to have a life interest in the abbey's estate of Gislingham (Sfk), with reversion to the abbey along with Wulfgeat's estate of Fakenham (Nfk) 'as fully and completely as Wulfgeat possesses it' (*so ful and so forth so Wlgeat it oh*).[130]

As Crick has noted, one factor common to almost all of these bequests is the absence of children.[131] The exception is the bequest of *Acleia* to Ramsey by Eadnoth and his wife, which stipulates that two pounds annually should be provided from the estate to provide clothing for their son Æthelric, for as long as he remained a monk there.[132] At least one couple were indeed childless at the time of their declaration: Æthelnoth and Gænburg make provision for the possibility that a child might yet be born to them.[133] However, it cannot necessarily be assumed that the remaining couples were also childless, since these bequests are specifically intended to earn spiritual benefit for the donors and those associated with the land in question. That these bequests were likely to have been supplemented by other dispositions is indicated by that of Ordnoth and his wife to the Old Minster, Winchester, which refers to their additional provision for a separate part of 'his' property (*æhta*) to be placed in the hands of friends (*freonda handa*), but no details are included.[134]

129 S1500/R3, *Christ Church* 39A; S1524/W5; S1235/*St Albans* 17; S1608, *ECEE* 133; S1232/R113. S1529/W36 and S1470/R100 do not specify that the donors are husband and wife. *LE* records joint bequests by Ordmær and his wife Ælde to King Edgar (II, 7/*Lib* 5) and by Lustwine and his wife Leofwaru to the monastery (II, 89). *CR* records joint bequests by Ærnketel and Wulfrun (S1493/*CR* 37/38), Ælfsige and Leva (*CR* 107, p. 174) and Eadnoth and wife (S1231/*CR* 107, at pp. 173–4). This group of wills is discussed by Crick, 'Women, posthumous benefaction', pp. 404–6. Two documents of uncertain integrity as they stand have been omitted: S1243/*St Paul's* 31; S1218, printed by C. R. Hart, *Early Charters of Essex* (Leicester, 1971), no. 30 (see *Wills*, p. 149). The bequests of land in the joint multi-gift wills of Brihtric and Ælfswith and Ulf and Madselin are discussed above at pp. 161–5 and Chap. 3, pp. 135–8 respectively.

130 S1470/R100. See also S1608, *ECEE* 133 and S1235/*St Albans* 17. The Latin text S1231/*CR* 107 (p. 173) uses the term *conventio* for a similar agreement. For reversionary agreements see Chap. 1, p. 36 above.

131 Crick, 'Women, posthumous benefaction', pp. 406–407.

132 S1231/*CR* 107 (p. 174). Æthelric's commitment to the monastic life seems to have been in doubt, since the donors envisage their son abandoning both habit and monastery, in which case the payments are to cease.

133 S1500/R3, *Christ Church* 39A.

134 S1524/W5.

It is in widowhood that women's individual voices emerge. Crick has shown that the majority of women may certainly or reasonably be described as widows at the time of their will-making.[135] Of the thirteen vernacular wills made by women, covering the ninth to the eleventh centuries, six women were certainly widowed.[136] Since a further four make bequests to children with no reference to a husband, it seems reasonable to assume that they, too, were widowed.[137] Of the remaining three, no evidence can be adduced for Siflæd, who mentions neither a husband nor children; Æthelflæd makes a bequest for her husband's soul, implying that she was a widow; and from the ninth century, Heregyth's status is unclear: her endorsement of her husband's will, written in a different hand, could imply that she had outlived him were it not for the fact that the food-rent which she bequeaths to Christ Church, Canterbury, is to take effect 'after her death and Abba's' (*ofer hire deg 7 ofer Abban*).[138] A similar pattern may be seen in the women's bequests recorded in the Ely and Ramsey chronicles: nine of the fourteen donors were widowed.[139] Further evidence comes from a writ of King Edward the Confessor, which, in the context of confirming her right to bequeath, describes Tole as Urk's widow (*lafe*).[140]

For women, therefore, it seems that widowhood was an important stimulus for will-making: it was at this point that a woman's marital agreements matured, and a variety of interests could be brought to bear upon her.[141] She was likely to forfeit her morning-gift if she remarried within a year of widowhood.[142] She might be subject to kindred pressures, as in the case of Æthelstan Mannessune's widow who, on the anniversary of his death, renegotiated the terms of his will with the Ramsey community *parentum inducta* (at the

135 Crick, 'Women, posthumous benefaction', pp. 407–10; this study appends a valuable list of bequests (pp. 419–21). For a portrait of a ninth-century Frankish widow see Nelson, 'The wary widow', pp. 82–113.

136 Ceolwynn (S1513/R17); Cynethryth (S1200/H7, *Christ Church* 90); Ælfflæd (S1486/W15); Æthelflæd (S1494/W14); Ælfgifu (S1484/W8); Æthelgifu (S1497/*St Albans* 7).

137 Wynflæd (S1539/W3); Wulfwaru (S1538/W21, *Bath and Wells* 21); Wulfgyth (S1535/W32, *Christ Church* 176); Leofgifu (S1531/W29).

138 Siflæd (S1525/W37, 38); Æthelflæd (S1495/W22, *St Paul's* 22); Heregyth (S1482/H2, *Christ Church* 70), which survives in a contemporary manuscript written in three hands: one scribe (Brooks' scribe 3) wrote the main text of Abba's will, a second scribe added the witness list, and a third scribe added Heregyth's bequest on the dorse: Brooks, *Early History*, p. 360, n. 70; BL Cotton Aug. ii 64 (*Facsimiles*, ed. Bond, II, no. 23).

139 See Appendix Two, nos. 6 (and 40: same donor), 12, 16, 19, 38, 46, 60; the vernacular wills of numbers 1 and 3 are extant: Ælfflæd (S1486/W15) and Ælfgifu (S1484/W8). A further two donors mention children, but no spouse (7, 14); three donors have living husbands (43, 44, 57).

140 S1064/ *Writs* 2.

141 Nelson, 'The wary widow', pp. 87–94; Crick, 'Posthumous obligation', pp. 203–205.

142 II Cnut, 73–73a. See also p. 147 above.

instigation of relatives).[143] In general, individual women appear in records of public activity in widowhood: for example, in the *Liber Eliensis* the widow Æscwyn of Stonea attends a meeting of two hundreds at Ely, along with relatives and neighbours, to declare her grant of land to Wulfstan of Dalham, the powerful East Anglian reeve, and the wife of Ælfwold the Fat enters the record because of her unsuccessful attempt to sell land inherited from her previous husband.[144]

Accounts of disputes from the tenth and eleventh centuries attest to the potential vulnerability of the widow's position, particularly to challenge by her late husband's kin. The dispute recounted in the tenth-century will of Æthelgifu may have been fuelled by the fact that a number of estates in Hertfordshire and Bedfordshire, probably the land which (the will tells us) Æthelgifu's husband had acquired and which he had granted to her with freedom of disposition, were bequeathed by her to the Church on his behalf and her own; the land would thus become alienated from his kindred.[145] Her principal heir, Leofsige, is to receive a life interest in one of those estates, Standon (Herts.) before its reversion to the church; although Leofsige's relationship with Æthelgifu is unstated, he is also to receive land in Northamptonshire which Æthelgifu probably inherited from her own family, suggesting that he was either her own kinsman, or a son or grandson resulting from her union with her husband as his second wife.[146] Whatever the truth of the matter, a complex kindred network seems involved, with conflicting claims on acquired land.[147]

Debate concerning the independence of women's landholding in the period before and after 1066 has raised questions about their rights of free disposition.[148] Some high-ranking women, such as Ælfgifu or Æthelflæd, held land by royal charter, but in most cases it was acquired from husbands, or from their own kindred, perhaps with freedom of disposition subject to a

143 *CR* 33; Crick, 'Posthumous obligation', p. 204.

144 *LE* II, 18/*Lib* 27; *LE* II, 11/*Lib* 14.

145 S1497/*St Albans* 7: Gaddesden, Munden, Standon, Westwick (Herts.); Langford (Beds.). *Æthelgifu*, pp. 28, 63–9. See Chap. 2, pp. 73–5 above for an account of the dispute.

146 *St Albans*, pp. 98–9; *Æthelgifu*, pp. 29, 63, with the suggestion that Offley may have been held on lease from St Alban's at p. 69.

147 Other disputes concerning similar challenges to women's rights in land are: S877/R63, *New Minster* 31 (996); S1511/W11, *Rochester* 35 (973x987); S1454/R66 (990x992); *LE* II, 11a / *Lib* 14. See also S1187/*EHD* I, no. 81 (804: see Chap. 1, pp. 44–6 above) and S1462/R78 (1016x1035), the Herefordshire Lawsuit (see Chap. 2, pp. 60–1 above).

148 The debate is outlined by Stafford, 'Women and the Norman Conquest', pp. 221–6; see also Stafford, 'Women in Domesday' for individual women landholders. Women's landholding is discussed by M. A. Meyer, 'Land charters and the legal position of Anglo-Saxon women', in *The Women of England from Anglo-Saxon Times to the Present*, ed. B. Kanner (London, 1980), pp. 57–82 (pp. 62–71) and Meyer, 'Women's estates'. Nelson, 'Wary Widow' and Crick, 'Women, posthumous benefaction' relate the issue specifically to the impact on women's bequests.

marriage agreement, but more often as usufruct.[149] The influence of husbands and fathers on women's bequests can be difficult to detect, but must be regarded as a potentially significant factor. The clearest example of a father's influence is in the tenth-century will sequence of Ealdorman Ælfgar and his two daughters. The survival of Ælfgar's will, which is first in the sequence, reveals that the subsequent wills of his daughters largely – if not entirely – reflect his intentions in bequeathing to the Church land which might otherwise appear to be their own independent bequests.[150] Making her own will in widowhood, Ælfgar's younger daughter, Ælfflæd, not only completes her father's bequests, but bequeaths to Ely, where her husband was buried, three estates 'which we both promised to God and his saints'.[151] It must therefore be borne in mind that other, apparently independent, bequests of land by women may in fact have been influenced by primary bequests of fathers, husbands or other kin.[152]

In terms of bequeathing land to kindred, women's wills show a strong focus on transmission in the direct line, or to their own collateral kin. Such bequests feature in the wills of nine of the twelve women donors who make bequests of land.[153] A case in point is the multi-gift will of Wynflæd, whose identity remains uncertain, although the possibility that she was King Edgar's grandmother is attractive.[154] Since no husband is mentioned, Wynflæd was probably widowed, with a surviving daughter and son (if it is accepted that Eadmær is indeed her son, as the context suggests) to whom she makes bequests.[155] One important aspect of this will is the distinction made between land which Wynflæd has the right to bequeath, and that over

149 For royal land held by Ælfgifu and Æthelflæd see Chap. 3, pp. 94–7 above. See *Shaftesbury*, no. 13 (S485) and p. xvi, n. 17 and Foot, *Veiled Women*, I, 136–7 for Wynflæd's possible links with royalty. A woman's acquisition of land in the Carolingian period has been discussed by Nelson, 'Wary Widow', pp. 85–90. For women's inheritance from husbands and fathers see pp. 146–50 above.

150 S1483/W2, 946x *c.* 951; S1494/W14, 962x991; S1486/W15, 1000x1002. See Chap. 6, pp. 235–7 below for a detailed account of this sequence of wills.

151 *Þe wit buta geheotan gode. 7 his halgan*: S1486/W15. One of these estates, Rettendon (Ex), had been her morning-gift. Her older sister, Æthelflæd, also fulfils the intention of her husband, King Edmund, in bequeathing Damerham to Glastonbury: S1494/W14; Chap. 3, n. 66 above.

152 *CR* 35 records Ælfhild's fulfilment in her own will of her husband's *viva voce* bequest.

153 S1513/R17; S1539/W3; S1521/W29; S1538/W21, *Bath and Wells* 21; S1535/W32, *Christ Church* 176; S1497/*St Albans* 7; S1484/W8; S1494/W14; S1486/W15. Madselin also bequeaths land to a kinswoman in the joint will W39/*Peterborough* 27. The exceptions are S1200/H7, *Christ Church* 90 (a ninth-century agreement); S1495/W22, *St Paul's* 22 (a single-gift bequest to the church, spurious in its present form); and S1525/W38 (which bequeaths two wagonloads of wood to the donor's brothers).

154 S1539/W3, *c.* 950. This text will be edited in the final volume of the British Academy charter series. For Wynflæd's identity see *Wills*, p. 109; *Shaftesbury*, p. xvi n. 17, xxvi–xxvii, no. 13 and pp. 56–7; Foot, *Veiled Women*, I, 136–9.

155 Eadmer is not explicitly referred to as Wynflæd's son: *Wills*, p. 110.

which she has no such right. For example, she bequeaths no land at Charlton (Dors.), but grants the men and stock to her daughter, reserving a pious gift. Similarly, her bequest of the estate at Chinnock (Som.) to the community at Shaftesbury distinguishes between the land itself, and the stock and men, which are distributed among Shaftesbury, her granddaughter and the church at Yeovil.[156] The terms of this bequest suggest that Chinnock is already the subject of an agreement with Shaftesbury:

> *7 be þan lande æt Cinnuc hit agon þa hiwan æt Sceaftesbyrig ofer hyre dæg 7 hio ah þæt yrfe 7 þa men.*
>
> (And with regard to the estate at Chinnock, the community at Shaftesbury possess it after her death, and she owns the stock and the men.)

It seems likely that Wynflæd is either holding a life interest in Chinnock from the community, or that she has only usufruct subject to a reversionary grant. Nelson's study of the will of the ninth-century Frankish woman Erkanfrida has demonstrated the complexity of the terms on which widows might hold land;[157] Wynflæd's bequests suggest similar complexity of tenurial rights.

One particular feature shared by the wills of Erkanfrida and Wynflæd is their bequest of land given to them by their husbands – *dos* and *morgengyfu* respectively – although they dispose of this property in different ways. Erkanfrida places most of her land, with the exception of that pertaining to the church of St Michael at Mersch, into the administration of a group of powerful lords. She is precise concerning the substantial payments to named churches which would allow her late husband's kin to acquire the property on her death, specifically excluding her *dos* – the church of St Michael and its land – from this agreement, since she has granted it to St Maximin of Trier in commemoration of herself and her husband.[158] The will ends with a reminder to her trustees that they must answer to God for their actions in relation to her dispositions.[159] Whereas Erkanfrida appears to have been childless, Wynflæd has direct heirs to whom she bequeaths her morning-gift:

> *7 hio an him eac þæs landes æt Faccancumbe þe hyre morgengyfu wes his dæg 7 ofer his dæg gyf Æþelflæd leng lybbe þonne he þonne fo hio to þam lande æt Faccancumbe and ofer hyre dæg ga hit eft an Eadwoldes hand.*
>
> (And she grants to him [Eadmær, probably her son] also the estate at Faccombe, which was her morning-gift, for his lifetime, and then after his death, if Æthelflæd [her daughter] survive him, she is to succeed to the

156 Wynflæd's bequests of movable wealth are discussed in Chap. 5 below.

157 Erkanfrida's rights in different estates are discussed by Nelson, 'Wary Widow', pp. 104–106.

158 Nelson, 'Wary widow', pp. 96–7 and pp. 99–101 for further documentary evidence for this grant.

159 Nelson, 'Wary widow', p. 109.

estate at Faccombe, and after her death it is to revert to Eadwold's possession [probably her grandson].)

Although her daughter, Æthelflæd, is to have a life interest in Faccombe (Hants.) the estate is to revert to the male line (Eadmær's son, Eadwold, was still a child at the time Wynflæd made her will).

It is unclear whether Wynflæd's decision to bequeath her morning-gift in this way was her own choice, or the result of a previous agreement. It has been shown above that the morning-gift was likely to be the subject of a marriage agreement, which could be ratified by the wills of male donors, and which might grant a woman free disposition of at least one estate: one of the marriage agreements is explicit in allowing the woman to hold land at Alton with the right to dispose of it as she chose during her life or on her death, and the will of Thurketel Heyng emphasises that his wife's *del* is at her own disposal.[160] We also learn from the will of Bishop Ælfric that the widow of Thurketel of Palgrave sold him the estate of Roydon (Nfk), which was the subject of her marriage agreement.[161]

That Wynflæd's bequest of her morning-gift, Faccombe, to her grandson Eadwold was an independent choice may seem more likely if the bequest is seen in terms of the subsequent clause:

> *7 gif god wille þæt Eadwold weorþe to þam gewexen an his fæder dæge þæt he land healdan mæge þene bid ic Eadmær þæt he him læte þara twega landa oþer to oþþe æt Colleshylle oð æt Eadburggebyrig 7 ofer his dæg buta.*
>
> (And if it is God's will that Eadwold be old enough in his father's lifetime to hold land, then I ask Eadmær to relinquish to him one of two estates, either Coleshill or Adderbury, and after his lifetime, both.)

This request directed to her son, relating to land over which she apparently has no control, indicates a concern for the land endowment of her grandson; this may well have influenced her bequest to him of Faccombe.

Wynflæd's bequests of land to her daughter, Æthelflæd, may also suggest some degree of independence. The first is an estate at Ebbesbourne (Wilts), bequeathed outright, with the title-deed, 'as perpetual inheritance to dispose of as she pleases' (*on ece yrfe to ateonne swa hyre leofosð sy*) and specifying the

160 See pp. 148–9 above. S1459/R76; S1528/W25. For a woman's rights in disposing of *dos* see Nelson, 'Wary widow', pp. 85–9; for tensions surrounding dowry in Francia, see Le Jan, *Famille et pouvoir*, pp. 366–71.

161 S1527/W24; S1489/W26. The widow of Æthelric of Bocking was also in a position to trade her morning-gift for the advocacy of the archbishop in persuading King Æthelstan to allow her husband's will to stand (S939/W16$^2$, *Christ Church* 137). The Fonthill letter (S1445/H18) records a woman's sale of her morning-gift. Æthelgifu refers to the land which her husband bequeathed to her 'for her to give to whom she wished' (*hire to sellanne þam þe hyo wolde*): S1497/*St Albans* 7.

inclusion of men and stock (reserving a pious gift for Wynflæd's soul).[162] The second bequest of land to her daughter shows that Wynflæd herself was holding a residence (*worþig*) inherited from her own mother; she grants it to Æthelflæd 'if the king grant it to her as King Edward granted it to Beorhtwynn, her mother' (*gif his hyre se cing an swa swa Eadweard cing ær his Byrhtwynne hyre meder geuþe*). Although Wynflæd's identity, and possible links with the royal house, remain uncertain, it is worth noting that a charter of King Edmund in favour of a nun named Wynflæd confirms her right to land at Cheselbourne (Dors.), which had been granted by his predecessors.[163] This particular charter may not be directly relevant to the Wynflæd whose will we have, but such a process of royal confirmation may underlie Wynflæd's bequest to her daughter of a homestead which had already passed in the female line across two generations.[164]

Æthelgifu seems also to have had at least some freedom of disposition over land which she may have inherited from her own kindred, a small and closely aligned group of estates in Northamptonshire.[165] Two of these estates, Watford and Thrupp, she bequeaths to her kinswoman Leofrun.[166] Watford is to pass in the female line: on Leofrun's death, it is to go to her daughter, Godwif, who is mentioned elsewhere in the will. However, a condition is attached to Æthelgifu's bequest of Thrupp: Leofrun will inherit this estate, presumably because she has a claim as a member of Æthelgifu's kin, but unless she agrees to abandon unreasonable claims (*on þa gerad þe heo selle hire wed 7 ælc yrre forgife*), she will not have the right of free disposal. If she agrees to Æthelgifu's terms, she will be able to grant the land 'within her own kindred'; if she does not, the estate will be divided among her children. Æthelgifu seems to have had sufficient autonomy over her bequest of this estate to manipulate a kinswoman into compliance.[167] The third Northamptonshire estate – Weedon – is granted to Æthelgifu's principal beneficiary, Leofsige, with the proviso that he subsidise the commemoration of her parents, her brother, herself and her lord with one barrel of ale annually from the estate,

162 The gift of the Ebbesborne estate is yoked with that of her engraved *beah* and a brooch, the significance of which as heirlooms is discussed below in Chap. 5, p. 204.

163 S485, *Shaftesbury* 13, dated 942. For discussion of the possible links between Wynflæd and the royal family see *Shaftesbury*, p. 56.

164 Ebbesborne, where Wynflæd also bequeaths land to her daughter, features in a number of royal charters in favour of laymen, but the connexion between the estate for which Wynflæd holds the *boc* and the land of the charters is unclear (S635, 956; S640, 957; S696, 961; S861, 986); perhaps this estate had been royal land.

165 S1497/*St Albans*, 7; *Æthelgifu*, pp. 28–9, 63; *St Albans*, p. 98.

166 Æthelgifu's relationship to Leofrun is unspecified; Leofrun's daughter, Godwif, is favoured in the will.

167 *LE* records Leofflæd's bequest of an estate to her daughter Leofwaru on condition that 'she remain in chastity or accept a lawful husband, lest she and our progeny be disgraced by the taint of fornication' (II, 88).

paid to an unspecified church. Again, Æthelgifu manipulates the succession: the estate will revert to Leofsige's child (*bearn*) if he should have one; if he does not, it will pass to his 'lawful kindred' (*riht cyn*). Although Leofsige's relationship to Æthelgifu is unstated, the responsibility for the commemoration of her family vested in him suggests that he was her own kin rather than her husband's. If this is so, Æthelgifu is ensuring that Weedon, like Watford and Thrupp, will revert to her own kindred.[168]

It is also conceivable that land bequeathed by Wulfgyth to her children may have been acquired from her own kindred.[169] Stisted (Ex) is to revert to Christ Church, Canterbury, after the lives of her two sons, in commemoration of her husband, herself and her children, but her children are to receive a further six estates in Norfolk and Suffolk.[170] Since most of the land bequeathed by Wulfgyth's brother, Edwin, lay in Norfolk, her own family property may have lain in this area.[171] Wulfgyth bequeaths Walsingham, Carleton and Harling (Nfk) to her sons Ælfketel and Ketel;[172] her daughters Gode and Bote are to share Somerleyton (Sfk) and Saxlingham (Nfk); and her daughter Ealdgyth is to receive Chadacre (Sfk) and Ashford (Kt?). Wulfgyth's will took effect before 1066; the pre-Conquest will of her son Ketel shows that he and his sisters were in possession of their inheritance.[173] His will also shows that two of the estates bequeathed by their mother – Walsingham and Somerleyton – as well as Ketel's estate at Ketteringham (Nfk) and Gode's estate at Preston (Sfk), were the subject of reversionary agreements between him and his sisters designed to ensure that this land would remain in the family, potentially passing in the female line.[174]

However, the overall pattern of women's bequests of land within the kindred suggests that, as for their male counterparts, preference of the male line was a critical factor. Nine of the documents are multi-gift wills.[175] Of these, three include bequests of land to sons, but none to male collateral kin.[176] Of the six which do not include bequests to sons, five feature bequests of land to male collateral kin.[177] In addition, two women making single-gift bequests

168 For an analysis of naming in this will which reveals Æthelgifu's recognition of her own kin, see Lowe, 'Problems of translation', pp. 30–1.

169 S1535/W32, *Christ Church* 176.

170 A further estate, *Essetesford*, is uncertainly identified as Ashford (Kt): *Christ Church* 176.

171 S1516/W33.

172 The text has *Wulkitele*, possibly an error for Ælfketel: *Wills*, p. 198.

173 S1519/W34.

174 See Chap. 6, pp. 257–9 below, for the association of this family and their land with local churches.

175 S1535/W32, *Christ Church* 176; S1539/W3; S1538/W21, *Bath and Wells* 21; S1497/ *St Albans* 7; S1521/W29; S1494/W14; S1486/W15; S1484/W8; S1525/W37, 38.

176 S1535/W32, *Christ Church* 176; S1539/W3, S1538/W21, *Bath and Wells* 21. Æthelgifu's relationship with her principal heir is uncertain (S1497/*St Albans* 7).

177 S1484/W8 (brothers); S1521/W29 (brother's son and unspec.); S1494/W14 (unspec.);

of land, Ceolwynn and Cynethryth, refer to kinsmen: Ceolwynn reserves a life interest for her brother's son in a hide of land belonging to an estate which she bequeaths to the Church, and Cynethryth, following her husband's instructions, transmits an estate to her late husband's closest relative: his brother's daughter's son.[178] Where both sons and daughters are named in women's wills, sons tend to receive more land. Wulfwaru's two sons receive a total of five and a half estates, while her elder daughter receives one, and her younger daughter is to have a half share of an estate, of which the other half is held by her older brother.[179] Further preference of the male line is suggested by Wynflæd's interest in the patrimony of her grandson, Eadwold: when he should reach the appropriate age, his father, Eadmær, is asked to relinquish to his son either Coleshill (Berks), which Wynflæd bequeaths to him, or Adderbury (Oxon), which is not otherwise mentioned in the will and which must already be in Eadmær's possession; Eadwold is to have both estates on his father's death, together with the reversion of Faccomb, Wynflæd's morning-gift. In contrast, Eadgifu, Eadwold's sister, is to receive only chattels. The fact that one daughter of Wulfgeat of Donington is privileged over another in his will may also be linked to the fact that she has a son: Wulfgifu is to receive Donington, which may be the main family estate, and a further estate which appears to have been bought with her mother's dowry or morning-gift (*mid hire moder golde geboht*); additionally, her son is to receive an estate. Wulfgeat's other daughter is to receive only one hide.[180]

While this apparent strategy designed to conserve land within a narrow range of kin does not exclude daughters or collateral kinswomen from inheriting, amounts bequeathed to them are small and the number of estates limited.[181] There is some evidence that a daughter might benefit from land derived from her maternal kin, as in Wynflæd's bequest of the *worþig* which seems to have passed in the maternal line, or Wulfgeat's bequest to his daughter of land bought with her mother's gold, but since it is often impossible to determine the origin of estates named in women's wills, this must

S1486/W15 (uncertain reading); S1497/*St Albans* 7 (sister's son). Siflæd bequeaths a wagonload of wood to her brothers (S1525/W38).

178 S1513/R17; S1200/H7, *Christ Church* 90. Ælfflæd (S1486/W15) may make a bequest of land to her husband's kinsman; a lacuna in the manuscript makes this reading uncertain.

179 S1538/W21, *Bath and Wells* 21. See also S1535/W32, *Christ Church* 176 and S1539/W3.

180 S1534/W19. See also S1483/W2 for Ealdorman Ælfgar's concern to protect the rights of grandchildren; the terms *child* and *bearn* used in his will are not gendered, but see n. 43 above. The relevant terminology is discussed by Lancaster, 'Kinship in Anglo-Saxon society', pp. 233–7.

181 Women's bequests of land to daughters: S1539/W3; S1535/W32, *Christ Church* 176; S1538/W21, *Bath and Wells* 21; S1497/*St Albans* 7; S1521/W29 (and see *LE* II, 88). To kinswomen: S1494/W14; S1486/W15; S1521/W29. Male *affines* may also be named in relation to kinswomen: S1494/W14; S1521/W29.

remain only a possibility. Nevertheless, women were an important factor in the transmission of land within the kindred, as shown by the reversionary agreements between Ketel and his sisters, discussed above. In addition, Ketel makes a similar reversionary agreement with his step-daughter concerning his estate at Onehouse (Sfk): the survivor will inherit the estate, which will ultimately revert to the church.[182] The joint will of Ulf and Madselin records reversionary agreements between Ulf and his mother, and between Madselin and a certain Ingemund, who may have been a kinsman.[183] On the evidence of these wills, the role of women in both the retention and circulation of land within the kin group was crucial.

Unlike the will of Erkanfrida, which sets out precise instructions concerning the amount to be paid to the church by her husband's kin if they wished to claim the land which she had inherited from him,[184] there is little evidence that the wills of Anglo-Saxon women were concerned with the transmission of land to their marital kin. In only one case is this demonstrable. Cynethryth, the widow of Ealdorman Æthelmod, inherited land at Chart (Kt) for her life, with reversion to Æthelmod's kinsman, his brother's son Osberht.[185] The latter clearly died before Cynethryth, since the document records that she had negotiated with her husband's closest surviving kinsman, Eadweald, the son of Æthelmod's brother's daughter; he was to 'give ten thousand' – presumably to the Church – for the land on her death, or, if he predeceased her, one of his children was to do so. Cynethryth followed to the letter her husband's instructions to dispose of the land 'as might be for them most just and charitable' (*swe hit him boem rehtlicast 7 elmestlicast were*). Æthelgifu bequeaths a life interest in land at Offley (Herts.) to her husband's daughter, presumably her own step-daughter, but the identification of the beneficiaries Ælfwold and Ælfnoth as her husband's kinsmen, who are to receive a life interest in land before its reversion to the Church, rests on the identification of the estates in question – Munden (Herts.) and Langford (Beds.) – as among the properties which Æthelgifu probably inherited from her husband.[186] Leofsige, who was to receive a life interest in Standon (Herts.), which Æthelgifu may also have inherited from her husband, seems more likely to have been her own kinsman.[187]

182 S1519/W34.

183 For reversionary agreements in the will of Ulf and Madselin (W39/*Peterborough* 27) see Chap. 3, p. 137 above. See also S1508/H10, *Christ Church* 96 and S1507/H11, *New Minster* 1 (and p. 153 above) for the practice of male kinsmen buying land from women who had inherited it from their fathers or husbands.

184 Nelson, 'Wary widow', pp. 96–7.

185 S1200/H7, *Christ Church* 90.

186 S1497/*St Albans* 7; *St Albans*, p. 98. Æthelgifu describes the estates which constituted her *ælmessa* as her husband's acquisitions (see Lord Rennell in *Æthelgifu*, pp. 63–74, and n. 145 above.).

187 *St Albans*, pp. 98–9; see p. 173 above.

Overall, women making their wills in widowhood seem to have been concerned primarily with the transmission of land to their own children and grandchildren, and to their own kin. It seems likely that the land which they bequeathed in this way was that which they had acquired through marriage agreement or inheritance from their own kin, over which they might claim some independence of disposition while avoiding the dispersal of land from the kin-group.

However, all but one of the extant women's wills also bequeath land to the Church.[188] It is possible that some of these bequests reflect the reversion of land predetermined by those from whom the donors had received it, as is demonstrated by the will of Ælfflæd, which fulfils the bequests of her father and husband to Stoke-by-Nayland and Ely.[189] The terms of women's bequests reveal their role in channelling land to the Church not only for their own spiritual benefit, but for that of others.[190] Husbands are often named: Wulfgyth, for instance, bequeaths the reversion of Stisted (Ex) to Christ Church, Canterbury, for her own soul and that of her husband, Ælfwine, as well as the souls of all her children.[191] Those to be commemorated may be those from whom the land originated, as in Wulfwaru's grant of land to the church 'for the souls of my ancestors from whom my property and my possessions came to me' (*for minra yldrena þe me min ar of com*).[192] Ælfflæd, bequeathing land to the community at Stoke-by-Nayland, refers to the fact that the property had previously been granted by her ancestors (*yldran*), who were buried there.[193] In the joint agreement which Æthelgyth and her second husband, Oswulf, made with St Alban's, the text indicates that Æthelgyth had negotiated with Oswulf that her first husband, Ulf, from whom she may have acquired the land, should be included with them in the commemoration which their gift would command, reflecting a woman's continuing obligation to commemorate her late husband, even after remarriage.[194] Even where women bequeath land to the church where they wish to be buried, the gift may refer to the commemoration of others: Leofgifu's bequest of two estates to Bury is made

188 The exception is S1200/H7, *Christ Church* 90.

189 See p. 169 above. Wynflæd's bequest of Chinnock to Shaftesbury may also refer to a prior arrangement (S1539/W3; see p. 170 above).

190 Neither S1525/W37, 38 nor S1539/W3 specify on whose behalf the gift is made.

191 S1535/W32, *Christ Church* 176. Husbands are included in S1497/*St Albans* 7; S1495/W22, *St Paul's* 22; S1521/W29; S1513/R17.

192 S1538/W21, *Bath and Wells* 21. See also S1497/*St Albans* 7 and p. 168 above for Æthelgifu's inheritance. *LE* II, 83 records a bequest by Godgifu of land inherited from her parents, and *LE* II, 10 describes Wulfflæd holding land following her father's death.

193 S1486/W15. For his daughters' delay in fulfilling Ælfgar's bequests see Chap. 6, pp. 236–7 below.

194 S1235/*St Albans* 17: *þ wif Athelið swyþost þis ðus begeat gedon æt hire hlaforde Oswulfe, for hire ærran hlafordes sawle Ulfes.*

not only for her burial, but 'for the redemption of my lord's soul and mine'.[195] The former queen Ælfgifu, bequeathing land to the Old Minster, Winchester, for her burial, as well as estates to other churches with royal associations, does so for the spiritual benefit of King Edgar.[196] The pattern of these bequests by women to the church suggests that their acquisition of land brought with it the responsibility for commemoration, a responsibility which is acknowledged in their wills.[197]

Some historians have seen will-making by women as evidence that Anglo-Saxon England was a Golden Age of women's independence, a view which has been both explored and challenged by Stafford.[198] It is certainly the case that women's independence in their bequests of land was often circumscribed by family constraints, or by the prior dispositions of husbands or fathers. Nevertheless, wills show clear evidence that while they had guardianship of land, women were capable of managing their estates. Ealdorman Ælfheah, for example, entrusted his wife with proper care of his estates after his death.[199] The multi-gift wills of two women – Leofgifu and Æthelgifu – reveal a thorough acquaintance with the property for which they were responsible.[200] The extent of Leofgifu's knowledge of her affairs is revealed in the meticulous detail of her opening dispositions; bequeathing two estates, Hintlesham and Gestingthorpe, to Bury as her burial gift, she continues:

> *... buten þat lond þat Ailsi hauede þat he at his lauerd ernede and at me. and ilc þridde aker on þan wude at Hintlesham habbe Ailri. and ingong and vtgong be feld and be fenne. and ic wille þat Ailric prest and Ailfric prest and Ailri diacon habben þat minstre at Colne. so here lofard it hem vthe. and ic wille þat Aylfric prest ben on þat ilke loh þe Aignoð was.*
>
> (... except the land which Æthelsige had, which he acquired from his lord and from me. And Æthelsige is to have every third acre in the wood at Hintlesham, and ingress and egress by open land and fen. And I desire that Æthelric the priest and Alfric the priest and Æthelsige the deacon shall have the minster at Colne as their lord granted it to them. And it is my wish that Ælfric the priest shall be in the same position in which Æthelnoth was.)[201]

195 S1521/W29: *mine louerdes soule to alisidnesse and mine.*

196 S1484/W8. For the possibility that this may have been royal land see Chap. 3, n. 90 above. The former queen Æthelflæd makes similar bequests on behalf of King Edgar and her late husband, King Edmund (S1494/W14).

197 For women's commemorative responsibility see below Chap. 5, pp. 224–5, and Chap. 6, pp. 276–7.

198 Stafford, 'Women and the Norman Conquest'.

199 S1498/W10, *New Minster* 25.

200 S1521/W29; S1497/*St Albans* 7.

201 For the term *ingong and utgong* see also S1528/W25. The *DOEC* reveals no other usage of this phrase in vernacular documents, although it occurs in literary sources; since both documents derive from Bury, this may be a local formula.

She knows of, and has participated in, her husband's largesse, designating precisely the amount of woodland which is to be allocated to Æthelsige, and asserting her right to confirm Ælfric the priest's position as a shareholder in the minster at Colne. She goes on to confirm the holdings of her stewards Godric, Ælfwig and Ælfnoth, and refers to the fact that she had leased land to her reeves, Æthelmær and Godric, as reeve-land (*to reflande*), which she now bequeaths to them. Leofgifu emerges as a woman who engaged with the running of her estates, and was as capable as her male counterparts of juggling the various claims on land. Æthelgifu's will is even more minutely detailed. A typical example is her bequest to a certain Ælfwold (possibly a kinsman of her late husband) of Munden (Herts.), which specifies the food-rent to be paid to local minsters during his tenure; the number of plough teams he is entitled to, with men and women; the manumission of named individuals; and the final reversion of the land to the minsters at Braughing and Welwyn (Herts.), with the stipulation that thirty masses are to be sung annually. No male donor is concerned with this amount of detail, suggesting that women's wills may have emerged from a process of careful inventory of the stock and men on the land, possibly made at the time of a husband's death.[202] Widows were also responsible for the payment of their husbands' heriot; the widow of Æthelric of Bocking is shown delivering his heriot payment at court, and pleading for her husband's will to stand in the face of accusations of his treachery.[203] That prompt payment was generally required is shown by a law of King Cnut, which permits a widow to make the payment within twelve months without incurring a fine if circumstances have prevented her from doing so earlier.[204]

In widowhood, at least, women had a public role to play: wills and other documents show them at meetings of the *witan*, the shire and the hundred where, in spite of their apparent need for male advocacy or their vulnerability to male influence, their significance in the process of transmitting land was recognised. The very fact that their *post obitum* dispositions were documented by the church acknowledges their social standing and their authority over the land which had been placed in their guardianship.

202 See *CR* 107 for the hint of an inventory underpinning the bequest of Thorgunnr. Since women often held land in usufruct, with responsibility for transmission with stock and men as they received it, careful accounting may have been particularly necessary. This issue is explored further in Chap. 5 below.

203 S939/W16$^2$, *Christ Church* 137.

204 II Cnut, 73.4.

## Tension and strategy

Patterns in the bequest of land reflect the tension between two imperatives for the lay nobility as they made their wills: that which prompted the pious gift to the Church, and that which resisted the alienation of land from the kin-group. This tension was exacerbated when acquired land passed by inheritance within the kindred for one or more generations, creating potential claims upon it by the collateral kin of the original holder.

For male donors, perhaps senior figures within a kin-group with responsibility for the prosperity of the wider kin as well as their immediate family, a judicious distribution of land among potential claimants was necessary to avoid dispute. For women, likely to be making their wills at a different point in the life-cycle, when a family unit was in transition, the bequest of land was an assertion of their own responsibilities, position and status, although not necessarily their own choices; their wills suggest that, at this point, women's links with their own kin were reasserted, and their relationship with the next generation adjusted.

Central to this process was the church, serving as a focal point for family identity in its provision of commemoration, and providing through the documentation of bequests the means by which donors could not only record their dispositions in advance of mortal illness, but could also institute complex strategies involving usufruct, reversion, contingency and proviso. For laymen and -women, written wills offered an opportunity to influence affairs beyond their own lifetime.

In the view of one legal historian, 'if the evidence of all Anglo-Saxon wills had survived ... bequests of land would be among the least common'.[205] The evidence of this and the previous chapter challenges this assumption, placing land squarely at the centre of Anglo-Saxon will-making. Nevertheless, for this elite group in Anglo-Saxon society, land was also a source of disposable wealth; it has been argued that, in the course of the ninth, tenth and eleventh centuries changes in agrarian organisation and an increasingly commercialised economy produced a new emphasis on conspicuous wealth as a means of asserting status.[206] The role of material goods in wills now needs to be considered.

205 Sheehan, *The Will*, p. 83.

206 The case for an increasingly commercialised economy and related increase in aristocratic consumption is argued by Fleming, 'The new wealth', esp. at pp. 1–4.

# CHAPTER FIVE

# The bequest of movable wealth

Since truncation of the text in the course of the transmission of wills is possible, and in one or two instances demonstrable, particularly in cartulary versions, it is more than likely that we do not have the full picture of donors' bequests of chattels, which were particularly vulnerable to omission.[1] No doubt Bede's deathbed distribution of his 'few treasures' (*quaedam preciosa*) among the priests of his monastery was a typical scenario for both laity and religious, usually unrecorded.[2] As the evidence stands, movable wealth features almost exclusively in multi-gift wills: three are royal wills, five are the wills of ealdormen, fifteen were made by thegns, nine by women, two jointly by husband and wife, and six by churchmen.[3] The three multi-gift wills dated to the ninth century bequeath considerable wealth, but largely in the form of coin or stock;[4] it is only in wills of the tenth and eleventh centuries that we find a wider range of movable wealth which might be characterised as personal property, including war-gear, clothing, furnishings, jewellery and items associated with hunting or travel. This chronological shift may be related to an increase in disposable wealth, but it is also likely to reflect the evolution of the written will, as tenth- and eleventh-century donors exploited its potential to encompass detailed and complex dispositions to a range of beneficiaries.

As Sheehan pointed out, the disposition of personal property was less damaging to the social group than the alienation of land.[5] This is well illustrated by the way in which donors bequeath stock, which was not in itself a prestige item, although it provided a valuable resource for both donors and beneficiaries. It is probable that estates, whether transmitted by *post obitum* or *inter vivos* arrangement, were usually transferred 'as stocked' (*eallswa hit*

1 See Chap. 1, pp. 20–1 above for the evidence for truncation, particularly of bequests of movable wealth.

2 *Ecclesiastical History*, ed. Colgrave and Mynors, pp. 584–5, and see Chap. 2 p. 165 above.

3 Movable wealth is bequeathed in 40 of the 43 extant multi-gift wills, and in the single-gift bequest S1499/W35; see Appendix 3.

4 S1482/H2, *Christ Church* 70: coin, stock, a horn, a sword; S1508/H10, *Christ Church* 96: stock, coin; S1507/H11, *New Minster* 1: coin, stock, a sword.

5 *The Will*, p. 101.

*stænt*).[6] Nevertheless, it seems that surplus stock which had accrued during the holder's tenure was regarded as distinct from the economic structure of the estate; [7] it could therefore be manipulated flexibly as a valuable asset. Stock was important for women, both as beneficiaries and donors. Ælfhelm, for example, bequeaths to his wife not only land, but also substantial interests in stock:

> *7 fo min wif to healuan þe on wealde is. 7 min dohter to healuan. 7 ic wylle þ min wif fo æfre to healuan æhtan on ælcan tune fo to lande se þe fo . swa . hio to forgyuen wæs.*
>
> (And my wife is to succeed to half of what is on the woodland, and my daughter to half. And I wish that my wife shall in all cases receive half the stock at each estate, whoever may succeed to the land, as it was granted to her.)[8]

Where a woman's right to alienate land was restricted, the freedom to bequeath stock was a particular advantage. Æthelflæd, whose disposal of land was circumscribed by her father's will, deployed stock for her own spiritual benefit:

> *7 ic wille … þ man dele æal healf þ yrue þ ic hæbbæ on ælcum tune for mire sawle.*
>
> (And I wish … that half the stock which I have on each estate be distributed for my soul.)[9]

Four women donors bequeath stock separately from land as an important element in their wills.[10] Wynflæd, for example, distributes stock to a number of local churches for her spiritual benefit, but in addition bequeaths stock from the estate at Chinnock (Dors.) to her granddaughter, Eadgifu, and that from Charlton (Som.) to her daughter, Æthelflæd.[11] Wynflæd seems to have held only a life interest in the estate at Charlton, perhaps inherited from

6 S1484/W8; Sheehan, *The Will*, pp. 101–102. For example: S1539/W3; S1512/W7; *LE* II, 11/*Lib* 10, 11; *LE* II, 31/*Lib* 41. *CR* 107 (pp. 175–6) specifies the day of inventory.

7 *LE* II, 34/*Lib* 45 shows Eadric specifically agreeing that stock accrued during his tenure of Swaffham (Cambs.) would revert to Ely – apparently an unusual circumstance. See Appendix 3 for wills bequeathing stock separately from land.

8 S1487/W13. The context supports Whitelock's translation of *æhtan* as 'stock' rather than 'property', but I have preferred the translation of *tun* as 'estate' to her 'village' (see also the next note). For Ælfhelm's bequest of land to his wife see Chap. 4, Table 3 above.

9 S1494/W14; Chap. 4, p. 169 above. I have adjusted the emphasis of Whitelock's translation, which reads: 'And I wish … that half the stock which I have be distributed in each village for my soul' (*Wills*, pp. 36–7, lines 31–2).

10 S1494/W14; S1593/W3; S1497/*St Albans* 7; S1525/W38.

11 S1539/W3. The will refers to a transaction involving Wynflæd's son, Eadmær, who is to give stock at Avon (Wilts., otherwise unmentioned in the will) to his son, Eadwold, who is to pay him an unspecified sum. A bequest is involved, possibly on the part of Wynflæd, but damage to the manuscript makes this interpretation uncertain.

her husband, since she does not refer to the destination of the land itself; Chinnock is to revert to Shaftesbury on her death, possibly in fulfilment of a previous arrangement.[12]

Since the bequest of land by churchmen was restricted by their terms of office, for them, too, accrued stock could be an important resource. This is most clearly seen in the will of Bishop Theodred, who distinguishes between stock which was on his episcopal estates when he came to office, and that which he added (*ic þerto bigat*); the latter he can dispose of for the sake of his soul:

> *7 Ic wille þat men nieme þat erfe þat at Hoxne stand. þat ic þerto bigeten habbe. and dele it man on to. half into þe minstre 7 dele for min soule. And lete men stonden so mikel so ic þeron fond.*
>
> (And it is my will that the stock which is at Hoxne, which I have acquired there, be taken and divided into two parts, half for the minster, and half to be distributed for my soul. And as much as I found on that estate is to be left on it.)

A similar arrangement was to be made for the estates which he held in relation to the bishopric of London.[13]

For these donors, the bequest of stock was a valuable means of fulfilling social obligations: in Wynflæd's case, this resource allowed her to endow the next generation of her family, while for Theodred, it subsidised the distribution of alms for the good of his soul and appropriate to his role as bishop.[14]

For laymen, it was also an advantage that stock could be used for pious bequests without the alienation of land. Ealdorman Alfred, in an extreme instance, bequeaths no land to the church, but leaves detailed instructions for his wife to distribute large numbers of swine to Christ Church, Canterbury, Chertsey and religious houses throughout his ealdormanry of Surrey and Kent, on behalf of his soul.[15] On a smaller scale, Wulfgeat of Donington bequeaths bullocks to the local churches of Leominster and Bromyard (both Hfds.), Clifton (Worcs.), Wolverhampton, Penkridge (Staffs.) and Tong

12 See Chap. 4, p. 170 above. Æthelgifu (S1497/*St Albans* 7) bequeaths to St Albans stock from Oakhurst (Herts.), otherwise unmentioned in her will, for her burial.

13 S1526/W1.This pattern is repeated for a further three estates, while a fourth is to be left as stocked. See also Bishop Ælfwold's bequest of wild horses on land at Ashburton, otherwise unmentioned in his will. Wulfric Spott distinguishes between the land held by the bishop, and the stock upon it which he can bequeath (S1536/W17, *Burton* 29). Sheehan, *The Will*, p. 102.

14 For the distribution of alms on the death of a bishop see Reuter, 'Testaments, hoards', pp. 17–18. For Bishop Wilfrid's distribution see *Life of Bishop Wilfrid*, ed. Colgrave, chap. 63.

15 S1508/H10, *Christ Church* 96.

(Shrops.), and Eadwine of Caddington bequeaths the best twenty oxen and cows from his property to St Alban's, where he was to be buried.[16]

The most comprehensive and detailed deployment of such resources is that of Æthelgifu, who enumerates the livestock to be given from her estates to St Alban's, various local minsters and a number of secular beneficiaries. She also makes provision that, once her bequests have been fulfilled, any surplus sheep from her estate at Langford are to be given to her priests, for the funding of vigils. However, livestock is not her only concern; she is equally specific in her bequests of men, women and children who provided the tied labour force on her estates.[17] She bequeaths more than sixty slaves, including some with specialised tasks: swineherds, shepherds, ploughmen and a *dæge*, probably a dairymaid.[18] They may be bequeathed to the Church, as in the case of the swineherd granted from Oakhurst to St Albans along with his herd, or to individual beneficiaries. Ælfwold, who also receives estates, is granted two plough-teams of oxen and four men, along with Oswig and his wife, Cinesige and his wife, Brihtwine, and Godere and his herd (*heord*).[19] The phrasing of one of Æthelgifu's bequests is particularly telling in equating human and animal resources:

> *7 Bogan hire preoste finde him mon of þære lafe anne gionne mannan gif þær sy gif ne selle mon of Offanlege ane cu.*
>
> (And for Boga her priest a young man is to be found from the remainder, if there be one; if not, a cow from Offley is to be given to him.)

But slaves were not only bequeathed in wills; they were also freed.[20] Churchmen can be seen responding to the statute of the Synod of Chelsea (816) which required that, on the death of a bishop, every man enslaved during his lifetime was to be freed.[21] The wills of four bishops put this statute into prac-

16 S1534/W19; S1517/*St Albans* 15. See also Ælfric Modercope's division of sheep between two estates bequeathed to different churches (S1490/W28). The final clause of S1504/H20 may be translated: 'all the stock I have on the land which I hold on lease, I wish that it should be distributed for my soul' (*7 eall þæt yrfe þæ ic hæbbe on lænelandum, þonne wylle ic þæt þæt sie gedeled for mine sawle*); compare Harmer: 'and I desire that a distribution of all the property which I hold on lease be made for the good of my soul' (*SEHD*, p. 64).

17 S1497/*St Albans* 7. Æthelgifu's bequests of stock to the church have been mapped schematically by J. Blair, 'Introduction: from minster to parish church', in idem, *Minsters and Parish Churches: the Local Church in Transition* (Oxford, 1988), pp. 1–19 (p. 5). I am particularly indebted in this discussion of the evidence for slavery in wills to the analysis by D. A. E. Pelteret, *Slavery in Early Mediaeval England* (Woodbridge, 1995), Chap. 4, (pp. 112–19 for this will). See Appendix 3 below for wills bequeathing slaves.

18 Pelteret, *Slavery*, p. 116; for his analysis of slaves bequeathed see his Table III, p. 114.

19 'Family' may be an alternative translation: Pelteret, *Slavery*, p. 333.

20 See Appendix 3 for wills freeing slaves.

21 Pelteret, *Slavery*, p. 120; *Councils and Ecclesiastical Documents Relating to Great Britain and Ireland*, ed. A.W. Haddan and W. Stubbs, 3 vols. (Oxford, 1869–79), III, 583.

tice, specifically freeing *witeþeowas* (those enslaved penally).[22] A further four lay donors stipulate the freeing of penal slaves on their estates,[23] but manumission also features in the wills of thirteen lay donors with no reference to penal enslavement, providing evidence, as both Pelteret and Faith have noted, for the extent to which the running of estates was dependent upon tied labour.[24] In addition to the sixty slaves whom she bequeaths, Æthelgifu grants freedom to a further seventy individuals and, in a number of instances, actually bequeaths slaves to those whom she has freed.[25] For example, Edwin, her priest, once freed, will receive Byrhstan's sister, Ælfswyth, and her children, and the miller's wife and her children. Wulfric the huntsman was probably already free, but his wife and family are to be freed, as are Mann the goldsmith and his wife and family;[26] in each case, husband and wife are allocated two men.

Donors were anxious to free enslaved men and women in order to gain spiritual benefits. Æthelgifu, for instance, specifically includes manumission among her alms (*heora ælmessa*). Nevertheless, as Pelteret has argued, donors also recognised the need to preserve the economic viability of the estates which they bequeathed. Some freed only those who had been penally enslaved, or a specific number of men.[27] Æthelstan Mannessune, whose will is preserved in the Ramsey Chronicle, specifies the freeing by lot of 'thirteen out of every thirty counted men, so that when they were at the crossroads they might journey wherever they wanted'.[28] Wulfgyth frees half the men on her estate at Stisted, but this is to take effect only once the estate had reverted to Christ Church, Canterbury, after the lives of her two sons.[29] Bishop Theodred makes a marked distinction between the estates he holds by right of office as bishop of London and Suffolk, where he stipulates full

22 Archbishop Ælfric: S1488/W18, *Abingdon* 133; Bishop Theodred: S1526/W1; Bishop Ælfsige: S1491/W4, *New Minster* 18; Bishop Ælfwold: S1492/N&S10. Pelteret, *Slavery*, pp. 120–2.

23 The ætheling Æthelstan (S1503/W20, *Christ Church* 142); Ælfgifu (S1484/W8); Ealdorman Ælfheah (S1485/W9); Wynflæd (S1539/W3).

24 Pelteret, *Slavery*, p. 116; Faith, *English Peasantry*, pp. 64–7.

25 See Pelteret, *Slavery*, Table II, p. 113 for an analysis of manumissions.

26 For Wulfric's status, see Pelteret, *Slavery*, p. 114. Excavations at Faccombe Netherton (Hants.), where Wynflæd held land as her morning-gift (S1539/W3), have revealed evidence of a goldsmith at work within the manorial complex during the tenth century (her will is dated *c.* 950): J. R. Fairbrother, *Faccombe Netherton: Excavation of a Saxon and Medieval Manorial Complex*, British Museum Occasional Papers 47, I (London, 1990), pp. 59–60, 269–72.

27 A specified number are freed in S1538/W21, *Bath and Wells* 21; S1532/*St Albans* 13; S1535/W32, *Christ Church* 176; S1534/W19. King Alfred allows his bondmen a choice (S1507/H11, *New Minster* 1). Pelteret, *Slavery*, pp. 110, 123–4.

28 *CR* 33: *et per omnes terras suas de xxx. hominibus numeratis xiii. manumisit, quemadmodum eum sors docuit, ut in quadrivio positi pergerent quocunque voluissent.*

29 S1535/W32, *Christ Church* 176.

manumission, and those he bequeaths in his own right to his kindred, on which only half of the men are to be freed.[30] Pelteret's analysis of Æthelgifu's deployment of manpower through her bequests reveals a strategy in estate management.[31] Since, on her death, her estates were to be dispersed among a number of beneficiaries, the full-time services of certain workers who had probably been part of Æthelgifu's household or demesne – the fuller, Mann the goldsmith, perhaps three women who had been her companions in religious observance, perhaps even Edwin the priest – were no longer necessary or sustainable. They were therefore freed.[32] On the other hand, workers such as the dairymaid, ploughmen, shepherds and swineherds were an economic necessity to the estates to which they were attached; those swineherds and shepherds who were freed were probably older men, replaced by younger men who remained enslaved.[33] At Standon, for example, Eadstan the swineherd and his family are to be freed, with the exception of his son, who is to have charge of the herd; this son, and the herd, are bequeathed to Leofsige.[34]

The will of Wynflæd, though less detailed than that of Æthelgifu, is the only other document to give such precise instructions concerning the deployment of slaves.[35] She, too, had slaves in her household, since she names Eadgifu and Æthelgifu, a weaver (*crencestre*) and seamstress (*semestre*) respectively; as in the case of Æthelgifu, they would have become redundant on her death, and she bequeaths them to her granddaughter, Eadgifu.[36] A third woman – Wulfflæd – is freed only on condition that she serve (*folgige*) Wynflæd's daughter, Æthelflæd, and Eadgifu; two further women are to be freed unconditionally. Wynflæd goes on to name twenty-seven individual men and women who are to be freed; in addition, her children are to be responsible for the freeing of further penal slaves on behalf of her soul.[37] The complexity of the relationship between the workforce and the land is demonstrated by Wynflæd's arrangements for her estate at Chinnock (Som.), which is to revert to Shaftesbury:

> *7 hio ah þæt yrfe 7 þa men þenne an hio þan hywum þara gebura þe on þam gafollande sittað 7 þera þeowra manna hio an hyre syna dehter Eadgyfe.*

30 S1526/W1.

31 Pelteret, *Slavery*, pp. 115–19.

32 Pelteret, *Slavery*, pp. 115–16; Faith, *English Peasantry*, pp. 64–6.

33 Pelteret, *Slavery*, pp. 116–17.

34 There are other bequests of younger men: Ælfnoth is to have the younger shepherd at Langford; Ælfgifu is to have the younger swineherd at Gaddesden; and the herd which Brihtelm was in charge of is bequeathed to Leofwine, together with Brihtelm's younger son (it is not clear whether the Byrhtelm freed at Weedon is the same man).

35 S1539/W3; her provisions are analysed in tabular form by Pelteret, *Slavery*, p. 127.

36 Leofgifu (S1521/W29) distinguishes between *men* in her household (*hirde*) and on the estate (*on tune*). Wynflæd bequeaths at least one further woman in a later section of the will, which has been damaged: *Wills*, p. 14, l. 6.

37 *7 gif þær hwylc witeþeow man sy butan þyson þe hio geþeowede hio gelyfð to hyre bearnon þæt hi hine willon lyhtan for hyre saulle*; Pelteret, *Slavery*, p. 127.

(And she owns the stock and the men; this being so, she grants to the community the peasants who dwell on the rented land, and the bondmen she grants to her son's daughter Eadgifu.)

Pelteret has suggested that the *gebura* could be bequeathed by Wynflæd because she had rights in the land which they occupied: in effect, she was bequeathing the rents and services which they owed, not their persons.[38] A similar situation seems to have pertained in Archbishop Ælfric's bequest of a life-interest in three hides of an estate at Dumbleton (Glos.) to Ælfnoth, with conditions:

*7 x. oxan 7 II. men he him becwæð 7 filgan hi þam laford scype þe þ land to hyre.*

(And he bequeathed him ten oxen and two men, and they are to be subject to the lordship to which the land belongs.)[39]

These men could therefore not be alienated from the land. In this respect they are distinct from Wynflæd's *þeowra manna,* who are tied to Wynflæd herself and are bequeathed, along with stock, to her granddaughter.

Realistically, the freedom granted to men and women in wills was probably limited. It is true that some donors grant not only freedom to their men, but also 'their' land, of which they already seem to have been in possession: Æthelgifu frees Liofing of Henlow and bequeaths to him 'his' land; Thurketel of Palgrave frees his men and 'each is to have his toft and his cow and his corn for food'.[40] However, in Faith's view it seems likely that such holdings 'were of a size well calculated to prevent them becoming self-sufficient'.[41] In effect, although they may have gained a change in legal status, these freedmen remained tied to the land.[42]

Valuable though the re-distribution of stock and human resources may have been, it is, as Sheehan noted, 'the bequest of more precious possessions, the sort, actually, that were once part of the endowment of graves, that finds most frequent mention in literary sources and in the Anglo-Saxon wills themselves'.[43] Since Sheehan wrote this, there has been a consider-

38 Pelteret, *Slavery*, pp. 127–8.

39 S1488/W18, *Abingdon* 133; Pelteret, *Slavery*, p. 122.

40 S1527/W24: *and ilk habbe his toft and his metecu 7 his metecorn*. See also S1525/W38. Ketel specifically excludes the land from his bequest to his freed men (S1519/W34). On the provision of land for slaves see Pelteret, *Slavery*, pp. 119, 124–5, 176 and Faith, *English Peasantry*, p. 69.

41 Faith, *English Peasantry*, p. 70.

42 The social and legal implications of these manumissions and their relation to the later serfdom are discussed by Pelteret, *Slavery*, pp. 121–9 and Faith, *English Peasantry*, pp. 69–70. See also T. M. Charles-Edwards, 'The distinction between land and moveable wealth in Anglo-Saxon England', in *English Medieval Settlement*, ed. P. H. Sawyer (London, 1979), pp 97–104 (pp. 102–104) for the gift of a dwelling as a means of subordination.

43 *The Will*, p. 101.

able development in our appreciation of the social significance of the goods deposited in graves of the fifth to eighth centuries, both in England and on the Continent. For example, the study by Halsall of grave deposits from the region of Metz in the sixth and seventh centuries has examined the display of material wealth in terms of the assertion of local power and prestige, the deposition of goods participating in what Halsall has termed 'the theatre of the cemetery'.[44] He has shown that the nature of grave deposits at Metz reflects complex social developments and conventions, influenced not only by factors of age and gender of the dead person, but also by the concomitant social conventions and obligations arising from the different stages in the life-cycle. The wealth and prestige of the family are closely bound up in the funerary ritual.[45] Similar patterns have been identified in a study by Stoodley of furnished burials in Wessex, which showed that choice of grave-goods may have been symbolic in terms of ancestry and ethnicity as well as gender and age, and that patterns changed over time, indicating a shift from the period of settlement (or 'frontier society') of the fifth to the early seventh centuries, which emphasised the establishment of relatively small social groups based on the wider household, to one which saw the emergence of a male elite symbolised by rich barrow burials, with a general decline in the wider deposition of rich grave-goods.[46]

The premise upon which such interpretations of archaeological evidence are based has been defined by Geake: 'material culture is meaningfully constituted, the result of conscious or unconscious self-expression'.[47] This premise is equally relevant to the deployment of movable wealth in Anglo-Saxon wills. Although the explanation for the cessation of furnished burial in the early years of the eighth century remains a subject for debate, the shift to written wills had a clear advantage: it provided an opportunity for display, while objects remained in circulation.[48] A study by La Rocca and Provero of the will of the Frankish nobleman Eberhard of Friuli and his wife Gisela, dated 863 or 864, has remarked on the shift from the use of burial deposits

44 G. Halsall, *Settlement and Social Organisation: the Merovingian Region of Metz* (Cambridge, 1995), p. 258. See also G. Halsall, 'Burial, ritual and Merovingian society', in *The Community, the Family and the Saint: Patterns of Power in Early Medieval Europe*, ed. J. Hill and M. Swan (Turnhout, 1998), pp. 325–38.

45 Halsall, *Settlement and Social Organisation*, pp. 246–8.

46 N. Stoodley, *The Spindle and the Spear: a Critical Enquiry into the Construction and Meaning of Gender in the Early Anglo-Saxon Burial Rite*, BAR British Series 288 (1999), especially at pp. 94–7, 139–41.

47 The quotation is from a survey of the theoretical approach by H. Geake, *The Use of Grave-Goods in Conversion-Period England c. 600–c. 850*, BAR British Series 261 (1997), pp. 3–4 (at p. 3).

48 Geake surveys the reasons for the decline in furnished burial: *The Use of Grave-Goods*, pp. 132–6. See also D. Bullough, 'Burial, community and belief in the early medieval west', in *Ideal and Reality in Frankish and Anglo-Saxon Society: Studies presented to J.M. Wallace-Hadrill*, ed. P. Wormald, with D. Bullough and R. Collins (Oxford, 1983), pp. 177–201.

to use of the written word as a testimony to the dead, and shown that, as in the case of grave-goods, items were selected for their social as well as personal resonance.[49] Count Eberhard and his wife were of the highest social rank: Eberhard's father is found among the witnesses of Charlemagne's will, and Eberhard himself served three successive Frankish kings; Gisela was a daughter of Louis the Pious.[50] The will distributes land and movable wealth among their nine children, showing careful selection and disposition of personal items, and books and other items belonging to their chapel.[51] Their bequests of movable wealth follow their dispositon of land, and are organised in two groups: in the first group, each son and daughter is named, followed by a list of personal items and items from the chapel designated for them; the second group comprises a similar disposition of books. La Rocca and Provero remark that items selected for inclusion in the will were a means of 'defining the social persona' of the current owners of the goods, while 'foreseeing and planning for the status of the new':[52] Eberhard's regalia, adorned with gold and jewels, mainly bequeathed to his son, Unroch, who was apparently his primary heir; his armour and weaponry, distributed among his sons; items associated with feasting, again often of precious metal; religious items, many of precious metal and richly adorned; and books for private devotion, as well as key religious texts and volumes on law and *rei militaris*.[53] All of the items bequeathed by Eberhard and Gisela were valuable, but Le Jan has argued that they also had a social function, to be displayed or used on occasions when the assertion of rank was appropriate, and in this respect they contributed to the system of social recognition and aristocratic exchange.[54] The goods bequeathed in Anglo-Saxon wills should not therefore be seen simply as personal possessions; instead, the term 'positional goods' used by Reuter to define items which 'represent status and power' is apposite.[55] Reuter also identified goods which qualified as 'noble' in the sense that they had value

49 La Rocca and Provero, 'The dead and their gifts', p. 232; Le Jan, *Famille et pouvoir*, pp. 61–2. For the beginning of the shift from temporary to permanent display, see G. Halsall, 'Social change around AD 600: an Austrasian perspective', in *The Age of Sutton Hoo: the Seventh Century in North-West Europe*, ed. M. O. H. Carver (Woodbridge, 1992), pp. 265–78 (pp. 269–70).

50 La Rocca and Provero, 'The dead and their gifts', pp. 235–8. The text of the will may be found in *Cartulaire de L'Abbaye de Cysoing*, ed. I. de Coussemaker (Lille, 1885), pp. 1–5.

51 *Cartulaire*, ed. Coussemaker, pp. 2–4; a summary of items and their distribution is given by La Rocca and Provero, 'The dead and their gifts', pp. 250–7.

52 La Rocca and Provero, 'The dead and their gifts', p. 251.

53 The will of Eccard, Count of Mâcon (876) bequeaths a similar range of equally valuable and impressive items: *Recueil des chartes de l'abbaye de Saint-Benoît-sur-Loire*, I, ed. M. Prou and A. Vidier, Documents publiés par la Société Historique et Archéologique du Gâtinais V (Paris, 1900), no. 25 (pp. 59–67); for a summary and discussion of Eccard's bequests of movable wealth see Kasten, 'Erbrechtliche Verfügungen', pp. 325–3.

54 Le Jan, *Famille et pouvoir*, p. 62.

55 For the term 'positional goods' see Reuter, 'Testaments, hoards', p. 23.

beyond the utilitarian, such as gold, silver, precious stones, fine textiles and war-gear.[56]

Such goods are to be found across the social spectrum in Anglo-Saxon wills, bequeathed as treasure by donors of thegnly status as well as those holding social positions which are readily recognisable – royalty, churchmen and ealdormen.[57] Clothing, furnishings, weaponry, horses, items associated with hunting or travel, and goods made of, or adorned with, precious metal reflect the aristocratic lifestyle of donors, indicating a society in which luxury items were available to an elite with sufficient disposable wealth to acquire them.[58] Occasional detail in wills highlights the value of these items: coloured clothing, rich textiles and fur, decorated cups or swords – donors often bequeath 'the best' of their possessions. The terms gold and silver feature regularly, silver contributing significantly to the display aspect of a number of wills, either in the description of an object or its valuation. Nevertheless, as Appendix Three shows, movable goods are not distributed evenly across the full corpus of multi-gift wills; women, in particular, bequeath a much wider range of items than laymen and most churchmen. Even allowing for the loss of evidence through the truncation of the original documents, such a discrepancy is sufficiently marked to require explanation.[59] In Sheehan's view, the bequest of these prestigious items in Anglo-Saxon wills was strongly influenced by gender:

> The wills of men dwell with 'loving precision' on war gear, horse furnishings, and the mounts themselves. Ships, too, sometimes fully equipped for war, are among their bequests. Bishops' wills show a special interest in relics, chalices, vestments and church equipment generally, though similar gifts were frequently made by the laity as well. In the wills of women, somewhat more concern with detail is shown. Jewellery, tapestries, gold and silver vessels, horns, bed furnishings, gowns, were of special interest of course; but occasionally the written wills reflect arrangements for the distribution of more common household items among sons, daughters and servants.[60]

56 The list of goods designated here as 'noble' is taken from T. Reuter, 'Plunder and tribute in the Carolingian Empire', *TRHS* 5th s., 35 (1985), 75–94 (p. 78).

57 Stafford has defined treasure as 'specially valued wealth, capable of bearing a special meaning and performing important social functions. It is that which is scarce, desirable and stored; yet it is also mobile, it can be given and negotiated': P. Stafford, 'Queens and treasure in the early Middle Ages', in *Treasure*, ed. Tyler, pp. 61–82 (pp. 62–3).

58 Fleming, 'The new wealth', p. 3.

59 Seven of the ten multi-gift wills made by male donors which survive in pre-Conquest manuscripts (including the eleventh-century cartulary copy of S1507/H11, *New Minster* 1, the will of King Alfred) bequeath movable wealth; of these, S1501/W16[1], *Christ Church* 136 includes only heriot, and S1508/H10, *Christ Church* 96 and S1534/W19 include coin and stock (see Appendix 3).

60 Sheehan, *The Will*, p 103, attributing the phrase 'loving precision' to D. Whitelock, *The Beginnings of English Society* (London, 1952), p. 95.

However, the gendered categories proposed by Sheehan have been challenged by Crick:

> First, men and women bequeath in unexpected ways ... the distribution of moveables does not follow anticipated gender divisions. Women bequeathed horses and weapons; men bequeathed clothes. Second, characterization of male and female property in older publications cannot be taken for granted; they may reflect the preconceptions of the author as much as that of his sources.[61]

The analysis of the bequest of movable wealth presented in this chapter suggests that, while for a number of Sheehan's categories the pattern is indeed more complex than he acknowledged, certain items bequeathed by men and women do indeed appear to have been strongly gendered, possibly reflecting long-established social symbolism of the masculine and feminine identity seen in the grave deposits of the fifth to the eighth centuries. These items will be considered first.

The movable wealth bequeathed by laymen is dominated by goods which are strongly male-gendered, associated with the public world of lordship and status. This is most clearly demonstrated by heriot clauses which, although they do not feature in the ninth-century multi-gift wills of Abba and Ealdorman Alfred, appear frequently in multi-gift wills spanning the tenth and eleventh centuries, almost exclusively in those of laymen and churchmen.[62] Since the origins and nature of heriot, with specific reference to the evidence of wills, have been fully explored in a definitive study by Brooks, only the key points will be summarised here.[63] Heriot payment has generally been seen as a derivation of the Germanic custom of the gift of arms to a retainer, with the return of the items on the death of the recipient.[64] For the later Anglo-Saxon period, Brooks has argued that heriot, consisting generally of an established quota of war-gear, horses and gold, according to the donor's status, 'take[s] us to the roots of the aristocratic society of late Anglo-Saxon England, to the bonds between the aristocracy and the king'.[65] The

61 Crick, 'Women, wills', p. 28. This valuable survey of issues surrounding the bequest of movable wealth raises questions which have been fundamental in prompting the discussion here.

62 Ealdormen: S1483/W2; S1485/W9; S1498/W10, *New Minster* 25*; S1504/H20*. Church: S1526/W1*; S1491/W4, *New Minster* 18* (unspecified); S1492/N&S 10. Thegns: S1487/W13; S1490/W28*; S1501/W16[1], *Christ Church* 136; S1505/W12, *New Minster* 29*; S1517/*St Albans* 15*; S1519/W34*; S1528/W25* (unspecified); S1531/W31*; S1534/W19; S1536/W17, *Burton* 29; S1537/W27. Joint: S1511/W11, *Rochester* 35. (* indicates that the term 'heriot' is mentioned in the will). Heriot appears in the wills of two women (S1484/W8; S1535/W32, *Christ Church* 176* [unspecified]), discussed below.

63 Brooks, 'Arms, status'.

64 Brooks, 'Arms, status', pp. 151–5.

65 Brooks, 'Arms, status', p. 155; for quotas, see ibid., pp. 144–51.

king bound men to him through the provision of equipment which symbolised their noble status – the helmet, the byrnie, the spear and the sword.[66] However, this was not merely a symbolic relationship: the aristocracy was expected to provide an armed retinue to fight in support of the king, as at the Battle of Maldon in 991.[67] On the death of such an arms-bearer, his war equipment was to be restored to the king, together with the payment of a specified amount in gold or silver.[68]

Heriot tariffs are set out in the law of Cnut, dating to *c.* 1020, probably drawing on rates in operation under King Æthelred.[69] They distinguish between ealdormen, king's thegns and lesser (*medemra*) thegns in the quantities of war-gear due, revealing important social distinctions. The lesser thegn is required to provide only one horse with saddle, and 'his weapons'. The king's thegn must provide one full set of weapons and armour (helmet, byrnie, sword, spear and shield) with a saddled horse, together with a saddled horse and equipment for a further lightly-armed man (without the helmet and byrnie), and, in addition, two unsaddled horses, with spears and shields to equip a further two men. The earl bears the heaviest burden: he is to provide saddled horses and equipment for four fully armed men, and four unsaddled horses, with spears and shields for a further four men.[70] Cnut's law makes a further distinction between rates which applied in the kingdom at large and those due within the Danelaw; here, only the king's thegn closest to the king (*he to ðam kyncge furðor cyððe hæbbe*) is required to supply war-gear (although at a lower rate than required elsewhere), while the king's thegn and the lesser thegn paid four pounds and two pounds respectively.[71]

It is not only in the quantities of war-gear that social distinctions are made. The payments due from the higher social ranks are expressed in gold: the earl is required to pay two hundred mancuses of gold, and the king's thegn and the king's thegn closer to the king in the Danelaw are required to provide fifty mancuses. These large amounts may commonly have been paid in the form

66 Brooks, 'Arms, status', pp. 140–1 and N. Brooks, 'Weapons and armour', in *The Battle of Maldon*, ed. Scragg, pp. 208–19, reprinted in Brooks, *Communities and Warfare*, pp. 162–74 (pp. 166–8). For the byrnie (coat of mail) see Brooks, 'Arms, status', pp. 156–9.

67 R. Abels, 'English tactics, strategy and military organisation', in *The Battle of Maldon*, ed. Scragg, pp. 143–55 (pp. 146–7); R. Abels, *Lordship and Military Obligation* (London, 1988), pp. 173–4.

68 Brooks, 'Arms, status', pp. 154–5.

69 II Cnut, 71–71.5; Brooks, 'Arms, status', pp. 144–7, 148; Wormald, *English Law*, pp. 361–2 and n. 441; P. Stafford, 'The laws of Cnut and the history of Anglo-Saxon royal promises', *ASE* 10 (1981), 173–90 (pp. 176–182). The account which follows is based on the analysis by Brooks, 'Arms, status', pp. 144–7.

70 Brooks points to the distinction shown on the Bayeux Tapestry between fully-armed thegns wielding swords as well as spears and shields, and those without armour carrying only shields and spears (possibly ceorls): 'Arms, status', p. 144 and fig. 27.

71 II Cnut, 71. 3–5; Brooks, 'Arms, status', pp. 146–7.

of *beagas* (rings), although they are specifically mentioned in only five wills.[72] Such rings feature in Old English poetry, with strong male associations: Beowulf gives Wiglaf his *hring* and *beah* at the point of death; in *The Battle of Maldon* the Viking leader demands *beagas* as a ransom, and they are the target of looters as the dead lie on the battlefield.[73] However, the amount due from lesser thegns, and king's thegns in the Danelaw, was given in pounds, suggesting that the heriot of lesser men was paid in silver, either as coin or in the form of *beagas*.[74]

Where heriot payments are itemised in wills, although correlation with the tariffs is rarely exact, most donors appear to pay at the rate of king's thegn or ealdorman.[75] Brooks has suggested that the evidence of wills reveals successive increases in heriot rates from the reign of King Edmund (939–946) to that of Æthelred (978–1016), with the rates enshrined in Cnut's law reflecting a response to the increasing threat of Viking attack during Æthelred's reign.[76] For example, Ealdorman Æthelwold (946x947) stipulates a heriot payment of four horses, four shields, four spears and four swords, while Ealdorman Æthelmær (971x983) stipulates eight horses (four with saddles and four without), with eight shields and spears, four swords, and four helmets and byrnies (both now appearing in a heriot clause for the first time).[77] It is possible that there was some flexibility in the elements constituting heriot; some clauses show a reduction in the amount of war-gear, with the shortfall made up with other items, as in the case of Wulfgeat (making his will *c.* 1000) who stipulates the payment due from a king's thegn of four shields, four spears and two swords, but only two horses and no mancuses; however, he adds ten mares and colts.[78] An intriguing case is that of Ælfgar,

72 *Beagas* are mentioned in the heriot payments of: S1483/W2; S1498/W10, *New Minster* 25; S1504/H20; S1505/W12, *New Minster* 29; S1511/W11, *Rochester* 35. Brooks, 'Arms, status', p. 146–7. For the distribution and value of extant *beagas* see D. A. Hinton, 'Late Anglo-Saxon metalwork: an assessment', *ASE* 4 (1975), 171–80 (pp. 177–8); D. A. Hinton, 'Late Saxon treasure and bullion', in *Ethelred the Unready*, ed. Hill, pp. 135–58 (pp. 138–41).

73 *Klaeber's Beowulf*, ed. R. D. Fulk, R. E. Bjork and J. D. Niles, 4th edn, based on the 3rd edn with first and second supplements of *Beowulf and the Fight at Finnsburg*, ed. F. Klaeber (Toronto, 2008), lines 2809–12; *The Battle of Maldon*, ed. and transl. D. Scragg, in *The Battle of Maldon*, ed. Scragg, pp. 14–36, lines 30–1, 160–1. *Beagas* are not found in grave deposits: E. Coatsworth and M. Pinder, *The Anglo-Saxon Goldsmith: Fine Metalwork in England: its Practice and Practitioners* (Woodbridge, 2002), p. 212.

74 The lesser thegn in Wessex might substitute his *healsfang* (a legal payment according to status) for weapons, or in Mercia and East Anglia pay two pounds. For the relative status of gold and silver see pp. 196–7 below.

75 The exception is Ketel (S1519/W34), whose heriot is that of a lesser thegn and is owed to Archbishop Stigand (see Chap. 3, pp. 133–4).

76 Brooks, 'Arms, status', p. 150–1; Stafford, *Unification and Conquest*, p. 142. On the inadequacy of English armour in the tenth century see Brooks, 'Weapons and armour', pp. 170, 172–4.

77 S1504/H20; S1498/W10, *New Minster* 25.

78 S1534/W19; Brooks, 'Arms, status', p. 148 on discretionary payments.

who became an ealdorman before 945, yet in his will, made between 946 and *c.* 951, the heriot payment cited appears to be that of a king's thegn under kings Edmund and Edgar (three horses, shields and spears, two swords and *beagas* worth fifty mancuses of gold); but for the right to make his will he adds a valuable sword given to him by King Edmund.[79]

These were substantial demands, subsidised in two wills by land transactions: Ælfhelm Polga bequeaths an estate to his kinsman Leofsige and his wife, who were required to pay one hundred mancuses of gold to the king as Ælfhelm's heriot; and Thurstan stipulates the sale of an estate, with his heriot of two marks to be taken from the proceeds.[80] As has been shown in Chapter Two, prompt payment, either by the widow or by one of the heirs, was expected in order for the will to stand, but payment alone would not be sufficient; King Æthelred refused to allow the will of Æthelric of Bocking to stand, in spite of the widow's arrival with the heriot, on the grounds that Æthelric had been guilty of involvement in treachery.[81] Ælfhelm Polga is careful to assert his own loyalty – probably to Æthelred – in his will, referring also to his service of King Edgar (father of both Æthelred and his predecessor Edward).[82] Such loyalty, together with the payment of the appropriate heriot, allowed donors to invoke the king's obligation to protect the dispositions of the will. Ælfgar does so explicitly, illustrating that the burden of responsibility lay with the regal office, not with the individual king:

> *And ic wille Bidden* [sic] *suilc louerd so þanne beth for godes luuen and for alle hise halegen. werken min bern þat he werken þat he nefre ne mugen forwerken mine quide þe ic for mine soule cueden habbe.*
>
> (And I beseech whoever may then be king, for the love of God and all his saints, that let my children do what they may, they may never set aside the will which I have declared for my soul's sake.)[83]

79 S1483/W2; *Wills*, p. 104; Brooks, 'Arms, status', pp. 150. On the giving of arms by the king to noble followers see Brooks, 'Arms, status', pp. 154–5.

80 S1487/W13; S1531/W31. Wulfric Spott bequeaths to Burton *heregeatland æt Suðtune*, from which his heriot payment of 200 mancuses of gold may have been due (S1536/W17, *Burton* 29). Godric also bequeaths Thorington (Sfk) to Ramsey for the discharge of heriot: *CR* 63. Stafford, *Unification and Conquest*, p. 160.

81 S939/W16², *Christ Church* 137: *he wære on þam unræde ꝥ man sceolde on Eastsexon Swegen underfon ða he ærest þyder mid flotan com.* See Chap. 4, p. 178 above for the payment of heriot.

82 S1487/W13 (975x1016). Although it is possible that Ælfhelm was addressing Æthelred's predecessor (Edward the Martyr, 975–978), his heriot payment accords with developments in Æthelred's reign, and his protestation of loyalty would be appropriate in the aftermath of the succession struggle which followed Edgar's death. Edgar granted Ælfhelm an estate (Wratting, Cambs.) which he bequeaths to Ely: *LE* II, 73; S794 (974). Ælfhelm (Polga) was also active as a lawman in East Anglia (*LE* II, 10/*Lib* 8; *LE* II, 11/ *Lib* 13. For the full text of this clause see Chap. 1, p. 24 above.

83 S1483/W2.

It is not only the dispositions which may be placed under the king's protection, but also – as in the case of Wulfgeat – the donor's dependants:

> *7 he geann his hlaforde .II. hors. 7 .II. sweord 7 .IIII. scyldas 7 .IIII. spera. 7 .x. mæran. mid .x. coltan. 7 he bit his hlaford for godes lufan þ he beo his wifes freond 7 his dohter.*
>
> (And he grants to his lord two horses and two swords and four shields and four spears and ten mares with colts. And he prays his lord for the love of God that he will be a friend to his wife and daughter.)[84]

Although, by the tenth century, heriot had become closely linked with inheritance, and by 1086 was equated with *relevium* (payment made by an heir to a lord for the right to inherit land), the ancient sense of the duty owed by a retainer to his lord, and that lord's reciprocal obligation, is present in wills.[85]

Where war-gear is bequeathed by laymen outside heriot, swords seem to have been of particular significance.[86] The long-standing role of the sword as a symbol of male prestige is suggested by its inclusion in high-status burial deposits of the fifth to eighth centuries, where it was likely to be accompanied by a significant number of other goods asserting the importance of the individual.[87] The swords bequeathed by Count Eberhard to his sons were richly adorned with gold, silver and ivory,[88] and there are hints in Anglo-Saxon wills that those bequeathed by royal or aristocratic Anglo-Saxon donors were also valuable, and highly adorned. For example, the sword which Ælfgar received from King Edmund, and which he now bequeaths to Edmund's successor, was worth a hundred and twenty mancuses of gold (*on hundtuelftian mancusas goldes*) with four pounds of silver on the belt (*four pund silueres on þam fetelse*).[89] The ætheling Æthelstan bequeaths a total of eleven swords,

84 S1534/W19.

85 Chap. 1, p. 40 above. See (for example) DB I, fol. 269v: 'If anyone wished to have his dead father's land he paid 40s death duty; if he did not wish to, the King had his dead father's land and all his goods'.

86 Additional items: Wulfsige bequeaths a byrnie to his kinsmen (S1537/W27); Ælfhelm bequeaths his longship (*scæð*) to be shared by the community and abbot of Ramsey (S1487/W13).

87 H. Härke, '"Warrior graves": the background of the Anglo-Saxon weapon burial rite', *Past and Present* 126 (1990), 22–43 (pp. 37–8); Geake, *The Use of Grave-Goods*, p. 72; Stoodley, *The Spindle and the Spear*, p. 104; Brooks, 'Weapons, armour', p. 212; H. R. Ellis Davidson, *The Sword in Anglo-Saxon England* (Oxford, 1962), pp. 8–13; Le Jan, *Famille et pouvoir*, pp. 64–5.

88 *Cartulaire*, ed. Coussemaker, pp. 3–4.

89 S1483/W2. Although Whitelock translates *fetels* as 'sheath', 'belt' is more likely: Ellis Davidson, *The Sword*, pp. 119–20; Eberhard bequeaths a number of richly-adorned belts (*baltheum*) together with swords and other war-gear (*Cartulaire*, ed. Coussemaker, pp. 2–3). See Dodwell, *Anglo-Saxon Art*, p. 190, with illustration of a silver sword-handle from the ninth century in Plates 51 (a and b), and *The Anglo-Saxons*, ed. Campbell, fig. 143 for a silver pommel inlaid with gold of *c.* 900, probably of English workmanship.

among which are three with silver hilts (the Anglo-Saxon Abingdon sword fragment, dating probably to the late-ninth or early-tenth century and now in the Ashmolean Museum, Oxford, perhaps gives some idea of their quality) and two *malswurd*, which may have been inlaid or pattern-welded.[90] Some had specific lineages attached to them; for instance, Æthelstan bequeaths to his brother a sword which he attributes to King Offa (which Whitelock is tempted speculatively to identify with that sent to Offa as a gift by Charlemagne),[91] along with one which Wulfric made, and another which had belonged to Withar.[92] Such bequests imply that some swords may have had heirloom status, or were at least strongly associated with individual owners or makers, and that the *Beowulf*-poet's description of the sword Hrunting as 'foremost of ancient treasures' (*foran ealdgestrēona*) was not entirely conventional.[93]

Although the bequest of a sword could be used to acknowledge a range of social relationships – for example, with the church, or male kin – it was particularly linked with lordship.[94] The role of swords in acknowledging lordship is most obviously demonstrated in their inclusion in heriot payments, but valuable swords are also bequeathed separately to the king by Ealdorman

90 S1503/W20, *Christ Church* 142. For the Abingdon sword see D. A. Hinton, *The Alfred Jewel and Other Late Anglo-Saxon Metalwork* (Oxford, 2008), pp. 52–58; *The Golden Age of Anglo-Saxon Art*, ed. J. Backhouse, D. H. Turner and L. Webster (Bloomington, 1984), no. 14. For pattern-welding see Ellis Davidson, *The Sword*, p. 120–2; Geake suggests that pattern-welding became less common in later Anglo-Saxon England, so such a sword may have been an antique (*The Use of Grave-Goods*, p. 71).

91 Whitelock, *Beginnings of English Society*, p. 95; see H. Härke, 'The circulation of weapons in Anglo-Saxon society', in *Rituals of Power*, ed. Theuws and Nelson, pp. 377–99 (p. 393, n. 64) for doubt as to the attribution to Offa, while acknowledging the probable antiquity of the sword; Charlemagne's letter to Offa referring to the gift is translated in *EHD* I, no. 197, pp. 848–9. For old swords in grave deposits, see Härke, 'The Anglo-Saxon weapon burial rite', pp. 34–5;

92 For swords bearing the names of makers or of workshops see Ellis Davidson, *The Sword*, pp. 45–8. Wulfric is credited elsewhere in the will as having made (*worhte*) a gold *beah* and belt (see n. 127 below).

93 *Klaeber's Beowulf*, ed. Fulk, Bjork and Niles, line 1458; Härke, 'The circulation of weapons', pp. 383–6. Geake suggests that the marked decline in sword-burials may be related to an increasing value for the antiquity of swords: *The Use of Grave-Goods*, p. 72.

94 King Eadred bequeaths two swords with golden hilts as part of his burial gift to the church (S1515/H21, *New Minster* 17), and the ætheling Æthelstan a silver-hilted sword to the Old Minster, Winchester (S1503/W20, *Christ Church* 142). Bequests to kinsmen: S1503/W20, *Christ Church* 142 (father and brothers); S1511/W11, *Rochester* 35 (a *handsecs* to a kinsman); Æthelwold bequeaths a *lecge* (?scabbard) to his son (S1505/W12, *New Minster* 29); possibly Abba's bequest of a sword to Freothomund (S1482/H2, *Christ Church* 70). The precise nature of the *lecg* is unclear: Æthelwold bequeaths a further two as part of his heriot, and Ealdorman Ælfheah bequeaths *handseax* with a gold-adorned *lecg* to the king (S1485/W9); for *lecg* see Ellis Davidson, *The Sword*, pp. 118–19, and *Golden Age*, ed. Backhouse, Turner and Webster, no. 94 for an inlaid *seax*.

Ælfgar, Ealdorman Ælfheah and the ætheling Æthelstan.[95] The fact that two ealdormen bequeath such swords, one of them returning a sword given to him by a previous king, suggests that they may have been symbols of office; it is perhaps in this context of conferring status that King Alfred bequeaths a sword worth one hundred mancuses to Æthelred, his son-in-law and Ealdormen of Mercia.[96] The ætheling Æthelstan bequeaths a silver-hilted sword to his father, King Æthelred, but also, in a display of patronage, distributes four swords among members of his household: his chaplain, seneschal (*discþegn*), sword-polisher (*swurdhwitan*) and his servant (*cniht*) Æthelwine.[97] The latter bequest is of particular interest because Æthelstan is returning to Æthelwine 'the sword which he gave to me before', indicating the circulation of swords from owner to owner.[98] The distinctiveness of such swords is illustrated by Æthelstan's bequest to a certain Eadric (identified only as the son of Wynflæd) of a sword 'on which the hand is marked'.[99]

If wills reflect the persistence of war-gear as an important aspect of the layman's noble persona, so do they illustrate the significance of the distribution of treasure in the form of gold and silver – a feature not identified by Sheehan as gender-specific. It is gold which seems to carry most prestige in wills, recurring particularly in the phrase *mancusa goldes*. It is often unclear whether the term 'mancus' is being used to refer to a gold coin or a weight in gold bullion, or as an equivalent to thirty silver pennies.[100] The mancus itself may have been in use as a unit of currency for specific, high-status transactions, such as the payment of heriot and other bequests to royalty, or land transactions, which are often expressed in mancus-value, but whether gold was actually employed other than as a means of establishing the value

95 S1483/W2; S1485/W9; S1503/W20, *Christ Church* 142.

96 S1507/H11, *New Minster* 1; La Rocca and *Provero* 'The dead and their gifts', p. 251. See also Chap. 2, n. 74 above. No such bequests of swords are recorded after the will of the ætheling Æthelstan (1012x1015), but no other wills of such prominent men survive from the eleventh century.

97 S1503/W20, *Christ Church* 142. Both Whitelock (*Wills* p. 172) and Ellis Davidson (*The Sword*, p. 120) comment on the fact that the bequest of a sword to a priest is inappropriate, unless it is perhaps to be regarded as an heirloom. Æthelstan's sword-polisher is to receive a *sceardan* (notched?) sword, perhaps needing skilled repair.

98 *þæs swurdes þe he me ær sealde*. Härke, 'The circulation of weapons', pp. 381–2, 392.

99 *þe seo hand is on gemearcod*. Ellis Davidson draws a comparison with the Hand of God coins of King Æthelred, and suggests that such symbols were added by the owner (*The Sword*, pp. 49–50, 121).

100 For the value of the mancus see M. Blackburn, 'Gold in England during the "Age of Silver"', in *Silver Economy in the Viking Age*, ed. J. Graham-Campbell and G. Williams (Walnut Creek CA, 2007), pp. 55–98 (pp. 57–9) with discussion of its use as a unit of weight for silver at p. 58. S1492/N&S10 refers to five mancuses of pennies'; S1519/W34 refers to 'one mark of gold or the equivalent' (*oþer þe wrth* [sic]). The term *mancusa goldes* is generally used in wills; an ore's weight of gold is bequeathed in S1537/W27, and a welter of terminology may be found in S1532/*St Albans* 13.

of any given transaction it is impossible to tell.[101] In contrast, where silver is to be distributed it often remains undesignated, specified only as 'pounds' or 'pence', in which it was commonly valued.[102] Where an amount is given in pounds it may not be clear whether it refers to weight or number (at 240 silver pennies to the pound).[103] That the literary accounts of lords amassing treasure and distributing it to their followers was far from a topos is illustrated by the arrangements made for the distribution of gold and silver by kings Alfred and Eadred.[104]

In making their wills, these Anglo-Saxon kings may have been influenced by that of Charlemagne, which was reported by Einhard in his biography of the king, a text known to Asser, Alfred's biographer.[105] According to Einhard, in 811 (three years before his death) Charlemagne shared out his treasure and other movable wealth, which included clothing, furnishings and vessels as well as gold and silver. This was done at a public ceremony during which two thirds of his wealth was apportioned in twenty-one parts, and each allocation placed in a coffer which was labelled with the name of the beneficiary. The beneficiaries were the metropolitan cities of the empire; each archbishop was to divide his portion, taking one third for his own church, and dividing the remaining two thirds among his bishops. Charlemagne kept the remaining third of his treasure for his own expenses; on his death, this was to be further divided into quarters, with one part added to the two thirds already allocated to the metropolitans, the second to be divided among his sons and daughters and the sons and daughters of his sons, the third part was to be given to the poor, and the fourth was to provide pensions for the servants of the royal palace. Einhard tells us that Charlemagne ordered the proceedings to be documented, and adds a list of the bishops, abbots and counts who were present. The weighting of Charlemagne's *divisio* suggests that such patronage

101 Blackburn, 'Gold in England', pp. 67, 77. For reference to gold in relation to land transactions see S1488/W18, *Abingdon* 133; S1534/W19; S1519/W34; W39/*Peterborough* 27. The ætheling Æthelstan (S1503/W20, *Christ Church* 142) seems to have paid for land in gold by weight (*be gewihte*).

102 Blackburn, 'Gold in England', p. 58. Fourteen wills use this non-specific terminology. S1532/*St Albans* 13 uses the phrase *marc gewegenes*, apparently in relation to silver. Only four wills use the word 'silver' in relation to distribution.

103 Occasionally a donor is specific: both Thurstan (S1530/W30, *Christ Church* 166; S1531/W31) and the ætheling Æthelstan refer to twelve pounds *be tale* (by number); Æthelgifu (*CR* 32) bequeaths two silver goblets of twelve marks 'according to the weight of the London hustings'(*ad pondus hustingiæ Londoniensis*). For items made of or adorned with silver, see below.

104 S1507/H11, *New Minster* 1; S1515/H21, *New Minster* 17. Reuter, 'Plunder and tribute', pp. 80–44; Le Jan, *Famille et pouvoir*, pp. 60–1 (on the significance of royal treasure).

105 For a translation of Charlemagne's will see *Two Lives*, transl. Thorpe, Book 5. The political implications of the will are discussed by Innes, 'Charlemagne's will', pp. 833–55. For Asser's familiarity with Einhard's text see Keynes and Lapidge, p. 254, n. 139. See Chap. 3, pp. 83–4 above for discussion of the will of King Æthelwulf, Alfred's father.

was intended to cement the relationship between the emperor and his imperial church.[106]

Neither Alfred nor Eadred bequeaths the range of high-status goods included in Charlemagne's will; their distribution focuses on gold and silver, and is expressed in values rather than the proportions favoured by Charlemagne.[107] Nevertheless, in each case considerable wealth is involved: Blackburn has estimated that Alfred's bequests amounted to about 1,700 mancuses of gold and 1,800 pounds of silver, and Eadred's to 5,000 mancuses of gold and 2,300 pounds of silver.[108] Alfred, having allocated his wealth, remarks that he is uncertain as to how much is available:

> *7 ic nat naht gewislice hwæðer þæs feos swa micel is, ne ic nat þeah his mare sy; butan swa ic wene. Gyf hit mare sy beo hit him eallum gemæne þe ic feoh becweden hæbbe. 7 ic wille þæt mine ealdormenn 7 mine þenigmenn þær ealle mid syndan 7 þis þus gedælan.*
>
> (I do not know for certain whether there is so much money, nor do I know whether there is more, though I suspect so. If there is more, it is to be shared among all those to whom I have bequeathed money; and I desire that my ealdormen and my officials shall all be involved and distribute it thus.)

The public nature of the division is emphasised here, as it is in the will of Charlemagne, and although their bequests lack the imperial perspective which influences those of Charlemagne, Alfred and Eadred recognise in their distribution of movable wealth a similar range of beneficiaries: both kings recognise the importance of generosity to those responsible for the stability of the realm; of pious gifts; of rewarding their retinue; and, in Alfred's case, of providing for his wife and children.

Gold bequeathed in mancuses is used by both kings to mark the status of important political and religious figures: Alfred bequeaths one hundred mancuses to each of his ealdormen and bishops, and Eadred one hundred and twenty mancuses, with two hundred for the archbishop. In addition, Eadred bequeaths gold to high-status members of his household (seneschal, chamberlain and butler);[109] the priests in charge of his relics are to receive fifty mancuses of gold, with a further five pounds of silver, while the other

106 Innes, 'Charlemagne's will', pp. 852–5; D. M. Deliyannis, 'Charlemagne's imperial tables: the ideology of an imperial capital', *EME* 12.2 (2003), 159–77.

107 But see *Asser*, chaps. 100–102 for an account of a proportional annual *divisio* by Alfred, again suggesting Asser's familiarity with Einhard's Life of Charlemagne. For the possible influence of canonical regulations concerning tithe on Charlemagne's *divisio* see Innes, 'Charlemagne's will', pp. 850–3.

108 Blackburn, 'Gold in England', p. 55, where Eadred's bequests are estimated as the equivalent of £2 million in modern values. See Keynes and Lapidge, p. 324, n. 97 for comments on the contemporary value of the two wills.

109 *Discðegn, hrægłðegn, biriele* (*byrle*): *New Minster*, p. 80.

priests are to receive only the silver. Alfred makes provision for two hundred pounds (presumably of silver) to be distributed among 'the men who serve me' (*þam mannum þe me folgiað*), to be allocated according to the rate established by his regular Easter distribution, which had just taken place. Alfred's private bequests to his family are also made in terms of silver; the bequests to his sons of five hundred pounds each outstrip in value the bequests in gold to political figures: as a very rough comparison, five hundred pounds is the equivalent of 120,000 silver pennies, while the one hundred mancuses granted by Alfred to the archbishop and each of his bishops is the equivalent of 3,000 silver pennies.[110] It therefore seems likely that the royal distribution in terms of gold among important public figures had a particularly powerful symbolic significance.

In general, silver, perhaps as the more practical option from the point of view of beneficiaries, seems to be preferred for wider distribution, as may be seen in the provision made by both kings for their souls.[111] Alfred bequeaths two hundred pounds 'to be distributed for my sake, for my father and the friends for whom he used to intercede and I intercede';[112] of this, fifty pounds constitute his burial gift, fifty are to be distributed to all the mass-priests in the kingdom, fifty to the 'poor servants of God' (*earmum Godes þeowum*) and fifty to the poor and needy (*earmum þearfum*).[113] Eadred bequeaths thirty pounds to each of the royal nunneries of Wilton, Shaftesbury and Winchester, as well as four hundred pounds to the church where he was to be buried.[114] However, Eadred goes on to make further provision in alms by distributing a considerable sum for the support of his people:

> *Þænne an he his sawla to anliesnesse 7 his ðeodscipe to þearfe sixtyne hund punda to þan ðæt hi mege magan hungor 7 hæþenne here him fram aceapian gif hie beþurfen.*
>
> (Then he gives sixteen hundred pounds for the redemption of his soul and for the good of his people, that they may be able to purchase for themselves relief from want and from the heathen army if they need to do so.)

Following the example of Charlemagne, he delegates responsibility for the wider distribution to his key churchmen: the archbishop of Canterbury is

110 Keynes and Lapidge, p. 324, n. 97. These calculations are based on 240 silver pennies to the pound and 30 to the mancus: Blackburn, 'Gold in England', p. 58. In addition, Alfred bequeaths 100 pounds each to his wife and three daughters.

111 Blackburn, 'Gold in England', pp. 66–7.

112 *For me 7 for minne fæder 7 for þa frynd þe he foreþingode 7 ic foreþingie.*

113 He also includes stock in his burial gift, 'such as may be and as is also appropriate and as you wish to give on my behalf' (*swa hit beon mæge 7 swa hit eac gerysne sy 7 swa ge me forgyfan wyllan*).

114 The church is unnamed. Eadred also bequeaths two golden crosses and two swords with golden hilts: see below pp. 213–14 for discussion of the bequest of religious items by laymen.

made responsible for the distribution of four hundred pounds among the people of Kent, Surrey and Berkshire; the bishop of Winchester, Ælfsige, receives two hundred pounds for Hampshire and one hundred each for Wiltshire and Dorset; Abbot Dunstan has responsibility for Somerset and Devon, for which two hundred pounds are allocated; four hundred pounds currently held by Bishop Wulfhelm is allocated to Mercia; and Bishop Ælfsige is to hold a further two hundred pounds, for allocation as necessary. Eadred then supplements this arrangement with a further bequest, this time of gold:

> *Þanne nime man twentig hund mancusa goldes 7 gemynetige to mancusan, 7 fo se ercebiscop to anum dæle, to oðrum Ælfsige biscop, to þriddan Oscytel biscop, 7 gedælen geond þa biscopricea Gode to willan 7 minre sawle to anliesnesse.*
>
> (Then gold to the value of two thousand mancuses is to be taken and coined into mancuses; and the archbishop is to receive one portion, and Bishop Ælfsige [of Winchester] a second, and Bishop Oscytel [of Dorchester] a third, and they are to distribute them throughout the bishoprics for the sake of God and for the redemption of my soul.)

Reuter described the distribution of treasures as a 'symbolic representation of the "institutions" which owned and controlled them', which was in tension with 'private', pious needs,[115] and it is indeed difficult to disentangle the 'institutional' aspect of this public display of royal munificence from the avowed pious motive. The bequest of gold here may, however, have a practical aspect: the fact that the gold is to be specially minted indicates that Eadred envisaged mancuses of a standard weight which could then be distributed and stored according to his instructions.[116] The beneficiaries were again public figures who might be entrusted with the safe-keeping and deployment of the gold; they had the facilities for storing it relatively safely (they seem to have had responsibility for storing Eadred's own personal wealth), and possibly had the means of converting the gold coins into silver-equivalent if the need arose.[117]

The public bequest of such wealth established the king at the head of the social hierarchy, distributing largesse. That both Alfred and Eadred chose to patronise through their bequests the secular lords and ecclesiastics on whose loyalty the smooth running of the kingdom depended reflects Charlemagne's use of his will to reinforce political affiliations.[118] The role played by gold, in particular, in these wills is significant, not only as a symbol of royal power,

115 'Testaments, hoards', p. 17.

116 Whatever that value may have been: see n. 100 above. It would presumably be easier to store 660 mancuses than the equivalent in silver pennies (approx. 20,000).

117 The arrangements for storing Eadred's treasure are related in *Memorials*, ed. Stubbs, pp. 29, 31.

118 See n. 105 above.

but because it demonstrates the way in which the written will could be used as a form of display; it was an effective means of publishing the wealth contained in the king's treasure-hoard, with the advantage of allowing the king to display his wealth and distribute it publicly while, at the same time, retaining the use of it for his lifetime.

Such distributions of gold and silver also feature in the wills of non-royal laymen.[119] That included in the tenth-century will of Ealdorman Æthelmær, with its patronage of Winchester institutions and others within Wessex, reflects Æthelmær's position as ealdorman and landowner in Hampshire: one hundred mancuses of gold and ten pounds of silver to the Old and New Minsters, Winchester; three pounds to Christ Church, Canterbury; two pounds each to the *Nunnaminster* (Winchester), St Augustine's (Canterbury), Rochester (Kt), Abingdon (Berks.), Romsey (Hants.), Wilton and Malmesbury (Wilts.), Shaftesbury (Dors.), Glastonbury (Som.); and one pound each to Bath (Som.), Cricklade (Wilts.) and Bourne (Hants?).[120] In addition, Æthelmær bequeaths two pounds to the priests' gild and one pound to the deacons' gild (the context suggests that both were Winchester based).[121] Although most of these foundations were high-status houses, a number with royal associations or closely associated with the religious reform movement, Æthelmær's bequests suggest a hierarchy of importance; he reserves gold for the two most prestigious, in one of which – the New Minster – he wished to be buried. Other laymen bequeath substantial distributions of coin to the church. Wulfric Spott bequeaths ten mancuses of gold to each archbishop, five to each bishop, abbot and abbess, and one pound (of silver pence) to each monastic foundation, beside his land endowment of Burton Abbey, while the reeve Abba makes provision for the distribution of one mancus of gold to every priest in Kent, one penny to every servant of God (*Godes ðiowe*) in Kent, and two thousand (pence?) for the payment of his wergild to St Peter's at Rome.[122] Noblemen, like kings, may also bequeath a distribution of gold or silver among the household or followers. Ealdorman Æthelmær bequeaths five pounds to be divided among his *hiredcnihtum*, and it seems likely that

119 Women also bequeath coin for pious distribution, but within a more limited range of beneficiaries: S1484/W8, S1539/W3.

120 S1498/W10, *New Minster* 25. The last named is probably St Mary Bourne (Hants.): *New Minster*, p. 120.

121 These gilds may have been formed in response to the need for priests to provide legal sureties: *New Minster*, p. 120; *Wills*, pp. 126–7.

122 S1536/W17, *Burton* 29; S1482/H2, *Christ Church* 70 (the denomination is unspecified here: see *Christ Church* 70 for discussion of the value of Abba's wergeld). Ealdorman Alfred (S1508/H10, *Christ Church* 96) makes provision for his two wergilds to be taken to St Peter's by his wife; Ulf bequeaths four marks of weighed silver to Rome 'for St Peter' and a further four marks of weighed silver for distribution among the principal minsters (*heh mynstran*) of this country (S1532/*St Albans* 13).

some of the beneficiaries named by Ulf, who are to receive gold or silver, were members of his retinue.[123]

If laymen's bequests of war-gear and precious metal reflect a social structure based on lordship, and are related to the position of both donor and beneficiary within a hierarchy, asserting status and establishing social relationships, women's multi-gift wills dispose of a range of items associated with domestic or personal display, endorsing Sheehan's emphasis on their bequest of vessels, domestic items, clothing and jewellery (see Appendix Three). Specific items are carefully allocated to beneficiaries, and sufficient detail is given to indicate that many were of considerable intrinsic value and were bequeathed as treasure.[124] The first category to be considered – jewellery – is difficult to define. It includes *beagas* which for women, as for men, seem to have functioned as an important means of both storing and transmitting wealth, since the often considerable mancus-value is usually given, and Wynflæd bequeaths a gold-adorned cup to her grandson, 'that he may enlarge his *beah* with the gold' (*þæt he ice his beah mid þam golde*); as Hinton points out, the pennanular design of the rings would have made this a straightforward process.[125] However, *beagas* were intended to be worn by women, as is illustrated by the *Beowulf*-poet's description Hrothgar's queen, Wealhtheow, as *bēaghroden* (ring-adorned).[126] Wynflæd bequeaths her *agrafenan* (engraved) *beah* to her daughter in the context of jewellery and clothing, suggesting that that it was regarded as an adornment; it is unclear whether the engraving was decorative or in the form of an inscription.[127] Ælfgifu's bequest to the queen distinguishes between a *beah*, which is given a value of thirty mancuses, and a *swyrbeah* (neck-ring or necklace) of twenty mancuses.[128] That they were

123 S1532/*St Albans* 13.

124 For the definition used, see n. 57 above.

125 S1539/W3; Hinton, *Gold and Gilt*, p. 147. *Beagas* are bequeathed by women to the church (S1538/W21, *Bath and Wells* 21); to the king (S1484/W8; S1486/W15); and to the ætheling (S1484/W8). In addition, they feature prominently in the joint will of Brihtric and Ælfswith (S1511/W11, *Rochester* 35).

126 *Klaeber's Beowulf*, ed. Fulk, Bjork and Niles, line 623.

127 S1539/W3. It is suggested by Coatsworth and Pinder that, since no mancus-value is given for this *beah*, it may have been a finger-ring such as the ninth-century gold ring inscribed + *ædred mec ah eanred mec agrof* (Ædred owns me, Eanred engraved me): *Anglo-Saxon Goldsmith*, pp. 213, 224 (catalogue no. 47). Only plaited or twisted examples of larger rings survive: a large gold ring from Brightlingsea (Ex) and a silver ring from Long Witenham (Oxon.) are illustrated by Hinton, *The Alfred Jewel*, p. 49. See also Hinton, *Gold and Gilt*, pp. 145, 147, and Dodwell, *Anglo-Saxon Art*, plate 5 (p. 28) for three *beagas* included in the temptations of Christ illustrated in the mid eleventh century manuscript BL Cotton Tiberius C VI fol. 10v. The ætheling Æthelstan refers to a *beah* which, together with a gold *fetelse* (belt), had been worked (*worhte*) by Wulfric, suggesting particular craftsmanship; Wulfric also made one of the swords bequeathed by Æthelstan (S1503/W20, *Christ Church* 142).

128 S1484/W8. Two *sweorbeagas* are bequeathed to the church in the joint will S1511/W11, *Rochester* 35 (see p. 210 below).

perceived as items of display is suggested by a passage from Ælfric's life of St Agnes, from the late tenth century, where Agnes rejects the worldly adornments offered by the young man who woos her, in favour of the spiritual gifts of Christ:

> *Ic hæbbe oðerne lufiend …*
> *seðe* [sic] *me bead bæteran frætegunga .*
> *and his geleafan hring me let to wedde .*
> *and me gefrætewode . mid un-asmeagendlicra wurðfulnysse .*
> *He befeng mine swiðran . and eac minne swuran .*
> *mid deorwurðum stanum . and mid scinendum gimmum.*
>
> (I have another lover …
> who has offered me better adornments,
> and has granted me for a pledge the ring of His faith,
> and has adorned me with unimaginable honour.
> He has encircled my right hand and also my neck
> with precious stones and with shining gems.)[129]

It seems possible, therefore, that at least some *beagas* were bequeathed by women, to other women, as items of adornment and display as well as bullion. That some *beagas* had specific associations, as well as being both valuable and distinctive, is suggested by Ælfflæd's bequest to Ely of a *beah* which was the pair or companion of one given as the burial fee for her husband, Ealdorman Byrhtnoth.[130]

Associated with, and difficult to distinguish from, the *beah* is the band (*bænde, binde, bend*), usually regarded as a headband or fillet, probably decorated. A *bend* of thirty mancuses of gold is bequeathed by Wulfwaru to her elder daughter in the context of jewellery and clothing, and Ælfgifu confirms the gift of a *bænd* which she has lent to her brother's wife, suggesting that it was an adornment.[131] Like *beagas*, bands were made of precious metal, or of gold thread, and could also be divided as bullion: Æthelgifu bequeaths five mancuses of gold to each of five beneficiaries, two of whom were male, to be cut (*ceorfe*) from her *bend*, and Wulfwaru bequeaths a *bend* worth twenty mancuses to four male servants, whom she names.[132]

129 Text and translation from Aelfric's *Lives of Saints*, ed. Walter Skeat, EETS OS 76 (London, 1881), pp. 172–3.

130 S1486/W15: *þes bæahges gemacan þe man sæalde minum hlaforde to sawlescæatte*; again no mancus value is given so these may have been finger-rings (see n. 127 above). A *beah* worth sixty gold mancuses is among Wulfwaru's gifts to Bath Abbey for her own soul and those of her *yldrena* (parents or ancestors), whom she cites as the source of her property and possessions (*þe me min ar of com. 7 mine æhta*).

131 S1538/W21, *Bath and Wells* 21; S1484/W8. Wynflæd (S1539/W3) bequeaths a *bindan* with her *halirift* (holy veil); Owen-Crocker, *Dress in Anglo-Saxon England*, pp. 224–5, 339.

132 S1497/*St Albans* 7; S1538/W21, *Bath and Wells* 21. A *bænd gyldene* is divided between two beneficiaries in S1511/W11, *Rochester* 35. See *LE* II, 62 for Byrhtnoth's gift of the bands of his cloak: *duabus laciniis palii sui, pretioso opere auri et gemmarum contextis* (two

However complex the role of *beagas* and bands may have been in the transmission and display of wealth, brooches pass in the female line, perhaps perpetuating the social symbolism suggested by the strong association of brooches with furnished female burials.[133] Wynflæd bequeaths two brooches (*preon*), one to her daughter and one to her granddaughter, and Wulfwaru bequeaths two brooches (*preon*) to her older daughter.[134] No description is given of these brooches, other than Wynflæd's reference to her *ealdan gewiredan preon*, which she bequeaths to her granddaughter, possibly as an heirloom; it was valued at six mancuses, suggesting that it was made of gold, or was at least gilt, and possibly incorporated filigree work.[135] The exceptional male donor – Wulfric Spott – bequeaths to his goddaughter a *bule*, a brooch (or pendant) which had belonged to her grandmother;[136] it is unclear why it should be in Wulfric's possession, but since its ancestry is specifically mentioned, the link across generations was clearly significant to both donor and beneficiary.

Clothing, too, was an important aspect of female identity. It features in the wills of four women, one of which – that of Æthelgifu – provides details which suggest an extensive, rich wardrobe designed to impress.[137] She owned gowns (*cyrtla*) in a variety of colours: blue, possibly purple (*godwebban*), and one, described as the brightest (*rotostan*) may have been yellow or red; others were brown, possibly of undyed wool, perhaps for everyday wear.[138] Since one is described as untrimmed below (*neaþene unrenod*), others may have been trimmed with embroidery or tablet-woven borders.[139] Æthelgifu's three *godwebbenan cyrtlas* may have been made of the precious imported fabric

borders of his cloak, woven with costly work in gold and gems): text and transl. from A. Kennedy, 'Byrhtnoth's obits and twelfth-century accounts of the Battle of Maldon', in *The Battle of Maldon*, ed. Scragg, pp. 59–78 (pp. 65, 68). Dodwell, *Anglo-Saxon Art*, p. 175 for discussion of gold-embroidered bands; Owen-Crocker, *Dress in Anglo-Saxon England*, pp. 224–6 for headbands, p. 59 for Kentish brocades of the fifth and sixth centuries, and p. 225 for the reclamation of gold from gold brocade.

133 Stoodley, *Spindle and Spear*, pp. 48, 136 (and see p. 222 below).

134 S1539/W3; S1538/W21, *Bath and Wells* 21.

135 Filigree work in Anglo-Saxon England is discussed by Dodwell, *Anglo-Saxon Art*, p. 208, and with a more technical approach by Coatsworth and Pinder, *Anglo-Saxon Goldsmith*, pp. 125–9. A silver brooch decorated with beaded wire survives from *c.* 960–975: Hinton, *Gold and Gilt*, p. 144, fig. 5.1, and pp. 143–4 for brooches generally.

136 The *bule* was worn at the neck, but precisely how is uncertain: Owen-Crocker, *Dress in Anglo-Saxon England*, p. 340; Coatsworth and Pinder, *Anglo-Saxon Goldsmith*, p. 211. For *bullae* found apparently worn as pendants in women's graves see Geake, *The Use of Grave-Goods*, pp. 36–7.

137 S1497/*St Albans* 7. Other women's wills bequeathing clothing are: S1539/W3; S1538/W21, *Bath and Wells* 21; S1535/W32, *Christ Church* 176.

138 For *cyrtel* see Owen-Crocker, *Dress in Anglo-Saxon England*, pp. 217, 337, and for colours, p. 211.

139 Bishop Theodred's chasuble (see below) is also described as *ungerenad*. *LE* II, 62 describes Byrhtnoth's gift of two borders of his cloak, richly decorated (see n. 132 above). Owen-

*purpura*, probably a type of silk (perhaps a shot taffeta) which was often purple, and which was much treasured in late Anglo-Saxon England.[140] She also bequeaths an unspecified number of 'best' headdresses (*heafodgewædo*). In contrast, the clothing bequeathed by Wynflæd is much less flamboyant. Her bequests of her *halirift* (holy veil) and *nunscrude* (nun's clothing) have prompted the suggestion that she may have taken vows of chastity in widowhood, living outside the cloister but in association with other religious women.[141] She refers to tunics (*tunecan*) in dull colours – brown and black – and identifies garments by fabric, such as *twilibrocenan* or *linnene*.[142] Many of the garments bequeathed in these wills were clearly of the highest quality, and much prized: Æthelgifu refers to her best headdresses, and Wynflæd to her best brown tunic and the better of her cloaks (*mentel*).[143]

Unsurprisingly, clothing was predominantly bequeathed by women, to women. Wulfwaru bequeaths a complete woman's outfit (*anes wifscrudes ealles*) to her older daughter, with her younger daughter receiving the remainder of her clothing. Æthelgifu's bequests follow a similar pattern: Wulfwynn, who receives the brightest kirtle, Ælfgifu and Godwif, who each receive a purple kirtle, are all identified as kinswomen, and are to inherit other goods, particularly furnishings (and, in Godwif's case, land, bondwomen and a portion of Æthelgifu's gold band). Beornwynn (who is to have the blue, untrimmed kirtle and best head-dress), Lufetat (a purple kirtle) and Wulfgifu (some of the brown kirtles) do not feature otherwise in the will; they may have been valued members of Æthelgifu's household, since she stipulates that her household women (*hiredwifmen*) are to divide the remainder of her clothing. It is likely that the female beneficiaries of clothing named by Wynflæd were also members of her household: Wulfflæd and Æthelgifu, for whom her daughter Æthelflæd is to provide from 'her nun's vestments' (*nunscrude*), may be, respectively, the woman freed by Wynflæd on condition that she serve her daughter and granddaughter, and the seamstress whom

Crocker, *Dress in Anglo-Saxon England*, pp. 171–2, 283–6. See Fleming, 'The new wealth', p. 9 for clothing deployed as conspicuous consumption.

140 Wulfgyth's bequest of a *pællene* kirtle to the church was probably of this textile: see Lowe, 'Will of Wulfgyth', 295–8 for an adjustment of Whitelock's reading; Dodwell, *Anglo-Saxon Art*, pp. 145–51; Owen-Crocker, *Dress in Anglo-Saxon England*, pp. 298–302; for Æthelgifu's bequest see Lord Rennell's comments in *Æthelgifu*, pp. 82–4.

141 It has been postulated that Æthelgifu may also have lived in a community of religious women, although the exotic nature of much of the clothing which she bequeaths does not add weight to the hypothesis: Foot, *Veiled Women*, I, 137–40; the *heafodgewædo* (headdresses) bequeathed by Æthelgifu, considered as possible evidence of veiling by Whitelock, could be secular apparel: *Æthelgifu*, p. 12, n. 10; Owen-Crocker, *Dress in Anglo-Saxon England*, pp. 219–23.

142 There is uncertainty about the meaning of *twilibrocenan*: G. R. Owen, 'Wynflæd's wardrobe', *ASE* 18 (1979), 195–222 (pp. 206–11).

143 Fleming, 'The new wealth', p. 9; Le Jan, *Famille et pouvoir*, p. 63.

she bequeaths to her granddaughter.[144] Wynflæd also refers to a *hræglcysð* (clothing chest) at the end of her disposition of clothing, but its intended destination is unclear.

However, rich clothing was also sufficiently prestigious to warrant its bequest to high-status beneficiaries irrespective of gender, as is illustrated by Æthelflæd's bequest of four garments (*pellas*) to the king.[145] Furthermore, Wulfgyth's bequest of her *pællene* kirtle to Ely show that such items were also appropriate as gifts to the church, perhaps to be recycled into vestments or altar covers, as is incidentally described by Gregory of Tours in his late sixth century account of a gift of a silken mantle given to the abbess of Tours:

> *Et inde partem abscidisset, unde quod vellet et faceret; de reliquo vero, quantum oportunum fuit, ad ornatum altaris pallam condignae condederit.*
>
> (She had cut off a portion of this for her own use. From what was left she had handed over as much as was necessary to make a suitable cloth for the altar.)[146]

Apart from the obvious intrinsic value of the clothing bequeathed by women, it is again the very specific allocation of individual items which is marked, often in acknowledgement of kinship or service within the household.

This is equally true of women's bequests of high-status goods which are related to the domestic environment, also regarded as specifically feminine items by Sheehan. Wulfwaru's will, for example, suggests a residence richly furnished with textiles.[147] She bequeaths hangings both for the hall and the chamber (*heallreafes* and *burreafes*), as well as a table-cover (*beodreafe*) and 'all the cloths (*hræglum*) which go with it'. Although seat-covers are not mentioned by Wulfwaru, they feature in a number of wills and would certainly have

144 Owen, 'Wynflæd's wardrobe', p. 219. Ceolthryth (unid.) is bequeathed her choice of Wynflæd's black tunics, best holy veil (*haliryft*) and band (*bindan*). Three further women are named in the will, but only Æthelflæd the White is to receive clothing: a gown, cap (*cuffian*) and band (*bindan*).

145 S1494/W14. The nature of these garments is unclear, but they were undoubtedly of the best quality – possibly *purpura* (see p. 205 above).

146 Gregory of Tours, *Historiae Francorum*, ed. W. Arndt and B. Krusch, MGH, *Scriptores Rerum Merovingicarum*, I, part 1 (Hanover, 1884), book 10, chap. 16; *Gregory of Tours: History of the Franks*, transl. L. Thorpe (London, 1974), p. 572. See Dodwell, *Anglo-Saxon Art*, pp. 179–81 for an account of the value of fabrics owned by both laity and church. See also *LE* II, 50 (p. 117) and *The Early History of Glastonbury: an Edition, Translation and Study of William of Malmesbury's 'De Antiquitate Glastonie Ecclesie'*, ed. and transl. J. Scott (Woodbridge, 1981), pp. 130–1 for the recycling of King Edgar's gifts of garments.

147 S1538/W21, *Bath and Wells* 21. E. Coatsworth, 'Cushioning medieval life: domestic textiles in Anglo-Saxon England', *Medieval Clothing and Textiles* 3 (2007), 1–12. Hangings, cushions etc. are illustrated in C. Fell, *Women in Anglo-Saxon England* (Oxford, 1984), pp. 46, 47, 57, taken from manuscripts and the Bayeux Tapestry (but see Coatsworth, 'Domestic textiles', p. 8 for the use of models rather than real life in some illustrations).

added to the brilliance and luxury of the décor.[148] That such textiles were a source of pride is indicated by Wynflæd's reference to her *betsþe bedwahrift* (best bed-curtain), and Æthelgifu designates the best wall-hanging and seat cover for St Albans.[149] Sets of bedclothes also add to the impression of luxury; one set, bequeathed by Wulfwaru to the church, also includes a hanging and a curtain which seem to have been integral, perhaps for use on special occasions.[150] Æthelgifu bequeaths not only bedding, but bedsteads, of which some seem to have been of particularly good quality: 'all the best bedsteads she has available' (*eal betstow swylce heo þærto betst hæfð*) are to go to her kinswoman Wulfwynn; Leofsige, her principal heir, is to receive a further two, and her kinswomen Ælfgifu and Godwif are to share the remainder. The few fragments which survive demonstrate how rich household textiles may have been, both in terms of materials and craftsmanship.[151] They were certainly sufficiently treasured not only to be bequeathed as heirlooms, but to be carefully stored. Wynflæd bequeaths to her granddaughter, Eadgifu, 'two chests, and in them her best bed-hanging and a linen covering and all the bed-clothing that goes with it'.[152]

The storage chest was an important item in the household. Its symbolism as part of a woman's household responsibilities is reflected in the law of Cnut, which holds her responsible if stolen goods should be found in a chest (*cyst*) for which she has the key.[153] The number of chests bequeathed by Wynflæd indicates a large household: four *mydrecan* containing bedding; two further large *mydercan*; one small chest described as a *towmyderce*, which has been interpreted as a spinning or weaving box;[154] and a *hræglcysð* (clothes chest). Wulfwaru's description of *anes godes casteneres wel gerenedes* (a good chest well

148 S1497/*St Albans* 7; S1539/W3; S1535/W32, *Christ Church* 176.

149 S1539/W3; S1497/*St Albans* 7.

150 *anes beddreafes mid wahryfte 7 mid hoppscytan*. Wynflæd bequeaths 'a set of bedclothing (*bedreaf*), all that belongs to one bed' (S1539/W3). See Coatsworth, 'Domestic textiles', p. 3 for the setting up of domestic spaces for different purposes. Manuscript illustrations show table- and bed-linen in use: Dodwell, *Anglo-Saxon Art*, plates 33–5 (pp. 142–3); BL Cotton MS Claudius B IV, fols. 27v, 32r, and MS Cotton Tiberius C VI, fol. 5v.

151 *LE* II, 63 refers to a hanging presented to Ely by Ælfflæd, widow of Ealdorman Byrhtnoth, which depicted his deeds. See Dodwell, *Anglo-Saxon Art*, pp. 139–41 and plates 19, 32–5, with discussion of literary references to hangings at pp. 133–6 and an account of the value of fabrics owned by both laity and church at pp. 179–81. For a survey of surviving fragments see M. Budny, 'The Byrhtnoth tapestry or embroidery', in *The Battle of Maldon*, ed. Scragg, pp. 263–78; M. Budny and D. Tweddle, 'The Maseik embroideries', *ASE* 13 (1984), 65–96 (pp. 84–9); E. Coatsworth, 'The embroideries from the tomb of St Cuthbert', in *Edward the Elder*, ed. Higham and Hill, pp. 292–306, with bibliography. Fleming, 'The new wealth', p. 10.

152 *twa mydrecan 7 þæraninnan hyre betsþe bedwahrift 7 linnenne ruwan 7 eal þæt bedref þe þærto gebyreð*.

153 II Cnut 76.1a. See Fell, *Women in Anglo-Saxon England*, pp. 59–61, for women's economic role in the household.

154 *Wills*, p. 114.

decorated) may suggest that the chest itself was ornate. As well as all these fine goods, there are Wynflæd's 'utensils and all the useful things', which she bequeaths to her daughter, Æthelflæd.[155] It is tempting to see such items as part of a woman's own dowry, particularly since, like textiles, they are likely to be bequeathed to kin: Æthelgifu bequeaths two chests (*mydercan*) to each of her kinswomen, Ælfgifu and Godwif, and Wynflæd two *mydrecan* each to her grandson and granddaughter.[156] Nevertheless, household women might also benefit: Wulfwaru's 'good chest well decorated' is bequeathed to her *hiredwifmannum* in common (*gemanum*); it is unclear whether the contents were to be shared, or whether it was intended for use in the women's quarters, or even to be sold and the profits distributed among them.[157]

The cups, bowls and horns found predominantly in the wills of women are also to be linked with domestic display, symbolic of the feasting culture which was an important feature of aristocratic life.[158] The vessels bequeathed by Eberhard and Gisela were luxury items indeed: dishes, ewers, goblets and spoons of gold and silver were to be distributed, testifying to the ostentatious display which accompanied aristocratic eating and drinking.[159] The limited descriptions of cups and other vessels provided in Anglo-Saxon wills indicates that they were also of considerable value, made of, or adorned with, precious metal. Some of these items were of silver, and some are valued as if they were silver, or had silver decoration, with such phrases as *on feower pund* (worth four pounds), or *on godum feo* (of good value).[160] That they might also be used as bullion is indicated by Wynflæd's bequest to her grandson of her wooden cup which has gold to the value of sixteen mancuses upon

155 *þara andlumena 7 ealra þera getæsa*; these are inside a receptacle, details of which are lost through manuscript damage.

156 S1497/*St Albans* 7; S1539/W3; S1538/W21, *Bath and Wells* 21. P. Skinner, 'Women, wills and wealth in medieval southern Italy', *EME* 2.2 (1993), 133–52 (pp. 138–9 for dowry, and p. 141 for a woman's right to bequeath); the period covered by these wills is *c.* 800–1100.

157 Fell, *Women in Anglo-Saxon England*, p. 45. Similar uncertainty arises with Wynflæd's bequest of hangings to her daughter, the smaller designated as fit to be given to 'her' women (Wynflæd's or her daughter's?).

158 Fleming, 'The new wealth', pp. 4–9 (at p. 4). For the role of feasting, see J. Campbell, 'England *c.* 991', in *The Battle of Maldon*, ed. Cooper, pp. 1–17, reprinted in Campbell, *The Anglo-Saxon State*, pp. 157–78 (pp. 162–3); D. A. Bullough, *Friends, Neighbours and Fellow-drinkers: Aspects of Community and Conflict in the Early Medieval West*, H. M. Chadwick Memorial Lecture 1 (Cambridge, 1990), esp. pp. 8–16; H. Magennis, *Anglo-Saxon Appetites: Food and Drink and their Consumption in Old English and Related Literature* (Dublin, 1999), Chap. 1.

159 *Cartulaire*, ed. Coussemaker, pp. 2–3; La Rocca and Provero, 'The dead and their gifts', p. 253.

160 S1538/W21, *Bath and Wells* 21. For silver vessels see S1497/*St Albans* 7, S1539/W3, S1486/W15 and the joint will S1511/W11, *Rochester* 35; *CR* records Æthelgifu's bequest of *duos ciphos argenteos de xii. marcis ad pondus hustingiæ Londoniensis* to Ramsey (*CR* 32).

it, so that he may enlarge his *beah* with the gold or receive its equivalent.[161] Other vessels were decorated: Wynflæd bequeaths a further two which are *gesplottude* (ornamented with dots?);[162] Wulfgyth bequeaths two horns which are *yboned* (ornamented, or perhaps burnished), and Ælfgifu bequeaths one which is *geræenodæs* (ornamented), recalling the horn, apparently edged with gold and with a decorated finial, shown on the Bayeux Tapestry, raised to the mouth of a member of Harold's party during the feast at Bosham.[163]

The social symbolism of such vessels seems to have had a long tradition, their inclusion in furnished burials serving as an important indicator of wealth.[164] Their proliferation in the wills of women seems to endorse the convention of Old English verse, where cups are associated with women serving warriors at feasts.[165] Wynflæd's bequests to her kindred are particularly complex. First, she bequeaths a lidded cup (*hlidfæsþe*) each to her son and daughter; she requests that they will 'furnish between them two fair goblets to the refectory for her sake, or augment her own ornamented cups [...] worth one pound'.[166] Each cup – presumably those presented to the refectory on her behalf – is then to be filled with half a pound of pence.[167] Wynflæd also stipulates that her grandson, Eadwold, is to be given back 'his own two silver cups' (*his agene .II. sylerenan cuppan*); perhaps she was holding them in trust for her young grandson as heirlooms, just as Wulfric Spott may have been holding his goddaughter's brooch, which had belonged to her grandmother.[168]

The joint will of Brihtric and Ælfswith, which is the only joint will to bequeath a significant amount of movable wealth, amalgamates the patterns

161 S1539/W3: *hyre goldfagan treowenan cuppan þæt he ice his beah mid þam golde oþþe hi mon æt him gehweorfe mid .XVI. mancussum reades reades* [sic] *goldes swa micel þær is to gedong* [sic].

162 Although see Hinton, *Gold and Gilt*, p. 322, n. 45 for the possibility of metal sheet held onto a wooden cup with rivets.

163 S1484/W8; S1535/W32, *Christ Church* 176. F. M. Stenton, *The Bayeux Tapestry* (London, 1957), plate 4. See also Dodwell, *Anglo-Saxon Art*, p. 39 for the seventh-century Taplow horn. Cups and vessels are shown in use at a feast in MS Cotton Tiberius C VI, fol. 5v (Dodwell, *Anglo-Saxon Art*, plate 34, p. 143).

164 Härke, 'The Anglo-Saxon weapon burial rite', pp. 37–8; Stoodley, *The Spindle and the Spear*, pp. 33, 108; Geake, *The Use of Grave-Goods*, pp. 83–4.

165 S1539/W3 (8); S1484/W8 (3); S1494/W14 (8); S1486/W15 (3); S1538/W21, *Bath and Wells* 21 (8); S1535/W32, *Christ Church* 176 (2); S1497/*St Albans* 7 (more than 6). The joint will of Brihtric and Ælfswith (S1511/W11, *Rochester* 35) bequeaths 5. See Fell, *Women in Anglo-Saxon England*, pp. 35–6, 50, and *Klaeber's Beowulf*, ed. Fulk, Bjork and Niles, lines 622–4 for the *bēaghroden cwēn* serving mead.

166 *findon betweox him twa smicere scencingcuppan into beodern for hi oþþe hyre ahgene ieredan cuppan geiccon hy sy* [lacuna in ms.] *an anon punde.*

167 *þonne wolde heo þæt man dyde innon ægþere cuppan healf pund penega.*

168 S1536/W17, *Burton* 29. Wynflæd seems to have been particularly concerned about her grandson's endowment: see Chap. 4, p. 171 above.

of men's and women's bequests which have been identified here.[169] The donors bequeath items of considerable value to royalty, the Church and kin.[170] The first dispositive clause, written in the third person singular, bequeaths Brihtric's heriot in all but name.[171] This is followed by a bequest to the queen of a *beah* of thirty mancuses and a stallion (*stede*), for her advocacy; although this is not specifically attributed to Ælfswith, it may have been made on her behalf, since such bequests to the queen are characteristic of women's wills, rather than those of laymen.[172] The will continues in the third person, the second dispositive clause bequeathing land to Rochester on behalf of Brihtric and his ancestors; this is followed by a similar gift in Ælfswith's name, in memory of her ancestors, which is immediately succeeded by a sequence of pious bequests of movable wealth 'for them' (*for hy*): the grammatical structure is ambiguous, but the gifts seem more likely to have been made on behalf of Brihtric and Ælfswith, rather than Ælfswith's ancestors:

> *7 þiderin for hy. ðrittig mancys goldes. 7 ænne sweorbeah. on .XL. mancysan. 7 ane cuppan seolfrene. 7 healfne bænd gyldenne. 7 ælce geare to heora gemynde. twegra daga feorme …*[173] *7 to Cristes circan .LX. mancys goldes .XXX. ðam biscope .XXX. ðam hirode. 7 ænne sweorbeah. on .LXXX. mancys. 7 twa cuppan seolfrene. 7 ðæt land æt Meapaham; 7 to Sancte Augustine. ðrittig mancys goldes. 7 twa cuppan seolfrene. 7 healfne bænd gyldenne.*
>
> (And to the same church [Rochester] on their behalf thirty mancuses of gold and a necklace of forty mancuses, and a silver cup and half a gold band; and each year in commemoration of them, two days' food-rent [from four estates]. And to Christ Church [Canterbury] sixty mancuses of gold, thirty for the bishop and thirty for the community, and a necklace of eighty mancuses and two silver cups, and the estate at Meopham. And to St Augustine's thirty mancuses of gold and two silver cups and half a gold band.)

These goods bequeathed to the church are familiar from the wills of individual women donors, occurring rarely in those of laymen. The only other items of movable wealth mentioned in the will are typically male-gendered: a *handsecs* worth three pounds and two spurs (*spuran*), each worth three pounds,

169 S1511/W11, *Rochester* 35; the will of Ulf and Madselin (W39/*Peterborough* 27) includes a distribution of coin.

170 See Chap. 4, pp. 161–5 above for the bequests of land in this will.

171 The heriot payment is that of a king's thegn: a *beah* of eighty mancuses of gold, a *handsecs* of the same value, four horses, two with harness, two swords and sheaths, two hawks and all *his* staghounds (my italics); the use of the masculine third person singular indicates that this bequest was made on Brihtric's behalf.

172 See n. 207 below.

173 I have here omitted the names of the four estates which were to provide food-rent to Rochester: *Hæslholt*, Wateringbury, Birling and Harrietsham; see Chap. 4, p. 165 above.

bequeathed to kinsmen. It seems that the bequests of movable wealth in this joint will represent the gender identity of both husband and wife.[174]

As might be anticipated, churchmen, too, appear to conform to Sheehan's stereotype in their bequests of movable wealth, showing 'a special interest' in religious items which they bequeath to their own churches or to favoured religious houses.[175] These items might be valuable personal possessions, as in the case of Bishop Theodred's gifts to his episcopal church at London:

> *And into sc̄e Paules kirke mine to beste messehaclen. þe ic habbe mid alle þinge þe þereto birið mid calice and on cuppe. and mine beste masseboc. and alle mine reliquias þe ic best habbe into Paules kirke.*
>
> (And to St Paul's church I grant the two best chasubles that I have, with all the things which belong to them, together with a chalice and one cup. And my best mass-book, and the best relics that I have [are to go] to St Paul's church.

In the same way, Archbishop Ælfric acknowledges his personal links with St Alban's by bequeathing to that house his books and his tent, and Bishop Ælfwold bequeaths to his episcopal church at Crediton three liturgical books and a mass vestment, and to Wilton a chalice and a paten of gold.[176] Theodred also makes bequests to his companions:[177]

> *And ic an Þeodred min wite massehakele þe ic on Pauie bouhte and al þat þerto bireð. 7 simbelcalice 7 þere messeboc þe Gosebricht me biquaþ. And ic an Odgar þere gewele massehakele þe ic on Pauie bouhte. 7 þat þerto bireð.*
>
> (And I grant to Theodred my white chasuble that I bought in Pavia, and all that belongs to it, and a chalice for festivals and the massbook which Gosebriht bequeathed to me. And I grant to Odgar the yellow chasuble which I bought in Pavia, and what belongs to it.)

Originating in Pavia, these garments were probably of Byzantine silk, the

174 See W39/*Peterborough* 27 for a similar shift in pronoun, where Ulf's bequests are in the first person, and Madselin's in the third person singular; their joint dispositions are in the third person plural.

175 Sheehan, *The Will*, p. 103. For celibate churchmen as constituting a third gender, see Crick, 'Women, wills', p. 28.

176 S1526/W1; S1488/W18, *Abingdon* 133 (for Ælfric's relationship with St Albans, see Chap. 3, p. 119 above); S1492/N&S10. At least some of the sumptuous gifts of Bishop Leofric to Exeter (1066x1072) may have been *post obitum*, but in its present form (a list written into the Exeter Book) only Leofric's *capella* is identified as such: *Charters*, Appendix I, no. 1, 1069x1072; Pelteret, *Catalogue*, no. 91; Ker, *Catalogue*, no. 116, fol. 1.

177 S1526/W1. The German derivation of the name Gosebriht, as well as those of Theodred's beneficiaries, suggests that these were close companions of Theodred, who may himself have been of German origin: *Wills*, p. 103; Whitelock, *Anglo-Saxon Bishops*, pp. 19–20.

yellow one at least decorated with embroidery, since Theodred bequeaths to Gundwine another yellow chasuble which is distinguished by its lack of ornamentation (*ungerenad*).[178] It is likely that the massbook which Theodred had inherited from Gosebriht had personal resonance for him. In contrast, Archbishop Ælfric's choice of beneficiaries for personal items may be politically significant: he bequeaths a pectoral cross, a *ring* – perhaps his episcopal ring – and a psalter to Archbishop Wulfstan, and a crucifix (*rode*) to Bishop Ælfheah of Winchester. These were men who would lead the church after his death: Wulfstan was the newly-appointed archbishop of York when the will was made, and Ælfheah became Ælfric's successor at Canterbury.[179]

The analysis presented here of the way in which movable wealth was bequeathed in the wills of these three social groups – laymen, women and churchmen – adds weight to Sheehan's view that donors were influenced in their dispositions by long-standing social conventions of gender symbolism, or the conventions of their social role. However, as Crick has perceived, these were not the only factors at work. The way in which a number of wills cross the gender boundaries in their bequests of movable items illustrates the way in which the worlds of male and female, secular and religious, intersected, and contributed to the complexity of dispositions. Sheehan himself recognised that his categories were permeable when he pointed out that lay as well as religious donors might bequeath religious items. Wynflæd and Æthelgifu, as has been suggested above, may have been living as vowesses in religious households: the former bequeaths the better of her offering cloths (*ofringsceat*) and her cross to the church, as well as *nunscrude* (nun's clothing) to various women; Æthelgifu, who has around her women upon whom she could rely to sing the psalter in her memory, bequeaths a book – presumably a religious text, perhaps adorned with precious metal – to St Alban's.[180] However, other women making such bequests, as well as laymen, may have been bequeathing treasures from a richly furnished private chapel, as did Eberhard and Gisela and Eccard, count of Mâcon.[181] Ælfgifu bequeaths her shrine (*scrin*) and relics to the Old Minster, Winchester, and a paten (*offringdisc*) to Nunnaminster; Wulfwaru bequeaths to Bath two gold crucifixes (*roda*), a set of mass-vestments (*mæssereaf*) and all that belonged to it, and a dorsal (*hrichrægl*); and Wulfgyth bequeaths a 'little gold crucifix' and a dorsal to Christ Church and

178 See Dodwell, *Anglo-Saxon Art*, pp. 149–53 for the significance of Pavia in the silk trade.

179 S1488/W18, *Abingdon* 133 is dated 1003x1005. Wulfstan was appointed to York in 1003; he is also named in the will as Bishop Wulfstan (possibly an error: *Abingdon*, part 2, p. 520), as joint executor with Ælfric's brother, Abbot Leofric.

180 S1539/W3; S1497/*St Albans* 7 (see p. 205 above). Two books bequeathed by Eberhard and Gisela are described as having gold writing (*cum auro scripto*): *Cartulaire*, ed. *Coussemaker*, pp. 2–4. Wynflæd also bequeaths 'books and other small things' to her daughter.

181 *Cartulaire*, ed. Coussemaker, pp. 2–4; *Recueil*, ed. Prou and Vidier, pp. 61–5. For Eccard, see n. 53 above.

St Augustine's, Canterbury, respectively.[182] The precise nature of the *hricghrægl* is unclear; the literal meaning of 'back-cloth' could refer to a garment, perhaps a cloak, or to a woven or embroidered curtain which hung behind the altar, as described in the eleventh-century Old English Vision of Leofric:

> *Ða wæs þær an þrilig wahrægl 7 swyðe þicce gewefen þæt hangode bæftan þam weofode.*
>
> (There was a triple-threaded wall-hanging, very thickly woven, that hung behind the altar.)[183]

It is possible that vestments and other textiles were produced in the households of aristocratic women, for whose skills in embroidery there is some evidence.[184] The *Liber Eliensis* records that the noblewoman Æthelswith became a nun at Coveney, near Ely, where 'in great seclusion she used to devote her time to gold embroidery and tapestry-weaving, in company with young girls, and, at her own expense, she made with her own hands a white chasuble, being very expert at this sort of craft'.[185] Wynflæd, after all, bequeaths both a seamstress and a weaver, suggesting that the production of textiles could take place within the household.

Three high-status laymen bequeath religious items, with the emphasis on precious metal.[186] King Eadred bequeaths two golden crosses, along with two golden swords, to the place of his burial; the ætheling Æthelstan bequeaths a silver cross to the *Nunnaminster*, Winchester, and to Bishop Ælfsige, a gold crucifix currently in the possession of Eadric, Wynflæd's son; and Ealdorman Æthelmær bequeaths to the New Minster, Winchester, his shrine (*scrin*).[187]

182 S1538/W21, *Bath and Wells* 21; S1484/W8; S1535/W32, *Christ Church* 176. Ælfwaru gave to Ramsey a chasuble, alb, priestly ornaments (*sacerdotalia ornamenta*) and a fine cross (*CR* 54).

183 Quotation and translation from M. McC. Gatch, 'Miracles and architectural settings: Christ Church, Canterbury and St Clement's, Sandwich in the Old English Vision of Leofric' *ASE* 22 (1993), 227–52 (p. 243 and n. 73). The full text is published in 'An Old English Vision of Leofric, Earl of Mercia', ed. and transl. A. S. Napier, *Transactions of the Philological Society* (1907–1910), 180–8. For the term see also S1535/W32, *Christ Church* 176; S1532/*St Albans* 13; S1492/N&S10. Coatsworth, 'Domestic textiles', p. 9, Table 1.1.

184 Budny and Tweddle, 'The Maseik embroideries', pp. 89–91; Owen-Crocker, *Dress in Anglo-Saxon England*, pp. 308–309.

185 *LE* II, 88: *ubi aurifrixorie et texturis secretius cum puellulis vacabat, que de proprio sumptu albam casulam suis manibus ipsa talis ingenii peritissima fecit.*

186 For *inter vivos* gifts by laymen see the reliquary cross presented to the church by two brothers in memory of a third illustrated in *Golden Age*, ed. Backhouse, Turner and Webster, no. 75, pp. 90–2, colour plate 23. *The Waltham Chronicle*, ed. Watkiss and Chibnall, records the gifts of Tovi (chaps. 11, 12) and Earl Harold (chaps. 16, 17); Fleming, 'The new wealth', pp. 13–14. See also Byrhtnoth's gifts to Ely on the eve of battle, which included two golden crosses (*LE* II, 62).

187 S1515/H21, *New Minster* 17; S1503/H20; S1498/W10, *New Minster* 25. For shrines of precious metal see Dodwell, *Anglo-Saxon Art*, pp. 196–7; for two wooden reliquary

Only Ulf bequeaths to St Alban's, where he wished to be buried, the range of religious items characteristic of women or churchmen: his best set of mass-vestments, a chalice, dish and mass-book, and his thickest dorsal. Not only this, he bequeaths two *pællene* kirtles, such as that bequeathed by Wulfgyth to Ely; the better one, which had belonged to Godgifu, was to go to St Alban's, and the other was to go to Ramsey.[188] The ambiguity of Ulf's bequests have led to debate as to whether he was lay or religious, since he is given no title in his will, nor is there a heriot clause; he bequeaths four marks for distribution among the principal minsters (*heh mynstran*) of the country, but also distributes gold and silver to a number of male beneficiaries, including four marks of gold to his *feolagan*, possibly business associates.[189] Perhaps, as Crick has suggested, the likeliest possibility is that Ulf was a nobleman who had entered into confraternity with a religious community in widowhood;[190] this would account for his pious bequests and, in this case, his *feolagan* might be his fellow religious.[191] Further speculation might suggest that Godgifu, whose *pællene* kirtle he bequeaths, may have been his late wife, and 'the child', for whose care he makes anxious arrangements, assigning responsibility for him to a certain Saxa, may have been his son.[192] If, however, it was acceptable for laymen to bequeath religious goods, the question remains why so few apparently chose to do so (see Appendix 3).

Just as the wills of lay donors include bequests of religious items, so those of churchmen often have a secular aspect. For example, although churchmen are not included in Cnut's tariffs, they may, like laymen, pay a form of heriot. Bishops Ælfsige, Theodred and Ælfwold refer to heriot payment: the first is unspecified, but Ælfwold lists horses, shields, spears, helmets and byrnies,

crosses of the early eleventh century adorned with precious metal see *Golden Age*, ed. Backhouse, Turner and Webster, nos. 75, 118 (colour plates XXIII, XXVI). One text of the Ramsey Chronicle records a wooden cross bequeathed by Æthelstan Mannessune: *CR*33 (p. 60, n. 4). Count Eccard's bequests included a golden reliquary cross containing a splinter from the Lord's cross, and a silver cross containing a nail from the crucifixion (Kasten, 'Erbrechtliche Verfügungen', pp. 327–8; *Recueil*, ed. Prou and Vidier, pp. 64, 65.

188 *Cyrtel* could refer to both male or female attire (Owen-Crocker, *Dress in Anglo-Saxon England*, p. 217); for *pællene*, see n. 140 above. The only other laymen to bequeath clothing are Æthelwold, who bequeaths two *crusnan* – probably fur robes (S1505/W12, *New Minster* 29), and Wulfsige, who bequeaths a cloak (*hakele* –S1537/W27). See Le Jan, *Famille et pouvoir*, p. 63 for the cloak as an element of display.

189 For the difficulty in identifying Ulf, see Keynes, 'The will of Wulf', p. 20; *St Albans*, pp. 203–4, with a review of Ulf's beneficiaries at p. 203. *Feolagan* usually appears in the context of a partnership in goods or land: see also S1531/W31 and S1519/W34; for the derivation from Old Icelandic *félagi*, and the possible meaning of 'comrade', see *Wills*, p. 193. Ulf's household servants 'who have no land' are each to receive a horse.

190 *St Albans*, pp. 203–4.

191 See S1505/W12, *New Minster* 29, where Æthelwold bequeaths twenty mancuses of gold 'for his brothers' (*his gebroþrune*) at Abingdon.

192 For such careful arrangements for a son in the case of the donor's widow remarrying, see S1517/*St Albans* 15.

as well as a fully equipped ship, and Theodred specifies war-gear and gold appropriate for an ealdorman.[193] In addition, Archbishop Ælfric refers to the money (*feoh*) which is to be made available to pay his heriot, while in a separate clause, not specified as heriot, he bequeaths to the king his best ship, and sixty helmets and byrnies.[194] Bishop Ælfwold also bequeaths six further byrnies: two to his brother-in-law, three to Wulfgar, his kinsman, and one (together with a helmet) to Cenwold, perhaps a kinsman or an important associate. Warrior bishops were not unknown, but it seems likely that churchmen, who often belonged to high-status kindred, were fulfilling their responsibilities as formidable landholders, as well as participating in the powerful, long-standing symbolism of aristocratic status based on a warrior society.[195] That they had the responsibilities of secular magnates is made clear in the will of Ærchbishop Ælfric, who not only grants ships to the people of Kent and Wiltshire, but writes off debts owed to him by three shires, probably as the result of payments to Danish raiders.[196] Similarly, bishops, in common with laymen, are likely to bequeath gold and silver for distribution both to the church and to members of their retinue and household. Bishop Ælfwold names a number of religious beneficiaries who also witnessed his will: the monk Ælfwold is to receive twenty mancuses, a horse and a tent; the priest Brihtmær also receives twenty mancuses and a horse; a second priest, Edwin, receives five mancuses and a cope; and since Ælfgar the scribe – presumably a member of the community – is to be paid one pound on Ælfwold's behalf, it is tempting to see him as the scribe who recorded the will.[197] In addition, Ælfwold acknowledges the secular members of his household with coin, bequeathing five pounds to be shared among his retainers (*hiredcnihton*) 'according to degree' (*be þam þe his mæð wære*).[198] Bishop Ælfric bequeaths

193 S1491/W4, *New Minster* 18; S1526/W1; S1492/N&S10. See the table in Brooks, 'Arms, status', p. 149.

194 S1488/W18, *Abingdon* 133.

195 *ASC* records bishops participating in expeditions against the Danes in 992, 1016, 1056. See the gift of two shields (*scuta*) and lances (*lances*) made by Boniface to King Æthelbald of Mercia 745x746: *Die Briefen des hl. Bonifatius und Lullus*, ed. M. Tangl, MGH, *Epistolae* III, *Epistolae Merowingici et Karolini aevi* I (Berlin, 1916), no. 69, p. 42; *The Letters of St Boniface*, transl. E. Emerton, ed. T. F. X. Noble (New York, 2000), no. 55, p. 101.

196 S1488/W18, *Abingdon* 133.

197 The layman Thurstan bequeaths gold from the sale of an estate to Earl Harold, Bishop Stigand, his partner Ulfketel and Sendi, all of whom are named as witnesses of his will (S1531/W31).

198 Other individuals receive gold, silver or a horse, but it is unclear whether they were members of Ælfwold's household. Ælfflæd, who is to receive five mancuses of pennies, is termed an *offestre*, probably a religious woman; the term is used in the phrase *nunne oððe offestre* in a version of the Benedictine Rule: *Die Winteney-Version der Regula S. Benedicti*, ed. A. Schröer, 1st edn (Halle, 1888), reprinted with appendix by M. Gretsch (Tübingen, 1978), chap. 60, p. 121, line 22; *DOEC*, no. 0551.

forty pounds to his servants (*cnihtas*) 'whom my stewards know' (*þa mina stiwardas witan*), four pounds to his cup-bearer (*fatfylre*) and five to his seamster (*sæmestre*).[199] A number of these bequests would not be out of place in the will of a secular lord.[200]

Further examples confirm that all donors might participate fully in all aspects of contemporary material culture, irrespective of gender. For example, women were not included in the heriot tariffs listed in Cnut's law, but it appears that they were expected to pay some form of inheritance tax; Wulfgyth refers to her *rihte heriet*, without further detail.[201] Among women donors only Ælfgifu bequeaths war-gear to the king; her payment of six horses, six shields and six spears, as well as a cup (*sopcuppan*) and three hundred and twenty mancuses in the form of *beagas*, has some correlation – minus the swords – with that bequeathed by a contemporary male aristocrat of the highest rank, perhaps reflecting her position as former queen.[202] Since Ælfgifu's will begins with a request to the king for permission to make her will, and concludes with a request that he should protect those of her men who commend themselves to him (*hine gesæcan*), her bequest invokes the reciprocal relationship with the king with which heriot is associated in the wills of her male counterparts.[203] Æthelflæd, also a former queen, bequeaths to the king the substantial gift of four *beagas* worth two hundred mancuses of gold (each?), four garments, four cups, four bowls and four horses, and her sister, Ælfflæd, bequeaths a rather smaller gift of two *beagas*, two cups and a silver vessel.[204] Æthelgifu, like Æthelflæd, bequeaths horses to the king (two *stedan*), and adds her staghounds (*header hundas*) to her gift.[205] That such bequests

199 S1489/W26.

200 For laymen's distribution of coin to the church and the household see p. 201 above.

201 S1535/W32, *Christ Church* 176; surviving in registers of the late thirteenth or early fourteenth century, although there seems no reason to doubt the integrity of this phrase (see *Christ Church* 176 for the general trustworthiness of the text, for the suggestion that by the mid-eleventh century heriot could be paid in cash and that women were required to pay it). See p. 194 above for the link between heriot and inheritance.

202 S1484/W8, 966x975. Ealdorman Æthelmær (S1498/W10, *New Minster* 25, 977x982) cites six horses, shields, spears and swords, plus 300 mancuses of gold and two vessels. See Chap. 3, pp. 95–6 above for Ælfgifu's identity, and her bequest of land to the king in addition to heriot.

203 A writ of King Edward appears to refer to a widow as 'Tole my man, Urk's widow' (*Tole min mann Urkes lafe*), suggesting that a widow could inherit her husband's obligation to the king (*Writs* 2); although the grammatical structure here may be ambiguous, Fell notes a similar usage in a Worcester lease, S1319 (*Women in Anglo-Saxon England*, p. 17). The occasional discovery of weapons in female graves has raised the possibility that such deposits reflect the social role of the individual, rather than the sex: Stoodley, *The Spindle and the Spear*, p. 29.

204 S1494/W14; S1486/W15.

205 S1494/W14; S1497/*St Albans* 7. Brihtric (S1511/W11, *Rochester* 35) bequeaths two hawks (*hafocas*) and all his staghounds (*heador hundas*) along with his heriot. These were highly appropriate gifts for a king: St Boniface provided hawks as gifts for King

to the king were closely associated with inheritance is shown by the will of Leofgifu, whose bequest of two marks of gold to the king carries the instruction, 'my heirs are to succeed to the inheritance, and pay the gold'.[206] Women might also bequeath movable wealth to the queen for her advocacy.[207] In spite of her bequest of gold to the king, Leofgifu places her will very firmly under the queen's protection, bequeathing her an estate at Belchamp (Ex):

> *And ic bidde mine leuedien for godes louen þat þu þolie þat ani man mine quide awende.*
>
> (And I pray my lady, for god's love, that you will [not] permit anyone to alter my will.)[208]

Although Leofgifu bequeaths land to the queen rather than movable goods, Ælfgifu's bequest to the queen of gold *beagas* and a drinking cup (*sopcuppan*) probably had the same purpose – to gain the queen's support for her will.[209] The will of Brihtric and Ælfswith includes a bequest to the queen of a *beah* of thirty mancuses of gold and a stallion (*stedan*), which may have been made on Ælfswith's behalf.[210] It seems that for women the warrior ethos of heriot did not generally apply, but high-status, valuable gifts reflecting the aristocratic life-style proved an appropriate substitute.

A further illustration of gender complexity is provided by the will of Bishop Ælfwold, who bequeaths goods which are strongly associated with women.[211] His kinsman Wulfgar is to receive not only byrnies, but also two wall-hangings (*wahryfta*) and two seat-covers (*setlhrægla*). His sister, Eadgifu,

Æthelbald of Mercia: *Briefen*, ed. Tangl, no. 69; *Letters*, transl. Emerton, no. 55, p. 101. For their acceptability as gifts see the king's request in *Briefen*, ed. Tangl, no. 105; *Letters*, transl. Emerton, no. 95, p. 157. For the aristocratic symbolism of hawking see G. Owen-Crocker, 'Hawks and horse-trappings: the insignia of rank', in *The Battle of Maldon*, ed. Scragg, pp. 220–37 (pp. 220–9).

206 S1521/W29: *for min eruenumen to 7 gealaeste þat gold.*

207 Two bishops bequeath gold to the queen, suggesting that for them, as for women, the queen may also have been regarded as a particularly appropriate advocate: S1526/W1; S1489/W26. The only layman to bequeath movable wealth to the queen is Wulfsige (S1537/W27), who grants half a mark of gold. Thurstan and Ulf bequeath gold to high-ranking laymen, perhaps for a similar purpose: S1531/W31; S1532/*St Albans* 13.

208 S1521/W29, 1035x1044. The will, uniquely, is addressed to the queen, probably the dowager queen, Emma, since it is possible that Leofgifu was in her service: see Stafford, *Queen Emma and Queen Edith*, p. 112, and p. 181, n. 95 for the suggestion that Belchamp was royal land held from the queen. If Emma was the addressee, the will was unlikely to have been made between 1037 and 1040, when she was in exile (see Stafford, *Unification and Conquest*, pp. 77–82 for a summary of the politics of this period).

209 Æthelgifu bequeaths the same amount of gold to the queen as to the king: 30 mancuses.

210 S1484/W8; S1497/*St Albans* 7; S1511/W11, *Rochester* 35 (see pp. 209–11 above for the distinction between the bequests of Brihtric and Ælfswith in this joint will).

211 S1492/N&S10. Crick notes this parallel in 'Women, wills', p. 28.

is to receive both a dorsal (*hrigchrægl*) and a seat-cover (*sethrægl*).[212] In addition, he bequeaths his bedding (*beddreaf*) to his chamberlains. These goods must have been his personal property, and it is difficult to know whether the possibility that this was a deathbed distribution makes his bequests of such conventionally feminine items uncharacteristic; they are certainly unique in churchmen's wills, but seat-covers, wall-hangings and *tæppedu* (carpets?), as well as a wealth of vestments and liturgical items, are included among the gifts to his episcopal church attributed to Bishop Leofric of Exeter.[213]

Examples multiply. For laymen, the bequest of cups and other vessels as prestigious gifts, or gifts within the kindred, seems perfectly acceptable, in defiance of the literary association of cups with women and their proliferation in women's wills: Abba bequeaths a horn to his brother; Æthelwold, a cup to his wife; the ætheling Æthelstan, a horn and a silver cauldron to the church. Vessels are also bequeathed to the king by two ealdormen, Æthelwold and Ælfheah, along with their heriot.[214] Ælfric Modercope's bequest to Bishop Ælfric, which was made in anticipation of a voyage (probably on pilgrimage), includes a tent and, that bastion of femininity, his bedding, 'the best that I had out on my journey with me' (*min bedreaf þat ic best hauede vt on mi fare mid me*); Wynflæd, on the other hand, emerges from conventional domesticity to bequeath her own red tent.[215]

The category of goods which most clearly illustrates these complex patterns of bequest is that of horses and riding-gear, a category identified by Sheehan as masculine. Sheehan's judgement may have been influenced by the will of the ætheling Æthelstan, whose bequests of horses and trappings occupy the world of male lordship.[216] Æthelstan bequeaths six individual horses, some of which are specifically identified. Those bequeathed to his father, for example,

212 For dorsal, see p. 213 above. Eadgifu is also to receive a *strichrægl*, a unique form; Whitelock (*EHD* I, p. 581, n. 3) suggests that *stric* may be an object which the *hrægl* would cover, or it may be a type of cloth (Old Norse *strik*). B&T Supp. suggests a cloth for rubbing; Boniface gives towels for foot-drying as gifts, e.g. *Briefen*, ed. Tangl, no. 63; *Letters*, transl. Emerton, no. 51 (I am grateful to Professor G. Owen-Crocker for this point). Coatsworth, 'Domestic textiles', p. 8, n. 26, proposes a possible derivation from Old English *strician*, to knit or net.

213 See Chap. 2, pp. 66–7 above for S1492/N&S10 as a deathbed will. For Leofric's gifts, see n. 176 above.

214 S1482/H2, *Christ Church* 70; S1505/W12, *New Minster* 29; S1503/W20, *Christ Church* 142; S1504/H20. Bishop Theodred (S1526/W1) bequeaths a cup to his episcopal church.

215 S1490/W28; S1539/W3. Tents are also bequeathed by Archbishop Ælfric and Bishop Ælfric (S1488/W18, *Abingdon* 133; S1492/N&S10).

216 S1503/W20, *Christ Church* 142. For a survey of the evidence for horse-breeding see S. Larratt Keefer, 'Hwær cwom mearh? The horse in Anglo-Saxon England', *Journal of Medieval History* 22 (1996), 115–34 (with discussion of terminology at pp. 128–9, and of this will at p. 127). For the symbolism of the horse, Le Jan, *Famille et pouvoir*, pp. 65–6; for the symbolism of riding-gear see Owen-Crocker, 'Hawks and horse-trappings', pp. 229–34.

had been given to Æthelstan by Thurbrand and Leofwine; Bishop Ælfsige, who witnessed Æthelstan's will, was to receive a black stallion (*blacne stedan*), as well as a gold crucifix, and Ælfmær the *discþegn* a dappled-grey stallion (*anes fagan stedan*).[217] War-gear might accompany the gift of a horse; both Ælfmær and Siferth receive a sword and shield, for example. Æthelstan's bequest of his own horse to his chaplain, Ælfwine, was accompanied by a fine sword, and included Æthelstan's own horse-trappings (*minon gerædon*), suggesting a more personal gift to a valued member of his household. A similar male context for the bequest of horses features in the will of Ulf, who, among bequests of horses to named beneficiaries, bequeaths 'a horse to each of my household servants who have no land', and Bishop Ælfwold, who grants a horse (*hors*) each to a series of named religious beneficiaries and kinsmen and 'to each retainer his steed, which he had lent him' – a resounding Napier and Stevenson translation.[218]

However strong this association of the horse with the aristocratic male may appear to be, women were not excluded. Æthelgifu, for example, bequeaths two *stedan* (stallions) to the king, and the bequest of a *steda* to the queen by Brihtric and Ælfswith emphasises that women could participate as beneficiaries as well as donors in the aristocratic symbolism of the horse. This is equally true of horse-trappings: Æthelgifu bequeaths her saddle-gear (*sadulgerædo*) to her kinswoman, Leofrun, and Ælfwaru bequeaths to Ramsey, in addition to vestments, furnishings and vessels, her saddle and horse-trappings.[219] We are given an incidental but vivid picture of such a woman in Lantfred's tenth-century account of the miracles of St Swithun, as she prepares for a journey (having failed to fulfil a promise to present gifts at St Swithun's tomb in return for a cure):

> *Haec dum post aliquod tempus cum proprio coniuge premeditaretur ad quasdam nuptias equitare, ministris optimos precepit cornipedes preparare. Qui postquam decentissime sunt ornati faleris, uir eius cum paucioribus antecessit clientibus; quem ipsa cum pluribus subsecuta est citius. Quae dum faleratum scanderet equum et dum equitaret post maritum, dolorem non sensit ullum nec penitus aliquam aegritudinis molestiam.*

> (When after some time she planned to ride with her husband to a wedding, she ordered her attendants to make ready the very best horses. After these horses had been pleasingly decked out with trappings, her husband went on ahead with a very few retainers; she herself followed quickly with

217 Whitelock translates *fagan* as 'pied', but see Larratt Keefer, 'The horse', p. 127 and n. 91.

218 S1532/*St Albans* 13 (*ælc minra hiredcnihta an hors þe nan land nabbað*); S1498/N&S10 (*ælcon hiredmen his onrid þe he alæned hæfde*).

219 S1497/*St Albans* 7; *CR* 54: *sellam suam cum omni equestri apparatu*. For the value of such items see Owen-Crocker, 'Hawks and horse-trappings', pp. 232–4.

many more. While she mounted the caparisoned horse and rode after her husband, she felt no pain and no trouble at all from her illness.)[220]

While women clearly travelled on horseback in considerable style, Æthelgifu's bequest of a *ferdwæn* (carriage) suggests that other modes of transport were also available.[221]

The horse was both a status symbol and an important economic resource in Anglo-Saxon England. Larratt Keefer has interpreted references to stallions as an indication that they were valued for their genetic significance in breeding and, as has been shown above in the case of stock generally, horses were also a commodity which could accrue, providing a surplus which was available to all donors independently of land. [222] There is evidence of horse-breeding in the bequest of studs (*stod*) by the ætheling Æthelstan and Ælfhelm Polga.[223] Wynflæd's bequest of *wildera horsa* indicates the management of unbroken horses, and the *wildra worfa* bequeathed by Bishop Ælfwold to the ætheling may also refer to untamed horses.[224] Wulfric Spott's bequest of 'a hundred wild horses and sixteen tame (or schooled) geldings' has prompted Larratt Keefer to suggest that he may have been breeding horses commercially.[225] The flexibility of horse-breeding as a resource is demonstrated by Ælfhelm's bequest of his stud, which is sited at Troston, an estate which he bequeaths to his brothers; he bequeaths the stud separately, half to his wife and half to 'the companions who ride with me' (*minon geferan … þe me mid ridað*). These horses represented a source of wealth which was not gender specific, available to all donors, to be deployed to maximum advantage in their wills, and appropriate for all beneficiaries.

This factor illustrates the further layer of complexity added to the gendering of movable wealth when the conventions governing its bequest are compared with those governing its inheritance. Some items such as swords, brooches

220 *Cult of St Swithun*, ed. Lapidge, pp. 290–3.

221 S1497/*St Albans* 7; a *firdwæn* (transl. 'military wagon') is among Bishop Leofric's gifts to Exeter (*Charters*, Appendix 1, no. 1, p. 228), but Whitelock suggests that *ferd* has here the sense of a journey without a military connotation (*Æthelgifu*, p. 12, n. 13).

222 For valuable bloodstock see Larratt Keefer, 'The horse', esp. at p. 127. For the value of the horse generally see J. Campbell, 'Was it infancy in England? Some questions of comparison', in *England and her Neighbours*, ed. M. Jones and M. Vale (London, 1989), pp. 1–17, reprinted in Campbell, *The Anglo-Saxon State*, pp. 179–99 (p. 193 and n. 79). For the importance of the horse for the king's administration, J. Campbell, 'Some agents and agencies of the late Anglo-Saxon state', in *Domesday Studies*, ed. J. C. Holt (Woodbridge, 1987), pp. 265–78 (pp. 201–18), reprinted in Campbell, *The Anglo-Saxon State*, pp. 201–25 (pp. 217–18). For stock generally, see pp. 180–3 above.

223 S1503/W20, *Christ Church* 142; S1487/W13.

224 S1539/W3; S1492/N&S10. Wynflæd's untamed horses are running with those of her son.

225 S1536/W17, *Burton* 29: *an hund wildra horsa. 7 sextena tame hencgestas;* Larratt Keefer, 'The horse', p. 126.

and bands, which are strongly gendered in patterns of bequest, generally remain so in patterns of inheritance: swords are granted solely to male and brooches and bands to female beneficiaries (although in two instances bands, items of feminine headgear, are to be shared by males as bullion).[226] But other items strongly associated, although not necessarily exclusively, with women's bequests are equally strongly associated with male beneficiaries. Cups and other vessels, for example, seem highly acceptable as prestigious gifts to the king and other male beneficiaries. Cups are bequeathed equally by Wulfwaru to her sons and daughters, who all receive two each.[227] Similarly, Wynflæd bequeaths cups to her son, Eadmær, her daughter, Æthelflæd, and Eadmær's son, Eadwold.[228] Ælfgifu bequeaths cups to the king, and two other male beneficiaries.[229] In addition, kinsmen are as likely as kinswomen to inherit household furnishings. Wynflæd's grandson has an equal share with his sister in their grandmother's hangings, bedding and chests, and this is not unique: Wulfwaru bequeaths such goods to her sons rather than to her daughters, and Æthelgifu bequeaths two bedsteads (*betstow*) as well as hangings and seat-covers to her principal heir, Leofsige.[230] Such items were clearly valued in terms of conspicuous wealth and luxurious living by both men and women, bequeathed as high-status goods commensurate with the wealth and status of both donors and beneficiaries, largely irrespective of gender.

The gendering of goods therefore cannot account for the fundamental anomaly that, outside heriot, women are more likely to include the bequest of movable wealth in their multi-gift wills than laymen and most churchmen, and bequeath a much wider range of items (see Appendix 3). One possible explanation is that this discrepancy reflects the likelihood, proposed in Chapter Four, that men and women tended to make their wills at different points in the lifecycle.[231] For laymen, often making their wills at the height of their family and public responsibilities, the bequest of heriot and land was crucial for the assertion of status both publicly and within the kindred, with significant quantities of movable items appearing in their multi-gift wills only rarely outside heriot, possibly as deathbed dispositions. For women, making their wills as widows, the bequest of valuable items of movable wealth was an equally important assertion of status at a time of vulnerability and adjustment; the careful allocation of such goods was a means of acknowledging their own personal networks of kin and household, as well as more public

226 S1538/W21, *Bath and Wells* 21; S1497/*St Albans* 7.

227 S1538/W21, *Bath and Wells* 21.

228 See p. 209 above for Wynflæd's bequests of vessels.

229 S1484/W8. Vessels are bequeathed to the king by Æthelflæd (S1494/W14); Ealdorman Æthelwold (S1504/H20); Bishop Theodred (S1526/W1); Ealdorman Ælfheah (S1485/W9).

230 S1539/W3; S1538/W21, *Bath and Wells* 21; S1497/*St Albans* 7.

231 Chap. 4, pp. 145–65, 167–9 above.

relationships with the church and the royal court. For a woman, therefore, this was a time of taking stock and of reorganisation, and perhaps of establishing herself in her new social role, which was likely to involve administrative responsibilities for family land as well as responsibility for the transmission of family property to the next generation, within the wider kindred and to the church.[232]

Widows' dispositions in their wills of high-status items may be interpreted in terms of 'the grammar of display', a phrase used by Halsall to describe the function of sixth-century burial deposits in the diocese of Metz.[233] The public display and ritual deposition of grave-goods may have represented a woman's status both within the immediate family, and in the wider social context.[234] Surveys of the evidence have shown that the nature of the depositions changed according to the point in a woman's life-cycle at which she died; for example, the graves of women aged between twenty and forty contained artifacts such as pottery vessels, reflecting their role within the home and family which focused on childbearing and motherhood, but a change in domestic status is suggested by the reduction in the items deposited in the graves of women past the age of forty.[235] A similar pattern may be identified for the deposition of jewellery in women's graves, which also reflected key points of change in a woman's life-cycle: the young woman of marriageable age acquired significant amounts of jewellery in her grave; for the young adult woman, jewellery was reduced in favour of domestic goods; and by the age of forty, a woman was buried with a drastically reduced number of goods. Old or worn jewellery found in the graves of young women may have been passed to them by older women as heirlooms when they reached marriageable age.[236] Such a convention may be reflected in Wynflæd's bequest of her old brooch to her granddaughter, and possibly Wulfric Spott's transmission to his goddaughter of the brooch which had belonged to her grandmother.

232 For a similar process see M. C. Howell, 'Fixing movables: gifts by testament in late medieval Douai', *Past and Present* 150 (1996), 3–45 (pp. 27–43). The signalling of status through the deposition of grave-goods may have been delegated to women in the Conversion period: Geake, *The Use of Grave-Goods*, p. 128. For women's administrative responsibilities for land see Chap. 4, pp. 177–8 above.

233 G. Halsall, 'Female status and power in early Merovingian central Austrasia: the burial evidence', *EME* 5 (1996), 1–24 (p. 13).

234 Halsall, 'Female status', pp. 18–19.

235 Halsall, 'Female status', pp. 17, 19–20; Stoodley, *The Spindle and the Spear*, pp. 111, 117–18.

236 Halsall, *Settlement and Social Organisation*, pp. 254–7; and Halsall, 'Female status', pp. 10–11, 18–21. For two repaired brooches in a seventh-century Anglo-Saxon context, and a brooch inscribed with the name Eadwynn which was at least a hundred years old when it was buried in a hoard *c.* 1070, see Hinton, *Gold and Gilt*, pp. 77 ( and Fig. 3.3), 143. On the longevity of jewellery and evidence of skilful repair see Coatsworth and Pinder, *Anglo-Saxon Goldsmith*, pp. 242–4.

For tenth- and eleventh-century widows, will-making may have been part of the process of acknowledging such a change of status within the family. The written will recorded not only a widow's dispositions of the land for which she had responsibility, but also her distribution of personal property and that to which she had a claim through her role within the conjugal unit, now to be dissolved. The claims of kinsmen and kinswomen – especially of the younger generation – were important, but clothing and domestic goods might be apportioned in recognition of loyal service within the household, particularly in the light of the reorganisation which would follow a widowed noblewoman's death. It is significant that, in contrast with laymen, who tend to reward their retinue with war-gear or a distribution of coin, women bequeath clothing or household goods for this purpose.[237] An inventory of movable wealth made at this transitional point in a woman's life may have been associated with her will-making.[238] There is a hint of an inventory of stock in the Ramsey Chronicle account of the bequest of Thorgunnr, in this case carried out at the first sign of her final illness; she bequeathed an estate to the abbey 'including everything which was on the land on the holy Easter day when the woman began to be ill'.[239] Such a process would account for the inclusion of specific detail in women's wills, from descriptions of items of clothing or the contents of chests, to the names of individual slaves, and the number of pigs and sheep on a given estate.

The process of inventory may also explain why the wills of some churchmen follow similar patterns to those of women, particularly in the bequest of stock and domestic items. A high-ranking churchman, putting his house in order in advance of death, was in an analogous position to that of a widow: just as a widow's property had to be defined in relation to the conjugal estate, so a churchman needed to differentiate between that which was his to bequeath, and that which was to be transmitted to his successor in office, who represented the next generation.[240] The tenth-century *Regularis Concordia*, while forbidding the accumulation of 'an earthly treasure-store' (*thesaurizaret terrenum*) by abbots and abbesses for the payment of heriot, implies that there was a procedure to be followed in order to identify any surplus when one of them died, and written inventories survive attesting to the meticulous detail with which this was done.[241] For individual religious

237 The exception is Wulfwaru, who bequeaths a gold band for division between four male servants (S1538/W21, *Bath and Wells* 21).

238 This may have been the case in the fifteenth-century wills from Douai: Howell, 'Fixing movables', pp. 7–8; Le Jan, *Famille et pouvoir*, p. 61 for an inventory compiled by a daughter on the death of her mother.

239 *cum omni investitura, sicut fuit in die sancto Paschæ quando cœpit mulier ægrotare; CR* 107 (pp. 175–6). In this case, Thorgunnr had a living husband at the time of her death.

240 See also S1526/W1 for Bishop Theodred's bequests of stock (p. 182 above).

241 *Regularis Concordia*, ed. Symons, chap. 69; for inventories of movable wealth see *LE* II, 114, 139 and III, 50; for a fragment from Bury on the accession of Abbot Leofstan

foundations, the death of an abbot or bishop was an opportunity, quite literally, to take stock; for women, the death of a husband may have prompted a similar review, with a redistribution of personal treasures and the family wealth in their guardianship through the written will.

The responsibility for commemoration vested in widows may well have contributed to their more frequent bequests of religious items but, although the church's institutional memory was long, all donors could hope, or even ask, for short-term memorialisation through their gifts to secular beneficiaries.[242] Æthelgifu's bequests of personal freedom to some of her women and her priest were specifically linked to formal commemoration by the donees in the form of psalm-singing or the offering of masses, but for women generally, brooches and fine outfits, bequeathed to their kinswomen or close companions, or the less valuable clothing to be distributed among their household women, carried with them, as long as they were worn, the memory of the donor.[243] For laymen, certain swords may have performed this function, as in the case of the ætheling Æthelstan's bequest to his father of a sword which had purportedly belonged to King Offa, and one which belonged to Ulfketel. However dubious the validity of the former claim, these weapons were imbued with the memory of previous owners, and now with that of Æthelstan.[244] Individual items might be personalised in wills, as in the case of Bishop Theodred, who refers to 'my' white chasuble, and describes how he bought both that and the yellow chasuble in Pavia, or Wynflæd's reference to her own wooden cup, and to Eadwold's silver cups, which are to be returned to him.[245] Other items, such as Wynflæd's *ealdan gewiredan preon*, bequeathed to her granddaughter, probably had heirloom status, with emotional resonance for both donor and beneficiary; Wulfric Spott's bequest to his goddaughter of her grandmother's *bule* confirms the significance of jewellery transmitted in the female line in perpetuating family memory.[246] It is impossible to know whether the wall-hangings bequeathed in a number of wills portrayed aspects of family tradition, as is suggested by the *Liber Eliensis* reference to a hanging depicting her husband's deeds presented to Ely by

(1044–1065) see *Charters*, no. 104, pp. 194–5. The list of Bishop Leofric's gifts to Exeter has been noted above (n. 176). Inventories are discussed briefly by J. Campbell, 'What is not known about Edward the Elder', in *Edward the Elder*, ed. Higham and Hill, pp. 12–24 (pp. 13–14).

242 The role of objects as 'pegs for memory' is discussed by E. Van Houts, *Memory and Gender in Medieval Europe* (London, 1999), Chap. 5. For the responsibilities of women for commemoration see Chap. 4, pp. 176–7 above and Chap. 6, pp. 276–7 below.

243 Van Houts, *Memory and Gender*, p. 104-9.

244 S1503/W20, *Christ Church* 142; see also Ælfgar's bequest to the king of the sword given to him by King Edmund (S1483/W2). Van Houts, *Memory and Gender*, pp. 109–10.

245 Van Houts, *Memory and Gender*, p. 103.

246 S1539/W3; S1536/W17, *Burton* 29, and see p. 222 above; Van Houts, *Memory and Gender*, pp. 106–9.

Ælfflæd, the widow of Ealdorman Byrhtnoth;[247] at the very least, displayed in the hall at the heart of a lordly residence, they represented family wealth and status, and commemorated those from whom that prosperity derived.

## Movable wealth, land and gift exchange

In certain respects the bequest of movable wealth differs from that of land. Whereas land was generally bequeathed to beneficiaries within a limited social range, movable wealth was likely to be distributed more widely, including beneficiaries from lower social groups.[248] In addition, while goods could be transferred physically into the possession of beneficiaries, land remained a fixed entity, allowing (in today's parlance) only a virtual transfer. Movable wealth also seems to have been free of the constraints which hedged the alienation of land, and could be bequeathed more freely, although certain items had longstanding cultural significance which is likely to have influenced donors in their dispositions. However, there are two common elements in the bequest of movable wealth and land: one is the social dimension of display, by which donors asserted their wealth and rank;[249] and the other is the deployment of property in order to achieve *memoria*, both for the individual donor and for close kin.[250] It is in these two respects that wills may most usefully be related to gift exchange.

The theory of gift exchange as a social mechanism in the early Middle Ages, stimulated by the seminal paper of Mauss published in 1925, continues to develop as a means of exploring relationships among the nobility, and between the laity and the Church.[251] Although the nature of wills means that the actual transfer of property was intended to be deferred until the death of the donor, that bequests were indeed perceived as gifts is attested by the phrase which recurs in wills, 'I give after my day'. The public nature of will-making lent immediacy to what, in reality, could be a protracted process of

247 *LE* II, 63; Budny, 'Byrhtnoth tapestry'; Van Houts, *Memory and Gender*, pp. 101-2. See Coatsworth, 'Domestic textiles', pp. 4–5 for secular narrative friezes. For the Continental evidence for tapestries linked with the commemorative responsibilities of women see Innes, 'Keeping it in the family', pp. 24–5.

248 Charles-Edwards, 'Land and moveable wealth', p. 104.

249 Le Jan, *Famille et pouvoir*, p. 60.

250 Le Jan, *Famille et pouvoir*, pp. 35, 45.

251 M. Mauss, 'Essai sur le don: forme et raison de l'échange dans les sociétés archaïques', *L'Année Sociologique* 1 (1923), 30–186, published in English as *The Gift: Forms and Functions of Exchange in Archaic Societies*, transl. I. Cunnison (New York, 1967). The literature is surveyed by A. J. A. Bijsterveld, 'The medieval gift as agent of social bonding and political power: a comparative approach', in *Medieval Transformations: Texts, Power and Gifts in Context*, ed. E. Cohen and M. B. De Jong (Leiden, 2001), pp. 123–56. See also the résumé by Rosenwein, *To Be the Neighbor*, pp. 125–43.

fulfilling the gift. Mauss described gift-giving as a social act, through which social relationships were negotiated.[252] Vernacular wills were social acts not only through the ceremonial aspect of the declaration or announcement of the dispositions, but through the nature of the dispositions themselves, which engaged with a range of social relationships, as this and previous chapters have shown. A crucial element in this social act is reciprocity, with the donee placed under an obligation to make a counter-gift as part of a continuing cycle of exchange.[253] Because donors were likely to make their dispositions in advance of mortal illness, the act of will-making could, through judicious distribution of property, contribute significantly to this process of reciprocation during the donor's lifetime, extending or reinforcing the network of secular and spiritual relationships essential to the social equilibrium.[254] A counter-gift on the death of the donor might, at the very least, take the form of support for the will, but it seems clear that an important concern for donors was to deploy property in order to gain commemoration for themselves and their kin.

The way in which the nature of property itself contributes to the commemorative aspect of bequests is illuminated by Mauss's concept that inanimate objects are imbued with the identity of the donor. Even when goods are alienated physically, they remain inalienable (*immeuble*) in essence, indelibly linked with their ancestry and forging a bond with the recipient.[255] This chapter has shown, for example, how certain items selected for bequest, such as clothing or swords, had personal associations with the donor; other items may have had heirloom status, invested with the memory of ancestors. Similarly, the evidence of wills for the bonds which could be forged through land between the laity and the Church, sometimes over several generations, has been outlined in Chapter Four.[256] Such bonds, established through the bequest of property by the laity and the offering of prayers by the church, are the subject of the next chapter.

In this chapter some degree of correlation has been noted between items bequeathed in wills and those chosen to accompany the furnished burials of an earlier period, but there is one significant difference: whereas goods deposited in graves were chosen by others – perhaps members of the kin group – to represent the social status and role of the deceased, donors of wills made their own choices, perhaps influenced to some degree by convention.

252 Mauss, transl. Cunnison, *The Gift*, p. 3; Bijsterveld, 'Medieval gift', p. 125.

253 Mauss, transl. Cunnison, *The Gift*, p. 5; Bijsterveld, 'Medieval gift', pp. 124–5

254 The key aspects of research into gift-giving to the church are outlined by Bijsterveld, 'Medieval gift', pp. 128–34, 137–43.

255 Mauss, transl. Cunnison, *The Gift*, pp. 9–10; Bijsterveld, 'Medieval gift', pp. 125–6, referring to the research of A. B. Weiner, *Inalienable Possessions: the Paradox of Keeping-While-Giving* (Berkeley, 1992).

256 See pp. 159–61. See also Chap. 6, pp. 233–7 below.

Therefore, through their bequests, donors were able to participate actively in the system of exchange described by Le Jan as 'le grand théâtre de la vie aristocratique';[257] they had the advantage of themselves constructing an individual persona. As a result, beyond the public image of heriot and conspicuous display, it is possible to glimpse private worlds, furnished with luxury goods which were not only treasure but treasured, and peopled by family, companions and servants who were often sufficiently valued by the donor to warrant a gift specifically chosen to acknowledge the relationship. In this respect, wills hint at a more personal aspect of gift-giving.

257 Le Jan, *Famille et pouvoir*, p. 77.

# CHAPTER SIX

# Wills, commemoration and lay piety

Previous chapters have established the significance of bequests to the church, particularly of land, as an aspect of social cohesion involving the interaction of donor, kindred, the king, the local network and beneficiary churches. Bequests of movable wealth were more personal in the sense that they represented the donor and the donor's family within the *locus sanctus* itself, on the altar or within the refectory. In the context of gift-giving, all bequests, even though deferred, posit a counter-gift. This chapter explores the spiritual benefits which donors might hope to receive in response to their gifts. In the wills themselves, such benefits are usually subsumed in the phrase 'for my soul', the precise nature of the contract apparently understood by both parties; only rarely is specific detail given. In order to gain a clearer understanding of the pious impulse which prompted bequests to the church, and the spiritual counter-gift which beneficiaries were likely to offer, it is once again necessary to draw on the wider historical context.

Vernacular will-making was stimulated by the contemporary religious ethos. Ninth-century wills, mainly focused on Christ Church, Canterbury, reflect the close relationship with the local nobility cultivated by at least two archbishops: Wulfred (805–832) and Ceolnoth (833–870).[1] It is also possible that the Viking raids of this period created a fear that Christianity itself was under threat; such a sentiment appears in Ealdorman Alfred's bequests of food-rents payable to the church 'so long as Christianity lasts in England'.[2] The sequence of wills which begins in the reign of Æthelstan (924/5–939) with the will of Wulfgar seems likely to be associated with the religious reform which gathered momentum in the early years of the tenth century.[3] King Alfred's education programme which followed the Viking wars, the beginnings made in establishing religious houses and the importation of both foreign scholars and Latin manuscripts laid important foundations for

1 Brooks, *Early History*, pp. 147–8, 151–2; Chap. 1, p. 13 above.

2 S1508/H10, *Christ Church* 96, 871x889: *ða hwile þe fulwihte sio on Angelcynnes ealonde*. The same phrase is found in the inscription recording the gift to Christ Church by Alfred and his wife of a ransomed gospel book: H9, *Cartularium*, ed. Birch, no. 634. For the same unease related to the upheavals of the final year of Æthelred's reign see S1503/W20, *Christ Church* 142 (*Wills*, p. 58, l. 25 and Chap. 3, pp. 97–8 above).

3 Dumville, *Wessex and England*, pp. 192–3, 203, and see Chap. 1, p. 15 above.

the renewal of religious life under his successors.[4] Diocesan reconstruction was carried out in the succeeding reign by Edward the Elder (899–924).[5] The political consolidation of Æthelstan's reign enabled him not only to expand the intellectual and religious life at court and in religious institutions, but also to disseminate the tenets of Christianity more widely through local churches with – perhaps – better educated clergy.[6] Dumville has argued that it was this period of activity which produced the reformers of the later tenth century, who were especially active under King Edgar.[7]

The religious climate of Æthelstan's reign is particularly likely to have contributed to the emergence of the sequence of vernacular wills which span the remainder of the Anglo-Saxon period. The piety demonstrated by Æthelstan himself set a precedent for the behaviour and attitudes of the aristocracy. He was an avid collector of books and relics, and was more generous in his gifts, particularly of land, to a range of churches than either of his predecessors.[8] Such piety may in part have had a political motive: Æthelstan's adherence to the cult of royal saints may have been deliberate policy to advance the influence of the royal house, and appears to have been continued by his half-brother and successor, King Edmund.[9] A further factor likely to have impinged strongly upon the aristocracy was the resurgence of the religious community, with particular emphasis on monasticism. The appointment of monastic bishops and abbots, first under Æthelstan and then under Edmund, provided the impetus for the reforms which would be brought to fruition in the reign of Edgar (959–975).[10]

There is evidence to suggest that these religious reforms permeated the laity. Gild statutes reveal burgeoning lay piety in the mid-tenth century: statutes survive from Exeter and Bedwyn, written in hands of the first half of the

4 Dumville, *Wessex and England*, pp. 193–5.

5 Dumville, *Wessex and England*, p. 162; A. Rumble, 'Edward the Elder and the churches of Winchester and Wessex', in *Edward the Elder*, ed. Higham and Hill, pp. 230–47 (pp. 238–44).

6 Dumville, *Wessex and England*, pp. 162–3.

7 Dumville, *Wessex and England*, pp. 164–5. A succinct account of the Carolingian reforms of the eighth and ninth centuries and their implications can be found in J. M. H. Smith, 'Religion and lay society', in *The New Cambridge Medieval History II*, ed. McKitterick, pp. 654–78.

8 J. A. Robinson, *The Life and Times of St Dunstan* (Oxford, 1923), pp. 51–80; D. Rollason, *Saints and Relics in Anglo-Saxon England* (Philadelphia, 1982), pp. 160–3; M. Wood, 'The Making of King Æthelstan's empire', in *Ideal and Reality*, ed. Wormald, pp. 250–72; S. Keynes, 'King Æthelstan's books', in *Learning and Literature in Anglo-Saxon England: Studies presented to Peter Clemoes*, ed. M. Lapidge and H. Gneuss (Cambridge, 1985), pp. 143–201 (pp. 143–7); Thacker, 'Dynastic monasteries', pp. 252–5 (but see the doubts of Dumville as to the integrity of some of the grants ascribed to Æthelstan: *Wessex and England*, p. 163, n. 148).

9 Thacker, 'Dynastic monasteries', pp. 255–6; Ridyard, *Royal Saints*, pp. 224–5, 250–1.

10 Dumville, *Wessex and England*, pp. 164–5, 175–6.

tenth century, stipulating commemorative and burial practice.[11] The motivation for the formation of the gilds arose from the laity, and the membership was predominantly lay.[12] Archaeology has shown that the building of estate churches by lay landholders was under way by the early years of the tenth century.[13] That churchmen were receiving gifts from the laity is demonstrated by the will of Bishop Theodred, appointed to the see of London by King Æthelstan, and possibly disposed to monastic reform; in it he refers to 'the souls of all the men for whom I intercede, and from whom I have received alms, and for whom it is fitting that I should pray'.[14]

One factor which is likely to have encouraged lay gifts to the Church was the increased emphasis on obedience to a strict monastic rule within religious foundations, contributing to the renewed sense of spiritual authority vested in them. Vows of poverty and chastity, and commitment to the regular cycle of prayer characterised these communities, whose role of intercession with the divine on behalf of the laity exerted considerable ideological power.[15] In addition, popular interest in relics was allied to the vigorous promotion by religious houses of saints' cults.[16] Spectacular ceremonies accompanied the translation of relics to purpose-built shrines, and the influence of the saints percolated into lay life through the use of relics in judicial procedures, the occurrence of saints' festivals throughout the year, penitential processions and the dedication of churches.[17] The prestige of a religious house was in part commensurate with its cult status.[18] A further important development was an increased interest in, and sense of responsibility for, the welfare of

11 For the dating of the gild statutes see Ker, *Catalogue*, nos. 194 (Exeter: s.x$^{1}$) and 6 (Bedwyn: s.x$^{1}$–s.x$^{med}$).

12 See G. Rosser, 'Anglo-Saxon gilds', in *Minsters and Parish Churches*, ed. Blair, pp. 31–4 (p. 31); Williams, 'Thegnly piety', pp. 22–3.

13 See Chap. 4, pp. 141–2 above, and below pp. 260–1.

14 *and for alle þe mannes soule þe ic forþingiae. And ic almesne vnderfongen habbe and me sie rithlike for to biddan*: S1526/W1, 942 x *c*. 951; Dumville, *Wessex and England*, pp. 164, 175; Whitelock, *Some Anglo-Saxon Bishops*, pp. 16–21.

15 McLaughlin, *Consorting with Saints*, pp. 227–30; P. Stafford, 'Queens, nunneries and reforming churchmen: gender, religious status and reform in tenth- and eleventh-century England', *Past and Present*, 163 (1999), 3–35 (pp. 6–10); C. Cubitt, 'Virginity and misogyny in tenth- and eleventh-century England', *Gender and History* 12.1 (2000), 1–32 (pp. 3–4); M. De Jong, *In Samuel's Image: Child Oblation in the Early Medieval West* (Leiden, 1996), pp. 140–2.

16 Dumville, *Wessex and England*, p. 161 with references.

17 Rollason, *Saints and Relics*, pp. 174–95. For processions, see M. Bradford Bedingfield, *The Dramatic Liturgy of Anglo-Saxon England* (Woodbridge, 2002), pp. 195, 206–207. For the dedication of churches, see J. Gage, 'The Anglo-Saxon ceremony of the dedication and consecration of churches, illustrated from a pontifical in the public library at Rouen', *Archaeologia* 25 (1834), 235–74; D. Rollason, *Two Anglo-Saxon Rituals: the Dedication of a Church and the Judicial Ordeal*, Fifth Brixworth Lecture (1988); Rollason, *Saints and Relics*, pp. 176–7.

18 A. Thacker, 'Saint-making and relic collecting by Oswald and his communities', in *St*

the dead, reflecting the belief that effective intercession on the part of those dedicated to God would assist in absolving the sins of the departed. The reformed monastic communities committed to a life of prayer bore responsibility for rituals surrounding commemoration of the dead, creating a spiritual milieu which gathered power, in many cases, from the physical presence of its saints. The liturgy encompassed rites for the dying and the dead, and for the process of long-term intercession for the souls of the departed.[19] The records of gilds surviving from the tenth and eleventh centuries suggest a strong lay concern with burial rites and commemoration. It seems likely that the development of a vernacular penitential system exerted a powerful influence on the eschatological thinking of both the laity and the clergy outside the reformed religious houses, with the emphasis on penitence in the legislation of Wulfstan intended to influence the laity, and impress individuals with a sense of responsibility for their souls' welfare.[20] The frequent use of charcoal burial at Winchester in the tenth and eleventh centuries has been linked with a more penitential spiritual climate, although it may also be seen in the context of the increasingly elaborate burial rites characteristic of the tenth and eleventh centuries.[21]

For wealthy donors, anxious to achieve a good death, the written will provided the opportunity to order both secular and spiritual affairs in advance of mortal illness.[22] A prayer surviving in eleventh-century manuscripts associated with Winchester, Canterbury and Worcester emphasises the importance of time for preparation:

> *7 min drihten ne læt me næfre færlicum deaðe of þissum earman life gewitan. Ac loc hwænne min tima beo 7 þin willa sy. þæt ic þis hlæne lif forlætan scyle. læt me mid gedefenesse mine dagas geendian.*
>
> (And my Lord, never let me suffer a sudden death from this wretched life, but look when my time comes, and it be your will that I must abandon this meagre life. Let me end my days with decency.)[23]

*Oswald*, ed. Brooks and Cubitt, pp. 244–68 (pp. 244–5); P. J. Geary, *Furta Sacra: Thefts of Relics in the Central Middle Ages* (Princeton NJ, revised 1990), pp. 15–22.

19 See below, pp. 251–4.

20 A. J. Frantzen, *The Literature of Penance in Anglo-Saxon England* (New Brunswick NJ, 1983), pp. 144, 146, 150; S. Hamilton, *The Practice of Penance 900–1050* (Woodbridge, 2001), Chap. 6, esp. at pages 182–3.

21 B. Kjølbye-Biddle, 'Dispersal or concentration: the disposal of the Winchester dead over two thousand years', in *Death in Towns*, ed. S. Bassett (Leicester, 1992), pp. 210–47 (pp. 228–33); Thompson, *Dying and Death*, pp. 118–22; D. M. Hadley and J. Buckberry, 'Caring for the Dead in Late Anglo-Saxon England', in *Pastoral Care*, ed. Tinti, pp. 121–47 (pp. 136, 147).

22 Binski, *Medieval Death*, pp. 36–7.

23 Quotation and translation taken from Thompson, *Dying and Death*, p. 60, n. 16, with manuscript details in n. 14: Cambridge, Corpus Christi College 391 (Ker, *Catalogue*, no.

This prayer was intended for use in the context of a religious community where, as Thompson has shown, to die *mid gedefenesse* was associated with the rites of the church, from confesson to burial.[24] She has also pointed to the uncertainty as to the general availability of such rites to the laity.[25] Nevertheless, that donors chose to make a written will to dispose of their property *for gode 7 for wurulde* (in the sight of God and the world)[26] suggests the influence of such spiritual concerns on lay thinking in Anglo-Saxon England; among the wealthy, will-making seems to have played a significant part in achieving a good end, in both spiritual and secular terms. By the reign of Cnut, at least, male intestacy seems to have been regarded as irresponsible.[27]

It was in this climate that the written vernacular will flourished. By the end of the tenth century the majority of religious communities which benefited from lay bequests were monastic foundations subject to the Benedictine Rule, although bequests were still made to houses of secular canons, some of which may have established a quasi-monastic life-style.[28] In addition, a number of donors show allegiance to local churches, perhaps served by a small community or a single priest. The spiritual benefits offered to benefactors by these two groups of beneficiary churches, which differed in wealth, size and status, will now be considered separately.

### Bequests to religious houses

Because the church was in a position to mediate between the living and the dead, it became 'an ideal component in family strategy for overcoming death'.[29] Gifts to a religious house maintained a bond between donors and their dead kin (who may have been the source of the property), but also encompassed the spiritual welfare of the donor and of the kin group.[30] This

67); BL Royal 2B. V (Ker, *Catalogue*, no. 249); BL Cotton Tiberius A. iii (Ker, *Catalogue*, no. 186).

24 Thompson, *Dying and Death*, p. 61. The rituals associated with the death of a monk are described in the tenth-century *Regularis Concordia*, ed. Symons, chap. 12, pp. 64–8.

25 Thompson, *Dying and Death*, pp. 62–3. See pp. 239–45 below.

26 S1487/W13. The phrase also occurs in S1524/W15 and S1503/W20, *Christ Church* 142 (*Wills*, p. 60, l. 40), but the sentiment is ubiquitous.

27 S1487/W13; II Cnut, 70, although this law need not refer to a written will (see Chap. 1, p. 48 above).

28 J. Barrow, 'Cathedral Clergy', in *Blackwell Encyclopaedia*, pp. 84–7; J. Barrow, 'English cathedral communities and reform in the late tenth and eleventh centuries', in *Anglo-Norman Durham*, ed. D. Rollason, M. Harvey and M. Prestwich (Woodbridge, 1994), pp. 25–39 (pp. 29–34); Williams, 'Thegnly piety', pp. 5–6. For Christ Church, Canterbury, see Brooks, *Early History*, p. 255.

29 Geary, 'Exchange and interaction', pp. 89–92 (the quotation from p. 91).

30 Ibid., pp. 77–83.

process has been described by McLaughlin in a study of the charters of French monastic houses between the eighth and eleventh centuries:

> It was not the church hierarchy or the church as a whole, but rather the local clerical community, the group gathered round the shrine of the local saint for collective prayer, that was viewed as the locus of salvation. That community was identified metonymically with the church as a whole and figuratively with the saints in heaven. It provided the gateway through which individual men and women could enter into those wider communities.[31]

Rosenwein's work on the charters of Cluny, which record land donations between 909 and 1049, has also demonstrated the significance of such gifts in establishing an ongoing 'family association' with the monastery; parcels of land might be given not just once, but re-donated by different donors over time, reaffirming previous gifts.[32] An important aspect of the gift of land was its immobility: that it remained visible to the donor and the neighbourhood. This shared knowledge of the land's ultimate destination contributed to its spiritual significance, bestowing upon it the character of a *locus sanctus*;[33] at the same time it could participate in the local economy through usufruct and leasehold. Such property transactions acted as 'a social glue ... which emphasized connections among people and between people and saints'.[34]

It has been shown in Chapter Four that the donors of Anglo-Saxon wills were granting land to the church on similar terms;[35] although the gift was, in the case of bequests, deferred, the publication of the will would identify the land as ultimately destined for the church, and confer upon it a role in establishing the spiritual bond between the donor's family and the beneficiary foundation.[36] The way in which the bequest of a single estate might contribute to the relationship between a family and a particular religious house is shown by Ealdorman Ælfheah's bequest of land at Batcombe (Som.) to Glastonbury (Som.).[37] Glastonbury was reformed under St Dunstan, who was appointed abbot *c.* 940; the house was favoured by kings Edmund and

31 McLaughlin, *Consorting with Saints*, p. 80.

32 Rosenwein, *To Be the Neighbor*, pp. 69–73, 122–5, and 49–65 for specific examples. See also Bouchard, *Sword and Miter*, pp. 96–8.

33 Rosenwein, *To Be the Neighbor*, p. 5.

34 Rosenwein, *To Be the Neighbor*, p. 202.

35 See pp. 159–61 above.

36 See Chap. 4, pp. 157–8 above.

37 S1485/W9, *c.* 968x971. The previous history of Batcombe is unclear (*Wills*, p. 125; Abrams, *Glastonbury*, p. 55). Twenty hides were granted by King Edmund to *Elswith*, described as the king's kinsman and minister (S462, 940); see Chap. 3, n. 163 above for the problems associated with this grant. For biographical details of the ealdorman and his wider bequests of land see Chap. 3, pp. 108–10 above.

Edgar, the former of whom had been buried there in 946.[38] Ælfheah was therefore investing in family commemoration at one of the most prestigious monasteries of the Benedictine Reform, possibly a royal *Eigenkloster*.[39] However, his bequest must also be seen in the context of other family links with Glastonbury. Williams has adduced evidence to show that one of his brothers, Ælfwine, may have married the daughter of Wulfric, reeve of the Glastonbury estates and brother of St Dunstan; Ælfwine seems to have inherited land from Wulfric and Wulfric's wife, which he gave to Glastonbury when he became a monk there, presumably as a widower.[40] Another brother, Ælfhere, Ealdorman of Mercia, was also a benefactor of Glastonbury, granting three estates and a collection of relics.[41] For his part, Ælfheah ensures in his will that, before Batcombe reverted to the church, his family would gain maximum benefit from the estate, bequeathing it in the first instance to his wife, Ælfswith:

> *And brucæ heo þæs landæs æt Batancumbæ hyræ dæg and æfter hire dæge ga hit an Ælfwærdes hand uncres suna gif hæ lifæs beo gyf hæ næ beo for mine broðorn to þa hwilæ þæ hi beon and after hyra dege ga into Glæstingabyrig for urnæ fædær and for uræ modor and for us eallæ.*
>
> (And [my wife] is to possess the estate at Batcombe for her time and after her death it is to pass into the possession of our son Ælfweard if he is still alive. If he is not, my brothers are to succeed to it for as long as they live, and after their death it is to go to Glastonbury for the souls of our father and mother and of us all.)[42]

The spiritual benefit of Ælfheah's bequest was to encompass three generations – his parents, his wife and siblings, and his son, reinforcing the relationship between a prestigious religious house and an aristocratic family of considerable wealth and power; yet he arranged that the family would continue to retain the land while investing in *familiaritas*, or close association, with the community which would ensure their commemoration after death.[43]

38 See B. Yorke, 'Introduction', in idem, *Bishop Æthelwold*, p. 2; Brooks, 'Career', pp. 22–3 refers to Edgar's grants to the abbey and its prestige; a summary of the abbey's land acquisitions between 943 and 1066 is given by M. Costen, 'Dunstan, Glastonbury and the economy of Somerset in the tenth century', in *St Dunstan*, ed. Ramsay, Sparks and Tatton-Brown, pp. 25–44 (pp. 36–7).

39 Dumville, *Wessex and England*, p. 176.

40 Williams, '*Princeps Merciorum gentis*', pp. 154–5; Brooks, 'Career', p. 8.

41 '*Princeps Merciorum gentis*', pp. 166–7.

42 Two of those brothers (Ælfhere and Ælfwine) are listed among the witnesses of the will. For this strategy of protecting family interests see Chap. 4, pp. 159–61 above. A third brother, Eadric, probably pre-deceased Ælfheah (Williams, '*Princeps merciorum gentis*', pp. 153–4; *Charters*, p. 339).

43 For the term *familiaritas* with the meaning of association or friendship, McLaughlin, *Consorting with Saints*, pp. 81–2.

There is some evidence to suggest that the names of Ælfheah, his brothers Ælfwine and Ælfhere, and Ælfswith (Ælfheah's widow) were recorded in a lost Glastonbury *liber vitae*.[44] Ælfheah's bequest was completed by his brother, Ælfhere, who was buried there in 983, and the abbey indeed held land at Batcombe in 1066.[45] It is unknown where Ælfheah himself was buried.

The extent to which the association between a noble family and a religious house had become an integral part of aristocratic identity by the mid-tenth century is illustrated by the relationship of Ealdorman Æthelwine of East Anglia and his family with Ramsey Abbey.[46] Together with Bishop Oswald, Æthelwine established the community *c.* 966, providing its initial land endowment (which was supplemented over time by the bequests of his immediate family) and building a fine stone church with two towers, one of which could be seen from some distance across the fens.[47] Not only was the building itself impressive, but the interior provided an opportunity for the display of treasure; when the church was rebuilt after the collapse of one of the towers, Æthelwine ordered a wooden altar frontal to be made, adorned with sheets of silver and jewels, and provided thirty pounds for copper organ pipes for use on feast days. We are told that the re-dedication ceremony was attended by many powerful laymen and churchmen, and was followed by a feast so great as to be beyond description.[48] The church may have acted as a family mausoleum, since both Æthelwine and his brother Ælfwold were buried within it.

The re-affirmation of a relationship with a religious community through re-donation of land, as identified at Cluny, can best be illustrated by the successive bequests of Ealdorman Ælfgar and his daughters, which spanned the latter half of the tenth century.[49] In his will, made between 946 and *c.* 951, Ælfgar bequeaths to his older daughter, Æthelflæd, a life interest in six estates which were to revert to the church on her death: Ditton (Cambs.) is to go to a religious house of her choice; Cockfield (Sfk) is to revert to Bury; and Lavenham (Sfk), Peldon, Mersea and Greenstead (Ex) are all to revert to

44 M. Blows, 'A Glastonbury obit-list', in *The Archaeology and History of Glastonbury Abbey: Essays in Honour of the Ninetieth Birthday of C. A. Ralegh Radford*, ed. L. Abrams and J. P. Carley (Woodbridge, 1991), pp. 257–69 (pp. 265–7, nos. 10, 15, 17 and 18); Ælfwine is probably the *Eilwinus, dux et monachus Glast.* recorded on vi. kl. Decembris. For *libri vitae* see pp. 251–3 below.

45 Williams, '*Princeps Merciorum gentis*', p. 167 and n. 115. DB I, fol. 90v.

46 See Wareham, *Lords and Communities*, Chap. 1. For a similar relationship in the eleventh century between the Earl Leofric and the church see Baxter, *Earls*, Chap. 5 (esp. pp. 195–203).

47 *CR* 22 (pp. 40–1); the bequests of Æthelwine and his kin are listed below in Appendix 2, nos. 38, 41, 43, 44, 47, 60.

48 *CR* 57, 58.

49 S1483/W2; S1494/W14; S1486/W15. These wills are discussed by Wareham, *Lords and Communities*, pp. 46–60, with religious benefactions set out in Table 6.

the community at Stoke-by-Nayland (Sfk).[50] Ælfgar's younger daughter and her husband, Ealdorman Byrhtnoth, are bequeathed a life interest in Eleigh (Sfk), with reversion to their child, if they should have one, or to Æthelflæd and then Christ Church, Canterbury, if no child should be born. Ælfflæd is also to have a life interest in Colne and Tey (Ex), with reversion either to a possible child, or to Byrhtnoth and then Stoke. In addition, Ælfgar bequeaths Baythorn (Ex) to Æthelflæd, with reversion to Ælfflæd, then (in the absence of a child) to Barking.[51] Conversely, Ælfgar bequeaths a life interest in Totham (Ex) to Ælfflæd and Byrhtnoth, with reversion to Æthelflæd's estate of Mersea (itself destined for Stoke).

Æthelflæd's will (made between 962 and 991, possibly after the death of King Edgar in 975) shows that she was in possession of the estates bequeathed to her by her father.[52] She bequeaths Ditton to Ely, the community of her choice, according to her father's instructions.[53] However, a number of estates (Cockfield, Lavenham, Peldon and Mersea and Greenstead) which, according to her father's will, should have reverted to the church on her death, are now diverted by Æthelflæd to her sister and brother-in-law for their lives before reversion to the churches designated by Ælfgar. Æthelflæd also bequeaths to Ælfflæd and Byrhtnoth, for their lives, a further six estates not mentioned by her father: three are to revert to Stoke,[54] one to Barking,[55] one to St Paul's (London),[56] and one to the local church of St Peter, Mersea.[57] In addition, one estate (Withermarsh, Sfk) is to pass directly to Stoke on her death.

Both sisters appear to have been childless, and it is Ælfflæd's will (1000x1002) which completes the sequence of family bequests to the church.[58] She refers to her ancestors' endowment of the community at Stoke with land from which it seems to have taken its name,[59] and confirms the dispositions of her father and sister. Her will lists the estates which 'my ancestors' (*yldran*) had bequeathed to Stoke, Christ Church, Canterbury, Barking and Bury. In spite of Æthelflæd's bequest of Withermarsh to Stoke, intended to take effect

50 Lavenham was to pass to Æthelflæd's son, should she have one.

51 This may have been a royal nunnery. Thurstan, who may have been distantly related to Ælfgar through Ælfflæd's marriage to Ealdorman Byrhtnoth (Thurstan's great-grandfather), also makes a bequest to Barking (S1531/W31), perhaps perpetuating the family connection into the fifth generation: Foot, *Veiled Women*, II, 30; J. Crick, 'The wealth, patronage and connections of women's houses in late Anglo-Saxon England', *Revue Bénédictine* 109 (1999), 154–85 (p. 170).

52 S1494/W14.

53 For the implications of this choice see Chap. 3, p. 110 above.

54 Polstead (Sfk); Stratford (Sfk); Balsdon (Sfk).

55 Woodham (Ex). See n. 51 above for the family links with Barking.

56 Hadham (Herts.).

57 Fingringhoe (Ex).

58 S1486/W15.

59 See Chap. 4, p. 58 above.

on her death, it is included in Ælfflæd's list of estates which would revert to Stoke on her own death, suggesting that the completion of Æthelflæd's bequest had been delayed. Ælfflæd also confirms the reversion of Fingringhoe to the church at Mersea as bequeathed by Æthelflæd and endorsed by her own husband Byrhtnoth.Thus it seems that this pattern of donation and re-donation maintained the family link with the beneficiary churches across two generations, with the ultimate reversion of designated estates deferred, in this case, until the demise of Ælfgar's direct line of inheritance.[60]

Any such bequests – whether unique or part of ongoing patronage – carried the social significance of gift-giving, involving the establishment and maintenance of extended social relationships.[61] A few wills expressly acknowledge God as the source of the donor's property, as in the case of Thurstan, who grants 'the things which God has lent me for as long as it shall be his will', with the implication that his bequests to the church could function as a form of counter-gift.[62] In their choice of beneficiary, donors may have been seeking the intercession of a powerful saint, whose relics were held by a religious house; bequests made to the saint, rather than to the community, of a religious house are a regular feature of wills which tends to be obscured by translation. It occurs most frequently in wills from the Bury archive, in which bequests are likely to be made to St Benedict at Ramsey or Holme, or to St Edmund at Bury, but it also occurs in documents from other archives: Wulfgyth's will, for instance, preserved in the archive of Christ Church, Canterbury, names St Edmund, St Æthelthryth (Ely), St Augustine (Canterbury), and St Osyth (Ex).[63] To what extent this is an expression of lay devotion to the saint, or a feature of the house style in drawing up the documents, it is difficult to say, but at the very least it suggests lay awareness of the saint's presence at the beneficiary house.[64] Donors certainly hoped for a spiritual return for their

60 The strategy of re-donation also appears in two wills which bequeath the same estate, Stisted (Ex), to Christ Church, Canterbury: S1535/W32, *Christ Church* 176, the will of Wulfgyth, and S1519/W34, that of her son, Ketel (see pp. 257–9 below). For the suggestion that reversion could be subject to re-negotiation by interested parties see Lowe, 'Nature and effect', pp. 42–4.

61 Rosenwein, *To be the Neighbor*, particularly at pp. 125–43, with references; Chap. 5, pp. 225–7 above.

62 *þe þing þe me god haueð lent so longe so his wille beth*: S1531/W31 (Bury archive). See also S1526/W1, S1516/W33, S1489/W26 (Bury); S1501/W16[1], S1535/W32, S1506/R32 (*Christ Church* 136, 176, 121). See S1532, S1517 (*St Albans* 13, 15) and S1504/H20 (Old Minster, Winchester) for bequests to God.

63 S1535/W32, *Christ Church* 176. See also S1503/W20, *Christ Church* 142 for the ætheling Æthelstan's bequests to *criste 7 sc̄e Petre* (the Old Minster, Winchester), and S1497, S1532 and S1517 (*St Albans* 7, 13 and 15) for bequests to *sancte Albane*. S1528/W25 bequeaths land to God, St Benedict and St Edmund.

64 Rosenwein, *To Be the Neighbor*, p. 137 for gifts made to God and St Peter.

gifts, and sought to establish a bond with a community dedicated to prayer.[65] Such a community might offer two particular counter-gifts to their benefactors: burial and commemoration.

**Burial *ad sanctos***

One way in which donors might gain spiritual benefit was through burial close to the resting place of a powerful saint with special intercessory powers.[66] The cult of saints had an increasing influence on the laity in the tenth and eleventh centuries: for instance, saints' festivals structured the year, and relics were an important element in legal procedures such as manumission and trial by ordeal.[67] It is also significant that the majority of religious houses cited as the burial places of donors were the centres of saints' cults, some possessing high-status relics of saints whose presence they promoted vigorously to attract pilgrims and benefactors: the Old Minster, Winchester, translated the relics of St Swithun to a new shrine with great pomp in 971, and the cult of the royal martyr St Edmund was well established at Bury by the late tenth century.[68] Relics might be owned by the laity; Ælfgifu bequeaths her relics, together with her shrine (*scrin*), to the Old Minster, Winchester, and

65 For the ritual function of donors as *offerentes* see McLaughlin, *Consorting with Saints*, pp. 141–2, and p. 142 for gifts as alms. The ideology of almsgiving is summarised with references by Bijsterveld, 'Medieval gift', pp. 128–9.

66 P. J. Geary, 'Sacred commodities: the circulation of medieval relics', first published in *Commodities and Culture*, ed. A. Appadurai (Cambridge, 1986), pp. 169–91, reprinted in Geary, *Living with the Dead*, pp. 194–218 (pp. 200–208).

67 Rollason, *Saints and Relics*, pp. 186–95. For the development of the cult of saints in the Carolingian Empire see McLaughlin, *Consorting with Saints*, pp. 190, 218; P. J. Geary, 'The uses of archaeological sources for religious and cultural history', published as 'Zur Problematik der Interpretation archäologischer Quellen für die Geistes- und Religionsgeschichte', *Archaeologia Austriaca* 64 (1980), 111–18, translated in Geary, *Living with the Dead*, pp. 30–45 (pp. 41–4); P. J. Geary, 'The saint and the shrine: the pilgrim's goal in the middle ages', first published in *Wallfahrt kennt keine Grenzen*, ed. L. Kriss-Rettenbeck and G. Möhler (Munich, 1984), pp. 265–74, reprinted in Geary, *Living with the Dead*, pp. 163–76 (pp. 167–71).

68 Rollason, *Saints and Relics*, p. 182; Gransden, 'Legends and traditions', p. 3; Ridyard, *Royal Saints*, p. 227. St Albans and Ely enshrined the ancient cults of St Alban and St Æthelthryth respectively (Rollason, *Saints and Relics*, pp. 12–14, 34–5). The new foundation of Ramsey acquired the relics of the Kentish royal princes Æthelred and Æthelberht before 992, and the bones of St Ivo which were miraculously discovered in a local field in 1001 (*CR* 29, 65). On the later tenth-century resurgence of the cult of St Alban, see *St Albans*, pp. 10–11. The New Minster, Winchester, held relics of St Judoc and St Grimbald: M. Biddle, '*Felix urbs Winthonia*: Winchester in the age of monastic reform', in *Tenth-Century Studies: Essays in Commemoration of the Millenium of the Council of Winchester and Regularis Concordia*, ed. D. Parsons (London, 1975), pp. 123–140 (p. 134); S. Keynes, *The Liber Vitae of the New Minster and Hyde Abbey, Winchester, British Library Stowe 944* (Early English Manuscripts in Facsimile, Copenhagen, 1996), Introduction, pp. 17–18, nn. 20–23, p. 29.

the *Liber Eliensis* records bequests of relics by Æthelgifu and Ælfwaru, those of the latter enclosed in a 'stepped reliquary' (*gradatum feretrum*).[69]

Burial *ad sanctos* brought the dead closer to a powerful source of intercession.[70] The introduction of a regular festival at Cluny to commemorate the dead – that of All Souls – illustrates an increasing sense of the Christian community's continuing responsibility for the welfare of the departed faithful.[71] The power of saints as intercessors for the soul on the Day of Judgement is reflected in a prayer included in the tenth-century customary known as the *Regularis Concordia*, introduced under the aegis of Bishop Æthelwold in the 970s with the aim of standardising the form of the Benedictine Rule used in English monasteries:

> *Satisfaciat tibi Domine Deus noster pro anima fratris nostri, N, beatae Dei Genetricis semperque uirginis Mariae et sancti Petri apostoli tui atque Sancti Benedicti confessoris tui omniumque sanctorum tuorum oratio et praesentis familiae tuae devota supplicatio, ut peccatorum omnium ueniam quam precamur obtineat.*
>
> (May the intercession of the Blessed and ever Virgin Mary Mother of God, of St Peter Thy Apostle, of St Benedict Thy Confessor, and of all Thy saints and the devout beseeching of this Thy present family make satisfaction unto Thee, O Lord our God, for the soul of our brother, N, that he may obtain that forgiveness of all his sins for which we pray.)[72]

Although this prayer was intended for use within the monastic fraternity, there is evidence from Continental monastic houses to suggest that rites for the dying and the dead, developed during the ninth and tenth centuries, could be adapted for the laity.[73]

69 S1484/W8; *LE* II, 59, 61. Ealdorman Æthelmær (S1498/W10, *New Minster* 25) bequeaths a shrine (*scrin*) to the New Minster; King Eadred (S1515/H21, *New Minster* 17) refers to the chaplains in charge of his relics (*reliquium*). Both S939/W16[2], *Christ Church* 137 and S1521/W29 refer to the storage of documents in the king's *haligdom*; Leofflæd's will is stored in the *thesaurus regis* (*LE* II, 88).

70 The development of this belief in Merovingian Gaul, with its implications for burial practice, is surveyed by B. Effros, 'Beyond cemetery walls: early medieval funerary topography and Christian salvation', *EME* 6.1 (1997), 1–23; B. Effros, *Caring for Body and Soul: Burial and the Afterlife in the Merovingian World* (University Park PA, 2002), pp. 75–8.

71 McLaughlin, *Consorting with Saints*, pp. 75–7; C. Cubitt, 'The tenth-century Benedictine Reform in England', *EME* 6.1 (1997), 77–94 (p. 81, with references); J. Gerchow, '*Societas et fraternitas*: a report on a research-based project based at the universities of Freiburg and Münster', *Nomina* 12 (1988–89), 153–71 (pp. 156–7).

72 *Regularis Concordia*, ed. Symons, chap. 68; for Æthelwold's authorship, M. Lapidge, 'Æthelwold as scholar and teacher', in *Bishop Æthelwold*, ed. Yorke, pp. 89–117 (pp. 98–101). See Thompson, *Dying and Death*, pp. 195–206 for an account of perceptions of the Last Judgement and the role of saints in intercession.

73 For example at Lorsch: Paxton, *Christianising Death*, pp. 196–200; and at Cluny: D. Poeck, 'Laienbegräbnisse in Cluny', *Frühmittelalterliche Studien* 15 (1981) 68–179, (pp. 68–80).

Gild statutes from the tenth and eleventh centuries show a similar concern on the part of the laity for appropriate burial rites.[74] Both the Cambridge and Abbotsbury statutes emphasise the responsibility of gild-members for ensuring that a dead gild-brother is buried appropriately in the place which he has designated. The Cambridge statutes stipulate that:

> *Gif hwilc gegilda forþfære gebrynge hine eal se gildscipe þær he to wilnie. 7 se þe þærto ne cume gylde syster huniges. 7 se gyldscipe hyrfe be healfre feorme þone forðferedan. 7 ælc sceote twegen pænegas to þære ælmæssan.*
>
> (If any gild-brother die, all the gildship is to bring him to where he desired, and he who does not come for that purpose is to pay a sester of honey; and the gildship is to supply half the provisions for the funeral feast in honour of the deceased; and each is to contribute twopence for the almsgiving.)[75]

It seems likely that most gild members would normally be buried at the minster with which the gild was associated, as the Abbotsbury statutes imply: if a gild-brother should die in the neighbourhood (*on neawyste*), the steward is to inform other members 'that they may come there and worthily attend the body and bring it to the minster, and pray earnestly for the soul' (*þæt he þærto cumon 7 þæt lic wurðlice bestandan 7 to mynstre ferian, 7 for ðære sawle georne gebiddan*).[76] Not only were three sets of the statutes – those of Cambridge, Bedwyn and Exeter – entered in gospel books in tenth-century hands, giving the responsibilities enjoined on members all the weight of the church, but the Cambridge statutes, in addition, refer to an oath of loyalty sworn on relics.[77]

This concern for appropriate burial, and for burial *ad sanctos* in particular, is reflected in wills. A number of donors make bequests – usually of land – to

74 The statutes from Cambridge, Exeter, Bedwyn and Abbotsbury are translated in *EHD* I, nos. 136–9; the Cambridge statutes are printed in *Diplomatarium*, ed. Thorpe, pp. 610–13, and those from Bedwyn by H. Meritt, 'Old English entries in a manuscript at Bern', *Journal of English and Germanic Philology* 33 (1934), 343–51 (pp. 344–5); the Exeter and Abbotsbury statutes are ed. and transl. in *C&S*, pp. 57–60 and 516–20 respectively. Williams, 'Thegnly piety', pp. 23–4.

75 *Diplomatarium*, ed. Thorpe, pp. 610–11; transl. *EHD* I, p. 604.

76 *C&S*, p. 519. This applies when the man dies in the neighbourhood (*on neawyste*); it is unclear whether the body will be brought to the minster if the man dies at a distance. See also the Abbotsbury statutes: *7 þa hine gebringon to ðære stowe þe he to gyrnde on his life* (and they are to bring him to the place which he desired in his life), which may refer to burial at the gild church (*C&S*, p. 519).

77 Exeter: written on a leaf of an eighth-century gospel book from Exeter, in a hand dated s.x$^{1}$ (Ker, *Catalogue*, no. 194 and p. xx for dating conventions); Cambridge: written on a leaf of an eighth-century Ely gospel book in a hand dated s.x$^{2}$ (Ker, *Catalogue*, no. 22); Bedwyn: written on a blank leaf of a gospel book (s.viii-s.ix) in a hand dated s.x$^{1}$-s.x$^{med}$ (Ker, *Catalogue*, no. 6). The responsibility of gilds for the rituals of death is discussed by Thompson, *Dying and Death*, pp. 112–15.

the religious house where they wish to be buried.[78] The gift may be referred to as *saulsceat* (burial dues, or mortuary); Ælfflæd, for example, refers to the *beah* which was given to Ely as *sawlescætte* for her husband, Byrhtnoth, who was buried there.[79] Other donors make explicit the link between a bequest of land and burial at a religious house, as does Leofgifu:

> *And ic kithe þe mine quide wat ic Crist an and his halegan mine louerdes soule to alisidnesse and mine into þe holy stowe þer ic self resten wille þat is at seynt Eadmundes byri. þat is þat lond at Hintlesham and þat lond at Gristlyngthorp.*
>
> (I declare to you my will, what I grant to Christ and his saints for the redemption of my lord's soul and mine, to the holy place where I myself wish to be buried, namely, Bury St Edmunds. That is, the estate at Hintlesham, and the estate at Gestingthorpe.)[80]

Leofgifu's reference to her lord's soul in relation to the bequest implies that he may already have been buried at the abbey, and it is possible that the maintenance of family links in death was an important factor in the burial ritual.[81] When Siferth of Downham visited the grave of his friend, Goding of Gretton at Ely, shortly before his own death, he is reported as saying that his *karissimi* and *fidelissimi* were already buried there, suggesting that there may have been a family plot where he, too, would be buried.[82] Burial within the church or cloister was the prerogative of founders and royalty, but it seems likely that religious communities provided a separate cemetery for other lay benefactors; at Cluny, such an arrangement was in place by the time of Bishop

78 S1482/H2, *Christ Church* 70; S1503/W20, *Christ Church* 142; S1498/W10, *New Minster* 25; S1484/W8; S1505/W12, *New Minster* 29; S1524/W5; S1521/W29; S1533/R26; S1506/R32, *Christ Church* 121; S1515/H21, *New Minster* 17; S1517/*St Albans* 15; S1532/*St Albans* 13; S1497/*St Albans* 7. *LE* II, 61, 62, 69, 89; *CR* 34, 38, 107. The wills which grant movable wealth only in return for burial are: S1482/H2, *Christ Church* 70 (stock and coin); S1505/W12, *New Minster* 29 (gold and a cup); S1517/*St Albans* 15 (stock only).

79 S1486/W15. Wulfgeat (S1534/W19) grants to God his *saulsceat*, but it is unclear where he intends to be buried. The will of Wynflæd (S1539/W3) uses the term *saulsceat* in the more general sense 'for my soul' without specific reference to burial. On soulscot in the context of other church dues see F. Tinti, 'The costs of pastoral care: church dues in late Anglo-Saxon England', in idem (ed.), *Pastoral Care*, pp. 27–51 (pp. 30, 34, 36, 42); J. Blair, *The Church in Anglo-Saxon Society* (Oxford, 2005), pp. 437–8, 446–7. See further at pp. 256–7 below.

80 S1521/W29.

81 Æthelgifu (S1497/*St Albans* 7) also bequeaths land and movable wealth to St Albans for her own burial, as well as commemoration of her husband who may already have been buried there. See also Scheibelreiter, 'The death of the bishop', p. 36 for episcopal concern about burial among kindred, and Alcuin's letter revealing his desire to be buried among those with whom he grew up: *Alcuini Epistolae*, ed. E. Dümmler, MGH, *Epistolae Karolini Aevi* 2 (Berlin, 1895), no. 42, p. 86; *Alcuin of York: his Life and Letters*, transl. S. Allott (York, 1974), Letter 1, p. 3. See also Bull, *Knightly Piety*, pp. 146–8; McLaughlin, *Consorting with Saints*, p. 1.

82 *LE* II, 11/*Lib* 12; see Chap. 2, p. 58 above for the full text.

Odilo (994–1049).[83] A plan dated 1165 from Christ Church, Canterbury, shows a wall with a door demarcating the *cimiterio laicorum*, which lay to the south of the church, with the monastic cemetery to the east of the wall, and excavation has revealed a similar internal division in the cemetery at St Augustine's, Canterbury, possibly dating to the eleventh century.[84] Such cemeteries may have been intended for the burial of lay brothers, but they may also have accommodated lay benefactors.[85] The obvious importance to donors of burial in close proximity to a powerful centre of prayer may have been one of the key factors which prompted the drawing up of a written will.

There are also occasional hints in wills which suggest that funerary arrangements might be negotiated with the community which was to be responsible for the burial. Ordnoth and his wife made an arrangement in the mid-tenth century with the community of the Old Minster, Winchester:

> *þ man unc gefecce. æt uncrum ændedege mid þes mynstres crafte 7 unc swylc legerstowe forescewian swylc unc for gode þearflice sy. 7 for weorulde gerysenlic.*
>
> (On the day of our death they will fetch us with the minster's resources and provide for us such resting-place as is necessary for us in God's sight and fitting in the eyes of the world.)[86]

The concern for appropriateness in burial rites is clear in the wording of the will: their burial place is to be spiritually appropriate (*for gode þearflice*), but also fitting in worldly terms (*for weorulde gerysenlic*).[87] This phrasing may be formulaic, but it is possible to imagine an impressive funeral procession as the corpse was conveyed to the Old Minster, and a marked grave appropriate to the wealth and social position of the deceased.[88] Gild statutes certainly imply dignified ceremonial, those of Abbotsbury requiring their members

83 Poeck, 'Laienbegräbnisse in Cluny', pp. 75–6.

84 R. Gilchrist and B. Sloane, *Requiem: the Medieval Monastic Cemetery in Britain*, (London, 2005), pp. 32, 35–6 and figs. 13 and 14.

85 For a possible lead coffin-plate hinting at the presence of a cemetery for lay benefactors at Bath see *Bath and Wells*, p. 17, n. 66; E. Okasha, *A Hand-List of Anglo-Saxon Non-Runic Inscriptions* (Cambridge, 1971), no. 7.

86 S1524/W5. For the suggestion that *cræft* might be interpreted as 'skill' rather than Whitelock's 'resources', with implications for the quality of the funerary service offered, see Thompson, *Dying and Death*, p. 104.

87 For discussion of the concept of 'dying with decency' (*mid gedefenesse*), see Thompson, *Dying and Death*, Chap. 3, esp. at p. 61, and pp. 231–2 above.

88 See S1386/*Writs* 27 from the Christ Church, Canterbury archive for the conjunction of the words *gerysenlic* and *þearflice*: ***þearflic** for Gode. 7 eac **gerysenlic** for worolde*. See also VI Æthelstan, 8.9. The term *cum custamento* used to describe the procedure to be adopted by the Ramsey community in collecting the corpses of Ærnketel and his wife, Wulfrun, for burial (*CR* 38) indicates a well-established custom. Evidence for grave-markers is reviewed by Hadley and Buckberry, 'Caring for the dead', pp. 140–3.

'worthily [to] attend the body and bring it to the minster'.[89] Descriptions of Ealdorman Æthelwine's funeral give a vivid picture of what may have been a grander version of common practice. The Ramsey Chronicle relates that, on being struck down by a fever at his nearby home, probably at Upwood (Hunts.), Æthelwine was given the last rites by Bishop Ælfheah of Winchester, who was in the neighbourhood.[90] Members of the Ramsey community attended the deathbed, joining Æthelwine in psalm-singing.[91] On his death, Æthelwine's body was carried to Ramsey – possibly by boat.[92] We are told that 'a huge crowd from almost the entire neighbourhood had gathered to accompany the venerable man's funeral procession' (*copiosa totius fere viciniæ turba, viri venerabilis exequias comitatura convenit*); the funeral procession must have provided considerable local spectacle, carried out, as it no doubt was, with great splendour.[93] Byrhtferth's account, incorporated into his Life of St Oswald written at Ramsey between 997 and 1002, provides what were probably eye-witness details:[94]

> *Perductum est corpus principis cum laude ad Ramesige, quo cum honore sepultum est. Delatum erat cum maximo honore ad locum dilectissimum; sed antequam ueniret, obuiam exierunt equestres et pedestres, inedicibilis multitudo. Exierunt et monachi cum cereis et crucibus et evangeliorum libris; qui tota nocte uigilias exercuerunt pro redemptione sue anime; et sic crastina die, omnibus rite peractis, reddiderunt terris, cuius animam commendauerunt Domino, ut eam redderet ciuibus superis.*
>
> (The body of the great man was taken with respect to Ramsey, where it was buried with honour. It was carried with the greatest veneration to his

89 *þæt lic wurðlice bestandan 7 to mynstre ferian* (*C&S*, p. 519; transl. *EHD* I, p. 607); up to thirty men could be involved in collecting the corpse. See also the Cambridge statute quoted above, p. 240.

90 *CR* 60 (p. 106). *CR* 28 refers to the hall and court (*aulam et curiam*) which Æthelwine kept at Upwood, apparently as a hunting lodge, when he granted the land to Ramsey (see Wareham, *Lords and Communities*, p. 26 for a possible location). Manuscript evidence for the administration of the last rites is surveyed by Thompson, *Dying and Death*, Chap. 3 (esp. pp. 67–81).

91 A *topos*: see accounts of psalm-singing at the deathbeds of Bede (*Ecclesiastical History*, ed. Colgrave and Mynors, pp. 583, 587) and Bishop Wilfrid (*Life of Bishop Wilfrid*, ed. Colgrave, chap. 65). See also Scheibelreiter, 'The death of the bishop', p. 37.

92 An earlier journey between Ramsey and Æthelwine's home was made by water (*CR* 60, p. 106, l. 10).

93 *CR* 60 (p. 107). Possibly also a *topos* (Scheibelreiter, 'The death of the bishop', pp. 38–9), but see the section of the Bayeux Tapestry depicting King Edward's funeral: *The Bayeux Tapestry*, ed. F. M. Stenton (London, 1957), pl. 35.

94 Byrhtferth, *Vita Oswaldi Archiepiscopi Eboracensis*, ed. J. Raine, *Historians of the Church of York*, 3 vols., Rolls Series 71 (London, 1879), I, part 5, 475. The text and translation here are taken from *Byrhtferth of Ramsey: the Lives of St Oswald and St Ecgwine*, ed. M. Lapidge (Oxford, 2009), pp. 200–201. See Lapidge, 'Byrhtferth and Oswald', pp. 80–1 for the incorporation of eye-witness accounts into the *vita*.

favourite place; but before it arrived, an inexpressible multitude, on horse-back and on foot, went to meet it. The monks too went out with candles and crosses and gospel books; they spent the entire night in vigils for the redemption of his soul. And thus, on the following day, when the funeral service had been duly completed, they returned him to the earth, whose soul they commended to the Lord, that He might convey it to the heavenly citizens.)

The funeral itself was conducted by Bishop Ælfheah, apparently before a large congregation who lamented their loss, before Æthelwine was buried 'in the house which he had wisely built for himself' (*in domo quam … sapienter sibi ædificaverat*), suggesting that, as the founder, he was interred in the church itself.[95] His brother, Ælfwold, also remembered as a patron, was buried at Ramsey with dignity equal to the obsequies of his brother.[96] Convention may have influenced these accounts, but there seems no reason to doubt that the occasion would have been impressive.

Those of lower status might also aspire to appropriate, if less spectacular, rites.[97] The Ramsey account of the death of Thorgunnr, for example, implies a funeral, or at least a commemorative ceremony, in the abbey church, in the course of which her bequest of land was fulfilled:

> *Vir ejus exanime conjugis corpus Ramesiam ad tumulandum deferri fecit, et terram prænominatam pro ipsius anima super majus altare coram abbate Alfwino et toto fratrum conventu obtulit.*
>
> (Her husband arranged for the lifeless body of his wife to be carried to Ramsey for burial, and offered the aforesaid land for her soul upon the high altar in the presence of Abbot Ælfwine and all the assembled brothers.)[98]

It seems likely that funeral processions were relatively frequent in the locale of great religious houses, perhaps sometimes covering considerable distances, as in a two instances from Gascony cited by Bull. An early twelfth century charter from the monastery of Sorde recounts how the monks administered the last rites to Bernard William of Lanne, and arranged for his body to be carried ten miles by water to the abbey for burial. Sometimes practical difficulties arose: a late eleventh century charter from the priory of St-Mont

95 *CR* 60. For Bishop Wilfrid's funeral see *Life of Bishop Wilfrid*, ed. Colgrave, chap. 66; for the funerals of bishops as *adventus* ceremonies see T. Reuter, 'Ein Europa der Bischöfe: das Zeitalter Burchards von Worms', in *Sonderdruck aus Bischof Burchard von Worms 1000–1025*, ed. W. Hartmann (Mainz, 2000), pp. 1–28 (pp. 1–5).

96 *CR* 34: *decus sibi egregium comparans sepulturæ.*

97 For lay aspirations for burial with full rites (*in honorifice*) at Cluny see Poeck, 'Laienbegräbnisse in Cluny', pp. 76–7; Bull, *Knightly Piety*, p. 147.

98 *CR* 107 (p. 176): my translation.

records a husband being prevented from carrying out his wife's wish to be buried there because snow made the ten-mile journey impossible.[99]

Such funerary rituals might be seen as the equivalent of the social display associated with the furnished burials of an earlier period and, like burial *ad sanctos*, may not have been available to all. However, the church had a further benefit to offer lay donors: the continuous cycle of prayer.

## Perpetual commemoration

The formula 'for my soul', often associated with bequests to religious houses, reflects two aspects of donation. The first is 'redemptive gift-giving'; that is to say, the distribution of worldly property in alms which would, in itself, earn a celestial reward.[100] The second is the belief of donors that their gifts would warrant active spiritual intercession on their behalf within the *societas orationum*, the community of prayer, not only in the aftermath of death, but in perpetuity.[101] Donors also acknowledged their obligation to commemorate their dead kin: such prayers recognised that the departed faithful remained members of the Church, and sought to fulfil on behalf of the dead 'the penitential obligations incurred by sin', creating a family memory which extended beyond the biological limit of three generations.[102] In their bequests of land to the living, as Chapter Four above has shown, donors were mainly concerned with the conjugal family and their collateral kin within limited degrees; however, in their pious bequests they also took account of ancestors.[103] By the ninth century, prayers for the dead, lay as well as religious, were being incorporated into the daily office, a practice reflected in the *Regularis Concordia*.[104] In addition, the annual feast for the dead, All Souls, became a feature of the calendar, elaborated particularly at Cluny in the tenth and eleventh centuries.[105] That the soul's welfare after death was at the heart of the contract between lay donor and beneficiary community is illustrated by the wording of a number of wills, spanning the mid-tenth to mid-eleventh

99 Bull, *Knightly Piety*, p. 152.

100 Rosenwein, *To Be the Neighbor*, p. 41.

101 For the significance of the term *societas orationum* see McLaughlin, *Consorting with Saints*, p. 81.

102 Paxton, *Christianizing Death*, p. 98 (for the quotation), pp. 134–7; Geary, 'Exchange and interaction', pp. 78–83, 86–7; McLaughlin, *Consorting with Saints*, pp. 62–6; Stafford, 'Kinship and women', p. 228; Le Jan, *Famille et pouvoir*, pp. 35–8. Belief in the effectiveness of prayer for the dead is explored in the *Dictionnaire d'archéologie chrétienne et de liturgie*, ed. F. Cabrol and H. Leclercq (Paris, 1903–53), VII, columns 443–5, 451.

103 See nn. 29, 30 above. For the recognition of a wider kin group for commemorative purposes than for those of inheritance, see P. Stafford, 'La mutation familiale: a suitable case for caution', in *The Community, the Family and the Saint*, ed. Hill and Swan, pp. 103–25 (p. 108).

104 This developing practice is described by McLaughlin, *Consorting with Saints*, pp. 67–79. The Horarium is shown schematically in *Regularis Concordia*, ed. Symons, pp. xliii–xliv.

105 For references, see n. 71 above.

centuries, which refer specifically to redemption, using variants of the phrase *heora saule to alysednesse*.[106] One example is the will of Edwin, from the Bury archive:

> *þis is þat frescet þe Eadwine haueð Crist vnnen and seynte Marie 7 alle Cristes halegen his sowle to alisidnesse and his sinne tor* [sic] *forgiuenesse.*
>
> (This is the free property which Edwin has granted to Christ and St Mary and all Christ's saints for the redemption of his soul and the forgiveness of his sins.)[107]

Some indication of what the provision for lay commemoration may have been at ninth-century Christ Church, Canterbury, is given by a document which, as it stands, may have been compiled in the 830s or 840s, but refers to an earlier *inter vivos* grant of land at Stanstead (Kt) by Ealdorman Oswulf and Beornthryth, his wife, to the community in the hope of salvation and confraternity.[108] The grant itself is followed immediately by a confirmation attributed to Archbishop Wulfred, which outlines the 'religious offices' (*godcundan god*) to be carried out on the anniversary of Oswulf's death on behalf of their souls:

> *Ðæt eghwilc messepriost gesinge fore Osuulfes sawle twa messan, twa fore Beornðryðe sawle; 7 æghwilc diacon arede twa passione fore his sawle, twa for hire; ond eghwilc Godes ðiow gesinge twa fiftig fore his sawle, twa fore hire.*
>
> (That every priest sing two masses for Oswulf's soul and two for Beornthryth's; and every deacon read two 'passions' for his soul and two for hers; and every servant of God sing two 'fifties' for his soul and two for hers.)[109]

In addition, alms were to be distributed and wax supplied for the church on behalf of their souls.[110]

A few wills specify the terms of the commemoration which donors anticipated would be carried out in return for their bequests. For example, between

106 Bury: S1516/W33, S1528/W25, S1490/W29, S1516/W33, S1608, *ECEE* no. 133; Canterbury: S1503/W20, *Christ Church* 142, S1234/R116, *Christ Church* 183; Winchester NM: S1515/H21, *New Minster* 17; Peterborough: W39/*Peterborough* 27.

107 S1516/W33, s.xi.

108 S1188/H1. The original transaction probably dates to 805x810. See Crick, 'Church, land' pp. 263–9 for the dating of the document and the attribution of the confirmation to Archbishop Wulfred. The document is discussed by R. Fleming, 'History and liturgy at pre-Conquest Christ Church', *Haskins Society Journal* 6 (1994), 67–83 (pp. 72–3).

109 A 'fifty' refers to a section of the psalter. Harmer suggests that *passione* may refer to sections of the Gospel concerned with Christ's passion (*SEHD*, p. 75); tales of martyrs is a further possibility: J. F. Niermeyer and C. Van De Kieft (ed.), *Mediae Latinitatis Lexicon Minus*, revised J. W. J. Burgers (Leiden, 2002), under *passio*, 7.

110 Land is bequeathed for the provision of lights (*to geleohtenne*) in S1501/W16[1], *Christ Church* 136. See Blows, 'A Glastonbury obit-list', pp. 257–8 for records of similar practice.

946 and 947 Ealdorman Æthelwold bequeathed twelve hides at Wiley (Wilts.) to God, and to the bishop and the community at the Old Minster, Winchester (at this time served by secular canons), 'for the provision of clothing, so that they may remember me in their prayers, as I believe they will'.[111] A century later, Edwin bequeathed a life interest in an estate at Thorpe (Nfk) to his nephew, Ketel, before its reversion to the recently refounded Bury, where daily masses were to be said for the souls of Edwin himself and his brother Wulfric, who held the land jointly.[112] Æthelgifu's will, bequeathing estates in Hertfordshire to St Albans, which was reformed *c.* 970 by Abbot, later Archbishop, Ælfric, sets out precisely the spiritual benefits which they were expected to earn (see Table 6).[113] The reference here to the thirtieth-day mass relates to established ritual procedures for commemoration: special masses were said on the third, seventh and thirtieth days after death, with a further commemorative mass on the anniversary, for which propers existed in early liturgical books.[114]

Food-rent, imposed by many donors on estates which they bequeathed, was an important factor in sustaining religious communities, and it might be specifically linked with commemoration, as Æthelgifu's bequests to St Alban's show: she bequeaths land at Weedon to Leofsige on condition that he provide one barrel of ale (the context suggests that St Albans is the beneficiary) for the souls of her parents, her brother, her husband and herself. Brihtric and Ælfswith, making a joint will between 973 and 987, stipulate an annual payment of two days' food-rent (*twegra daga feorme*) from each of four estates bequeathed to kinsmen; it is to be paid to Rochester for their commemoration (*to heora gemynd*). In each case, those inheriting the land are involved in the ongoing process of commemoration.[115] As well as prayer, commemoration might involve distribution of alms, made on the donor's behalf. The ætheling Æthelstan specifies that annually, on the feast of St Æthelthryth, a food-rent is to be paid (from unidentified estates which he bequeaths to his brother) to the

111 *þæt hi me on heora gebeddredenne hæbben, swa swa ic him to gelyfe*: S1504/H20. See also S1532/*St Albans* 13, S1608, *ECEE* no. 133 and *LE* II, 60 for similar references.

112 S1516/W33.

113 Æthelgifu's will is currently dated 956x1002 (*St Albans*, pp. 92–4); the detailed references to commemoration may suggest that it was drawn up after Ælfric's reforms, since before that time the house may have been in disarray (*St Albans*, pp. 17–18).

114 McLaughlin, *Consorting with Saints*, pp. 51–3, 71, 224, 243; Paxton, *Christianising Death*, pp. 136–7; see *Dictionnaire*, ed. Cabrol and Leclercq, VII, col. 453 for the designated days for commemoration. The gild statutes from Exeter and Bedwyn refer to the funding of masses for dead brothers, and Exeter stipulates the singing of a mass for the departed at each gild meeting (Exeter: *C&S*, p. 59; Bedwyn: Meritt, 'Old English entries', pp. 344–5, *EHD* I, p. 605).

115 S1511/W11, *Rochester* 35. Other wills including references to food-rent: S1484/W8; S1506/R32, *Christ Church* 121; S1483/W2; S1538/W21, *Bath and Wells* 21. See Crick, 'Posthumous obligation', p. 200 for the acquisition of land as the trigger for commemorative obligations.

**Table 6.** Æthelgifu's bequests to St Alban's for commemoration (S1497/*St Albans* 7)

| Commemoration | Bequest |
|---|---|
| burial | 2 estates (Westwick and Gaddesden), stock[1] |
| 30 masses & 30 psalters annually (for her and her lord) | reversion of 1 estate (Standon) after 2 lives, stock |
| *ditto* | 3 days' food-rent annually, or the specified equivalent, from 3 estates (Offley, Tewin and Standon) |
| *ditto* | possible reversion of 1 estate (Offley) after 1 life |
| 30th day | 1 measure of wine, 20 cheeses, 6 swine, 1 bullock from Gaddesden and other estates |

1 Æthelgifu also bequeaths to St Alban's slaves from Langford, two silver cups, two horns, a book, a hanging and a seat cover for her and for her lord's soul, without reference to specific commemoration.

community at Ely, with one hundred pence, for the feeding of one hundred needy people (*þearfena*); this is to be paid in perpetuity by anyone holding the land, which is to revert to Ely should the obligation be ignored.[116] Such distributions may have been arranged to coincide with the anniversary of the donor's death. Archbishop Wulfred's confirmation of the gifts of Oswulf and Beornthryth lists the provisions due, via the collecting point at Lympne, from the estate at Stanstead which they granted to Christ Church, and stipulates that one hundred and twenty *gesufl* loaves should be distributed on the anniversary of the donors, for their souls, from the resources of the community; in addition, the archbishop's estate at Bourn is to provide one thousand loaves (and as many *sufla*) for distribution on that day, on his behalf, and on behalf of Oswulf and Beornthryth.[117] The food-rent payable from Stanstead was considerable, as is that from two estates for which details are given by Æthelgifu:

> *Selle man Leofsige þ land æt Offanlege 7 eal þ seo boc tæcð. 7 þ lond æt Twingum him to swinlande on þa gerad þe he gefeormige of þam twam tunum þone hired æt*

116 S1503/W20, *Christ Church* 142.

117 S1188/H1. The precise meaning of *gesufl* is unclear, but Harmer suggests a derivation from *sufl*, food to accompany bread (*SEHD*, pp. 74, 75). Archbishop Wulfred requested a distribution on his anniversary of bread with either cheese or lard (*caseum, aut lardum*): S1414/*Christ Church* 64.

> *sce Albane .iii. dagas ælce gere oððe .xvi. mittan mealtes 7 .iii. melwes 7 anne sester huniges of Offanlege mid þam lon feo. 7 .viii. weþeras 7 .vi. lomb 7 an slegeryþer 7 .xxx. cysa. 7 of Standune anne oman wines 7 .xx. cysa 7 .vi. swin. 7 an hryðer 7 nyme man of æghwylcum tune to þam þryttyguþan dæge gelice mycel ge of Gætesdene ge of eallum þam oþrum þe þær on lande sint.*
>
> (The land at Offley, and all that the title-deed directs, is to be given to Leofsige, and the land at Tewin as swine-pasture for him, on condition that he provide from those two estates for the community at St Albans three days' food-rent each year, or sixteen measures of malt, and three of meal and one sester of honey from Offley with the rent,[118] and eight wethers and six lambs, and one bullock for slaughter and thirty cheeses; and from Standon one measure of wine and twenty cheeses and six swine and one bullock.)

Laconic references to food-rent in many of the wills may refer to similar rates of provision.[119]

The bequest of an annual food-rent could also be linked to the provision of special meals for the monks, usually on the anniversary of the donor's death. The principle of the commemorative repast is expressed in an eleventh-century charter from Cluny, which records a gift by Geoffrey in memory of his father:

> This *refectio* should be prepared in a most praiseworthy manner for the lords of Cluny, so that the brothers may keep his memory more willingly in all their divine services.[120]

In the same vein, the Latin will of Æthelgifu *comitissa* (the second wife of Ealdorman Æthelwine), recorded in the Ramsey Chronicle, bequeaths one mark of gold, half of which was to be used for the requirements of the monastery (*in usus monasterii necessarios*):

> *De altera vero medietate refectio fratribus procuretur; et duos ciphos argenteos de xii. marcis ad pondus hustingiæ Londoniensis, ad serviendum fratribus in refectorio, quatinus dum in eis potus edentibus fratribus ministratur memoria mei eorum cordibus arctius inculcetur.*
>
> (And from the other half provisions for the brothers may be purchased, and two silver goblets of twelve marks according to the weight of the London hustings for serving the brothers in the refectory, so that when drink is

118 Whitelock suggests that this is a payment representing the abbey's claim to reversion (*Æthelgifu*, p. 10, n. 2); in legal terms, this amounts to *precaria remuneratoria* (see Chap. 1, n. 148).

119 A similarly detailed account is found in Heregyth's endorsement to the ninth-century will of her husband, Abba (S1482/H2, *Christ Church* 70): payment is enjoined upon those holding the estates in question after her death, and is to be made annually 'when the community is bled' (*to higna blodlese ymb twelf monað agefan*).

120 Quoted by McLaughlin, *Consorting with Saints*, at p. 151.

> provided in them to the brothers at meals my memory will be impressed upon their hearts more strongly.)[121]

Liturgical and alimentary commemoration are linked with food-rent in the ninth-century vernacular will of Badanoth Beotting; those in possession of the land were to be responsible for payment.[122] He places his wife and children into the protection of Christ Church, Canterbury, giving them a life interest in 'my heritable land' (*min ærfe lond*).[123] During their lifetime they are to 'provide the community with a food-rent at my anniversary, as good as they can afford, and the community shall commemorate us in their divine services, as shall be beneficial for us and charitable in them'.[124] The land is then to pass to Christ Church, for the refectory (*to heora beode*), and Badanoth enjoins the community to ensure that whoever holds the lease of the land should 'fulfil the same condition for providing a feast on my anniversary as my successors shall have instituted it beforehand and for divine benefit for my soul'.[125]

By the tenth century, such commemorative meals might take the form of monastic *caritas*, an additional allowance of food or drink served on special occasions: the *Regularis Concordia* refers to the brothers receiving *caritas* in the refectory each Saturday, apparently accompanied by reading.[126] Accounts show that on some occasions, monastic feasting, like that of the lay gilds, could be both grand and bibulous, often with the presence of lay guests;[127] in such a context, Æthelgifu's silver cups would seem entirely appropriate. Campbell suggests that anniversary commemorations may have provided a context for the reading of such celebratory works of art as the poem *The Battle of Maldon*, recording the death of Ealdorman Byrhtnoth in 991, and display

121 *CR* 32.

122 S1510/R6, *Christ Church* 78, 845x853. A meal for the community (*higna suesendum*) is included in the annual commemoration of Oswulf and Beornthryth, according to Archbishop Wulfred's confirmation of their gift of land to Christ Church, Canterbury (S1188/H1).

123 Robertson's translation; see Wormald, 'Kingship and royal property', pp. 265–6 for detailed discussion of the term *ærf*.

124 *gefeormien to minre tide swæ hie soelest ðurhtion megen 7 higon us mid heora godcundum godum swe gemynen swæ us arlic 7 him ælmeslic sie.*

125 *ða ilcan wisan leste on swæsendum to minre tide 7 ða godcundan lean minre saule mid gerece swe hit mine ærfenuman ær onstellan.*

126 *Regularis Concordia*, ed. Symons, chap. 26 (pp. 22–3). See also *Briefen*, ed. Tangl, no. 91 (*Letters*, transl. Emerton, no. 75, p. 147) for St Boniface's reference to the two casks of wine which he was sending to Archbishop Ecgbert of York to provide a 'merry day' for the community.

127 Campbell, 'England', pp. 162–4. Bullough, *Friends, Neighbours*, pp. 8–11, with reference to Alcuin's description of *caritas quae in pleno potatur calice* (the allowance which is drunk from a full cup) at n. 17. Funeral feasting is specified in the Cambridge gild statutes (*Diplomatarium*, ed. Thorpe, p. 611; transl. *EHD* I, p. 604).

of the tapestry recording his deeds presented to Ely by his widow.[128] But they might also be fraught with contention: the Ramsey Chronicle records that it was on the anniversary of Æthelstan Mannessune that a dispute arose concerning his bequests.[129] However distant such occasions may seem from intercession for departed souls, they kept the memory of benefactors alive within the religious community. In enjoining the Christ Church community to observe the anniversary of Oswulf and Beornthryth, Wulfred reminds them that they should do so 'that you may be blessed with worldly benefits in the sight of the world, just as their souls are blessed with religious benefits'.[130]

The institutional memory of the church meant that the association of benefactors with the cycle of prayer was assured in perpetuity.[131] There are occasional hints in wills that some donors may have entered into confraternity with the community of a religious house, as is implied by the eleventh-century agreement of Oswulf and Æthelgyth with St Albans:

> *Hig geafan an pund þam abbode Leofstane 7 eallum gebroþrum to karitate þa þa hig eodon þær on broðorrædene.*
>
> (They give one pound to Abbot Leofstan and to all the brethren for charity when they go there in confraternity.)[132]

In the latter tenth century Æthelwold bequeathed twenty mancuses of gold to Abingdon *his gebroþrun* (to or for his brothers), which may suggest that he had entered into a formal arrangement with that house.[133] Necrologies, organised in calendar form, recorded the anniversaries of individual donors, whose names were read out in the monastic Chapter on the appropriate day; *libri memoriales*, or *libri vitæ*, were books recording the names of benefactors which could be placed on the altar during the Mass, symbolically bringing those

128 Campbell, 'England', pp. 166, 171–2. See *LE* II, 63 (p. 136) for the tapestry: *cortinam gestis viri sui intextam atque depictam in memoriam probitatis eius.*

129 *CR* 33.

130 *ðætte ge for ueorolde sien geblitsade mid ðem weoroldcundum godum 7 hiora saula mid ðem godcundum godum* (S1188/H1).

131 Geary, 'Exchange and interaction', pp. 90–1.

132 S1235/*St Albans* 17. On confraternity between religious communities and the admission of lay members see McLaughlin, *Consorting with Saints*, pp. 82–90; Bull, *Knightly Piety*, pp. 160–3. See also *SEHD*, p. 72.

133 S1235/*St Albans* 17; S1505/W12/*New Minster* 29. See also S1482/H2, *Christ Church* 70; S1510/R6, *Christ Church* 78. Ulf's bequest to his *feolagan* may also suggest that he had entered into confraternity (S1532/*St Albans* 13; Chap. 5, p. 214 above). The *Regularis Concorda* includes prayers for *familiares* following those to be offered for the king and queen, making no distinction between those who may have been *confratres*, lay or religious, or *benefactores* (ed. Symons, p. 12, n. 7); see McLaughlin, *Consorting with Saints*, pp. 81–2 for the possible referents of *familiares.*

named into the heart of the liturgy.[134] The preface to the eleventh-century New Minster *Liber Vitae* describes how 'by the making of a record on earth [of the names of brethren and benefactors] in this written form, they may be inscribed on the pages of the heavenly book'.[135] The book itself is actually depicted in the opening pages of the manuscript, which have been analysed by Gerchow.[136] In the frontispiece, King Cnut and Queen Emma are shown presenting a great cross at the altar; below, a monk in the midst of the praying community holds the memorial book, while Christ, above in a mandorla, holds the heavenly equivalent, the Book of Life.[137] The following double page shows a vivid Last Judgement scene.[138] On the right-hand page, in the middle register, the *liber* is shown being held open by an angel, for consultation by St Peter, while Peter himself is engaged in striking out at the devil, who himself holds the book of sinners. On the left, a group of the elect are led by angels towards heaven, represented in the upper register of the right-hand page where Christ sits in a mandorla and Peter waits to welcome them.

In recording the bequests of the widow Ælfwaru, the *Liber Eliensis* compiler remarks:

> *Corpus vero eius in Ely delatum reconditur et nomen illius super sanctum altare descriptum cum fratrum nominibus perpetuam in ecclesia memoriam habet.*
>
> (Her body, having been brought to Ely, is, in fact, buried here, and her name has a perpetual memorial in the church having been inscribed above the holy altar with the names of the brothers.)[139]

The New Minster preface describes how those whose names were included in the book were commemorated on a daily basis:

134 For the development and use of necrologies and *libri memoriales/libri vitae*, see McLaughlin, *Consorting with Saints*, pp. 91–5. On confraternity books generally see Cubitt, 'Tenth-century Benedictine Reform', p. 81 and references; the English evidence is collected by J. Gerchow, *Die Gedenküberlieferung der Angelsachsen mit einem Katalog der Libri Vitae und Necrologien*, Arbeiten zur Frühmittelalterforschung 20 (Berlin, 1988). See also *Liber Vitae*, ed. Keynes, 'Introduction', pp. 49–65.

135 Transl. *Liber Vitæ*, ed. Keynes, 'Introduction', p. 83. For the Latin text see *Liber Vitae: Register and Martyrology of New Minster and Hyde Abbey, Winchester*, ed. W. de Gray Birch, Hampshire Record Society (London, 1892), pp. 11–12: *per temporalem recordationem scripture istius in celestis libri conscribantur pagina.*

136 London, BL Stowe 944, fols. 6r, 6v, 7r. J. Gerchow, 'Prayers for King Cnut: the liturgical commemoration of a conqueror', in *England in the Eleventh Century*, ed. C. Hicks (Stamford, 1992), pp. 219–38 (pp. 230–1).

137 *Liber Vitæ*, ed. Keynes, fol. 6r (Plate V); Gerchow, 'Prayers for King Cnut', pp. 230–1; Thompson, *Dying and Death*, p. 203.

138 *Liber Vitæ*, ed. Keynes, fols. 6v, 7r (Plates VI, VII); Gerchow, 'Prayers for King Cnut', p. 231; Thompson, *Dying and Death*, pp. 203–6.

139 *LE* II, 61.

*Et omnium qui se eius orationibus ac fraternitati commendant. hic generaliter habeantur inscripta. Quatinus cotidie in sacris missarum celebrationibus. vel psalmodiarum concentibus eorum commemoratio fiat. Et ipsa nomina per singulos dies a subdiacono ante sanctum altare ad matutinalem seu principalem missam presentur et ab ipso prout tempus permiserit in conspectu altissimi recitentur. Postque oblatem Deo oblationem dextra manu cardinalis qui missam celebrat sacerdotis.*

(And may the names be entered here of all those who commend themselves to [the community's] prayers and its fraternity, in order that there may be a commemoration of them every day, in the holy solemnities of Mass or in the harmonies of psalmody. And may the names themselves be presented by the sub-deacon every day before the holy altar at the Morrow or principal Mass, and may they be read out by him in the sight of the Most High, as time permits. And, after the offering of the oblation to God, placed on the altar at the right hand of the principal priest who is celebrating Mass.)[140]

In addition, individual items donated by benefactors, some of which may have borne their names, were probably used in church on their anniversary; William of Malmesbury records in his twelfth-century *De Antiquitate Glastonie* what may have been tenth- and eleventh-century practice:

*In anniuersiariis uero regum, episcoporum, abbatum et ducum qui Glastonie ecclesiam construxerunt debent fratres per singula altaria pro eorum animabus missas celebrare et maxime in communi conuentu honorifice coram positis ornamentis que huic ecclesie dederunt.*

(On the anniversary of kings, bishops, abbots and ealdormen who helped build the church, the brethren were obliged to celebrate mass for their souls at each altar, and, in particular, in the presence of the whole convent, to do so using the ornaments that they had given to the church.)[141]

Some donors can be identified in extant memorial lists. For example, in the lists of Christ Church, Canterbury, Ælflæd and her husband Byrhtnoth are recorded alongside one of the estates that Ælflæd bequeathed in her will, and Wulfgyth is recorded alongside Stisted, which she bequeathed to Christ Church.[142] A similar list may underlie the brief references to donations incorporated by the Ramsey chronicler in his *liber benefactorum*.[143]

140 *Liber Vitae*, ed. Birch, p. 12; transl. *Liber Vitæ*, ed. Keynes, 'Introduction', p. 83.

141 Scott, *Early History*, chap. 80, p. 162; Blows, 'A Glastonbury obit-list', pp. 256–7; Chap. 5, pp. 212–14 above. See also Æthelgifu's gift of silver goblets to the refectory (*CR* 32, discussed above, pp. 249–50).

142 S1486/W15; S1535/W32, *Christ Church* 176; S1519/W34. Fleming, 'Christ Church's sisters and brothers', under G 3Id Aug. and 3Id Mar. respectively; for the family of Ealdorman Alfheah commemorated at Glastonbury, see n. 44 above.

143 *CR* 107 appears in part to draw on such a list. For the importance of monastic memory in establishing and protecting the endowment see Geary, *Phantoms of Remembrance*, pp.

The aspirations of donors and religious houses have been summarised in relation to Christ Church, Canterbury, by Fleming:

> Lay benefactors craved the spiritual benefits offered by commemorative ritual, and Christ Church's *familia*, for its part, wished to encourage the flow of benefactions by offering such services and protecting additions to their patrimony by enmeshing them in awesome ritual.[144]

Surrounding the process of donation was 'a mythology of permanence, both of prayers and patrimony', built around the community's primary need to protect their endowment.[145] Myth this may have been, as historical perspective shows, but in their wills donors committed their property, their own spiritual welfare and that of their kindred to the care of the church in an age when its buildings and rituals provided powerful symbols of stability.

## Bequests to local churches

However significant burial and commemoration at prestigious religious houses may have been for the soul's welfare, wills also reveal allegiance on the part of donors to local churches. As Blair has pointed out, the diversity within this category makes definition difficult, but for the purpose of the discussion here I have assumed a local church to be one which is unlikely to appear in the historical record outside the wills, and if recorded in Domesday Book is shown to have limited and local land endowments.[146] Some of these churches may have been served by small communities of secular clergy. This was clearly the case at Ealdorman Ælfgar's Stoke-by-Nayland (Sfk), since he refers to 'the community' (*hired*) there in his will, and at Wulfgar's Kintbury (Berks.), since he bequeaths land to the 'servants of God' (*Godes þeowum*) in that place; Leofgifu's will refers to the deacon and two priests serving the church at Colne (Ex).[147] Other churches, possibly served by a single priest, are likely to have been of the type which began to proliferate in the tenth and eleventh centuries as the result of the economic changes related to increased

117–18. For the *obit* lists at Christ Church, Canterbury, see Fleming, 'Christ Church's sisters and brothers', and Fleming, 'History and liturgy'.

144 Fleming, 'History and liturgy', p. 72.

145 Fleming, 'History and liturgy', pp. 80–1.

146 Blair, *The Church*, p. 372–3. The typical endowment of a 'lesser' church in a European context is described by S. Wood, *The Proprietary Church in the Medieval West* (Oxford, 2006), p. 438. This section is particularly indebted to Blair, *The Church*, Chap. 7: 'The birth and growth of local churches'.

147 S1483/W2; S1533/R26; S1521/W29. Bishop Theodred (S1526/W1) bequeaths land to the community at Mendham (Sfk). See also W39/*Peterborough* 27 (a bequest to *sc̄e Marian Stowe*, a community of canons re-endowed by Earl Leofric of Mercia and his wife 1053x1055: S1478/R115); S1522/N&S9 (to the community at Notley).

manorialisation and the emergence of a new landed aristocracy prepared to establish churches on their estates.[148]

Such estate churches were significant for thegnly status, becoming sufficiently numerous by the time of King Edgar's second law-code, promulgated at Andover *c.* 960, to warrant clarification of their relationship with the mother-churches which were responsible for the delivery of pastoral care over a designated area, termed in later legislation the *rihtscriftscir* – literally, the district within which the clergy of the mother-church must hear confession.[149] Edgar's law seeks to protect the payment of tithes to the old churches to which obedience is due (*to ðam ealdum mynstrum þe seo hyrnes tohyrð*), while recognising the existence of churches on bookland:

> 2. *Gif hwa þonne þegna sy þe on his boclande circan hæbbe þe legerstow on sy, gesylle þone þriddan dæl his agenra teoðunga into his circan.*
> §1. *Gif hwa circan hæbbe þe legerstow on ne sy, do he of þam nigoðan dæle his preoste þæt þæt he wille.*
> §2. *7 ga ælc cirisceat into ðam ealdan mynstre be ælcum frigan heorðe.*
>
> (If, however, there is a thegn who, on the land which he holds by title-deed, has a church to which is attached a graveyard, he shall pay a third part of his own tithes to his church.
> §1. If anyone has a church to which there is no graveyard attached, he shall pay what he will to his priest out of the nine parts.
> §2. And every church-due for every free household shall go to the old church.)[150]

By the time of King Æthelred's eighth code of 1014, the hierarchy of churches is expressed as the *heafodmynster* (principal minster); *medemra mynster* (minster of medium rank); one *git læssan* (still smaller – possibly the thegn's estate church with a graveyard); and the *feldcircan* (field church).[151] That burial in local churchyards indeed took place in some areas is most clearly demonstrated by the distribution of funerary monuments in Lincolnshire in the tenth and early-eleventh centuries, where the pattern of small numbers of carved stone slabs occurring at many churches has been interpreted by Stocker as indicating sites for elite family burial over a number of genera-

148 Chap. 4, pp. 141–2 above; Blair, *The Church*, pp. 368–70, with references which place this phenomenon in a European context. See also J. Blair, 'Local churches in Domesday Book and before', in *Domesday Studies*, ed. Holt, pp. 265–78 (p. 270); Barrow, 'Survival and mutation', pp. 166–7; Faith, *English Peasantry*, pp. 165–7; Barlow, *The English Church 1000–1066*, pp. 183–7.

149 Tinti, 'Church dues', p. 34 and n. 27; Blair, *The Church*, pp. 429–30. For estate churches as symbols of thegnly status, see Chap. 4, pp. 140–1 above.

150 II Edgar, 1.1- 2.2. The phrase *þam nigoðan dæle* is clarified in the law of Cnut as *ðam nigon dælum*: I Cnut, 11.1.

151 VIII Æthelred, 5.1; see also I Cnut, 3.2 for more detailed distinction between the last two. Blair, *The Church*, pp. 368–9.

tions.[152] Similarly, the graveyard at Raunds Furnells (Northants.) may have contained a founder's grave marked by a cabled slab, possibly with a cross at the head, with the presence of a number of stone coffins suggesting the high local status of the cemetery.[153] It is also possible that some thegnly estates were at an inconvenient distance from minster churches holding rights of burial, which was the reason given for the establishment in 1080 of a chapel at Whistley (Berks.), three miles from the mother-church at Sonning.[154] However, as far as the wills are concerned, there is no unequivocal evidence that any donor intended to be buried in a local churchyard, or even that of a mother-church; those wills which refer to the place of burial invariably name religious houses.[155]

A further clause, inserted into King Edgar's second code by Archbishop Wulfstan, probably in 1008, suggests that a mother-church (*mynster*) had a claim to the *saulsceat*, or burial dues, of those within its district.[156] The term *saulsceat* is used in four wills dated before or around the year 1000, and therefore pre-dating this clause. The will of Æthelwold bequeaths 'for his soul, twenty mancuses of gold to the new Minster, and a cup as his soul-scot', suggesting that this was where he expected to be buried.[157] Ælfflæd, whose will refers to the burial of her husband, Byrhtnoth, at Ely, bequeaths to that house a *beah* identical to that given on behalf of her husband *to sawlescæatte*.[158] Wulfgeat of Donington grants to God his *sawelsceattas*, but it is unclear to which church it is to be paid.[159] In contrast, Wynflæd uses the term repeatedly, in relation to gifts both to churches and to members of an unnamed religious community, with no apparent reference to burial.[160] The use of the term *saulsceat* in these wills suggests that tenth-century practice had been the payment of dues to the church (or, in Wynflæd's case, churches) of the donor's choice

152 D. Stocker, 'Monuments and merchants: irregularities in the distribution of stone sculpture in Lincolnshire and Yorkshire in the tenth century', in *Cultures in Contact*, ed. Hadley and Richards, pp. 179–212 (pp. 181–3). A survey of burial forms may be found in Hadley and Buckberry, 'Caring for the dead', pp. 132–43.

153 Boddington, *Raunds Furnells*, p. 67; R. Cramp, 'The monumental stone', in Boddington, *Raunds Furnells*, pp. 102–112 (pp. 111–112); Blair, *The Church*, pp. 467–71.

154 Blair, 'Introduction', pp. 8–9; Blair, *The Church*, p. 385.

155 The only reference in a will which may refer to burial in a local graveyard is ambiguous: see the opening clause of S1534/W19, *c.* 1000, which may refer to burial at Donington church.

156 II Edgar, 5.2; Wormald, *English Law*, p. 314, 332.

157 *For his sule xx mancusas goldes into niwan menstre* [sic] *and ane cuppan him to sawelsceatte*: S1505/W12, *New Minster* 29 (after 987).

158 S1486/W15 (1000x1002).

159 S1534/W19 (*c.* 1000).

160 S1539/W3 (? *c.* 950). *Saulsceat* is designated for Milbourne (Dors.), Yeovil (Som.), Wantage (Berks.), and possibly Coleshill (Berks.), probably small local communities (Blair, *The Church*, pp. 302, 326 n. 180, 338 n. 229).

for funerary obsequies.[161] Æthelred's fifth code of 1008 makes it clear that *saulsceat* was due to the parish (*rihtscriftscir*) to which the deceased belonged, even if burial took place elsewhere.[162] Although bequests continue to be made in eleventh-century wills in return for burial at religious houses, there are no discernible bequests to mother-churches which might be construed as *saulsceat*. It is therefore unclear to what extent such payments were enforced where donors expressed a clear preference, and made financial provision, for burial elsewhere.

The distribution of local churches across England suggested by the Domesday survey shows a preponderance in eastern counties.[163] This is reflected in wills, with the majority of beneficiary churches distributed within a similar geographical area (mainly in Suffolk, Norfolk, Essex and Bedfordshire: see the list in Appendix Four); however, the fact that wills which include such bequests (or otherwise refer to local churches) are mainly preserved in the archives of Bury (Sfk), St Albans (Herts.) and Christ Church, Canterbury (Kt) may distort the evidence.[164] Only two lay donors bequeathing land to a local church are ranked above king's thegn,[165] with such bequests tending to occur in wills which have a strong local focus, in contrast to the vast, widespread estates bequeathed by the magnates of the tenth century. Bequests to local churches therefore often seem to reflect local, relatively small-scale prosperity, which was itself related to the distinct social development of the region.[166]

One family group of wills illustrates how significant the patronage of these churches had become in East Anglia. At some point between 1042 and 1053, Wulfgyth, widow of Ælfwine, made her multi-gift will, bequeathing the estate at Stisted (Ex) to Christ Church, Canterbury, after the lives of her two sons. She also bequeaths land to the local church:

161 Blair, *The Church*, pp. 446–7

162 V Æthelred, 12.1; see also I Cnut, 13.1. Eleventh-century wills citing religious houses as burial places: S1503/W20, *Christ Church* 142; S1521/W29; S1517/*St Albans* 15; S1532/*St Albans* 13.

163 For the discussion of the implications of this and architectural evidence for the building of estate churches before *c.* 1050, see Blair, *The Church*, pp. 417–21.

164 Bury: S1531/W31; S1525/W37, 38; S1516/W33; S1519/W34; S1527/W24; S1494/W14; S1486/W15; S1521/W29. Christ Church, Canterbury: S1482/H2, S1501/W16[1], S1535/W32, S1234/R116 (*Christ Church* 70, 136, 176, 183). St Albans: S1497; S1517; S1235 (*St Albans* 7, 15, 17). S1522/N&S9 (Westminster) bequeaths land in Essex. Other bequests to local churches: S1511/W11, *Rochester* 35; S1539/W3 (Shaftesbury?); S1533/R26 (Old Minster, Winchester); S1498/W10, *New Minster* 25; S1534/W19 (Worcester).

165 The exceptions are Ealdorman Ælfgar (S1483/W2) and Ealdorman Æthelmær (S1498/W10, *New Minster* 25).

166 Blair, *The Church*, pp. 421–2; Faith, *English Peasantry*, pp. 153–5.

> *A[n]d ic yan into þare chereche at Stistede to þan þe ic on liue yuþe Eldemesland and þertohycken þet þer sy alles vifty ekeres on wude and on velde efter mine forthsiþe.*
>
> (And I grant to the church at Stisted, besides what I granted during my life, *Eldemesland* and so much in addition that there shall be in all fifty acres of woodland and of open country after my death.)[167]

Although the location of the property marked out for the local church is now beyond recovery, the context suggests that it formed part of the main estate of Stisted. The same process of reserving a portion of land from the main bequest seems to be at work in one of Wulfgyth's bequests to her daughters:

> *And ic yan minen twam doytren. Gode and Bote. Sexlingham and Sumerledetune and into þere chereche at Sumerledetune sixtene eker londes and enne eker med.*
>
> (And I grant to my two daughters, Gode and Bote, Saxlingham (Nfk) and Somerleyton (or Somerton, both Sfk). And to the church at Somerleyton sixteen acres of [arable] land and one acre of meadow.)

The family association with the local churches of Stisted and Somerleyton is pursued in the will of Wulfgyth's son, Ketel, made between 1052 and 1066.[168] He has inherited Stisted, and reiterates his mother's bequest of the reversion of the estate to Christ Church, reserving a life interest for the reeve, Mann, in his holding. The following clause also appears to relate to Stisted, indicating that parts of the estate were held by others, possibly for their lives:

> *And ic an into þere kirke þat lond þat Withrich hauede vnder hande and Lewine and Siric and Goding so so geard goð to Leueriches hyge.*
>
> (And I grant to the church the land which Wihtric had in his possession, and Leofwine and Siric and Goding, to where the fence reaches Leofric's hedge.)

As so often, the phrasing is ambiguous, but the context suggests that 'the church' in question was Stisted church, which was to receive this land reserved from the bequest of the main estate to Christ Church; it is unclear whether this was an independent bequest by Ketel, or related to *Eldemes* land bequeathed by his mother, but continuing family patronage of a local church is evident. Such patronage also appears in Ketel's reciprocal bequest-agreement with his sister Gode: if Gode should outlive him, Ketel will inherit her estate of Preston (Sfk); if he should outlive her, she will inherit Ketel's estate at Walsingham (Nfk), from which he reserves ten acres for the church – again, by implication, that related to the estate. A similar agreement with his sister, Bote, concerning Somerleyton ensures that the land should remain

167 S1535/W32, *Christ Church* 176.

168 S1519/W34.

in the family. Bote has inherited the estate at Somerleyton from her mother (who had reserved land for Somerleyton church); if Bote should outlive Ketel, she is to inherit his estate at Ketteringham (Nfk), but if he should outlive her, he will inherit Somerleyton. This series of bequests and bequest-agreements, designed to preserve family estates and ensure the prosperity of churches linked with those estates, illustrates the way in which, in East Anglia at least, churches could be closely associated with, and endowed from, the estates upon which they had been established.

The pattern of these bequests, establishing a strong link between the local churches and the estates from which they were endowed, is repeated in a further family will, that of Edwin, brother of Wulfgyth and uncle of Ketel.[169] He bequeaths estates not only to Bury, Ely and St Benedict at Holme, but also reserves land from those estates for a series of local churches (see Table Two above).[170] This proliferation of churches within a limited area indicates a high degree of saturation. It is possible that many of the churches which benefit under Edwin's will may have been relatively new, since Wreningham is distinguished as the 'old church' (*ealde kirke*); it is to receive eight acres reserved from the estate, which is more than that designated for Fundenhall and Nayland (two acres each), and may therefore have had greater prestige or parochial responsibilities.[171] This pattern of endowing a local church with land reserved from another bequest is found in other wills, two of which use the term *tunkirke*, translated as 'village church' by Whitelock but perhaps more appropriately rendered in this context as 'estate church'.[172] It is also remarkable that, in general, such churches are not identified by dedication, as the religious foundations discussed above so often are, but in relation to the estate with which they are associated.[173]

While bequests of land were particularly important in establishing local churches on a permanent footing, making them valuable in the eyes of the Domesday commissioners, stock was undoubtedly an important asset.[174]

169 S1516/W33, s.xi$^{med}$; for this will see Chap. 3, pp. 131–2 above.

170 The estates at Thorpe and Great Melton were subject to an agreement between Edwin and his nephew, Ketel, but although Ketel confirms the reversion of the estates to Bury and Holme, he does not include details of land reserved from these two estates by his uncle for local churches.

171 See II Edgar, 1.1 for the term *ealdum mynstrum* to which tithes are due (p. 255 above).

172 S1531/W31 (1043x1045) and S1525/W38 (s.x$^2$-s.xi); for *tunkirke* see Blair, 'Local churches', p. 271; Blair, *The Church*, p. 502; Faith, *English Peasantry*, pp. 165–7.

173 See p. 237 above. Exceptions are: S1234/R116, *Christ Church* 183, which bequeaths the church of All Hallows; S1494/W14, which bequeaths the reversion of an estate to St Peter's Church, Mersea (Ex); S1486/W15 and S1501/W16$^1$, *Christ Church* 136, both bequeathing land to St Gregory's, Sudbury (Sfk); S1535/W32, *Christ Church* 176, a bequest to St Osyth at Chich. See also S1525/W38 for bequests to Christ Church and St Mary's Church, Norwich.

174 For estate churches as economic assets see Blair, *The Church*, p. 409; Wood, *Proprietary Church*, Chap. 14.

Æthelgifu, for example, bequeaths both land and stock: churches at Braughing and Welwyn (both Herts.) are to share the reversion of her estate at Munden, as well as an allocation of stock; her estate at Langford is to revert to Hitchin (Herts.); and a further four churches – Ashwell (Herts.), Bedford, Flitton and Henlow (Beds.) – are to receive stock from Langford.[175] Wynflæd, similarly, bequeaths stock to six local churches: Milbourne (Dors.), Yeovil (Som.), Wantage, Shrivenham, Coleshill and Childrey (Berks.).[176]

Since so many of the local churches of this period underlie modern parish churches, it is possible to envisage a landscape dotted with small churches embedded within the agricultural system, as they remain in the countryside today, and as Thurketel of Palgrave's bequest to the church of the middle furlong at Roydon Hill, *Scortland*, and the priest's toft so vividly suggests.[177] Wills are mostly silent on the nature of the buildings themselves, since they were available for all to see, although the likelihood that many were of wooden construction is endorsed by the bequest-agreement of Oswulf and Æthelgyth with the abbot and community of St Albans, dated 1053x1066. This records that, in return for their bequest of Studham (Beds.), the abbot would provide timber for the building of a church. This indeed seems to have taken place since the document refers to a public dedication.[178] Excavation is revealing evidence of pre-Conquest timber phases beneath later stone churches, and the timber church at Greenstead (Ex), dated 1063x1100, may give some sense of the nature of these buildings.[179] Other churches were built in stone, as excavations on a number of sites have shown. At Raunds, the earliest church was constructed in the course of the tenth century, adjacent to the enclosed residence and straddling the ditch which had been partially back-filled to accommodate it. It was a simple building, roughly eight metres by three, with walls of rough-hewn limestone and a clay floor, with a possible bell-cote at the west end. In the early years of the eleventh century changes were made to enlarge and enhance the church: the eastern end acquired a small chancel, and the floor was paved.[180] A similar pattern is emerging from other sites, such as Goltho (Lincs.), providing a physical context for King

175 S1497/*St Albans* 7.

176 S1539/W3. The bequests of Æthelgifu and Wynflæd are shown in diagrammatic form in Blair, 'Introduction', p. 5, fig. 2.

177 S1527/W24. Blair, *The Church*, p. 369, 498–504; Barlow, *The English Church 1000–1066*, p. 184.

178 S1235/*St Albans* 17; *St Albans*, pp. 224–5.

179 Blair, *The Church*, p. 392; R. Morris, *Churches in the Landscape* (London, 1989), p. 149.

180 The site was initially published by Boddington, *Raunds Furnells;* see also M. Audouy and A. Chapman, *Raunds: the Origin and Growth of a Midland Village AD 450–1500* (Oxford, 2009). For a summary of key features relating to the church see Blair, *The Church*, pp. 391–2, and Audouy and Chapman, *Raunds*, pp. 85–7. For the possible bell-cote, see Boddington, *Raunds Furnells*, p. 24, fig. 24 and pp. 64–5.

Edgar's strictures on the payment of church dues.[181] It also seems likely that local churches were adorned. Architectural sculpture survives from the tenth-century church at Barton-upon-Humber (Lincs.), and from parish churches in southern England, some of which may have begun life as estate churches.[182] Even the unassuming church at Raunds acquired plaster on the outer walls and on the inner walls of its chancel, while fragments of architectural sculpture suggest decorated surrounds for door and windows.[183] The stone tower at Earl's Barton (Northants.), with its ground-floor chapel and first-floor residence, represents in its architectural detail all that ostentation could achieve in the early years of the eleventh century, marking the trend which straddled the Conquest of building or re-building churches in stone.[184] The dedication stone at Kirkdale (Yorks.), which records the re-building of St Gregory's Minster by Orm Gamalsson between 1055 and 1065, illustrates the sense of pride attendant upon such an enterprise.[185]

It is difficult to say how many donors of wills had a proprietary interest in the churches to which they make bequests, or were contributing to churches endowed by others.[186] Given the increasing archaeological and topographical evidence of the proximity of thegnly residence and church, proprietary interest must be considered, particularly where estates are bequeathed with the reservation of land for 'the church' apparently related to that estate. Whereas both Siflæd and Eadwine of Caddington refer to 'my' church,[187] some donors make such proprietary interest clear by bequeathing the churches themselves in

181 A. Reynolds, *Later Anglo-Saxon England: Life and Landscape* (Stroud, 1999), pp. 128–34 and figs. 55–58; Blair, *The Church*, pp. 387–92. For Edgar's law see p. 255 above.

182 W. Rodwell and K. Rodwell, 'St Peter's Church, Barton-upon-Humber', *Antiquaries Journal* 62 (1982), 283–315 (pp. 308–10); P. Everson and D. Stocker, *The Corpus of Anglo-Saxon Stone Sculpture V: Lincolnshire* (Oxford, 1999), pp. 101–105 and plates 17–33; D. Tweddle, 'The development of sculpture *c.* 950–1100', in *The Corpus of Anglo-Saxon Stone Sculpture IV: South-East England* (Oxford, 1995), ed. D. Tweddle, M. Biddle and B. Kjølbye-Biddle, pp. 62–7 and plates.

183 Boddington, *Raunds Furnells*, p. 8; Audouy and Chapman, *Raunds*, p. 85.

184 Blair, *The Church*, pp. 411–17 on the the problems of identifying pre-Conquest churches. Earl's Barton is discussed and illustrated by Reynolds, *Later Anglo-Saxon England*, p. 96, plates 8–10. Wood, *Proprietary Church*, p. 455.

185 The inscription is reproduced in Blair, *The Church*, p. 359.

186 I use the term proprietary in the sense of donors having an economic interest in the church and its endowments; the term, its relationship with the German *Eigenkirche*, and its application are discussed in detail by Wood, *Proprietary Church*, pp. 1–4. See also Reynolds, *Fiefs and Vassals*, pp. 61, 418. On churches as an economic asset, Barlow, *The English Church 1000–1066*, pp. 186–7. On the various ways in which local churches might originate see Blair, *The Church*, pp. 374–407; on multiple endowment, Blair, 'Local churches', pp. 270–1, and *The Church*, pp. 409–10; on the development of a community role, Blair, *The Church*, pp. 501–2.

187 S1525/W37; S1517/*St Albans* 15.

their wills, in most cases to a religious house.[188] A proprietary interest is also implied by donors' patronage of the clergy who staff the churches. Æthelgifu's freeing of the priest Edwin is conditional upon his maintenance of the church and commemoration of her and her husband. Leofgifu confirms her late husband's gift of the minster at Colne to the deacon and two priests serving there 'as their lord granted it to them' (*so here lofard it hem vthe*) and designates the priest Ælfric as guardian (*mund*) of the minster.[189] Ketel's bequest of an estate to *Alfric mine prest and mine cuthen*, where *cuthen* could be translated 'relation' or 'friend', suggests a more personal relationship.[190]

A vignette of this relationship between a lay donor and a local church is provided by the two wills of Siflæd, preserved in the thirteenth-century Bury cartulary and datable only in broad terms to the late tenth century, or first half of the eleventh.[191] Even the relationship between the two documents cannot be determined. Both are concerned with the bequest of Siflæd's estate at Marlingford (Nfk) to St Edmund (at Bury), but there are subtle differences in emphasis between them.

The document printed first by Whitelock as W37 sets out how Siflæd's *aihte* (property) is to be distributed *ouer hire day* (after her day – a characteristic will phrase). The initial focus is on her bequest of Marlingford to St Edmund for her soul, excepting twenty acres, two wagonloads of wood and the woods to the north, the destination of which is not given. But at the heart of the document is the fate of 'her' church:

> *7 min kirke be fre. And Wlmer prest singe þerat. and his bearntem so longe. so he þen to þen hode. and fre leswe into þere kirke. and mine men fre. And be seynt Eadmund mund þer ouer þen freschot.*

> (And my church is to be free and Wulfmær the priest is to sing at it, he and his issue, so long as they are in holy orders. And free meadow to the church. And my men are to be free. And may St Edmund be guardian there over the free property.)

Siflæd is anxious to protect the independence of both the church and its incumbent and emphasises the freehold of the meadow which she bequeaths

188 S1234/R116, *Christ Church* 183; S1525/W37, 38; S1497/*St Albans* 7; S1521/W29; *CR* 51; *CR* 54. S1608/*ECEE* no. 133 is garbled, but implies that there were churches on the estates bequeathed to Bury by Oswulf and Leofrun.

189 S1497/*St Albans* 7; S1521/W29 (and Blair, *The Church*, p. 363 on these as possible prebendal appointments). For unfree clergy see Wood, *Proprietary Church*, pp. 525–7, and for tenant priests, pp. 551–5.

190 Thurstan also refers to *Þurstan mine hirdprest* and *Ordeh mine hirdprest*, who are to share an estate with the priest Ælfwig (S1531/W31).

191 S1525/W37, 38; these dating parameters are proposed by Whitelock on stylistic grounds (*Wills*, p. 206).

to the church; Bury's guardianship perhaps applied to the church's overall endowment.[192]

The document printed second by Whitelock, W38, was drawn up in anticipation of Siflæd's journey 'across the sea' (that is, on pilgrimage). Her first concern in this will is to endow the *tunkirke on Mardingforð* with five acres, a toft, two acres of meadow and two wagonloads of wood. Together with a number of small bequests, and the grant of homesteads to her *landsethlen* (tenants), this endowment is reserved from the bulk of the Marlingford estate; she grants to Bury 'all that may happen to be left of my property' (*al þat þere to lafe gesceotte*) in Marlingford, which is then itemised as 'house and homestead, with wood and open land, meadow and livestock'.[193] This has all the ingredients of a thegnly estate, complete with residence and church; although the provision made by Siflæd for the church is relatively small compared with the acreage granted to individual churches by Edwin, for example, it is sufficiently varied that it could generate a reasonable living for the incumbent priest and allow for maintenance.[194]

It seems possible that W37 and W38 reflect the same transaction – made in advance of Siflæd's pilgrimage – recorded in separate documents for different beneficiaries, as has already been suggested for the two versions of Thurstan's single-gift bequest.[195] Although W37 is presented as a pious benefaction, its assertion of the priest's rights and emphasis on the independence of the estate church, together with the limitation placed on Bury's claim on the property, would have been of particular value to the priest himself as evidence of Siflæd's intentions.[196] W38, on the other hand, would have been of more relevance to Bury, anticipating the acquisition of the estate; Siflæd sets out her dispositions concerning Marlingford in more detail, specifying the property which she reserves for the church (which may have been the means of establishing its independence), the small bequests of chattels to other beneficiaries, and the allocation of tofts to her *landsethlen*, before

192 Both Æthelgifu and Leofgifu bequeath churches to clergy: S1497/*St Albans* 7, S1521/W29; Blair, *The Church*, pp. 493–4. For inherited churches: Blair, *The Church*, p. 521; Barlow, *The English Church 1000–1066*, pp. 188–90; F. Barlow, *The English Church 1066–1154* (London, 1979), pp. 51–2. See VIII Æthelred, 30 for the directive that priests should not marry. For *mund*, see n. 237 below.

193 *Hus and hom. 7 wude and feld. 7 on medwe. and on yrue.* Other bequests made from the estate are: a wagonload of wood for each (*either*) of her (two?) brothers; cattle to Christ Church and St Mary's churches at Norwich, and to an unidentifiable beneficiary (*mine duzme*). Her men are to be free, and her *landsethlan* are given their tofts.

194 See Thurketel's bequest to Roydon church (S1527/W24); Blair, *The Church*, p. 492 and nn. 298–9 on the holdings of priests; Wood, *Proprietary Church*, pp. 443–4.

195 S1530/W30, *Christ Church* 166: Chap. 1, n. 49 above.

196 For possible documentation of such arrangements see S1446/H15 (Chap. 1, pp. 49–50 above).

bequeathing the residue to Bury.[197] The suggestion that this was indeed the dominant record of Siflæd's transaction with Bury is supported by the fact that it is in this document that she reserves her own rights in the estate: 'If I come home again, then I wish to occupy that estate for my life, and after my death the will is to take effect'.[198]

Many of the priests mentioned in wills, such as Siflæd's Wulfmær, probably belonged to the category defined in the law of Æthelred as the *folciscne mæssepreost ... þe regollif næbbe* (the secular priest who does not live according to a rule).[199] The pastoral letters of Ælfric, monk and later of abbot of Eynsham, written between 992 and 1006, adopt the voice of a bishop addressing members of the secular clergy, whose standards of behaviour and liturgical observance appear often to have fallen short of the monastic ideal; they are presented as morally lax, ignorant and ill-disciplined.[200] Allowance must be made for the fact that Ælfric and those who commissioned his letters – Bishop Wulfsige of Sherborne and Wulfstan, Bishop of Worcester and Archbishop of York – were intent on promoting the monastic ideal in the secular church. Nevertheless, the Ramsey monk Byrhtferth uses the phrase *uplendisca preost* (rustic priest) several times to refer to priests with little education, and an eleventh-century text associated with Archbishop Wulfstan accepts that it might be necessary to ordain a 'half-educated man, who knows all too little' (*samlæredne þe ealles to lytel cann*).[201]

Limited evidence survives for the responsibilities of such priests. The

197 For the significance of Siflæd's endowment of the church see Wood, *Proprietary Church*, p. 552. W37 is vague about the endowment of the church, referring to the 'free meadow', but two wagonloads of wood, reserved in this text without a beneficiary, are allocated to the church in W38; the 20 acres and 'woods to the north' which are also not allocated in W37 may be related to the more precise allocation to the church and *landsethlen* of W38.

198 *And gif ic hom cume: þanne wille ic sitten on þat londe mine day. and after mine day: stonde þat cuide.* DB shows that Bury held what was probably Siflæd's land in 1066 (DB II, fol. 209v), but remarks laconically that 'others held there' (see DB II, fol. 145v).

199 VIII Æthelred, 21.

200 J. Hill, 'Monastic reform and the secular church', in *England in the Eleventh Century*, ed. Hicks, pp. 103–117 (pp. 104–105, 110–11). Ælfric's letters are printed in *Die Hirtenbriefe Ælfrics*, ed. B. Fehr, Bibliothek der angelsächsischen Prosa IX (Hamburg, 1914, repr. Darmstadt, 1964); reference here will be made to the text and transl. in *C&S*, pp. 191–226, 255–301. See also *The Northumbrian Priests' Law* (*c.* 1023) for a code of practice implying serious misdemeanours in the secular church: *C&S*, pp. 449–68, where Whitelock notes correspondences with the works of Archbishop Wulfstan; Wormald, *English Law*, pp. 208–10, 396–7 doubts Wulfstan's authorship but recognises his influence.

201 *Byrhtferth's Enchiridion*, ed. Baker and Lapidge, at (for example) Book II, chap. 3, lines 237–41 (pp. 120–1). For full references see Blair, *The Church*, p. 491, n. 287, and G. Rosser, 'The cure of souls in English towns before 1000', in *Pastoral Care Before the Parish*, ed. J. Blair and R. Sharpe (Leicester, 1992), pp. 267–84 (p. 283 and n. 86). The text 'On the examination of candidates for ordination' is printed with transl. in *C&S*, pp. 422–7

regular duties which might be expected of them – perhaps idealistically – are summed up by Ælfric in his pastoral letter addressed to Bishop Wulfsige:

> *Nu gebyrað mæssepreostum 7 eallum Godes þeowum þæt hi healdan heora cyrcum mid halgum þeowdome, 7 þa seofon tidsangas gesyngon þærinne þe him gesette synd, swa swa se sinoð hi gedihte: uhtsang 7 primsang, undernsang 7 middægsang, nonsang 7 æfensang 7 nihtsang seofoðan. 7 hi sceolon gebiddan geornlice for þone cyning 7 for heora bisceop 7 for þa þe him god doð 7 for eall Cristen folc ... Se mæsse preost sceal secgan Sunnandagum 7 mæssedagum þæs godspelles angyt on englisc þam folce; 7 be þam paternostre 7 be þam credan eac, swa he oftost mage.*
>
> (Now it befits mass-priests and all God's servants that they maintain their churches with holy service, and sing the seven canonical hours therein which are appointed for them just as the synod regulated them: nocturns and prime, tierce and sext, nones and vespers and compline the seventh. And they are to pray zealously for the king and for their bishop and for those who do good to them, and for all Christian people ... The mass-priest shall tell to the people on Sundays and festivals the meaning of the gospel in English; and about the paternoster and about the creed also, as often as he can.)[202]

Use of the verb *singan* in Siflæd's will, referring to the priest Wulfmær's responsibilities at her church of Marlingford, suggests some compliance with Ælfric's stipulations concerning the daily office, and even the smallest estate churches could provide a sacred space appropriate for the liturgy; at Raunds, for instance, a bench placed against the east wall of the chancel has been interpreted as a clergy bench, and it is possible that a pottery vessel placed adjacent to the altar was used as a sacrarium.[203] Pontificals show that relics were inserted into a cavity in the altar during the dedication of a church by a bishop.[204] No complete manual for priests has survived, but the increasing use of the vernacular in liturgical books of the late-tenth and eleventh centuries to complement the Latin text indicates that material was being disseminated to guide those responsible for delivering pastoral care.[205] Thompson

(quotation at p. 425); the association with Wulfstan is discussed by Whitelock, *C&S*, pp. 422–3.

202 Ælfric's pastoral letter for Wulfsige III, *C&S*, pp. 206–209 (chaps. 48–51, 61); Hill, 'Monastic reform', pp. 103–104.

203 See D. Parsons, 'Liturgical and social aspects', in Boddington, *Raunds Furnells*, pp. 58–66 (pp. 63–4) for the liturgical implications of the chancel arrangements at Raunds, and pp. 59–63 for the possible sacrarium found in association with the first phase of the church; the architectural evidence for developments in liturgical space is surveyed by R. Gem, 'How much can Anglo-Saxon buildings tell us about liturgy?', in *The Liturgy of the Late Anglo-Saxon Church*, ed. H. Gittos and M. Bradford Bedingfield (London, 2005), pp. 271–90.

204 For church dedication see n. 17 above.

205 For a survey of this development see D. N. Dumville, *Liturgy and the Ecclesiastical History of Late Anglo-Saxon England* (Woodbridge, 1992), pp. 127–132. See also Beding-

has also drawn attention to the existence of detailed and elaborate rituals, either written or glossed in the vernacular, for confession, the administration of extreme unction and preparation of the body for burial.[206] The particular interest of the manuscript known as The Red Book of Darley, probably produced at Sherborne or the New Minster, Winchester, *c.* 1061, has been demonstrated by Gittos.[207] Although not a manual *per se*, it is of portable size (194x129 mm), containing among other items material of considerable use to a priest, including the Canon of the Mass; several special masses; prayers and blessings (including that for marriage); rites for baptism, visiting the sick and burial; and the offices of matins, vespers and lauds, and for the dead.[208] The vernacular is used for headings and rubrics, but appears more extensively in the manual section, in some instances indicating that Old English was actually spoken in the course of certain rites – particularly important in the rite for the visitation of the sick, where confession was crucial.[209]

Priests were also expected by Ælfric to be properly equipped for their *gastlicum cræfte to Cristes þenungum* (spiritual craft for Christ's services):[210]

> *Mæssepreost sceal habban mæsseboc 7 pistelboc 7 sangboc 7 rædingboc 7 saltere 7 handboc 7 penitentialem 7 gerim; 7 þa beon wel gerihte; 7 clæne mæssereaf to Cristes þenungum ... Beo his calic geworht of ecum antimbre, gylden oþþe sylfren, glæsen oþþe tinen. Ne beo he na hyrnen ne huru treowen ... 7 his weofod beo clæne 7 wel gescryd æfre, na mid musa tyrdlum ne mid meoxe befiled.*
>
> (A mass-priest must have a missal and a book of the epistles, and a hymbook and a reading-book and a psalter and a manual and a penitential and a

field, *Dramatic Liturgy*, pp. 20–1. Ælfric refers to a manual (*handboc*) in his first letter to Wulfstan, quoted below.

206 Thompson, *Dying and Death*, Chap. 3, esp. pp. 67–81, 87–9.

207 Cambridge, Corpus Christi College 422; Ker, *Catalogue*, no. 70B. The account here follows H. Gittos, 'Is there any evidence for the liturgy of parish churches in late Anglo-Saxon England? The Red Book of Darley and the status of Old English', in *Pastoral Care*, ed. Tinti, pp. 63–82. See also S. Larratt Keefer, 'Manuals', in *The Liturgical Books of Anglo-Saxon England*, ed. R. W. Pfaff, Old English Newsletter, *Subsidia* 23 (Kalamazoo, 1995), pp. 99–109 (pp. 99–100, 102, 104–106); Dumville, *Liturgy*, pp. 74–5; H. Gneuss, 'Liturgical books in Anglo-Saxon England and their Old English terminology', in *Learning and Literature*, ed. Lapidge and Gneuss, pp. 91–141 (pp. 134–5). Links between this manuscript and both Worcester and Winchester are made by C. Hohler, 'The Red Book of Darley', in *Nordisk Kollokvium, 2: I Latinsk liturgi forskning*, ed. H. Slott (Stockholm, 1972), pp. 39–47.

208 Gittos, 'The liturgy of parish churches', pp. 67–70.

209 Gittos, 'The liturgy of parish churches', pp. 77–8. See also V. Thompson, 'The pastoral contract in late Anglo-Saxon England: priest and parishioner in Oxford, Bodleian Library, MS Laud Miscellaneous 482', in *Pastoral Care*, ed. Tinti, pp. 108–118; Thompson, *Dying and Death*, pp. 67–81. On provision for hearing confession in the vernacular see S. Hamilton, 'Penance and excommunication', in *Pastoral Care*, ed. Tinti, pp. 83–105 (pp. 87–9).

210 Ælfric's first letter to Wulfstan *c.* 1006, *C&S*, p. 293 (chap. 171).

computus; and they are to be well corrected; and clean mass-vestments for Christ's service ... His chalice is to be made from imperishable material, of gold or silver, glass or tin. It is never to be of horn, and especially not of wood ... and his altar is always to be clean and well draped and never soiled with mouse-droppings or with dung.)[211]

The wills include no bequests to local churches of religious items such as these, but given the bequests by lay donors of vestments, vessels, hangings and books to religious houses, it is likely that at least those local churches of some pretension would have been equipped with items which would enhance the status of their patrons. The eleventh-century inventory of the treasures belonging to the church of Sherburn-in-Elmet (Yorks.) lists not only vestments, vessels and bells, but a number of books, including two gospel books, two epistle books (*pistolbec*), a missal, a hymn book (*ymener*) and a psalter.[212] Even where the supply of books was limited, it is possible that Ælfric's vernacular homilies were available for use by local priests; they were widely copied and disseminated as a means of instructing both the laity and semi-educated priests as part of a regular cycle of preaching.[213]

In spite of the negative view of the secular clergy presented by Ælfric, local priests seem to have impressed lay benefactors sufficiently to warrant inclusion in their wills as beneficiaries. The livelihood of Wulfmær and priests like him, serving in small local churches, must in large part have depended on lay patronage such as that of Siflæd. King Edgar's law-code of *c.*960 assumes that a thegn with a church on his bookland will be responsible for the payment of 'his' priest.[214] Some priests feature in wills as the incumbents of churches which are to receive land reserved from other bequests, as in the case of Æthelric's bequest to Bocking:

*7 ic geann Leofwynne minan wife ealles þæs þe ic læfe hire dæig. 7 ofor hire dæg. gange þ land on Boccinge into Cristes circean þam hirede for uncera saule 7 for mines fæder þe hit ær begeat eall buton anre hide ic gean into þære cyrcean þam preoste þe þar gode þeowaþ.*

(And I grant all that I leave to my wife for her lifetime; and after her death the estate at Bocking is to go to the community at Christ Church, for our

211 *C&S*, pp. 291–3 (chaps. 157–9, 161–2, 164), and see discussion of manuals above.

212 For the Sherburn inventory see *The York Gospels*, ed. N. Barker (London, 1986), fol. 161r (and transl. pp. 96–7); *Charters*, Appendix 2, no. 2. Sherburn, which was in the demesne of the Archbishop of York, had two churches and two priests in 1066 (DB I, fol. 302v). For inventories from ninth-century Carolingian country churches see C. Hammer, 'Country churches, clerical inventories and the Carolingian renaissance in Bavaria', *Church History* 49 (1980), 5–17. Wood, *Proprietary Church*, pp. 454–7.

213 J. Wilcox, 'Ælfric in Dorset and the landscape of pastoral care', in *Pastoral Care*, ed. Tinti, pp. 52–62, (pp. 59–62).

214 II Edgar, 2–2.2; see p. 255 above for this clause.

souls and that of my father who obtained it; all except one hide which I give to the church for the priest who serves God there.)[215]

Other priests may have been members of thegnly households, as was the priest supplied by the secular community at Christchurch (Hants.) to serve the church built at Milford (Hants.) between 1079 and 1087 by Ælfric the Small; 'he should have his food allowance at Ælfric's table when he should be resident there'.[216] This may have been the case where the possessive is used in wills to refer to a priest, who is often bequeathed land: Æthelflæd, for example, bequeaths two hides each to 'her' priests (*preost*) Ælfwold and Æthelmær, and Thurstan bequeaths an estate at Kedington (Sfk) to be shared between the priest Ælfwig and 'my' chaplains (*hirdpreost*), Thurstan and Ordheah.[217] Æthelgifu's bequests to the clergy are more difficult to interpret. The priest, Edwin, is to be freed, and to have a life interest in the church at Stondon and is to receive a number of slaves; the fact that Byrhstan's sister is to be given to Stondon for Edwin (*into Standune Eadwine*) may indicate that land from that estate supported the church.[218] In addition, Æthelgifu refers to 'her' priests, who were apparently under her patronage, and were to receive surplus stock; as Blair suggests, the intention may have been to devolve them from her household on her death to serve local churches.[219]

It seems likely that donors may have wished to create for themselves and their families local rituals of commemoration which would complement those implemented by the prestigious religious houses. The sparsity of bequests to local churches explicitly made for the welfare of the donor's soul may reflect the drafting of wills in the scriptoria of religious houses, which had a vested interest in promoting their own special claims to the power of prayer, rather than lay dissatisfaction with local liturgical provision.[220] The will of Æthelgifu

215 S1501/W16[1], *Christ Church* 176. Similar bequests referring to priests: S1527/W24; S1497/*St Albans* 7; S1521/W29.

216 *debet habere corrodium suum ad mensam Alverici quotienscumque inibi esset residens*; text and translation from the fourteenth-century Christchurch cartulary are taken from Blair, *The Church*, p. 518 (and see p. 384). P. H. Hase, 'Mother churches of Hampshire', in *Minsters and Parish Churches*, ed. Blair, pp. 45–66 (pp. 54–6).

217 S1494/W14; S1531/W31. Other wills using the possessive: S1487/W13; S1521/W29; S1519/W34; S1503/W20, *Christ Church* 142. *CR* 35 (Ælfhild's bequest of a life interest in land to *capellano meo*). *Hirdpreost* also occurs in S1521/W29. See Blair, 'Local churches', pp. 269, 271 for discussion of the staffing of estate churches.

218 Stondon (Beds.) is not bequeathed in the will. Half of a hide was held there by Ramsey *TRE* (DB I, 210) – perhaps the land which supported the church: see Lord Rennell in *Æthelgifu*, p. 74.

219 Blair, *The Church*, p. 383; Blair, 'Local churches', p. 270.

220 References to local commemoration occur in S1497/*St Albans* 7 and possibly S1234/R116, *Christ Church* 183 (see pp. 271–2 below); S1539/W3 includes Wynflæd's bequests to local churches *to saulsceat*.

is again unique in detailing the commemorative practice donors could expect from their priests:

> *Byrhstanes swustur into Standune Eadwine on þa gerad þe heo 7 hire hlaford habban ælce gere on ælcere wucan .iii. mæssan 7 a heora gebedrædenne arære.*
>
> (Byrhstan's sister (is to be given) to Stondon, for Edwin (the priest), on condition that she and her lord have every year three masses a week and that he ever raise intercession for them.)

In addition, in arranging for the distribution of the surplus (*oforeacan*) of her Langford estate, Æthelgifu stipulates that 'with the surplus one is to think about the vigils'.[221] The Latin term *vigilia* (*neht wæccan* in the will) is used in the *Regularis Concordia* for Nocturns, the nine psalms, lessons and responds which, we are told, should be said daily for one week after the burial of a monk. Ælfric's instructions for priests in his first letter to Archbishop Wulfstan, *c.* 1006, include a similar reference to nocturns:

> *7 sceolon singan Sunnanuhtan 7 mæsseuhtan æfre nigan repsas, æfre mid nigon rædingon.*
>
> (And on Sunday nocturns and festival nocturns you must always sing nine responses, always with nine lessons.)[222]

Ælfric's scheme of prayer may reflect monastic practice, but Æthelgifu's will suggests that lay patrons of local churches could anticipate at least some form of religious commemoration from the incumbent clergy.

Where donors had a proprietary interest in a church and its endowment, their wills may include clauses which seek to protect them. Wulfric Spott invokes the support of great men for his newly-founded abbey at Burton-on-Trent:

> *7 ic wylle þ se cyning beo hlaford. þæs mynstres ðe ic getimbrede. 7 þæra landara þe ic ðyderinn becweden hæbbe gode to lofe. 7 to wurðmynta minan hlaforde 7 for minra sawla. 7 Ælfric arceƀ. 7 Ælfhelm min broðor. þ hig beon mund. 7 freond. 7 forespreocan. into ðære stowe wið ælcne geborenne mann. heom to nanre agenre æhta. butan into sanctus Benedictus regole.*
>
> (And I desire that the king be lord of the monastery which I built and the estates which I have bequeathed to it to the glory of God and the honour of my lord and for my soul; and that Archbishop Ælfric and my brother Ælfhelm be protectors and friends and advocates of that foundation against

221 *Geþence mon þa neht wæccan mid þam oforeacan*; I have followed Whitelock's translation of this elliptical passage.

222 *Regularis Concordia*, ed. Symons, chap. 66 (p. 65); Ælfric's first OE letter to Wulfstan, *C&S*, p. 292 (chap. 160). For the Continental monastic practice of vigils for the dead before and after burial, see McLaughlin, *Consorting with Saints*, pp. 44, 75, 89.

any man born, not as their own possession, but [as belonging] to St Benedict's order.)[223]

Both Ælfric and Ælfhelm are named as beneficiaries elsewhere in the will, the former granted land 'in the hope that he may be a better friend and supporter of the monastery which I have founded'.[224] Neither is assigned proprietorial rights; the word *mund* has implications of guardianship, and *forespreca* of advocacy with the sense of spokesman rather than legal representative.[225] The integrity and independence of the monastery and its estates are emphatically asserted, and placed under the protection of the king who, as the will reminds him, would be honoured by the community in the course of the daily cycle of prayer (as set out in the *Regularis Concordia*).[226] An acknowledgement of royal responsibility for the protection of such foundations and their endowment is expressed in a writ of King Edward, granting to the widow Tole the right to bequeath her property to the monastery at Abbotsbury which was refounded by her and her late husband, Urk:

> *7 ic me sylf wille beon geheald. 7 mund þer ofer. 7 ofer þa are þe þar inn to hirð. 7 ic nelle nanan menn geþafian ꝥ þar geutige ænig þæra þinga þæs þe hig þider inn gedon habbað.*
>
> (And I myself will be protector and guardian over it and over the property that belongs to it. And I will not permit anyone to alienate from it any of the things that they [Urk and Tole] have bestowed upon it.)[227]

Ælfflæd, too, sought the king's protection for the foundation at Stoke-by-Nayland associated with her family, and bequeathed land to Ealdorman Æthelmær in return for his advocacy.[228] She seems to have been unfortunate in her choice of *forespreca*; Ealdorman Æthelmær retired from the court of King Æthelred, *c.* 1005, perhaps a victim of political machinations, depriving Stoke of its strongest advocate at a crucial moment in its history.[229] The religious community at Stoke seems to have died out before 1066, perhaps overwhelmed by the advancing tide of religious reforms, which saw houses such

223 S1536/W17/*Burton* 29. The verb *getimbrede* may reflect use of timber for some estate churches: see p. 260 above.

224 *wið þan þe he freond. 7 fultum. ðe betere sy into þære stowe þe ic geworht hæbbe.*

225 Wood, *Proprietary Church*, p. 410 for the definition of advocacy; for the monastic advocate in eleventh- and twelfth-century Burgundy, Bouchard, *Sword, Miter*, pp. 125–8.

226 Wood, *Proprietary Church*, pp. 410–11, points out that King Æthelred's confirmation of Wulfric's will (S906/*Burton* 28) explicitly acknowledges his responsibility for protecting the freedom of the foundation.

227 S1064/*Writs* 2, 1058x1066. Royal protection was renewed under William I (*Writs*, pp. 119–20). Tole's bequest was made in the context of previous agreements (*forewearda*).

228 S1486/W15; see Chap. 2, pp. 77–8 above.

229 Keynes, *Diplomas*, pp. 211–14.

as Ely and Ramsey attracting increased patronage;[230] only a church, with sixty acres of free land, is mentioned in Domesday Book.[231]

In general, local churches with relatively small endowments were unlikely to command such high-ranking lay support.[232] As in the case of Siflæd's Marlingford, proprietors might seek security for their churches in the guardianship of a religious house, in the hope not only that the endowment would be protected, but that the established religious observance, and perhaps their family commemoration, should continue. This is made explicit in a late bequest-agreement, dated 1052x1070, between Brihtmær of Gracechurch and Archbishop Stigand, and the dean and community of Christ Church, Canterbury:

> *Þet is þanne þet he vþe Xp̄e into Xp̄es chereche þane homstal þet he on set . and alre halegene cheriche efter his dage . and efter Eadgefan his ybedden . and efter his childrene dage . Edmeres and Eþelwines swo hi hit alþerbest ygodeden . vor hire saule . alesednesse . and swo þet se hired sholde witen . þet se þeudom ne adeswen . þe into þare cheriche belimpcht ne ne atfalle al be þan . þe si chereche were ygoded.*
>
> (He has granted to Christ, to be held by Christ Church after his day and that of Eadgifu his wife and after his children's day, Eadmær and Æthelwine, the homestead which he occupies and the church of All Hallows with all the endowments which they have bestowed upon it, for the redemption of their souls, on these terms, that the community shall see to it that the service which belongs to the church neither ceases (?) nor falls off in view of the endowments of the church.)[233]

Both Blair and Robertson point out the likelihood that All Hallows was an estate church in an urban context: modern Gracechurch Street (London) runs from the Monument to the junction of Leadenhall Street and Cornhill, with a church dedicated to All Hallows at the halfway point on its western side.[234] The terms in which the community's responsibilities are expressed are difficult to interpret,[235] but it appears that a direct link is being made between the bequest of the property and the liturgical cycle of the church associ-

230 Stafford, *Unification and Conquest*, p. 189.

231 DB II, fol. 401r. See Chap. 2, n. 114 for the fate of Stoke's endowment.

232 It is unclear to whom Leofgifu assigns *mund* over the church at Colne (S1521/W29): *And be se mund ofer þan minstre þe is ofer alle oþere* (and may he be guardian over the minster who is over all others). This is unlikely to refer to the priest Ælfric, who is the subject of the previous clause; it is more likely that Leofgifu is placing the church in the guardianship of the king (named as beneficiary in the next clause), or conceivably the bishop or archbishop.

233 S1234/R116, *Christ Church* 183, 1052x1070.

234 Blair, *The Church*, p. 403; *Charters*, p. 469.

235 The query is Robertson's, but I believe that the sense is caught by her translation; *DOEC* records no other occurrence of *adeswen*. The term *þeudom* (service) used here refers to the liturgy: B&T, *þeow-dom* Ia: service of the church, divine service.

ated with the estate of Gracechurch. The agreement implies that Brihtmær was seeking to transfer to the Christ Church community responsibility for ensuring the continuity of appropriate religious observance, and perhaps associated commemoration, at the church which his family had endowed.[236] It is likely that Siflæd also envisaged that religious observance at her church at Marlingford and the appointment of priests would devolve upon Bury through the reversion of the church's proprietary rights when her priestly dynasty lapsed.[237] Ælfwaru's bequest of land at Holywell (Hunts.) to Ramsey included no mention of a church; however, that she, too, had secured for the priest Gode a life interest, perhaps with reversion to Ramsey on his death, is suggested by his subsequent bequest of the church and its endowments to the abbey.[238] Most local churches are bequeathed to religious houses by widows, perhaps anticipating the vulnerability of their endowments as the founder's family died out. Brihtmær's bequest is to take effect on the death of the final member of his conjugal family. Other factors prompting such bequests may have been a changing religious climate, or the expense of maintaining (or rebuilding in stone) churches which had stood for a generation.[239] For these donors, perpetuity was vested not in the independence of their churches, but in the institutional protection of the great monastic houses.

## Wills as evidence for lay piety

Lay wills attest to the church's successful permeation of late Anglo-Saxon society, from royalty, via earls and bishops, to thegns. The influence of dynamic churchmen, themselves often of noble status, was fundamental in ninth-century Kent, where Archbishop Wulfred won local patronage, and in later tenth-century England, where the reforming bishops, with royal support, transformed and regularised the church, stimulating the endowment and patronage of religious communities. The impulse which lay behind lay bequests to the church was, no doubt, multi-faceted, perhaps as likely to be

236 S1608, *ECEE* no. 133 shows similar concern (although in rather garbled form) to ensure that the liturgy should continue. Both S1608 and S1234/R116, *Christ Church* 183 survive in much later copies: the former from the fifteenth century, the latter from the fourteenth.

237 Barlow, *The English Church 1066–1154*, pp. 131–2, describes how such churches became subsumed by monasteries; for the implications of *mund* for fostering a proprietary claim see Wood, *Proprietary Church*, p. 410; for a dispute arising from the lapsing of a priestly dynasty see S1446/H15 (and Chap. 1, pp. 49–50 above).

238 *CR* 54, 55. The abbot held nine hides at Holywell *TRE*, including both a church and priest: DB I, fol. 204. Ælfwaru also bequeathed both land and church (of which she was *avocata*) at Elsworth (Cambs.) to Ramsey.

239 Wood, *Proprietary Church*, p. 455; Bouchard, *Sword, Miter*, pp. 179–81, Blair, *The Church*, pp. 412–17.

influenced by social, family or political strategy as spiritual concerns.[240] The noble persona seems to have acquired a religious dimension by the time of Bede, whose letter to Archbishop Ecgbert of York in 734 describes the building of *monasteria* by laymen on land acquired by charter, with – at least from Bede's point of view – disastrous loss of spiritual integrity.[241] Lay bequest of land both to religious houses and to local churches reflects this long-standing tradition, particularly where relationships between noble families and individual foundations extended over several generations. Arrangements made in wills to maintain a family interest in estates before their reversion to the church indicate the tension which existed between religious commitment on the part of the laity and the need to restrict the alienation of family land.

Wills reflect the fact that the rituals of the Church had replaced the furnished burial as a means of funerary display for this elite group, and since it is likely that the wills were drawn up under the aegis of beneficiary religious communities, a degree of institutional piety in their expression might be suspected. The concern expressed in lay wills for the welfare of the donor's soul, and the sense of responsibility for promoting intercession for the souls of the dead, may reflect the origins of the documents in scriptoria; nevertheless, these sentiments were at least endorsed by donors, indicating that such preoccupations were deeply embedded in tenth- and eleventh-century society.

There are, however, hints in the wills of a more personal piety, in spite of the formulaic style of the documents. References to the employment of one or more personal priests, for example, may indicate a commitment by donors to private devotion. Bishop Theodred's will includes commemoration of 'the souls of all the men for whom I intercede, and from whom I have received alms, and for whom it is fitting that I should pray', suggesting that lay benefactors valued his personal intercession.[242] In addition, the pilgrimages mentioned in a number of wills appear to have been undertaken with the intention of visiting shrines at Rome, in the case of Ketel and his step-daughter, or Jerusalem, in the case of Ulf and Madselin.[243] Some donors,

240 As suggested in Chaps. 3 and 4 above. In another context (*State and Society*, p. 25) Innes has pointed out that 'a society in which rural elites were increasingly prepared to invest in a local church or a family monastery was one in which they might also be prepared to make donations to large-scale monastic foundations to build up their local prestige.'

241 Blair, *The Church*, pp. 100–108; 'Epistola Bede ad Ecgbertum Episcopum', in *Baedae Opera Historica*, 2 vols., ed. C. Plummer (Oxford, 1896, repr. 1946 in one vol.), pp. 405–23; transl. *EHD* I, no. 170.

242 S1526/W1: *and for alle þe mannes soule þe ic foreþingiæ. And ic almesne vnderfongen habbe and me sie rithlike for to bidden.*

243 S1519/W34; W39/*Peterborough* 27. See also S1500/R3, *Christ Church* 39A (*suð for*); S1535/W38 and S1490/W28 (*ouer se ferde*). S1482/H2, *Christ Church* 70 refers to the possibility of a wife travelling south, and S1508/H10, *Christ Church* 96 to the widow's payment of her husband's two wergilds to St Peter – presumably at Rome. See also S1187/*EHD* I, no. 81 for Æthelric's visit to St Peter and St Paul which prompted the disposition of his land and title-deeds.

on the other hand, may have lived quasi-religious lives in retirement from the world, as has been proposed for the widows Wynflæd and Æthelgifu,[244] and possibly Ulf.[245] The bequest of two estates to Thorney by Mantat 'the anchorite', although unreliable in its present form, may preserve a genuine record of the reversion of estates – perhaps leased from the abbey – which had supported a religious recluse.[246]

It also seems likely that private chapels furnished many of the religious items bequeathed in wills, as was the case in the wills of the Frankish aristocrats Eberhard and Eccard.[247] As well as providing a context for lay ownership of liturgical vestments and vessels and the crucifixes of precious metals bequeathed by donors, such chapels may have housed relics in richly-worked shrines.[248] The wills of both Eberhard and Eccard suggest that the chapel was the focus of the library. Eberhard possessed a psalter and a lectionary written in gold, but there is no indication in Anglo-Saxon wills that such books were owned by the laity, or bequeathed as treasure. The fine gospel book, now known as the Codex Aureus, ransomed in the late ninth century 'with their pure gold' by Ealdorman Alfred and his wife from the Viking Army, was presented by them to Christ Church, Canterbury *inter vivos*, as a pious gift, the inscription attesting to the devotion of the donors who stipulated that readings from the book should be made monthly on their souls' behalf.[249] Few books feature in vernacular wills, the majority in the wills of churchmen.[250] However, it seems likely that the lay nobility in Anglo-Saxon England possessed libraries similar to those of their Carolingian counterparts, typical of 'la bibliothèque de fonctionnaires carolingiens, soldats, grands propriétaires et chrétiens'.[251] The books listed in the ninth-century will of Eberhard and Gisela represent such a library; they include a Bible, multiple psalters, a penitential, works of St Augustine and Isidore, a bestiary, a cosmography, a royal capitulary (*librum de constitutionibus principum et edictis imperatorum*),

244 S1539/W3; S1497/*St Albans* 7. See J. L. André, 'Widows and vowesses', *Archaeological Journal* 49 (1892), 69–82; Foot, *Veiled Women*, I, Chap. 5.

245 S1532/*St Albans* 13; Chap. 5, n. 190 above.

246 S1523/W23; *Wills*, p. 177; *ECEE*, p. 205. The daughter of Thurketel Heyng was a recluse at St Benedict at Holme (see Chap. 4, p. 144 above).

247 See Chap. 5, pp. 212–13 above.

248 Chap. 5, p. 212 above.

249 H9, *Cartularium* ed. Birch, no. 634. The manuscript is now in Stockholm, Royal Library MS A. 135 (Ker, *Catalogue*, no. 385). See S1202/H8, *Christ Church* 95 and S1508/H10, *Christ Church* 96 for Ealdorman Ælfred's bequests to Christ Church. For gifts of valuable books see Dodwell, *Anglo-Saxon Art*, pp. 202–203; Fleming, 'The new wealth', pp. 13, 15.

250 S1488/W18, *Abingdon* 133 ('books' and a psalter); S1526/W1 (missals, one of which was inherited); S1492/N&S10 (service books, a missal, a benedictional, an epistle-book, a copy of Hrabanus and a martyrology).

251 P. Riché, quoted by R. McKitterick, *The Carolingians and the Written Word* (Cambridge, 1989), pp. 249–50.

books of law, and one concerning *rei militaris*.[252] While some of the religious books bequeathed in this will were richly adorned and intended for display, others were clearly functional: for example, one of the psalters was for 'our' personal use – presumably that of Eberhard and his wife;[253] and one of the missals is described as 'the missal for everyday use which we have always had in our chapel'.[254] Æthelweard, Ealdorman of the Western Provinces (died *c.* 998), is likely to have had such a library; Ælfric of Eynsham records that Æthelweard commissioned the translation of a range of works from the Latin, and was to receive a personal copy of a collection of Ælfric's homilies; the topics addressed by Ælfric in his Lives of Saints, written at the instigation of Æthelweard and his son, may well reflect the interests of an Anglo-Saxon nobleman and royal official.[255]

There are occasional glimpses in wills of such lay libraries. Bishop Ælfwold's bequest to Ordulf (probably the son of Ealdorman Ordgar of Devon) of a copy of Hrabanus and a martyrology suggests that Ordulf, too, may have had a collection of didactic and devotional books.[256] Ulf, who may have been a pious nobleman, bequeaths a missal to St Albans.[257] Other references to books in lay hands are non-specific, and found in the wills of women: Æthelgifu bequeaths a book to St Albans, and Wynflæd bequeaths *bocum 7 an swilcum lytlum* (books and such small things) to her daughter, Æthelflæd.[258] Since both Æthelgifu and Wynflæd may have been vowesses, these books are likely to have been devotional, and as those bequeathed by Wynflæd are classed as 'small things' hers, at least, may have been functional, psalters or prayer-books for use in private devotions, or even collections of homilies for private reading; Eberhard's will specifically mentions a psalter and commentary used by Gisela.[259] The ninth-century Frankish noblewoman Dhuoda, writing a manual for her son between 840 and 843, had access – perhaps

252 *Cartulaire*, ed. Coussemaker, pp. 3–4; McKitterick, *Carolingians and the Written Word*, pp. 246–8; La Rocca and Provero, 'The dead and their gifts', pp. 256–7. A similar range of books is bequeathed by Eccard: *Recueil*, ed. Prou and Vidier, pp. 65–6. For a summary see Kasten, *Verfügungen*, pp. 332–3; McKitterick, *Carolingians and the Written Word*, pp. 248–9.

253 *Quod ad nostrum opus habuimus*: *Cartulaire*, ed. Coussemaker, p. 4.

254 *missale cotidianum, quod semper in nostra capella habuimus*: *Cartulaire*, ed. Coussemaker, p. 4; La Rocca and Provero, 'The dead and their gifts', pp. 256–7.

255 Æthelweard was also the author of the Latin version of the Anglo-Saxon Chronicle. His interest in books is summarised in *Æthelweard*, ed. Campbell, pp. xiv-xv; his interest in the noble persona is discussed by Baxter, *Earls*, pp. 79–85. See the article by M. R. Godden, 'Ælfric of Eynsham', in *Blackwell Encyclopaedia*, pp. 8–9 for a summary of Ælfric's themes.

256 S1492/N&S10.

257 S1532/*St Albans* 13.

258 S1497/*St Albans* 7; S1539/W3.

259 *Cartulaire*, ed, Coussemaker, p. 4: *psalterium cum sua expositione habeat, quem Gisla ad opus suum habuit*. It has been suggested that Ælfric's homilies may have provided for

through *florilegia* – to a range of religious and moral works which informed her text.[260] It is unclear to what extent either noblemen or -women were likely to have been sufficiently literate to read such texts independently; bequests to chaplains and household priests may reflect their significance as librarians and secretaries, as well as spiritual guides.[261]

Wills make it clear that, along with property, women inherited responsibility for family commemoration.[262] This is made explicit in the will of Wulfgar, whose widow, Æffe, is to have a life interest in the estate at Inkpen.[263] In return, she is expected to take responsibility for ensuring not only her husband's commemoration but also that of his father and grandfather through an annual payment of three days' food-rent.[264] Ealdorman Ælfgar bequeaths a life interest in several estates to his older daughter, Æthelflæd, 'on condition that she be the more zealous for my soul and of her mother's soul and of her brother's soul and of her own',[265] or 'on condition that she does the best she can for the community at Stoke for the sake of my soul and of our ancestors' souls'.[266] That women took this responsibility seriously is illustrated by the will of Æthelgifu, which stipulates that commemorative masses and psalters for herself and for her lord should be said or sung by the priest Edwin, to whom she bequeaths a life interest in the church at Stondon (Beds.), and the community at St Albans, to whom she bequeaths a number of estates.[267] Dhuoda's instructions to her son also place emphasis on the commemoration of her husband's family, 'who handed down their goods [to his father] in legitimate inheritance'.[268] However, Anglo-Saxon women also used their

the pious laity the equivalent of the later medieval Book of Hours: Wilcox, 'Ælfric in Dorset', p. 55.

260 For an overview of Dhuoda's reading see McKitterick, *Carolingians and the Written Word*, pp. 224–5, and for a detailed analysis, *Dhuoda: Manuel pour mon fils*, ed. P. Riché and others, 2nd edn (Paris, 1997), pp. 32–7.

261 On the various roles of royal priests see S. Keynes, 'Regenbald the chancellor (*sic*)', *ANS* 10 (1987), 185–222 (pp. 189–92).

262 See Chap. 4, pp. 176–7 above.

263 S1533/R26.

264 See Chap. 4, p. 158 above.

265 S1483/W2: *on þe red þat heo be þe bet for mine soule. and hire moder soule 7 for hire brother soule. 7 for hire seluen.*

266 *on þe red þat heo do þan hirde so wel heo best may into Stoke for mine soule and for ure aldre.* In holding Greenstead she is to do her best for the souls of Wiswith and Æthelweard, probably Ælfgar's wife and son. For the fulfilment of Ælfgar's bequests to the church by his younger daughter, Ælfflæd, see pp. 236–7 above.

267 S1497/*St Albans* 7; see p. 247 and Table 6 above. Reference to commemoration of husbands is also made in: S1200/H7, *Christ Church* 90; S1494/W14; S1486/W15; S1495/W22, *St Paul's* 22; S1521/W29. For the role of women in commemoration in a Carolingian context see M. Innes, 'Keeping it in the family: women and aristocratic memory 700–1200', in *Medieval Memories: Men, Women, and the Past, 700–1300*, ed. E. Van Houts (Harlow, 2001), pp. 17–35 (pp. 23–9).

268 *Qui illi res suas in legitima dimiserunt hereditate*: *Manuel*, ed. Riché, Book 8.14, ll. 1–2;

wills to bequeath property to the Church on behalf of their own kin. Æthelgifu's bequest of Weedon (Northants.), which probably derived from her own kindred, to Leofsige, her principal heir, requires him to provide a barrel of ale to an unspecified church in commemoration of her own parents and brother, as well as of herself and her lord.[269] In each of these cases, the gift of land is to earn spiritual reward for those from whom it originated.

The fact that women's wills are more likely than those of laymen to include bequests of religious goods to the Church may also reflect their responsibility for family commemoration. Gifts such as crosses, liturgical vessels or adornments for the Church, made in the hope of commemoration, were important in bringing the memory of donors and their ancestors into the *locus sanctus* and involving them in the cycle of prayer. Both Wulfwaru and Ælfswith bequeath movable wealth in commemoration of their ancestors, and Æthelgifu's bequest of vessels, furnishings and a book to St Alban's were made 'for her and for her lord's soul' (*for hio 7 for hire hlafordes sawle*).[270] Some items may have borne the names of those in whose memory the gifts were given, as in the case of the inscription on a fine early eleventh century reliquary cross, now in Brussels: 'Æthelmær, and Æthelwold his brother, ordered this cross to be made for the glory of Christ [and] for the soul of Ælfric their brother'.[271]

Dhuoda's instructions to her son, composed in the early 840s, place the responsibility for family commemoration firmly on his shoulders. She provides her son with a list of his father's relatives for whom he should pray, and adds:

> When a member of your family passes on, this does not befall except through God's power. When the lord so commands ... you who survive must effect that his name be written down among the others, and you must pray for him.[272]

She goes on to request that, on her own death, her name should be added.[273] However, by the tenth century such commemoration appears increasingly

transl. C. Neel, *Handbook for William: a Carolingian Woman's Counsel for her Son* (Lincoln NE, 1991), p. 87. C. Bouchard, *'Those of My Blood': Constructing Noble Families in Francia* (Philadelphia, 2001), pp. 62–4.

269 For the origin of this estate see Chap. 4, p. 172 above. Women also bequeath property on behalf of their own kin in S1486/W15, S1538/W21, *Bath and Wells* 21.

270 S1538/W21, *Bath and Wells* 21; S1511/W11, *Rochester* 35; S1497/*St Albans* 7. See Chap. 5, pp. 212–14 above and Appendix 3 for bequests of religious items.

271 *Þas rode het Æþlmær wyrican 7 Aðellwold hys beroþor Criste to lofe for Ælfrices savle hyra beroþor*: *Golden Age*, ed. Backhouse, Turner and Webster, no. 75, Plate XXIII.

272 *Quisquis de tua migrauerit stirpe, quod non est aliud nisi in potestate Dei, quando iusserit ipse ... rogo, tu si superstes fueris, nomen illius cum praescriptis personis supra iube transcribi, orando illum*: *Manuel*, ed. Riché, Book 10. 5, ll. 11–15; transl. Neel, *Handbook for William*, p. 100.

273 *Manuel*, ed. Riché, chap. 10.6; transl. Neel, *Handbook for William*, p. 101.

to have become the province of the church.[274] Anglo-Saxon wills played an important part in that process, providing a vehicle for the transfer of property to the church to invoke that perpetual institutional intercession which would transcend family memory. This was not an abdication of responsibility on the part of the living, but a commitment to the contemporary religious ethos by an elite who had wealth to invest in the best spiritual welfare available. Fragmentary though the evidence for personal piety may be, there seems little reason to doubt that, for many of the donors, the formula 'for my soul' meant precisely that.

274 On the shift of responsibility for commemoration see Geary, *Phantoms of Remembrance*, pp. 48–51, and Innes, 'Keeping it in the family', *passim*.

# CONCLUSION

## Why make a written will in Anglo-Saxon England?

The phenomenon of the Anglo-Saxon written will was associated with a wealthy elite. The extent to which the documentation of *post obitum* disposition became customary among the nobility in the tenth and eleventh centuries cannot now be known, although (as Chapter One has shown) it seems likely that the procedure was more widely embraced than the number of surviving wills suggests. More amenable to discussion is why such an instrument came to be valued and used in a society which by custom privileged oral testimony and procedures.

There can be little doubt that the documentation of bequests had its roots in the inveterate record-keeping of the Church. Lay bequest of bookland appears to have become established as an important element in the relationship between the nobility and the Church at least by the time that the main sequence of wills begins in the tenth century, and for beneficiary religious houses, familiar with the form and function of the Latin charter as well as a range of vernacular documents, it was a particular advantage to hold a written record of the terms of a deferred gift. However, the significance of these records for the laity is implied by the use of the vernacular, and in the expansion of the documents to include a range of bequests which were of no direct interest to the house responsible for drawing up individual wills.

One secular aspect of the multi-gift will is that it seems to have become a factor in the relationship between the nobility and the royal court. Wills may be addressed to the king (or, in one case, the queen), requesting royal permission for the dispositions to stand. The inclusion of such a clause reflected not only the interest of the donor in gaining royal support for the will, but also that of the church which stood to benefit when the bequests were implemented. When King Æthelred refused to allow the will of Æthelric of Bocking to stand on grounds of his treachery, the claim of Christ Church, Canterbury, to the estate of Bocking was as much in jeopardy as the inheritance of Æthelric's widow, requiring the intervention of Archbishop Ælfric to convince the king to change his mind.[1]

[1] See Chap. 2, pp. 70–1.

The evidence, as it stands, suggests that the responsibility of transmitting acquired land was a key factor in prompting will-making by both lay and religious donors. In Chapter One I showed that many of the estates bequeathed in wills were held by *boc*, with freedom of disposition; where this is not actually demonstrable, it is probable. Churchmen used their wills to distinguish and distribute land which they held in their own right, as opposed to that which they held by right of office. Laymen held acquired land which had significance for family wealth and status, with the attendant responsibility of satisfying potential claims upon it from within the kindred. In Chapter Four I argued that some multi-gift wills may represent the outcome of family negotiations as to its distribution, rather than the unilateral decisions of the donor, particularly where bookland had been acquired by a previous generation and passed by inheritance at least once, and where alienation to the church was in question. If this was indeed the case, the bequest of bookland by laymen among collateral kin as well as within the conjugal family represents a family strategy for its transmission, protecting the interests of the kin-group while alienating land to the church on its behalf. The wills of women, as widows and daughters, had an important part to play in this transmission process.

For wealthy donors faced with the disposition of considerable amounts of property, one significant advantage of the multi-gift will was its capacity to enshrine and preserve in an organised way a series of extremely complex arrangements. Since wills were intended to be read aloud at court and in other public forums, the language, style and structure of the documents were designed to make the contents readily accessible to a lay audience. In addition, the production of wills in multiple copies indicates their archival value. Copies were held by the church which drew up the will, possibly by other beneficiary churches, and occasionally in the royal archive; invariably one was held by the donor or donors, implying the existence of lay archives which may also have stored landbooks and other administrative documents. In having a copy of the will in an archive, the donor metaphorically held the reins of family assets.

The inclusion in the document by a monastic scribe of bequests to the donor's kindred which were of no interest to his own or any other house may suggest that, in drawing up multi-gift wills, the scriptorium accepted a secretarial function, compiling a full list of dispositions in return for the bequest of land. However, Chapter Four also refers to the way in French religious houses anxiously garnered support for a gift of land from potential claimants within a kin-group: the *laudatio parentum*. If bequests of land to the Church made by Anglo-Saxon donors were contingent upon similar kindred support, given in return for an acceptable share in family property, it would be in the interest of a beneficiary church to record and file details of such a distribution. From a lay perspective, the presence in the monastic archive, within the *locus sanctus*, of a multi-gift will naming key beneficiaries among the donor's kindred cemented the bond between members of the kin-group as benefactors and the religious house which offered them commemoration in perpetuity. Such a location also reinforced the anathema which already gave spiritual protection to the document.

I have argued (particularly in Chapter Five) that the process of will-making was valued by the laity as a means of display, analogous to the earlier practice of depositing grave-goods. Since the oral declaration of the donor's intentions which preceded documentation was likely to be crucial in establishing wealth and status, the precise contribution of the written will in this context is difficult to define. The written will could hardly achieve more in terms of display than a public declaration or, in the case of clothing, war-gear or household goods, ostentatious parade on public occasions. What the multi-gift will *could* provide, however, was a map of the nexus of gift exchange which was crucial to maintaining the equilibrium of social relationships in Anglo-Saxon society, and to which the bequest of property made a significant contribution. Since wills were, in general, likely to be made in advance of mortal illness, deferred gifts allowed donors to participate strategically in the exchange mechanism which established or confirmed their status within a series of complex social networks, while retaining the property which symbolised that status. In this respect, the written will encapsulated each donor's social identity as he or she perceived it.

The written will may have fallen out of favour with the lay aristocracy in the first half of the eleventh century. No wills of royalty or the aristocracy are extant after that of the ætheling Æthelstan, datable to 1014. This may be an accident of survival but, as Chapter Three suggests, it may also reflect the political changes which followed the accession of Cnut in 1016, which disrupted the long-standing relationship between aristocratic families, the king and the Church detectable in the wills of tenth-century ealdormen.[2] The particularly rich Bury archive shows that it was not ealdormen who embraced the written will under the new regime, but wealthy thegns whose local status and allegiance is evident in their dispositions. To what extent this is a phenomenon local to East Anglia, or part of a wider pattern, further research may show.

However, the demise of the Anglo-Saxon written will after 1066 must be linked in part to the social changes which followed William's accession. It has been argued that, within twenty years, the majority of land had been transferred to new lordship, and it seems likely that most Englishmen held land in subordination to such lords.[3] The symbiotic relationship between king, church and lay nobility, within which the circulation of property was an important factor, had been fragmented, and with it the network of social relationships which had been augmented by the judicious bequest of prop-

2 Chap. 3, pp. 111–12.
3 The case is put by Fleming, *Kings and Lords*, Chap. 4; Lewis, 'Domesday jurors'.

erty. The patterns of land transmission demonstrated by vernacular wills were based on notions of personal and spiritual allegiance which played little part in post-Conquest tenurial re-organisation.[4] Furthermore, in their use of English the documents reflect the role of the written vernacular in government, law and a wide range of transactions, employed by both church and laity. After the Conquest, Latin displaced English as the language of literacy.[5] When the multi-gift will re-appeared in the early years of the thirteenth century, it was written in Latin.[6]

The disposition of property *mortis causa* continued after the Conquest, but no evidence survives of the type of wide-ranging, detailed bequests of goods and land to both religious and secular beneficiaries characteristic of the Anglo-Saxon multi-gift will.[7] The cartularies of religious houses record *post obit* gifts of land, often with elements of contract, probably to be equated with the single-gift bequest as it has been described in this book.[8] It was in the course of the twelfth century that the study of Roman law began to generate renewed interest in the documentation of *post obitum* disposition, with wills eventually being placed under the aegis of ecclesiastical courts and the evolution of complex rules to define and govern such matters as the rights of the heir, the role of the executor and limitations on the disposal of property.[9] By the early thirteenth century, the written will was becoming widely used, with the pious gifts and bequests to family and household characteristic of its Anglo-Saxon predecessor.[10] The process of will-making may have become subject to a developing legal concept of inheritance, but it was still within the province of the Church, and thirteenth-century donors shared with their tenth- and eleventh-century counterparts the desire to dispose of their property *for gode and for worulde*.

I began this book by quoting Pollock and Maitland who, from the perspective of Roman law and the canonical will, saw the Anglo-Saxon vernacular will as 'ill-defined'.[11] It has been my purpose to challenge that view, and to show that the documents, generated by a specific concatenation of political, economic and social circumstances, were remarkably successful in adapting contemporary documentary forms and the resources of the vernacular in order to encompass what were often complex dispositions. The written

4 Fleming, *Kings and Lords*, p. 143.

5 Clanchy, *From Memory to Written Record*, p. 27.

6 Sheehan, *The Will*, pp. 192–3.

7 This may reflect differences between England and Normandy in conventions related to the transmission of land: J. C. Holt, 'Feudal society and the family in early medieval England: I. The revolution of 1066', *TRHS* 5th s., 32 (1982), 193–212 (esp. pp. 195–200).

8 Sheehan, *The Will*, pp. 107–15.

9 These developments are described by Sheehan, *The Will*, Chaps. 5 and 6, particularly at pp. 135–47 for the canonical will in England.

10 Sheehan, *The Will*, pp. 144, 258–65.

11 Introduction, n. 1.

will may have remained subservient to the oral act which it recorded, but it engaged with all aspects of contemporary life and allows the emergence of voices which are otherwise largely silent in the historical record. Although the Anglo-Saxon will could not survive the severing of key social relationships by the Conquest, the significance accorded to individual documents by monastic archivists, of the twelfth century in particular, ensured their preservation, complemented in some instances by enthusiastic forgery. The old order had changed, but its memory lingered on into the new.

# APPENDIX 1

# The corpus of Anglo-Saxon wills

(arranged chronologically by latest date)[1]

## 1A: Vernacular wills surviving in pre-Conquest manuscripts

| Date | Sawyer/Ed. | Name(s) | Archive | B.A. vol/no. | Type[2] |
|---|---|---|---|---|---|
| 805x824 | S1500/R3 | Æthelnoth & Gænburg | CCC | 18/39A | sg* |
| 833x839 (?835) | S1482/H2 | Abba & Heregyth | CCC | 18/70 | mg* |
| 845x853 | S1510/R6 | Badanoth Beotting | CCC | 18/78 | sg * |
| 867x870 | S1200/H7 | Cynethryth | CCC | 18/90 | agr* |
| 871x889 | S1508/H10 | Eald. Alfred | CCC | 18/96 | mg* |
| ?896x899 | S1507/H11 | King Alfred | NMW | 9/1 | mg |
| 931x939 | S1533/R26 | Wulfgar | OMW | | mg |
| *c.* 950 | S1539/W3 | Wynflæd | ?Shaftesbury | | mg |
| 941x958 (?958) | S1506/R32 | Æthelweard | CCC | 18/121 | agr* |
| 962x991 (?after 975) | S1494/W14 | Æthelflæd | Bury | | mg |
| *c.* 960x995/6 | S1501/W16[1] | Æthelric of Bocking | CCC | 18/136 | mg[3] |
| 998 | S1522/N&S9 | Leofwine | Westminster | | mg |
| *c.*1000 | S1534/W19 | Wulfgeat | Worcester | | mg |

1 Archive abbreviations: CCC (Christ Church, Canterbury); NMW and OMW (New and Old Minsters, Winchester); St Aug. (St Augustine's, Canterbury). Type of will: mg (multi-gift); sg (single-gift); agr (bequest-agreement).

2 An asterisk added to this column indicates a witness list. (Both copies of S1503/W20 and S1530/W30 include witness lists.)

3 S1218 is a Latin version of one bequest from this will (land to Christ Church, Canterbury). C. R. Hart, *Early Charters of Essex: The Norman Period* (Leicester, 1957), no. 31.

| Date | Sawyer/Ed. | Name(s) | Archive | B.A. vol/no. | Type |
|---|---|---|---|---|---|
| 956x1002 | S1497 | Æthelgifu | St Alban's | 12/7 | mg |
| 1000x1002 | S1486/W15 | Ælflæd | Bury | | mg |
| *c*.985x1006 | S1455/R62 | Ealdred | St Aug. | 4/31 | agr* |
| 1014 | S1503/W20 | Æthelstan ætheling | CCC | 18/142 | mg* |
| 1011x1015 | S1492/N&S10 | Bishop Ælfwold | Exeter | | mg* |
| 975x1016 | S1487/W13 | Ælfhelm Polga | Westminster | | mg |
| 1035x1040 | S1489/W26 | Bishop Ælfric | Bury | | mg |
| 1042x1043 | S1530/W30 | Thurstan | CCC | 18/166 | agr* |
| *c*. 1045 | S1471/R101 | Æthelric Bigga | CCC | 18/170 | agr* |

## 1B: Vernacular wills surviving in post-Conquest manuscripts

| Date | Sawyer/Ed. | Name(s) | Archive | B.A. vol/no. | Type |
|---|---|---|---|---|---|
| 855 | S1514/R9 | Dunn | Rochester | 1/23 | sg |
| 870x888 | S1202/H8 | Eald. Alfred | CCC | 18/95 | agr* |
| *c*. 900 | S1513/R17 | Ceolwynn | OMW | | sg |
| 932x939 | S1509/R27 | Alfred (thegn) | NMW | 9/11 | sg* |
| 946x947 | S1504/H20 | Eald. Æthelwold | OMW | | mg |
| 946x*c*.951 | S1483/W2 | Eald. Ælfgar | Bury | | mg |
| 942x*c*.951/3 | S1526/W1 | Bishop Theodred | Bury | | mg |
| 946x953 | S1418/R28 | Æthelnoth priest | NMW | 9/14 | sg |
| 947x955 | S1419/R29 | Eadwulf priest | NMW | 9/16 | mg |
| 951x955 | S1515/H21 | King Eadred | NMW | 9/17 | mg |
| 951x958 | S1491/W4 | Bishop Ælfsige | NMW | 9/18 | mg |
| 957x*c*.958 | S1496/W6 | Æthelgeard | NMW | 9/21 | sg |
| *c*.968x971 | S1485/W9 | Eald. Ælfheah | OMW | | mg* |
| 966x975 | S1484/W8 | Ælfgifu | OMW | | mg |
| 964x980 | S1512/W7 | Brihtric Grim | OMW | | sg* |
| 977x982 | S1498/W10 | Eald. Æthelmær | NMW | 9/25 | mg |
| 975x987 | S1511/W11 | Brihtric & Ælfswith | Rochester | 1/35 | mg* |
| after 987 | S1505/W12 | Æthelwold | NMW | 9/29 | mg |
| ?s.x | S1524/W5 | Ordnoth & wife | OMW | | sg |

| Date | Sawyer/Ed. | Name(s) | Archive | B.A. vol/no. | Type |
|---|---|---|---|---|---|
| s.x$^2$-s.xi | S1525(a)/ W37,38 | Siflæd | Bury | | mg |
| *c.* 1000 | S1495/W22 | Æthelflæd | St Paul's | 10/22 | sg* |
| 984x1001 | S1538/W21 | Wulfwaru | Bath | 13/21 | mg |
| 1002x1004 | S1536/W17 | Wulfric Spott | Burton | 2/29 | mg |
| 1002x1005 | S1488/W18 | Archbishop Ælfric | Abingdon | 8/133 | mg |
| s.xi (after 1020?) | S1528/W25 | Thurketel Heyng | Bury | | mg |
| 1035? | S1465/R86 | Eadsige (priest) | CCC | 18/153 | agr* |
| 1017x1035 | S1523/W23 | Mantat | Thorney | | mg |
| s.xi (pre-1038?) | S1527/W24 | Thurketel of Palgrave | Bury | | mg |
| *c.*1040 | S1224/R92 | Stigand (priest?) | Bury | | agr* |
| 1022x1043 | S1537/W27 | Wulfsige | Bury | | mg |
| 1042x1043 | S1490/W28 | Ælfric Modercope | Bury | | mg |
| 1035x1044 | S1521/W29 | Leofgifu | Bury | | mg |
| 1043x1044 | S1468/R97 | Æthelmær (priest) | Bury | | agr |
| 1043x1045 | S1531/W31 | Thurstan | Bury | | mg* |
| 1026x1046 | S1532 | Ulf | St Alban's | 12/13 | mg |
| 1043x1047 | S1470/R100 | Wulfgeat & wife | Bury | | agr |
| 1042x1066 (*c.*1050?) | S1517 | Eadwine of Caddington | St Alban's | 12/15 | mg |
| s.xi$^{med}$ | S1516/W33 | Edwin | Bury | | mg |
| s.xi$^{med}$ | S1529/W36 | Thurkil & Æthelgyth | Bury | | sg |
| 1044x1052 | S1608/ *ECEE* 133 | Oswulf & Leofrun | Bury | | mg |
| 1044x1053 (?1046) | S1535/W32 | Wulfgyth | CCC | 18/176 | mg |
| 1052x1066 | S1519/W34 | Ketel | Bury | | mg |
| 1053x1066 | S1235 | Oswulf & Æthelgyth | St Alban's | 12/17 | agr |
| 1066x1069 | W39 | Ulf & Madselin | Peterborough | 14/27 | mg |
| 1047x1070 | S1499/W35 | Bishop Æthelmær | Bury | | sg |
| 1052x1070 | S1234/R116 | Brihtmær | CCC | 18/183 | sg* |

## 1C: Wills and bequests recorded in Latin (excluding those recorded in *LE* and *CR*)

| Date | Sawyer[4] | Name(s) | Archive | B.A. vol/ no. | Type |
|---|---|---|---|---|---|
| 762 | S1182/ *EHD*I 72 | Dunwald | St Aug. | 4/12 | sg |
| 793x796 | S146/*EHD*I 78 | King Offa | Worcs. | | sg |
| *c.* 801 | S157 | Swithhun | Rochester | 1/16 | sg |
| 804(?) | S1187/ *EHD*I 81 | Æthelric | Worcs. | | mg |
| 833 | S1414 | Werhard | CCC | 18/64 | sg |
| s.ix² | S1652 | Æthelferth | St Aug. | 4, p. 184, iii | sg |
| 1048x1050 | S1502 | Æthelric Bigga | St Aug. | 4/38 | sg[5] |

4 The texts of these wills, with the exception of S1652, are available on the database of the *Regesta Regum Anglorum*, available via the Anglo-Saxon charters home page at www.trin.cam.ac.uk/chartwww/

5 A separate bequest by the donor of the vernacular bequest-agreement with Christ Church, Canterbury (S1471/R101).

# APPENDIX 2

## The evidence for wills and will-making in the *Liber Eliensis* and *Chronicon Abbatiæ Rameseiensis*

A number of the references to wills or will-making listed here are made in passing by the compiler of the chronicle. In some cases there is no direct reference to a written will; in one case (no. 41) a bequest was made orally. References to the documentation of bequests in the *Liber Eliensis* are indicated by an asterisk in the 'Bequest' column; in four cases (nos. 7, 8, 21 and 27) the documents are said to have been written in English. The Ramsey compiler's claim to be drawing on vernacular documents is discussed in Chapter One.[1] Where a vernacular will is extant for a donor, the reference appears in square brackets in the 'Bequest' column.

Since the evidence for dating is generally tenuous, donors are listed alphabetically for each chronicle.[2] Numbers allocated in Sawyer's list are given where appropriate. Those gifts which are specified as *post obitum* are included, as well as those given for the benefit of the donor's soul or as payment for burial, where the context implies that they are to take effect on the death of the donor. Occasionally wider contextual evidence has been used to determine *post obitum* intention; any doubt is indicated by a question mark added to the 'Bequest' column. Where donors appear in both chronicles, or are related to other donors, links have been indicated by cross-referencing the Appendix numbers.

1 See p. 38 above.

2 The dates given follow Hart, *ECEE*, unless otherwise stated.

## *LIBER ELIENSIS* (Book II)

| Donor | Chapter | Date | Sawyer | Bequest |
|---|---|---|---|---|
| 1. Ælfflæd (wid. of 10) | 63 | 1000x1002 | | land to Ely [S1486/W15] |
| 2. Ælfgar of *Multune* | 35/*Lib* 46 | *c.* 924x*c.* 975[3] | | land to Wulfstan of Dalham |
| 3. Ælfgifu | 47/*Lib* 58 | 966x975 | | land to Kg Edgar [S1484/W8] |
| 4. Ælfhelm Polga | 73 | 975x1016[4] | | land to Ely (see also 37) [S1487/W13] |
| 5. Ælfmær (br. of 18) | 70 | 996x1001 | | share of estate held with br. to Ely (brother's share to Ramsey: 54)* |
| 6. Ælfwaru (? eldest d. of 9/45)[5] | 61 | *c.* 1007 | | d. bed; land and movables to Ely (see 40 for bequest to Ramsey)* |
| 7. Æthelgifu (of Thaxted) | 59 | *c.* 1000[6] | | land and movables to Ely* |
| 8. Æthelric ? br. of 27, 30 | 68 | *c.* 1000 | | land and movables to Ely; son>monk* |
| 9. Æthelstan Mannessune (?f. of 6/40) | 13 | 986 | | land to Ely (see also 45, 46) |
| 10. Byrhtnoth (eald; husb. of 1, f. of 19) | 62 | 991 | | land, movables to Ely (see 50) |
| 11. Byrhtsige | 11/*Lib* 10 | *c.* 970x984[7] | | silver cup to Bp Æthelwold (d. bed?) |
| 12. Eadgifu (g. mother of Kg Edgar) | 31/*Lib* 41 | 961x964? | | land to *nobili matrone* Ælfthryth |
| 13. Eadric the Tall | 27/*Lib* 38 | *c.* 975 | | land to Kg Edgar; unpaid heriot* |
| 14. Eanflæd | 21/*Lib* 32 | ? | | land to Ely and Wine |
| 15. Eadric | 34/*Lib* 45 | *c.* 970x984[8] | | reversion of land to Ely |

3 During the lifetime of Wulfstan, fl. 924/39x973/5 (Wareham, *Lords and Communities*, p. 34).

4 *Wills*, p. 133. Hart gives 989, based on a Ramsey record of Ælfhelm's death (*ECEE*, p. 31).

5 Hart, 'Eadnoth', p. 614.

6 Æthelgifu was attended by Abbot Ælfsige, whose dates are uncertain: *c.* 999–1016x1022 (Blake, *LE*, p. 411).

7 During Bishop Æthelwold's activities at Ely (*c.* 970–984).

8 See n. 7.

| Donor | Chapter | Date | Sawyer | Bequest |
|---|---|---|---|---|
| 16. Godgifu | 81, 83 | 1022x1029 | | land to Ely; additional d.bed bequest* |
| 17. Goding, monk | 26/*Lib* 37 | *c.* 970–984[9] | | land to Ely |
| 18. Godwine (br. of 5) | 69 | 975x978[10] | | d.bed bequ. of land to Ely (see 54 for bequ. to Ramsey)* |
| 19. Leofflæd (wid of 27, d. of 10) | 88 | 1017x1035 | 1520 | bequ. to Ely and daughters; tripartite chirograph* |
| 20. Leofric | 10/*Lib* 7 | *c.* 971 | | ref. to bequ. to sisters |
| 21. Leofwine | 60 | 1002x*c.* 1016 | | multiple estates: penance; son>monk* |
| 22. Lustwine & Leofwaru | 89 | 1017x1049 | | multiple estates to Ely; parents of Thurstan [S1531/W31]* |
| 23. Ogga of Mildenhall | 18/*Lib* 27 | *c.* 955 | | attempted oral bequ. to Ely |
| 24. Ordmær & Ealde | 7/*Lib* 5 | 959x975[11] | | land to Kg Edgar (with charter) |
| 25. Oskytel Bp of Dorchester | 22/*Lib* 33 | before 972 | | land to Bp Æthelwold |
| 26. Osmund Hocer | 12/*Lib* 16 | 970x*c.* 999[12] | | reversion agreement with Ely |
| 27. Oswi (br. of 8,30; husb. of 19) | 67 | 995x1001 | | land *ad vestimentum* with son>monk; reversion to Ely* |
| 28. Siferth of Downham | 11/*Lib* 12 | 975x978[13] | | land to Ely and daughter; account of d.bed will-making* |
| 29. Thurcytel Abbot of Bedford | 31/*Lib* 41 | before 984[14] | | land to St Paul's (for entry to community) |
| 30. Ufi (br. of 8, 27) | 66 | 996x1001 | | land to Ely* |

9 See n. 7.
10 During the reign of Edward the Martyr.
11 During the reign of King Edgar.
12 The abbacy of Abbot Byrhtnoth.
13 See Chap. 2, p. 56 above.
14 *St Paul's*, pp. 96–7.

| Donor | Chapter | Date | Sawyer | Bequest |
|---|---|---|---|---|
| 31. Wulfric the reeve | 32/*Lib* 42 | s.x$^{med.}$ [15] | | land to nephew (priest) |
| 32. Wulfsige, Mawa & son, Ælfsige | 15 | 970x*c.* 999[16] | | land to Ely |
| 33. Wulfstan of Dalham | 7, 55/*Lib* 5 | d. *c.* 973x975[17] | | land to Ely |
| 34. *ditto* | 10/*Lib* 9 | d. *c.* 973x975[18] | | bequest to daughter? |
| 35. Unnamed mother of Ælfric & Leofwine | 11/*Lib* 13 | *c.* 970–984[19] | | land to sons |
| 36. unnamed | 11/*Lib* 14 | *c.* 970–984[20] | | land bequeathed to the widow of Ælfwold the Fat by her late husband? |

## *CHRONICON ABBATIÆ RAMESEIENSIS*

| Donor | Chapter | Date | Sawyer | Bequest |
|---|---|---|---|---|
| 37. Ælfhelm & Æffe | 34 | 975x1016?[21] | 1807 | land to Ramsey [S1487/W13] (see 4) |
| 38. Ælfhild (wid. of 41) | 35 | 990x *c.*1000 | 1808 | confirms husband's bequest; estate with son > monk |
| 39. Ælfsige & Leva | 107 | 1043x1066 | | land to Ramsey after death of both |
| 40. Ælfwaru. (?eldest d. of 9/45) | 54 | *c.* 1007 | | land, church & movables to Ramsey (see 6) (?protects tenure of priest: see 52) |
| 41. Ælfwold (br. of 47) | 34 | *c.* 990 | | land to Ramsey *viva voce* res. usufruct x2 for wife (see 38) |
| 42. Ærnketel & Wulfrun | 37, 38 | 978x1016[22] | 1493 | land, coin, chattels (unspec.) to Ramsey for burial |

15 The chronology of this chapter is convoluted.
16 See n. 12.
17 See n. 3.
18 See n. 3.
19 See n. 7.
20 See n. 7.
21 See n. 4 above, and Chap. 1, pp. 39–40.
22 C. R. Hart, *The Early Charters of Northern England and the North Midlands* (Leicester, 1975), no. 116 (pp. 112–13).

| Donor | Chapter | Date | Sawyer | Bequest |
|---|---|---|---|---|
| 43. Æthelflæd (1st wife of 47) | 28 | *c.* 977 | | land to Ramsey for burial |
| 44. Æthelgifu (2nd wife of 47) | 32 | *c.* 985 | 1809 | land, coin & movables to Ramsey |
| 45. Æthelstan Mannessune (f. of 6/40) | 33 | 986 | | multigift will: land to Ramsey, Ely & kin; manumission; ? wooden cross to Ramsey (see 9) |
| 46. Widow of 45 | 33 | 987 | | reversionary agreement with Ramsey |
| 47. Æthelwine (eald.) | 28 | *c.* 992 | | d.bed bequest of fishery etc. |
| 48. Æthelwine Niger | 103 | 1049[23] | | d. bed bequ. of land to Ramsey; disputed by kinsman |
| 49. Berric | 51 | before 992[24] | | bequ. of land to Ramsey |
| 50. Byrhtnoth (eald.) | 68 | 991 | | bequ. of land to Ramsey & Ely before battle (see 10) |
| 51. Eadnoth & uxor | 106/7 | 1043x1065 | | land to Ramsey to clothe son > monk; manumission |
| 52. Gode, priest | 55 | *c.* 1007 | | land, church to Ramsey; ? life tenure from 40 |
| 53. Godric (br. of Abbot Eadnoth) | 62, 63 | *c.* 1007 | 1518 | multigift will: land to br. & son; other gifts not detailed |
| 54. Godwine (br. of 5) | 53 | 969x979 | | his share of estate held with br. (see 5) to Ramsey. Reversion of 2nd estate. See 18 for bequ. to Ely |
| 55. Kinemund, priest | 28 | before 992[25] | | ref. to bequ. of land to 47 |
| 56. Ralph, Earl of Hereford[26] | 105 | *c.* 1053x1057 | | reversionary agreement with Ramsey |
| 57. Thorgunnr | 107 | *c.* 1055x 1066 | | d.bed bequ. of land to Ramsey for burial |
| 58. Tostig | 107 | *c.* 1050x1065 | | land to Ramsey for burial |

[23] *CR*, p. 169.
[24] Witnessed by Bishop Oswald and Ealdorman Æthelwine, both d. 992.
[25] Death of the beneficiary, Ealdorman Æthelwine.
[26] Barlow, *The English Church 1000–1066*, p. 61.

| Donor | Chapter | Date | Sawyer | Bequest |
|---|---|---|---|---|
| 59. Wach | 172 | *c.* 1054 | | fishery to Ramsey?[27] |
| 60. Wulfgifu (3rd wife of 47) | 30, 31 | 995x1001 | 1810 | land to Ramsey; tripartite chirograph |
| 61. Wulfwine (son of Ælfwine) | 89 | *c.* 1044 | | reversionary agreement with Ramsey |
| 62. parents of 47 | 28 | s.x.$^{med.}$ | | ref. to land inherited from both parents |
| 63. father-in-law of 54 | 53 | s.x.$^{med.}$ | | ref. to d.bed bequ. of land to daughter, wife of 54 |

27 Perhaps given in return for confraternity: Hart, *ECEE*, p. 235.

# APPENDIX 3

## The bequest of movable wealth

| Vernacular Wills | Heriot[1] | Coin (Distr.) | Coin (Individ. Gift) | Stock | Slaves | Horses | Riding Gear | Sword(s) | Seax | Byrnie(s) | Belt | Ship(s) | *Beagas* | Band(s) | Brooch(es) | Clothing | Vessels | Furnishings | Rel. Items | Books | Tent | Trumpet | Hawks | Hounds | Wagon | Manumission | Other |
|---|---|---|---|---|---|---|---|---|---|---|---|---|---|---|---|---|---|---|---|---|---|---|---|---|---|---|---|
| ***Royal*** | | | | | | | | | | | | | | | | | | | | | | | | | | | |
| S1507/H11 | | ✓ | | ✓ | | | | ✓ | | | | | | | | | | | | | | | | | | ✓ | |
| S1515/H21 | | ✓ | ✓ | | | | | ✓ | | | | | | | | | | | ✓ | | | | | | | | |
| S1503/W20 | | ✓ | ✓ | | | ✓ | ✓ | ✓ | | ✓ | ✓ | | ✓ | | | | ✓ | | ✓ | | | ✓ | | | | ✓ | |
| ***Ealdormen*** | | | | | | | | | | | | | | | | | | | | | | | | | | | |
| S1508/H10 | | ✓ | | ✓ | | | | | | | | | | | | | | | | | | | | | | | |
| S1504/H20 | ✓ | | | ✓ | | | | | | | | | | | | | ✓ | | | | | | | | | | |
| S1483/W2 | ✓ | | | | | | | ✓ | | | | | | | | | | | | | | | | | | | |
| S1485/W9 | ✓ | | ✓ | | | | | ✓ | ✓ | | | | | | | | ✓ | | | | | | | | | ✓ | |
| S1498/W10 | ✓ | ✓ | ✓ | | | | | | | | | | | | | | | | ✓ | | | | | | | | |

1 Heriot includes specified war-gear, horses and coin/*beagas* at the appropriate rate. Brackets indicate that the term is used in the will without further details.

| **Vernacular Wills** | Heriot | Coin (Distr.) | Coin (Individ. Gift) | Stock | Slaves | Horses | Riding Gear | Sword(s) | Seax | Byrnie(s) | Belt | Ship(s) | *Beagas* | Band(s) | Brooch(es) | Clothing | Vessels | Furnishings | Rel. Items | Books | Tent | Trumpet | Hawks | Hounds | Wagon | Manumission | Other | |
|---|---|---|---|---|---|---|---|---|---|---|---|---|---|---|---|---|---|---|---|---|---|---|---|---|---|---|---|---|
| ***Thegns*** | | | | | | | | | | | | | | | | | | | | | | | | | | | | |
| S1482/H2 | | ✓ | | ✓ | | | | ✓ | | | | | | | | | ✓ | | | | | | | | | | | |
| S1505/W12 | ✓ | | ✓ | | | | | ? | | | | | | | | ✓ | ✓ | | | | | | | | | | | |
| S1487/W13 | ✓ | | | ✓ | | ✓ | | | | | | ✓ | | | | | | | | | | | | | | | | |
| S1501/W16[1] | ✓ | | | | | | | | | | | | | | | | | | | | | | | | | | | |
| S1536/W17 | ✓ | ✓ | | ✓ | | ✓ | | | | | | | | | ✓ | | | | | | | | | | | | | |
| S1534/W19 | ✓ | ✓ | ✓ | ✓ | | ✓ | | | | | | | | | | | | | | | | | | | | ✓ | ✓ | A brewing of malt |
| S1527/W24 | | | | | | | | | | | | | | | | | | | | | | | | | | ✓ | | |
| S1528/W25 | (✓) | | ✓ | | | | | | | | | | | | | | | | | | | | | | | ✓ | | |
| S1537W27 | ✓ | | ✓ | | | ✓ | ✓ | | | ✓ | | | | | | ✓ | | | | | | | | | | ✓ | | |
| S1490/W28 | ✓ | | ✓ | ✓ | | | | | | | | | | | | | | ✓ | | | ✓ | | | | | | | |
| S1531/W31 | ✓ | ✓ | ✓ | | | | | | | | | | | | | | | | | | | | | | | ✓ | | |
| S1516/W33 | | | | | | | | | | | | | | | | | | | | | | | | | | ✓ | | |
| S1519/W34 | ✓ | | | | | | | | | | | | | | | | | | | | | | | | | ✓ | | |
| S1532/ *St Albans* 13 | | ✓ | ✓ | | | ✓ | | | | | | | | | | ✓ | ✓ | | ✓ | ✓ | | | | | | ✓ | | |
| S1517/ *St Albans* 15 | ✓ | | | ✓ | | | | | | | | | | | | | | | | | | | | | | ✓ | | |

| Vernacular Wills | Heriot[1] | Coin (Distr.) | Coin (Individ. Gift) | Stock | Slaves | Horses | Riding Gear | Sword(s) | Seax | Byrnie(s) | Belt | Ship(s) | *Beagas* | Band(s) | Brooch(es) | Clothing | Vessels | Furnishings | Rel. Items | Books | Tent | Trumpet | Hawks | Hounds | Wagon | Manumission | Other | |
|---|---|---|---|---|---|---|---|---|---|---|---|---|---|---|---|---|---|---|---|---|---|---|---|---|---|---|---|---|
| ***Women*** | | | | | | | | | | | | | | | | | | | | | | | | | | | | |
| S1539/W3 | | ✓ | ✓ | ✓ | ✓ | ✓ | | | | | | | ✓ | | ✓ | ✓ | ✓ | ✓ | ✓ | ✓ | ✓ | | | | | ✓ | | |
| S1484/W8 | ✓ | ✓ | ✓ | | | | | | | | | | ✓ | ✓ | | | ✓ | | ✓ | | | | | | | ✓ | | |
| S1494/W14 | | | | ✓ | | ✓ | | | | | | | | | | ✓ | ✓ | | | | | | | | | ✓ | | |
| S1486/W15 | | | | | | | | | | | | | ✓ | | | | ✓ | | | | | | | | | | | |
| S1538/W21 | | | ✓ | | | | | | | | | | ✓ | ✓ | ✓ | ✓ | ✓ | ✓ | ✓ | | | | | | | ✓ | | |
| S1521/W29 | | | ✓ | | | | | | | | | | | | | | | | | | | | | | | ✓ | | |
| S1535/W32 | (✓) | | ✓ | | | | | | | | | | | | | ✓ | ✓ | ✓ | ✓ | | | | | | | ✓ | | |
| S1525/W37,38 | | | | ✓ | | | | | | | | | | | | | | | | | | | | | | ✓ | ✓ | wagonloads of wood |
| S1497/ *St Albans* 7 | | | ✓ | ✓ | ✓ | ✓ | ✓ | | | | | | | ✓ | | ✓ | ✓ | ✓ | | ✓ | | | | ✓ | ✓ | ✓ | | |
| ***Joint*** | | | | | | | | | | | | | | | | | | | | | | | | | | | | |
| S1511/W11 | ✓ | ✓ | | | | ✓ | ✓ | | ✓ | | | | ✓ | ✓ | | | ✓ | | | | | | ✓ | ✓ | | | | |
| W39/ *Peterb.* 27 | | ✓ | | | | | | | | | | | | | | | | | | | | | | | | | | |
| ***Church*** | | | | | | | | | | | | | | | | | | | | | | | | | | | | |
| S1526/W1 | ✓ | ✓ | ✓ | ✓ | | | | | | | | | | | | | ✓ | | ✓ | ✓ | | | | | | ✓ | | |
| S1491/W4 | (✓) | | | | | | | | | | | | | | | | | | | | | | | | | ✓ | | |
| S1488/W18 | (✓) | | | ✓ | ✓ | | | | | ✓ | | ✓ | | | | | | | ✓ | ✓ | ✓ | | | | | ✓ | ✓ | helmets |
| S1492/N+S10 | ✓ | ✓ | ✓ | | | ✓ | | | | ✓ | | ✓ | | | | | | ✓ | ✓ | ✓ | ✓ | | | | | | ✓ | ploughteam helmet |
| S1489/W26 | | | ✓ | | | | | | | | | | | | | | | | | | | | | | | | | |
| S1499/W35 | | | ✓ | | | | | | | | | | | | | | | | | | | | | | | | | |

| The Chronicle Evidence | Heriot | Coin (Distr.) | Coin (Individ. Gift) | Stock | Slaves | Horses | Riding Gear | Sword(s) | Seax | Byrnie(s) | Belt | Ship(s) | *Beagas* | Band(s) | Brooch(es) | Clothing | Vessels | Furnishings | Rel. Items | Books | Tent | Trumpet | Hawks | Hounds | Wagon | Manumission | Other | |
|---|---|---|---|---|---|---|---|---|---|---|---|---|---|---|---|---|---|---|---|---|---|---|---|---|---|---|---|---|
| ***LE*** | | | | | | | | | | | | | | | | | | | | | | | | | | | | |
| Byrhtsige II, 11 | | | | | | | | | | | | | | | | | ✓ | | | | | | | | | | | |
| Byrhtnoth[2] II, 62 | | ✓ | | | | | | | | | | | | | | ✓ | | | ✓ | | | | | | | | | |
| Æthelgifu II, 59 | | | | | | | | | | | | | | | | | | | ✓ | | | | | | | | | |
| Ælfwaru II, 61 | | | | | | | | | | | | | | | | | | | ✓ | | | | | | | | | |
| ***CR*** | | | | | | | | | | | | | | | | | | | | | | | | | | | | |
| Æthelstan 33 | | | | | | | | | | | | | | | | | | | ✓[3] | | | | | | | ✓ | | |
| Æthelgifu 32 | | ✓ | | | | | | | | | | | | | | | | | ✓ | | | | | | | | | |
| Ælfwaru 54 | | ✓ | | | | | ✓ | | | | | | | | | | ✓ | ✓ | ✓ | | | | | | | | | |
| Ærnketel & Wulfrun 37, 38 | | ✓ | | | | | | | | | | | | | | | | | | | | | | | | | ✓ | unspecified chattels |
| Godric 63 | (✓) | | | | | | | | | | | | | | | | | | | | | | | | | | | |
| Eadnoth & wife 107 | | | | | | | | | | | | | | | | | | | | | | | | | | ✓ | | |

2 *LE* gives an account of Ealdorman Byrhtnoth's bequests to Ely on the eve of the Battle of Maldon.
3 This bequest features in only one ms of the Chronicle: Mackay, *Chronicon*, p. 60, n. 4

# APPENDIX 4

# Local churches mentioned in wills[1]

## 4A: Local churches as beneficiaries (arranged by archive)

In some cases, donors refer specifically to a beneficiary church associated with a particular place. Where bequests are made for the donor's soul to a particular place without mention of a church, the presence of a local church is implied. Where neither is the case, it has been assumed that when bequests were made to a specified place, they were intended to benefit a local church. An asterisk indicates a reference to a community.

| **Bury** | |
|---|---|
| S1526/W1 | Mendham (Sfk)* |
| S1483/W2 | Stoke-by-Nayland (Sfk)* |
| S1494/W14 | Stoke-by-Nayland (Sfk)* |
| | Hadleigh (Sfk) |
| | Mersea (Ex) |
| S1486/W15 | Stoke-by-Nayland (Sfk)* |
| | St Gregory's, Sudbury (Sfk) |
| | Mersea (Ex) |
| S1527/W24 | Roydon (Nfk) |
| S1531/W31 | Wetheringsett (Sfk) |
| | Weston, Bromley, Henham, Dunmow (Ex) |
| S1516/W33 | Multiple beneficiaries in Norfolk[2] |
| S1519/W34 | Stisted (Ex) |
| | E. Harling (Nfk) |
| | Walsingham (Nfk) |
| S1525/W37, 38 | Marlingford (Nfk) |
| | Christ Church and St Mary's Church (Norwich) |

[1] For the criteria used in this study to define a local church see Chap. 6, p. 254 above.

[2] See Table 2, p. 132 above.

**Christ Church, Canterbury**

| | |
|---|---|
| S1482/H2, *Christ Church* 70 | Folkestone, Lyminge (Kt)*[3] |
| S1501/W16[1], *Christ Church* 136 | Bocking (Ex)<br>St Gregory's, Sudbury (Sfk) |
| S1535/W32, *Christ Church* 176 | Stisted (Ex)<br>Somerleyton (Nfk)<br>St Osyth's (Ex)[4] |

**St Albans**

| | |
|---|---|
| S1497/ *St Albans* 7 | Stondon, Bedford, Henlow, Flitton (Beds.)<br>Hitchin, Hertingfordbury, Welwyn, Ashwell, Braughing (Herts.) |
| S1517/ *St Albans* 15 | Sundon (Beds.) |

**Worcester**

| | |
|---|---|
| S1534/W19 | Leominster,[5] Bromyard (Hfds.)<br>Clifton-upon-Teme (Worcs.)<br>Penkridge (Staffs.), Tong (Shrops.) |

**Westminster**

| | |
|---|---|
| S1522/N&S9 | Notley (Ex)* |

**Rochester**

| | |
|---|---|
| S1511/W11, *Rochester* 35 | *Wolcnesstede* (Godstone, Sy) |

**Shaftesbury?**

| | |
|---|---|
| S1539/W3 | Milbourne (Dors.), Yeovil (Som.), Wantage, Coleshill, Shrivenham, Childrey (Berks.) |

**Old Minster, Winchester**

| | |
|---|---|
| S1533/R26 | Kintbury (Berks.)* |

**New Minster, Winchester**

| | |
|---|---|
| S1498/W10, *New Minster* 25 | Cricklade (Wilts.)<br>Bourne (Hants?)[6] |

3 I have included these communities as having primarily a local focus, although as royal foundations (Brooks, *Early History*, p. 183) they may have had a higher status than other churches listed here.

4 The status of St Osyth's is unclear: see Foot, *Veiled Women*, II, 159–62.

5 The status of Leominster is unclear: see Foot, *Veiled Women*, II, 103–7.

6 The church at Cricklade was sited in a royal burh (Blair, *The Church*, p. 331); the identification of Bourne is uncertain (*New Minster*, ed. Miller, p. 120).

## 4B: Wills bequeathing churches

| | |
|---|---|
| S1526/W1 (Bury) | Mendham (Sfk)[7] |
| S1521/W29 (Bury) | Colne (Ex)* |
| S1497/*St Albans* 7 | Stondon (Beds.)[8] |
| S1234/R116 (Christ Church) | All Hallows, Gracechurch (London) |
| *CR* 54 | Elsworth (Cambs.) |
| *CR* 55 | Holywell (Hunts.) |

## 4C: Other references to local churches

| | |
|---|---|
| S1235/ *St Albans* 17 | Studham (Beds.): a church built on land bequeathed to St Albans |
| S1608/*ECEE* 133 (Bury) | Dickleburgh and Semer (Nfk): churches placed in *mund* |

7 Bishop Theodred bequeaths the estate at Mendham to his nephew, reserving one hide and the minster (*mynstre*) for the church (*kirke*). Theodred's bequest presumably granted rights in the minster itself to a community already established there (see next note).

8 Æthelgifu bequeaths a life interest in the church to her priest, whom she frees, requiring him to sing commemorative masses and to maintain the church. These terms may reflect those on which donors bequeath the churches at Mendham and Colne: see Chap. 6, pp. 271–2.

# APPENDIX 5

# Note on unpublished material by Patrick Wormald

The untimely death of Patrick Wormald prevented the completion of his important work *The Making of English Law*, of which only Volume One was published.[1] Volume Two would have brought to fruition his views on Anglo-Saxon wills.

Wormald's thoughts on land tenure and inheritance evolved over many years and were explored in a number of his published works, most notably in the present context *Bede and the Conversion of England: the Charter Evidence*, Jarrow Lecture (1984);[2] 'Charters, law and the settlement of disputes in Anglo-Saxon England' (1986);[3] and '*On þa wæpnedhealfe*: kingship and royal property from Æthelwulf to Edward the Elder' (2001).[4] In addition, among the series of Wormald's unpublished lecture notes which contain material preparatory to the second volume of *The Making of English Law* there is an outline of his provisional ideas on inheritance and tenurial issues.[5] These notes have been deposited with the remainder of his papers in the archives of King's College, London, and may be obtained there or by contacting Dr Stephen Baxter.

For the purposes of this book I have restricted my references to Wormald's published works without attempting to engage with or expound on these unpublished notes. However, I am grateful to Dr Baxter for making this material available to me, and for drawing my attention to the key aspects of Wormald's research relevant to the study of wills which are summarised here. Wormald's published works (as cited above) develop the suggestion that the land bequeathed in wills may have been mostly bookland, which had been granted in the first place with freedom of disposition, and which was not, therefore, necessarily subject to any customary inheritance practice. The holder therefore had the right, at least in theory, to bequeath such land outside the kin-group (usually to the church) undisputed by kin.[6] However,

1 P. Wormald, *The Making of English Law: King Alfred to the Twelfth Century* (Oxford, 1999).

2 Reprinted in Wormald, ed. Baxter, *The Times of Bede*, pp. 135–66.

3 First published in *Settlement of Disputes*, ed. Davies and Fouracre, pp. 149–68, reprinted in Wormald, *Legal Culture*, pp. 289–311.

4 Published in *Edward the Elder*, ed. Higham and Hill, pp. 264–79.

5 This outline may be found in the lecture notes entitled 'The Making of English Law, VII: The Nature of Title'.

6 These views are most clearly set out in his 'Kingship and royal property', pp. 264–8.

Wormald's unpublished notes indicate that he was exploring further points relevant to the understanding of wills which lacked full elucidation at his death, in particular questioning the extent to which wills may be seen as representative of Anglo-Saxon inheritance practice if they are primarily concerned with the transmission of bookland.[7] His analysis of laymen's wills[8] led him to note that sons rarely feature as significant beneficiaries, whereas women do; he proposed that wills may have been used to provide for sons who were not provided for by other means, and for female kin.[9] The surprising corollary is that Anglo-Saxon wills may reveal relatively little about Anglo-Saxon inheritance patterns. To compensate for this, Wormald planned to examine other evidence for bequests, including Domesday Book. His provisional hypothesis was that partible inheritance among sons was practised, perhaps with some prominence given to the eldest son, before primogeniture became established.[10]

It is very much to be hoped that a later generation of scholars working on Anglo-Saxon law, land tenure and inheritance practice will explore the wealth of ideas contained in Wormald's unpublished notes and build on the foundations which he laid.

7 Lecture VII, sections 1b, 4b. This view is in contrast with that of Holt, 'Feudal society', to which Wormald refers in 4b.

8 Lecture VII, table E.

9 Lecture VII, sections 4a, 4b.

10 Lecture VII, section 6.

# BIBLIOGRAPHY

## Editions of vernacular wills additional to those included in the List of Abbreviations


'A new edition of the will of Wulfgyth', ed. and transl. K. A. Lowe, *Notes and Queries* n.s., 36 (1989), 295–8.

'The will of Eadwine of Caddington', ed. and transl. S. Keynes, appended to 'A lost cartulary of St Alban's Abbey', *ASE* 22 (1993), 253–79 (pp. 275–9).

'The will of Wulf', ed. and transl. S. Keynes, *Old English Newsletter* 26.3 (1993), 16–21.


## Other primary sources


Ælfric, *Lives of Saints*, ed. W. Skeat, EETS OS 76 (London, 1881).

*Alcuini Epistolae*, ed. E. Dümmler, MGH, *Epistolae Karolini Aevi* 2 (Berlin, 1895).

Allott, S. (transl.), *Alcuin of York: his Life and Letters* (York, 1974).

Backhouse, J., D. H. Turner and L. Webster (ed.), *The Golden Age of Anglo-Saxon Art* (Bloomington, 1984).

*Baedae Opera Historica*, ed. C. Plummer, 2 vols. (Oxford, 1896, repr. in one volume 1946).

*The Battle of Maldon*, ed. and transl. D. Scragg, in Scragg (ed.), *The Battle of Maldon*, pp. 14–36.

*The Bayeux Tapestry*, ed. F. M. Stenton (London, 1957).

Bede, *Ecclesiastical History of the English People*, ed. and transl. B. Colgrave and R. A. B. Mynors (Oxford, 1969).

Blows, M., 'A Glastonbury obit-list', in *The Archaeology and History of Glastonbury Abbey*, ed. Abrams and Carley, pp. 257–69.

*Die Briefen des hl. Bonifatius und Lullus*, ed. M. Tangl, MGH, Epistolae III, *Epistolae Merowingici et Karolini aevi*, I (Berlin, 1916).

Byrhtferth, *Vita Oswaldi Archiepiscopi Eboracensis*, in *The Historians of the Church of York and its Archbishops*, ed. J. Raine, Rolls Series 71, 3 vols. (London, 1879–94), I, 399–475.

*Byrhtferth's Enchiridion*, ed. P. S. Baker and M. Lapidge, EETS SS 15 (Oxford, 1995).

Byrhtferth of Ramsey, *The Lives of St Oswald and St Ecgwine*, ed. and transl. M. Lapidge (Oxford, 2009).

Campbell, A., 'An Old English will', *Journal of English and Germanic Philology* 37 (1938), 133–52.

*Cartulaire de L'Abbaye de Cysoing*, ed. I. de Coussemaker (Lille, 1885).

*Cartularium Saxonicum: a Collection of Charters Relating to Anglo-Saxon History*, ed. W. de Gray Birch, 3 vols. (London, 1885–99).

*The Chronicle of Æthelweard*, ed. and transl. A. Campbell (London, 1962).

*Codex Diplomaticus Aevi Saxonici*, ed. J. Kemble, 6 vols. (London, 1839–48).

*The Corpus of Anglo-Saxon Stone Sculpture IV: South-East England*, ed. D. Tweddle, M. Biddle and B. Kjølbye-Biddle (Oxford, 1995).

*The Corpus of Anglo-Saxon Stone Sculpture V: Lincolnshire*, ed. P. Everson and D. A. Stocker (Oxford, 1999).

*Councils and Ecclesiastical Documents Relating to Great Britain and Ireland*, ed. A.W. Haddan and W. Stubbs, 3 vols. (Oxford, 1869–79)

*The Cult of St Swithun*, ed. and transl. M. Lapidge, Winchester Studies 4, ii (Oxford, 2003).

*Dhuoda: Manuel pour mon fils*, ed. P. Riché, 2nd edn (Paris, 1997).

*Diplomatarium Anglicum Aevi Saxonici: a Collection of English Charters from the Reign of King Æthelstan of Kent AD 605, to that of William the Conqueror*, ed. and transl. B. Thorpe (London, 1865).

*The Early History of Glastonbury: an Edition, Translation and Study of William of Malmesbury's 'De Antiquitate Glastonie Ecclesie'*, ed. and transl. J. Scott (Woodbridge, 1981).

*The Ecclesiastical History of Orderic Vitalis: Vol. II, Books III and IV*, ed. and transl. M. Chibnall (Oxford, 1969).

Einhard and Notker the Stammerer: *Two Lives of Charlemagne*, transl. L. Thorpe (Harmondsworth, 1969).

*Facsimiles of Ancient Charters in the British Museum*, ed. E. A. Bond, 4 vols. (London, 1873–78).

*Facsimiles of Anglo-Saxon Manuscripts*, ed. W. B. Sanders, Ordnance Survey, 3 vols. (Southampton, 1878–84).

*Facsimiles of English Royal Writs to AD 1100: presented to V. H. Galbraith*, ed. T. A. M. Bishop and P. Chaplais (Oxford, 1957).

Fehr, B. (ed.), 'Altenglische Ritualtexte für Krankenbesuch, heilige Ölung und Begräbnis', in *Texte und Forschungen*, ed. Boehmer, pp. 26–67.

Fleming, R., 'Christchurch's sisters and brothers: an edition and discussion of Canterbury *obit* lists', in *The Culture of Christendom*, ed. Meyer, pp. 115–153.

Geary, P. J., *Aristocracy in Provence: The Rhône Basin at the Dawn of the Carolingian Age* (Stuttgart, 1985).

*Die Gesetze der Angelsachsen*, ed. F. Liebermann, 3 vols. (Halle, 1898–1916).

Gregory of Tours, *Historia Francorum*, ed. W. Arndt and B. Krusch, MGH, *Scriptores Rerum Merovingicarum*, I, part 1 (Hanover, 1884).

——, *The History of the Franks*, transl. L. Thorpe (London, 1974).

*Handbook for William: a Carolingian Woman's Counsel for her Son*, transl. C. Neel (Lincoln NE, 1991).

*Heremanni Archidiaconi Miracula Sancti Eadmundi*, ed. F. Liebermann, *Ungedruckte Anglo-Normannische Geschichtsquellen* (Strasbourg, 1879), pp. 203–81.

*Die Hirtenbriefe Ælfrics*, ed. B. Fehr, Bibliothek der Angelsächsischen Prosa IX (Hamburg, 1914).

*Klaeber's Beowulf*, ed. R. D. Fulk, R. E. Bjork and J. D. Niles, 4th edn, based on the 3rd edn with first and second supplements of *Beowulf and the Fight at Finnsburg*, ed. F. Klaeber (Toronto, 2008).

*The Letters of St Boniface*, transl. E. Emerton, ed. T. F. X. Noble (New York, 2000).

*Liber Eliensis: a History of the Isle of Ely from the Seventh Century to the Twelfth*, transl. J. Fairweather (Woodbridge, 2005).

*The* Liber Vitae *of the New Minster and Hyde Abbey, Winchester, British Library Stowe 944*, ed. S. Keynes, Early English Manuscripts in Facsimile 26 (Copenhagen, 1996).

*Liber Vitae: Register and Martyrology of New Minster and Hyde Abbey, Winchester*, ed. W. de Gray Birch, Hampshire Record Society (London, 1892).

*The Life of Bishop Wilfrid by Eddius Stephanus*, ed. and transl. B. Colgrave (Cambridge, 1927).

*Memorials of St Dunstan*, ed. W. Stubbs, Rolls Series 63 (1874).
Meritt, H., 'Old English entries in a manuscript at Bern', *Journal of English and Germanic Philology* 33 (1934), 343–51.
Napier, A.S. (ed.), 'An Old English vision of Leofric, Earl of Mercia', *Transactions of the Philological Society* (1907–10), 180–8.
Okasha, E., *A Hand-List of Anglo-Saxon Non-Runic Inscriptions* (Cambridge, 1971).
*Ramsey Abbey's Book of Benefactors Parts I and II*, transl. S. B. Edgington and others (Huntingdon, 1998 and 2001).
*Recueil des chartes de l'abbaye de Saint-Benoît-sur-Loire*, ed. M. Prou and A. Vidier, Documents publiés par La Société Historique et Archéologique du Gâtinais V (Paris, 1900).
*Regularis Concordia Anglicae Nationis Monachorum Sanctimonialiumque*, ed. and transl. T. Symons (London, 1953).
*Vita Ædwardi Regis qui apud Westmonasterium requiescit*, ed. and transl. F. Barlow (London, 1961).
*The Waltham Chronicle*, ed. L. Watkiss and M. Chibnall (Oxford, 1994).
Webster, L. and J. Backhouse (ed.), *The Making of England: Anglo-Saxon Art and Culture 600–900* (London, 1991)
William of Malmesbury, *Gesta Pontificum Anglorum*, ed. and transl. M. Winterbottom and R. M. Thomson (Oxford, 2006).
William of Malmesbury, *Gesta Regum Anglorum*, ed. and transl. R. A. B. Mynors, R. M. Thomson and M. Winterbottom (Oxford, 1998).
*Die Winteney-Version der Regula S. Benedicti*, ed. A. Schröer, 1st edn (Halle, 1888), reprinted with appendix by M. Gretsch (Tübingen, 1978).
Wulfstan of Winchester, *The Life of St Æthelwold*, ed. and transl. M. Lapidge and M. Winterbottom (Oxford, 1991).
*The York Gospels*, a facsimile with introductory essays by J. Alexander, P. McGurk, S. Keynes and B. Barr, ed. N. Barker (London, 1986).

## Secondary Sources

Abels, R., 'English tactics, strategy and military organisation in the late tenth century', in *The Battle of Maldon*, ed. Scragg, pp. 143–55.
——, *Lordship and Military Obligation in Anglo-Saxon England* (London, 1988).
Abrams, L., *Anglo-Saxon Glastonbury: Church and Endowment* (Woodbridge, 1996).
Abrams, L. and J. P. Carley (ed.), *The Archaeology and History of Glastonbury Abbey: Essays in Honour of the Ninetieth Birthday of C. A. Ralegh Radford* (Woodbridge, 1991).
André, J. L., 'Widows and vowesses', *Archaeological Journal* 49 (1892), 69–82.
Archer, E. R. and B. E. Ferme, 'Testamentary procedure with special reference to the executrix', *Reading Medieval Studies* 15 (1989), 3–34.
Atherton, I., E. Fernie, C. Harper-Bill and H. Smith (ed.), *Norwich Cathedral: Church, City and Diocese* (London, 1996).
Audouy, M. and A. Chapman, *Raunds: the Origin and Growth of a Midland Village AD 450–1500* (Oxford, 2009).
Balzaretti, R., 'The monastery of Sant' Ambrogio and dispute settlement in early medieval Milan', *EME* 3.1 (1994), 1–18.
Barlow, F., *Edward the Confessor* (London, 1970).
——, *The English Church 1000–1066* (London, 1963).
——, *The English Church 1066–1154* (London, 1979).
Barrow, J., 'Cathedral clergy', in *Blackwell Encyclopaedia*, pp. 84–7.

——, 'The chronology of forgery production at Worcester from *c.* 1000 to the early twelfth century', in *St Wulfstan*, ed. Barrow and Brooks, pp. 105–22.
——, 'English cathedral communities and reform in the late tenth and eleventh centuries', in *Anglo-Norman Durham*, ed. Rollason, Harvey and Prestwich, pp. 25–39.
——, 'How the twelfth-century monks of Worcester perceived their past', in *The Perception of the Past*, ed. Magdalino, pp. 53–74.
——, 'Survival and mutation: ecclesiastical institutions in the Danelaw in the ninth and tenth centuries', in *Cultures in Conflict*, ed. Hadley and Richards, pp. 155–76.
Barrow, J. and N. P. Brooks (ed.), *St Wulfstan and his World* (Aldershot, 2005).
Bassett, S. (ed.), *Death in Towns* (Leicester, 1992).
Baxter, S., 'Archbishop Wulfstan and the administration of God's property', in *Archbishop Wulfstan*, ed. Townend, pp. 161–205.
——, *The Earls of Mercia: Lordship and Power in Late Anglo-Saxon England* (Oxford, 2007).
Bedingfield, M. Bradford, *The Dramatic Liturgy of Anglo-Saxon England* (Woodbridge, 2002).
Beresford, G., 'Goltho Manor, Lincolnshire: the buildings and their surrounding defences *c.* 850–1150', *ANS* 4 (1981), 13–136.
Biddle, M., '*Felix urbs Winthonia*: Winchester in the age of monastic reform', in *Tenth-Century Studies*, ed. Parsons, pp. 123–40.
Bijsterveld, A. J. A., 'The medieval gift as agent of social bonding and political power: a comparative approach', in *Medieval Transformations*, ed. Cohen and De Jong, pp. 123–56.
Binski, P., *Medieval Death* (London, 1996).
Blackburn, M., 'Gold in England during the "Age of Silver" (eighth–eleventh centuries)', in *Silver Economy in the Viking Age*, ed. Graham-Campbell and Williams, pp. 55–98.
Blair, J., *The Church in Anglo-Saxon Society* (Oxford, 2005).
——, 'Hall and chamber: English domestic planning 1000–1250', in *Manorial Domestic Buildings*, ed. Meirion-Jones and Jones (ed.), pp. 1–16.
——, 'Introduction: from minster to parish church', in Blair, *Minsters and Parish Churches*, pp. 1–19.
——, 'Local churches in Domesday Book and before', in *Domesday Studies*, ed. Holt, pp. 265–78.
—— (ed.), *Minsters and Parish Churches: the Local Church in Transition* (Oxford, 1988).
——, 'Ramsey Abbey', in *Blackwell Encyclopaedia*, pp. 385–6.
Blair, J. and R. Sharpe (ed.), *Pastoral Care Before the Parish* (Leicester, 1992).
Boddington, A., *Raunds Furnells: the Anglo-Saxon Church and Churchyard*, English Heritage Archaeological Report 7 (London, 1996).
Boehmer, H. and others, *Texte und Forschungen zur Englischen Kulturgeschichte: Festgabe für Felix Liebermann* (Halle, 1921).
Bouchard, C., *Sword, Miter and Cloister: Nobility and the Church in Burgundy, 980–1198* (Ithaca NY, 1987).
——, *'Those of My Blood': Constructing Noble Families in Medieval Francia* (Philadelphia, 2001).
Boynton M. and S. Reynolds, 'The author of the Fonthill letter', *ASE* 25 (1996), 91–5.
Brooks, N. P., 'Anglo-Saxon charters: the work of the last twenty years', *ASE* 3

(1974), 211–31, reprinted with a post-script in Brooks, *Anglo-Saxon Myths*, pp. 181–215.
——, *Anglo-Saxon Myths: State and Church* 400–1066 (London, 2000).
——, 'Arms, status and warfare in late-Saxon England', in *Ethelred the Unready*, ed. Hill, pp. 81–103, reprinted in Brooks, *Communities and Warfare*, pp. 138–61.
——, 'The career of St Dunstan', in *St Dunstan*, ed. Ramsay, Sparks and Tatton-Brown, pp. 1–23.
——, *Communities and Warfare 700–1400* (London, 2000).
——, *The Early History of the Church of Canterbury* (Leicester, 1984).
——, 'Treason in Essex in the 990s: the case of Æthelric of Bocking', forthcoming.
——, 'Weapons and armour', in *The Battle of Maldon*, ed. Scragg, pp. 208–19, reprinted in Brooks, *Communities and Warfare*, pp. 162–74.
Brooks, N. and C. Cubitt (ed.), *St Oswald of Worcester: Life and Influence* (Leicester, 1996).
Budny, M., 'The Byrhtnoth tapestry or embroidery', in *The Battle of Maldon*, ed. Scragg, pp. 263–78.
Budny, M. and D. Tweddle, 'The Maseik embroideries', *ASE* 13 (1984), 65–96.
Bull, M., *Knightly Piety and the Lay Response to the First Crusade: the Limousin and Gascony, c. 970–1130* (Oxford, 1993).
Bullough, D., 'Burial, community and belief in the early medieval West', in *Ideal and Reality*, ed. Wormald, pp. 177–201.
——, *Friends, Neighbours and Fellow-Drinkers: Aspects of Community and Conflict in the Early Medieval West*, H. M. Chadwick Memorial Lecture, 1 (Cambridge, 1991).
Cabrol, F. and H. Leclercq (ed.), *Dictionnaire d'archéologie chrétienne et de liturgie*, 15 vols. (Paris, 1903–53).
Campbell, J. (ed.), *The Anglo-Saxons* (London, 1982).
——, *The Anglo-Saxon State* (London, 2000).
——, 'The East Anglian sees before the Conquest', in *Norwich Cathedral*, ed. Atherton et al., pp. 3–21, reprinted in Campbell, *The Anglo-Saxon State*, pp. 107–27.
——, 'England *c.* 991', in *The Battle of Maldon*, ed. Cooper, pp. 1–17, reprinted in Campbell, *The Anglo-Saxon State*, pp. 157–78.
——, 'Some agents and agencies of the late Anglo-Saxon state', in *Domesday Studies*, ed. Holt, pp. 201–18, reprinted in Campbell, *The Anglo-Saxon State*, pp. 201–25.
——, 'Was it infancy in England? Some questions of comparison', in *England and her Neighbours*, ed. Jones and Vale, pp. 1–17, reprinted in Campbell, *The Anglo-Saxon State*, pp. 179–99.
——, 'What is not known about Edward the Elder', in *Edward the Elder*, ed. Higham and Hill, pp. 12–24.
Carver, M. O. H. (ed.), *The Age of Sutton Hoo: the Seventh Century in North-West Europe* (Woodbridge, 1992).
Cavallo, S. and L. Warner (ed.), *Widowhood in Medieval and Early Modern Europe* (Harlow, 1999).
Charles-Edwards, T. M., 'The distinction between land and moveable wealth in Anglo-Saxon England', in *English Medieval Settlement*, ed. Sawyer, pp. 97–104.
Clanchy, M. T., *From Memory to Written Record: England 1066–1307*, 2nd edn (Oxford, 1993).
Classen, P. (ed.), *Recht und Schrift im Mittelalter* (Sigmaringen, 1977).
Coatsworth, E., 'Cushioning medieval life: domestic textiles in Anglo-Saxon England', *Medieval Clothing and Textiles* 3 (2007), 1–12.

——, 'The embroideries from the tomb of St Cuthbert', in *Edward the Elder*, ed. Higham and Hill, pp. 292–306.

Coatsworth, E. and M. Pinder, *The Art of the Anglo-Saxon Goldsmith: Fine Metalwork in England: its Practice and Practitioners* (Woodbridge, 2002).

Cohen, E. and M. B. De Jong (ed.), *Medieval Transformations: Texts, Power and Gifts in Context* (Leiden, 2001).

Cooper, J. (ed.), *The Battle of Maldon: Fiction and Fact* (London, 1993).

Costen, M., 'Dunstan, Glastonbury and the economy of Somerset in the tenth century', in *St Dunstan*, ed. Ramsay, Sparks and Tatton-Brown, pp. 25–44.

Cramp, R., 'The monumental stone', in Boddington, *Raunds Furnells*, pp. 102–12.

Crawford, S. and H. Hamerow (ed.), *Anglo-Saxon Studies in Archaeology and History* 15 (Oxford, 2008).

Crick, J., 'Church, land and local nobility: the case of Ealdorman Oswulf', *Bulletin of the Institute of Historical Research* 61 (1988), 251–69.

——, 'Men, women and widows: widowhood in pre-Conquest England', in *Widowhood in Medieval and Early Modern Europe*, ed. Cavallo and Warner, pp. 24–36.

——, 'Offa, Ælfric and the refoundation of St Albans', in *Alban and St Albans*, ed. Henig and Lindley, pp. 78–84.

——, 'Posthumous obligation and family identity', in *Social Identity in Early Medieval Britain*, ed. Frazer and Tyrell, pp. 193–208.

——, 'The wealth, patronage and connections of women's houses in late Anglo-Saxon England', *Revue Bénédictine* 109 (1999), 154–85.

——, 'Women, posthumous benefaction and family strategy in pre-Conquest England', *Journal of British Studies* 38 (1999), 399–422.

——, 'Women, wills and moveable wealth in pre-Conquest England', in *Gender and Material Culture from Prehistory to the Present*, ed. Donald and Hurcombe, pp. 17–37.

Cubitt, C., *Anglo-Saxon Church Councils c. 650–c. 850* (Leicester, 1995).

——, 'Monastic memory and identity in early Anglo-Saxon England', in *Social Identity*, ed. Frazer and Tyrell, pp. 253–76.

——, 'The tenth-century Benedictine Reform in England', *EME* 6.1 (1997), 77–94.

——, 'Virginity and misogyny in tenth- and eleventh-century England', *Gender and History* 12.1 (2000), 1–32.

Danet, B. and B. Bogoch, 'From oral ceremony to written document: the transitional language of Anglo-Saxon wills', *Language and Communication* 12 no. 2 (1992), 95–122.

——, 'Orality, literacy and performativity in Anglo-Saxon wills', in *Language and the Law*, ed. Gibbons, pp. 100–35.

——, '"Whosoever alters this, may God turn his face from him at the day of judgement": curses in Anglo-Saxon legal documents', *The Journal of American Folklore* 105 no. 416 (1992), 132–65.

Davies, W. and P. Fouracre (ed.), *Property and Power in the Early Middle Ages* (Cambridge, 1995).

——, *The Settlement of Disputes in Early Medieval Europe* (Cambridge, 1986).

Davis, G. R. C. (ed.), *Medieval Cartularies of Great Britain: a Short Catalogue* (London, 1958).

De Jong, M., *In Samuel's Image: Child Oblation in the Early Medieval West* (Leiden, 1996).

Deliyannis, D. M., 'Charlemagne's imperial tables: the ideology of an imperial capital', *EME* 12.2 (2003), 159–77.

Dodwell, C. R., *Anglo-Saxon Art: a New Perspective* (New York, 1982).

Donald, M. and L. Hurcombe (ed.), *Gender and Material Culture from Prehistory to the Present* (London, 2000).
Draper, S., 'The significance of OE *burh* in Anglo-Saxon England', in *Anglo-Saxon Studies*, ed. Crawford and Hamerow, pp. 240–53.
Dumville, D. N., 'The ætheling: a study in Anglo-Saxon constitutional history', *ASE* 8 (1979), 1–33.
——, *Liturgy and the Ecclesiastical History of Late Anglo-Saxon England* (Woodbridge, 1992).
——, *Wessex and England from Alfred to Edgar: Six Essays on Political, Cultural and Ecclesiastical Revival* (Woodbridge, 1992).
Effros, B., 'Beyond cemetery walls: early medieval funerary topography and Christian salvation', *EME* 6.1 (1997), 1–23.
——, *Caring for Body and Soul: Burial and the Afterlife in the Merovingian World* (University Park PA, 2002).
Ellis Davidson, H. R., *The Sword in Anglo-Saxon England* (Oxford, 1962).
Epstein, S., *Wills and Wealth in Medieval Genoa* (Cambridge, 1984).
Fairbrother, J. R., *Faccombe Netherton: Excavation of a Saxon and Medieval Manorial Complex*, British Museum Occasional Papers 47, I (London, 1990).
Faith, R., *The English Peasantry and the Growth of Lordship* (Leicester, 1997).
Fell, C., *Women in Anglo-Saxon England* (Oxford, 1984).
Fleming, R., 'History and liturgy at pre-Conquest Christ Church', *Haskins Society Journal* 6 (1994), 67–83.
——, *Kings and Lords in Conquest England* (Cambridge, 1991).
——, 'The new wealth, the new rich and the new political style in late Anglo-Saxon England', *ANS* 23 (2000), 1–32.
Fletcher, R., *Bloodfeud: Murder and Revenge in Anglo-Saxon England* (London, 2003).
Flight, C., 'Four vernacular texts from the pre-Conquest archive of Rochester Cathedral', *Archaeologia Cantiana* 115 (1995), 121–53.
Foot, S., *Veiled Women*, 2 vols. (Aldershot, 2000).
Frantzen, A. J., *The Literature of Penance in Anglo-Saxon England* (New Brunswick NJ, 1983).
Frazer, W. O. and A. Tyrell (ed.), *Social Identity in Early Medieval Britain* (London, 2000).
Gage, J., 'The Anglo-Saxon ceremonial of the dedication and consecration of churches, illustrated from a pontifical in the public library at Rouen', *Archaeologia* 25 (1834), 235–74.
Garrison, M., 'Letter collections', in *Blackwell Encyclopaedia*, pp. 283–4.
——, '"Send more socks": on mentality and preservation context of medieval letters', in *New Approaches*, ed. Mostert, pp. 69–99.
Gatch, M. Mc., 'Miracles and architectural settings: Christ Church, Canterbury and St Clement's, Sandwich in the Old English vision of Leofric', *ASE* 22 (1993), 227–52.
Geake, H., *The Use of Grave-Goods in Conversion-Period England, c. 600–850*, BAR British Series 261 (1997).
Geary, P. J., 'Exchange and interaction between the living and the dead in early medieval society', published as 'Echanges et relations entre les vivants et les morts dans la société du haut Moyen Age', *Droit et Cultures* 12 (1986), 3–18, translated in Geary, *Living with the Dead*, pp. 77–92.
——, *Furta Sacra: Thefts of Relics in the Central Middle Ages*, revised edn (Princeton NJ, 1990).
——, *Living with the Dead in the Middle Ages* (Ithaca NY, 1994).
——, *Phantoms of Remembrance* (Princeton NJ, 1994).

——, 'Sacred commodities: the circulation of medieval relics', first published in *Commodities and Culture*, ed. A. Appadurai (Cambridge, 1986), pp. 169–91, reprinted in Geary, *Living with the Dead*, pp. 194–218.

——, 'The saint and the shrine: the pilgrim's goal in the Middle Ages', first published in *Wallfahrt kennt keine Grenzen*, ed. L. Kriss-Rettenbeck and G. Möhler (Munich, 1984), pp. 265–74, reprinted in Geary, *Living with the Dead*, pp. 163–76.

——, 'The uses of archaeological sources for religious and cultural history', published as 'Zur Problematik der Interpretation archäologischer Quellen für die Geistes- und Religionsgeschichte', *Archaeologia Austriaca* 64 (1980), 111–18, translated in Geary, *Living with the Dead*, pp. 30–45.

Gem, R., 'How much can Anglo-Saxon buildings tell us about liturgy?', in *The Liturgy*, ed. Gittos and Bedingfield, pp. 271–90.

Gerchow, J., *Die Gedenküberlieferung der Angelsachsen: mit einem Katalog der Libri Vitae und Necrologien*, *Arbeiten zur Frühmittelalterforschung* 20 (Berlin, 1988).

——, 'Prayers for King Cnut: the liturgical commemoration of a conqueror', in *England in the Eleventh Century*, ed. Hicks, pp. 219–38.

——, '*Societas et Fraternitas*: a report on a research project based at the universities of Freiburg and Münster', *Nomina* 12 (1988–89), 153–71.

Gibbons, J. (ed.), *Language and the Law* (London, 1994).

Gilchrist, R. and B. Sloane, *Requiem: the Medieval Monastic Cemetery in Britain* (London, 2005).

Gittos, H., 'Is there any evidence for the liturgy of parish churches in late Anglo-Saxon England? The Red Book of Darley and the status of Old English', in *Pastoral Care*, ed. Tinti, pp. 63–82.

Gittos, H. and M. Bradford Bedingfield (ed.), *The Liturgy of the Late Anglo-Saxon Church* (London, 2005).

Gneuss, H., 'Liturgical books in Anglo-Saxon England and their Old English terminology', in *Learning and Literature*, ed. Lapidge and Gneuss, pp. 91–141.

Godden, M. R., 'Ælfric of Eynsham', in *Blackwell Encyclopaedia*, pp. 8–9.

Graham-Campbell, J. and G. Williams (ed.), *Silver Economy in the Viking Age* (Walnut Creek CA, 2007).

Gransden, A., *Historical Writing in England c. 550-c. 1307* (London, 1974).

——, 'The legends and traditions concerning the origins of the Abbey of Bury St Edmunds', *EHR* 100 (1985), 1–24.

Hadley, D. M. and J. Buckberry, 'Caring for the dead in late Anglo-Saxon England', in *Pastoral Care*, ed. Tinti, pp. 121–47.

Hadley, D. M. and J. D. Richards (ed.), *Cultures in Contact: Scandinavian Settlement in England in the Ninth and Tenth Centuries* (Turnhout, 2000).

Halsall, G., 'Burial, ritual and Merovingian society', in *The Community, the Family and the Saint*, ed. Hill and Swan, pp. 325–38.

——, 'Female status and power in early Merovingian central Austrasia: the burial evidence', *EME* 5 (1996), 1–24.

——, *Settlement and Social Organisation: the Merovingian Region of Metz* (Cambridge, 1995).

——, 'Social change around AD 600: an Austrasian perspective', in *The Age of Sutton Hoo*, ed. Carver, pp. 265–78.

Hamilton, S., *The Practice of Penance 900–1050* (Woodbridge, 2001).

——, 'Remedies for "Great Transgressions": penance and excommunication in late Anglo-Saxon England', in *Pastoral Care*, ed. Tinti, pp. 83–105.

Hammer, C., 'Country churches, clerical inventories and the Carolingian renaissance in Bavaria', *Church History* 49 (1980), 5–17.

Härke, H., 'The circulation of weapons in Anglo-Saxon society', in *Rituals of Power*, ed. Theuws and Nelson, pp. 377–99.
——, '"Warrior graves": the background of the Anglo-Saxon weapon burial rite', *Past and Present* 126 (1990), 22–43.
Harper-Bill, C. and R. Harvey (ed.), *Medieval Knighthood* IV (Woodbridge, 1992).
Hart, C. R., 'Athelstan "Half-King" and his family', *ASE* 2 (1973), 115–38, 143–4, revised and reprinted in Hart, *The Danelaw*, pp. 569–604.
——, 'Eadnoth, first abbot of Ramsey and the foundation of Chatteris and St Ives', *Proceedings of the Cambridge Antiquarian Society* 56–7 (1964), 61–7, revised and reprinted in Hart, *The Danelaw*, pp. 613–23
——, 'The ealdordom of Essex', in *An Essex Tribute: Essays presented to Frederick G. Emmerson*, ed. K. Neale (London, 1987), pp. 57–73, 76–85, revised and reprinted in Hart, *The Danelaw*, pp. 115–40.
——, *The Early Charters of Essex* (Leicester, 1971).
——, *The Early Charters of Essex: The Norman Period* (Leicester, 1957).
——, *The Early Charters of Northern England and the North Midlands* (Leicester, 1975).
——, 'The Eastern Danelaw', in Hart, *The Danelaw*, pp. 25–113.
——, 'The Mersea charter of Edward the Confessor', *Essex Archaeology and History* 12 (1980), 94–102, revised and reprinted in Hart, *The Danelaw*, pp. 495–508.
——, 'The St Paul's estates in Essex', in Hart, *The Danelaw*, pp. 205–20.
——, 'The will of Ælfgifu', in Hart, *The Danelaw*, pp. 455–65.
Hartmann, W. (ed.), *Sonderdruck aus Bischof Burchard von Worms 1000–1025* (Mainz, 2000).
Hase, P. H., 'The mother churches of Hampshire', in *Minsters and Parish Churches*, ed. Blair, pp. 45–66.
Hazeltine, H. D., 'Comments on the writings known as Anglo-Saxon wills', in *Wills*, ed. Whitelock, pp. vii–xl.
Heidecker, K., 'Communication by written texts in court cases: some charter evidence (*ca* 800–*ca* 1100)', in *New Approaches*, ed. Mostert, pp. 101–26.
Henig, M. and P. Lindley (ed.), *Alban and St Albans: Roman and Medieval Architecture, Art and Archaeology*, The British Archaeological Association Conference Transactions 25 (Leeds, 2001).
Hicks, C. (ed.), *England in the Eleventh Century: Proceedings of the 1990 Harlaxton Symposium* (Stamford, 1992).
Higham, N. J., *The Death of Anglo-Saxon England* (Stroud, 1997).
Higham, N. J. and D. H. Hill (ed.), *Edward the Elder* (London, 2001).
Hill, D., *An Atlas of Anglo-Saxon England* (Oxford, 1981).
—— (ed.), *Ethelred the Unready: Papers from the Millenary Conference*, BAR British Series 59 (1978).
Hill, J., 'Monastic reform and the secular church', in *England in the Eleventh Century*, ed. Hicks, pp. 103–17.
Hill, J. and M. Swan (ed.), *The Community, the Family and the Saint: Patterns of Power in Early Medieval Europe* (Turnhout, 1998).
Hinton, D. A., *The Alfred Jewel and Other Late Anglo-Saxon Decorated Metalwork* (Oxford, 2008).
——, *Gold and Gilt, Pots and Pins: Possessions and People in Medieval Britain* (Oxford, 2005).
——, 'Late Anglo-Saxon metalwork: an assessment', *ASE* 4 (1975), 171–80.
——, 'Late Saxon treasure and bullion', in *Ethelred the Unready*, ed. Hill, pp. 135–58.
Hohler, C., 'The Red Book of Darley', in *Nordisk Kollokvium* 2, ed. Slott, pp. 39–47.
Holt, J. C. (ed.), *Domesday Studies* (Woodbridge, 1987).

——, 'Feudal society and the family in early medieval England: I. The revolution of 1066', *TRHS* 5th s., 32 (1982), 193–212.
Hooke, D., *The Landscape of Anglo-Saxon England* (Leicester, 1998).
Howell, M. C., 'Fixing movables: gifts by testament in late medieval Douai', *Past and Present* 150 (1996), 3–45.
Innes, M., 'Charlemagne's will: piety, politics and the imperial succession', *EHR* 112 (1997), 833–55.
——, 'Keeping it in the family: women and aristocratic memory 700–1200', in *Medieval Memories*, ed. Van Houts, pp. 17–35.
——, *State and Society in the Early Middle Ages: the Middle Rhine Valley 400–1000* (Cambridge, 2000).
Insley, C., 'Where did all the charters go? Anglo-Saxon charters and the new politics of the eleventh century', *ANS* 24 (2001), 109–127.
John, E., 'The end of Anglo-Saxon England', in *The Anglo-Saxons*, ed. Campbell, pp. 214–39.
——, *Land Tenure in Early England*, 2nd edn (Leicester, 1964).
——, *Orbis Britanniae and Other Studies* (Leicester, 1966).
Jones, M. and M. Vale (ed.), *England and her Neighbours, 1066–1453: Essays in Honour of Pierre Chaplais* (London, 1989).
Kanner, B. (ed.), *The Women of England: From Anglo-Saxon Times to the Present* (London, 1980).
Kasten, B., 'Erbrechtliche Verfügungen des 8/9. Jahrhunderts', *Zeitschrift der Savigny-Stiftung für Rechtsgeschichte, germanistische Abteilung* 107 (1990), 236–338.
Kelly, S. E., 'Anglo-Saxon lay society and the written word', in *Uses of Literacy*, ed. McKitterick, pp. 36–62.
Kennedy, A., 'Byrhtnoth's obits and twelfth-century accounts of the Battle of Maldon', in *The Battle of Maldon*, ed. Scragg, pp. 59–78.
——, 'Disputes about *bocland*: the forum for their adjudication', *ASE* 14 (1985), 175–95.
——, 'Law and litigation in the *Libellus Æthelwoldi Episcopi*', *ASE* 24 (1995), 131–83.
Ker, N. R. (ed.), *Catalogue of Manuscripts Containing Anglo-Saxon* (Oxford, 1957).
——, 'Hemming's cartulary: a description of the two Worcester cartularies in Cotton Tiberius A. XIII', in *Studies in Medieval History presented to F. M. Powicke*, ed. R. W. Hunt, W. A. Pantin and R. W. Southern (Oxford, 1948), pp. 49–75, reprinted in *Books, Collectors and Libraries: Studies in the Medieval Heritage*, ed. A. G. Watson (London, 1985), pp. 31–59.
Keynes, S., 'Charters and writs', in *Blackwell Encyclopaedia*, pp. 99–100.
——, 'Cnut's earls', in *The Reign of Cnut*, ed. Rumble, pp. 43–88.
——, 'Crime and punishment in the reign of King Æthelred the Unready', in *People and Places*, ed. Wood and Lund, pp. 67–81.
——, *The Diplomas of King Æthelred 'the Unready' 978–1016* (Cambridge, 1980).
——, 'Edward, King of the Anglo-Saxons', in *Edward the Elder*, ed. Higham and Hill, pp. 40–66.
——, 'Ely Abbey 672–1109', in *A History of Ely Cathedral*, ed. Meadows and Ramsay, pp. 2–58.
——, 'England *c.* 900–1016', in *The New Cambridge Medieval History III*, ed. Reuter, pp. 456–84.
——, 'The Fonthill letter', in *Words, Texts and Manuscripts*, ed. Korhammer, pp. 53–97.
——, 'King Athelstan's books', in *Learning and Literature*, ed. Lapidge and Gneuss, pp. 143–201.

——, 'The power of the written word: Alfredian England 871–899', in *Alfred the Great*, ed. Reuter, pp. 175–97.

——, 'Regenbald the chancellor (*sic*)', *ANS* 10 (1987), 185–222 (pp. 189–92).

——, 'Royal government and the written word in late Anglo-Saxon England', in *The Uses of Literacy*, ed. McKitterick, pp. 226–57.

——, 'A tale of two kings: Alfred the Great and Æthelred the Unready', *TRHS* 5th s., 36 (1986), 195–217.

——, 'The West Saxon charters of King Æthelwulf and his sons', *EHR* 109 (1994), 1109–49.

King, V., 'St Oswald's tenants', in *St Oswald*, ed. Brooks and Cubitt, pp. 100–16.

Kirby, D. P., *The Earliest English Kings* (London, 1991).

Kjølbye-Biddle, B., 'Dispersal or concentration: the disposal of the Winchester dead over 2000 years', in *Death in Towns*, ed. Bassett, pp. 210–47.

Korhammer, M. (ed.), *Words, Texts and Manuscripts: Studies in Anglo-Saxon Culture presented to Helmut Gneuss* (Cambridge, 1992).

Lancaster, L., 'Kinship in Anglo-Saxon society', parts 1 and 2, *British Journal of Sociology* 9 (1958), 230–50, 359–77.

Lapidge, M., 'Æthelwold as scholar and teacher', in *Bishop Æthelwold*, ed. Yorke, pp. 89–117.

——, 'Byrhtferth and Oswald', in *St Oswald*, ed. Brooks and Cubitt, pp. 64–83.

Lapidge, M. and H. Gneuss (ed.), *Learning and Literature in Anglo-Saxon England: Studies presented to Peter Clemoes* (Cambridge, 1985).

La Rocca, C. and L. Provero, 'The dead and their gifts: the will of Eberhard, Count of Friuli, and his wife Gisela, daughter of Louis the Pious (863–864)', in *Rituals of Power*, ed. Theuws and Nelson, pp. 225–80.

Larratt Keefer, S., 'Hwær cwom mearh? The horse in Anglo-Saxon England', *Journal of Medieval History* 22 (1996), 115–34.

——, 'Manuals', in *Liturgical Books*, ed. Pfaff, pp. 99–109.

Lawson, M. K., *Cnut: the Danes in England in the Early Eleventh Century* (London, 1993).

Le Jan, R., *Famille et pouvoir dans le monde franc (vii^e-x^e siècle): essai d'anthropologie sociale* (Paris, 1995).

Lewis, C. P., 'The Domesday Jurors', *Haskins Society Journal* 5 (1993), 17–44.

Loades, D. (ed.), *The End of Strife* (Edinburgh, 1984).

Locherbie-Cameron, M. A. L., 'Byrhtnoth and his family', in *The Battle of Maldon*, ed. Scragg, pp. 253–62.

——, 'The men named in the poem', in *The Battle of Maldon*, ed. Scragg, pp. 238–49.

Lowe, K. A., '"As fre as thowt"?: some medieval copies and translations of Old English wills', *English Manuscript Studies 1100–1700* 4 (1993), 1–23.

——, 'Latin versions of Old English wills', *Legal History* 20.1 (1999), 1–24.

——, 'Lay literacy in Anglo-Saxon England and the development of the chirograph', in *Anglo-Saxon Manuscripts*, ed. Pulsiano and Traherne, pp.161–204.

——, 'The nature and effect of the Anglo-Saxon vernacular will', *Legal History* 19.1 (1998), 23–61.

——, 'Never say *nefa* again: problems of translation in Old English charters', *Neuphilologische Mitteilungen* 94 (1993), 27–35.

——, 'Two thirteenth-century cartularies from Bury St Edmunds: a study in textual transmission', *Neuphilologische Mitteilungen* 93 (1992), 293–301.

——, 'William Somner, S1622, and the editing of Old English charters', *Neuphilologus* 83 (1999), 291–7.

——, 'Wills', in *Blackwell Encyclopaedia*, pp. 478–80.

Loyn, A.R., *The Governance of Anglo-Saxon England 500–1087* (London, 1984).

Mack, K., 'Changing thegns: Cnut's conquest and the English aristocracy', *Albion* 16 (1984), 375–87.

Magdalino, P. (ed.), *The Perception of the Past in Twelfth-Century Europe* (London, 1992).

Magennis, H., *Anglo-Saxon Appetites: Food and Drink and their Consumption in Old English and Related Literature* (Dublin, 1991).

Maitland, F. W., *Domesday Book and Beyond: Three Essays in the Early History of England* (Cambridge, 1897, repr. 1907).

Mauss, M., 'Essai sur le don: forme et raison de l'échange dans les sociétés archaïques', *L'Année Sociologique* 1 (1923), 30–186, published in English as *The Gift: Forms and Functions of Exchange in Archaic Societies*, transl. I. Cunnison (New York, 1967).

McKitterick, R., *The Carolingians and the Written Word* (Cambridge, 1989).

—— (ed.), *The New Cambridge Medieval History II: c. 700-c. 900* (Cambridge, 1995).

—— (ed.), *The Uses of Literacy in Early Medieval Europe* (Cambridge, 1990).

McLaughlin, M., *Consorting with Saints: Prayer for the Dead in Early Medieval France* (Ithaca NY, 1994).

Meadows, P. and N. Ramsay (ed.), *A History of Ely Cathedral* (Woodbridge, 2003).

Meirion-Jones, G. and M. Jones (ed.), *Manorial Buildings in England and Northern France* (London, 1993).

Meyer, M. A. (ed.), *The Culture of Christendom: Essays in Medieval History in Memory of Denis L. T. Bethell* (London, 1993).

——, 'Land charters and the legal position of Anglo-Saxon women', in *The Women of England*, ed. Kanner, pp. 57–82.

——, 'Women's estates in later Anglo-Saxon England: the politics of possession', *Haskins Society Journal* 3 (1991), 111–29.

Miller, E., *The Abbey and Bishopric of Ely: the Social History of an Ecclesiastical Estate from the Tenth to the Early Fourteenth Century* (Cambridge, 1951).

Miller, S., 'Eadred', in *Blackwell Encyclopaedia*, p. 150.

Morris, R., *Churches in the Landscape* (London, 1989).

Mostert, M. (ed.), *New Approaches to Medieval Communication* (Turnhout, 1999).

Mynors, R. A. B. and R. M. Thomson, *Catalogue of Manuscripts of Hereford Cathedral Library* (Cambridge, 1993).

Nelson, J. L., 'The Frankish kingdoms 814–898: the West', in *New Cambridge Medieval History II*, ed. McKitterick, pp. 110–41.

——, 'Reconstructing a royal family: reflections on Alfred, from Asser, chapter two', in *People and Places*, ed. Wood and Lund, pp. 47–66.

——, 'The wary widow', in *Property and Power*, ed. Davies and Fouracre, pp. 82–113.

Niermeyer, J. F. and C. Van De Kieft (ed.), *Mediae Latinitatis Lexicon Minus*, revised J. W. J. Burgers (Leiden, 2002).

Nonn, U., 'Merowingische Testamente: Studien zum Fortleben einer römischen Urkundenform im Frankreich', *Archiv für Diplomatik* 18 (1972), 1–129.

Owen, G. R., 'Wynflæd's wardrobe', *ASE* 18 (1979), 195–222.

Owen-Crocker, G. R., *Dress in Anglo-Saxon England*, revised edn (Manchester, 2004).

——, 'Hawks and horse-trappings: the insignia of rank', in *The Battle of Maldon*, ed. Scragg, pp. 220–37.

Parkes, M. B., 'A fragment of an early-tenth-century Anglo-Saxon manuscript and its significance', *ASE* 12 (1983), 129–40.

Parsons, D., 'Liturgical and social aspects', in Boddington, *Raunds Furnells*, pp. 58–66.

—— (ed.), *Tenth-Century Studies: Essays in Commemoration of the Millennium of the Council of Winchester and Regularis Concordia* (London, 1975).
Paxton, F. S., *Christianising Death: the Creation of a Ritual Process in Early Medieval Europe* (Ithaca NY, 1990).
Pelteret, D. A. E., *Catalogue of English Post-Conquest Vernacular Documents* (Woodbridge, 1990).
——, *Slavery in Early Medieval England* (Woodbridge, 1995).
Pestell, T., *Landscapes of Monastic Foundation: the Establishment of Religious Houses in East Anglia c. 650–1200* (Woodbridge, 2004).
Pfaff, R. W. (ed.), *The Liturgical Books of Anglo-Saxon England*, Old English Newsletter, Subsidia 23 (Kalamazoo MI, 1995).
Poeck, D., 'Laienbegräbnisse in Cluny', *Frühmittelalterliche Studien* 15 (1981), 68–179.
Pollock, F. and F. W. Maitland, *The History of English Law Before the Time of Edward I*, 2 vols., 2nd edn (Cambridge, 1911).
Pulsiano, P. and E. M. Traherne, (ed.), *Anglo-Saxon Manuscripts and their Heritage* (Aldershot, 1998).
Rackham, O., *The History of the Countryside: the Classic History of Britain's Landscape, Flora and Fauna* (London, 1986; reprinted London, 2000).
Raftis, J. A., *The Estates of Ramsey Abbey* (Toronto, 1957).
Ramsay, N., M. Sparks and T. Tatton-Brown (ed.), *St Dunstan: his Life, Times and Cult* (Woodbridge, 1992).
Reuter, T. (ed.), *Alfred the Great: Papers from the Eleventh-Centenary Conferences* (Aldershot, 2003).
——, 'Ein Europa der Bischöfe: das Zeitalter Burchards von Worms', in *Sonderdruck*, ed. Hartmann , pp. 1–28.
—— (ed.), *The New Cambridge Medieval History III: c. 900-c. 1024* (Cambridge, 1999).
——, 'Plunder and tribute in the Carolingian Empire', *TRHS* 5th s., 35 (1985), 79–94.
——, '"You can't take it with you": testaments, hoards and moveable wealth in Europe, 600–1100', in *Treasure in the Medieval West*, ed. Tyler, pp. 11–24.
Reynolds, A., *Later Anglo-Saxon England: Life and Landscape* (Stroud, 1999).
Reynolds, S., 'Bookland, folkland and fiefs', *ANS* 14 (1992), 211–27.
——, *Fiefs and Vassals: the Medieval Evidence Reinterpreted* (Oxford, 1994).
Ridyard, S., *The Royal Saints of Anglo-Saxon England: a Study of West Saxon and East Anglian Cults* (Cambridge, 1989).
Robinson, J. A., *The Life and Times of St Dunstan* (Oxford, 1923).
Rodwell, W. and K. Rodwell, 'St Peter's Church, Barton-upon-Humber', *Antiquaries Journal* 62 (1982), 283–315.
Rollason, D., *Saints and Relics in Anglo-Saxon England* (Philadelphia, 1982).
——, *Two Anglo-Saxon Rituals: the Dedication of a Church and the Judicial Ordeal*, Fifth Brixworth Lecture (1988).
Rollason, D., M. Harvey and M. Prestwich (ed.), *Anglo-Norman Durham* (Woodbridge, 1994).
Rosenwein, B., *To Be the Neighbor of St Peter: the Social Meaning of Cluny's Property 909–1049* (Ithaca NY, 1989).
Rosser, G., 'The Anglo-Saxon gilds', in *Minsters and Parish Churches*, ed. Blair, pp. 31–4.
——, 'The cure of souls in English towns before 1000', in *Pastoral Care Before the Parish*, ed. Blair and Sharpe, pp. 267–84.
Rumble, A. R., 'Edward the Elder and the churches of Winchester and Wessex', in *Edward the Elder*, ed. Higham and Hill, pp. 230–47.

——, 'The purposes of the *Codex Wintoniensis*', *ANS* 4 (1981), 153–67.
——, (ed.), *The Reign of Cnut, King of England, Denmark and Norway* (London, 1994).
Sawyer, P. H., *English Medieval Settlement* (London, 1979).
Scheibelreiter, G., 'The death of the bishop in the Early Middle Ages', in *The End of Strife*, ed. Loades, pp. 32–43.
Scragg, D. (ed.), *The Battle of Maldon AD 991* (Oxford, 1991).
Sharpe, R., 'The use of writs in the eleventh century', *ASE* 32 (2003), 247–91.
Sheehan, M. M., *The Will in Medieval England* (Toronto, 1963).
Sims-Williams, P., *Religion and Literature in Western England, 600–800* (Cambridge, 1990).
Skinner, P., 'Women, wills and wealth in medieval southern Italy', *EME* 2.2 (1993), 133–52.
Slott, H. (ed.), *Nordisk Kollokvium 2: I Latinsk Liturgi Forskning* (Stockholm, 1972).
Smith, J. M. H., 'Religion and lay society', in *The New Cambridge Medieval History II*, ed. McKitterick, pp. 654–78.
Smith, M. F., 'Archbishop Stigand and the eye of the needle', *ANS* (1994), 199–219.
Smyth, A. P., *King Alfred the Great* (Oxford, 1995).
Spreckelmeyer, G., 'Zur rechtlichen Funktion frühmittelalterlicher Testamente', in *Recht und Schrift*, ed. Classen, pp. 91–113.
Stafford, P., '*Cherchez la femme*: Queens, queens' lands and nunneries: missing links in the foundation of Reading Abbey', *History* 85 (2000), 4–27.
——, 'Eadgifu', in *Blackwell Encyclopaedia*, p. 149.
——, 'Ealdorman', in *Blackwell Encyclopaedia*, pp. 152–3.
——, 'The king's wife in Wessex 800–1066', *Past and Present* 91 (1981), 3–27.
——, 'Kinship and women in the world of Maldon: Byrhtnoth and his family', in *The Battle of Maldon*, ed. Cooper, pp. 225–35.
——, 'The laws of Cnut and the history of Anglo-Saxon royal promises', *ASE* 10 (1981), 173–90.
——, 'La mutation familiale: a suitable case for caution', in *The Community, the Family and the Saint*, ed. Hill and Swan, pp. 103–25.
——, *Queen Emma and Queen Edith: Queenship and Women's Power in Eleventh Century England* (Oxford, 1997).
——, 'Queens, nunneries and reforming churchmen: gender, religious status and reform in tenth- and eleventh-century England', *Past and Present* 163 (1999), 3–35.
——, 'Queens and treasure in the early middle ages', in *Treasure*, ed. Tyler, pp. 61–82.
——, 'The reign of Æthelred II: a study in the limitations on royal policy and power', in *Ethelred the Unready*, ed. Hill, pp. 15–37.
——, 'Succession and inheritance: a gendered perspective on Alfred's family history', in *Alfred the Great*, ed. Reuter, pp. 251–64.
——, *Unification and Conquest: a Political and Social History of England in the Tenth and Eleventh Centuries* (London, 1989).
——, 'Women in Domesday', *Reading Medieval Studies* 15 (1989), 74–94.
——, 'Women and the Norman Conquest', *TRHS* 6th s., 4 (1994), 221–49.
Stocker, D., 'Monuments and merchants: irregularities in the distribution of stone sculpture in Lincolnshire and Yorkshire in the tenth century', in *Cultures in Contact*, ed. Hadley and Richards, pp. 179–212.
Stoodley, N., *The Spindle and the Spear: a Critical Enquiry into the Construction and Meaning of Gender in the Early Anglo-Saxon Burial Rite*, BAR British Series, 288 (1999).

Tabuteau, E. Z., *Transfers of Property in Eleventh-Century Norman Law* (Chapel Hill NC, 1988).
Taylor, H. M., 'The Anglo-Saxon church at Canterbury', *Archaeological Journal* 126 (1969), 101–29.
Thacker, A., 'Dynastic monasteries and family cults: Edward the Elder's sainted kindred', in *Edward the Elder*, ed. Higham and Hill, pp. 248–63.
——, 'Saint-making and relic collecting by Oswald and his communities', in *St Oswald*, ed. Brooks and Cubitt, pp. 244–68.
Theuws, F. and Nelson, J. L. (ed.), *Rituals of Power from Late Antiquity to the Early Middle Ages* (Leiden, 2000).
Thompson, V., *Dying and Death in Later Anglo-Saxon England* (Woodbridge, 2004).
——, 'The pastoral contract in late Anglo-Saxon England: priest and parishioner in Oxford, Bodleian Library, MS Laud Miscellaneous 482', in *Pastoral Care*, ed. Tinti, pp. 108–18.
Thomson, R. M., *The Archives of the Abbey of Bury St Edmunds* (Woodbridge, 1980).
Tinti, F., 'The costs of pastoral care: church dues in late Anglo-Saxon England', in Tinti, *Pastoral Care*, pp. 27–51.
——, 'From episcopal conception to monastic compilation: Hemming's Cartulary in context', *EME* 11.3 (2002), 233–61.
—— (ed.), *Pastoral Care in Late Anglo-Saxon England* (Woodbridge, 2005).
——, *Sustaining Belief: the Church of Worcester from c. 870 to c. 1100* (Farnham, 2010).
Townend, M. (ed.), *Wulfstan, Archbishop of York: the Proceedings of the Second Alcuin Conference* (Turnhout, 2004).
Tweddle, D., 'The development of sculpture *c.* 950–1100', in *Corpus of Anglo-Saxon Stone Sculpture IV*, ed. Tweddle, Biddle and Biddle, pp. 62–7.
Tyler, E. M. (ed.), *Treasure in the Medieval West* (York, 2000).
Van Houts, E. (ed.), *Medieval Memories: Men, Women, and the Past, 700–1300* (Harlow, 2001).
——, *Memory and Gender in Medieval Europe* (London, 1999).
Wareham, A., *Lords and Communities in Early Medieval East Anglia* (Woodbridge, 2005).
——, 'Saint Oswald's family and kin', in *St Oswald*, ed. Brooks and Cubitt, pp. 46–63.
——, 'The transformation of kinship and the family in late Anglo-Saxon England', *EME* 10.3 (2002), 375–94.
Welby, A. C. E., 'Ulf of Lincolnshire before and after the Conquest', *Lincolnshire Notes and Queries* 14 (1917), 196–200.
White, S., *Custom, Kinship and Gifts to Saints: the* laudatio parentum *in Western France, 1050–1150* (Chapel Hill NC, 1988).
Whitelock, D., *The Beginnings of English Society* (London, 1952).
——, *Some Anglo-Saxon Bishops of London* (London, 1975).
Wilcox, J., 'Ælfric in Dorset and the landscape of pastoral care', in *Pastoral Care*, ed. Tinti, pp. 52–62.
Williams, A., '"A bell-house and a burh-geat": lordly residences in England before the Norman Conquest', in *Medieval Knighthood IV*, ed. Harper-Bill and Harvey, pp. 221–40.
——, *The English and the Norman Conquest* (Woodbridge, 1995).
——, 'Land and power in the eleventh century: the estates of Harold Godwineson', *ANS* 3 (1980), 171–87.
——, 'Land tenure', *Blackwell Encyclopaedia*, pp. 277–8.
——, '*Princeps Merciorum gentis*: the family, career and connections of Ælfhere, ealdorman of the Mercians', *ASE* 10 (1981), 143–72.

——, 'Some notes and considerations on problems connected with the English royal succession, 860–1066', *ANS* 1 (1978), 144–67.
——, 'The spoliation of Worcester', *ANS* 19 (1996), 383–408.
——, 'Thegnly piety and ecclesiastical patronage in the late Old English kingdom', *ANS* 24 (2001), 1–24.
Willis, R., *The Architectural History of Canterbury Cathedral* (London, 1845).
Wood, I. and N. Lund (ed.), *People and Places in Northern Europe 500–1600: Studies presented to Peter Hayes Sawyer* (Woodbridge, 1991).
Wood, M., 'The making of King Æthelstan's empire: an English Charlemagne?', in *Ideal and Reality*, ed. Wormald, pp. 250–72.
Wood, S., *The Proprietary Church in the Medieval West* (Oxford, 2006).
Wormald, P., *Bede and the Conversion of England: the Charter Evidence*, Jarrow Lecture (1984), reprinted in Wormald, ed. Baxter, *The Times of Bede*, pp. 135–66.
——, 'Charters, law and the settlement of disputes in Anglo-Saxon England', in *Settlement of Disputes*, ed. Davies and Fouracre, pp. 149–68, reprinted in Wormald, *Legal Culture*, pp. 289–311.
——, 'Giving God and king their due: conflict and its regulation in the early English state', *Settimana di Studio del Centro Italiano di Studi sull' alto Medioevo* 44 (1997), 549–90, reprinted in Wormald, *Legal Culture*, pp. 333–57.
——, 'A handlist of Anglo-Saxon lawsuits', *ASE* 17 (1988), 247–81, reprinted in Wormald, *Legal Culture*, pp. 253–87.
——, *Legal Culture in the Medieval West: Law as Text, Image and Experience* (London, 1999).
——, *The Making of English Law: King Alfred to the Twelfth Century* (Oxford, 1999).
——, 'The ninth century', in *The Anglo-Saxons*, ed. Campbell, pp. 132–59.
——, '*On þa wæpnedhealfe*: kingship and royal property from Æthelwulf to Edward the Elder', in *Edward the Elder*, ed. Higham and Hill, pp. 264–79.
——, ed. S. Baxter, *The Times of Bede: Studies in Early English Christian Society and its Historian* (Oxford, 2006).
Wormald, P. (ed.), with D. Bullough and R. Collins, *Ideal and Reality in Frankish and Anglo-Saxon Society: Studies presented to J. M. Wallace-Hadrill* (Oxford, 1983).
Yorke, B., 'Æthelwold and the politics of the tenth century', in Yorke, *Bishop Æthelwold*, pp. 65–88.
—— (ed.), *Bishop Æthelwold: his Career and Influence* (Woodbridge, 1988).
——, 'Edward as ætheling', in *Edward the Elder*, ed. Higham and Hill, pp. 25–39.

## Unpublished works

Lowe, K. A., 'The Anglo-Saxon Vernacular Will: Studies in Texts and their Transmission' (unpublished doctoral thesis, University of Cambridge, 1990).
Tollerton Hall, L., 'Wills and Will-Making in Late Anglo-Saxon England' (unpublished doctoral thesis, University of York, 2005).
Wareham, A., 'The Aristocracy of East Anglia *c.* 930–1154: a Study of Family, Land and Government' (unpublished doctoral thesis, University of Birmingham, 1992).
Wormald, P., unpublished lecture notes containing material preparatory to the second volume of his two-volume study *The Making of English Law* (deposited in the archives of King's College, London): Lecture VII.

# INDEX

*Page numbers in italics refer to illustrations*

## YORK MEDIEVAL PRESS: PUBLICATIONS

*God's Words, Women's Voices: The Discernment of Spirits in the Writing of Late-Medieval Women Visionaries*, Rosalyn Voaden (1999)

*Pilgrimage Explored*, ed. J. Stopford (1999)

*Piety, Fraternity and Power: Religious Gilds in Late Medieval Yorkshire 1389–1547*, David J. F. Crouch (2000)

*Courts and Regions in Medieval Europe*, ed. Sarah Rees Jones, Richard Marks and A. J. Minnis (2000)

*Treasure in the Medieval West*, ed. Elizabeth M. Tyler (2000)

*Nunneries, Learning and Spirituality in Late Medieval English Society: The Dominican Priory of Dartford*, Paul Lee (2000)

*Prophecy and Public Affairs in Later Medieval England*, Lesley A. Coote (2000)

*The Problem of Labour in Fourteenth-Century England*, ed. James Bothwell, P. J. P. Goldberg and W. M. Ormrod (2000)

*New Directions in later Medieval Manuscript Studies: Essays from the 1998 Harvard Conference*, ed. Derek Pearsall (2000)

*Cistercians, Heresy and Crusadse in Occitania, 1145–1229: Preaching in the Lord's Vineyard*, Beverly Mayne Kienzle (2001)

*Guilds and the Parish Community in Late Medieval East Anglia, c. 1470–1550*, Ken Farnhill (2001)

*The Age of Edward III*, ed. J. S. Bothwell (2001)

*Time in the Medieval World*, ed. Chris Humphrey and W. M. Ormrod (2001)

*The Cross Goes North: Processes of Conversion in Northern Europe, AD 300–1300*, ed. Martin Carver (2002)

*Henry IV: The Establishment of the Regime, 1399–1406*, ed. Gwilym Dodd and Douglas Biggs (2003)

*Youth in the Middle Ages*, ed. P. J. P. Goldberg and Felicity Riddy (2004)

*The Idea of the Castle in Medieval England*, Abigail Wheatley (2004)

*Rites of Passage: Cultures of Transition in the Fourteenth Century*, ed. Nicola F. McDonald and W. M. Ormrod (2004)

*Creating the Monastic Past in Medieval Flanders*, Karine Ugé (2005)

*St William of York*, Christopher Norton (2006)

*Medieval Obscenities*, ed. Nicola F. McDonald (2006)

*The Reign of Edward II: New Perspectives*, ed. Gwilym Dodd and Anthony Musson (2006)

*Old English Poetics: The Aesthetics of the Familiar in Anglo-Saxon England*, Elizabeth M. Tyler (2006)

*The Late Medieval Interlude: The Drama of Youth and Aristocratic Masculinity*, Fiona S. Dunlop (2007)

*The Late Medieval English College and its Context*, ed. Clive Burgess and Martin Heale (2008)

*The Reign of Henry IV: Rebellion and Survival, 1403–1413*, ed. Gwilym Dodd and Douglas Biggs (2008)

*Medieval Petitions: Grace and Grievance*, ed. W. Mark Ormrod, Gwilym Dodd and Anthony Musson (2009)

*St Edmund, King and Martyr: Changing Images of a Medieval Saint*, ed. Anthony Bale (2009)

*Language and Culture in Medieval Britain: The French of England c.1100–c.1500*, ed. Jocelyn Wogan-Browne et al. (2009)

*The Royal Pardon: Access to Mercy in Fourteenth-Century England*, Helen Lacey (2009)

*Texts and Traditions of Medieval Pastoral Care: Essays in Honour of Bella Millett*, ed. Cate Gunn and Catherine Innes-Parker (2009)

*The Anglo-Norman Language and its Contexts*, ed. Richard Ingham (2010)

*Parliament and Political Pamphleteering in Fourteenth-Century England*, Clementine Oliver (2010)

*The Saints' Lives of Jocelin of Furness: Hagiography, Patronage and Ecclesiastical Politics*, Helen Birkett (2010)

*The York Mystery Plays: Performance in the City*, ed. Margaret Rogerson (2011)

**York Studies in Medieval Theology**

I *Medieval Theology and the Natural Body*, ed. Peter Biller and A. J. Minnis (1997)

II *Handling Sin: Confession in the Middle Ages*, ed. Peter Biller and A. J. Minnis (1998)

III *Religion and Medicine in the Middle Ages*, ed. Peter Biller and Joseph Ziegler (2001)

IV *Texts and the Repression of Medieval Heresy*, ed. Caterina Bruschi and Peter Biller (2002)

**York Manuscripts Conference**

*Manuscripts and Readers in Fifteenth-Century England: The Literary Implications of Manuscript Study*, ed. Derek Pearsall (1983) [Proceedings of the 1981 York Manuscripts Conference]

*Manuscripts and Texts: Editorial Problems in Later Middle English Literature*, ed. Derek Pearsall (1987) [Proceedings of the 1985 York Manuscripts Conference]

*Latin and Vernacular: Studies in Late-Medieval Texts and Manuscripts*, ed. A. J. Minnis (1989) [Proceedings of the 1987 York Manuscripts Conference]

*Regionalism in Late-Medieval Manuscripts and Texts: Essays celebrating the publication of 'A Linguistic Atlas of Late Mediaeval English'*, ed. Felicity Riddy (1991) [Proceedings of the 1989 York Manuscripts Conference]

*Late-Medieval Religious Texts and their Transmission: Essays in Honour of A. I. Doyle*, ed. A. J. Minnis (1994) [Proceedings of the 1991 York Manuscripts Conference]

*Prestige, Authority and Power in Late Medieval Manuscripts and Texts*, ed. Felicity Riddy (2000) [Proceedings of the 1994 York Manuscripts Conference]

*Middle English Poetry: Texts and Traditions. Essays in Honour of Derek Pearsall*, ed. A. J. Minnis (2001) [Proceedings of the 1996 York Manuscripts Conference]

**Manuscript Culture in the British Isles**

I *Design and Distribution of Late Medieval Manuscripts in England*, ed. Margaret Connolly and Linne R. Mooney (2008)

II *Women and Writing, c.1340–c.1650: The Domestication of Print Culture*, ed. Anne Lawrence-Mathers and Phillipa Hardman (2010)

III *The Wollaton Medieval Manuscripts: Texts, Owners and Readers*, ed. Ralph Hanna and Thorlac Turville-Petre (2010)

**Heresy and Inquisition in the Middle Ages**

*Heresy and Heretics in the Thirteenth Century: The Textual Representations*, L. J. Sackville (2011)

Printed and bound by CPI Group (UK) Ltd, Croydon, CR0 4YY

13/09/2026

14961004-0002